The Complete Court Cases
of Magistrate Frederick Stewart
as Reported in *The China Mail*
July 1881 to March 1882

Compiled and Edited by
Gillian Bickley

Proverse Hong Kong, 2021

THE COMPLETE COURT CASES OF MAGISTRATE FREDERICK STEWART AS REPORTED IN *THE CHINA MAIL* JULY 1881 TO MARCH 1882 proides sources, commentary and analaysis, useful for historians and students of colonial law and colonial administration, Hong Kong (China) legal and social history. The book contains a carefully edited and annotated transcription of newspaper reports of magistrate's court cases at a particularly lively period in Hong Kong history, with analyses and background documentation of specific offences, detailed references to historical Ordinances, and a careful index. The book: illuminates the interface and parallels between the establishment of a colonial education system and the introduction of colonial law; extends our knowledge and understanding of nineteenth century Hong Kong family and social life, law, policing, and court practice; provides information about hundreds of individuals; and throws additional light on the Irish Roman Catholic Governor of the time, John Pope Hennessy and the Founder of Hong Kong Government Education, Frederick Stewart.

"Together [these brief reports] do even more for the modern reader than put him in the armchair of someone who took the *China Mail* in Victorian Hong Kong— although that alone would be interesting enough. They provide him with a seat at the back of Mr Stewart's court, alive again and in session."
—**The Hon. Mr Justice Bokhary PJ.**

GILLIAN BICKLEY is the biographer of the magistrate whose court cases are transcribed and discussed here, Frederick Stewart. She has been studying and publishing well-received scholarly books and academic articles on 19th century Hong Kong history for over twenty years. She has also been actively engaged in presenting her material to the general public through talks, historical walks, radio interviews and media feature articles. Her work is now additionally being used as a resource by heritage groups to support various campaigns.

The Complete Court Cases

of
Magistrate
Frederick Stewart

as Reported in
The China Mail
July 1881 to March 1882

Compiled, Edited, Written
by Gillian Bickley

Proverse Hong Kong

The Complete Court Cases of Magistrate Frederick Stewart
as reported in *The China Mail*, July 1881 to March 1882.
Compiled, edited and written by Gillian Barbara Bickley
Published in Paperback in Hong Kong
by Proverse Hong Kong, February 2021.
ISBN-13: 978-988-8228-77-5
Copyright © Gillian Bickley 2021
1st published in CD format in Hong Kong
by Proverse Hong Kong, December 2008.
Reissued, March 2016.
ISBN-13: 978-988-17724-1-1
Copyright © Gillian Bickley 2008

Distribution (Hong Kong and worldwide):
The Chinese University Press of Hong Kong,
The Chinese University of Hong Kong,
Shatin, New Territories, Hong Kong SAR.
Email: cup@cuhk.edu.hk; Web: www.cup.cuhk.edu.hk

Distribution (United Kingdom): Stephen Inman, Worcester, UK.
Enquiries to: Proverse Hong Kong,
P.O. Box 259, Tung Chung Post Office,
Lantau, NT, Hong Kong SAR, China.
Email: proverse@netvigator.com; Web:
www.proversepublishing.com

Book cover image: The Clock-Tower, Hong Kong,
Courtesy, Gillian and Verner Bickley collection

British Library Cataloguing-in-Publication Data
A catalogue record is available
from the British Library

Moral Rights

The right of Gillian Bickley to be identified as the editor of, "The Complete Court Cases of Magistrate Frederick Stewart as reported in *The China Mail*, July 1881 to March 1882", and as the author of the following parts of this book – "Editor's Introduction", "Cases brought for alleged Offences against 'The Excise Ordinance (Opium) 1858-1879, Amendment Ordinance 1879', their results, the sentences given and notes on the relevant legislation", "Gamblers' encounters with the police and the magistrate's court, forms of gambling, gambling venues and equipment: information derived from the gambling and gambling-related cases heard before Frederick Stewart, July 1881 to March 1882. With quotations from relevant ordinances"; and of all "Tables" with related commentaries, and of the Appendix, "The Excise Ordinance (Opium) 1858-1879, Amendment Ordinance 1879: Selections to explain the opium and opium-related cases before Frederick Stewart, July 1881 to March 1882" – has been asserted by her in accordance with the Copyright, Designs and Patents Act 1988.

The right of Ian Grant to be identified as the author of, "Comparing the work of Frederick Stewart and his equivalent Scottish contemporaries", in accordance with the Copyright, Designs and Patents Act 1988.

The right of Kemal Bokhary to be identified as the writer of the, "Preface", has been asserted by him in accordance with the Copyright, Designs and Patents Act 1988.

Preface

Some cases hit the headlines. They come to feature in major law reports and influential law books. Indeed they may even eventually find a place in history books. Other cases are made of more common clay. Nevertheless they can – taken together over a period and carefully analysed – provide valuable insight into the nature of judicial justice. To a greater or lesser extent, they can even tell us something about life in general at a particular time and place. Harvesting the information that such cases contain is by no means easy. It is however possible, and can be very rewarding. Dr Gillian Bickley has shown the way. She has done so as the editor of two scholarly and readable works. This set of reports is the second. *A Magistrate's Court in Nineteenth Century Hong Kong: Court in Time* (2005) is the first.

The court dealt with is that of Frederick Stewart, Esq. (1836 – 1889) who sat as a magistrate in Hong Kong from July 1881 to March 1882. Dr Bickley and her contributors have dealt with Mr Stewart's cases in a very interesting way. So much so that there has grown a great demand to know more about those cases. Hence this welcome set of reports.

Dr Bickley's choice of court and era is, if I may say so, a good one. The Treaty of Nanking formally ceding Hong Kong to Britain was entered into in 1842 and ratified in 1843. Such cession had however been agreed in principle by the so-called Convention of Chenpui in January 1841. Acting on that agreement in principle, Britain immediately entered into occupation of Hong Kong. This was quickly followed by the Bremer-Elliot Proclamation of 1 February 1841 which assigned a very special role to magistrates. It did so by declaring that pending Her Majesty's pleasure, the Chinese inhabitants of Hong Kong would be governed according to Chinese laws, customs and usages by village elders, subject to the control of a British magistrate. Before long, Hong Kong's law came to be applied generally to everybody here. That did not diminish, rather did it increase, the importance of magistrates. The Magistrate's Court is at the frontline of the administration of justice. It occupied that position before and during Mr Stewart's time, and has occupied it ever since.

To understand the law as it stands and assess how it ought to develop, it is generally useful and sometimes essential to know what the law had been in the past. That is, I tend to think, as true in regard to legal systems as it is true of substantive law. And in each instance, the lawyer's work must be carried out in a complete social context. The law may have a lot more to do with history and anthropology than is generally realised within each of those three disciplines.

Many of the offences for which people were tried in Mr Stewart's court are still in existence. One of the cases shows him imposing a sentence of two months' imprisonment with hard labour for pickpocketting. Nowadays this offence normally attracts a sentence of twelve to fifteen months' imprisonment – but of course without hard labour. Some of the offences for which people were tried in Mr Stewart's court have been abolished. So have some of the penalties which he imposed. These were offences like being without light or pass and penalties like exposure in the stocks. In fairness to Mr Stewart, it should be recognised that they were very much more a reflection on his times than on himself. Moreover, there is this important thought to bear in mind when judging the past. We must pause to wonder if everything being done today will without exception enjoy the unalloyed admiration of future generations. I doubt that it will. It is not in the nature of progress that it should.

To the extent revealed in these reports, Mr Stewart's judicial behaviour was well up to the standard demanded today. He appears to have maintained order and kept things moving along with a firm but not heavy hand. When he felt it necessary to elicit more detailed testimony from a witness, he appears to have done so without putting ideas into the witness's head let alone words into his mouth.

Each of these reports is brief. But together they do even more for the modern reader than put him in the armchair of someone who took the *China Mail* in Victorian Hong Kong – although that alone would be interesting enough. They provide him with a seat at the back of Mr Stewart's court, alive again and in session.

The Hon. Mr Justice Bokhary PJ
 Court of Final Appeal
2008

Acknowledgements

Warm thanks go to Khemal Bokhary for contributing the "Preface" and Ian Grant for contributing his essay, comparing the work of Frederick Stewart and his equivalent Scottish contemporaries.

Verner Bickley, my husband, is always patient, helpful, encouraging and supportive. He is particularly thanked for his constant interest as in-house, "research supervisor", for his labour in creating the index and for his own research skills in finding several relevant and helpful materials.

I acknowledge support for this publication from the Council of The Lord Wilson Heritage Trust.

The co-operative work of Verner Bickley, Christopher Coghlan, Timothy Hamlett, Geoffrey Roper and Garry Tallentire, in contributing to *A Magistrate's Court in Nineteenth Century Hong Kong: Court in Time* has been fundamental. Without this, the database of court case material, previously gathered during the eight years research for *The Golden Needle: The Biography of Frederick Stewart (1836-1889),* discussed and partly published in *A Magistrate's Court in Nineteenth Century Hong Kong,* would not have seen the light of day. The chapters contributed to *A Magistrate's Court in Nineteenth Century Hong Kong* by Verner Bickley, Christopher Coghlan, Timothy Hamlett, Geoffrey Roper and Garry Tallentire, together with additional Tables compiled by Geoffrey Roper, have been of ongoing assistance in understanding the significance of this material and hence in editing and writing the present work.

Many years ago, Mildred Marney and Lilith Yin Wai Lee reduced the labour of inputting the text of the original database.

I am grateful for replies to research enquiries from Bernard Hui and other Colleagues at the Hong Kong Public Records Office, for help from Colleagues at Hong Kong Baptist University Library and The University of Hong Kong Libraries, to

Danny K. C. Chow, Nicole Ho, Kam Keung Lee, May Lee, Henry So and S. H. Tong of Hong Kong Baptist University, Angelina Wong of the Chinese University of Hong Kong Press, N. K. Wong, Curator of the Hong Kong Police Museum and to Margaret McBryde and Elizabeth Buckley of the National Archives of Scotland.

I salute the generous co-operative assistance and supportive work of the late Carl Smith.

All are remembered and thanked.

Gillian Bickley
Honorary Research Fellow
Centre of Asian Studies, University of Hong Kong
2008

Table of Contents

Editor's Introduction

Hong Kong

The history of Hong Kong, a British Crown Colony since 1843, which was returned to the Government of Mainland China at midnight, 30 June 1997, is fascinating as an example of what happens when two very different cultures meet, collide and gradually accommodate to each other, producing a separate and identifiable new culture. Hong Kong's story is of course also important for the part it has played in the history of Mainland China itself and in the history of those European and other countries and institutions, which have found it a useful basis for their operations in China and elsewhere in Asia.

The study of Hong Kong history has been and to an extent still is an occupation — even a vocation — embraced by enthusiasts. But each additional work makes it more possible that the subject will be taken up into the main stream of world studies, where it deserves to be included and where it could certainly have useful synergy with the whole.

Because of its small size — particularly true of nineteenth century Hong Kong, before the acquisition in 1898 of the New Territories — the study of Hong Kong history is a finite task. It is also a task where, paradoxically — and not only because of the part Hong Kong has played and plays in the history of much larger political entities and groups of people — there is always more; something interesting, novel, illuminating and useful, to be discovered and done.

Value of contemporary Reports of Cases heard in Magistrates' Courts

The general value of reports of cases heard in magistrates' courts is implied, shown and discussed in *A Magistrate's Court in Nineteenth Century Hong Kong* (Proverse, 2005), in the chapters contributed by Gillian Bickley, Verner Bickley, Christopher Coghlan, Timothy Hamlett, Geoffrey Roper and Garry Tallentire, and by Sir T. L. Yang in his historical Preface. Taken as a whole, the contributed and editorial discussions in *A Magistrate's Court* bring out the different cultural backgrounds and assumptions, not only as between a colonial administration and the administered people, or between legal professionals and those coming into professional contact with them, but between domestic employers and their servants, merchants and employees, providers and users of public transport, street-wise and street-innocent, travellers and residents, adults and children, urban, rural and sea-dwelling people, teachers and taught, formally educated and uneducated, ambitious and accepting, honest and criminal, mentally sound and unsound, conformists and non-conformists, individuals and family-members, adherents of different religions, and many other different groupings and callings of people. No wonder, when so many differences are shaken up in the same pot, misunderstandings and conflicts arise between people with so very many differences from each other.

Access to these materials informs not only our understanding of specific periods and places in the past, but of our own varied lives and circumstances today. Certainly, these newspaper reports of Court Cases from a specific period of time, July 1881 to March 1882, in the specific place, colonial Hong Kong, enrich our understanding of Hong Kong and Mainland China, not only at that specific time, but at other periods, giving at times a sense of historical perspective to our lives today. — How often, reading the newspapers "today", do we find reports of cases very similar in nature or in spirit to those that former readers saw in their much earlier newspapers a century and a quarter ago!

In 2006, the *South China Morning Post* reported, "the first known case of child slavery in Hong Kong in 50 years . . . revealed when an 11-year-old mainland girl was admitted to hospital with multiple injuries. Doctors said the case strongly resembled the long-outlawed practice of *mui tsai*, in which rich

Hong Kong families would acquire a child servant directly from poor parents or by kidnapping."[1]

In 2008, a news item about an event on the Chinese Mainland, captioned, "Nine boys rescued from trafficking ring",[2] echoes the cases of child trafficking in Hong Kong in the 1880s among these *China Mail* court case reports.[3]

In another story from 2008, about a couple who had come to Hong Kong from the Mainland twenty years previously, a husband reportedly told police that his wife, who had threatened to commit suicide, had been unhappy, "After con artists cheated her out of HK$300,000 in a blessing scam in September". This story also would not have been out of place in *The China Mail* of the 1880s.[4]

In this case it is a "new" arrival, who fell victim to a scam. A letter-writer to the *South China Morning Post*, Elaine Chan of North Point identified a different group — the elderly — as likely victims. She wrote, "Mainly mainlanders come here as tourists but some aim to 'earn' money, using their sophisticated skills to deceive Hong Kong residents, especially the elderly. Many of the elderly fall victim to con artists because of their traditional thinking. The old people really believe the fraudsters can bring blessings for their families and therefore are willing to hand over large sums of money".[5]

The Secretary for Security, Ambrose Lee Siu-kwong, is quoted on this topic in the *South China Morning Post* in January 2007. As reported, he said that, "Many street scams were old ruses and most fell into three categories: scam artists promising to provide 'blessings' for a fee, 'borrowing' mobile phones and pretending to have dropped money on the

---

[1] SCMP, 9 December 2006, p. 1, cc. 1-7. See CC Nos 20. 93, 235, 238 and CC 37.
[2] SCMP, 4 January 2008.
[3] See CC Nos 20, 93, 235, 238 and CC 37.
[4] Clifford Lo, "Train fare cheat, 61, threatens death leap", SCMP, 4 January 2008.
[5] SCMP, 12 January 2007, p. C2, c. 5.

floor."[6] — It seems from the court cases reported in the present publication that there was more variety in nineteenth-century street scams.

In the early 1880s, it might be a rural visitor from the Chinese Mainland who might fall victim to a Hong Kong urban sharper. Court Case 180 ("A Goose Plucked") speaks of a "poor simpleton", a "farmer fool", who fell for a trick. But today in the early 2000s, it can be even relatively sophisticated international visitors from overseas, or expatriate residents, who are taken in, while Chinese residents "know the score". Clifford Lo's article, "Fake monks scam alms from unwary expats", quotes a police comment that, "local residents are aware of the scam and don't give them [the fake monks] money."[7]

These reports of a Hong Kong Magistrate's Court Cases from the early 1880s can enrich our understanding of human social relations in other places and other times as well as in Hong Kong at this specific period, not only in similar contexts, but — with some application of lateral thinking — in any society at all. For example, when traveling in Malaysia in 2006, the present writer read an article, "Bogus exorcist jailed, caned for molesting woman" in *The Straits Times*.[8] The simplicity of the woman who was duped was very reminiscent of some of the people we come across in these Hong Kong court cases from a century and a quarter ago.

---

[6] Robin Kwong, "Most scam artists come from the mainland", SCMP, 11 January 2007, p. C3, c. 7.
[7] SCMP, 8 March 2008, City, C3.
[8] *The Straits Times*, 16 May 2006, p. H2.

What is the specific contribution to Hong Kong studies, including studies of Hong Kong society and the Hong Kong legal and penal system, of the source material contained in, "The Complete Court Cases of Magistrate Frederick Stewart, as Reported in *The China Mail*, July 1881 to March 1882"?

There is a particular reason why information about the legal and penal system during the Governorship of John Pope Hennessy is both interesting and useful as an aid to study. He was a Governor who was controversially active in this sphere. So inflamed did public opinion become among "foreign residents", as a result of his early initiatives, that, on Monday, 7 October 1878 (a mere half year after Hennessy arrived in Hong Kong in April 1877), a meeting was called, "to consider the present state of insecurity of life and property in the Colony, and to pass such resolutions as may be deemed advisable".[9] (Frederick Stewart was absent on his only home leave at the time.) The event made such a stir that, three years later, *The China Mail* made a point of reminding its readers of this event.[10]

Hennessy certainly introduced some changes. Some were perceived by some members of the community as wantonly liberal. One of these was the abolition of public flogging. (The *China Mail* of 3 March 1882 reports that, "The much-abused and lately neglected whipping post near the Harbour Master's Office is now in course of removal."[11])

In apparent contradiction, other changes evidently made for greater strictness. For example, in 1879, Hennessy commenced a system of increased strictness of gaol discipline. The system of deportation was resumed, and a rule was made that all old offenders should be tried in the Supreme Court, where they might receive sentences

---

[9] CM, 27 September 1878, p. 3, c. 3.

[10] CM, Friday, 7 October 1881, p. 2, c. 6.

[11] CM, p. 3, c. 3.

commensurate with habitual indulgence in crime, instead of the frequent short sentences inflicted by the Police Magistrates.[12]

The more information that can become current, which can throw light on the truth or otherwise of statements made by Governor John Pope Hennessy and in relation to Governor John Pope Hennessy by contemporaries, as well as by later writers necessarily relying on what data is available to them, the more accurate our discussions of nineteenth-century Hong Kong, including its legal history, will be.

Between the lines of the following extract from the *China Mail* Report of a Legislative Council meeting, we receive a taste of how the Governor himself represented some of his interventions.

Of Ordinance No. 3 of 1881, the Penal Laws Amendment Ordinance, we find this:

> "It repeals or amends 10 ordinances, some of them of exceptional severity and particularly directed against one race only. The ordinances they have passed were part of a policy which the Royal prerogative enabled him to enforce for some years past in spite of some little local criticism. Henceforth it will be illegal to brand[13] any criminals in this colony and it will also be illegal to punish by public flogging, and it will not allow of flogging in Hong Kong except for such offenses as are punished by flogging in England. This impolitic system abolished by the Queen and Legislature of this Colony had actually manufactured a criminal population and increase of crime. This abolition has

---

[12] E. J. Eitel, *Europe in China: the History of Hong Kong, from the beginning to the year 1882*, Hong Kong, Oxford University Press, 1983 (first published by Kelly and Walsh, Ltd., 1895), p. 545. Referred to below as, "E. J. Eitel, *Europe in China*".

[13] For details about branding (in effect, tattooing), see *A Magistrate's Court in Nineeenth Century Hong Kong*, Ed. Gillian Bickley, Proverse Hong Kong, 2005, pp. 26, 36, 37, 60-61, 62, 66, 67, 68, 70, 72, 138. Referred to after this as, "*A Magistrate's Court in 19th Century Hong Kong*".

been followed by a decrease of crime, and the returns now bear witness to the increased security of life and property in Hong Kong. . . . statistics . . . Another class of crime . . . kidnapping. With reference to that crime the law instructed him to approve in his name a Chinese Society called the Po Leung Kuk, which acting in concert with the Captain Superintendent of Police had done much to stamp it out. The consequence was that the smallest number of cases of kidnapping that had occurred in the four years he had already referred to occurred in 1881. He found that the change was owing to the operation of the Society and the skill and energy of the Police Force and the effect of giving proper sentences when they were brought before the Court. . . ."[14]

Seventeen days later, an editorial in the same newspaper responded, matching rhetoric with rhetoric:

"The disregard of the evil consequences to society that must ensue from laxity of prison discipline, in this Colony, does not give Sir John Pope Hennessy the slightest concern. His "popularity" has been purchased at rather an expensive cost to the community of Hong Kong. His exceptional action with reference to the local gaol reflects on his predecessors in office — directly charging them with gross neglect of duty, and such inhumane tendency as to totally incapacitate them from further administrative employment under the Crown. On public grounds, it would be better to err on the side of discipline than that of undue leniency. We all know practically, in what Governor Hennessy's over-indulgence of

---

[14] Proceedings of the Legislative Council, CM, 7 February 1882, p. 2, c. 7 - p. 3, cc. 1 - 3.

prisoners has resulted — both to himself and the Colony. He has found favour with those sensationalists called "horror-mongers" at home, and his reputation bids fair in consequence, to rank prominently among the humanitarians of the day! But what of Hong Kong? Its prisoners grow fat and insolent; and rampant crime, fostered by a benign Government, is perpetrated with greater vigour than ever. The evil-doers escaping from punishment reduces a certain class of convictions, and the immunity from detection, escape from apprehension, is wonderfully utilised by Governor Hennessy to his own credit — in first increasing the efficiency of the local Police Force, and next in the enhanced moral tone of the Chinese population engendered from his humane views and superior treatment! [15] His Excellency is certainly clever. We have always given him credit for abilities, although some of them are of a very negative order. With some folks figures may be made to provide anything; but with others they are worthless unless supported by facts. Stern reality is the rock on which Sir John will split — his assertions wreck; and, in the meanwhile, we have to accept the inevitable — the injurious consequences arising from the unscrupulous exercise of power by one vested with a little brief authority, who maintains, fully, the unenviable reputation acquired elsewhere."[16]

---

[15] Indirectly, the writer is stating that it is by not punishing criminals that the statistics of crime give the false impression that crime has dropped, together with the equally false impression (to those who do not know the reality), of increased efficiency by the Police Force. The writer's points are that crime has not been reduced, although the punishment of crime has become less; and that any increased efficiency of the Police Force is not proved by these particular statistics.

[16] "Editorial Notes", CM, 24 February 1882, p. 3, c. 2.

Writing as published in 1895, E. J. Eitel repeats these views even more directly.[17] — It is clear that we need as much information as possible and as much careful analysis of that information as possible, in order to discuss the events of Governor John Pope Hennessy's term of office and its ramifications.

Additionally important as a further justification of the value of the source materials presented in *The Complete Court Cases*, is the appeal to facts as a true test of the Governor's statements, made in the *China Mail* editorial just quoted. These court case reports provide an abundance of facts, including facts about the implementation of the legal and penal system during one concentrated period within Pope-Hennessy's governorship, July 1881 to March 1882.

Contemporaries have put on record their observation that the Governor was active in suppressing information about the work of the Police. E. J. Eitel — often described as the first chronicler (if not historian) of Hong Kong under British administration — has asserted that the annual reports of the Superintendent of Police for the four years 1878-1881 were suppressed and for them were substituted, by order of the Governor, bare statistics of crimes committed. Eitel comments also that the statistics show increases of serious crimes. In 1877, the increase was 12.86% and in 1878 it was 32.31 per cent. In 1879, there was a decrease of 8.19 per cent, and in 1880 of 14.43 per cent. In 1881, however, there was a fresh increase of serious crimes, amounting to 13.55 per cent.[18]

The present writer has found no reason to object to these statements or to the supposition that the Governor's reasons for changing the previous practice included at least the desire to be as free as possible to interpret any published facts in ways that suited his political advantage. Indeed, the research for this book revealed another change in the release of

---

[17] E. J. Eitel, *Europe in China*, pp. 541-542.

[18] E. J. Eitel, *Europe in China*, p. 545.

information. "The Criminal Calendar", published in the *Hong Kong Government Gazette*, monthly, in 1881 and up to April 1882, ceased to be published for the remainder of 1882. Because of this, the results of some of the cases which Frederick Stewart referred to the Supreme Court have been impossible to trace, a consequence that doubtless had an impact on contemporaries also. Is this another example of a deliberate suppression of information?

Even where information was not actively suppressed, published Government statistics of the time were noticed by contemporaries as imperfectly complete. In March 1882, *The China Mail* made the following sharp criticism on Government returns.

> In the *Gazette* of last Saturday is a return of serious and minor offences committed during the year 1881[19] from which there seems [*sic*] to be some omissions. Under the heading of piracy there are no cases reported in the months of August, or September, although on the 25th of August a case was opened before Mr Wodehouse, and continued at intervals up till the 10th of September, when the three men charged were committed to gaol pending the Governor's orders. There is nothing whatever to show what has become of these men, whether they are still in gaol or whether they had been discharged. This peculiar way of making up returns is calculated to throw doubt on anything coming from the same source.[20]

The detailed and specific information, provided by the present edition of newspaper reports of court cases in Hong Kong in the early 1880s, can certainly supplement such published material even from a

---

[19] The return referred to can be found in HKGG, 11 March 1882, p. 259. The particular omission which the *China Mail* gives as an example can clearly be seen.

[20] "Local and General", CM, 16 March 1882, p. 2, c. 7.

governmental and therefore supposedly authoritative source.

Historians often prefer and may indeed, in some circumstances, have no choice but to use data which has previously been analysed and summarised. However, when available, detailed and specific information is valuable as a check on the accuracy of such analyses and summaries, whether these have been obtained from specific doubtful sources, or in general.

Other original sources are also of course capable of misleading, including newspaper commentary and reporting, particularly when statements from an apparently authoritative source are reproduced without any correction. Particularly relevant to any discussion of Hong Kong crime and the Hong Kong penal system at this period is the following comment by *The China Mail* relating to a speech by Governor John Pope Hennessy about "the crime and penal system of Hong Kong", which had been reported in *The Daily Press*.

> "Some of the errors into which H. E. Governor Hennessy so frequently falls are inexplicable, while others are probably caused by a too eager desire "to find it so." The misconceptions and misrepresentations of which he is the author usually tend to accomplish a certain amount of harm to some one; but now and again a lunge into inaccuracy is taken when apparently no such desire exists. In case, however, any future chronicler of events should attempt to construct a history out of the materials supplied in Governor Hennessy's public utterances, it is our duty as journalists to note the unreliability of some of his data." [21]

The China Mail makes the point that this particular speech that it objected to had not been published in

---

[21] CM, 9 June 1881, pp. 2-3?

The Hong Kong Government Gazette (which would have exposed it to informed discussion).

This example demonstrates the care with which even contemporary sources need to be addressed. Picking a single point or fact, here or there, can be highly unreliable.

What is the specific contribution of this edition of, "The Complete Court Cases of Magistrate Frederick Stewart, as Reported in *The China Mail*, July 1881 to March 1882"?

The mere location, obtaining of working copies, filing, accurate transcription and editing of these rare and often barely legible source materials is a task which is more expensive in time, skill and financial expense than anyone who has not done similar work can even begin to imagine. Simply presenting the material in clean, readable and reliable text is a valuable contribution on its own. But there are additional features provided by the editing.

Among the 726 Reports, twenty-nine cases are reported more than once, in continuing hearings; some as many as four or five times.[22] One case was heard over a period of four months and ten were heard over a period of two months. The identification of these groups of reports, relating to one case but where personal and place names may appear in very different spellings, lays the ground for easier analysis of this material, which it is hoped will be useful to others.

Similarly, among the 682 cases,[23] thirty-two were referred to the Criminal Sessions for trial. Almost all have been successfully traced in the

---

[22] See the Table below, "Court Cases heard by Frederick Stewart and Reported more than once in *The China Mail*".

[23] Among the 726 Reports, twenty-nine cases are reported on more than once, accounting, between them, for a total of seventy-three reports. (See the Table below, "Court Cases heard by Frederick Stewart and Reported more than once in *The China Mail*".) The total number of cases is thus 682 cases.

monthly Criminal Calendars and the verdicts and sentences found there are recorded in the notes. In a few cases also, a newspaper report of the Criminal Sessions trial is transcribed in a note as supplementary material. This additional material in particular, together with this supplementary material, increases the value of *The Complete Court Cases* for those who have a particular interest in the Hong Kong legal system, whether at this specific period or comparatively over time.

Hong Kong Ordinances
Certain Ordinances are mentioned within the Reports. The text of the Ordinance has been found and then any part, relevant to the cases reported here, has been identified and (usually) quoted, either in the notes, or in a separate discussion.

There is a new and useful resource, not available when the present writer began work in this area. This is, "The Historical Laws of Hong Kong Online", described on a University of Hong Kong Library website as, "a full-text image database providing access to past revised editions of Hong Kong Laws". As the same source states, "The database comprises a total of six consolidations of the laws of Hong Kong: 1890, 1901, 1912, 1923, 1937, 1950, and 1964 (last updated to 1989)."

This online resource is very useful indeed, providing access to rare materials of otherwise very limited accessibility. It is most valuable if used in addition to, and not in place of, a careful search of the Ordinances as they first appear, from late 1853, in *The Hong Kong Government Gazette*. The University of Hong Kong Libraries has made the *Gazettes* also accessible online as part of "Hong Kong Government Reports Online (1853-1941)"; and again a parallel physical search of the complete originals is recommended.

A significant advantage to the collected retrospective printed editions of the Ordinances (and of the online digitised versions of these also therefore) is that they direct readers to the history of each Ordinance, indicating the dates when parts or the whole of an Ordinance were repealed. (The points should not be taken as totally accurate, however, and should always be checked.) The *Hong Kong Government Gazettes* themselves also quite often reprint Ordinances many years after their first passage and, when they do so, often give an account of any subsequent amendment or repeal.

As mentioned, the first *Hong Kong Government Gazette* appeared in the late 1853. Before this date, we can search for the original text of Ordinances in the Hong Kong Government Blue Books.

"The Historical Laws of Hong Kong Online" is a compilation of six consolidations of the laws of Hong Kong, and one downside is that it inevitably reproduces any errors or omissions in these previous consolidations.

Other limitations are indicated by the University of Hong Kong Libraries website. Under the heading, "Data provenance and limitations", the website explains that, "The text source of this database is the print copies of the revised editions of Hong Kong laws held in the Lui Che Woo Law Library of the University Libraries. All are original copies except v. 2 of 1904 edition, and v. 1 and v. 3 of 1923 edition, which are reprographic copies. Image capture and text creation were done by scanning and OCR (Optical Character Recognition)." It continues:

> "Except for the 1964 edition, the physical condition of some of the earlier revised editions did not lend themselves well to the scanning and OCR process. Because of its dated nature, we did not work from perfect original documents. The changes in paper colour, from a white to a yellowed or foxed background made it sometimes difficult for text to be accurately created by OCR. All editions except the 1964 were bound in book format. Scanning was painstakingly done, page by page without breaking these

bindings. This together with the brittle
condition of some of them has resulted in
some text occasionally blocked off in the
gutter area."

Both the original *Hong Kong Government Gazettes*
and working copies made of them by various
despoitories or individuals for private study, have
similar imperfections; but, to the extent that it is the
originals which are being worked from, less (or
different) material may be illegible or lost.

Some of the original sources have manuscript notes,
which have been made by informed readers or
official users of the materials. This manuscript
material is most helpful as an additional source. The
University of Hong Kong website states that this
additional material was deliberately omitted:

"As laws were amended, updated or repealed,
the original printed text may include
marginalia, hand-written annotations or
typewritten slips pasted in. These have been
toned down or excluded as much as possible
during scanning in order to capture the
original printed text as it was first
published."

Fortunately, quite of bit of manuscript material still
remains in the online material in their digital
databases.

Both the original sources and the online
resources are useful and the best results can be
achieved from using all of them.

Locating and identifying the relevant Ordinances

The *Hong Kong Government Gazettes* sometimes
includes Indices, which in some cases can help
readers to identify the subject content of various
Ordinances. The University of Hong Kong website
also includes useful Indices. Again these two sources
should be used alongside the search possibilities of
the online databases in their present form. In due

course, an online keyword search may be available,[24] and this hopefully will make it very much easier to identify the relevant Ordinances than any of the presently available aids.

The Ordinances and their application in policy and in the magistrate's court

The documentation of the ordinances given in the present publication, using all the above resources, provides the opportunity to compare the text of the ordinances mentioned in the Court Case Reports presented here, with the application of the ordinances in court.

Sentencing

Apart from this, the present publication makes it possible to compare the sentencing among different cases, tried under the same Ordinance or group of Ordinances. For example, seven reports concern cases tried under "The Market Ordinance"[25] (CCs 83, 123, 134, 135, 226, 227 and 261). In five cases, the sentence is explicitly stated to be a one dollar fine, or, failing that, four days in gaol. In one case the penalty was "similar" and in another it was, "nominal" — that is, probably also a one dollar fine. The Table of the very much larger number of cases, "Showing gambling and gambling related cases, the numbers involved, the results of the cases, the sentences

---

[24] The University of Hong Kong online commentary on the *Historical Laws of Hong Kong Online* states, "The present first release of the Historical Laws of Hong Kong Online database allows searching for text in these particular field(s) only: Chapter or Ordinance Number, Chapter or Ordinance Title, and Edition. With further enhancement, it is expected that the second release will incorporate full text keyword search of all Chapters or Ordinances."

[25] There is a "Markets [*sic*] Ordinance 1867", No. 5 of 1867. (HKGG, 25 May 1867, pp. 179-180.)
Specific offences under "The Market Ordinance", which are recorded in these Reports, include: selling on the street salt fish (CC 134), blood (CC 227), congee (CC 227) and worms (CC 261).

given", provides the basis for a similar comparison, briefly included in the discussion of this table below, which additionally includes quotations from the relevant ordinances. The many cases where a defendant was sentenced as a "Rogue and Vagabond" make it possible to explore how one particular magistrate used the discretion magistrates were given under the relevant Ordinances and which E. J. Eitel called to the attention of Governor Pope Hennessy in a paper, dated 22 April 1880.[26] A brief comment on the sentencing in relation to offences against the "Opium Ordinance", made below in discussing these cases,[27] provides some response to Eitel's implicit assertion that too much discretion was given to Police Magistrates in Hong Kong. The mass of material published here can be mined for useful analyses of other groups of interesting data.

Confirming and extending our picture of Nineteenth Century Hong Kong

The testimony of the Market Ordinance cases and the gambling and gambling-related cases is consistent with what has previously been described about life and the law in Hong Kong during the early period of British administration, but adding detail, life and emotion. In contrast, the twenty or so cases concerning offences against "The Opium Ordinance"[28] add substance to the existing discussion. Like the Market Ordinance cases, the opium cases have also been analysed in some detail. The discussion, "Cases brought for alleged Offences against 'the Opium Ordinance', their results, the sentences given and notes on the relevant legislation",

---

[26] "Treatment of Paupers in Hong Kong", 22 April 1880, in HKGG, 9 June 1880, pp. 466-473.
[27] "Cases brought for alleged Offences against 'The Excise Ordinance (Opium) 1858-1879, Amendment Ordinance 1879': their results, the sentences given and notes on the relevant legislation."
[28] The Excise Ordinance (Opium) 1858-1879, Amendment Ordinance 1879.

together with the Appendix, "The Excise Ordinance (Opium) 1858-1879, Amendment Ordinance 1879: Selections to explain the opium and opium-related cases before Frederick Stewart, July 1881 to March 1882", contains a level of detail with which the general student of Hong Kong history or even the general student of the history of opium and opium use itself may not yet be entirely familiar, as some of the information seems not to have been discussed in recent times.

It is hoped that the results of these analyses as presented here will be found valuable in themselves and that they will also suggest ways in which others may use this data.

Individuals

As for the documentation of the lives of individuals, these Court Case Reports provide the names of hundreds of individuals which might otherwise never and certainly not easily be found. For example, at this period, even in the Index to Establishments published in the annual Hong Kong Blue Book issued by the Hong Kong Government and yearly sent to the Colonial Office in London, no Police Constable or Police Sergeant is named, only those of Inspectorial rank or above. But many Police Sergeants and Police Constables (including Indian, Chinese as well as European members of these ranks) are named in these Reports. We also find the names of members of "the detective force", informers, Po Leung Kuk detectives, district watchmen and watchmen in private employment. There is a clear benefit for those interested in the history of the Hong Kong Police Force, the history of security (including private security) and of other related occupations and groups in Hong Kong. It is through gathering together these reports that a revision can be suggested of the existing record, painstakingly compiled by the late admired Kevin Sinclair, of the members of the Hong Kong Police Force, killed during the performance of their duty. [29] Easur Singh, Constable No. 693, murdered in the execution of his duty on 27 November 1881, should appear as the second on the "Roll of Honour", after PC Lall Khan (August 1863) and before PC Ameer Singh (November 1884). [30] Kevin Sinclair points out, in his book, that it was not possible to list all the names that doubtless should appear on this Roll of Honour, because it was very difficult to research them. I am sure he would have been pleased to know of this addition.

Among the other names, perhaps most refer to individuals from very humble spheres, whom we would not expect to find documented anywhere else at all. Indeed, Jung-Fang Tsai has commented on the scarcity of scholarly publications on Hong Kong working people during the period 1842-1913. (*Hong Kong in Chinese History: Community and Social Unrest in the British Colony, 1842-1913,* New York, Columbia University Press, 1993, p. 103.) But who knows? To European contemporaries in Hong Kong, and until his trial in June 1886, Li Afan was simply a detective in the Hong Kong Police Force. But in the event, he proved to be the head of the Triad Society and had a violent and spectacular end on the Chinese Mainland. (See *A Magistrate's Court in Nineteenth Century Hong Kong*, pp. 219-222.) Maybe there are other surprises in store as to the identity of others who appeared in Magistrate Frederick Stewart's Court and who, at the moment, appear to be obscure and private individuals. If future studies identify and focus on these, this court case material will provide useful additional information to fill in the picture of their lives too.

---

[29] Kevin Sinclair and Nelson Ng Kwok-cheung, *Asia's Finest Marches On: Policing Hong Kong from 1841 into the 21st century*, Hong Kong, Kevin Sinclair Associates Limited, 1997, p. 227. (Earlier version, Kevin Sinclair, *Asia's Finest*, Hong Kong, Unicorn, 1983.)

[30] See *A Magistrate's Court in 19th Century Hong Kong*, p. 474, note 563.

Family and Social Life

Although many of these reports concern those who apparently had no family life in Hong Kong (a common situation at the time, doubtless among the causes of at least a proportion of the offences that occurred), the testimony of witnesses in certain cases includes a clear description of family life, which gives valuable and interesting insight into how people lived with their families in Hong Kong, and this is, as far as the present writer's knowledge goes, unique.[31]

The law, policing and practice of the courts. Behaviour and habits of the people.

The testimony of these court case reports extends our knowledge and understanding of Hong Kong law, policing and the practice of the courts in nineteenth century Hong Kong and about the behaviour and habits of various types of people. Some of the groups of cases on a particular subject have been analysed by means of extracting some of the data from each court case report to construct a Table, and then describing and considering the results.

The Table, "Showing gambling and gambling related cases, the numbers involved, the results of the cases, and the sentences given", and the discussion, "Gamblers' encounters with the police and the magistrate's court, forms of gambling, gambling venues and equipment: information derived from the gambling and gambling-related cases heard before Frederick Stewart, July 1881 to March 1882. With quotations from relevant ordinances", provide a concrete picture of the Hong Kong gambling scene then: — where and at what time of day and night people gambled, what games they played, what gaming equipment they used, what emotions were aroused, what encounters there were between gamblers and the law and some details of how the law was applied in practice.

---

[31] See e.g. CC 485.

Similarly, the discussion, "Cases brought for alleged Offences against 'the Opium Ordinance', their results, the sentences given and notes on the relevant legislation", which relies on both a Table (not included) [32] and the Appendix, "The Excise Ordinance (Opium) 1858-1879, Amendment Ordinance 1879: Selections to explain the opium and opium-related cases before Frederick Stewart, July 1881 to March 1882", gives a different focus on the preparation, sale and use of opium in Hong Kong at a time after the opium trade had been legalized, as well as explaining some details of the relevant law and its application. It was a world of informers, Excise Officers, search warrants and central locations where people could be seen, "laying about smoking opium".[33] Nowhere among these court case reports is there any mention of the deleterious effects of the habit.[34]

---

[32] The Table created as a step towards this analysis is not included in the present publication, as it is very lengthy.

[33] CC 371.

[34] Reading the *Hong Kong Government Gazettes*, as well as the observations of historians, it seems that the Hong Kong administration was mainly concerned with the use of the opium trade as a means of raising revenue and it seems that the "Opium Farm" and the "Spirit Farm" are spoken of in similar terms. (See for example, a Bill to establish a Spirit Farm, HKGG, 11 June 1879, pp. 305-330.)

Regulations for constructing opium furnaces and boiling houses were published by the Government. (See e.g. HKGN No. 87, which refers to Sections II and III of Ordinance No. 2 of 1858. -- HKGG, 31 July 1869, p. 335.)

More than this, with effect from 21 February 1883, a Public Factory at Sai On Lane, Saiyingpun, was designated as the place where all opium had to be boiled and prepared. (HKGN No. 67, dated 21 February 1883, signed by "Frederick Stewart, Acting Colonial Secretary", HKGG, 21 February 1883, p.122.) However, HKGN No. 67 of 1883 also states, "Special arrangements will be made for persons wishing to boil large quantities, so as to enable them to boil in their own premises under Government supervision." All these operations would be carried out by proper persons, authorized by licence from the Governor in Council. Such persons could boil and prepare opium, and sell and retail opium so boiled and prepared, with effect from 1 March 1883.

The tables, "The 'Light and Pass' Rules in Frederick
Stewart's Court, 1881-1882" and "Sentences to the
Stocks (or Cangue) in Frederick Stewart's Court,
1881-1882", which formed the basis for discussions
in *A Magistrate's Court in Nineteenth Century Hong
Kong*, are also included in the present publication,
with some additional data.

**How representative of the whole are the cases
heard by Frederick Stewart as recorded in *The
Complete Court Cases of Magistrate Frederick
Stewart as Reported in "The China Mail", July
1881 to March 1882*?**

In answer to this question, we may state as follows.
The cases recorded in *The Complete Court Cases of
Magistrate Frederick Stewart as Reported in "The
China Mail", July 1881 to March 1882*, represent a
13.01% sampling by *The China Mail* from the whole
number of cases heard in the two concurrent Police
Magistrates' Courts during that period. The sampling
was most probably based on a variety of constraints,
including the time the *China Mail* reporter was able
to be present in court, the timing of the hearing, the

HKGN No. 67 of 1883 also states, "Sealed tenders will
be received up to the 27th instant [February 1883], at noon, for
the farming of opium Dross within the Colony."
 The "Conditions made by the Governor in Council,
under the provision of the Excise Ordinances (Opium), 1858-
1879", which follow HKGN No. 67 of 1883, are carefully
composed in detail, so as to control these and other related
activities. It may not be too fanciful to see in them (as well,
perhaps, as in the earlier, "Supplementary Conditions made by
the Governor in Council, to which Licenses granted under the
Excise Ordinances (Opium), 1858-1879, are to be subject",
which were passed by the Executive Council on 27 April 1882
and published in the *Hong Kong Government Gazette* on 13 May
1882 (HKGG, 13 May 1882, pp. 475-476) the careful hand of
Frederick Stewart, informed by his recent experience sitting as
Magistrate in the Police Magistrate's Court and now again (as
from the end of March 1882) occupying the position of Acting
Colonial Secretary. (See "Police Intelligence", CM, 28 March
1882, p. 2, cc. 6, 7; p. 3, c. 1. See also *A Magistrate's Court in
19th Century Hong Kong*, p. 34.)

number of column inches available and competing stories in any single issue of the newspaper, as well as perceived intrinsic interest to readers. To the extent that Frederick Stewart, with his competence in Cantonese, may have heard quite a number of the proceedings at least partly in Cantonese, this also could have had an impact on the cases reported in *The China Mail*. The reporter assigned to court-reporting duties on any particular day may or may not have had the language ability to understand some of the cases heard in Stewart's court and may have selected the cases to attend and report with this constraint in mind. As for the thirty-two cases sent to the Supreme Court by Magistrate Frederick Stewart, these represent an 18.6% sampling from the whole number of cases, sent from the Police Magistrates' Court to the Supreme Court in these years.

Taken together, the nature and extent of these samples suggest how far the cases recorded in *The Complete Court Cases of Magistrate Frederick Stewart as Reported in "The China Mail", July 1881 to March 1882*, may be representative of the whole. [35]

---

[35] In 1881, the total number of cases, "brought under cognizance at the Police Magistrates' Court", was 8,203, of which 240 (2.92%) were sent before the Supreme Court. In 1882, the total number of cases was 7,567, of which 276 (3.64%) were sent before the Supreme Court. ("Abstract of Cases brought under Cognizance at the Police Magistrates' Court during a period of Ten Years, from 1st January 1875, to 31st December, 1882, inclusive", HKGG, 7 April 1883, p. 315.)
Of the 15,770 cases heard in the Magistrates' Court in the entire years 1881 and 1882 taken as a whole, the 684 cases — as mentioned elsewhere in the present publication, some of the cases are reported twice and others up to five times in *The China Mail* — reported in *The Complete Court Cases of Magistrate Frederick Stewart as Reported in "The China Mail", July 1881 to March 1882*, are 4.33% of the whole. The thirty-two of these that were sent before the Supreme Court are 6.2% of the total of 516 cases that were sent before the Supreme Court in these two years.

The actual part of the two years 1881 and 1882, during which Stewart occupied his substantive position as magistrate was rather small: — the eight months from 26 July1881 to 29 March

Creating an archival image of Hong Kong

These reports create an intangible archive of a particular period in Hong Kong's past. Hong Kong has been well-served by accomplished photographers such as John Thomson (*Illustrations of China and its People, 1873-1874*) and by artists, illustrators and map-makers. Nevertheless, words are a useful additional source for storing the heritage of a place; for delaying the receding of memory as to who and what was here.

Who was Frederick Stewart, the Magistrate whose reported court cases are collected in this publication?

A detailed biography of Frederick Stewart appeared in 1997, the year when the sovereignty of Hong Kong was handed back to the Government of Mainland China, and readers are referred to this book. [36] However, the main points are these. Frederick Stewart (1836-1889) arrived in Hong Kong in 1862, to take up concurrent posts as the first Headmaster of

---

1882. These statistics are based on a monthly average derived from annual totals.

Another table, "Return of Serious and Minor Offences reported to have been committed during the Year . . . [N], with the Results of such Reports" (e.g. HKGG, 11 March 1882, p. 259) lists its data by month. However, it may not be possible, from this data, to reach reliable conclusions about the specific months when Stewart was sitting in court. As mentioned elsewhere in the present text, some of the cases were heard more than once. In fact, one case was heard over four months and ten cases were heard over two months. There is no indication of when a case is included in the statistics — the first time; the last time? — or indeed whether or not a case is included each time it is heard. Additionally, it is this very table for 1881, "Return of Serious and Minor Offences reported to have been committed during the Year 1881, with the Results of such Reports" (HKGG, 11 March 1882, p. 259), which gave rise to contemporary criticism for incompleteness at least.

[36] Gillian Bickley, *The Golden Needle: the Biography of Frederick Stewart (1836-1889)*, David C. Lam Institute for East-West Studies, Hong Kong Baptist University, 1997, pp. 232-235. Referred to after this as, *"The Golden Needle"*.

the Central School (now Queen's College) and Inspector of Schools. A few years later, he was appointed as the first Head of the Government Education Department. His work in education was recognised by contemporaries as extraordinarily important and successful and indeed they acknowledged him as, "The Founder of Hong Kong Government Education". But, following a period of friction with Governor John Pope Hennessy (during which the Colonial Office in London privately supported Stewart but publicly had to support the Queen's representative), Stewart resigned from the headship of this school, still important today and highly respected, to take up work in the substantive post of Police Magistrate.

During his term as substantive Police Magistrate, Frederick Stewart resumed another position he had previously held, that of Acting Colonial Secretary. In time, he accepted the substantive position of Registrar General and Protector of Chinese. In this position also, for a long period, he again acted as Colonial Secretary. Finally, he was appointed substantive Colonial Secretary (head of the Hong Kong Civil Service), remarkably the first person chosen for this post from among the permanent members of the Hong Kong Civil Service. In this position, he acted for short periods on several occasions as Administrator or Acting Governor of Hong Kong.

In spite of this range of important appointments, however, Frederick Stewart is mainly remembered today, for his work in Education, partly because so many former pupils of his own, or of the school at later periods, rose to prominence and gave distinguished service themselves in many different spheres. Most well known of these are Sir Robert Ho Tung, the first Eurasian resident of Hong Kong to be knighted by the British Crown, who attended the school during Stewart's peiod as Headmaster, and Sun Yat-sen, Father of the Chinese Republic, who attended the school while Frederick Stewart indeed still played a commanding role in Hong Kong education but when the headmaster of the renamed "Victoria College" (later renamed again "Queen's College") was George Bateson Wright.

Among contemporaries, Stewart was recognized for ability, courtesy, conscientiousness, efficiency and dedication to duty, as well as considerable modesty. He was considered to have a close understanding of the Chinese population and noted for his good skill in spoken Chinese. He was repeatedly recommended for the award of the CMG, a high honour; but this was never conferred. The reason was that Stewart, aware of and later, guessing, that a repeat recommendation would be made, wrote privately to London, requesting that the honour not be conferred. "I hope you will not think me either ungrateful to my Chief or a despiser of dignities which my betters value very highly. By no means: but such things are entirely unsuited and uncongenial to a man of my solitary way of living. My ambition is to be allowed to do my work and be left unknown to the World at large."[37]

On his death at the relatively young age of fifty-two, three weeks short of his fifty-third birthday, *The China Mail* wrote, "As an official, Dr Stewart was a model public servant. . . . he perhaps understood better than any public man who has ever served here, the relations which ought to subsist between the various races which compose our somewhat heterogeneous community."[38] As educator, registrar general and police magistrate, Frederick Stewart would have had continous daily face-to-face connection with this, "heterogeneous community". Studying his life in context is a good means of understanding the nature of Hong Kong society at this time and the attitudes of various groups within it.

---

[37] Quoted in *The Golden Needle*, pp. 232-235.
[38] Quoted in *The Golden Needle*, p. 256.

Why are the court cases of Frederick Stewart of particular value?

Frederick Stewart's service in court as acting and substantive Police Magistrate occupied two relatively short periods of time. He was Acting Police Magistrate and Coroner for the five months from 7 August 1876 to 3 January 1877, during the time when substantive Police Magistrate James Russell was Acting Attorney General. Stewart himself performed the duties of substantive Police Magistrate for the eight months from 26 July1881 to 29 March 1882. As is evident from the title of the present publication, it is the *China Mail* Reports of the court cases from this *second* period only which are transcribed, edited and commented on here.

To the extent that knowledge of the cases that Frederick Stewart heard throws additional light on a prominent and admired official, who has left little personal information behind, the cases have a biographical value. They also illuminate the interface and parallels between the establishment of a colonial education system and the introduction of colonial law. Frederick Stewart's earlier period as Police Magistrate (1876-1877) and his earlier period as Coroner ran parallel with part of his direct service within the sphere of Hong Kong Government Education (1862-1881). If a mere coincidence, it is a particularly provocative coincidence. But perhaps it was more than coincidence? — Similar skills and personality were required in all three of these areas of work, and in each of them Stewart's study and knowledge of Cantonese and Chinese customs were of well-recognised value. It may be that there was a general understanding of the mutual impact of education and law at this time. Certainly, it would be useful to explore the synergy between these two areas as well as contemporary attitudes towards their inter-relations. This court case material is useful for this purpose.

There is a more detailed discussion of the particular value of the court cases of Frederick

Stewart in "Magistrate Frederick Stewart", in *A Magistrate's Court in Nineteenth Century Hong Kong* (pp. 33-73).

It is appropriate to conclude the discussion here with a *China Mail* editorial published on the same day that Frederick Stewart served as Police Magistrate for the last time, 29 March 1882. This makes very clear one aspect of the relationship between the penal system and the education of youth, namely the need for reformatories to put on the right track those, who had either never known it or had strayed away from accepted paths.

> "The fact that a boy of fourteen years of age has been today sentenced to one-year's imprisonment and twelve strokes on the breech, suggests one or two remarks. As we have all along maintained, contrary to the utterances of Governor Hennessy, the punishment of flogging has not been removed from our local statute-book except in regard to enactments which had practically become inoperative, or had never come into force, — such, for instance, as mendicancy, refusal to aid at fires, being out without a pass, etc. While regretting, therefore, that occasion should have arisen for the exercise of severity on the part of Mr Justice Snowden, it is reassuring to find that certain powers still remain to the Bench with which to meet such cases. After the sentence was passed, the Crown Solicitor observed that there was no penitentiary in Hong Kong, which might be utilised for prisoners such as this youth appears to be. The Puisne judge remarked that it was a pity there was no institution to which the young offender could be consigned. This is a consideration which may by and by receive the careful attention of the Executive. In the meantime, there is no reason why the Gaol should not be so arranged that special accommodation be

given to such offenders; and had the separate system been carried out, or some other means been adopted by which the hardened criminals had been dealt with and disposed of, there would have been ample room for providing special cells for this class of offenders. As it is, all the talk in favour of separate systems and reformatories, and against more forcible repressive measures, has ended in nothing [as] the Gaol is now full, the separate system has not been carried out, and reformatory accommodation is exactly where it was five years ago."[39]

A month later, on 24 April 1882, Anthony Santos Spencer, a former pupil of Frederick Stewart's Hong Kong Government Central School for Boys, received a not dissimilar sentence: — twelve months with hard labour (three months for each of four counts); the first week and last month of imprisonment to be passed in solitary confinement. He was also to be "once privately whipped fifteen strokes with a rattan on the breach."

~~~~~~~

Background to the present publication, "The Complete Court Cases of Magistrate Frederick Stewart, as Reported in *The China Mail*, July 1881 to March 1882"

An initial survey of the court cases of Frederick Stewart was part of the eight-year period of research for the biography of Frederick Stewart, *The Golden Needle: the Biography of Frederick Stewart (1836-1889)*, which focuses mainly on Stewart's work in Hong Kong Government education. This was published by the David C. Lam Institute for East

---

[39] Editorial, CM, 29 March 1882, p. 2, c. 1.

West Studies, Hong Kong Baptist University, in 1997, shortly after the sovereignty of Hong Kong was returned to and resumed by China.

Shortly after this, the more than seven hundred newspaper reports of court cases, heard by magistrate Frederick Stewart during the period, 26 July 1881-29 March 1882, were gathered together, transcribed, edited and annotated in the unpublished typescript (ed. Gillian Bickley, 1998-1999), "Before Frederick Stewart, Esq: The Court Cases of Frederick Stewart, Police Magistrate, Hong Kong, July 1881-March 1882, as published in *The China Mail*".

This typescript was used by a group of scholars, writers and legal professionals for work leading to the publication of, *A Magistrate's Court in Nineteenth Century Hong Kong: Court in Time* (Proverse Hong Kong, May 2005). It incorporates information about a hundred or so selected cases, in transcriptions of about 120 newspaper reports.[40] As stated in *A Magistrate's Court*, the typescript was the contributors', "Main source for all commentary on Frederick Stewart's Court Cases, for references to cases and newspaper reports on cases, and for quotations from the reports in *The China Mail*".[41]

Both *The Golden Needle* and *A Magistrate's Court in Nineteenth Century Hong Kong: Court in Time* have been well received.

However, conscious of the value of these source materials, which provide considerable information and insight into nineteenth century Hong Kong as to both social conditions and legal practices, some scholars and commentators expressed the wish that all 700 or so reports of Frederick Stewart's Court Cases that appeared in *The China Mail* might be made available to them.

In response to this interest, the complete database of material has now been further edited and polished, and is now published as, *The Complete*

---

[40] *A Magistrate's Court in 19th Century Hong Kong*, p. 20.
[41] *A Magistrate's Court in 19th Century Hong Kong*, p. 435.

Court Cases of Frederick Stewart. Scholars and students who are interested in or studying Hong Kong history, particularly social and law-court history, have access, in this, to a full set of edited and indexed usable and valuable source materials, with references to the previously published book, *A Magistrate's Court in Nineteenth Century Hong Kong.*

~~~~~~~~~~

How do *A Magistrate's Court in Nineteenth Century Hong Kong* and *The Complete Court Cases of Frederick Stewart* complement each other?

Complementarity
The Complete Court Cases of Frederick Stewart stands on its own, but nevertheless the two publications complement each other. It is suggested that (before consulting other sources or reference material) readers first seek in one of these two publications answers to questions which might arise while reading or consulting the other, including, for example, questions of detail such as transcription accuracy and conventions, personal and place names, glossing of words, comment on linguistic usage, as well as details and more general commentary relating to social and location background.

Graphic material
Unlike in *A Magistrate's Court in Nineteenth Century Hong Kong*, there is no graphic material in *The Complete Court Cases of Frederick Stewart.* Reference is recommended to the archival photographs, cartoons and documents in the first edition of *A Magistrate's Court in Nineteenth Century Hong Kong.* These do more than illustrate, supplying helpful information for understanding the context of specific Court Cases as well as for placing in their social, historical, physical and political context, the Court Cases as a whole. Also portrayed

by images are named individuals, including both Magistrate Frederick Stewart himself and Ng Choy (1842-1922), also known as Wu Ting Fang, the first Chinese Barrister and Member of the Legislative Council in Hong Kong, who was as well, for a brief period, acting Magistrate. Photographs showing a group of Tung Wah Hospital officials, Chinese, European and Indian police posing with village leaders, young boys in a field, as well as unnamed Chinese merchants, shroffs, pedestrians, British soldiers and others, serve to populate and create visual images, complementing the written records published in *The Complete Court Cases of Frederick Stewart*. A map of the Hong Kong Central District of the time, where many of the events which led to court appearances took place, is particularly helpful.

Following a slightly updated E-book publication in 2006 (available through Mobipocket E-book base and elsewhere) of the first (print) edition of *A Magistrate's Court in Nineteenth Century Hong Kong* (2005), a second edition of *A Magistrate's Court in Nineteenth Century Hong Kong*, available from 2009 as an E-book, replaces the previously included archival photographs and maps. It includes more modern photographs, showing the heritage buildings which formerly held the Central Magistracy, the Central Police Station, Victoria Prison and the Supreme Court. The former Central Magistracy building, completed in 1914, replaced the Magistracy built in 1847, but on the same site where nineteenth-century magistrates heard their cases. Some of the complex of former Central Police Station buildings existed at the time of these Court Cases, and the Victoria prison buildings are certainly places where many of those named in these Court Case Reports spent "time". The photographs in this E-book publication make it also, therefore, a useful supplement to the CD publication of *The Complete Court Cases of Frederick Stewart*.

Indexing

Similar to the Index to *A Magistrate's Court in Nineteenth Century Hong Kong,* the Index to this complete set of over 700 cases lists the names of people, places, ships, companies, buildings, streets and street addresses, with many details of how individuals were described and identified.

~~~~~~~

Numbering and sequence of presentation of the Court Case Reports: 1

"Before Frederick Stewart, Esq: The Court Cases of Frederick Stewart, Police Magistrate, Hong Kong, July 1881-March 1882, as published in *The China Mail*" and *The Complete Court Cases of Frederick Stewart*

In the unpublished typescript, "Before Frederick Stewart, Esq: The Court Cases of Frederick Stewart, Police Magistrate, Hong Kong, July 1881-March 1882, as published in *The China Mail*", the court case reports transcribed are numbered in chronological sequence of publication, each report being given a number. Hence "Court Case 1" is the first in the sequence; "Court Case 50" the fiftieth. The text now presented in *The Complete Court Cases of Frederick Stewart* is an improved and expanded version of this unpublished typescript. It incorporates three Court Case reports (CCs 296, 300 and 388), which were added to the typescript, during the course of the contributors' work for *A Magistrate's Court in Nineteenth Century Hong Kong*, and some additional material, not then available to contributors, including Nos 255a, 635a, 674a, added at a late stage of work). Court Case No. 255a does not appear in the "Police Intelligence" column in *The China Mail*, but its content is closely related to the reporting of one of the cases (CC 251).

In *The Complete Court Cases of Frederick Stewart*, the reports are presented in sections, according to the months when the cases were heard, as shown below:

MONTH & YEAR	CASES	MONTH & YEAR	CASES
July 1881	1-27	December 1881	430-518
August 1881	28-104	January 1882	519-587
September 1881	105-235	February 1882	588-656; with 635a
October 1881	236-339, with 255a	March 1882	657-723, with 674a
November 1881	340-429		

Numbering and sequence of presentation of the Reports: 2

A Magistrate's Court in Nineteenth Century Hong Kong and *The Complete Court Cases of Frederick Stewart*

There are differences in the sequence of presentation of the reports between *A Magistrate's Court in Nineteenth Century Hong Kong* and *The Complete Court Cases of Frederick Stewart*. Nevertheless, all numbers for court case reports in *The Complete Court Cases of Frederick Stewart* are consistent with those used in the book, *A Magistrate's Court in Nineteenth Century Hong Kong*.

In *A Magistrate's Court in Nineteenth Century Hong Kong*, the reports of the hundred or so selected cases, which are included, are grouped, either according to the persons who appeared in court ("Sailors", "Soldiers", "Police", "Teachers and Men of the Cloth", "The Domestic Scene: Wives & Husbands, Amahs & Cooks, Widows & Protected Women, Sons & Adopted Daughters, Burglars",

"Prostitutes, their Associates and Clients", "Kidnappers and Traffickers in Human Beings", "Children and Students", "Gamblers and Informers") or according to the location where the originating events occurred ("Urban Life", "Rural Life" and "Pirates and Life at Sea").

Additionally, in *A Magistrate's Court in Nineteenth Century Hong Kong*, each case is treated as a whole. Where there is more than one report for a single case, the first and all subsequent reports of the same case (or once, of a related case)[42] are grouped together. This means that the second or later reports of the same case may appear in the book *before* reports for other cases, which may have been heard at earlier dates.

As in, "Before Frederick Stewart, Esq: The Court Cases of Frederick Stewart, Police Magistrate, Hong Kong, July 1881-March 1882, as published in *The China Mail*", the complete database of all the cases heard by Frederick Stewart and reported in *The China Mail*, presented in *The Complete Court Cases of Frederick Stewart*, strictly preserves the chronological order in which the reports of the cases originally appeared. As a result, some sense of what each day in court was like at this time for Frederick Stewart, and doubtless for his fellow police magistrate, H. E. Wodehouse, is conveyed.[43]

A few examples of narratives, references or discussion of these cases, found outside the "Police Intelligence" section of the newspaper, are also included in this sequence, and indicated as "Additional" and/or "Editorial".

In *A Magistrate's Court in Nineteenth Century Hong Kong* the 120 or so cases presented appear in the second part of the book. The first part of the book

---

[42] See "Mr Driscoll's Amah Again", in "Wives and Husbands, Amahs and Cooks, Widows and Protected Women, Sons and Adopted Daughters. Burglars. The Domestic Scene", below.
[43] For a brief list of 19th century Hong Kong Police Magistrates, please see, "*A Magistrate's Court in 19th Century Hong Kong*", p. 435, n. 3.

contains chapters by contributors, who use their varying professional experience, applied to their reading of the whole set of over 700 reports as made available to them,[44] to discuss aspects of these 700 plus reported cases and their significance. Students and practitioners will now have a similar opportunity to analyse the whole set of reports from their own perspective, as directed by their own interests and professionalism.

Structure of the Hong Kong legal system

For the general reader, it would be helpful, before reading the text of these Complete Court Case Reports, to know the broad structure of the Hong Kong legal system in the 1880s and, for the sake of comparison, at the time of writing. Readers are referred to the Contributors' essays in *A Magistrate's Court in Nineteenth Century Hong Kong* (Proverse Hong Kong, 2005), including those by barrister Christopher Coghlan, former Assistant Commissioner of Police Geoffrey Roper, and then Principal Magistrate Garry Tallentire, where many of the details found in these 1881-1882 court cases are highlighted, explained or compared with practices today.

As explained by Christopher Coghlan and Garry Tallentire, the Hong Kong Courts today, are: 1) The Magistrates' Courts, with their associated tribunals — Small Claims, Labour, Obscene Articles and Coroners' Court; 2) District Courts; 3) Court of First Instance; 4) Court of Appeal; and 5) Court of Final Appeal. Both now and in the past, all criminal cases begin in the Magistrates' Courts. Today, more serious cases are referred to the District Courts and the most serious — such as murder, rape, etc. — are referred

---

[44] The cases included in the second part of *A Magistrate's Court in 19th Century Hong Kong* were chosen independently and do not necessarily include any or all of those the distributors discuss in their chapters.

to the High Court.[45] In the 1880s, magistrates referred cases such as manslaughter, murder, theft of goods over a certain value, to the Criminal Sessions.

Specific details are also helpful. For example, Christopher Coghlan has commented on the fact that policemen acted as prosecutors in the magistrates' courts during the 1880s, and also made the interesting point that this practice had only very recently died out.[46] A contemporary article published in *The China Mail* confirms the former observation, stating, "We have always looked upon the Head of the Police, and his Inspectors, as Public Prosecutors, and generally found them to be ever ready to undertake such a duty."[47]

These cases also refer to informers, to the detective force and to detectives of the Women and Children's Protection Society, the Po Leung Kuk. They testify to the use of the poor box and the handing out as a reward to informers or members of the police force of part of the fines ("if paid"), all points discussed by the contributors.[48]

~~~~~~~~~~~

Note On the Text Of *The China Mail* Court Case Reports
Broadly speaking, the same editorial practices have been followed in *The Complete Court Cases of Magistrate Frederick Stewart as Reported in "The China Mail" July 1881 to March 1882* as in *A Magistrate's Court in Nineteenth Century Hong Kong.*

---

[45] Christopher Coghlan, "White Gloves and Patience", in, *"A Magistrate's Court in 19th Century Hong Kong*, p. 90.
[46] Christopher Coghlan, "White Gloves and Patience", in, *"A Magistrate's Court in 19th Century Hong Kong*, p. 92.
[47] This article is quoted at more length in, *A Magistrate's Court in 19th Century Hong Kong*, note 251.
[48] For example, Christopher Coghlan comments on the use of the Poor Box in, "White Gloves and Patience", in, *A Magistrate's Court in 19th Century Hong Kong*, p. 89.

Organisation and Sources of the Court Reports

All reports in the main text of *The Complete Court Cases of Magistrate Frederick Stewart as Reported in* "The China Mail" *July 1881 to March 1882* are, as the title implies, from *The China Mail*. In most of the relevant issues of *The China Mail* — perhaps all except one or two (e.g. CCs 360/366, CC 415)— the court cases reported were those heard earlier on the same day. The date given in the main text is that of the <u>day of the court proceedings</u> and the date of publication of the report in *The China Mail* is given in the notes. The two dates are, obviously, usually the same. On the rare occasions when the report appeared on a later day than the hearing, this is signalled. On the two occasions where there is an error in the date given in the newspaper,[49] this is commented on.

The date is given only once for each particular day; before the text of the first report of that day. The source reference is repeated (in a footnote) only when the details (e.g. page or column details) change. Occasional exceptions are when a switch is noted between a case being heard before one magistrate and a case being heard before two magistrates or *vice versa*.

In *The China Mail* at this time, the regular columns dealing with magistrates' court cases are captioned, "Police Intelligence", and usually appear on page three — rarely, page two — of the newspaper.

Occasionally, a report from the Police Courts was given greater prominence, either in the "Local and General" columns (on page two, page three, or pages two to three of *The China Mail*), or by being given its own caption, or from elsewhere in the newspaper.

With a very few exceptions, all the reports of cases reproduced here are from the "Police Intelligence" section of *The China Mail*.

---

[49]. Wednesday, 13 September 1881, erroneously given for 14 September 1881. (See "Larceny of Jewelry", Court Case 153.)

Occasionally, a comment is included from a different part of the newspaper. These two types of content are distinguished as follows. For the former, the date is given in capital letters; in the latter, in both upper and lower case letters. For the latter, the source, "The China Mail" is stated in the caption to the case in question.

Modifications of the Original Text

In his essay, "Reporting the Cases of Frederick Stewart", which appears in *A Magistrate's Court in Nineteenth Century Hong Kong*, Tim Hamlett explains how both the structure of the reports and the sprinkling of printing errors are a product of the pressures of time under which the reporter and then the type-setters, compositors and proof-readers worked. There are errors in syntax. There are the occasional seemingly implausible statements that the currency in which a fine was to be paid was sterling. There is the embedding of direct speech in reported speech with no use of quotation marks. Sometimes, complete lines are omitted. Errors in substance include phrases like, "Reserving his offence" for "reserving his defence",[50] and the use of the word, "deceased's", for "witness's".[51] Such errors as these have been corrected in the text given here, but for those who are interested in this topic, this is indicated in the notes.

In general, however, the body of the text of the original *China Mail* reports is here reproduced exactly. Minor printing errors (for example, "u"s for "n"s, and similar) and some larger ones (for example, imperfect layout) are corrected silently. Some punctuation has also been silently improved or corrected, for example: misuse of apostrophes; when a comma appears after the name of a person, even when no complement follows; and when sentences in the original are separated by a comma only. When

---

[50]. CC 131.
[51]. "The Tai Tam Attack", CM, 14 December 1881.

additional punctuation has been added, this may be indicated by square brackets.

Frequently, in the originals, reported speech is not given in inverted commas; and on occasion, these have been supplied, sometimes with, sometimes without indicating that this has been done.

In a few cases, errors in case have also been silently corrected, as well as obvious typographical errors such as spelling.

The names of ships are italicised or not, according to whether or not this is done in the original. On occasion, italics are added when the *China Mail* reports the questions and answers in the court-room in the same way as dialogue is laid out in the script of a play.

Abbreviations

Some abbreviations are spelt out in full. (For example "Geo." is spelt out as "George", "Aug" as "August", "P. C." as "Police Constable ", "Ins" or "Ins." as "Inspector", "Lieu." as "Lieutenant, "P. S." as "Police Sergeant", "Sergt." as "Sergeant"; "Co." as "Company", "No." as "Number" (except when used as part of an address), "cts" as "cents", "Oct." as October. Some numbers are given as words, rather than figures, and some money symbols are also given as words. When time is indicated, using the word, "o'clock", preceding figures are given in words. Some typographical features (for example, typeface, font, decorative lines) are modified. "Inst.", "Ult." and "Prox." are spelt out in full, and italicised.

Place and Personal Names

"Hongkong" is given as "Hong Kong". Otherwise, place names are given as in the originals, preserving the original variations. When a personal name is given in several versions, these variations also are preserved, and, after rechecking the often difficult originals for any misreading or misconception, if cross-identifications still seem inarguable, a note is given of all variations for each report or group of reports as follows: when any one of the variations appears for the first time, or — when several names have variations — in the first of a group of reports on the same case.

There are frequent variations in the spelling of personal names as between the Magistrate's Court Report(s) of a case and any Criminal Sessions report, whether in HKGG or in *The China Mail*. These differences have <u>not</u> been noted by the word "[sic]". The present editor has checked carefully to ensure that the same person is meant by these variations. (When any doubt remains, this is noted.) Different spellings as between different Magistrate's Court Reports of the same case have, however, often been indicated.

Comments on and Explanations of the Text

In addition to the comments and explanations given in the endnotes, some comments and explanations may be given in the main text, enclosed in square brackets. (These are always used in this book to indicate editorial intervention in those reports, which are reproduced, as well as within any other quotations.) On occasion, errors in the originals are corrected (as indicated by square brackets), and a note is given, stating how the original reads. For example, for one case, the main text is given as follows: "with [intent][52] to commit a felony on the 8th instant". And an endnote states, "The original reads "intend" [*sic* for "intent"]." Omissions or illegible portions of the originals may be supplied in square brackets, but with no further comment.

Layout of text

In Reports from the Supreme Court, the general caption to the reports of the day's cases may not have been followed immediately by the report transcribed

---

[52]. See, "Assault with Intent", CM, 10 December 1881, Court Case 454.

here. No indication is made of this in the present publication.

Some of the conventions used in the original reports need comment. When information is given in response to a question, the reporter does not necessarily indicate this. Sometimes, in describing the dialogue in court, he writes, "By [so-and-so]", meaning, "in reply to a question from the particular person named". Sometimes the reporter simply provides the answer to such a question, leaving it to the reader, first to deduce that a question had been asked, and also to work out what the question had been. An example of this is the report of the "Assault" on 22 October 1881, where we read, "He did not know defendants and none of them were concerned in a case recently in which complainant was fined fifty cents". [53] Another is, "Public Obstruction", reported on 16 November 1881. Doubtless in response to a question or an implied accusation, the Police Constable is reported as saying, "He never at any time kicked defendant's empty baskets about."[54]

---

[53]. "A Raid on Gamblers", CM, 22 October 1881, Court Case 311.
[54]. "Public Obstruction", CM, 16 November 1881, Court Case 387.

Editor's Note

[] means editorial comment, explanation, additional information, the supply of letters or words missing due to deficiencies in any of the following — the copy of the original newspaper seen, or the the working photocopy or hard-copy from microform made from the original newspaper.

📖 This symbol means that a transcription from *The China Mail* also appears in *A Magistrate's Court in Nineteenth Century Hong Kong.*

Index To Captions Of Court Case Reports

The following index of captions lists the reports in *The China Mail* of the court cases heard by Frederick Stewart in the same chronological sequence as that in which they were published.

In a few instances, a report is of a case which Frederick Stewart heard, sitting with his fellow Police Magistrate, H. E. Wodehouse.

The heading, **BEFORE FREDERICK STEWART, ESQ.**, is repeated at the head of the list for each of the months July 1881 to March 1882 and also whenever an intervening report concerns a case heard by both magistrates sitting together.

The symbol 📖 indicates that an edited and annotated transcription of the *China Mail* report of the case has previously been included in *A Magistrate's Court in Nineteenth Century Hong Kong: Court in Time* (Proverse, 2005).[55] The page number following this

---

[55] *A Magistrate's Court in Nineteenth Century Hong Kong: Court in Time*, edited by Gillian Bickley, indexed by Verner Bickley, with chapters contributed by Gillian Bickley, Verner Bickley, Christopher Coghlan, Tim Hamlett, Geoffrey Roper and Garry Tallentire, and with a Preface by former Hong Kong Chief Justice Sir T. L. Yang, published in Hong Kong by Proverse

symbol refers to the first (and sometimes only) page number in *A Magistrate's Court* where the transcribed newspaper report appears.

The name of the section in *A Magistrate's Court in Nineteenth Century Hong Kong* where any of these reports appears is also indicated.

If a case was referred to the Criminal Sessions of the Supreme Court, this is indicated.

Where a case was heard more than once in Frederick Stewart's Magistrate's Court, this is indicated in the footnotes, and is not added as an additional point in the Index to Captions. Sometimes *The China Mail* used the same or a similar caption for a second or third report. On other occasions, the same caption is used for a different case entirely and this can be confusing.

General Index

Many of the personal names are very similar and sometimes it may appear that the original contains a misspelling or typgraphical error. On occasion, the entries for similar names are merged; sometimes not. Those readers who are particularly interested in some individual bearing a name similar to that which appears in the general index may like to look carefully at the notes where appear some careful discussions of which entries relate to the same individual and which do not.

Hong Kong in 2005, ISBN-10: 9628557041, ISBN-13: 9789628557042. Referred to in notes below as, "*A Magistrate's Court in 19th Century Hong Kong*".

INDEX TO CAPTIONS OF REPORTS
IN THE *CHINA MAIL*
OF THE COMPLETE COURT CASES
OF MAGISTRATE FREDERICK STEWART
JULY 1881 TO MARCH 1882

COURT CASES: JULY 1881

BEFORE FREDERICK STEWART, ESQ.

TUESDAY 26 JULY 1881
Without a License [No. 1]
Assault [No. 2]
Cruelty to a Dog [No. 3]
Theft of an Umbrella [No. 4]
A Medicine Man [No. 5]
Earring Snatching [No. 6]
Buying a Soldier's Greatcoat [No. 7]

WEDNESDAY 27 JULY 1881
Furious Driving [No. 8]

THURSDAY 28 JULY 1881
Theft [No. 9]
Rogue and Vagabond [No. 10]
Unlawful Possession [No. 11]
Assault [No. 12]
Theft of Shoes [No. 13]
Gambling [No. 14]
[Gambling] [No. 15]
Larceny from the Person [No. 16]
Pickpocket [No. 17]

FRIDAY 29 JULY 1881
Rogue and Vagabond [No. 18]
[Being in Possession of Opium without a Licence]
[No. 19]
Detaining a Boy [No. 20] **KIDNAPPERS &
TRAFFICKERS** 📖 **p. 301**

SATURDAY 30 JULY 1881
Fighting in the Streets [No. 21]
Assaults [No. 22]
[Assaults] [No. 23]
Disorderly Conduct [No. 24]
Gambling [No. 25]
Memento Mori [No. 26]
Drunk and Disorderly [No. 27]

COURT CASES: AUGUST 1881
BEFORE FREDERICK STEWART, ESQ.

MONDAY 1 AUGUST 1881
Disorderly Conduct [No. 28]
Theft of Clothing [No. 29]
Selling Fresh Pork [No. 30]
Throwing Rubbish into the Harbour [No. 31]
Damaging Trees [No. 32]
Without a Certificate [No. 33]
[Disobedience] of Orders [No. 34]
Indecent Assault [No. 35]
Theft of Clothing [No. 36]

TUESDAY 2 AUGUST 1881
Kidnapping [No. 37] **KIDNAPPERS &
TRAFFICKERS 📖 p. 305** (To Criminal Sessions)

WEDNESDAY 3 AUGUST 1881
Street Gambling [No. 38]
[Street Gambling] [No. 39]
Larceny [No. 40] (**To Criminal Sessions**)

FRIDAY 5 AUGUST 1881
Theft of Two Water Buckets [No. 41]
Theft of an Anchor [No. 42]
Gambling [No. 43]
Cutting Trees [No. 44]
Theft [No. 45]

MONDAY 8 AUGUST 1881
Rogue and Vagabond [No. 46]
At Large Without a Light [No. 47]
Assault [No. 48] **PROSTITUTES, Etc. 📖 p. 277**

TUESDAY 9 AUGUST 1881
Drunk [No. 49]
Theft of Clothing [No. 50]
Joss Pidgin [No. 51]
Assault [No. 52]

WEDNESDAY 10 AUGUST 1881
More Bonfires [No. 53]
Attempted Theft [No. 54]
A Frisky Seaman [No. 55]
Drunks [No. 56]
[Drunks] [No. 57]
Public Gambling [No. 58]
A Curious Rogue and Vagabond [No. 59]
The Kicking Case [No. 60]

THURSDAY 11 AUGUST 1881
Alleged Traffic in Girls [No. 61]
Larceny of Clothing [No. 62]
The 'Ricksha Nuisance [No. 63]
A Dangerous Nuisance [No. 64]
The Kicking Case [No. 65] (**To Criminal Sessions;
but not tried there.**)

SATURDAY 13 AUGUST 1881
Unlawful Possession [No. 66]
[Unlawful Possession] [No. 67]
Drunk [No. 68]
Rogue and Vagabonds [No. 69]
[Rogue and Vagabonds] [No. 70]
Defiling a Stream [No. 71]
Throwing Rubbish into the Harbour [No. 72]

MONDAY 15 AUGUST 1881
Watchman, What of the Night? [No. 73]
Mariners Bold [No. 74]
Stabbing [No. 75]

TUESDAY 16 AUGUST 1881
Charges of Creating a Disturbance
in a Dwelling House [No. 76]
Larceny from the Person [No. 77]
Larceny of a Box of Clothing, &c. [No. 78Penitent
Servants [No. 79]

WEDNESDAY 17 AUGUST 1881
Drunk [No. 80]
[Drunk] [No. 81]
Refusing to Pay Hire [No. 82]
Breach of Market Ordinance [No. 83]
Theft of a Pair of Trousers [No. 84]
Theft of Clothing [No. 85]
Alleged Assault [No. 86] **THE DOMESTIC
SCENE** 📖 **p. 243**

THURSDAY 18 AUGUST 1881
Alleged Assault [No. 87] **THE DOMESTIC
SCENE** 📖 **p. 243**

FRIDAY 19 AUGUST 1881
Drunk [No. 88]
Assault [No. 89]
Mendicancy [No. 90]
Unlicensed Opium [No. 91]
An Airy Costume [No. 92]
Traffic in Children [No. 93] **KIDNAPPERS &
TRAFFICKERS** 📖 **p. 301**

SATURDAY 20 AUGUST 1881
Alleged Assault [No. 94] **THE DOMESTIC
SCENE** 📖 **p. 248**

TUESDAY 30 AUGUST 1881
[Stealing] [No. 95]
Larceny [No. 96]
[Larceny] [No. 97] **PROSTITUTES, Etc.** 📖 **p. 277**

WEDNESDAY 31 AUGUST 1881
Larceny [No. 98]
Theft of a Jacket &c. [No. 99]
Drunk and Disorderly Conduct [No. 100]
Sleepy Watchman [No. 101]
Larceny from the Person [No. 102]
Theft of a Passage Ticket [No. 103]
Theft of Seven Jackets [No. 104]

COURT CASES: SEPTEMBER 1881
BEFORE FREDERICK STEWART, ESQ.

FRIDAY 2 SEPTEMBER 1881
Theft of Chair Poles [No. 105]
Obstruction [No. 106]
Unlawful Possession of Old Iron [No. 107]
Rogue and Vagabond [No. 108]
Larceny of Clothes [No. 109]
Unlawful Possession of Coal [No. 110]
Unlawful Possession of Opium [No. 111]
Theft of a Watch, Etc. [No. 112] **POLICE 📖 p. 225**
Silly Billy [No. 113]

SATURDAY 3 SEPTEMBER 1881
Fighting [No. 114]
Unlawful Possession [No. 115]

MONDAY 5 SEPTEMBER 1881
Street Gambling [No. 116]
[Street Gambling] [No. 117]
Unlawful Possesion [No. 118]
Assaults [No. 119]
[Assaults] [No. 120]
Nuisance [No. 121]

TUESDAY 6 SEPTEMBER 1881
Mendicancy [No. 122]
Breaches of Market Ordinance [No. 123]
Without a Permit [No. 124]
Street Gambling [No. 125]
[Street Gambling] [No. 126]
Theft from the Person [No. 127]
Watchman to Gamblers [No. 128]
Theft of a Jacket [No. 129]
Unlawfully Using a Registration Ticket [No. 130]
All is not Gold that Glitters [No. 131] **URBAN
LIFE, 📖 p. 347 (To Criminal Sessions)**

THURSDAY 8 SEPTEMBER 1881
The Chair Nuisance [No. 132]
Drunk [No. 133]
Breach of Market Ordinance [No. 134]
[Breach of Market Ordinance] [No. 135]
Unlawful Possession of a Boat [No. 136]
Larceny [No. 137]
Cutting Earth in Hospital Road [No. 138]
Pocket Picking [No. 139]

FRIDAY 9 SEPTEMBER 1881
Refusal to Perform their Duty [No. 140]

SATURDAY 10 SEPTEMBER 1881
Theft of Copper Nails [No. 141]
Larceny from the Person [No. 142] **CHILDREN &
RETURNED STUDENTS** 📖 **p. 323**
Unlawful Possession of Coal [No. 143]
Larceny of a Door [No. 144]
Disorderly Conduct and Assault [No. 145]
Public Gambling [No. 146] **GAMBLERS &
INFORMERS** 📖 **p. 339**
Rogue and Vagabond [No. 147]

MONDAY 12 SEPTEMBER 1881
Rogues and Vagabonds [No. 148]
Drunk [No. 149]
Unlawful Possession [No. 150]
Watchman to Gamblers [No. 151]
Theft of Sweet Potatoe [sic] Sprouts [No. 152]

WEDNESDAY 14 SEPTEMBER 1881
Larceny of Jewellery [No. 153] **PROSTITUTES,
Etc.** 📖 **p. 277**
Theft [No. 154]
Without a Light [No. 155]

THURSDAY 15 SEPTEMBER 1881
Theft of a Clock [No. 156] (**To Criminal Sessions**)

THURSDAY 22 SEPTEMBER 1881
Theft of Clothing [No. 181]
Sweet Sleep [No. 182]
Cutting Trees [No. 183]
Assaulting the Police [No. 184]
Rogue and Vagabond [No. 185]
Theft of a Silver Button [No. 186]
Pocket-picking [No. 187]

FRIDAY 23 SEPTEMBER 1881
The Tables Turned [No. 188]

SATURDAY 24 SEPTEMBER 1881
Disorderly Conduct [No. 189] **PROSTITUTES, Etc.**
    📖 **p. 278**
Rogue and Vagabond [No. 190]
The Burglary at Bellevue [No. 191] **THE**
      DOMESTIC SCENE 📖 **p. 255**
Unlawful Possession [No. 192]
A Bean Curd Makers' Row [No. 193]
False Weights and Measures [No. 194]
The Boot on the Other Leg [No. 195]
Theft of a Box, Clothing and Money [No. 196]

MONDAY 26 SEPTEMBER 1881
Using Abusive Language [No. 197]
Rogue and Vagabond [No. 198]
Street Gambling [No. 199]
A Thieves' Friend [No. 200]
Snatching [No. 201]
Theft by a Servant [No. 202]
Unlawful Possession [No. 203]
Fighting, Petty Assaults, Hawking against the
Regulations,
Obstruction [No. 204]

TUESDAY 27 SEPTEMBER 1881
Habitually Ill Treating a Little Girl [No. 205] **THE**
      DOMESTIC SCENE 📖 **p. 254**
Short Weights and Measures [No. 206]

WEDNESDAY 28 SEPTEMBER 1881
Employer and Servant Case [No. 207]
Street Gambling [No. 208]
A Kind Uncle [No. 209]
Unawful Possession of Opium [No. 210]
Rogues and Vagabonds [No. 211]
Stealing Roots [No. 212]
A Needy Customer Provided For [No. 213]
Loafing at the Dock [No. 214]
Love Me, Love My Cat [No. 215]
Drink [sic] Again [No. 216]
Obstructions [No. 217]

THURSDAY 29 SEPTEMBER 1881
Larceny [No. 218]
Pickpocket [No. 219]

FRIDAY 30 SEPTEMBER 1881
Theft [No. 220] **URBAN LIFE 📖 p. 348 (To Criminal Sessions)**
Larceny from the Person [No. 221] **URBAN LIFE 📖 p. 349 (To Criminal Sessions)**
Street Gambling [No. 222]
Hawking without a License [No. 223]
Drunk [No. 224] **SAILORS 📖 p. 174**
Theft of a Hair Pin [No. 225] **URBAN LIFE 📖 p. 349**
Breach of the Market Ordinance [No. 226]
[Breach of the Market Ordinance] [No. 227]
Suspicious Character [No. 228]
Disturbance [No. 229]
Disorderly Conduct [No. 230]
Street Gambling [No. 231]
Unlawful Possession [No. 232]6 **CHILDREN & RETURNED STUDENTS 📖 p. 323**
Serious Assault [No. 233] **SAILORS 📖 p. 173**
Alleged Indecent Assault [No. 234]
Wholesale [Decoying] of Boys and Girls [No. 235] **KIDNAPPERS & TRAFFICKERS 📖 p. 302**

COURT CASES: OCTOBER 1881
BEFORE FREDERICK STEWART, ESQ.

SATURDAY 1 OCTOBER 1881
The Robbery from Bellevue [No. 236] **THE DOMESTIC SCENE 📖 p. 257**
The Serious Assault Case [No. 237] **SAILORS 📖 p. 174**
The Abduction Case [No. 238] **KIDNAPPERS & TRAFFICKERS 📖 p. 305**

MONDAY 3 OCTOBER 1881
Assault [No. 239]
Unlawful Possession [No. 240]
Theft of a Jacket [No. 241]

TUESDAY 4 OCTOBER 1881
The "Bolton Abbey" -- False Report [No. 242]
SAILORS 📖 p. 174
Rogue and Vagabond [No. 243]
Larceny from the Person [No. 244]
Obstruction [No. 245]
[Obstruction] [No. 246]
Indecent Assault [No. 247]
Dispatch of a Steamer without Woman [No. 248]

WEDNESDAY 5 OCTOBER 1881
Leaving His Employer's Service Without Notice [No. 249]
The "Bolton Abbey" [No. 250] **SAILORS 📖 p. 175**
The China Mail, 6 October 1881
"Local and General", re students returned from America case [ADDITIONAL 251]
CHILDREN & RETURNED STUDENTS 📖 p. 324. See also 📖 p. 325.

THURSDAY 6 OCTOBER 1881
[Leaving his Employer's Service without Notice] [No. 252]
Theft [No. 253]

FRIDAY 7 OCTOBER 1881
Rogue and Vagabond [No. 254]
The Naval Yard Embezzlement Case [No. 255]
POLICE 📖 p. 226

SATURDAY 8 OCTOBER 1881
Gambling [No. 256]
[Gambling] [No. 257]
The Rickshaw Question [No. 258]
The Moon Feast [No. 259]
Rogue and Vagabond [No. 260]
Contraventions of Market Ordinance [No. 261]
Curious Case [No. 262]
A Night on Shore [No. 263]
Breach of the Opium Ordinance [No. 264]
Assault [No. 265]

MONDAY 10 OCTOBER 1881
Theft [No. 266]
No Pass Or Light [No. 267]
Incapable [No. 268]
[Incapable] [No. 269]
[Incapable] [No. 270]
Theft [No. 271]
Row in a Boarding House [No. 272]

TUESDAY 11 OCTOBER 1881
Assault [No. 273]

WEDNESDAY 12 OCTOBER 1881
Theft [No. 274]
Without a Light [No. 275]
Disorderly Conduct [No. 276] **PROSTITUTES, Etc.**
    📖 p. 278
Rogue and Vagabond [No. 277]
False Evidence [No. 278] **PROSTITUTES, Etc.**
    📖 p. 279
Throwing Rubbish into the Harbour [No. 279]
Committal [No. 280]

THURSDAY 13 OCTOBER 1881

WEDNESDAY 26 OCTOBER 1881
A Suspicious Case [No. 323]
Breach of the Opium Ordinance [No. 324]
Obstruction [No. 325]
Larceny [No. 326]
Another Opium Case [No. 327]

[THURSDAY] 28 OCTOBER 1881
Breach of Ordinance [No. 328]
Breach of Opium Ordinance [No. 329]
Larceny [No. 330]
A Raid on Gamblers [No. 331]
Trespassing on the Race Course [No. 332]
Larceny from the Person [No. 333]

FRIDAY 29 OCTOBER 1881
A Rogue and Vagabond [No. 334]
Assault with a Lethal Weapon [No. 335]
PROSTITUTES, Etc. 📖 p. 280

MONDAY 31 OCTOBER 1881
Providing for a Rainy Day [No. 336]
Embezzlement [No. 337]
Larceny from a Dwelling House [No. 338]
Assault [No. 339] **PROSTITUTES, Etc. 📖 p. 281**

COURT CASES: NOVEMBER 1881
BEFORE FREDERICK STEWART, ESQ.

THURSDAY 3 NOVEMBER 1881
Assaulting a Constable [No. 340]
Found in a House for a Supposed Unlawful Purpose
[No. 341]

FRIDAY 4 NOVEMBER 1881
Committed for Trial [No. 342] (**To Criminal Sessions**)
Alleged Trafficking in Human Beings [No. 343]
KIDNAPPERS & TRAFFICKERS 📖 p. 307
(**To Criminal Sessions**)

SATURDAY 5 NOVEMBER 1881
Unlawful Possesssion [No. 344]
Pugilistic Seamen [No. 345]
Drunk and Incapable [No. 346]
Wilfull Damage to a Garden [No. 347] **COUNTRY
LIFE 📖 p. 367**

MONDAY 7 NOVEMBER 1881
A Batch of Drunk and Incapables [No. 348]
[A batch of Drunk and Incapables] [No. 349]
[A batch of Drunk and Incapables] [No. 350]
[A batch of Drunk and Incapables] [No. 351]
[A batch of Drunk and Incapables] [No. 352]
Watchman to Gamblers [No. 353]
Disorderly Conduct [No. 354] **SAILORS 📖 p. 182**

TUESDAY 8 NOVEMBER 1881
Unlawful Pawning [No. 355]

WEDNESDAY 9 NOVEMBER 1881
Wilful Damage to a Garden [No. 356] **COUNTRY**
     LIFE 📖 **p. 368 (To Criminal Sessions)**
Damaging a 'Ricksha [No. 357]
Jack Ashore [No. 358] **SAILORS** 📖 **p. 183**
A Taste for Legal Documents [No. 359]
Attempted Suicide [No. 360]
Robbery from the Person [No. 361]
A Disturbance in Court [No. 362]

THURSDAY 10 NOVEMBER 1881
A Refractory Servant [No. 363] **THE DOMESTIC**
     SCENE 📖 **p. 258**
Disorderly Conduct [No. 364] **PROSTITUTES, Etc.**
     📖 **p. 281**
Theft of Public Documents [No. 365] **CHILDREN**
     & RETURNED STUDENTS 📖 **p. 325**

FRIDAY 11 NOVEMBER 1881
Attempted Suicides [No. 366]
Drunk and Disorderly [No. 367]
Bribing a Constable [No. 368] **URBAN LIFE**
     📖 **p. 354**
Gamblers [No. 369]
Unlawful Possession [No. 370]
Breach of Opium Ordinance [No. 371]

SATURDAY 12 NOVEMBER 1881
A Dangerous Lunatic [No. 372]
Drunk and Disorderly [No. 373]
Disorderly Conduct on Board a Steamer [No. 374]
TEACHERS AND MEN OF THE CLOTH
     📖 **p. 231**

MONDAY 14 NOVEMBER 1881
Breach of the Opium Ordinance [No. 375]
Selling Spirits without a License [No. 376]
Attempted Suicide [No. 377]
A Rogue and Vagabond [No. 378]

TUESDAY 15 NOVEMBER 1881
Drunk and Disorderly [No. 379]
Drunk and Incapable [No. 380]
Watchman to Gamblers [No. 381]
Larceny [No. 382]
Creating a Disturbance [No. 383]
Obstructionists [No. 384]
A Lunatic [No. 385]
Breach of the Opium Ordinance [No. 386]

WEDNESDAY 16 NOVEMBER 1881
Public Obstruction [No. 387] **URBAN LIFE**
       📖 **p. 354**
<u>**The China Mail**</u>, 16 November 1881
Stabbing Case on Board the Helen Marion Committal
for Murder [No. 388] **SAILORS (To Criminal**
       Sessions) 📖 **p. 181**

THURSDAY 17 NOVEMBER 1881
Larceny of Clothing [No. 389] **URBAN LIFE**
       📖 **p. 357**
Attempted Suicide [No. 390]
Drunk and Disorderly [No. 391]
A Riotous Youth [No. 392]
No Light or Pass [No. 393]
Larceny from the Person [No. 394]

SATURDAY 19 NOVEMBER 1881
A Rogue and Vagabond [No. 395]
Two Old Card Sharpers [No. 396]
A Feeble Charge [No. 397]
Mendicants [No. 398]
A Raid on Gamblers [No. 399]

MONDAY 21 NOVEMBER 1881
Drunk and Disorderly [No. 400]
Drunk and Incapable [No. 401]
Larceny [No. 402]
Drunk and Creating a Disturbance [No. 403]
Theft of Clothing [No. 404]

WEDNESDAY 23 NOVEMBER 1881
Another Raid on Gamblers [No. 405]
Obstructionists [No. 406]
[Obstructionists] [No. 407]
A Public Nuisance [No. 408]
Only Two Drinks [No. 409]
A Rogue and Vagabond [No. 410]
Street Gambling [No. 411]

FRIDAY 25 NOVEMBER 1881
Unlawful Possesssion [No. 412]
Causing an Obstruction [No. 413]
A Rogue and Vagabond [No. 414]
Street Gamblers [No. 415]
Larceny [No. 416]

SATURDAY 26 NOVEMBER 1881
Street Gambling [No. 417]
Obtaining Money under False Pretences [No. 418]
URBAN LIFE 📖 **p. 357**
Stealing a Gold Finger Ring [No. 419]
Passing Counterfeit Coin [No. 420] (**To Criminal
        Sessions**)
Wilfull Damage on Board Ship [No. 421] **SAILORS**
        📖 **p. 184**

MONDAY 28 NOVEMBER 1881
The Armed Attack at Tai Tam [No. 422] **COUNTRY
        LIFE** 📖 **p. 369 (See also** 📖 **p. 370-373.)**
A Rogue and Vagabond [No. 423]
Larceny by a Servant [No. 424]

TUESDAY 29 NOVEMBER 1881
A Sleepy Watchman [No. 425]
Drunk and Disorderly [No. 426]
Rogues and Vagabonds [No. 427]
Obtaining Goods under False Pretences [No. 428]
In Possession of Counterfeit Coin [No. 429]

COURT CASES: DECEMBER 1881
BEFORE FREDERICK STEWART, ESQ.

THURSDAY 1 DECEMBER 1881
Intent to Commit a Felony [No. 430]
Attempted Larceny [No. 431]
Larceny of Clothing [No. 432]

FRIDAY 2 DECEMBER 1881
Counterfeit Coin [No. 433]

SATURDAY 3 DECEMBER 1881
Breach of the Opium Ordinance [No. 434]
Drunk and Disorderly [No. 435]
Too Much Samshu [No. 436]
Unawful Possession [No. 437]
A Porter Bath [No. 438]
An Informer [No. 439]

MONDAY 5 DECEMBER 1881
Stealing, and Receiving Stolen Property [No. 440]
Theft of Wood [No. 441]
Public Gambling [No. 442]
Larceny on Board Ship [No. 443]
The Attack at Tai-tam [No. 444] **COUNTRY LIFE**
    📖 **p. 373**

WEDNESDAY 7 DECEMBER 1881
Breach of Opium Ordinance [No. 445]
Creating a Disturbance [No. 446]
Robbery from the Person [No. 447]
Wilfull Damage [No. 448] **SAILORS** 📖 **p. 185**
Obtaining Goods under False Pretences [No. 449]

FRIDAY 9 DECEMBER 1881
Obtaining Goods under False Pretences [No. 450]
Wachman to Gamblers [No. 451]

SATURDAY 10 DECEMBER 1881
Piracy on the High Seas [No. 452] **PIRATES &
    LIFE AT SEA** 📖 **p. 385**
Double Assault [No. 453]
Assault with Intent [No. 454] **SOLDIERS** 📖 **p. 205**
Robbery from the Person [No. 455] (**To Criminal
    Sessions**)

MONDAY 12 DECEMBER 1881
Alleged Assault with Intent [No. 456] **SOLDIERS**
    📖 **p. 205**
Damaging a Street Chair [No. 457]

MONDAY 12 DECEMBER 1881
Rogues and Vagabonds [No. 458]
[Gambling] [No. 459]
Larceny [No. 460] **PROSTITUTES, Etc.** 📖 **p. 282**
Unlawful Possession [No. 461]

TUESDAY 13 DECEMBER, 1881
Preparing for Christmas [No. 462]
Improper use of a Householder's Certificate [No. 463]
Street Gambling [No. 464]
[Street Gambling] [No. 465]
Unlawful Possession [No. 466]
[Unlawful Possession] [No. 467]
Assault [No. 468] **CHILDREN & RETURNED
    STUDENTS** 📖 **p. 326**
Drunks [No. 469]
[Drunks] [No. 470]
Theft from the Docks [No. 471]
Straying Cattle [No. 472] **TEACHERS AND MEN
    OF THE CLOTH** 📖 **p. 232**

WEDNESDAY 14 DECEMBER 1881
The Tai Tam Attack [No. 473] **COUNTRY LIFE**
    📖 **p. 373**

THURSDAY 15 DECEMBER 1881
Larceny [No. 474]
Public Gambling [No. 475]
An Incorrigible Rogue and Vagabond [No. 476]
No Jurisdiction [No. 477]
A Pickpocket [No. 478] **URBAN LIFE** 📖 **p. 358**

SATURDAY 17 DECEMBER 1881
Drunk and Disorderly [No. 479]
Larceny [No. 480]
Drunk and Refusing to Pay Chair-hire [No. 481]
The Tai-tam Attack [No. 482] **COUNTRY LIFE**
　　📖 **p. 375**
Piracy on the High Seas [No. 483]1 **PIRATES &**
　　LIFE AT SEA 📖 **p. 385**

MONDAY 19 DECEMBER 1881
An Unfounded Charge [No. 484] **GAMBLERS &**
INFORMERS [Keeping a public gambling
　　house]📖 **p. 340**
Gambling Informers [No. 485] **GAMBLERS &**
　　INFORMERS 📖 **p. 340**
Sunday Carousals [No. 486]
[Sunday Carousals] [No. 487]
[Sunday Carousals] [No. 488]

TUESDAY 20 DECEMBER 1881
Theft of Clothing [No. 489]
An Unjust Accusation [No. 490] **SAILORS**
　　📖 **p. 186**
The Tai Tam Case [No. 491] **COUNTRY LIFE**
　　📖 **p. 376 (To Criminal Sessions)**

WEDNESDAY 21 DECEMBER 1881
Breach of the Opium Ordinance [No. 492]
A Batch of Gamblers [No. 493]
A Pickpocket [No. 494] **PROSTITUTES, Etc.**
　　📖 **p. 283**
Unlawful Possession [No. 495]
A Rogue and Vagabond [No. 496]

FRIDAY 23 DECEMBER 1881
Alleged Attempted Suicide [No. 497]

SATURDAY 24 DECEMBER 1881
Attempting to Steal a Gold Bangle [No. 498]
TEACHERS AND MEN OF THE CLOTH
     📖 **p. 233**
Gambling [No. 499]

TUESDAY 27 DECEMBER 1881
Throwing a Parcel into Gaol [No. 500]
Street Gambling [No. 501]
Snatching Caps [No. 502]
Stealing Two Jackets and a Dollar Bank Note
     [No. 503]
A Pick Pocket [No. 504]
Rogue and Vagabond [No. 505]
Theft of Part of the "Dragon" [No. 506]

WEDNESDAY 28 DECEMBER 1881
Assault [No. 507]
Piracy on the High Seas [No. 508] **PIRATES &**
     LIFE AT SEA 📖 **p. 389**

THURSDAY 29 DECEMBER 1881
Alleged Unlawful Possession [No. 509]

FRIDAY 30 DECEMBER 1881
Cutting and Wounding [No. 510] **THE**
     DOMESTIC SCENE 📖 **p. 258**
Illegal Possession of Opium [No. 511]
Obtaining Money by False Pretences [No. 512]
Rogues and Vagabonds [No. 513]
[Rogues and Vagabonds] [No. 514]

SATURDAY 31 DECEMBER 1881
Rogue and Vagabond [No. 515]
Pickpocket [No. 516]
Assault [No. 517]
Theft of Silk [No. 518]

COURT CASES: JANUARY 1882
BEFORE FREDERICK STEWART, ESQ.

WEDNESDAY 4 JANUARY 1882
Disobedient Chair Coolies [No. 519]
Piracy [No. 520] **PIRATES & LIFE AT SEA**
     📖 **p. 389 (To Criminal Sessions)**
Cutting and Wounding [No. 521]
A Determined Gaol Bird [No. 522] **(To Criminal
     Sessions)**

FRIDAY 6 JANUARY 1882
Blue Jackets on the War Path [No. 523] **SAILORS**
     📖 **p. 187**
Theft of Trousers [No. 524]
Counterfeit Coin [No. 525] **URBAN LIFE** 📖 **p. 359**

SATURDAY 7 JANUARY 1882
Robbing a Shipwrecked Seaman [No. 526]
SAILORS 📖 **p. 189**
Stealing Clothing [No. 527]

MONDAY 9 JANUARY 1882
Drunk and Assaulting the Police [No. 528]
Counterfeit Coin [No. 529] **URBAN LIFE**
     📖 **p. 360 (To Criminal Sessions)**
Assault and Robbery [No. 530]

TUESDAY 10 JANUARY 1882
Disobedient Servant [No. 531]
Aiding and Abetting Gamblers [No. 532]
A Chair Coolie in Liquor [No. 533] **TEACHERS
     AND MEN OF THE CLOTH** 📖 **p. 234**
Larceny of Clothing [No. 534]

THURSDAY 12 JANUARY 1882
Breach of the Opium Ordinance [No. 535]
Unlawful Possession of Warlike Stores [No. 536]
Drunk and Incapables [No. 537]
A Straggler [No. 538]
A Pickpocket [No. 539]
A Sleepy Watchman [No. 540]

SATURDAY 14 JANUARY 1882
Throwing Bricks [No. 541]
Stealing Copper Nails [No. 542]
A Straggling Sailor [No. 543]

MONDAY 16 JANUARY 1882
Wholesale Theft [No. 544]
A Batch of Rogues [No. 545]
Theft of Trousers [No. 546]
Theft by an Actor [No. 547]
An Opium Case [No. 548]

TUESDAY 17 JANUARY 1882
Larceny and Unlawful Possession [No. 549]

WEDNESDAY 18 JANUARY 1882
A Collector of Herbs [No. 550]
Counterfeit Coin [No. 551]

THURSDAY 19 JANUARY 1882
Vagabonds and Incapables [No. 552] **TEACHERS
AND MEN OF THE CLOTH** 📖 **p. 234**

FRIDAY 2O JANUARY 1882
Theft from the Barracks [No. 553]
Stealing a Sampan [No. 554]
Unlawful Possession [No. 555]
Rogue and Vagabond [No. 556]

SATURDAY 21 JANUARY 1882
Robbery [No. 557] **PROSTITUTES, Etc.** 📖 **p. 283**
Stealing a Coverlet [No. 558] (**To Criminal Sessions**)

MONDAY 23 JANUARY 1882
Larceny [No. 559]
Unlawful Possession of a Jacket [No. 560]
A Novel use of a Queue [No. 561]
Theft of Wood [No. 562]

TUESDAY 24 JANUARY 1882
An Offence under the Post Office Regulations
[No. 563]
Theft of Twenty Cents [No. 564]
Theft of Scales [No. 565]
Unlawful Possession of Rice [No. 566]
Robbery from the Person [No. 567] (**To Criminal Sessions**)
Passing Counterfeit Coin [No. 568]

WEDNESDAY 25 JANUARY 1882
Opium Case [No. 569]

THURSDAY 26 JANUARY 1882
Larceny [No. 570] **CHILDREN & RETURNED STUDENTS** 📖 **p. 326**
A Gambler's Haunt [No. 571]
Damaged Trees at the Race Course [No. 572]
A Vagrant [No. 573]

FRIDAY 27 JANUARY 1882
Larceny [No. 574]
Kidnapping [No. 575] **KIDNAPPERS & TRAFFICKERS** 📖 **p. 308**
Attempted Larceny of a Sampan [No. 576]

SATURDAY 28 JANUARY 1882
Committal of Nuisance [No. 577] **URBAN LIFE** 📖 **p. 361**
Drunk and Disorderly [No. 578]
Theft of Jackets [No. 579]
[Theft of Jackets] [No. 580]
[Theft of Jackets] [No. 581]
Unlawful Possession [No. 582]

MONDAY 30 JANUARY 1882
Drunk and Incapables [No. 583]
Unlawful Possession [No. 584]
Rogues and Vagabonds [No. 585]
[Rogues and Vagabonds] [No. 586]

TUESDAY 31 JANUARY 1882
Alleged Kidnapping [No. 587] **KIDNAPPERS & TRAFFICKERS** 📖 **p. 310**

COURT CASES: FEBRUARY 1882
BEFORE FREDERICK STEWART, ESQ.

WEDNESDAY 1 FEBRUARY 1882
An Unlicensed Vegetable Hawker [No. 588]
Assault on Board the "Glenelg" [No. 589]
Obtrusive Chair Coolies [No. 590]
Destruction of Trees [No. 591]
Theft of a Piece of Wood [No. 592]
Robbery [No. 593] **PROSTITUTES, Etc.** 📖 **p. 285**
Assault [No. 594] **PROSTITUTES, Etc.** 📖 **p. 285**
A Destitute Seaman [No. 595]
The Tables Turned [No. 596]

THURSDAY 2 FEBRUARY 1882
Alleged Robbery of $100 [No. 597]

FRIDAY 3 FEBRUARY 1882
The Attractions of a Clothes Line [No. 598]
An Old and Dangerous Offender [No. 599]

SATURDAY 4 FEBRUARY 1882
Alleged Kidnapping [No. 600] **KIDNAPPERS &**
          TRAFFICKERS 📖 **p. 311**
Attemped Suicide [No. 601]

MONDAY 6 FEBRUARY 1882
Destroying Trees [No. 602]
A Straggler [No. 603]
[Robbery] [No. 604]

TUESDAY 7 FEBRUARY 1882
Larcenies [No. 605]
[Larcenies] [No. 606]
Unlawful Possession [No. 607]

THURSDAY 9 FEBRUARY 1882
A Seamen's Fight [No. 608]
Street Gambling [No. 609]

FRIDAY 10 FEBRUARY 1882
Unlawful Possession [No. 610]
Breach of Recognizance [No. 611] **SAILORS**
    📖 **p. 190**

SATURDAY 11 FEBRUARY 1882
Drunk and Disorderly [No. 612]
[Drunk and Disorderly] [No. 612]
[Drunk and Disorderly] [No. 614]
Mendicancy [No. 615]
A Youthful Pickpocket [No. 616] **CHILDREN &**
    RETURNED STUDENTS 📖 **p. 327**
Rogue and Vagabond [No. 617]
Assault by a Ship Captain [No. 618] **SAILORS**
    📖 **p. 191**
Alleged Kidnapping [No. 619] **KIDNAPPERS &**
    TRAFFICKERS 📖 **p. 312 (Apparently**
sent To Criminal Sessions)

MONDAY 13 FEBRUARY 1882
The Cracker Nuisance [No. 620]
Unlawful Possession [No. 621]
Theft of an Anklet [No. 622]
Larceny [No. 623]
A Drunken Chinaman [No. 624]
Theft of Cotton [No. 625]

TUESDAY 14 FEBRUARY 1882
Alleged Theft in the Police Quarters [No. 626]

WEDNESDAY 15 FEBRUARY 1882
Snatching Dollars from a Stall [No. 627]
Gambling [No. 628]
Obtaining Watches by False Pretences [No. 629]
An Evasive Passenger [No. 630]
An Unhappy Inmate of a Brothel [No. 631]
    PROSTITUTES, Etc. 📖 **p. 286**
Night Prowlers [No. 632]
A Dangerous Fishmonger [No. 633] (**To Criminal**
    Sessions)

THURSDAY, 16 FEBRUARY 1882
Larceny of Pipes [No. 634] (**To Criminal Sessions**)

FRIDAY 17 FEBRUARY 1882
["Local and General"] [Cutting and Wounding]
    [No. 635] **SAILORS** 📖 **p. 192**
["Local and General"] [ADDITIONAL 635a]

MONDAY 20 FEBRUARY 1882
Theft [No. 636]
Rogues and Vagabonds [No. 637]
Pickpocket [No. 638] **CHILDREN & RETURNED**
    STUDENTS 📖 **p. 327**
Drunk [No. 639]
A Juvenile Thief [No. 640] **CHILDREN &**
    RETURNED STUDENTS 📖 **p. 328**

TUESDAY 21 FEBRUARY 1882
Theft of Lucifers [No. 641]
Obstructionists [No. 642]
Attempted Larceny from the Person [No. 643]
CHILDREN & RETURNED STUDENTS
    📖 **p. 328**
[Gambling] [No. 644]

WEDNESDAY 22 FEBRUARY 1882
Unlawful Possession [No. 645]

FRIDAY 24 FEBRUARY 1882
Breach of Opium Ordinance [No. 646]

SATURDAY 25 FEBRUARY 1882
[Stealing] [No. 647]
Straggler [No. 648]
A Violent Lascar [No. 649]

MONDAY 27 FEBRUARY 1882
Stealing a Cotton Jacket and Four Silver Buttons
     No. 650]
Riotous Seamen [No. 651]
Theft of Matches [No. 652]
Creating a Disturbance [No. 653]
Larceny [No. 654]
Alleged Attempted Shooting [No. 655]1 **SAILORS**
     📖 **p. 193**

BOTH MAGISTRATES SITTING

MONDAY 27 FEBRUARY 1882
Theft at the Races [No. 656]

COURT CASES: MARCH 1882
BEFORE FREDERICK STEWART, ESQ.

WEDNESDAY 1 MARCH 1882
Assaulting a House-boy [No. 657]
Larceny [No. 658]
[Larceny] [No. 659]
Attempted Shooting [No. 660] **SAILORS** 📖 **p. 194**
   (**To Criminal Sessions**)

FRIDAY 3 MARCH 1882
An Old Man's Troubles [No. 661] **THE**
   DOMESTIC SCENE 📖 **p. 259**
Drunk and Incapable [No. 662]
Larceny [No. 663]
Stealing his Master's Goods [No. 664]
Charge of Stealing Cotton Jackets [No. 665] (**To**
   Criminal Sessions)
Unlawful Possession [No. 666]
Assault by a Constable [No. 667]

MONDAY 6 MARCH 1882
Gambling [No. 668]

TUESDAY 7 MARCH 1882
Firing Crackers [No. 669]
Drunks [No. 670]
[Drunks] [No. 671]
Unlawful Possession [No. 672]
Theft [No. 673]
Gamblers [No. 674]

THURSDAY 9 MARCH 1882
EDITORIAL [ADDITIONAL 674a]
   PROSTITUTES, Etc. 📖 **p. 286**

FRIDAY 10 MARCH 1882
Rogue and Vagabond [No. 675]

SATURDAY 11 MARCH 1882
Chinese Female Rowdies [No. 676]
A Mischievous Seaman [No. 677]
Robbing a Widow [No. 678]
Abusing a Friend's Hospitality [No. 679]

TUESDAY 14 MARCH 1882
The Attack on the Police Sergeant [No. 680]
Stealing a Shipmate's Clothing [No. 681]

WEDNESDAY 15 MARCH 1882
Larceny [No. 682]
Alleged Assault [No. 683] **PROSTITUTES, Etc.**
 📖 **p. 287**
Larceny of Clothing [No. 684]
Unlawful Possession [No. 685]
A Drunk and Violent Darkie [No. 686]
A Frequent Offender [No. 687] (**To Criminal
 Sessions**)

THURSDAY 16 MARCH 1882
Rogue and Vagabond [No. 688]
Theft of Copper [No. 689]

FRIDAY 17 MARCH 1882
Larceny of a Boat [No. 690]
Bangle Stealing [No. 691] **CHILDREN &
 RETURNED STUDENTS** 📖 **p. 329**
A Bad Fit [No. 692]
Alleged Assault and Robbery [No. 694]
TEACHERS AND MEN OF THE CLOTH
 📖 **p. 235** (**To Criminal Sessions**)
Friday 17 March 1882 [No. 695]
[Disturbance at the Supreme Court] **URBAN LIFE**
 📖 **p. 361**

MONDAY 20 MARCH 1882

BOTH MAGISTRATES SITTING
Theft at the Sailors' Home [No. 696] **SAILORS**
 📖 **p. 195**

MONDAY 20 MARCH 1882

BEFORE FREDERICK STEWART, ESQ.
Assault on a Constable [No. 697]

MONDAY 20 MARCH 1882
Unlawful Possession of Branches [No. 698]
Hard up for a Drink [No. 699]
Insensibly Drunk [No. 700]
No Permit [No. 701]
Theft of an Umbrella [No. 702]
Theft of Rice [No. 703]

TUESDAY 21 MARCH 1882
Drunk [No. 704]
Drunk [No. 705]
An Habitual Loiterer [No. 706]
Larceny of Wood [No. 707]
An Ineffectual Attempt to Escape [No. 708]
A Needy Hawker [No. 709] **TEACHERS AND MEN OF THE CLOTH 📖 p. 236**
Theft from the Naval Yard [No. 710]

THURSDAY 23 MARCH 1882
Thefts [No. 711]
[Thefts] [No. 712]

SATURDAY 25 MARCH 1882
Larceny [No. 713]
More Pay [No. 714]

MONDAY 27 MARCH 1882
Leaving Service without Notice [No. 715]
A Disorderly Amah [No. 716] **THE DOMESTIC SCENE 📖 p. 260 (See also 📖 p. 262.)**
Drunk [No. 717]
Larceny [No. 718]
Disturbers of the Peace [No. 719]
Attempted Robberies on Board the *Mary Tathan* [No. 720]

TUESDAY 28 MARCH 1882
Spencer Committed for Trial [No. 721] (**To Criminal Sessions**)
[Obtaining Goods on False Pretences] [No. 722]

WEDNESDAY 29 MARCH 1882
Gamblers' Watchman [No. 723]

~~~~~~~

THE COMPLETE COURT CASES OF MAGISTRATE FREDERICK STEWART, AS REPORTED IN *THE CHINA MAIL*, JULY 1881 TO MARCH 1882

THE EDITED, ANNOTATED TEXT OF THE CHINA MAIL REPORTS

BEFORE FREDERICK STEWART, ESQ.,
July 1881

TUESDAY 26 JULY 1881[56]
WITHOUT A LICENSE
CC Number 1

Ngai To Tsa, for hawking without a license and attempting to bribe the constable who arrested him, was fined $2 or four days' imprisonment.

ASSAULT
CC Number 2

Leong Au was charged with assaulting a private in the 27th Inniskillings.

Complainant said that six Chinamen had been engaged to bury a horse which had died at the barracks, for which they were to get $1. They came back and demanded more money, and while complainant was endeavouring to get them to go away, defendant struck him on the shoulder with his bamboo.

Fined $2 or ten days in gaol with hard labour.

CRUELTY TO A DOG
CC Number 3

Lai Akwai, for throwing hot water over a dog belonging to Sergeant Gamble,[57] was fined $1 or four days in gaol.

---

[56] "Police Intelligence", CM, Tuesday, 26 July 1881, p. 3, cc. 3 - 4.

[57] Sergeant Gamble was in the news again, in November the same year: " . . . Paymaster Sergeant Gamble, of the Royal Inniskilling Fusiliers, who a while since was selected for a Com? the Field-Marshal Commanding has passed a very successful examination to qualify him for promotion to the rank of Lieutenant. We heartily congratulate him on his well-merited success, . . him every prosperity in his new . . which will, we are sure, be re? by his many friends in the Colony." (CM, 29 November 1881, p. 3. c, 1.) [LH column obscure.]

THEFT OF AN UMBRELLA
CC Number 4

Wong Ahong, who (as he alleged) only went into the house of the complainant to inquire for a friend who was at the U.S. Consulate, and departed in company with an umbrella belonging to the occupant, was relieved of the necessity of having an umbrella by getting six weeks' imprisonment with hard labour.

A MEDICINE MAN
CC Number 5

Lai Angau [*sic*], whose devotion to medicine led him to damage some trees at Wong Nei Chong, suffered martyrdom to the extent of $5 or ten days with hard labour.

EARRING SNATCHING
CC Number 6

Lau Amau [*sic*] was charged with larceny of one pair of gold earrings from the person of Kok Akum, kept woman.

Complainant said she and another woman were walking last night in Queen's Road, near the Central Market, when some one snatched her earrings. She turned and saw defendant making off. She gave chase, calling out "Thief." Defendant was arrested by a police constable, but she did not see this.

Police Constable 175 said he saw defendant who was standing under a verandah go across the street in the direction of the two women. He immediately heard the cry of "thief." He gave chase. Ultimately defendant was caught by a Parsee in Graham Street, and witness took him to the Station. Nothing was found on him.

The woman who was walking with complainant gave corroborative evidence.

Defendant was a coolie, and was looking for a friend. Why the constable should have taken him into custody was to him an unfathomable mystery.

Three months' imprisonment with hard labour.

BUYING A SOLDIER'S GREATCOAT
CC Number 7

Lau Afook, remanded from the 23rd, charged with buying a soldier's uniform greatcoat, was again before the Court to-day.

Charles Nelson, an unemployed seaman, said that last Friday evening, between nine and ten o'clock, he was standing in a street in Tai-ping-shan sheltering himself from the rain. The soldier, Greaves, came and stood beside him. He had a dark blue greatcoat on his arm, which he wanted to sell. This was near the defendant's shop. The coat was sold to him for 50 cents. Witness and Greaves then adjourned to two public houses in Queen's Road, where defendant treated him to brandy and beer. He made Greaves' acquaintance in gaol.

Defendant was fined £5, and $10.96, being three times 15/2 1/2d [fifteen shillings and two pence and one half-penny] the present value of the greatcoat; in default six weeks' imprisonment.

WEDNESDAY 27 JULY 1881[58]
FURIOUS DRIVING
CC Number 8

The case in which a jinricksha coolie was charged with running down a young Chinese girl was to-day dismissed, complainant not appearing, and the evidence being very doubtful.

THURSDAY 28 JULY 1881[59]
THEFT
CC Number 9

Chan Among, remanded from yesterday, charged with stealing 25 mat suits, was again before the Court to-day. The suits had been laid on the beach to dry, at

---

[58] "Police Intelligence," CM, Wednesday, 27 July 1881, p. 3, c. 3.
[59] "Police Intelligence," CM, Thursday, 28 July 1881, p. 3, c. 3.

Wanchai. Defendant said he was passing when some one remarked that these coats were of use, why should they be there? Defendant didn't see how they should, and picked up some of them.

He got one week's imprisonment with hard labour.

ROGUE AND VAGABOND
CC Number 10
Leong Awong was convicted, on the evidence of Police Constable 188, of being a rogue and vagabond, and was sentenced to six weeks imprisonment with hard labour.

UNLAWFUL POSSESSION
CC Number 11
Tsoi Asam, remanded from yesterday, charged with being in unlawful possession of 12 catties of copper nails was to-day sentenced to a fine of $10 or six weeks' imprisonment with hard labour.

ASSAULT
CC Number 12
Ip Alui was charged with assaulting his wife. The assault had arisen out of a domestic quarrel. Defendant had cut her across the fingers with a fan-dagger. He was sent to gaol for two months with hard labour.

THEFT OF SHOES
CC Number 13
Chan Atsun was charged with stealing a pair of shoes from a coolie who had been lying sleeping in a shed at the wharf. Complainant had got information where the shoes were, and found them in a pawnshop.

Sentence — six weeks' imprisonment with hard labour.

GAMBLING
CC Number 14

Chung Acheung was charged with street gambling and causing an obstruction.

A Police Constable said that this morning he saw defendant and a number of others gambling in Po Yan Street. He apprehended defendant.

Six weeks' imprisonment with hard labour as rogue vagabond [sic].

[GAMBLING]
CC Number 15

Another Chinaman, charged with gambling, was convicted and sent to gaol for fourteen days with hard labour as a rogue [and] vagabond.

LARCENY FROM THE PERSON
CC Number 16

Wong Chung Shing was charged with stealing a hair pin from the person of a Chinese girl.

Complainant had been walking down Ladder Street, when defendant snatched a hair pin from her hair.

Defendant merely picked up the pin.

Six weeks' imprisonment with hard labour, and six hours in stocks.

PICKPOCKET
CC Number 17

Lau Afu, remanded from the 25th of June charged with attempting to pick another Chinaman's pocket, in the Recreation Ground, was again before the Court.

Complainant stated that while at that place he felt some one's hand in his pocket, and this turned out to be defendant's.

Six months' imprisonment with hard labour and six hours in the stocks.

FRIDAY 29 JULY 1881[60]
ROGUE AND VAGABOND
CC Number 18

Chung Acheung, 25, coolie, for causing an obstruction by gambling, was sent to six months' hard labour, as a rogue and vagabond. Cash 155, seized from the place on the public street where the prisoner and some ten others were gambling, was ordered to be paid into the poor box.

[BEING IN POSSESSION OF OPIUM WITHOUT A LICENCE][61]
CC Number 19

For being in possession of prepared opium (3 taels and 4 taels dross) without a valid certificate from the Opium Farmer, Lau Afat, 32, unemployed, was fined $15, with the alternative of five days' imprisonment, the opium to go to the Farmer.

---

[60] "Police Intelligence," CM, Friday, 29 July 1881, p. 3, c. 4.
[61] There are several local Hong Kong Ordinances relating to opium, including Ordinance No. 21 of 1844, No. 5 of 1845, No. 4 of 1853, No. 2 of 1858, No. 7 of 1858, No. 1 of 1879, No. 7 of 1879, No. 4 of 1883, No. 8 of 1883, No. 1 of 1884, No. 17 of 1886, No. 22 of 1887.
The Ordinance applicable to these 1881-1882 court cases is clearly Ordinance No. 7 of 1879, "The Excise Ordinance (Opium) 1858-1879, Amendment Ordinance 1879".

DETAINING A BOY[62]
CC Number 20 📖 p. 301

Tong Achi, 42, a marine hawker, and Wong Ang, 52, wife of one Li Au, were charged with forcibly detaining two boys and three girls for an unlawful purpose on the 7th *instant*. They were first before the Court on the 15th, when they were simply remanded for a week, and again on the 22nd when they were remanded till to-day. Mr. Tonnochy was then on the Bench.[63]

Dr. Stewart now proceeded with the case.

Police Sergeant Fisher spoke to having gone to Number 4 Cheng On Lane, Sai Ying Pun, on the 14th in company with a Chinese constable No. 192 and an informer named Wong Way Fu who pointed out the defendant and the three children whom he would produce. He told the informer that he wanted two more children. Found two more children. He asked for a remand, as the police were in communication with the Po Leung Kuk (Society for the Protection of Women and Children) who were taking the usual steps in the matter.

---

[62] The following is the complete set of reports in connection with this case as found in "The Complete Court Cases of Magistrate Frederick Stewart as reported in *The China Mail*, July 1881 to March 1882" [henceforth referred to as *"The Complete Court Cases"*]: CC Nos 20, 93, 235, 238. CC No. 37 may possibly also be related to this group of cases.

There are some differences among the different reports in the spelling of place names ("Cheung Lane" is variably given as "Cheng On Lane") and personal names ("Li Au" is also given as, "Li Aü"; "Police Sergeant Fisher" as "Detective Sergeant Fisher"; "Wong Ang" as "Wong a Ng"; "Wong Way Fu" as "Wong Man Yu", "Wong Man In" (CC 238). This last appears in reports of other cases as well, where his name is also given as, "Wang Man Yu" (CC37).

It is interesting that, within CC report 235, one person is described differently in connection with evidence provided by different people: "informer", when the evidence of the western detective sergeant is being reported and, "detective of the Po Leung Kuk", when his own evidence is being reported.

[63] The case is not reported among Tonnochy's cases in *The China Mail* on either 15 or 22 July 1881.

Remanded till August 5th.[64]

SATURDAY 30 JULY 1881[65]
FIGHTING IN THE STREETS
CC Number 21

Five Chinamen were charged with fighting and creating a disturbance on the public streets yesterday.

Police Constable 137 said that last night he was on duty in Battery Road when he saw a number of people fighting in the street. With the assistance of other Constables the five defendants were arrested. It seemed there had been a crowd of 300 or 400 people, 30 or 40 of whom (rice-pounders) were fighting. After the defendants had made statements, they were each fined $5, or ten days in gaol, and to find one surety each in $25 to keep the peace for two months or be imprisoned for a further term of ten days.

ASSAULTS
CC Number 22

Ching Atsun was charged with assaulting Lam Acheung, a rice- pounder, being armed with a deadly weapon.

Complainant said he was a rice-pounder. Yesterday he saw defendant fighting with another man, and went to separate them. Defendant had two iron bars, with one of which he struck complainant on the head and knocked him down. Witness, however, succeeded in getting hold of his queue, and detaining him. Complainant was taken to the hospital, and had his wound dressed. According to one of the witnesses, this disturbance had no connection with the late row amongst the rice-pounders.

Defendant was sent to prison for fourteen days with hard labour.

---

[64] *The Complete Court Cases* contains no report of this case on this date. CC 235 states that the case had not been before the Court since 15 July.

[65] "Police Intelligence," CM, Saturday, 30 July 1881, p. 3, c. 3.

[ASSAULTS]
CC Number 23
Manuel Gomes was charged with assaulting Ching Alai, a boatman.

Complainant said that to-day about 11 a.m., he was sitting in the Parade Ground when defendant came up and struck him on the arm. Defendant also hit him on the head with a stone and cut him. He then gave him into custody.

Defendant asked complainant if he did not steal his bundle and bread, to which the complainant answered in the negative.

A police constable deposed as to arresting prisoner, who was drunk.

Defendant said that he was sitting this morning at St. John's Cathedral and had with him a bundle containing some clothing and bread, which complainant picked up and ran off with. As defendant was not able to overtake him he threw a stone which hit him. He was perfectly sober. He had been in gaol before.

He got six weeks' imprisonment with hard labour.

DISORDERLY CONDUCT
CC Number 24
Wong Ashing was charged with disorderly conduct and assaulting a Police Constable.

Police Constable 321 said that to-day about 10.45, while on duty outside the charge-room gate, defendant wanted to pass. Witness pushed him back, when defendant struck him thrice on the breast with his fist.

He was fined $5 or seven days' imprisonment.

GAMBLING
CC Number 25

Three Chinamen were charged with gambling on the street on the 29th *instant*.

Acting Sergeant No. 590 said that yesterday afternoon he saw defendants and about thirteen others playing at Fan Tan in Marketing Street, Tai-ping-shan. When witness came near them the men ran. He and another constable pursued and caught the defendants. The money in Court was found in the hands of the first and third defendants, and in the rain-hat [*sic*] in Court.

Sentence — first and third defendants six weeks in gaol with hard labour as rogues and vagabonds; and second defendant, who had been in gaol before, three months, with hard labour also, as a rogue and vagabond.

MEMENTO MORI
CC Number 26

Lau Ahing was charged by a forest guard with cutting shrubs at Lap Sap Wan.

Defendant was merely clearing the shrubs from a friend's grave, but the forest guard was sure there was no grave at the spot.

The Court could not appreciate his reverence for the departed, and sentenced defendant to pay $1 or two days' imprisonment with hard labour. Guard to be paid $1.

DRUNK AND DISORDERLY
CC Number 27

Gustav Akaaersund, fireman on board the steamship *Octava*, was charged with being drunk and disorderly. From the evidence it appeared that defendant had got drunk and gone to buy a cap, which he retained without paying for it. Defendant was sorry for what had happened.

Fined $2 or two days in gaol.

BEFORE FREDERICK STEWART, ESQ.,
August 1881[66]

MONDAY 1 AUGUST 1881[67]
DISORDERLY CONDUCT
CC Number 28

Lok Achun, Kun Asu, and Choi Ming Hing were charged with disorderly conduct at Queen's Road East yesterday.Police Constable 667 said the first defendant, who was a public coolie, was in the habit of placing his chair on the footpath. He was sitting beside it on a large stone. Witness told him to remove the chair and the stone, which he refused to do. Witness seized him, when defendant struck him on the chest three times. Second defendant then came up, called out "Ta," and seized witness by the arm. Third defendant was also there, and also called out "Ta." On the arrival of Police Constable No. 3, third defendant bolted. Witness gave first and second

---

[66] **Notes on the Reports for August 1881.**
<u>Related matters reported in</u> *The China Mail.* On 1 August 1881, *The China Mail* refers to Frederick Stewart's resignation as Acting Colonial Secretary and his assumption of his substantive appointment as Police Magistrate (p. 3, c. 1). On the same day, *The China Mail* also has an item on the returns (i.e. statistical reports) relating to gambling (p. 3, c. 1).

     The Legislative Council was sitting on Tuesday and Wednesday, 23 and 24 August 1881, and also on Monday and Tuesday, 29 and 30 August 1881. Reports of the proceedings of the Council appeared on Tuesday, Wednesday and Monday, 23, 24 and 30 August 1881 and take up space, some of which might otherwise have been allocated to reports from the Police Magistrates' courts. Indeed, on Tuesday, 23 August 1881, there is no report from either of the Police Magistrates' courts on p. 3, where these reports usually appeared. And although there is a report from the court of H. E. Wodehouse on 24 August (p. 3), there is none from Stewart's.

     There are related articles, however. On Monday, 29 August 1881, *The China Mail* (p. 2, c. 5) has a summary of prisoners; a separate narrative of an escape from prison, and -- another separate item -- the request for increased pay for police clerks. The Report of the Legislative Council Proceedings (29 August 1881, p. 3, cc. 1-2) includes material on the police.
[67] "Police Intelligence," CM, Monday, 1 August 1881, p. 3, cc. 3 - 4.

defendant into custody of the other constable, and then pursued and arrested third defendant. A large crowd gathered and there was much excitement.

Police Constable No. 3 corroborated.

The first defendant accused the first witness of striking and kicking him. Second defendant merely advised the first to go quietly to the station, and the third said he knew nothing about the first and second defendants; he was merely passing.

First defendant was fined $5, or seven days in prison with hard labour; and the second and third $2 each or two days' imprisonment with hard labour.

THEFT OF CLOTHING
CC Number 29

Chan Akau was charged with stealing one quilt and one jacket on the 30th *ultimate*.

Ip Akwai said he was a bricklayer working at Praya Central. On the 30th *ultimate* he heard a disturbance and saw defendant in charge of a Police constable. Defendant had his quilt and a jacket belonging to his brother. His quilt had been left in the house next to the one in which he was working.

Police Constable 129 said he saw the defendant and another man walking about in a suspicious manner. He saw defendant go into a house, while the other man remained outside, apparently watching. Witness went up the house when the other man walked off, and on defendant coming out with a bundle he arrested him.

Defendant said his brother used to work in the house. He was now sick. This brother told him he had left a quilt and jacket behind him, and defendant went to secure these, which he did. He admitted having been in gaol before for a similar offence.

Sentence—6 months in gaol with hard labour.

SELLING FRESH PORK
CC Number 30

A Chinaman was fined $2 or four days' imprisonment for selling fresh pork in the street.

THROWING RUBBISH INTO THE HARBOUR
CC Number 31
Ng Afo admitted having committed this offence, and was fined $1 or four days' in gaol with hard labour.

DAMAGING TREES
CC Number 32
Wong Apin was charged with cutting trees on the Hill-side on the 30th *ultimate*. A Constable gave evidence as to seeing defendant and another man breaking off the shrubs and fruit produced.
Defendant was fined $1 or four days' imprisonment with hard labour—$1 to go to the Constable.

WITHOUT A CERTIFICATE
CC Number 33
Chai Awing admitted having been in possession of some prepared opium, and was fined $5, or seven days' imprisonment—the opium to go to the Farmer.

[DISOBEDIENCE] OF ORDERS
CC Number 34
Tam Wang Sing was charged by Ramon Maurente, merchant, with refusing to obey orders.

Complainant said that the defendant was his coolie. On several occasions he had asked defendant to go to his office and remove an article of furniture. On several occasions he had told him to do this, but he had paid no attention. On Saturday when asked to do so he became very impudent. Witness sent for a constable.

Defendant said what he was asked to do was no part of his work. Complainant had struck him [on] the mouth.

Prisoner was fined $5 or seven days in gaol.

INDECENT ASSAULT
CC Number 35
Chang Aheung was charged by To Amui, a married woman, with indecently assaulting her.

After evidence had been heard, the defendant, who said he was drunk and accidentally stumbled against complainant, was sent to gaol for six weeks with hard labour.

THEFT OF CLOTHING
CC Number 36
Lum Alap was charged with stealing some clothing on the 25th of June.

Leung Fat said he was a bricklayer. He had reported the theft of some clothing on the 25th of June. He had not seen defendant since till last night.

Defendant admitted having stolen the clothing and was sentenced to six weeks' imprisonment with hard labour.

TUESDAY 2 AUGUST 1881[68]
KIDNAPPING[69]
CC Number 37 📖 p. 305
Chan Ang, 50, a widow and Asam, 61, also a widow, were charged with bringing into the Colony one Tang Tung Yau, a boy aged 11 years, with intent to sell him, on the 26th *instant*.

Wang Mun Yu,[70] a detective of the Po Leung Kuk,[71] gave evidence of the boy having been offered to him for sale, and subsequently to a friend, who agreed to pay $42 for him. The two women in the dock were trying to sell the child, who they said had been given to them by his uncle for sale. He sent

---

[68] "Police Intelligence," CM, Tuesday, 2 August 1881, p. 3, cc. 3 - 4.

[69] Possibly, this case is linked with other cases in *The Complete Court Cases*: i.e.: CC Nos 20, 93, 235, 238.

[70] CC 238 spells this name differently, as, "Wong Man In".

[71] In *The China Mail*, 16 January 1878, p. 2, c. 5, Lai Shik Kai (apparently employed within the Registrar General's Department) is named as "the kidnapping detective".

them away to get a bill of sale, and meanwhile went for a constable to whom he gave them in charge on their return.

To-day the first witness was the boy whose sale was the subject of the charge. He said he was twelve years of age. Had no parents. Had lived with his uncle at the Man Kong village, Pun U District.[72] Some day last month—he forgot the exact day—his maternal uncle came to the house of the uncle with whom he resided and said to his uncle that he wanted to take the boy to Whampoa to get employment as a servant boy. His uncle said "very good." His maternal uncle took him to Whampoa and to the house of a relative there, where there were some women. He remained in the house for some fifteen days. His uncle then went away leaving him there. At the end of the fifteen days the woman with whom he was living called in the two defendants and made him go along with them to get employment. Defendants on the 25th of last month brought him down to Hong Kong, and took him to a house where he remained about ten days, during which he heard the defendants trying to sell him to various people. One day defendants took him to witness' house and tried to sell him. The second defendant asked $50 for him. He was then sold for $42. First witness then said to come to the station and get the money. Then we all went to the Central Station.[73] Was now living in the Tung Wah Hospital.

The Police Constable who apprehended the women gave evidence corroborating that of the first witness. He said that he also heard the woman say in the Central Police Station that they had brought the boy for sale. They were cautioned by Inspector Mathieson,[74] but repeated that it was true. They also said they had paid $36 for him, and only made $6 for

---

[72] Pun Yu is a district in Canton Province, not far from Canton itself.

[73] Direct speech is here embedded in reported speech!

[74] The name is also given as "Inspector Matheson" in these Reports.

their trouble. The bill of sale was put in, and the defendants were duly committed to take their trial at the Supreme Court,[75] reserving their defence.

WEDNESDAY 3 AUGUST 1881[76]
STREET GAMBLING
CC Number 38 📖

In a case in which Fak Acheong and Leung Atsin, coolies, aged 28 and 26 years respectively, were charged with street gambling in Gilman's Bazaar, the offence was proved, the first being fined $2 or seven days' imprisonment with hard labour, and the second, who was convicted in March last of keeping a public gambling-house, was now sentenced to six weeks' hard labour.

[STREET GAMBLING]
CC Number 39

Kwan Atsan, 28, a coolie, was fined $2 for street gambling.

LARCENY
CC Number 40

Chan Achung, unemployed, and two other men (charged with the larceny of clothing and divers other articles to the value of $30) whose case has been two or three times before the Court already, and lengthy

---

[75] This case was not heard at the August Criminal Sessions which took place on 19 and 20 August 1881. In the report of the Criminal Sessions held on 19 August, it states that the Attorney General had stated that two cases only would be brought before the Court on the following day. This implies that there were cases outstanding. It is also not listed in the Criminal Calendar September, October, November or December 1881 Sessions, or the January, February, March, April 1882 sessions. The "Return of Serious and Minor Offences reported to have been committed during the Year 1881, with the Results of such Reports" (HKGG, 11 March 1882, p. 259) does list two cases of Kidnapping for August 1881, and states that three persons were discharged and none convicted. Presumably this case has contributed to these statistics.

[76] "Police Intelligence," CM, Wednesday, 3 August 1881, p. 3, c. 2.

evidence been taken in it, were now finally disposed of.

Inspector Cameron gave some final evidence closing the case, and they were, reserving their defence, committed to the Supreme Court.[77]

FRIDAY 5 AUGUST 1881[78]
THEFT OF TWO WATER BUCKETS
CC Number 41

Wan Acheun was charged with stealing two water buckets the property of U Fong.

Complainant said that yesterday he had gone to the hydrant at Number 5 Station, but there being no water he sat down under the verandah, leaving his buckets sitting there.

Defendant took up his buckets and walked off with them.

Police Constable 641 said he saw the defendant with two buckets. He had just passed him when the complainant came running up and accused the defendant of stealing his buckets.

Defendant was merely washing his feet with water out of the buckets. He had been in gaol before.

---

[77] Possibly No. 3 in Criminal Calendar - August Sessions, 1881. (HKGG, 3 September 1881, p. 817.) The name is given as "Chau A-cheung" and there are two other men accused (Ng A-chun and Fu A-lung). The day of the trial, before Acting Chief Justice, Francis Snowden, was 19 August 1881 and sentence was given on 23 August 1881. All three were charged on two counts: 1) Entering a dwelling house at night with intent to commnit a felony, and committing a felony therein; 2) Receiving stolen goods. The first and second prisoners were found guilty on the first count only and sentenced to nine calendar months' imprisonment with hard labout. The third prisoner was found guilty on the second count and not guilty on the first count and sentenced to one year's imprisonment with hard labour. However there is a remark, "There was not sufficient evidence to support a conviction in this case against Chau A-cheung or Ng A-chun. I have addressed a letter to His Excellency recommending the release of these two prisoners." Unfortunately, the "Return of Serious and Minor Offences reported to have been committed during the Year 1881, with the Results of such Reports" (HKGG, 11 March 1882) throws no additional light on this case.
[78] "Police Intelligence," CM, Friday, 5 August 1881, p. 3, c. 2.

Sentence—three months' imprisonment with hard labour.

THEFT OF AN ANCHOR
CC Number 42

Un Atai was charged with the theft of an anchor from Wong Kum Tsun.

Defendant had, while in a small boat, pulled up and taken the anchor of the complainant's boat. He pursued, but did not at the time succeed in catching him. He afterwards saw him and gave him into custody.

Defendant denied the charge.

He was sent to gaol for twenty-one days with hard labour.

GAMBLING
CC Number 43

Luk Akin was convicted on the evidence of Police Constable 569 of gambling in the street, and was sentenced to six weeks' imprisonment with hard labour as a rogue and vagabond.

CUTTING TREES
CC Number 44

Tsang Aman was charged with damaging trees, convicted on evidence, and fined $1, or one day's imprisonment with hard labour.

THEFT
CC Number 45

Ip Akin admitted having stolen a blanket from Tuk Hing Shun, and was sent to gaol for twenty-one days with hard labour.

MONDAY 8 AUGUST 1881[79]
ROGUE AND VAGABOND
CC Number 46

Leung Wah Tik was charged with being a rogue and vagabond, convicted on the evidence of W. M'Leane, Police Constable 76, and ordered to find security in the sum of $25 to be of good behaviour for six months, in default to be committed.

AT LARGE WITHOUT A LIGHT[80]
CC Number 47

Leong Ashui was charged by Police Constable 266 with being at large in the streets without a light. It appeared from the evidence that defendant had been found by complainant sleeping on a mat. He had neither pass nor light. Defendant had been twice in gaol before. Sentenced to three weeks' imprisonment with hard labour.

ASSAULT
CC Number 48 📖 p. 277

Two Chinamen charged with assaulting an inmate of a licensed brothel, creating a disturbance, and smashing crockery ware, &c., were sentenced to pay a fine of $1 each or four days' imprisonment, and ordered to pay 20 cents for damage, or two days' additional imprisonment.

TUESDAY 9 AUGUST 1881[81]
DRUNK
CC Number 49

F. Culbyering, a native of Ireland, was convicted of being drunk and incapable, and was sentenced to pay a fine of 25 cents or one day's imprisonment.

---

[79] "Police Intelligence," CM, Monday, 8 August 1881, p. 3, c. 3.
[80] For a discussion of the Hong Kong "Light and Pass" Rules, see Gillian Bickley in, *A Magistrate's Court in Nineteenth Century HongKong*, pp. 99-116.
[81] "Police Intelligence," CM, Tuesday, 9 August 1881, p. 3, cc. 1 - 2.

THEFT OF CLOTHING
CC Number 50
Mong Sing Chan was charged with stealing clothing to the value of $15.

It appeared from the evidence that defendant had been to a house along with complainant, and during complainant's absence he had taken the opportunity of stealing this quantity of clothing.

Defendant said he paid his debts with the money he got from the pawning of the clothes.
He was sentenced to six months' imprisonment with hard labour.

JOSS PIDGIN
CC Number 51
Three Chinese were charged with unlawfully making a bonfire in the public street. The defendants admitted having done so, and were each sentenced to pay a fine of $2 or two days' imprisonment.

ASSAULT
CC Number 52
Lam Achu, charged with assaulting another Chinaman, was convicted on evidence and sentenced to pay a fine of $3 or seven days' imprisonment with hard labour, and ordered to find personal security in the sum of $20 to be of good behaviour for two months.

WEDNESDAY 10 AUGUST 1881[82]
MORE BONFIRES
CC Number 53
Twenty Chinese admitted having made bonfires in the public streets, and were each fined $1 or four days' imprisonment. This is in connection with the festival of All Souls, which we noticed in last issue.

---

[82] "Police Intelligence," CM, Wednesday, 10 August 1881, p. 3, cc. 2 - 3.

ATTEMPTED THEFT
CC Number 54

Fung Ahing was charged with attempting to steal some clothing. Complainant said that this morning about daylight defendant, who had a bamboo,[83] thrust it through his open window and then tried to lift some clothing off a rail.

Fourteen days' imprisonment with hard labour.

A FRISKY SEAMAN
CC Number 55

Charles Higgins was charged with refusing to pay chair-hire, assaulting the police, and damaging their uniform. It seemed that four Police Constables were required to take this doughty seaman to the Station. He was fined $2 for assaulting the police or four days' imprisonment with hard labour, to pay $3 for the torn uniform or other two days, and to pay the chair-coolie40 cents or one day more in Gaol.

DRUNKS
CC Number 56

Pellici Louis, a seaman on board the *Adonis*, admitted being drunk and incapable, and was fined 25 cents or one day in Gaol.

[DRUNKS]
CC Number 57

Herve Jeun, another seaman belonging to the *Adonis*, was fined $1 or two days' imprisonment for being in a similar state to his fellow seaman.

PUBLIC GAMBLING
CC Number 58

Lim Ashing was charged with the above offence.
Inspector Matheson gave evidence as to visiting the house No. 22, Lower Lascar Road. On

---

[83] "A bamboo": a bamboo cane, which he regularly used, perhaps, for carrying things over his shoulder(s).

going up the stair he heard the noise of a trap door falling. He met defendant on the staircase, and told some of the constables to arrest him. He could not force open the trap door. By going up the street a distance of some five houses he got into the roof of a chandler's shop. He then managed to enter the house 22 by an escape. He found a number of gambling implements and money.

Evidence was given by the informers as to gambling going on there. Some papers found in the place had relation to gambling.

Defendant was fined $50 or three months' imprisonment with hard labour. The articles found in the house to be forfeited. Informers to be allowed $5 each.

A CURIOUS ROGUE AND VAGABOND
CC Number 59

A personage rejoicing in the name of Alexander William Eversley, was charged by Mr. J. Y. V. Vernon with being a rogue and a vagabond. The defendant is steward on board the British ship P.C. [sic] Carvill, and is apparently of an exceedingly amorous temperament. According to his statement, on Sunday he had observed a handkerchief waving from complainant's villa, and, no doubt thinking this might have been a signal from some love lorn damsel who had seen him from afar, he proceeded to the place and inquired for a Miss Goodwin. He was told no such person lived there. On the Monday the signal again floated in the breeze, and he again proceeded to inquire after Miss Goodwin, and with the same success. The signal was again hoisted yesterday upon the west side of the villa, and the result of his visit this time was that a Police Constable took charge of him. It seemed defendant was perfectly quiet and sober,

On promising to go on board at once defendant was cautioned and discharged.

THE KICKING CASE[84]
CC Number 60

This case in which two Chinamen were charged with causing the death of a third was before the Court to-day.

Mr. Mossop appeared for the second prisoner.

Lau Akwai, a Chinese woman, gave evidence substantially similar to that she gave at the inquest.

The woman's eyesight which seemed to be somewhat defective, was tested by Mr. Mossop by placing three men before the witness, and asking the colour of their coats. In the first instance she was wrong, but in the other two correct. He also examined her on some other points of her story.

Police Constable 210 said he was on duty in Southern Street on the day in question. From what he heard about a man being killed near the Salt Fish Lan he went there. No one told him anything about how the man had come by his death.

The witness had gone about his duty in so cautious a manner that the Magistrate told him that if he had gone a little more expeditiously about it, there possibly being some life in the man, there was no knowing, but the man might have been saved. His conduct had not been like what a constable's behaviour should be.

Witness's story differed considerably from that of the woman. He had only arrested the second defendant after he had been pointed out to him by the first. The people in the Lan said he did not kill the man. He afterwards arrested the second defendant, who thereupon told him he had better arrest the first defendant, which he did. When the first defendant pointed out the second he said he was the man who struck deceased. The witness said that during a period

---

[84] The following is the complete set of reports in connection with this case in *The Complete Court Cases*: CC Nos 60, 65. The two accused are not named in either. The dead man is named in the report of the Inquest, held before H. E. Wodehouse, as "Lam Akwong".

extending over a quarter of an hour he stood by and examined the body. He did nothing else. All this time there was no one answered any questions.

The Magistrate said he could hardly believe this lukong. He could understand them skulking work, but why he should stand there all this time and do nothing, and that no one would answer any question was almost beyond belief.

A long time was spent in trying to get at the bottom of what was the truth of this witness's statement.

Mr. Mossop cross-examined witness as to the evidence given at the inquest, and his answers were most conflicting. To the Magistrate he swore one thing and was equally ready to do a similar favour to Mr. Mossop.

One more witness gave evidence, but did not throw much new light on the matter.

Adjourned till half past two to-morrow afternoon.

THURSDAY 11 AUGUST 1881[85]
ALLEGED TRAFFIC IN GIRLS
CC Number 61

The case in which Shik Tai Ping, a widow, was charged with unlawfully bringing complainant's daughter, twenty-five years of age, into the Colony for the purpose of selling her, was again before the Court, having been remanded from the 4th *instant*.

Wong Tsan [*sic*], Police Constable 197, stated that he was in the detective branch of the Police Force. He had made enquiries now for several weeks about the case, but had discovered nothing, and had no expectation of getting any evidence. He had no clue as to the whereabouts of the missing woman.

Defendant, who stated that the charge was a false one, was discharged.

---

[85] "Police Intelligence," CM, Thursday, 11 August 1881, p. 3, c. 2.

LARCENY OF CLOTHING
CC Number 62
Chun Tai Hing, 25 rice-pounder, against whom two previous convictions were proved, was convicted of stealing a jacket and pair of trousers, the property of Ng Ang, a stone-cutter, on the 11th instant, and was sentenced to be imprisoned for six months with hard labour.

THE 'RICKSHA NUISANCE
CC Number 63
Sixteen jinricksha coolies were convicted of driving their vehicles in a reckless manner, and not observing the rules of the road, and were fined 50 cents each, with the alternative of two days' imprisonment.

A DANGEROUS NUISANCE
CC Number 64
Nine Chinamen were fined $1 each, or four days' imprisonment for lighting bonfires on the public streets.

THE KICKING CASE[86]
CC Number 65
The kicking case in which two Chinamen are charged with causing the death of a third was resumed this afternoon.

Mr. Mossop appeared for the second defendant.

Dr. Marques, Assistant Superintendent at the Civil Hospital, gave evidence similar to that he had given at the inquest.

Chan Aluk, also a witness at the inquest, was examined. He did not see the woman U Nga on the Praya at the time the man was killed; he first saw her following to the Station. He did not see the witness Lau Afui either, except at Number 7 Station. Cross-examined by Mr. Mossop, witness said he was quite

---

[86] The following is the complete set of reports in connection with this case in *The Complete Court Cases*: CC Nos 60, 65.

certain that it was neither of the prisoners who struck deceased; he would know the man if he saw him. The first prisoner might have been in the crowd. When the Constable arrested the second defendant witness said, "that is not the man," and repeated this at Number 7 Station.

Mr. Mossop reserved his defence on behalf of the second prisoner, and applied for bail to be allowed, but did not press the application, as his Worship[87] thought it was not a case in which he could accept it, the case being purely one for the Supreme Court.

The prisoners have been duly cautioned, reserved their defence, and were committed for trial at the next Sessions of the Supreme Court.[88]

---

[87] Magistrates in Hong Kong are still addressed as, "Your Worship".

[88] The August 1881 Criminal Sessions are reported in *The China Mail* on 19 August 1881, p. 3, c. 4 and 20 August 1881, p. 3, c. 3, On 19 August, the report concludes with the statement that, "Three cases remain on the Calendar, but the Attorney General stated that two only would be brought before the Court." This case appears to be the one that was not brought before the Court at this time.

Subsequently, on Tuesday, 23 August 1881, *The China Mail* (p. 3, c. 6, captioned "The Kicking Case") gave a further report of the Criminal Sessions held at the Supreme Court on the same day, "(Before His Honour the Acting Chief Justice, F. Snowden, Esq.)", stating that, "The two men who had been remitted from the Police Court, charged with causing the death of a third, were not tried, owing to insufficiency of evidence."

The two accused are named in neither Court Case Report. They are not named in the report of the Inquest hearing on 5 August 1881, said to be an adjourned hearing (the first inquest hearing report that has been found) either. In the report of the 5 August hearing, the inquest, was reported to be further adjourned to Monday 8 August. However, no report of any hearing on this date or any other later date has been found.

For a report of the adjourned inquest on this man, named as Lam Akwong, (CM, Friday, 5 August 1881, p. 3, c. 2), see Gillian Bickley, ed, "The Kicking Case", in, "Some Nineteenth Century Hong Kong Court Cases", 2009/2010.

SATURDAY 13 AUGUST 1881[89]
UNLAWFUL POSSESSION
CC Number 66

Leung Ahai was charged as above.

Marcus Prehn said he was a ship carpenter, residing in the German Tavern. On going to his tool chest yesterday he missed some tools. He afterwards found the tools on defendant's stall.

Defendant stated that he bought the hammer, but was fined $2 or seven days' imprisonment with hard labour.

[UNLAWFUL POSSESSION][90]
CC Number 67

Leung Awan and Tam Ayu were charged with being in unlawful possession of tools belonging to Marcus Prehn. The article had been found on first defendant's stall.

The first defendant said he bought it from the second defendant ten days ago.

Second defendant said that about ten or twenty days ago he bought the chisel. He afterwards sold it to the first defendant.

The first defendant was fined $2 or seven days' in gaol with hard labour, and the second defendant discharged.

DRUNK
CC Number 68

Henry Kenny, seaman, admitted being drunk and incapable, and was fined twenty-five cents, or one day's imprisonment.

---

[89] "Police Intelligence," CM, Saturday, 13 August 1881, p. 3, c. 3. The following is the complete set of reports in connection with this case in *The Complete Court Cases*: CC Nos 66, 67.

[90] The following is the complete set of reports in connection with this case in *The Complete Court Cases*: CC Nos 66, 67.

ROGUE AND VAGABONDS
CC Number 69
Police Constable 566 said he saw the defendant Ko Afui, and four others, gambling with dice. He caught defendant. Prisoner of course said he was innocent, but notwithstanding this protestation was sent seven days to gaol with hard labour.

[ROGUE AND VAGABONDS]
CC Number 70
Li Afai was convicted on the evidence of Police Constable 289 of playing at Fantan along with others near the Harbour Office, and was sentenced to seven days' imprisonment with hard labour.

DEFILING A STREAM
CC Number 71
Salomon Ramma, and Juan Bantista, admitted the above offence, and were each fined 50 cents or five days' in gaol with hard labour.

THROWING RUBBISH INTO THE HARBOUR
CC Number 72
Three Chinamen were convicted of throwing rubbish into the harbour, and each fined $1, or four days' imprisonment with hard labour.

MONDAY 15 AUGUST 1881[91]
WATCHMAN, WHAT OF THE NIGHT?
CC Number 73
Hassam Bux, a watchman at Kowloon Docks, admitted having yielded to the influence of "nature's great nurse" and got fined $2 or seven days' imprisonment with hard labour.

---

[91] "Police Intelligence," CM, Monday, 15 August 1881, p. 3, c. 2.

MARINERS BOLD
CC Number 74

Thomas Phillips, seaman, American ship *Invincible*, George Waugh, British barque *John C. Munro*, Emile Knap, engineer steamship *Africa*, and Frederick Smith, seaman of the same ship, had evidently been enjoying themselves yesterday. The first defendant was found drunk and incapable by a Sikh constable in East Street. He attempted to arrest defendant, when he was set upon by the other defendants, and it was only after the arrival of some European policemen that these high spirited tars were conveyed to the Station.

First defendant was fined 50 cents or two days in gaol for being drunk and disorderly; second $2 or four days with hard labour for assaulting the police, and to pay $1 compensation for damaging a turban, or two days' additional imprisonment; third $1 or two days with hard labour for assaulting the police; fourth $1 or two days with hard labour for assaulting the police, and $1 for damaged turban, or an additional two days' imprisonment.

STABBING
CC Number 75

Lo Lai Hi and Lo Aloi, fisherman, remanded from the 3rd instant, were again in Court to-day, complainant having been discharged from the Civil Hospital this morning. According to complainant's story he had engaged the boat belonging to a woman of the name of Lai Mi Kiu for amusement. As the tide was strong he tied the boat to a buoy. While lying there the two defendants pulled alongside in a sampan, jumped on board, beat the complainant with their fists, and then stabbed him in the right side. Defendants were arrested by the police boat. The case was again remanded to the 18th instant.

TUESDAY 16 AUGUST 1881[92]
CHARGES OF CREATING A DISTURBANCE IN A DWELLING HOUSE
CC Number 76

Leung Anam, coolie, appeared on remand from the 13th *instant*, charged with creating a disturbance in the house of Mr. J. A. Gutierres [*sic*], Number 5, Elgin Street, on the 12th *instant*.

Augusto Aureliano Gutierrez [*sic*], recalled, gave some further evidence, to the effect that defendant was not at the front door of complainant's house when the amah was there with her box; he entered the house by the back door. Beyond his entering the house, witness knew of no disturbance created by defendant.

Complainant, recalled, stated that it was while going from the back to the front door that defendant made a noise; he called out Ta! Ta!

No further evidence being produced, the prisoner was discharged.

LARCENY FROM THE PERSON
CC Number 77

Ho Afuk, 25, coolie, remanded from the 13th *instant*, was again[93] before the Court on a charge of stealing a pair of gold earrings, worth $24 from the person of a married woman named Loong Ai.

The latter gave further evidence to the effect that it was at the corner of Stanley and Pottinger Street that the rings were taken. The moon was not shining at the time, but the street lamps were alight. Defendant was behind witness when he took the rings from her. She had not the least doubt that defendant was the man who snatched her earrings. The servant who was with complainant corroborated this evidence, and said that she saw his face distinctly and identified the prisoner as the man who stole the

---

[92] "Police Intelligence," CM, Tuesday, 16 August 1881, p. 3, cc. 2 - 3.
[93] There is no account of this earlier appearance in *The Complete Court Cases*.

earrings from her mistress. He had on a brown jacket at the time, and witness did not see him throw it off.

Defendant again denied the charge, and said he had no jacket, and had no earrings in his possession when arrested, but was convicted and sentenced to three months' imprisonment with hard labour.

LARCENY OF A BOX OF CLOTHING, &C.
CC Number 78

Tsang Akin, who was remanded on the 13th *instant*, on a charge of stealing a box with a number of articles of clothing, and an umbrella, in value altogether about $50, the property of Luk Apong, on the 12th *instant*, was again brought up.

Complainant was recalled, and stated that he had heard defendant's statement on the last occasion they were before the Court, to the effect that he, witness, had told the defendant that he was to collect debts and pay money. Witness gave defendant no instructions about moving his property. Defendant desired him to go to Singapore, but he declined.

Defendant was sentenced to be imprisoned for two months with hard labour.

PENITENT SERVANTS
CC Number 79

The case of Fong Akum and two other chair coolies in the employ of Mr J.D. Hutchison, merchant, who were remanded on the 9th *instant*, to see if they would obey the orders of their employee [*sic* for employer], was again called, and, complainant stating that the culprits had since obeyed orders, the case was dismissed.

WEDNESDAY 17 AUGUST 1881[94]
DRUNK
CC Number 80

George Brecket, seaman, was charged with being drunk and refusing to pay [chair]hire, and on the evidence of the coolie was convicted, and sentenced to pay 50 cents for hire or two days' imprisonment, and give complainant $1 for his jacket or [two] days' additional imprisonment. Defendant had torn the coolie's jacket.

[DRUNK]
CC Number 81

John Allen, a Scotchman, was convicted on the evidence of Police Constable 562 and Inspector Mathieson of being drunk and incapable. Defendant, who had been discharged from gaol on Saturday, and who had been five times previously convicted, was fined $1 [or] four days' imprisonment.

REFUSING TO PAY HIRE
CC Number 82

Francis Victor was convicted on evidence of refusing to pay chair hire, and was [or]dered to pay 50 cents for hire or two days' imprisonment, and to pay a further 25 cents as compensation for loss of time, or one day additional in gaol.

BREACH OF MARKET ORDINANCE
CC Number 83

Lung Ahing admitted this charge, and was fined $1 or four days in gaol.

THEFT OF A PAIR OF TROUSERS
CC Number 84

Li Akwai was convicted of stealing a pair of trousers from Hung Ahok, a widow living in Queen's Road. Complainant had hung her trousers out to dry, and

---

[94] "Police Intelligence," CM, Wednesday, 17 August 1881, p. 2 c. 7, p. 3 c. 1.

defendant, who had been on the adjoining verandah, put round his hands and took them away. Fourteen days with hard labour.

THEFT OF CLOTHING
CC Number 85
The complainant in this case said he was a cook on board the steamer *Tung Ting*, now in the harbour. This morning, while asleep in bed in his house in Chuk Hing Lane, his wife woke him up and said a thief was pulling away his clothes with a bamboo. He got up and pursued the defendant, who dropped some articles of clothing. Defendant was given into custody. Prisoner admitted having been in gaol. He had been four times in that building. Sentenced to six months' imprisonment with hard labour, and exposure in the stocks for two hours.

ALLEGED ASSAULT[95]
CC Number 86 📖 p. 243
James Joseph M'Breen, a clerk, belonging [to] Ireland, and George Blake, staff ser[geant] were charged with assaulting Jane M'Breen, wife of the first defendant.

Mr Mossop, who appeared for the complainant, asked that the summons against the second prisoner might be amended to [aiding] and abetting, and he produced a letter from first defendant to complainant. Mr Mossop requested that the summons might be withdrawn against the first defendant if he would consent to return her clothes, jewellery and money and agree to separation.

Remanded till to-morrow at 2 p.m. to see if the parties could come to some arrangement.

---

[95] The following is the complete set of reports in connection with this case in *The Complete Court Cases*: No 86, 87, 94.

THURSDAY 18 AUGUST 1881[96]
ALLEGED ASSAULT[97]
CC Number 87 📖 p. 243

The case in which James Joseph M'Breen, a clerk, and George Blake, staff sergeant, were charged with assaulting the wife of the first defendant, was resumed this afternoon.

Mr. Mossop, who appeared on behalf of the complainant, said that his client was Mrs. James M'Breen, wife of the first defendant. About nine months ago the two had been married, and since then they had lived most unhappily together. The first defendant at the time of the marriage was out of employment, and was for some time entirely supported by complainant; about four months ago he obtained employment in the Commissariat, as a clerk, and from the time of his securing this clerkship up to now, he had ceased to live with the complainant, and ceased to allow her anything for her support, but had lived with the second defendant. Complainant had requested her husband to live with her, but this he refused to do while in the house she then occupied. Accordingly rooms were taken at the Blue Buildings. Defendant when asked to pay the rent by complainant, said he had not got the money. The two had gone to some Chinese friend and borrowed the money. Defendant however had not used this money to pay the rent, and on the evening of Sunday, the 7th, complainant had bitterly reproached him for appropriating the money to his own uses. On the evening of that day defendant had attacked her fiercely, struck her, knocked her down and jumped upon her, leaving some very severe marks on her body. She left the house in Blue Buildings and returned to the one she had formerly occupied, to which place first defendant had gone and taken away a box containing personal clothing, jewellery, and

---

[96] "Police Intelligence," CM, Thursday, 18 August 1881, p. 3, cc. 3 - 4.

[97] The following is the complete set of reports in connection with this case in *The Complete Court Cases*: CC Nos 86, 87, 94.

money, by force. As his Worship had suggested yesterday with a view to an arrangement, the box had been opened in the presence of Mr. Parker,[98] when it was found that not only the money and jewellery, but also some of the personal clothing, had been removed.

Complainant then went into the box.

Jane Francis M'Breen said she was the wife of the first defendant. She was married to him nine months ago. When witness married him, she was living in Number 208, Queen's Road Central. First defendant, after marrying witness, left the police force, where he had been, and came and lived with witness. For four or five months witness entirely supported the first defendant. He got employment about four months ago in the Commissariat Department. The first day he got employment there he stopped in the Sergeants' Mess. Since he had got work he had never given her any money. First day he got paid he had given her $30, but the next day he took them back. The second moon [sic] he gave her $11 and took away $5. Every evening he came up to see witness, she had to pay his 'rickshaw and give him cigar money. The third month he gave witness $20, but he asked her to take the gold ring out of pawn. For this she paid about $5 for the redemption. The ring, for which she had paid, costs about $10. This was all the money she had received. In the latter part of July he asked witness to take lodgings so that they might live together. He took rooms next door to the American Consulate. Witness moved with her private effects. First defendant [M'Breen] sometimes came and lived with her there. She asked him when rent was due to pay it. This was the week before last. He told her he had no money. First defendant asked

---

[98] Each of Court Cases No. 463 and No. 716 states that Mr Parker was Chief Clerk of the Magistracy. In *The Complete Court Cases*, he features in four cases. Three involve women who each possess a European surname: Mrs M'Breen, Mrs Driscoll and the prostitute Dolly Johnson. The fourth case concerns impersonation by a Chinese male.

witness to go to a friend's house and borrow the money for him. She and her husband went and borrowed the money from Mrs Aku, who handed the money to him. He did not pay the rent with this money. On the 7th *instant* the first defendant came to her house, when she asked him to pay $20 of house rent, but he said he had spent the money. First defendant came there about 9 p.m. that evening, and as witness described it he was proper drunk. He gave her a slap in the face, knocked her down and jumped upon her. Witness called out for her cook to come and save her life.[99] The cook came and pulled the first defendant away from her. Her arms and legs were bruised. After this the first defendant went away. On the 14th of August the two defendants came to 208 Queen's Road, where she was then living. The first defendant said he must have a large box, which witness said belonged to her; she was quite agreeable to let him have a smaller one, but first defendant said he would take anything he liked; he was "boss" of the house. Four or five coolies came upstairs, but witness dismissed them, and then sent for an Indian Police Constable. First defendant said witness had stolen the boxes. The whole party then went to the Central Station. The Inspector said he had nothing to say in the matter. They went down into Pottinger Street, when Sergeant Blake said to the husband "You take hold of her hands and I'll take the box." Her husband held her hands behind her back, and she cried out for police. A constable came from the charge room, and then her husband let her go. She and the two defendants proceeded as far as the Naval yard; two coolies carried the boxes—second defendant following. At this place witness got out of the chair and took hold of her own box. Her husband again held her hands, while the second defendant helped the coolies to put the box into a jinrickshaw. Afterwards she saw the second defendant take the

---

[99] It seems that she shouted out, "Save Life!" This seems to be a translation from Cantonese.

box from the vehicle and put it into his house. In the box were one gold watch, value $35; one silver watch, $10; one gold chain, $30; one neck chain, $15; one pair earrings, $5.30; one brooch, $4; 2 $25 notes; 30 mexican dollars; and a quantity of clothes, value about $120. There were two shirts which had been left with her for redemption for $3. There was nothing of her husband's in the box. The box was opened in the Magistracy office yesterday, and witness examined it. All her clothes were not there, and the jewellery and the money were gone.

Neither of the defendants wished to ask any questions at present.

Mr. Mossop said they had no right to cross-examine the witness at a later stage, unless his Worship gave special permission.

His Worship agreed with this view, and First[100] defendant [i.e. M'Breen] wished to know from witness how he came to leave the police,[101] and witness answered that she wished to employ him to manage the tavern,[102] and requested him to leave the police force. She did not offer him $200 or 300 to leave.[103] Defendant asked if he gave her any money while employed in the Daily Press. Witness said, Yes, but that he had got it all back. Witness knew nothing about a stipulation by the Commissary General that on getting the appointment in the Ordnance Store he should leave Queen's Road. During the week they stopped in the Blue Buildings, first defendant came home every night. The cook boy complained of want of food, after witness left the

---

[100] The lay-out of the text here (a paragraph ending with the word "and" and a new paragraph beginning with the word "First") is given as in the original.

[101] The answer to this question gives an explanation of the relationship between this couple, which is helpful for understanding the narrative elsewhere. It is also interesting for the light it throws on social customs in Hong Kong at this time.

[102] Perhaps the tavern was located at the "208, Queen's Road" address given elsewhere in the reporting of this case.

[103] This statement is obviously in response to a question which is omitted from this report.

house. She did not strike him with a chair on the Sunday night. The gentleman and lady living on the second floor asked defendant, not witness, whether the latter had been beaten. Witness did tear his shirt, but did not force him from the house. He did furnish a house for her, and she did leave it. She took away a number of things.

Re-examined:—The things she took away were witness's own property. She took away three chairs which her husband had bought. The only furnishing her husband provided consisted of five chairs. When first defendant could not pay for things he would have liked her to do so.

By the second defendant [Blake], on the 4th of August, when the boxes were taken to the Central Station witness had no wish to go, but the policeman made her. The Police Constable did not tell second defendant to fetch the coolies, the second defendant told the Constable to do so. She did not hear her husband tell the Constable to call the coolies. Witness did not hear her husband ask the second defendant to help him to carry the box. Second defendant asked the Constable to carry the box. She did not push the box while being taken downstairs—she pulled it. It was her husband who told the coolies to put the box in the 'rickshaw. Witness was close to the 'rickshaw when her husband took hold of her hands.

Chan Asan, cook to the plaintiff, gave evidence as to the assault committed on the evening of the 7th *instant*.

Joseph Ramsay, Constable of the Naval Yard Police, said he was on duty at the gate in the 14th. He saw the first defendant holding complainant by the arms. She was shouting police. This was on the side-path about thirty yards from the gate. Witness did not see second defendant there.

By the second defendant:—Witness did not see two boxes being put into a rickshaw.

Re-examined:—Second defendant might have been there, but he did not see him.

The case was adjourned till half-past two on Saturday.

FRIDAY 19 AUGUST 1881[104]
DRUNK
CC Number 88
John Anderson admitted being drunk and incapable, and was fined 25 cents or one day's imprisonment.

ASSAULT
CC Number 89
Wong Apak was charged with assaulting R. Love, Police Constable No. 32, and tearing his cape on the 18th instant. He was convicted on the evidence of the Police Constable and fined 50 cents for assault or two days in gaol with hard labour, and to pay 25 cents for damage done to the constable's cape or an additional day's imprisonment.

MENDICANCY
CC Number 90
Three Chinamen, charged with mendicancy, were sentenced, — the first to be sent to the Tung Wah Hospital, and the second and third to their native country.

UNLICENSED OPIUM
CC Number 91
Tai Asam, was charged with having a quantity of prepared opium in his possession without a certificate.

Inspector Perry said he went to the top floor of Number 8 Shin Hing Lane, and made a search. There were found a pot containing about 7 or 8 taels of opium, and a smaller one containing about 2 taels. He also found five small horn opium boxes each of which contained a small quantity of prepared opium. He also found a boiling pan, as also 33 balls of Malwa opium and 2 balls of Patna.

---

[104] "Police Intelligence," CM, Friday, 19 August 1881, p. 3, c. 2.

An excise officer and an informer gave corroborative evidence.

Defendant was fined $25 or one month's imprisonment, the whole of the opium found in the house to be delivered to the Opium Farmer.

AN AIRY COSTUME[105]
CC Number 92

Mooideen, a seaman, belonging to Malacca, was found by a constable at an early hour this morning, below the Wellington Barracks, in a state of nudity, with the exception of an apron of green leaves, and was taken to the Number 2 Police Station pair of trousers. Defendant stated that he would get his own trousers when he got to Bangkok. There being doubt as to his sanity, the defendant was remanded until tomorrow for report of the Colonial Surgeon as to his mental condition.

TRAFFIC IN CHILDREN[106]
CC Number 93 📖 p. 301

The case in which Tong Achi and Wong a Ng were charged with forcibly detaining two boys and three girls for an unlawful purpose, was again called, but Detective Sergeant Fisher having stated that the four men sent to make enquiries regarding the children in the neighbouring province not having yet returned, it was further remanded till the 26th *instant*.

---

[105] The following is the complete set of reports in connection with this case in *The Complete Court Cases*, are: CC Nos 92, 113. In CC 113, "Mooideen" is spelt, "Moodien".

[106] The following is the complete set of reports in connection with this case in *The Complete Court Cases*: CC Nos 20, 93, 235, 238. CC No. 37 may also be related to this group of cases.

SATURDAY 20 AUGUST 1881[107]
ALLEGED ASSAULT[108]
CC Number 94 📖 p. 248

The case in which Joseph James M'Breen, clerk, and George Blake, staff sergeant, were charged, the former with assaulting his wife, and the latter with aiding and abetting therein, was finished this afternoon.

Mr Mossop, who again appeared for the complainant, applied that all witnesses leave the Court.[109]

His Worship drew attention to the fact, [that] the second defendant had nothing to do with the assault said to be made on 7th instant.

First defendant [M'Breen] stated that the boxes were his property, and the Magistrate said that [as th]e husband of plaintiff he could not [deny] that,[110] whereupon Mr. Mossop observed that if the boxes were not returned the case would not end in this Court.

Further evidence was then called.

C.A. Paterson, Police Constable 20, said he went down to Pottinger Street having heard a noise there. He saw the complainant get out of a chair and try to prevent the coolies from taking the boxes away. First defendant took hold of complainant's arms. Witness [Paterson] told him to let go and he did so. [First] defendant seemed to be stopping her from preventing the coolies taking the boxes.

---

[107] "Police Intelligence," CM, Saturday, 20 August 1881, p. 3, cc. 1 - 2.

[108] The following is the complete set of reports in connection with this case in *The Complete Court Cases*: CC Nos 86, 87, 94.

[109] In represented cases, it is the duty of prosecuting counsel to ensure all prosecution witnesses are out of court and [it is the duty of] defence counsel [to ensure] all defence witnesses [are out of court]. This is to ensure witnesses give honest evidence not evidence tailored to other accounts. (Note supplied courtesy, Magistrate Garry Tallentire.)

[110] The Magistrate is presumably referring to the fact that a wife's property automatically belonged to her husband at this time.

By second defendant [Blake]:—Witness [Paterson] did not hear him say anything to the first defendant.

This closed the case for the prosecution.

The first defendant [M'Breen] wished to call Mr. Parker[111] to explain about the means he took to come to an arrangement.Mr. Mossop said he would object to that. Carl Siemund [*sic*][112] said he saw first defendant and his wife on the night of the 7th about nine o'clock. He heard a dreadful noise as though somebody's throat had been cut. He went half way down stairs. The noise was simply disgraceful. The voice was a woman's. The woman was howling like a maniac. The first defendant was sitting as quiet as could be smoking his pipe. Witness [Mr Siemund] asked him what was the matter, and whether she was drunk. He said no. The screaming was something about $25. First defendant said there had been no fighting whatever. The noise was most disgraceful, and latterly he went to the Police Station to see if he could get a policeman. She tried to incite [him t]o strike her.

Mr Mossop:—Be careful.

Witness [Mr Siemund]: There is no careful about it. She said "You likee flog me." Witness is quite certain about the words. When he went downstairs he found a European constable looking in at the window; he [s]ent to the Station. Witness said first defendant was as drunk now as he was then (meaning that he was sober). Complainant had a couple of youngsters sitting howling in company with her, and the noise was dreadful. On the morning of the [8]th, the yelling by complainant commenced again. Witness did not see complainant throw anything at first defendant.

By Mr. Mossop:—Complainant did try to incite defendant to flog her. The words were "You wanchee flog my; You likee flog my."

---

[111] Mr Parker was Chief Clerk at the Magistracy.
[112] The variations, "Siemund" and "Seimund", appear in the reporting of this case.

Inspector Adams [113] said he was in first defendant's house on the evening of the 7th August On that day he was in first defendant's house. He was there seeing him and his wife. She was pulling and hauling about. It seemed to him that it was in earnest. It was about $25. This witness did not understand. Witness then left in disgust, as he did not think such conduct proper.

Mr. Mossop objected to any evidence of anything that took place before the affair.

The Magistrate admitted the evidence.

Witness [Inspector Adams]:— About eleven o'clock that night — he stopping next door to first defendant, — heard Mrs M'Breen calling her husband very filthy names. (Witness, at Mr Mossop's request, repeated one or two of them.) He heard first defendant say keep quiet. This continued for two or three minutes.

By Mr. Mossop: — Witness would not give his opinion as to whether it was surprising, that if complainant had been assaulted at nine o'clock, she should have been abusing him at eleven o'clock.

Mr Mossop: I think you said something about them walking away.

Witness [Inspector Adams]: I think you have made a mistake.

Mr Mossop: Perhaps I have; you may correct it.

Witness [Inspector Adams]: No I won't.

Mr Mossop: Be careful; you are in a Court of Justice.

Witness [Inspector Adams]: I think you had better be careful.

Mr Mossop again cautioned witness, who thanked him for his advice. [114]

---

[113] Possibly M. J. Adams, Inspector of Nuisances, Surveyor General's Department. ("List of Officers", HKBB1882, Section I3.)

[114] The witness is being sarcastic.

The Magistrate said Mr Mossop had a very delicate duty to perform,[115] and Mr Adams should answer the question properly.

This witness then did.

Subject to Mr Mossop's objection, complainant was examined by her husband.

Mrs M'Breen, on being shown a ring, said it did not belong to her husband. It was the ring she had taken out of pawn.

First defendant [M'Breen] then made a statement in defence. Complainant on the afternoon of the day in question asked him to go to Happy Valley. They went there; and when there complainant threw herself down upon a grave. He remained there for two hours, but she would not come away.

The Magistrate: Was the deceased any relative?

First defendant [M'Breen] said he did not know. She said it was her late husband. Directly she came home she assaulted him violently, and kept up such a disagreeable row that he left and that night slept in the house of a friend. With regard to the taking of the box, his wife, when she left him, had taken away all the articles of furniture, food, and clothing, all his wearing apparel, and some of his linen, as also some articles he had got from Mr Cassumbhoy, also two or three pairs of white trousers. She had afterwards gone and taken away the small box. He was rather doubtful of going to the house himself, and so he asked if second defendant would kindly go with him. Prior to this he had asked the Captain Superintendent of Police to send a policeman with him for his protection, but he said he could not do this. When first defendant arrived there he wished to remove the small box, but she sat down on the top of it and began screaming. He said if she did not be quiet he would not only take the small box but the large one. An Indian Constable came, and

---

[115] By being is being polite and conciliatory, Frederick Stewart is able to persuade the witness to answer the question properly.

first defendant [M'Breen] asked him to get coolies to remove the boxes. The boxes ultimately were taken to the Central Station. The Inspector there would have nothing to do with the matter. In Pottinger Street he asked the second defendant [Blake] to take charge of the boxes. He held his wife, who was screaming police.[116] When the constable came he let go and walked by the side of her chair as far as the Hotel de l'Univers. He next saw her beyond the Dock-yard gate, where she was violently abusing the second defendant. The boxes were taken away solely under his superintendence.

The second defendant [Blake] said he would like to say a few words about an assertion made by Mr Mossop in his opening speech, which seriously affected his character as a military man. He referred to the statement that the first defendant [M'Breen] had lived with him.[117] As he had only one room, and he was a married man, this would not have been decent, and beside he was not allowed to keep lodgers.

The Magistrate said he was sure that Mr Mossop[118] would do nothing which was not proper. Of course Mr Mossop was acting under instructions, which was quite a different thing from what Mr Mossop might do individually.[119] It was a delicate matter, and he was bound to say that Mr Mossop had conducted the case very properly.

Mr Mossop said that he did not think that the complainant meant to infer[120] that first defendant lived in the same room with the Sergeant.

Mr Mossop then addressed his Worship on the case. He thought it was a most imprudent thing on the part of a Staff Sergeant — a man who ought to

---

[116] That is, she was screaming out, "Police!"

[117] See above.

[118] *Sic* for Mr Blake? Or is the text in fact correct?

[119] Frederick Stewart is again being polite and conciliatory. But he may also really feel that Mr Mossop had conducted the case very properly.

[120] "Infer": *sic* for "imply".

have known better — to go into his client's private room and aid in taking away these boxes. He had no hesitation in saying that the evidence of the complainant did not support the assertion that first defendant had lived with the Sergeant.

The Magistrate said as far as the Sergeant[121] was concerned the summons was dismissed. His Worship was sorry he had got into this disagreeable affair. If he had known then what he knew now, probably he would never have been mixed up in it. With regard to the assault on the 7th, the evidence given today had put a very different complexion upon it. Besides, the corrections made upon her own evidence had led him to doubt the complainant's truthfulness. Although there was much in the case which should not have been, yet he could not say that the assault had been proved against the first defendant. Mr Seimund [*sic*][122] had said that, though complainant was screaming like a maniac, the husband was calmly smoking his pipe. Altogether he could not convict the first defendant of the assault; and therefore the summons would be discharged.

TUESDAY 30 AUGUST 1881[123]
[STEALING]
CC Number 95

Ng Ajuk, 26, a rice pounder, for stealing two pieces of clothing and an opium pipe value $3 on the 28th inst, he having been four times previously before the Court, — once for giving false evidence in Dec. 1879; once for larceny in May, 1880; once as a rogue and vagabond, Aug 5th, 1880, and once for house breaking Dec. last year — was sentenced to six months' imprisonment with hard labour, the same sentence as was imposed on him on his immediately preceding conviction.

---

[121] "The Sergeant": i.e. George Blake.
[122] The variations, "Siemund" and "Seimund", appear in the reporting of this case.
[123] "Police Intelligence," CM, Tuesday, 30 August 1881, p. 3, cc. 5- 6.

LARCENY
CC Number 96
Li Akin, 35, a coolie, for larceny of a coverlet value $1 was sent to Gaol for fourteen days with hard labour.

[LARCENY]
CC Number 97 📖 p. 277
Lan Aping, 29, boatman, was sentenced to three months' imprisonment with hard labour for stealing clothing and jewellery to the value of $22.50 from the inmate of a brothel.

WEDNESDAY 31 AUGUST 1881[124]
LARCENY
CC Number 98
Ip Afu was charged with stealing a jacket and a purse. It seemed that the complainant had awakened this morning on hearing some one in the room. He struck a light and saw defendant running out of the room. Complainant and others ran after defendant, who was arrested. Defendant admitted the charge and also having been in gaol before. Three months' imprisonment with hard labour.

THEFT OF A JACKET &C.
CC Number 99
Tam Aman was charged with stealing a variety of articles from Wong Ahi a tailor. Defendant had been sleeping in complainant's house, had risen during the night, and taken away with him the property. Complainant made a report at the station. This was on the 13th of July. On the 30th inst, defendant was seen by complainant going into a house in Square Street. He called a Police Constable and had him arrested. Defendant admitted that some of the property was in a certain pawnshop.

---

[124] "Police Intelligence," CM, Wednesday, 31 August 1881, p. 3, cc. 3 - 4.

Defendant admitted the charge, and was sent [for] four weeks to gaol with hard labour.

DRUNK AND DISORDERLY CONDUCT
CC Number 100

Manuel Villarocencious [*sic*] was accused of the above offences. Police Constable 559 said that an European gentleman asked him to take defendant, who was very drunk, into custody. When taking him to the station he was very violent. Witness blew his whistle and another Police Constable came to his assistance. Defendant struck the second Constable and broke his chain whistle.

Police Constable 527 gave evidence to the same effect.

Defendant said the Constables clubbed him and kicked him in the ribs.

Inspector Lindsay gave evidence as to the disorderly conduct of the prisoner in the charge room, where he struck and kicked all round.

Patrick Crokeny gave evidence as to the prisoner abusing him. He gave him into charge.

Defendant was convicted of disorderly conduct, and fined $5 or ten days in gaol with hard labour.

A SLEEPY WATCHMAN
CC Number 101

Yung Ahan was convicted on the evidence of Police Constable 647 of being asleep on duty at some military bungalows at Wanchai, and was fined $5 or ten days' imprisonment. He had been fined for a similar offence before.

LARCENY FROM THE PERSON
CC Number 102

Tan Cheung charged Leung Yeung with picking his pocket of $1 while at the Harbour Master's Office, when he gave the defendant into custody. Defendant stated that it rained, and that he accidentally ran up against complainant, who seized and beat him. He had been in gaol before. He was sentenced to two months' imprisonment with hard labour.

THEFT OF A PASSAGE TICKET
CC Number 103

U Apui, farmer, a passenger bound for California, said that to-day while outside the Harbour Master's Office, defendant snatched his passage ticket from his hand. He pursued and caught him. His parents paid the $50 for the ticket.

Police Constable 585 said he saw defendant snatch the ticket.

Defendant, who had been in gaol before, was sent there for three months with hard labour.

THEFT OF SEVEN JACKETS
CC Number 104

Chung Wan I and Ho Aman were charged with stealing seven jackets.

Tu Ayau, a gardener, said that on the morning of the 30th, he got up and missed a jacket. His fellow-workmen missed six others. From information received second defendant was first arrested, and ultimately first defendant. Second defendant admitted having pawned three of the jackets, and three others were produced by the first defendant. After further evidence had been heard the prisoners were sentenced to two months' imprisonment each with hard labour.

BEFORE FREDERICK STEWART, ESQ.,
September 1881[125]

FRIDAY 2 SEPTEMBER 1881[126]
THEFT OF CHAIR POLES
CC Number 105

Leong Ahi, 36, a coolie, was charged with stealing two chair poles, value 70 cents, the property of two chair coolies, one of whom was the complainant. He was sentenced to ten days' hard labour in gaol.

OBSTRUCTION
CC Number 106

For leaving a quantity of rattans on the footpath, Queen's Road West, Pang San Kong was fined $10 with the alternative of seven days' imprisonment.

UNLAWFUL POSSESSION OF OLD IRON
CC Number 107

Cheung Afuk, 41, a boatman, for unlawful possession of a quantity of old iron of the value of $1.25, was fined $2, with the alternative of seven days' imprisonment with hard labour.

ROGUE AND VAGABOND
CC Number 108

Li Afu, 38, a hawker, was sentenced to fourteen days' imprisonment with hard labour, for being a rogue and vagabond and indulging in street gambling on the 1st *instant*.

---

[125] **Note to September reports.** Although there is a report of cases heard before P.G. Wodehouse in the 1 September 1881 *China Mail*, there is none of cases heard before Frederick Stewart. Similarly there is no report of cases heard before Frederick Stewart in the Tuesday, 7 September, Tuesday, 13 and Tuesday 21 September *China Mail*.

[126] "Police Intelligence," CM, Friday, 2 September 1881, p. 3, c. 5.

LARCENY OF CLOTHES
CC Number 109

Mung Ahing, 35, unemployed, was charged with stealing two jackets of the value of $6, on the 1st instant, also one pair of trousers value 60 cents, on the 29th August at Stanley. He was convicted and sentenced to six weeks' imprisonment with hard labour; four weeks on the first charge, and two on the second.

UNLAWFUL POSSESSION OF COAL
CC Number 110

For unlawful possession of about half a ton of coal, value $5, on board a boat in the harbour, Li Acheung, 27, unemployed, was fined $10, with the alternative of 21 days' imprisonment with hard labour.

UNLAWFUL POSSESSION OF OPIUM
CC Number 111

Chai Aping, 68, unemployed, for being found in unlawful possession of prepared opium without a valid certificate from the opium farmer, was fined $10, with the alternative of fourteen days' imprisonment, the opium to be forfeited to the farmer.

THEFT OF A WATCH, ETC.
CC Number 112 📖 p. 225

Ahmed, a Malacca-man, 25, a seaman, was charged with stealing a watch and chain, 60 cents in money, a knife, a handkerchief, and some beads, all of the value of $12.25, on the 30th *ultimate*.

Ameer Khan deposed that he was formerly in the Police Force, from which he was dismissed. He had had no employment for a year. Saw the defendant for the first time in the Mahomedan Cemetery. Went there, about 12.30 p.m. to pray. Defendant was in the compound at the time. Took off his long coat, in the pocket of which he had 60 cents in silver, a knife worth 50 cents, a handkerchief worth 10 cents., and some beads worth 10 cents. Also took off his belt, to which his silver watch and chain were attached. Went to a well to wash his hands and feet before saying his prayers. Left his coat and belt on the table in the Mosque. Was away about 10 or 15 minutes. When he came back he found the coat and belt there, but the other property described was amissing.[127] Went out at once; but defendant was not to be seen. Went to Number 2 Station and reported the matter and gave the constable a description of the man. To-day, saw defendant in Lascar Row; when defendant saw him (witness) defendant ran away. Ran after him and the Constable stopped him. Had not recovered any of his property.

To the Court the complainant said the only other person within the gate was the gardener, who was at work. Witness, recalled later on in the case, stated that the watch and chain produced were his property.

Other evidence was given connecting the defendant with the pawning of the watch and chain thus identified.

Prisoner was sentenced to four weeks' imprisonment with hard labour.

SILLY BILLY[128]
CC Number 113

Moodien, 40, a Malacca-man, seaman, was charged with indecently exposing himself in Queen's Road East, on the 19th *ultimate*.

Police Constable No.1 (J. Foley) spoke to finding the accused wandering about near the Wellington Barracks, nothing on but a sort of apron of leaves. Believed the man was insane; he was quite quiet.

Defendant said he would be able to get trousers when he got to Bangkok.

---

[127] "Amissing": missing. This colloquialism is used several times in *The Complete Court Cases*.

[128] The following is the complete set of reports in connection with this case in *The Complete Court Cases*: CC Nos 92, 113.

A written certificate was put in from Dr. Ayres that defendant was unsound of mind.

Defendant stated that Abung Baba, Upper Lascar Row, is a friend of his; and further that he is a British subject and a native of Malacca.

Case adjourned to allow of Abung Baba being in attendance and enquiries being made as to whether some arrangement cannot be made to get the defendant to Malacca.

Abung Hadie Baba said the defendant lived next door to him. He had been a seaman but was now of unsound mind. Had no one to take care of him. Was a countryman of witness. Defendant's brother was in the P.& O. steamer *Malacca*. Defendant got his food from various ships. Often got clothing also, but always threw it away.

Baba, assistant serang, Malacca said defendant, who was from the same village as him, was 38 years of age, and was once a seaman. Had been one year out of employment. He used to stop for a few days in witness' house, and would then disappear. Was sometimes very quiet and sometimes very violent. Has plenty of relations in Malacca.

The case was remanded till the 9th instant, the Colonial Surgeon having no available accommodation in the Asylum at present.

SATURDAY 3 SEPTEMBER 1881[129]
FIGHTING
CC Number 114

Chan Aluk and Lam Aching were convicted on the evidence of Police Constable 651, of creating a disturbance at a hydrant, in Third Street, and each fined 50 cents or two days' imprisonment.

---

[129] "Police Intelligence," CM, Saturday, 3 September 1881, p. 3, c. 2.

UNLAWFUL POSSESSION
CC Number 115
Leong Asam was charged with being in unlawful possession of a quantity of coal.

G. MacDonald [*sic*], Police Constable 82,[130] said that this morning while on duty in a police boat off Wanchai, he saw a small boat passing, in which were two men, one of whom was the defendant. As soon as they saw the police boat they pulled ashore among some junks. Defendant was caught, but the other man got off. In the boat were found some coals.

Defendant said he bought the coals from a small boat. He did not know where the boat was now. A long time ago he had been fined for being in possession of stolen property.

Fined $10 or twenty-one days with hard labour; the boat to be confiscated.

MONDAY 5 SEPTEMBER 1881[131]
STREET GAMBLING
CC Number 116
Cheung [*sic*] and Li Achi were convicted, on the evidence of Police Constable No. 199, who said that on the 3rd instant, he saw defendants and forty or fifty others playing fantan near the Harbour Office. He arrested the defendants. They were playing with small stones and square pieces of tile. Sentence fourteen days' imprisonment with hard labour as rogues and vagabonds.

[STREET GAMBLING]
CC Number 117
Li Aun was charged with this offence. Police Constable 199 said that on the evening of the 3rd instant, he saw defendant and some others playing fantan near the Harbour Office. Sent to gaol for fourteen days as a rogue and vagabond.

---

[130] Police Constable No. 82 appears both as "G. McDonald" and "G. MacDonald" in *The Complete Court Cases*.

[131] "Police Intelligence," CM, Monday, 5 September 1881, p. 3, c. 2.

UNLAWFUL POSSESSION
CC Number 118
Ng Sui Ko, remanded from 31st August, on a charge of stealing clothing, was before the Court to-day, when he was sentenced to a fine of $5 or fourteen days in gaol with hard labour.

ASSAULTS
CC Number 119
Chan Afuk was charged with assaulting U Akum. Complainant said that this morning defendant and another man were fighting by throwing stones at each other. One of the stones struck complainant on the face. Fined $1, or four days' imprisonment with hard labour.

[ASSAULTS]
CC Number 120
Mak Alui charged Li Asau, a hawker, with assaulting him. It seemed that complainant had been told by his brother that defendant had beat him. Complainant asked him why he had done so. As answer defendant took up a pole and hit him over the head, with such effect that the wound had to be dressed at the Civil Hospital.

Defendant said that complainant and he had a quarrel, and that the complainant's brother threw a stone which hit the complainant on the head. He was fined $1, or seven days' imprisonment with hard labour, and ordered to pay $1 amends to complainant, or three days' additional imprisonment.

NUISANCE
CC Number 121
Wong Shing Wan, remanded from a previous day, charged with allowing noisome matter in the neighbourhood of his house, was brought up to-day, he having taken no steps to remove the nuisance. Fined $2, or four days in gaol.

TUESDAY 6 SEPTEMBER 1881[132]
MENDICANCY
CC Number 122
Chun Ayui admitted the charge of mendicancy, but stated that she had been twenty years in the Colony. She was cautioned and discharged, and ordered to get $1 from the poor box to pay for a license and buy a stock of cakes so that she might hawk.

BREACHES OF MARKET ORDINANCE
CC Number 123
Leong Ai and Li Ai admitted this charge and were fined $1 each or four days' imprisonment.

Wang Afung admitted the same charge and was similarly sentenced.

WITHOUT A PERMIT
CC Number 124
Ng Alui was charged with being in possession of crude opium without a certificate.

J. Smith Police Constable 31, said that he entered Number 51 Wanchai Street on the 5th *instant*. He searched the place and found three jars containing opium. He also found two jars of opium dross, and two balls of raw opium. There were also four brass pans, two ladles and five empty tins in one of which there were traces of prepared opium.

An informer gave evidence as to purchasing opium from defendant, informing the Opium Farmer, and laying an information.

Defendant said he had nothing to do with opium. He let part of his house to another man to whom the opium belonged.

Fined $25 or twenty one days' imprisonment. The opium to be given to the Opium Farmer.

---

[132] "Police Intelligence," CM, Tuesday, 6 September 1881, p. 3, cc. 2 - 4.

STREET GAMBLING
CC Number 125
Fu Akwai and Un Aon were charged with this offence.

Police Constable 279 said that on the 5th *instant* he went to Market Street and saw defendants playing fantan. There were five or six others. Witness arrested first defendant and Police Constable 235 apprehended the second. He found some implements of gambling at the spot.

First defendant denied the gambling, but admitted having been in gaol twice before. Second defendant was not gambling either, of course.

First defendant was sent to gaol for six weeks with hard labour as a rogue and vagabond, and second defendant for two weeks, also as a rogue and vagabond.

[STREET GAMBLING]
CC Number 126
Chan Ahing and Kwok Ayeung were charged with gambling on the street.

Police Constable 181 said that on the evening of the 5th inst, he saw defendants and thirteen or fourteen others playing at fantan on the Praya. Witness arrested first defendant and Police Constable 243 arrested the second.

Both defendants denied having had anything to do with the gambling.

They were sentenced to fourteen days' imprisonment with hard labour each as rogues and vagabonds. Money found to go to the poor box.

THEFT FROM THE PERSON
CC Number 127
Lai Asan was charged with stealing an opium box from Cheung Yuk Sing in the 5th *instant*. Complainant said that he went into a fortune-teller's shop to hear what was going on. He felt a touch at his purse, and on looking missed his opium box. He ran

after defendant who was caught by a Police Constable.

Prisoner was sent to gaol for twenty-one days with hard labour.

WATCHMAN TO GAMBLERS
CC Number 128

Lam Ayan was charged as above.

Police Constable 221 said that on the 5th inst, while near Market Street, he saw the defendant standing at the corner of the street with a bamboo hat on. When he saw witness he made a signal with the hat and called out "here's a special constable coming." Witness arrested defendant.

Fourteen days in gaol with hard labour.

THEFT OF A JACKET
CC Number 129

Shui Akam was charged with stealing a jacket from a Chinese woman. The jacket had been hanging at a back window.

Police Constable 692 said he saw defendant putting the jacket under his arm. He took him to complainant's house to see to whom the jacket belonged, when she claimed it.

He was sentenced to four weeks' imprisonment with hard labour.

UNLAWFULLY USING A REGISTRATION TICKET
CC Number 130

Wong Yuk Tsun was charged with this offence.

Li Hong Mi, second clerk at the magistracy, said that to-day defendant came and offered himself as bail for a prisoner in gaol. He produced a registration ticket, and witness asked him if he was the actual holder of it. He said he was. Witness asked him how long he had held the ticket, and he said twenty years. Having been taken to the first clerk's office, he said his father's name was Wong U and not his.

Defendant denied having said his name was Wong U. He was fined $10 or one month's imprisonment.

ALL IS NOT GOLD THAT GLITTERS
CC Number 131 📖 p. 347

Chan Asai, trader, was charged with obtaining $21.60, one pair ear-rings, and one gold hair-pin, valued at $37.60, by false pretences, on the 3rd instant.

Mr. Wotton appeared for the defendant.

Chung Atong, widow, said that on the 3rd *instant*, about noon, while in the Queen's Road, near the Central Market, a man, apparently a bricklayer, came to her and asked the way to Wanchai. She told him to go eastward. He them went up to another man and they spoke together. Afterwards defendant came up to her and said "That man has taken gold from Wanchai; don't tell anybody." Defendant asked her to follow him, and they went to the lane between Crosby's store and the Supreme Court. The bricklayer them took out five pieces of yellow metal and showed them to her and the defendant. Defendant said she had better buy some, and she retorted that he had better buy some himself. He said he had no money. The bricklayer said they were $5 a-piece. Defendant then took her aside and said "he does not know they are good; you had better buy some." He got them at Wanchai while building a house. He does not know the value of them. They are worth $30 a-piece. You had better offer him $4. She had $21 in notes, and handed them to the defendant, who gave them to the bricklayer. In return she got five pieces of the metal produced. Four more pieces were produced, and she having no more money, took her earrings and gold hair-pin and handed them to the defendant, who passed them to the bricklayer. She gave defendant six 10-cent piees, which went to the same receptable. Defendant asked her if she had got a handkerchief. She gave him one, and he wrapped up the nine pieces of metal in it, and told her not to let people see them.

He told her to take some of them to a goldsmith's shop, and exchange them for $80. By this means she would be able to get money, which she could give to the bricklayer, and then he would give her back her earrings and hair-pin. She must get silver dollars, as the bricklayer did not want bank notes. Defendant said "I will stop and watch the bricklayer; you hurry up and get back soon." She went to a money changer's stall and asked if he wanted gold. He said "Yes." She then produced a few of her pieces; but the money changer said he did not want such gold as that. She went back to the lane, but the defendant and the bricklayer had disappeared. She showed the pieces to a large number of people. The police them came, and she went to the Police Court and made a report. She afterwards went to the Macao steamer and saw defendant there. She said to him "Now I have changed the gold for money; come along with me." But defendant denied all connection and said she must be mistaken. A constable then arrested him.

Mr. Wotton cross-examined.

Several witnesses were examined for the defence.

The prisoner having reserved his offence[133] was committed for trial at the Criminal Sessions.[134]

---

[133] *Sic* for "defence".

[134] The case is reported as Number Five in the Criminal Calendar -- September Sessions, 1881. "Chan A-sai" was tried by Francis Snowden, Acting Chief Justice, on 20 September 1881, for "Obtaining money by false pretences", and found "Not guilty". ("Criminal Calendar -- September Sessions, 1881", HKGG, 1 October 1881, p. 875.)

The hearing is reported in *The China Mail*. (20 September 1881, p. 3, cc. 1 - 2.)

"Obtaining Money by False Pretences

"Chan Asai was charged with falsely obtaining from Chan Afook a certain sum of money and some jewellery by selling to her certain pieces of metal which he led her to believe were gold.

"Prisoner pled [*sic*] not guilty.

"The following Jury was impanelled:--

Bail in two sureties of $200 each.

THURSDAY 8 SEPTEMBER 1881[135]
THE CHAIR NUISANCE
CC Number 132
Eight chair coolies for annoying strangers, who had landed at Peddar'sWharf, [136] were each fined 25 cents, or one day's imprisonment with hard labour.

DRUNK
CC Number 133
Joseph Howard, an American seaman, was fined 25 cents, or one day's imprisonment, for being drunk and incapable on the 7th *instant*

"D. H. Billia, H. C. Maclean, R. dos Remedios, Erich Georg, Charles L. Gorham, E. Herbst, and Harry Wicking.

"The Attorney General went over the circumstances of the case as already detailed and said that he believed the defence was mistaken identity. [The original has "identify".]

"Evidence was heard for the prosecution, in which it came out that on the prisoner being searched two $10 notes, two $5 notes, and a $1 note -- the exact values of the notes given by the woman to prisoner -- were found.

"Mr Hayllar who, instructed by Messrs Brereton and Wotton, appeared for the prisoner, said his case would be one of mistaken identity. The evidence against the prisoner depended entirely upon the woman. He held that the similarity of the notes was merely a coincidence. It was obvious that the woman had been trying to cheat too. He would call witnesses (opium dealers) to prove that prisoner during the whole of the period during which the offence was said to have been committed was in their shop.

"Lam Afat salesman [The original has "salesmen".] in an opium shop in Wing-lok Street, gave evidence as to the prisoner being there, and as to his having large transactions with him. The master of the shop gave similar evidence.

"Mr Hayllar addressed the Jury and the Attorney General replied. His Lordship having gone over the evidence, the jury returned a verdict of not guilty.

"Prisoner discharged."

[135] "Police Intelligence," CM, Thursday, 8 September 1881, p. 3, c. 3.

[136] *Sic* for "Pedder's". "Peddar" was the name of a one-time Hong Kong Harbourmaster and the wharf was named after him. The spelling, "Peddar's Wharf" later changed to, "Pedder's Wharf".

BREACH OF MARKET ORDINANCE
CC Number 134
U Awa admitted selling salt fish on the street on the 7th *instant*, and was fined $1 or four days' imprisonment.

[BREACH OF MARKET ORDINANCE]
CC Number 135
Sin Alum, for a similar offence, was similarly sentenced.

UNLAWFUL POSSESSION OF A BOAT
CC Number 136
Li Ato was charged with being in unlawful possession of a boat and four baskets of coal. From the evidence of Police Constable312, it appeared that on the 8th *instant*, witness had seen defendant in a boat, which contained some coals coming to Ship Street Wharf, Wanchai. Witness took boat and coals to the Station. Prisoner was fined $5 or fourteen days' imprisonment. Boat to be confiscated.

LARCENY
CC Number 137
Chan Asing was charged with being in unlawful possession of a pair of shoes. On the evidence of Police Constable 157, and An Tah Yung, he was convicted of larceny, and sentenced to fourteen days with hard labour.

CUTTING EARTH IN HOSPITAL ROAD
CC Number 138
Hing Achan, and Tang Achiu, were charged as above.

Mr. Watts of the Survey Department, said that while standing in Queen's Road he saw eight or ten people cutting earth below Hospital Road. They were undermining the retaining wall, lately built at considerable expense. The earth-cutters had exposed several coffins, and destroyed two young trees. They had to keep a constant watch on the spot. The second defendant made a trade of earth-cutting, but witness did not know the first defendant.

Sentenced to pay $1 each, or fourteen days' imprisonment with hard labour, and to be each exposed in the stocks for 6 hours.

POCKET PICKING
CC Number 139

Chow Atuk was charged with picking the pocket of Chiu Uhing.

Complainant said that while in the Po Lok Theatre defendant took 30 cents from his purse. He followed defendant and accused him of picking his pocket. Defendant said to him "Don't say anything, and I'll give it you back."

Prisoner was sent to gaol for six weeks with hard labour.

FRIDAY 9 SEPTEMBER 1881[137]
REFUSAL TO PERFORM THEIR DUTY
CC Number 140

Wong Ping Nam and Tong Aki were charged at the instance of Jose Maria Pinto Cunha Teixeira [sic], with refusing duty, on the 8th.

The case again came before the Court to-day.

Mr Jose Loureiro, Portuguese Consul, said that in the morninghe found his room had not been tidied nor the water changed. He sent for defendants but they said there [sic for "they"] were going away. Witness said he would send for a Police Constable, which he did, and gave them into custody.

The first defendant said that he was merely a substitute for a week, and that he had worked for nine days. The regular servant told him he need do so no more.

---

[137] "Police Intelligence," CM, Friday, 9 September 1881, p. 3, c. 1.

First defendant fined $1 or four days' imprisonment; and the second defendant $3, or seven days' imprisonment.

THEFT OF COPPER NAILS
CC Number 141
Lo Atin was charged with stealing about 2 lbs. of copper nails, the property of the Hong Kong and Whampoa Dock company.

Ismail, a watchman, said that while searching the prisoner he ran away, jumped into the water, and dropped the handkerchief containing the nails. Defendant was arrested. He was sentenced to twenty-one days' imprisonment with hard labour.

SATURDAY 10 SEPTEMBER 1881[138]
LARCENY FROM THE PERSON
CC Number 142 📖 p. 323
Chan Akan was charged with stealing from the person of Leung Mi Chenn, a Chinese girl, jewellery of the value of $2.70.

Complainant said that on the morning of the first *instant*, she went to a shop to get cucumber. She met defendant in the street and he offered to take her up the hill to get bamboo shoots. She went up the hill with defendant, and then he took away her silver bangle and a set of silver buttons, and a silver anklet. He then ran away. Witness was crying and a Police Constable took her to the station. On the 9th *instant* she saw defendant in First Street and told a Police Constable to arrest him.

Defendant denied the charge, but was sentenced to three months' imprisonment with hard labour.

UNLAWFUL POSSESSION OF COAL
CC Number 143
Lam Aking and Lum Atsoi were charged with being in unlawful possession of coal.

---

[138] "Police Intelligence," CM, Saturday, 10 September 1881, p. 3, cc. 2 - 3.

G. McDonald, Police Constable 82 [*sic*], said that while on duty in a police boat off Wanchai he saw a small boat in which were the two defendants, pulling towards the shore. He pulled after them, and overtook them. There were five baskets of coal in the boat. Both defendants denied the charge. They were fined £5 [*sic*], or two months' imprisonment each with hard labour. Boat to be confiscated.

LARCENY OF A DOOR
CC Number 144
Wong Hi was charged with stealing a door, the property of Leung Ashu, a carpenter.

Complainant said that there was a new building being erected in Circular Pathway, near which the door in question was standing. Witness found defendant in a watchman's custody, charged with stealing the door.

Su Atai, a district watchman, said he saw defendant carrying the door in Circular Pathway. Upon calling on the defendant to stop, he throw [*sic* for "threw"] the door down, and ran. Witness ran after and caught him.

Defendant only took the door to sleep on, and as it came on to rain, he was removing it to a more sheltered spot, when the watchman arrested him. He was once in Gaol before. One month's imprisonment with hard labour.

DISORDERLY CONDUCT AND ASSAULT
CC Number 145
Ip Asin was charged as above. It appeared from the evidence of Police Constable 627, that defendant and a number of others had been in the habit of playing chess and making a noise under a verandah, near the Commissariat. On his telling them to remove they took no notice, so he took defendant by the shoulder. He attempted to strike witness with a bamboo and did strike him with his bamboo hat[139] on the hand.

---

[139] This small detail of the bamboo hat helps to paint the scene.

Defendant denied this.

He was sentenced for disorderly conduct to four hours in the stocks at Commissariat,[140] and for assaulting the Police Constable fined $1 or four days in gaol with hard labour.

PUBLIC GAMBLING[141]
CC Number 146 📖 p. 339

Twenty-two Chinamen were charged with public gambling on the 9th *instant*.

G. Rae, Police Sergeant No. 69,[142] said that about noon on the 9th he went with a party of police to Number 11 Centre Street. He found the house secured. He entered from the roof. He saw third defendant sitting on a stool near the landing with a fan-dagger beside him. Witness jumped through a hole in the roof, and then opened the trap-door, which was a strong one with a spring lock. He unlocked it to allow the constables to come up. He arrested all the defendants with the exception of the 8th defendant who was now in hospital. In the house he found a table and mat, four stools, $10 scattered on the floor, a quantity of cash-cards, dice, counting-stick, pen and ink cups, square, scales, three daggers, one sword, one strong door with spring lock, two ladders, and two fighting irons. The game being played was fantan.

A couple of informers gave evidence as to playing in the house in question, and as to the first defendant counting the cash, the second receiving and paying the money, and the third being watchman with a dagger in his hand.

First, second, and third defendants fined $100 or four months' imprisonment with hard labour;

---

[140] The man was sentenced to spend time in the stocks at the Commissariat, because this was where he had committed the offence for which he was being punished.

[141] The following is the complete set of reports in connection with this case as found in *"The Complete Court Cases"*: CC Nos 146, 157.

[142] *Sic.*

the remainder were fined $20 or six weeks' imprisonment with hard labour. All gambling implements to be forfeited. Informers to receive $10 each from fines.

Eighth prisoner remanded.[143]

ROGUE AND VAGABOND [Public Gambling]
CC Number 147

Li Aho was convicted on the evidence of Police Constable 188 of having been playing at fantan and was sentenced to fourteen day's imprisonment as a rogue and vagabond with hard labour.

MONDAY 12 SEPTEMBER 1881[144]
ROGUES AND VAGABONDS
CC Number 148

George Kirby and William Cottrall were charged by T. Beattie, Police Constable No. 2, with misbehaving themselves in front of the London Mission Chapel in Queen's Road on the morning of the 11th. First defendant had been in gaol thrice before, and the second defendant once.

The first prisoner was sentenced to six weeks' imprisonment as a rogue and vagabond, and the second to three weeks' imprisonment also as a rogue and vagabond.

DRUNK
CC Number 149

Manuel Gomes admitted having been drunk and having been twice in gaol before, and was fined $1 or ten days' imprisonment with hard labour.

UNLAWFUL POSSESSION
CC Number 150

---

[143] CC No. 157 explains what happened to the Eighth prisoner, but we have to guess why he was in hospital, as stated in CC No. 146.
[144] "Police Intelligence," CM, Monday, 12 September 1881, p. 3, cc. 2 - 3.

Kan Aun was charged by Police Constable 654 with having in his possession five pieces of iron of which he could give no satisfactory account, and after the evidence of the Police Constable had been heard, prisoner was fined 10 shillings or seven days' imprisonment.

WATCHMAN TO GAMBLERS
CC Number 151
Police Constable 518 said that on the 12th *instant* while on duty in Market Street he saw a crowd of people gambling on the footpath. Witness heard prisoner (Un Aman) call out "Police coming, be off." Witness arrested the defendant but the others escaped.

Sentence, — fourteen days in gaol with hard labour.

THEFT OF SWEET POTATOE [*sic*] SPROUTS
CC Number 152
Leung Akam was charged with stealing sweet potatoe [*sic*] sprouts from a field belonging to Li Tai Shing, a fisherman living at To-kwa-wan. Complainant saw defendant in the field cutting the sprouts, arrested him, and handed him over to a Police Constable.

Defendant admitted having stolen the vegetables, but denied that they belonged to complainant. He had been in gaol three times previously.

Sentenced to three months' imprisonment with hard labour.

WEDNESDAY 13 [*Sic* for 14], SEPTEMBER 1881[145]
LARCENY OF JEWELLERY
CC Number 153 📖 p. 277
Sun Yeung Mun was charged by the inmate of a brothel with stealing a quantity of jewellery.

---

[145] "Police Intelligence," CM, Wednesday, 14 September 1881, p. 3, c. 3, Report relating to "Wednesday 13" [*sic* for "Wednesday 14"] September 1881.

After evidence had been heard defendant was sent to gaol for four months with hard labour.

THEFT
CC Number 154

Sin Akiu was charged by Man Achin with stealing one pair of shoes and two jackets. Complainant had gone to sleep, his shoes and jackets being close to him. He awakened and saw the defendant running from his room. He got up and seized the defendant.

Defendant was sentenced to six weeks' imprisonment with hard labour.

WITHOUT A LIGHT[146]
CC Number 155

Four Chinamen were charged by G. Hennessy, Police Sergeant No. 6, with being at large at 3.10 a.m. this morning without a light or pass.

The defendants had been arrested in Queen's Road Central; the first had been three times in gaol, the second three times, the third once, and the fourth no less than nine times. When arrested all the defendants pretended to be asleep.

They were sentenced to pay a fine of $10 or three months imprisonment with hard labour each, and for being rogues and vagabonds other three months with hard labour. Sentences cumulative.

THURSDAY 15 SEPTEMBER 1881[147]
THEFT OF A CLOCK
CC Number 156

Li Aki was charged by Yeung Aping on the 6th instant, with having stolen a clock from him. Defendant has been several times before the Court; and today after the receiving officer of the gaol had

---

[146] The following is the complete set of reports in connection with CC No. 155 in *The Complete Court Cases*: CC Nos 155, 165.
[147] "Police Intelligence," CM, Thursday, 15 September 1881, p. 3, c. 5.

testified to his having been in gaol five times, he was committed for trial at the next Criminal Sessions.[148]

FRIDAY 16 SEPTEMBER 1881[149]
GAMBLING[150]

---

[148] The case of Li A-ki is No. 1 in the Criminal Calendar -- October Sessions, 1881. (HKGG, 29 October 1881, p. 950). He was tried on three counts: 1) Larceny in a dwelling house; 2) Previous conviction (summary); 3) Previous conviction (summary). He was found Guilty on the first count, unanimously, and sentenced to seven years' penal servitude. A *Nolle prosequi* was entered by the Attorney General on the 2nd and 3rd counts.

The following report appears in *The China Mail*, Tuesday, 18 October 1881, p. 3, c. 4.
"Supreme Court
"In Criminal Sessions (Before the Acting Puisne Judge, Hon. J. Russell.)
"Tuesday, 18 October 1881
"Larceny in a dwelling house

"Lu Achee [*sic*] was charged with stealing a clock valued at $30, on the 3rd September.

"Mr Francis, under instructions from the Attorney General, prosecuted.

"The jurors were Messrs J. W. Crocker, R. Steil, A. S. Garfit, A. F. Gonsalves, T. H. E. Lorberg, E. Vogel, and S. V. dos Remedios.

"It appeared that on the 3rd of September defendant had gone to a house in Wing On Lane, looking for some one who had formerly lived there. While leaving he was observed to be carrying a clock which had been hanging in an inner room. He was not caught at the time, but was subsequently apprehended, and the clock which had been pawned was redeemed.

"The Jury returned a verdict of guilty.

"There were four previous convictions against the prisoner, and his Lordship said it was his duty to protect the community from such persons. The sentence of the Court would be that the prisoner be kept in penal servitude for seven years."

[149] "Police Intelligence," CM, Friday, 16 September 1881, p. 3, cc. 3 - 4.

[150] The following is the complete set of reports in connection with this case as found in "*The Complete Court Cases*": CC Nos 146, 157.

CC Number 157
The eighth prisoner in the gang of twenty-two, who were arrested the other day, was before the Court this day, when he was fined $10 or three weeks' imprisonment with hard labour.

THEFT FROM THE PERSON
CC Number 158
Ip Ui was charged with stealing $2 from the person of Tsoi Awan.

Complainant said he was at the Harbour Master's Office today for the purpose of getting his ticket to Singapore signed, when he felt a hand at his bag, and turning saw defendant taking his hand from under his jacket. He handed him over to a Police Constable.

Prisoner was sentenced to six months' imprisonment with hard labour. He had been in gaol before.

LARCENY OF IRON
CC Number 159
Wong Agan was charged with stealing some iron the property of a Chinese builder. The iron had been left inside the railing of a building in course of erection. The complainant, a coolie in the builder's service, saw defendant in the act of taking away some of the iron. Witness pursued and a Police Constable arrested defendant.

Prisoner had been eight times in gaol before, and was now sentenced to imprisonment for four months' with hard labour.

ASSAULT
CC Number 160 📖 p. 277
Nocheum Greenstang and Benjamin Flin were charged by Joseph Greenberg with assaulting him.

Complainant said he was a merchant residing in Pottinger Street. He had gone into a brothel where the defendants were. They set upon him and beat him, and the first defendant also beat him on the left hand. After calling "Police"[151] two constables came to his assistance. After some more evidence had been heard both defend ants were fined $2 each or four days in gaol with hard labour.

ATTEMPTED RESCUE OF A PRISONER
CC Number 161
Wong Aping was charged with attempting to rescue a prisoner from the custody of Police Constable 221.

He admitted the charge, and was fined $5 or ten days in gaol.

HIGHWAY ROBBERY
CC Number 162
The four Chinamen charged with highway robbery on the Pok-foo-lum [*sic*] Road, were today after some further evidence had been taken, committed for trial at the Criminal Sessions.[152] Mr. Wotton appeared for the defendants, and reserved their defence. They were allowed out on bail each in two sureties of $100 each.

THEFT
CC Number 163
Li Ayeung was charged by Emma Webb, with stealing on the 1st of September a $25 note. The case was before the Court yesterday, and again to-day,[153] when the prisoner was committed for trial at the Criminal Sessions.[154]

---

[151] The original report simply states, "after calling Police", with no inverted commas. In either case, there is an error in syntax, because it is the complainant who called for the Police and not the two constables themselves.

[152] The only case in the Criminal Calendar for the September Sessions, 1881, where there are four accused, was heard on 20 September. (HKGG, 1 October 1881, p. 875.) The charge was "Conspiracy", however. No other apparently more appropriate listing appears in any later Criminal Calendar seen by the present writer.

[153] The case was not reported in CM on Thursday, 15 September 1881.

[154] The case of Li A-yung is No. 9 in the Criminal Calendar -- September Sessions, 1881. (HKGG, 1 October 1881, p. 875.) The

SATURDAY 17 SEPTEMBER 1881[155]
THEFT
CC Number 164

Li Atak was charged on the 16th with having stolen a piece of brass from Mr. Armstrong's Auction rooms. The case was resumed to-day, and the Receiving Officer of the gaol having proved five previous convictions against the prisoner, he was committed for trial at the Criminal Sessions.[156]

---

charge was Larceny and the date of the trial was 19 September 1881,

The following report appears in *The China Mail*, Monday, 19 September 1881, p. 3, c. 2
"Supreme Court
"In Criminal Sessions
"(Before His Honour the Acting Puisne Judge, J. Russell, Esq.)
"Saturday [*sic* for "Monday"], 19 September 1881

"Theft of a $25 note

"Li Ayeung admitted stealing a $25 from Emma Webb, but said the crime was committed at the instigation of his fellow servant who spent part of the money. He was eighteen years of age.

"His Lordship said that by his crime he had laid himself open to fourteen years' imprisonment, but he was a young boy, and the evidence had shown nothing against him. He had done well in admitting the matter instead of braving it out; but as a breach of trust had been committed, he must go to gaol for nine months with hard labour. If he behaved himself in gaol he might get off a portion of his time. The Governor had the power to release them, and generally did release them, before their time was up."

[155] "Police Intelligence," CM, Saturday, 17 September 1881, p. 3, c. 3.

[156] The case of Li A-tak is No. 3 in the Criminal Calendar -- October Sessions, 1881. (HKGG, 29 October 1881, p.950.) He was tried on 18 October on three counts: 1) Larceny; 2) Previous conviction (summary); 3) Previous conviction (felony) and pleaded guilty on all counts. He was sentenced to seven years' penal servitude.

The following report appeared in *The China Mail*, Tuesday, 18 October 1881, p. 3, c. 4.
"Supreme Court
"In Criminal Sessions (Before the Acting Puisne Judge, Hon. J. Russell.)

[SATURDAY 17 SEPTEMBER 1881][157]
SENTENCE AMENDED[158]
CC Number 165

Four Chinamen who were sentenced on the 14th inst, for having no pass, to pay a fine of $10 each or three months' imprisonment with hard labour, and for being rogues and vagabonds to three months in gaol with hard labour (sentences to be cumulative), to-day had their sentences amended in accordance with Section 11 of Ordinance 5 of 1850[159] to a fine of $10 each or three months' imprisonment with hard labour for having no pass.

MONDAY 19 SEPTEMBER 1881[160]
THEFT OF HAM
CC Number 166 ⌨ p. 278

Un Afuk was charged by Chan Alam with stealing a piece of ham from him on the 17th *instant.*

Complainant said he was a cook in a brothel. He saw defendant put his hand in at the window and lift the ham. Witness ran out and found him in the custody of a Police Constable.

"Tuesday, 18 October 1881
"Theft of Brass

"Lai Atak pleaded guilty to stealing a piece of brass, the property of Mr J. M. Armstrong, on the 16th *instant.* There were six previous convictions against him. He had also been reported [*sic* for "deported"]. He was sentenced to penal servitude for seven years."

[157] "Police Intelligence," CM, Saturday, 17 September 1881, p. 3, c. 3.

[158] The following is the complete set of reports in connection with CC No. 155 in *The Complete Court Cases*: CC Nos 155, 165.

[159] See Ordinance Number 5 of 1850 in *The Ordinances of Hong Kong for the years 1847-1859*. [HKU Law Library. KT 4351 H7 S1]. Section 11 of this "Ordinance to regulate Proceedings before Justices of the Peace" reads as follows: "Be it further enacted and ordained, That the adjudicating Justice may at any time reverse or amend his decision or appoint the case to be reheard by himself or another Justice, should it appear that such decision was erroneous or unjust."

[160] "Police Intelligence," CM, Monday, 19 September 1881, p. 3, c. 3.

Sentenced to fourteen days in gaol with hard labour.

THEFT OF A CLOCK
CC Number 167

Wong Afuk was charged by Li Su Wan with appropriating a clock belonging to him.

Complainant said he was a furniture dealer at 108 Hollywood Road. On the 17th instant he saw defendant outside his shop-door. He suddenly put his hand in and snatched the clock from the counter and bolted. Witness pursued and defendant dropped the clock. A Police Constable stopped defendant, and the thief was taken to the Station. Defendant said he was going to buy cigars, a man ran against him, and a Police Constable completed the catastrophe by apprehending him.

Sentenced to twenty-one days' imprisonment with hard labour.

DISORDERLY BEHAVIOUR – WITCHERY
CC Number 168

Abdoola Fukeera (at whose instance the charge was brought) said that the defendant, Ameer Khan, had, owing to witness advising his relations to discontinue going to defendant's classes, since greatly annoyed him and his family. On the 15th and 16th *instant*, he sat on a mat behind defendant's house, with a censer, the Koran, and another book. This was done to bewitch.

Fined $5 or seven days' imprisonment with hard labour and to give securities, two sureties of $40 to keep the peace towards complainant for three months, or be committed for a further period of fourteen days.

TUESDAY 20 SEPTEMBER 1881[161]
HABITUALLY ILL-TREATING A LITTLE GIRL[162]
CC Number 169 📖 p. 253

Li Achoy, 56, of Shanghai, wife of Fung Awai, was charged with assaulting and ill-treating a female named An Asam, at different times during the last seven days.

An Kam Yan, Police Constable 311, said that today about 10 a.m., he saw defendant beat the little girl she was charged with ill-treating. She slapped the girl's face very severely. The girl cried and some of the neigbours made witness arrest the defendant, as she had beaten the girl before. Did not know defendant. The girl is betrothed to defendant's son. Defendant lives in Tank Lane.

Lam Yun, broom maker, Tanner Lane, Tai-ping-shan, about 7 a.m. saw the girl jump into a well in the Lane; ran to her and took her out; she said— "I don't want to be taken out, I want [sic] go ho[me, I] rather die here." The girl's clothes were all wet. Took her home and saw defendant there; defendant slapped her face.

I Azs, wife of Ching Agan, living in the second floor of the house, the second of which is occupied by the defendant though the one enters from Caine Road [and] the others from Tank Lane, said the defendant often beat the little girl. Witness often heard her crying bitterly. Saw the girl fished out of the well and taken home. Defendant is a wife [sic] of a marine hawker.

Leung Kam Yew, widow living in Tank Lane said that this morning she saw the little girl jump into the well, and saw first witness run out and save her. Witness said it was the common talk of the neighbourhood that the defendant habitually ill treats the little girl.

---

[161] "Police Intelligence," CM, Tuesday, 20 September 1881, p. 2, c. 7 - p. 3, c. 1.
[162] The following is the complete set of reports in connection with this case in *The Complete Court Cases*: CC Nos 169, 205.

Li Along, coolie, living in San Lane, off Caine Road, next door to defendant said he often saw the defendant beating the girl. Had seen defendant beat the girl unmercifully with firewood. The girl often cried bitterly. Defendant sometimes beat her as often as four or five times a day. Last saw the girl beaten four or five days ago, when a bamboo was used.

The girl herself, An Asam, said she was 15 years of age. Her mother was dead. Her father gave her to the defendant to be her adopted daughter, about 6 years ago. She cut her lips when she accidentally fell into the well this morning.

The case was adjourned, without the girl's evidence being further gone into until the 27th *instant*, the defendant being admitted to bail in $50, two householders in $25 each.

RECEIVING STOLEN GOODS[163]
CC Number 170
Leung Ang, 52, licensed opium dealer was charged with receiving stolen goods on the 19th, at Yau-mah-ti, British Kowloon.

Inspector Cameron, having reason to believe that he would be able to arrest thieves applied for a remand.

Case remanded till Monday, bail, two householders in $20 each.

TWENTY ONE DAYS SEVENTY CENTS
CC Number 171 📖 p. 323
Three Chinese boys, two 14 years old, one little customer aged 11, were each sentenced to seven days' solitary confinement for stealing a jacket value 70 cents.

---

[163] The following is the complete set of reports in connection with this case in *The Complete Court Cases*: CC Nos 170, 200.

"JACK" PAID OFF
CC Number 172

Andrew Lange, 22, ship's carpenter, Norwegian, was paid off yesterday, and got drunk, after which his record of what happened became underperable [*sic*]. Two or three constables, however, who had had their work cut out for them, in running and jumping walls after him to arrest him for knocking down a man in Peterson's boarding house, gave quite a graphic account of how he had behaved, and Andrew admitted that there might be some truth in it. He was fined $2 for his drunkenness and disorderly conduct (in default 2 days' imprisonment) and was ordered to pay $1 amends (in default an additional two days in gaol... to Police Constable 508, who being off duty was called in by his brother constable 599 to secure the turbulent Lange, and got his jacket so torn that it would take 35 cents to mend it, lost his handkerchief, containing 20 cents in the struggle, got his turban knocked off and his hair torn up by the roots, hair triumphantly produced in Court in aggravation of the amount of compensation to be awarded). A friend of Lange who had made some strong protest against his arrest, but was not proved to have attempted to rescue him, was cautioned to mind his own business in future and allowed to go.

THE STONE-DRESSING NUISANCE
CC Number 173

For dressing granite at the scene of some building operations, in Hollywood Road, when it could properly have been dressed at the quarry, Tin Ang was fined $2, in default 2 days' imprisonment.

UNLAWFUL POSSESSION
CC Number 174

Li Akow, 41, hawker, was charged with unlawful possession of 2 1/2 baskets of partially burnt coal, 3 baskets of small coal, and a boat, value $4.

Defendant's tale was that the so-called coal was cinders which he bought from a steam launch for 30 cents.

The Magistrate fined him £2, the boat to be forfeited.

LARCENY
CC Number 175

Wong Alin, 34, hawker, for stealing a lock and a pair of trousers was sentenced to 14 days' hard labour in gaol.

THE SEQUEL OF A GAMBLING RAID[164]
CC Number 176

Wong Ayau was charged with haunting[165] a gambling house in Gilman's Bazaar, Number 4. This house was entered on the 25th ultimo and seventeen gamblers were seized, brought before the Court and fined. Defendant jumped some 50 feet at least out of a window and was found lying insensible, with a dagger in his hand. He had been in Hospital since. His legs were yet swollen, and he walked with difficulty. Another man, who also jumped with him, is still ill in hospital.

Ordered to find two householders, each to be surety in $20 to be of good behaviour for two months, in default 14 days' imprisonment.

DIRTY LINEN
CC Number 177

William Samuel, watchman, Surveyor General's Department, charged Maria Mathias, 24, wife of one Lorenço Mathias, and Antonia Lopes, 48, a widow, both Macaoese [sic], with using insulting and indecent language towards him whereby a breach of the peace might have been occasioned.

---

[164] There is no previous report of this case in *The Complete Court Cases*.

[165] "Haunting" a place of gambling is specifically mentioned in Ordinance No. 9 of 1876, para. 5. The maximum fine was $50.

Complainant, who lives in Number 6 Station, Tai-ping-shan Street, occupying the upper floor of the house of which defendants had the lower floor, said that at 8.30 a.m. he was in the lane in front of his door, when the first defendant abused him. Witness had asked this woman why she had complained to the landlord's agent of witness disturbing her when he went to draw water in the morning. At the same time defendant came out and used exactly the same expressions. She also threatened witness with a broomstick and said she would thrash him.

First defendant admitted that she called the complainant by a low name. She told complainant politely not to look into her house in her husband's absence. He continued to do so after she had spoken to him, and this was why she abused him. The complainant called her by a bad name. Did not complain to her husband because she feared a quarrel.

Second defendant denied the charge.

Defendants were ordered to give personal securities in $10 each, to keep the peace towards the complainant for two months.

OPIUM CASE
CC Number 178

Chan Cheung Fat, master of the licenced fishing junk No. 2184, was charged with being in unlawful possession of a quantity of prepared opium without a valid certificate from the Farmer, on the 19th instant, on board a junk in Shau-ki-wan Bay.

Inspector Swanston made the seizure, on board, of a tin tray, opium lamp and pipe, 2 sets of scales bearing traces of opium, two horn boxes nearly full of prepared opium, a pillow box con taining other three [sic] horn boxes, nearly full of prepared opium; also another opium pipe, 5 earthenware jars containing more or less opium; a tin box with opium dross, and a piece of raw opium, about 4 oz.; 3 opium pipes and shades, several empty pots containing traces of prepared opium; a small box three parts full of prepared opium; a strainer containing opium refuse; a brass pan, and a large horn box containing about 3 taels of opium. Had known defendant for two years as the master of the junk.

Mr. Santos also gave evidence; there was about 10 or 20 taels of prepared opium, worth about $10 and 3 taels of raw opium worth about $1. Defendant had no permit from the Opium Farmer.

Defendant said the opium belonged to his son, who bought it from the Opium Farmer. Produced two tickets showing the purchase of 2 taels, 6 mace, 3 candareens on August 11, and 1 tael, 2 mace on August 26th. There was another ticket for 2 taels in June. The pan was only used when they were at sea.

Fined $20, in default 14 days' imprisonment; opium, raw and prepared, to go to the Farmer.

PREVENTION BETTER THAN CURE
CC Number 179

Leong Akai, 29, a coolie, for being at large without a light or pass on the streets on the 19th, and for being in possession of a house-breaking implement, was sentenced, under Ordinance 7 of 1865, Sec. 46,[166] to

---

[166] Ordinance Number 7 of 1865, dated 3 June 1865, is entitled, "An Ordinance to consolidate and amend the Enactments in Force in this Colony relating to Larceny and similar Offences". (HKGG, 24 June 1865, pp. 355-373.)
Section 46 reads as follows: "Whoever shall be found by Night armed with any dangerous or offensive Weapon or Instrument whatsoever, with Intent to break or enter into any Dweing House, or other Building whatsoever, and to commit any Felony therein, or shall be found by Night having in his Possession without lawful Excuse (the Proof of which Excuse whall lie on such Person) any Picklock Key, Crow, Jack, Bit, or other Implement of Housebreaking, or shall be found by Night having his Face blackened or otherwise disguised with Intent to commit any Felony, or shall be found by Night in any Dwelling House, or other Building whatsoever with Intent to commit any Felony therein, shall be guilty of a Misdemeanor, and being convicted thereof shall be liable, at the Discretion of the Court, to be kept in Penal Servitude for the Term of three Years, -- or to be imprisoned for any Term not exceeding Two Years, with or without Hard Labour, and with or without Solitary Confinement."

3 months' imprisonment with hard labour. He admitted having previously been in gaol for 6 months for breaking into a dwelling house.

A GOOSE PLUCKED
CC Number 180

Lai Asau, 32, a stonecutter, and Yau Afat, 25, a trader were charged with obtaining $7 under false pretences, from a farmer, Wong Afun.

Complainant in this case was a gullible young man from the country on his way to California to seek his fortune. The very ancient trick was played on him of getting him to buy out his two partners in a gold ring picked up on the street, in which the poor simpleton was allowed to have a share having seen it picked up. The farmer fool paid the rogues all the money he had with him, $7; and was inviting them to come to the place where he was staying so that he might give them more money, when a lukong came upon the scene, spoiled their little game, and took the two rascals in charge. The moral of this story is that even Sikh policemen are not always awanting when their good offices are serviceable. The ring was now proved to be worth 8 cents; the "gold" was proved to be of the same quality as that wherewith brass candle-sticks are made.

Second defendant admitted having been in gaol before for six months.

Sentenced,--6 months' imprisonment with hard labour, save for the first and last fortnights, during which time the prisoners will be relegated to solitary confinement.

Ordinance Number 7 of 1865 is referred to in Ordinance No. 2 of 1875, *q.v.* It is also referred to in Draft Ordinance . . . to amend and repeal certain ordinances relating to branding and to the punishment of flogging. (HKGG, 19 November 1881, pp. 1006-1007.)

Although paragraph 87 of Ordinance Number 7 of 1865 refers to loitering at night, there is no reference to, "being at large without a light or pass on the streets", as charged in CC 179.

For a discussion of "The Hong Kong 'Light and Pass' Rules", see, *A Magistrate's Court in 19th Century Hong Kong*, pp. 99-116.)

THURSDAY 22 SEPTEMBER 1881[167]
THEFT OF CLOTHING
CC Number 181

[...] Akin was charged with stealing a pair of trousers and a jacket from Li Achiu. Complainant said that on the 21st *instant*, [he missed] from his house the jacket and [trousers] in Court. From certain information he got he went on the search for defendant, whom he found and seized in [Queen]'s Road. The clothes were in his [...]. Defendant who had been twice [in ga]ol before was sentenced to four months with hard labour.

SWEET SLEEP
CC Number 182

[...] Smith, Police Constable No. 47, said that between [...] and two this morning he was on duty [at] Kowloon Dock, when he found defendant (Abdoolah Man), a watchman, asleep [on] duty and arrested him. Defendant had [...] in July last for the same offence. Fined $5, or ten days' imprisonment with hard labour.

CUTTING TREES
CC Number 183

[...]ong Ayan was convicted of cutting [trees] on the 21st *instant* at Shau-ki-wan, [was?] fined $2 or four days' in gaol with hard labour. The Police Constable who arrested him to get [...].

ASSAULTING THE POLICE
CC Number 184

[...]ak Ayan and Shin Afui were charged [with] being without a pass or light.

[...] MacDougall, Police Constable 50, said that about [...] this morning he met the two defendants in Robinson Road. When asked for [their] pass or light, they gave him no satisfactory answer.

---

[167] "Police Intelligence," CM, Thursday, 22 September 1881, p. 3, c. 1.

Complete Court Cases   178

Witness attempted to arrest the first defendant when he pushed [witness]. He arrested them both.

First defendant was fined $1 for assaulting the Police Constable or four days' imprisonment, [...] the second defendant was discharged.

ROGUE AND VAGABOND
CC Number 185

[...]ung Afui was charged with being a rogue and vagabond and obstructing the [public] street.

Police Constable 236 said that while in First Street [he s]aw about nine men playing at fantan. Witness arrested the defendant.

He was sent to gaol for fourteen days [with] hard labour as a rogue and vagabond.

THEFT OF A SILVER BUTTON
CC Number 186

[...]ak Asho was charged with stealing a silver button from a boatwoman.

Complainant said that, about 5.30 p.m., she went to Wanchai market to buy fish. While there she felt some one touch her pocket. She looked down and saw defendant with the knife in his hand. She seized defendant.

A Police Constable said that defendant and other [...]s were in the habit of prowling about [the] Praya and the markets.

Twenty one days' imprisonment with hard labour.

POCKET-PICKING
CC Number 187

[...] Achi, fisherman, charged Tam Afat [with] abstracting from his pocket a pawn [ticket] and 60 cents.

Complainant said he came to Hong Kong [on] the 13th *instant* to look for work. On the [...] *instant* he went to a theatre. Witness [felt] a hand at his pocket. He turned, saw defendant, and seized him. He missed his pawn ticket and money. A Police

Constable arrested defendant. Sentence, — one month's imprisonment with hard labour.

FRIDAY 23 SEPTEMBER 1881[168]
THE TABLES TURNED
CC Number 188

Three Chinamen were charged by Wong Achu with having robbed him of five dollars.

According to the story of the plaintiff two of the defendants had assaulted and robbed him. Later on he accused a third man of holding his queue while the others were beating him. Third defendant said he had been called as a witness, but had been accused. After a deal of contradictory evidence, complainant was placed in the dock as prisoner for making a false charge. He admitted he had made a false charge, and asked for mercy. He was fined $15, in default six weeks' imprisonment with hard labour. The other three parties to find security in $10 each to be of good behaviour for two months, or be committed for fourteen days.

SATURDAY 24 SEPTEMBER 1881[169]
DISORDERLY CONDUCT
CC Number 189 📖 p. 278

Four Chinamen were charged with disorderly conduct and damaging the roof of a house. It appeared that defendants had been for one or two nights past sleeping on the roof of Number 25, East Street, had got to skylarking and displaced some of the mortar from the tiles. The complainant, mistress of a brothel, complained of the noise, and the defendants were arrested.

They were each fined $2 or seven days' in gaol with hard labour.

---

[168] "Police Intelligence," CM, Friday, 23 September 1881, p. 3, c. 5.

[169] "Police Intelligence," CM, Saturday, September 24, p. 3, cc. 4 - 5

ROGUE AND VAGABOND
CC Number 190

Police Constable 523 said that on the 23rd *instant*, he went to First Street, where he found a number of men gambling. When they saw witness they ran. Defendant (Mok Chin Ki) took up the dice and cup and bolted into a house. Witness arrested him.

Defendant admitted having been in gaol before, and was sentenced to six weeks' imprisonment with hard labour, as a rogue and vagabond.

THE BURGLARY AT BELLEVUE[170]
CC Number 191 📖 p. 255

Ng Aking, 33, wife of one Wong Fuk, was charged yesterday, with the unlawful possession of a gold watch value $40, burglariously stolen from the residence (Bellevue) of Mr. George Scott, manager of the O.B.C., on the 20th July last.

Inspector Perry formally charged the defendant on the 16th instant, when a remand was granted to enable him to find the defendant's husband.

Mr. Scott's evidence was now taken. He identified the watch as his wife's and stated: On 7th July, between two and three o'clock a.m. a travelling clock worth about $45, a pencil case worth $25 or $30, and the watch in court worth about $50, were taken from his bed-room. Attached to the watch by a ribbon were a key and the pencil case; the key was a Chubb's one and belonged to a cash box. His bedroom opened on to the verandah facing the harbour. All the doors were open. Any person entering must have come from the cook-house roof. He was disturbed by the barking of a dog in his room. At 10 minutes past two o'clock the clock was in its place; he knew this because his wife got up then to look at the time. At 3.15 the clock was gone; he knew

---

[170] The following is the complete set of reports in connection with this case in *The Complete Court Cases*: CC Nos 191, 236.

this because he got up then to look at the time. It was between these two times that the barking of the dog took place. At 3.15 he missed the watch and its appendages, as well as the clock. He went into the verandah in consequence of the barking of the dog. Saw nothing there; it was when he came in again that he missed the clock, watch, &c.; went down stairs and roused the servants. The house-coolie brought up a light and he found the mark of a bare foot on the balustrade of the verandah just above the roof of the cook- house, which was easily accessible from the ground at the back. Did not know the defendant.

Ting Apik, accountant in the Ki Hing pawn-shop at the corner of Queen's Road and Wing On Lane, said that on July 20th, about noon, defendant brought the watch in court to witness; asked her to whom it belonged. Defendant said it belonged to a woman named Asam who asked her to bring it to the pawn-shop. The defendant said she wanted a loan on it of $10. He gave her the money and pawn-ticket No. [5,037]; defendant gave the name of Ng Ting residing in Number 75 Fung Man Lane. Told one of his men to follow the defendant when she left the shop, and he did so. Never saw defendant before. About 11 or 12 days ago the police came to his shop looking for a watch. Showed them the one in Court; was asked who pawned it. He told them the name and the address the woman had given. The Inspector said there was no such number as 75 there. Witness said he did not know the number but knew the house; went there and found Asam, who said she knew who pawned the watch, but denied that it belonged to her. Had no doubt whatever that the defendant was the woman who pawned the watch. Was taken into the gaol about a week ago, and picked out the defendant from amongst six or seven women who were prisoners.

I Awan, coolie in the same pawnshop, said that on the 20th ulto., after the defendant had pawned the watch now in Court, or one very like it, receiving 8 taels, he followed her by order of the last witness and found that she went into a house in Tung-Man-Lane which he could point out; went back and told last witness that on the ground floor of the house this woman went into was the Kwong Sun Lung shop. Last witness wrote that on the paper in which the watch was wrapped up. Was positively certain that the defendant pawned a gold watch on the date he had mentioned; was taken into the gaol about a week ago and picked out the defendant from among six or seven women.

The case was remanded till the 1st proximo.[171]

UNLAWFUL POSSESSION
CC Number 192
Wong Aon, 23, a coolie, was charged with the theft of a piece of iron, value 30 cents, the property of the Hong Kong and Whampoa Dock Company, Limited, on the 23rd instant, at Hung Ham [sic]. The Company's watchman deposed to finding the iron under the man's jacket, and across his chest. He was coming from the yard when the watchman stopped him and searched him. Prisoner said he was very tired and took the iron to sit down upon to rest him self. He had been twice previously convicted of larceny, and once of disorderly conduct. He was now found guilty of unlawful possession, and was fined £1 [sic], with the alternative of 21 days' hard labour.

A BEAN CURD MAKERS' ROW
CC Number 193
Lo a Ip, and two other coolies, two hawkers, and a woman were charged with fighting and creating

---

[171] The finding of the watch was commented on separately in the paper. See CM, 15 September 1881, p. 3, c. 3. "Some praise is due to the vigilance of the police that the lady's gold watch stolen from the villa "Bellevue" about two months ago has now been recovered. Facts such as this show that, although cases may drop from the notice of the public, they remain green in the memory of the ubiquitous policeman. The watch was found in a pawnshop, the No. having been carefully erased."

disturbance in Tai Ping Lane and also with assaulting one Hu Asheung, bean curd manufacturer, on the 23rd. The male defendants were young men of from 22 to 28, the woman 45 years of age, wife of one Li Tsun.

The statement against the prisoners was that they, with some 25 others, had combined against the bean-curd maker by whom this woman, Hu Asheung, was employed, pelted her in his shop with bricks, struck her with bamboos, broke the pots and tubs, scattered the stock of bean-curds all over the floor, and so on, all because the objectionable bean-curd maker, Chan Kau, was taking away their custom by making better bean-curd than they did. Chan Kau was formerly employed by Lo Afu, he said; and this Lo Afu had set on these men and the others to attack his place of business. One of the prisoners, Pun Afat, was the partner of the complainant; he was arrested by mistake.

The defence was that Chan Akau had cut off Lo Afu's water, whereupon they had a quarrel. Lo Afu then engaged a number of men to go and beat Chan Akau. One of the prisoners said he was trying to separate the rioters when he was arrested. Another was a peacemaker. No. 5 was the partner of the man whose house was attacked. He said he was arrested by mistake.

The case was remanded till the 26th, and defendants released in bail on $10 each.

FALSE WEIGHTS AND MEASURES
CC Number 194

Eighteen cases in which Chinese store-keepers were charged with being found in possession of weights or measures not in accordance with the Government standard, were down for hearing, but had to be held over till Tuesday next, the 27th instant, at 9 a.m., through press of business in Court, and want of time.

THE BOOT ON THE OTHER LEG[172]
CC Number 195

Ping Alung, a hawker, was charged with assaulting and robbing the complainant of 32 cents on the 23rd instant. Complainant gave evidence that he was walking on Tai-ping-shan Street, when the defendant with some other men came up to him and asked him if he had any money. He said he had not. Defendant then seized him and held him, and with some of the other men took two cents from off his person.

Asked by the Magistrate why he had given information that this man stole 32 cents from him, the complainant explained that he had included 30 cents which the defendant had taken from him some time ago.

From the evidence of the police constable it turned out that the complainant had originally charged the prisoner with stealing ten cents from him.

The defendant further explained to the Court that when the constable arrested him he was just going up to the constable to call on him to arrest the complainant for stealing $1 from him some time ago.

This was too much for the Magistrate, who ordered the complainant into custody, and remanded the whole matter till the 28th instant, when the present complainant will be charged with wilfully making a false charge.

THEFT OF A BOX, CLOTHING AND MONEY
CC Number 196

Wong Chan Ki, a bird-cage maker, was charged with stealing a box, containing clothing to the value of $20 and $50 in money, the property of one Li Ashi, on the 19th *instant*.

Complainant arrived here by the Penedo which came in the other day. He took his box to the house of the complainant who is a friend of his. It was all right there until the 20th when he had a change of clothes; the next day it was gone.

---

[172] Today, we normally say "The boot is on the other *foot*".

Defendant said somebody must have taken it and advised him to go round the pawn- shop, which he did not do.

The case was adjourned till the 28th *instant*.

MONDAY 26 SEPTEMBER 1881[173]
USING ABUSIVE LANGUAGE
CC Number 197

Lo Yuk Yung was convicted on the evidence of the complaint, Mr Adams, Inspector of Nuisances, with using abusive language to him, and was fined $1, or three days' imprisonment.

ROGUE AND VAGABOND
CC Number 198

Chan Agan was charged by Police Constable 192 with being a rogue and vagabond and suspicious character.

Complainant said that on the night of the 25th *instant*, he saw defendant following a woman in Hollywood Road in a suspicious manner. On seeing witness defendant ran. Witness arrested him.

Defendant, who had been five times in gaol, was sentenced to three months' imprisonment with hard labour as a rogue and vagabond.

STREET GAMBLING
CC Number 199

Lau Ashing was convicted on the evidence of Police Constable210 of street gambling on the 25th instant, and was sent to gaol for fourteen days as a rogue and vagabond.

A THIEVES' FRIEND[174]
CC Number 200

Leong Ang, 52, a licensed opium dealer was charged with receiving stolen goods on the 19th at Yau-mah-ti.

---

[173] "Police Intelligence," CM, Monday, September 26, p. 3, c. 4.
[174] The following is the complete set of reports in connection with this case in *The Complete Court Cases*: CC Nos 170, 200.

Man Ali, 70 years of age, living at Number 63 Temple Street, Yau-mah-ti, deposed to three men coming to the clansman's house which he was looking after there, to one of them seizing him by the throat, rubbing his face with pepper, from the intended consequences of which[175] he saved himself by shutting his eyes, the other two men meantime proceeding to ransack the house, taking with other goods some of his property. The man who seized him and assaulted him tied a cravat round his throat and nearly strangled him. Identified the property in Court as a portion of that then stolen. A silk jacket and a pipe were missing. The property in Court consisted of a silk jacket, a blanket and a quilt, value together some $3.20. A head coolie identified these articles as belonging to him.

Defendant keeps an opium divan at 45, Praya, into which the thieves went after committing the theft. These goods were found in defendant's possession and he refused to say who brought them or to give any information to the police to enable them to get hold of the thieves. He says it would cause too much trouble.

Defendant was sentenced to six weeks' imprisonment with hard labour.

SNATCHING
CC Number 201

Cheung Aking, 25, unemployed, was sentenced to six months' imprisonment with hard labour for stealing from Ching Kung, wife of Cheung Muk, one pair of earrings value $1.50. He was also charged with assaulting Police Constable 201 in the execution of his duty, on the 25th *instant*. This was one of the ordinary cases of snatching; the thief was taken with the articles which he had stolen in his hand. He had a knife in his hand when the Constable caught him, and attempted to cut the Constable and get away. A

---

[175] The intended consequence, presumably, was blinding, either temporary or permanent.

packet of pepper was found in the thief's pocket when he was searched at the Station.

The prisoner explained most innocently that he had a bad cough which troubled him in the night time, and he always carried pepper with him to alleviate his sufferings. He received no further sentence for the alleged assault. He had been once previously convicted.

THEFT BY A SERVANT
CC Number 202
For stealing $8 in notes from a steam launch just returned with a shooting party[176] from Deep Bay on Sunday, Lum Ahun, servant to Mr Jupiter Ungher [sic], commercial traveller, was sentenced to two months' imprisonment with hard labour. The money stolen belonged to Mr. D.K. Griffiths, photographer, one of the party, and had been abstracted from his pocket while his clothes were hung up on deck to dry.

UNLAWFUL POSSESSION
CC Number 203
Ip Afun, 21, Ng Asun, 35, Ip A-I, 39, boat people and Leong Atsun, 28, shop-coolie, were charged with the unlawful possession of five pieces of sapan wood on the 23rd *instant*, on board a small cargo boat in the harbour, and being convicted were ordered to find security in two householders in $10 each to be of good behaviour for two months, in default to be committed for 14 days each.

---

[176] It seems there may be a (quite nicely composed) photo of this shooting party in the Hong Kong Museum of History photographic collection (ref. no. P1968.0024; title, "Picnic and Hunting Party, c. 1880". (There are a few other photographs of similar subjects, catalogued with nearby reference numbers.)

Complete Court Cases   188

[FIGHTING, PETTY ASSAULTS, HAWKING AGAINST THE REGULATIONS, OBSTRUCTION]
CC Number 204

There were between 30 and 40 cases before the Magistrates today of the usual Monday-morning type, fighting, petty assaults, hawking against the regulations, obstruction and so on; but only the above were of any public interest.

TUESDAY 27 SEPTEMBER 1881[177]
HABITUALLY ILL TREATING A LITTLE GIRL[178]
CC Number 205 📖 p. 254

Li Achoy, 56, of Shanghai, wife of one Fung Awai, was charged with assaulting and ill-treating a female named An Asam, at different times during the last seven days.

The case was last before the court on the 20th, when it was fully reported in our columns.

An Asam's evidence was now continued. She said: Defendant treats me very badly; she sometimes beats me with firewood. I jumped into the well, because I was hungry, because I do not get enough to eat. Sometimes I get no food, but I had had a meal early that morning. Whenever I take anything to eat, defendant beats me. Defendant slapped my face when I was taken out of the well.

To defendant: — No one taught me what to say here.

Defendant said: The people above let dirty water run down into my room, and I scolded them for this. They have, for revenge, taught the girl to accuse me. I thanked the man who took the girl from the well, and gave him 200 cash as tea money. I do not know why the girl jumped into the well. I was not out

---

[177] "Police Intelligence," CM, Tuesday, 27 September 1881, p. 3, cc. 5 - 6.
[178] The following is the complete set of reports in connection with this case in *The Complete Court Cases*: CC Nos 169, 205.

of bed when it happened. I slap the girl when she is naughty.

The Magistrate sentenced the woman to fourteen days' imprisonment with hard labour.

SHORT WEIGHTS AND MEASURES
CC Number 206

The following eighteen cases, in which Inspector Orley[179] prosecuted, were disposed of:—

1. Ching Shui, master of the Fuk Lun draper's shop, Number 2, Jervois Street, for unlawfully having in his shop, on September 22nd, 47 covid or chek measures,[180] the same being false and deficient, and not according to Government standard;

2. Chan Leung, master of the Hang Cheung shop, Number 4, Jervois Street; a similar charge in respect of two false covid measures;

3. Lam Akat, master of the Kwong Cheong Tai draper's shop, Number 6, Jervois Street in respect of 13 false covid measures;

4. Lan Shing and Leung Po, of the I-cheung shop,[181] Number 8, Jervois Street, in respect of two false covid measures;

---

[179] Inspector Orley was Inspector of Markets, Registrar General's Department; Inspector of Dangerous Goods; and Foreman, Fire Brigade. ("List of Officers", HKBB1882, Section I3.)

[180] "Covid": "A lineal measure formerly used in India: its length varied, at different times and places, from 36 to 14 inches" (*The Oxford English Dictionary*). The dictionary entry gives as one example of use, "A Chinese Covet". See also *A Magistrate's Court in 19th Century Hong Kong*, p. 433. "Chek" seems to have the same meaning.

[181] It seems that, "I-Cheung" or "I-ts'z" is a place to house death tablets and coffins awaiting shipment. This was a service provided in Hong Kong particularly by the Tung Wah Hospital. Historically, Chinese people living overseas wished their remains to be returned in China. When they died outside China, including in Hong Kong, their remains were stored, waiting for arrangements to be made for their final resting-place in their family home in China.
The Rates Assessment, Valuation and Collection Book of 1881 (HKPRO, HKRS 38-2-36) clearly shows these draper's shops. (Courtesy, Mr Bernard Hui, HKPRO.)

5. Leung Sing, of the Hing Cheung and Wing Li shops, Nos. 10 and 12, Jervois Street, in respect of three false covid measures;

6. Lun Heong, of the Fung Tai old-clothes shop, Number 14, Jervois Street, in respect of three false covid measures;

7. Pun Lun, of the Lim Cheung old-clothes shop, Number 18, Jervois Street, in respect of three false covid measures;

8. Ng Tong, of the Ku Cheung old clothes shop, Number 20, Jervois Street, in respect of three false covid measures;

9. Leung Pui Ling, of the Kwong Tai draper's shop, Number 24, Jervois Street, in respect of three false covid measures;

10. Liu Nam, of the Mi Cheung and Mi Cheung Chan shops, Number 26 and 28, Jervois Street, in respect of three false covid measures;

11. Pun Yeuk, of the Shing Ki draper's shop, Number 30, Jervois Street, in respect of two false covid measures;

12. Lai Yuk Chan of the Yan Cheung old clothes shop Nos. 32 and 34, Jervois Street, in respect of three false covid measures;

13. Wong Yat Hing, of the Tung Cheung shop, Number 36, Jervois Street, in respect of one false covid measure;

14. Leong Fong Shek of the Hang Cheong shop, Number 38, Jervois Street, in respect of two false covid measures;

15. Chan Lam, of the Wing Un draper's shop, Number 40, Jervois Street, in respect of one false covid measure;

16. Lai Ming Yew and Mok Shi, of the Yin Cheung old clothes shop, 42, Jervois Street, in respect of two false covid measures;

17. Tse Tak, of the Lee Yau draper's shop, Number 44, Jervois Street, in respect of one false covid measure; and

18. Mak Lung, of the Fuk Tai, old clothes shop, Number 44a, Jervois Street, in respect of two false covid measures.

In the first case, 47 measures produced. Evidence given that defendant sells measures; every one of the 47 covid measures was either too long or too short; not one of them the standard length; they were from one-eighth of an inch short to three-fourths of an inch too long.

Defendant said his measures were correct according to Chinese standard; they were the Pai-tain chek and Kai-ng chek.

With regard to the other cases, it was proved that 51 measures, single covid and double covid, were found in the shops named, all of which were *over* (not less than) the standard in length, the difference being one-eighth to seven-eights of an inch.

The Magistrate sentenced each defendant to pay a fine of 50 cents for each measure in use in their shops, all the measures in Court to be confiscated, including the 45 measures exposed for sale as well as the 2 in use in the case of the first defendant, and the 12 measures exposed for sale in the Kwong Cheong Tai Shop; a moiety of the fines to go to the informer. His Worship said he inflicted this nominal penalty, as the trade had been representing to the Government a "custom" not recognised by Ordinance.[182] He did not

---

[182] From the very beginning of the British administration in Hong Kong, there had been a concern to permit the continuation of existing Chinese customs.

The first number of *The Hong Kong Government Gazette* (1 May 1841), only three months after Commodore Bremer of HMS *Sulphur* hoisted the Union Flag at Possession Mound (26 January 1841), announced the appointment of the first Chief Magistrate of Hong Kong. He was to exercise authority over all non-Chinese inhabitants (those of the Army and Navy excepted) according to the customs and usages of British police law, and over all Chinese inhabitants – as far and as closely as possible – according to the laws, customs [present writer's emphasis] and usages of China, "every description of torture excepted".

know that the "custom" would ever be recognised by the Legislature, but he hoped the Ordinance would be translated[183] and circulated so as to remove all doubt as to what the Law on the subject really was.

WEDNESDAY 28 SEPTEMBER 1881[184]
EMPLOYER AND SERVANT CASE
CC Number 207

Kwong Achu servant to a woman named Dolly Johnson,[185] residing at Number 15, Graham Street, charged his mistress and a certain foreigner called Peter with assault. The woman appeared on a

---

"It was intended that the Chinese on the island should be subject to Chinese law, though this caused problems. . . . The Hong Kong constitution . . . was designed to safeguard trade and protect native customs." (E. J. Eitel, *Europe in China*, pp. 227-228.)

(For the relationship between Hong Kong and British law, see also Christopher Coghlan, "Thoughts about the Practice of Law in Hong Kong," in *A Magistrate's Court in 19th Century Hong Kong*, pp. 87-97.)

From this comment in, CC 206, *The Complete Court Cases*, it appears that, in 1881, Chinese customs needed to be recognized by Ordinance in order to be acceptable as a basis for a legal defence.

[183] The Ordinance in question was Ordinance No. 22 of 1844, entitled, "An Ordinance for Establishing Standard Weights and Measures, and for preventing the Use of such as are false and deficient", dated 30 December 1844.

A week after Frederick Stewart made this remark, apparently in direct response to what he said, a Chinese translation of the Ordinance was published. (HKGG, 8 October 1881, pp. 915-919.)

The later report of a case heard in October 1881 [CC. No. 285], refers to the fact that the translation had appeared.

For further discussion and documentation of this case, see Gillian Bickley, ed, "Weights and Measures", in, "Some Nineteenth Century Hong Kong Court Cases", 2009/2010.

[184] "Police Intelligence," CM, Wednesday, September 28, p. 3, cc. 5 - 6.

[185] Some months later, Wednesday 22 March (CM, p. 3, cc. 6-7), H. W. Wodehouse heard a case in which Un Wa Chung, servant, wsa charged with having stolen articles, the property of Dolly Johnson and Kate Douglas, "Single women [i.e. according to the terminology of the time, "prostitutes"] residing in Graham Street".

summons, warrant was issued on the 24th for the man's arrest; but "Peter" has not yet been found.

The boy's story was that he was cook. At one o'clock in the morning his mistress had a visitor, who drank all the beer in the house. Complainant would not go for more beer to a shop because he had no pass. Defendant went herself; and afterwards abused complainant for not going. Peter, whom witness described as defendant's "master," came and ordered complainant off at once. He answered that he would go in the morning. In the morning he made tea for his mistress and Peter; and when he asked for his wages after that, preparatory to leaving, Peter held his queue and the woman struck him twice with her fists. He had no marks. He called out "Save life," but Peter stopped him by seizing him by the throat. When they had done with him he came to the Magistracy and took out a summons. Defendant had since paid him his wages, $8, in the Magistracy, Chief Clerk's office. She also offered him $2 to go away and say nothing more about the matter; this offer he refused.

The assault was denied.

A Police Constable, No. 164, spoke to serving summons on the female defendant. She told him Peter was asleep and could not be disturbed. Posted up the summons on an inner door; the woman tore it down. Witness then posted it up on an outer. Defendant said she would summon him for seizing her by the dress.

Mr. Parker[186] gave evidence as to the woman having given the boy his wages, $8, and $2 to drop the case; he agreed on taking the dollars to do so.

Case dismissed.

STREET GAMBLING
CC Number 208

Lum Ashing and Chin Aying were charged on the 26th *instant* with gambling, when Police Constable 518 said that on the 25th he was in Market Street,

---

[186] Mr Parker was Chief Clerk at the Magistracy.

where he saw about the [*sic* for "ten"?] men playing with dice. He arrested first defendant, and another Police Constable apprehended the second defendant.

Today no further evidence was produced, and prisoners were sentenced to one months' imprisonment with hard labour as rogues and vagabonds.

A KIND UNCLE
CC Number 209

Lam Acho, 54, coolie, was charged with assaulting one Lam Akin also a coolie, on the 27th *instant*.

Complainant's story was that at 11 a.m. in Third Street, Sai- ying-poon, defendant beat him with an iron bar (shows bruises on arm.) Believed defendant had mistaken him for some other person, who resembled him. He denied, in answer to defendant, that he was defendant's nephew.

Defendant said that the complainant was his nephew and he had had occasion to chastise him for idling and gambling. He wanted complainant to work and he would not.

Complainant added in explanation that defendant had made an immoral charge against him, and demanded $2 hush money. He would not pay him, whereupon defendant struck him.

Complainant and defendant were ordered to give personal security in $10 to keep the peace towards each other for three months.

UNLAWFUL POSSESSION OF OPIUM
CC Number 210

Lum Akan, 22, unemployed, for being found in possession of about 8 taels of prepared opium without a valid certificate from the opium farmer, which he said some friends had brought from Macao and given to him, was fined $20, with the alternative of 21 days' imprisonment, and the opium was ordered to be given to the Farmer.

ROGUES AND VAGABONDS
CC Number 211

Un Asoi, 36, and Chun Aleong, 28, jin-ricksha coolies, who were found playing cards with several others in an empty house in St. Francis Street, were sentenced as rogues and vagabonds to fourteen days' imprisonment with hard labour; and 20 cents money found at the place where they had been gambling was paid into the poor box.

STEALING ROOTS
CC Number 212

Ho Achoi, 30, a coolie, for stealing taroes and lilly [*sic*] roots, value 20 cents, from the door of a fruit lan in Bonham Strand, was sentenced to two months' imprisonment with hard labour. He was last convicted of larceny in February.

A NEEDY CUSTOMER PROVIDED FOR
CC Number 213

Wong Asing, 18, washerman, was found guilty of stealing a jacket which was spread out on the hill side to dry. Defendant said he had no employment and no regular fixed place to live in. He got a meal now and again from a friend. The Magistrate pitying,[187] the poor fellow's case, ordered that he should be fed and clothed and provided with a regular fixed place to live in for the next fourteen days.

---

[187] It is difficult to know what the tone is here. It is shown in *A Magistrate's Court in 19th Century Hong Kong* that a homeless person might commit an offence deliberately, in order to be sentenced to prison and so obtain a bed for the night, often with the magistrate fully understanding the situation. Here the offender is sentenced to *fourteen* days in prison and his offence is theft, not the common, "committing a nuisance", often done for this purpose. The magistrate could well feel compassion for a person as bereft as the offender seems to be. But that might have nothing to do with the sentence. On the whole, it seems that the reporter is speaking, tongue-in-cheek.

LOAFING AT THE DOCK
CC Number 214

Tam Atai, 32, a hawker who has been in gaol before for larceny, was ordered to find security, two householders in $10 each, to be of good behavior for three months, in default to be committed, he having been found on the premises of the Dock Company[188] with intent to commit a felony, at Lap-sap-wan, on the 27th *instant*.

LOVE ME, LOVE MY CAT[189]
CC Number 215

Ackrumm [*sic*], 40, a Calcutta-man, was charged with threatening Chan Achiu with intent to provoke a breach of the peace.

The Chinaman is the owner of a cat which defendant's son beat, while it was sitting quietly purring at complainant's door. Complainant called defendant's wife to see the cat, and told her she should punish the boy. She said it was only a cat after all; and treated the matter lightly. The complainant reasoned with her, arguing that the cat had a life, that it was wrong to beat a cat, because the cat might be killed, that it was wrong to take the life of a cat and so on. Defendant's wife, woman-like, met his argument by calling him a gaol bird and such like. Then defendant came with a stick and tried to beat the complainant. Defendant took two of complainant's men to the Police Station, but the Inspector sent them away. Defendant then told complainant that he was too saucy and told him he would take an early opportunity of stabbing him.

Defendant's story ran in another form. He heard complainant abusing his (defendant's) son for stealing a cat, and telling the lad he had killed the cat, and so he would kill him. Went out and saw the cat there, alive and well. Complainant told defendant that

---

[188] "Company" replaces the short version, "Coy", in the original.
[189] The usual saying is, "Love me, Love my Dog". The writer is intending us to note the variation as a means of catching the reader's attention.

if the cat died he would see defendant's son promptly hung. Defendant carried it further and told complainant that if he did that he would himself be hanged. Complainant's comrades then assaulted defendant.

Bound over in $20 to keep the peace towards complainant for two months.

DRINK AGAIN
CC Number 216
John Fitzpatrick, steward, from Australia, paid 25 cents for having been foolishly persuaded to take a little more than he could carry.

OBSTRUCTIONS
CC Number 217
Eleven Chinese were fined $1, with the alternative of two days' imprisonment, for leaving goods, stalls, &c., on the footway, so as to obstruct foot passengers.

THURSDAY SEPTEMBER 29, 1881[190]
LARCENY
CC Number 218
Wong Chan Ki, charged on remand with stealing a box value $70 was again before the Court today. Some further evidence was heard, and the case was remanded till 6th October. Bail as before.

PICKPOCKET
CC Number 219
Lum Among, charged on remand with picking the pocket of Tong A-in, a trader, was today convicted, after further evidence, and was sentenced to two months' imprisonment with hard labour.

---

[190] "Police Intelligence," CM, Thursday, September 29, p. 3, c. 3.

FRIDAY 30 SEPTEMBER 1881[191]
THEFT
CC Number 220 📖 p. 348

Chiu Ayau was charged on remand, with having stolen an umbrella the property of Cheung Akwai, cook.

On the 17th *instant*, complainant had been buying some sugar water, and while doing so put his umbrella against the hawker's stall. When finished drinking, he found the umbrella gone. He saw defendant running off with it in his hand. Complainant called out "Police" when defendant dropped the umbrella. A constable arrested him.

Defendant had been four times previously convicted. He was cautioned, reserved his defence, and was committed for trial at the Criminal Sessions.[192]

---

[191] "Police Intelligence," CM, Friday, 30 September 1881, p. 3, cc. 2 - 3, c. 4.

[192] The case of Chan A-yau is No. 6 in the Criminal Calendar -- October Sessions, 1881. He was tried on 18 October 1881 on three counts: 1) Larceny; 2) Previous conviction (summary); 3) Previous conviction (summary). He was found guilty on the first count, unanimously, and pleaded guilty on the second and third counts. He was sentenced to three years' penal servitude.

The following report appears in *The China Mail*, Tuesday, 18 October 1881, p. 3, c. 4.
"Supreme Court In Criminal Sessions (Before the Acting Puisne Judge, Hon. J. Russell.)
"Tuesday, 18 October 1881
"Theft of an Umbrella

Mr Francis, under instructions from the Attorney General, prosecuted.

The jurors were Messrs J. W. Crocker, R. Steil, A. S. Garfit, A. F. Gonsalves, F. H. G. Lorberg, E. Vogel, and S. V. dos Remedios.

"Chan Ayau was charged with stealing an umbrella on the 17th Sept. It will be recollected that complainant had set his umbrella down at the side of a stall near the Harbour-master's office while drinking some sugared water. Defendant took it up and ran, but

Complete Court Cases   199

LARCENY FROM THE PERSON
CC Number 221 📖 p. 349

Lum Amui was charged by Lo Aping with stealing a bundle of clothing.

Complainant, a dealer in second-hand clothes had gone to Station Street to hawk clothes. His bundles were put on the ground, while he was bargaining with a customer. He missed a bundle, and made a report at Number 7 Station. Afterwards he was sent for, and went to the station, where defendant was in custody. He went with a police constable to a pawnshop in Yau-mah-ti, where he found the articles amissing.

Leung Ching, servant to the first witness, said he saw defendant pick up the bundle and run. Witness went to Kowloon, and saw defendant pawning some of the clothing. Defendant got away, but afterwards he saw him in Hong Kong, and asked him to deliver up the pawn-tickets which he did.

Defendant, who had been three times previously convicted, was cautioned, reserved his defence, and was committed for trial at the Criminal Sessions.[193]

---

was stopped by a Police Constable. Prisoner was also charged with a previous conviction.

"The Jury found him guilty.

"His Lordship said he was a bad boy. Although only seventeen years of age he had been convicted a great many times. It was only a waste of time to go on giving him short punishments. The sentence would be three years' penal servitude."

[193] The case of Lam A-mui is No. 5 in the Criminal Calendar -- October Sessions, 1881. He was tried on three counts: 1) Larceny; 2) Previous conviction (summary); 3) Previous conviction (summary). He was found guilty on the first count, unanimously, and pleaded guilty on the second and third counts. He was sentenced to five years' penal servitude.

The following report appeared in *The China Mail,* 18 October 1881, p. 3, c. 4.
"Supreme Court In Criminal Sessions
"(Before the Acting Puisne Judge, Hon. J. Russell.)
"Tuesday, 18 October 1881

FRIDAY 30 SEPTEMBER 1881[194]
STREET GAMBLING
CC Number 222

Un Asing was charged with the above offence.

Police Constable 519 said that on the 30th instant, about 8 a.m., while in Market Street he saw ten or twelve people gambling. He went up and arrested defendant. The others ran away. At the place he found the mat, counting stick, cup, and bad cash in Court. Witness also found seven cents in good cash. He was quite sure defendant was gambling.

Defendant said he was merely passing. He had the cents and cash in his hand. He was going to get his jacket mended.

Prisoner was sentenced to fourteen days' imprisonment with hard labour as a rogue and vagabond. Cents and good cash to go to poor box.

HAWKING WITHOUT A LICENSE
CC Number 223

Tsing Aluk admitted having been hawking sweetmeats without a licence; and was fined 50 cents or two days' imprisonment.

"Larceny

"Lum Amui was charged with the theft of twenty-two articles of clothing and two red handkerchiefs on the 6th *instant*. The circumstances of the case were that the owner (a hawker) had gone to Station Street to sell his wares. He had a boy to carry them. While engaged in completing a bargain the bundles were set on the ground, and one of them was lifted by prisoner, who was seen doing so by the boy. The goods had been pawned at Kowloon by the prisoner. The pawn tickets were found on him.

"His Lordship, in sentencing prisoner to five years' penal servitude, remarked that it would be cheaper for the ratepayers to keep him in gaol than to have him prowling about in the Colony."
[194] "Police Intelligence," CM, Friday, 30 September 1881, p. 3, cc. 2 - 3, c. 4.

DRUNK[195]
CC Number 224 📖 p. 174

George Cameron, [196] seaman, American ship "Twilight", was convicted of being drunk and incapable.

Defendant said he was sorry. He had had a little too much.

Prisoner was fined 25 cents or one day's imprisonment.

THEFT OF A HAIR PIN
CC Number 225 📖 p. 349

Au Apo was charged at the instance of Mok Awa, a boatman in the employ of the Harbour Department, with stealing a silver hair pin from Chan Mui, a widow living in Square Street. It seemed that on the 29th about 3 p.m., while she was on the Praya, a man snatched her silver hair pin. She turned and saw defendant running away.

She called out thief, and defendant was stopped by one of the Harbour Office boatmen. She was sure defendant was the man. Her son was there.

Mok Awang said he was twelve years of age. On the day in question, he was a little behind his mother on the Praya when he saw defendant pass him and snatch his mother's hair pin. Witness called out "robbery," and defendant ran. He was stopped by a boatman.

Mok Awa said he was a boatman in the Harbour Department. On the 29th he was on the Praya, when he heard a cry of "robbery." He saw defendant running towards him with the last witness after him. Witness stopped the defendant; no hair pin was found on him.

---

[195] The complete set of reports in connection with this case in *The Complete Court Cases*, are: CC Nos 224, 242, 250. See also Gillian Bickley, ed., "Bolton Abbey", in, "Some Nineteenth Century Hong Kong Court Cases", 2009/2010" for Reports of a Marine Court of Enquiry.

[196] The following versions of this name appear in this series of reports: "Cannron", "Cameron", "Cannon".

Prisoner denied the theft, but was sentenced to twenty-one days' imprisonment with hard labour.

BREACH OF THE MARKET ORDINANCE
CC Number 226
Lo Li Ui admitted this charge and was fined $1 or four days' imprisonment.

BREACH OF THE MARKET ORDINANCE]
CC Number 227
Leung Awai admitted having sold blood in the street and having sold congee without a license, and was fined $1 or four days' imprisonment.

SUSPICIOUS CHARACTER
CC Number 228
Tong Awai said he was master of the Sz Chin chandler's shop, Pound Lane. On the 29th instant about 10 p.m. he went up stairs where his family lived. On getting to the first floor, which was unoccupied, he heard a noise. He went in and saw defendant in the cook room. He gave him into custody. Witness did not know defendant. The door of the first floor had its lock broken. A few nights ago witness had got some bed boards stolen from the first floor.

Prisoner was ordered to find security (2 householders) in $20 each to be of good behaviour for two months, in default to be committed.

DISTURBANCE
CC Number 229
Four Chinamen was [*sic* for "were"] charged by Police Constable 594 with creating a disturbance.

According to the evidence of the constable, the second, third, and fourth defendants had their stalls on the foot path in Centre Street on the 29th. First defendant was standing at the door of a house close by where an auction was going on. Some coolies removing furniture knocked against one of the stalls and over turned it. The second, third, and fourth defendants seized first defendant, and said that as he had hired the coolies he must pay for the damage. They came to blows; the first defendant did not strike any body.

First defendant was discharged. Second, third, and fourth fined 25 cents or one day's imprisonment each.

DISORDERLY CONDUCT
CC Number 230

Capitulino Priamo Marçal said that he was a compositor at present unemployed. On the 29th he engaged defendant's (Chang Amui's) jinricksha to take him from near the Central Market to the Tang-lung-chow Temple and back. When they came opposite the old Sugar Refinery at East Point defendant stopped and asked for payment. Complainant refused to pay until he had completed the journey agreed on. Defendant said if Europeans had tempers Chinese had tempers too.[197] A crowd of coolies gathered round him and insulted him. Defendant took him as far back as Number 2 Station, and there complainant gave him in charge.

Defendant was fined 50 cents, or two days imprisonment.

STREET GAMBLING
CC Number 231

Police Constable 683 said that on the 29th he was on duty near Park Wharf where he saw defendants (Wong Ayau and Lum Kwai Mui), with two others

---

[197] It is a little unclear what the situation is. It is clear that the rickshaw driver asked for payment before he would complete the journey. It seems that the passenger reacted angrily and that the driver responded in kind, and a crowd gathered. It seems also that, following this, the passenger asked the driver to take him to a different destination, Police Station no. 2, in order to charge him. If this is the correct interpretation, it is interesting that the driver did do this, knowing what the purpose was. The comment about tempers highlights the consciousness of racial difference which at least some people felt, and which was here apparently exacerbated in response to friction arising from another cause.

not in custody gambling with cards. When witness seized defendant he had money in his hand, but this he threw in the water.

Sentence seven days' imprisonment with hard labour as rogues and vagabonds.

UNLAWFUL POSSESSION
CC Number 232 📖 p. 323

Wong Ayeung was charged by Police Constable 197 with being in unlawful possession of two jackets and one blanket on the 29th *instant*.

Police Constable 197 said that this morning just after midnight he got information about a man taking two bundles to an opium divan in Square Street. Witness went to the house and found defendant on a bed with the blanket in court for a pillow. Witness asked him where the other bundle was, and he answered under the bed. It contained two jackets. On being asked to whom the articles belonged defendant pointed to a blind boy, but this person denied the ownership. Defendant was often seen prowling about the streets.

Defendant, who had been in gaol three times before, was sent to that place again for a period of thirty days with hard labour, with the option of 15 shillings of a fine.

SERIOUS ASSAULT[198]
CC Number 233 📖 p. 173

Charles Naylor,[199] second officer of the Kang Chi, was charged with assaulting one Apo of the age of 17 years, so as to cause him to jump overboard in Victoria Harbour on the 29th of September.

Ho Asing said he was boatswain on the Kang Chi. On the 29th about 7.30 p.m., he was below on the 'tween decks when he heard a noise on deck. He went up to see what was the matter. He saw the boat

---

[198] The reports in connection with this case in *The Complete Court Cases*, are: CC Nos 233, 237.

[199] The name, "Naylor", is also given as "Taylor" in reports of this case.

boy jumping from the deck to a cargo boat on the star board side of the vessel. Defendant went into the cargo boat after Apo, who jumped into the water. Witness after some delay got a boat and looked for him, but could find no trace of the lad. The other Chinese on the vessel looked round the vessel with lamps. Witness had not seen the boy since. He did not know why defendant was following Apo. Witness made a report at 9 p.m. on the 29th. The steamer left for Haiphong this morning. She was lying about 50 England[200] [*sic*] yards from the shore. Witness did not know if the boy could swim. Before Apo joined the steamer he was a boat boy. By Mr. Wotton: He had been once at Shanghai. He did not know what the "Shanghai dodge" was. The boy was strong and had the use of all his limbs. He was an active lad and in good health.

The case was adjourned to Tuesday first at half-past two, and defendant was admitted to bail in one householder of $1,000, or two of $500 each.

ALLEGED INDECENT ASSAULT[201]
CC Number 234

[Cheang Asz], 42, described as a coolie, but certified by the Dep. Inspector General as being at present employed as head nurse in the Royal Naval Hospital, and residing at Number 7, Hing Han Street, was charged with entering the room of a married woman, one Yan Kiu, wife of one Cheong Ng, residing on the same floor, and with indecently assaulting her.

Case was remanded till the 4th proximo.

---

[200] "England" for "English".

[201] The following is the complete set of reports in connection with this case in *The Complete Court Cases*: CC Nos 234, 247.

WHOLESALE [DECOYING] OF BOYS AND GIRLS[202]

CC Number 235 📖 p. 302

A case comes before the Court tomorrow, on remand, which, although it has already been before the Court several times has not yet been noticed in either of the papers.[203] As it will probably be finally disposed of tomorrow, so far as the Magistrate's concern with it goes, it may very properly be briefly stated here:—

Tong Achi, 42, of Nam-hoi, marine hawker, and Wong Ang, 52, of Samshui, wife of Li Aü were charged with forcibly detaining two boys and three girls for an unlawful purpose on July 7th. This case has been before the Court since July 15th. The following is a summary of the evidence, up to the present stage in the case.

Detective Sergeant Fisher stated that on July 14th, by virtue of two warrants[,] he went to Number 4 , Cheung Lane, Sai-ying-pun, in company with Chinese Police Constable No. 192, and an informer named Wong Man Yu, who pointed out the two defendants to him and the three children he would produce at a subsequent stage of the proceedings. Told the informer, a Chinese and in presence of the defendants, he wanted three more children. The informer said there *were*[204] five but he could not find the other two. Searched the other rooms and in them found two more children. The informer told him these were the children he was in search of; and he took the defendants and the children to the Station. The Po Leung Kuk had taken the usual steps in the case and endeavoured first to find out and communicate with the parents. Every effort had been

---

[202] The following is the complete set of reports in connection with this case in *The Complete Court Cases*: CC Nos 20, 93, 235, 238. CC No. 37 may also be related to this group of cases. CC No. 235 aims to give the complete reporting on the case as a whole, based on the various earlier hearings.

[203] This statement that this case had not been reported in either of the papers before is not correct. It was reported twice previously in *The China Mail* itself, on 29 July and 19 August.

[204] The italics appear in the original.

made, but nothing could be discovered about these five children, although the case had been adjourned from July 15, week by week, till August 12th, to give ample opportunity for everything being done. Several people had come but no one had yet claimed them. On account of the floods in the neighbouring province about that time people were prevented from coming to see the children. Then another week's remand was granted. Four men were sent out to make enquiries regarding the children and every effort was made to obtain some information concerning them. The case was remanded from week to week, awaiting the return of these men, until the 3rd Sept. when,

[205]Wong Man Yu detective of the Po Leung Kuk, gave evidence. On the 13th July, he received certain information from one Fung Kwok Tai, in consequence of which he went with his informant to Number 4 Cheung On Lane where he saw the five children concerned in this case. Defendants and several other persons were in the house. Asked second defendant "Have you got boys for sale?" She said "Yes," and pointed out the boy Amui, for whom she wanted $65 and Ahing for whom she wanted $55. First defendant said, — "At that price they are cheap." Second defendant then said, — "These three girls (pointing to Amui, Asan and Aut) are also for sale." Did not ask the price of these three, but said he would see about it and come back again. He then left. Next day he came to the Magistracy and laid an information (information put in and ac knowledged).

In reply to the first defendant, the witness said he was quite sure he saw him in the house on the 13th July last. To the second defendant he said he did not know anyone called Tan Afau or Tsoi Acheong.

Kwong Kwok Tai, a doctor, living in Tai Kwai Lane, deposed to having, on certain information received from one Kwan Atsu, went [sic for "gone"] with that man to house Number 4,

---

[205] The comma after "when" and the break after it to the next line accurately reflect the original report.

Cheung On Lane where he saw second defendant and some other women and the five children now in Court. Said to her — "Are these children for sale?" She said "Yes." He asked the price of the two boys Ahing and Amui. She said "The younger (Amui) is $65 and Ahing is $55." He said "very well"; my master may want to buy them. He and the man with whom he had gone to the house then left. Last day he gave information to the last witness and went with him to the house.

To first defendant witness said he was quite sure he was in the house.

To second defendant, witness denied that he had gone to her house on the 8th July just to borrow money, one Afau being with him at the time. Did not return with Afau on the 10th July. Did not threaten that if the second defendant did not give him money he would give her trouble. Did not go to her house with Afau on the 14th, and demand 10 taels.

Kwong Acheung, Police Constable 192, said he went with Sergeant Fisher to Number 4 Cheung On Lane on the 14th July about 4.30 p.m., and saw the defendants and the children there. Asked the first defendant where the children came from, and he said he did not know. Witness said — "You live here and do not know?" Defendant said "I go out every day to collect old wares". Then asked second defendant, and she looked very much afraid and gave no answer. In another room were two of the children and a woman. This woman also said she did not know where the children were from. This woman further said in the hearing of both defendants that one of the children had been in the house two months, and the other about ten days. Showed the defendants his warrant for arresting them, and they both said they knew nothing about it. He took the defendants and the children to the Central Station.

Wong Man Yu, recalled, said a man from Sam Shui came to the Tung Wa Hospital and identified one of the boys, Chan Hing, as his nephew who had been missed as far back as June last. That man had gone away to get the boy's mother. He had said he had to go to Lo Fan, in the Sam Shui District; he would take about three days to go to the place. At the last date, this uncle of the boy Chan Hing had not returned, and the case is now down for tomorrow, when if he is forthcoming, his evidence will be taken.

BEFORE FREDERICK STEWART, ESQ.,
October 1881[206]

SATURDAY 1 OCTOBER 1881[207]
THE ROBBERY FROM BELLEVUE[208]
CC Number 236 📖 p. 257

The case in which a Chinese woman named Ng Aking was charged with being in unlawful possession of a gold watch belonging to Mr George O. Scott, was resumed today.

Inspector Perry was recalled and detailed the circumstances of the finding of the watch, and the arrest of the prisoner.

Defendant said that on the 11th *ultimate* she met Police Sergeant Pang Loi[209] in the street. He asked her if she had become rich, and asked her for the loan of a few dollars. She said she was too poor to do so. The Sergeant said "all right" and went away. On the 15th the Sergeant returned and arrested her in Tai Wai Street. She was put in gaol, and in a line with several others. Before doing this Sergeant Pang Loi told the witness that the woman who had lost two front teeth was the person wanted. In this way, the witness pointed her out. She had nothing more to say.

Prisoner was fined L10 [*sic* for $10?], in default three months in gaol with hard labour.

---

[206] **Note on October 1881 court case reports as a whole**. On 19 October 1881, nothing is reported in *The China Mail* as "Before Frederick Stewart, Esq."

[207] "Police Intelligence," CM, Saturday, 1 October 1881, p. 3, c. 3.

[208] The following is the complete set of reports in connection with this case in *The Complete Court Cases*: CC Nos 191, 236.

[209] Aka Pang Alui.

THE SERIOUS ASSAULT CASE[210]
CC Number 237 📖 p. 174

The case in which C. Taylor, second officer of the Kang Chi, was charged with assaulting a Chinese boy and causing him to jump overboard, was reduced this morning to very slight dimensions. The boy who was said to be amissing, came up to the Magistracy yesterday afternoon, and was examined this morning. He had had no intention of reporting the matter to the police. Defendant had challenged him for leaving the shop too soon with the boat for the purpose of bringing off the Captain. Defendant ordered him forward, and slapped him in the face. The boy said he got frightened and jumped into the cargo-boat. He was frightened to go back. He had no wish to press the charge.

Defendant was fined $1, or one day's imprisonment.

THE ABDUCTION CASE[211]
CC Number 238 📖 p. 305

The case in which Fong Achi [sic] and Wong Ang were charged with the abduction of five children, was resumed today, when

[212]Mok Kai, detective in the employment of the Po Leung Kok [sic for "Kuk"], said that Wong Man In,[213] the other detective, had gone to Tung Kin to make further inquiries regarding the parents of the children. He was not sure when he would return.

Remanded till 8th instant.

---

[210] The following is the complete set of reports in connection with this case in *The Complete Court Cases*: CC Nos 233, 237.

[211] The following is the complete set of reports in connection with this case in *The Complete Court Cases*: CC Nos 20, 93, 235, 238. CC No. 37 may also be related to this group of cases.

[212] The line break at this position (between "when" and "Mok") is the same as in the original report.

[213] For variations in the reporting of this name, see note to CC 20.

MONDAY 3 OCTOBER 1881[214]
ASSAULT
CC Number 239

Chu Kun, a cook on board the Thales, complained that on the 1st instant, when the steamer arrived here, the defendant came on board, and began fighting with some people. Complainant thought it was his duty to preserve order on board and in his endeavour to do so lost one of his front teeth, which was displaced by defendant. A police constable on board arrested defendant.

> Sentence —Ten days' imprisonment with hard labour.

UNLAWFUL POSSESSION
CC Number 240

Police Sergeant 199[215] said that on the 1st instant, a little after midnight from information he received he went up to defendant in Hollywood Road, and asked him what he had in his hand. Defendant had the watch produced. On being asked where he got it he said he picked it up on the street. He offered the watch to the Police Sergeant to overlook the matter. After arresting defendant he found the owner of the watch. The owner of the watch, a seaman unemployed, said that while looking at a Chinese funeral procession, he lost the watch in Court.

> Defendant denied the theft, but was sentenced to three months' imprisonment with hard labour for larceny from the person.

THEFT OF A JACKET
CC Number 241

Chang Asing was convicted of stealing a jacket, the property of Chan Asang, on the 1st *instant*, and was sentenced to two months' imprisonment. He had been in gaol before. The jacket had been left by the owner

---

[214] "Police Intelligence," CM, Monday, 3 October 1881, p. 3, c. 2.
[215] We know from CC 308 that this is Pang Loi aka Pang Aloi.

Complete Court Cases   213

in his tool chest (he being a carpenter) and was picked up by the defendant.

TUESDAY 4 OCTOBER 1881[216]
THE "BOLTON ABBEY" -- FALSE REPORT[217]
CC Number 242 📖 p. 174

George Cannron,[218] of the ship Twilight, was accused of being a rogue and vagabond.

Mr Maconachie said he was manager of the firm of Messrs. Gilman & Company; on the 27th ultimo he was informed that the British ship Bolton Abbey, had been spoken by the Twilight about 300 miles from Hong Kong. On the afternoon of the 20th defendant came to witness' office and represented himself as the boatswain of the Bolton Abbey. He told witness the ship had been anchored near the Cape D'Aguilar and Cape Collinson lights. Witness asked why he came instead of the Captain. He said the Captain and the Chief Officer were sick, and had been so, prisoner said, since the big typhoon. Defendant said he had been sent to report the ship's arrival. On the strength of the defendant's report, witness sent a telegram to Lloyd's that the ship had arrived in Hong Kong Harbour. The defendant on finishing his story said he had been sent ashore without money or food. Witness told him that Lloyd's were not the people to provide him with such things. Witness had to send a telegram to Lloyd's contradicting his former one.

The prisoner made a statement in the graphic words appended: —I can't swear whether I did it or whether I did it not. I was drunk, and when drink is in wit is out. I was before you the other day and was fined 25 cents, and I have been drunk most every day

---

[216] "Police Intelligence," CM, Tuesday, 4 October 1881, p. 3, cc. 3 - 4.

[217] The following is the complete set of reports in connection with this case in *The Complete Court Cases*: CC Nos 224, 242, 250. See also note to CC No. 224 above.

[218] The following versions of this name appear in this series of reports: "Cannron", "Cameron", "Cannon".

since I came here by the Twilight. I know I passed the Bolton Abbey, and that is all I know about her.

The case was remanded till the 5th *instant*.

ROGUE AND VAGABOND
CC Number 243

John Perry was convicted on the evidence of Police Sergeant John Butlin of begging in Queen's Road. He had been convicted previously, and was sentenced today to twenty-one days' imprisonment with hard labour as a rogue and vagabond.

LARCENY FROM THE PERSON
CC Number 244 📖

Complainant in this case said he got a five dollar note to go and get $2.70 change and left the $5 note as security. While getting back the defendant (Li Ahok) snatched the money from his hand. A district watchman caught the defendant.

Defendant was sentenced to three months' imprisonment with hard labour.

OBSTRUCTION
CC Number 245

Fang Chu Wa was convicted on the evidence of Police Sergeant 524 of leaving boxes on the footway and was fined $5 or four days' imprisonment. Prisoner admitted the charge.

[OBSTRUCTION]
CC Number 246

Seven other Chinamen were convicted on the evidence of Police Constable 568 of leaving articles in the footpath to the obstruction of passengers, and were each fined $3 or four days' imprisonment.

INDECENT ASSAULT[219]
CC Number 247
This case in which a Chinese woman charged a Chinaman with indecently assaulting her was dismissed.

DISPATCH OF A STEAMER WITHOUT WOMAN
CC Number 248
U Wan Cho was charged by Mr Lister, Post-master General, with omitting to give notice of the departure of the steamer China. Several people had been put to serious inconvenience.

Defendant admitted that he had not given notice, and was fined $25 or twenty-one days' imprisonment.

WEDNESDAY 5 OCTOBER 1881[220]
LEAVING HIS EMPLOYER'S SERVICE WITHOUT NOTICE
CC Number 249
Lai Atin said he was a baker at house Number 57, Queen's Road East. Defendant (Lau Mun) was in his employ. Defendant had been employed as a deliverer of bread for him, and on the 2nd instant, he came back with about half of the bread. Complainant asked how he had brought back so much bread, and defendant said the customers had gone to Macao. From the story of the complainant, it turned out that the defendant had appropriated money belonging to his master, and Lau Mun was thereupon today convicted of embezzlement, and sentenced to six months' imprisonment with hard labour; the first and last fortnight to be in solitary confinement.

---

[219] The following is the complete set of reports in connection with this case in *The Complete Court Cases*: CC Nos 234, 247.

[220] "Police Intelligence," CM, Wednesday, 5 October 1881, p. 3, c. 3.

THE "BOLTON ABBEY"[221]
CC Number 250 📖 p. 175

In this case, today; Captain Thomsett gave evidence. He said defendant (Cannon)[222] came to him and told him a rambling story about his ship having passed a village on a river. Witness thought the ship had got among some islands; the ship according to defendant's story was dismasted, and the fall of the masts had carried away the deck house.

Defendant said he would rather go to Gaol than go back to his ship. As he had lost three wives, he had been driven to drink.

He was sentenced to three months' imprisonment with hard labour, as a rogue and vagabond.

The China Mail, 6 October 1881[223]
"Local and General"[?],
re students returned from America case[224]
ADDITIONAL 251 📖 p. 325

[Before] Dr Stewart today there began a [case] which promises to develop some [interesting] features. Two Chinamen, said to [be stud]ents returned from America, dressed [in Europ]ean style, were placed in the dock, [] by one Wong Yuen Woi Chuen, [] in Yokohama, and who it is said is [the employer] of the first prisoner, with stealing [a travell]ing box, containing over $2,000 [] of bank drafts; Chinese documents; [] blankets and a watch and clock.

---

[221] The following is the complete set of reports in connection with this case in *The Complete Court Cases*: CC Nos 224, 242, 250. See also note to CC No. 224, above.

[222] The following versions of this name appear in this series of reports: "Cannron", "Cameron", "Cannon".

[223] "Local and General"[?], CM, Thursday, 6 October 1881, p. 3, c. 1.

[224] The following is the complete set of reports in connection with this case in *The Complete Court Cases*: CC Nos 251, 255a.

See also Gillian Bickley, ed., "Chinese Students Returned from America", in, "Some Nineteenth Century Hong Kong Court Cases", 2009/2010, for a documented transcript of the complete original sources on this case from *The China Mail*.

[Hors]pool gave evidence as to receiving [] from H.M. Consul at Nagasaki []g the prisoners as mentioned above, []nd under Mr Horspool's directions Inspector Perry arrested the prisoners. The [Govern]ment had been communicated with, [] was asked for. The first prisoner who could talk English fluently with a[n] American accent, said he had no ques[tions] until the arrival of the plaintiff, [but he] would ask whether they would be [let] out on bail or not. Dr Stewart [said it] was a very serious charge, and until [he hea]rd from the Government he could [not ta]ke the responsibility upon himself. []nt prisoner said it was a charge [] proof, and thought if the law were []ly enforced that bail would be allowed. "We," he said, "are placed in [your h]ands." His Worship assured them [if he c]ould grant them bail he would, but [that in] the circumstances he did not con[sider] himself justified in doing so. As far [as he] was concerned he would endeavour [to see] the case pushed through as soon as [possible]. The case was remanded until [tomor]row, and if any communication was [receiv]ed from the Government, the application for bail would be decided on.

THURSDAY 6 OCTOBER 1881[225]
[LEAVING HIS EMPLOYER'S SERVICE WITHOUT NOTICE]
CC Number 252

Li Akiu was charged by Emil von Otto with leaving his employment without notice and was convicted, and fined $10 or seven days' imprisonment.

THEFT CC Number 253

Ng Achan was charged by Wong Tai Ngan with stealing a jacket and a pair of trousers. It appeared from the evidence that the clothes had been steeping in a tub amongst water, and that defendant had taken them from that place. Defendant had been formerly

---

[225] "Police Intelligence," CM, Thursday, 6 October 1881, p. 3, c. 5.

employed to take away kitchen refuse, but since this occurred had never returned. Complainant reported the matter to the Station. He had not seen his jacket or trousers since.

Another witness spoke to the defendant taking away the jacket. Defendant had been previously convicted, and was sentenced to three months' imprisonment with hard labour.

FRIDAY 7 OCTOBER 1881[226]
ROGUE AND VAGABOND
CC Number 254

Chan Ahing was accused by Police Constable No. 579 with being a rogue and vagabond. It appeared from the evidence that the defendant had been trying to do the ring trick. Lang A-Au saw him at this with the ring in his hands, and accused him of picking pockets, when he ran away. Complainant pursued, and caught him, and gave him into custody.

Prisoner was sent to gaol for three months with hard labour.

THE NAVAL YARD EMBEZZLEMENT CASE[227]
CC Number 255 📖 p. 226

Cornelius Conner, charged with embezzling money belonging to the Naval Yard Canteen, was today committed for trial at the Criminal Sessions.[228]

---

[226] "Police Intelligence," CM, Friday, 7 October 1881, p. 3, c. 4.
[227] The following is the complete set of reports in connection with this case in *The Complete Court Cases*: CC Nos 255, 292, 293.
[228] CC No. 255 was re-opened (CC 292) and, because of a technicality, was not sent up to the Criminal Sssions. See CC 293 below.

***The China Mail*,**
Friday 7 October 1881[229]
[Students returned from America][230]
ADDITIONAL **255a**

The case, in which two Chinamen were arrested on board the *City of Peking*, came again before Dr Stewart today. Mr Horspool (recalled) said he had no further evidence to produce. His Worship said he had been considering the case, and his opinion had been confirmed that he had no jurisdiction in the matter. The defendants were then discharged.

SATURDAY 8 OCTOBER 1881[231]
GAMBLING
CC Number 256

Mah Achiu, a servant, for gambling with dice in Peel Street, with some other men, was fined $1, with the alternative of seven days' imprisonment.

[GAMBLING]
CC Number 257

Li Amah, for gambling with cards, with some other men, in the public street, this morning, was sentenced to fourteen days' imprisonment, as a rogue and vagabond.

---

[229] CM, Friday, 7 October 1881, p. 2, c. 7.
[230] The following is the complete set of reports in connection with this case in *The Complete Court Cases*: CC Nos 251, 255a.

See also Gillian Bickley, ed., "Chinese Students Returned from America", in, "Some Nineteenth Century Hong Kong Court Cases", 2009/2010, for a documented transcript from several original sources, related to this case and related topics.
[231] "Police Intelligence," CM, Saturday, 8 October 1881, p. 3, c. 4.

THE 'RICKSHAW QUESTION[232]
CC Number 258

Herman Hunter, a steward from San Francisco, was charged with refusing to pay hire to and with assaulting a 'rickshaw coolie. The case was one of the ordinary cases of an European from on board ship engaging a 'rickshaw when he was more or less under the influence of liquor, and when called upon to pay for it, not only refusing to give the coolie his cents, but assaulting him as well. The prisoner was fined fifty cents, and was further ordered to pay 25 cents to the coolie.

THE MOON FEAST
CC Number 259

Pong Atin was fined $1 for firing crackers on the street in celebration of the moon pidgin of last night.

ROGUE AND VAGABOND
CC Number 260

Lo Ayau, described as a coolie, was sentenced, as a rogue and vagabond, to three months' imprisonment with hard labour, having been previously convicted more than once. He had been apprehended this time selling lottery tickets to a crowd of people in Lascar Row.

CONTRAVENTIONS OF MARKET ORDINANCE
CC Number 261

Several men were fined in nominal sums for breaches of the Market Ordinance, one for selling worms.

CURIOUS CASE
CC Number 262

Tsan Afan went up to the Central Police Station, early this morning, in a most excited state, and could

---

[232] See Gillian Bickley, ed., "Rickshaws: A 19th Century Traffic Problem", in, "Some Nineteenth Century Hong Kong Court Cases", 2009/2010, for a documented transcript of original sources about problems caused by the introduction of rickshaws.

not contain himself long enough to tell what he had to complain of. He did not seem to know what he wanted. When the constables wanted to put him out he hung on to a lamp-post and would not be put out. He continued jabbering away at an enormous rate when given in charge for creating a disturbance. He was fined $2, with the alternative of seven days' imprisonment.

A NIGHT ON SHORE
CC Number 263
William Kennedy, engineer, S.S. Lorne, for being drunk and incapable was fined 50 cents and was ordered to pay 25 cents to the chair coolies who had carried him about.

BREACH OF THE OPIUM ORDINANCE
CC Number 264
Li Ayan, cook, for being in unlawful possession of two taels of opium, was fined $20, with the alternative of fourteen days' in gaol.

ASSAULT
CC Number 265
Li Tun Lan and Wong Aloi, for assaulting another Chinaman, hitting his head so that he had to be sent to the hospital to have it dressed, were each fined $1 and were further ordered to be exposed in the stocks for six hours. The fight arose through a difference as to whose turn it was first at a public hydrant; and at the same hydrant the unfortunates will be duly exposed in the stocks to warn the other coolies who have traffic there.

MONDAY 10 OCTOBER 1881[233]
THEFT
CC Number 266

Ho Akwong, chair coolie, was convicted on the evidence of his employer, Charles F. Degenaer, of stealing a piece of brass, complainant's property. Prisoner was convicted, and sentenced to seven days' imprisonment with hard labour.

NO PASS OR LIGHT
CC Number 267

Three Chinamen who were seen, about a quarter past ten p.m. on the 9th *instant*, on the street without pass or light were to-day convicted and fined $2 each or six days' imprisonment with hard labour.

INCAPABLE
CC Number 268

John Murray of the steamer Anjer Head[234] was sentenced to pay a fine of 25 cents, or one day's imprisonment.

[INCAPABLE]
CC Number 269

James Made [*sic*] was convicted of a similar offence, and refusing to pay 'rickshaw, and was fined $2 or ten days' imprisonment, and ordered to pay 20 cents to coolies or one day's imprisonment.

[INCAPABLE]
CC Number 270

Alfred Henderson was convicted of being drunk and fined $1 or four days in gaol.

---

[233] "Police Intelligence," CM, Monday, 10 October 1881, p. 3, c. 3.
[234] CM, 7 October 1881, p. 3., c. 2, states: "The "Anjer Head", Captain A. Roper, from Singapore and Saigon, September 30, reports: —Experienced heavy weather and high cross-seas, from the 2nd to the 5th of October; wind veering round during the gale from north-west, round by the southward, to the south-east and then moderating. Bar. 29.60."

THEFT
CC Number 271

Lui Tung, a carpenter, Hollywood Road, said on the 9th *instant*, he washed his trousers and hung them out to dry. Complainant heard a cry of "thief" raised. Complainant ran out, and defendant was caught by a Police Constable. Defendant admitted the charge, and got fourteen days' imprisonment with hard labour.

ROW IN A BOARDING HOUSE
CC Number 272

Frederick Fredreson charged John Sutherland with assaulting him in Petersen's Boarding House. From the evidence it appeared the affair had been a sort of a general row, but it tended to show the defendant had been to blame, and he was fined $1 or four days' imprisonment.

TUESDAY 11 OCTOBER 1881[235]
ASSAULT
CC Number 273

Luck Atsin, remanded from the 8th *instant*, charged with assaulting Kwong Akwai, was today sent to prison for seven days with hard labour. Complainant said he accidentally knocked against defendant, who struck him on the head with an iron bar. Defendant said complainant first tried to assault him. Defendant then took the bar from him and struck him.

WEDNESDAY 12 OCTOBER 1881[236]
THEFT CC Number 274

Wung Alun admitted stealing a jacket from a dwelling house on the night of the 11th *instant*. From the evidence it appeared that defendant had gone fishing for the jacket, which was hung from a window to dry. He had gone on to the roof and let down a line with hook attached, by which he caught

---

[235] "Police Intelligence," CM, Tuesday, 11 October 1881, p. 3, c. 5.
[236] "Police Intelligence," CM, Wednesday, 12 October 1881, p. 3, c. 3.

the jacket. Complainant saw this operation and went to the roof and caught defendant.

Prisoner had been in gaol before, and was again sent there for four months with hard labour.

WITHOUT A LIGHT
CC Number 275

Hu Asai and Chung Aki were charged with being at large without a light on the night of the 11th *instant*.

Police Constable 591 said he found both defendants in Caine Road without a light or pass. He apprehended them.

First defendant said he was merely sitting at the door when he was arrested. He had been in gaol before. Second said he was a chair coolie to the Hon. Mr. Johnson. They were fined $2 each or seven days' imprisonment.

DISORDERLY CONDUCT
CC Number 276 📖 p. 278

Nine inmates of a brothel were convicted of making a noise on the street, and were sentenced —the mistress of the brothel, who formed one of the party, to be fined $5 or seven days' imprisonment; and the other defendants 50 cents or two days' imprisonment each.

ROGUE AND VAGABOND
CC Number 277

Tsang Afuk, remanded from the 10th to allow the gaol authorities to produce previous convictions, was today convicted on the evidence of Thomas Grozart, Police Constable 24, of sleeping in a cave on the hillside. He was sent to prison for three months with hard labour, this making his sixth conviction.

FALSE EVIDENCE
CC Number 278 📖 p. 279

Shu Ahi, a fireman, was charged by Ho Ayau, a Chinese female, with snatching her earrings, but after evidence had been heard, it turned out that complainant kept a brothel, where defendant had been. She was put in the box and fined $25 or two months in gaol. Shu Ahi was discharged.

THROWING RUBBISH INTO THE HARBOUR
CC Number 279

Lam Afat was convicted of throwing rubbish into the harbour, and was fined $10 or seven days in gaol. The defence was that as the wind and tide were against him he threw some rubbish overboard.

COMMITTAL CC Number 280

Chan Afuk, remanded from the 10th charged with detaining a girl named Chan Quai Lang, was today committed for trial at the Sessions.

THURSDAY 13 OCTOBER 1881[237]
CUTTING EARTH WITHOUT A LICENSE
CC Number 281 📖 p. 350

Tong Achi was charged by H. Gustave with cutting earth without a license.

Complainant said that he was a scholar at St. Joseph's College.[238] On the 11th *instant* defendant and several others began to cut earth close to his house. Some of the earth fell and struck some of the diggers. They came next day, when complainant gave them in charge. The foundation of the garden wall was left bare.

William Watts, an overseer in the Survey Department, said he inspected the cuttings which were to the extent of fifteen feet by twenty feet. The retaining wall of Inland Lot 420[239] was undermined and caused damage to the extent of twenty dollars.

---

[237] "Police Intelligence," CM, Thursday, 13 October 1881, p. 3, cc. 3 - 4.

[238] It was common at this time for adults to attend school. Many at the Government Central School were married, and some had sons at school at the same time as they themselves attended it.

[239] To register ownership, Hong Kong Island was separated into Lots, including Inland Lots and Marine Lots. The "Plan of the City of Victoria", reproduced in A Magistrate's Court, pp. 424-427, includes the relevant lot numbers. The Lots are also referred

Fined five dollars or fourteen days' imprisonment with hard labour and six hours in the stocks at the place.[240]

THURSDAY 13 OCTOBER 1881[241]
OBSTRUCTION CC Number 282

Tong Akwong, for leaving a number of oil buckets on the Praya in front of his shop, was fined $5 or seven days' imprisonment.

[OBSTRUCTION]
CC Number 283

For a similar offence Lai Tsun Ning was fined $3 or three days' imprisonment.

[OBSTRUCTION]
CC Number 284

Chan Nam, similarly charged, was fined $1 or two days in gaol.

FALSE MEASURE
CC Number 285 📖 p. 351

Lul Singh, Police Constable 530, said that on the 8th *instant* he went to Li Kwo Ching shop, 11 Jervois Street, and bought four yards of flannel. When he went to a tailor's he was told that the cloth did not measure four yards.

Inspector Orley said he was examiner of weights, and measures. The cloth was four yards and two inches over. The measure was half an inch short. Some of the inch marks were too short, and some too long.

---

to in other documentation relating to property, such as sale and purchase, rent and rates.
[240] It was a common practice at the time for a person to serve time in the stocks at the same place as he committed the offence. These movable stocks may have been the "cangue", a wooden collar, rather than the wooden contraption in which the two legs are locked.
[241] "Police Intelligence," CM, Thursday, 13 October 1881, p. 3, cc. 3 - 4.

Defendant said he had applied for a new measure on the 6th. He had heard of the translation of the order,[242] but had been absent.

Prisoner was fined $1 or two days' imprisonment for having an insufficient yard measure. A moiety of the fine, if paid, to go [to] the examiner.

ASSAULT AND ROBBERY
CC Number 286 📖 p. 351

Yep Ahing was charged, with two others not in custody, by Chiu Ayuk, with assaulting and robbing him of some money.

Complainant said he was a cook unemployed. He came here ten days ago, and had been stopping at Wanchai. On the 12th instant on his way to the theatre, and when near the guard house opposite Ha Wan Market, he met defendant and five others. Two of the defendants seized complainant by the arms, and defendant put his hand into complainant's pocket, and took out a parcel containing money. Defendant struck him on the back of the hand with a stick. Complainant called out "robbery," and when a police constable came the men ran. Defendant went into a house and locked the door. Defendant was arrested. Complainant was walking with another man Li Atsai, but was in some doubt as to the whereabouts of this personage, when the assault and robbery was committed.

Li Atsai corroborated. Police Constable 133 gave evidence as to the arrest of the defendant.

Another Chinese Constable deposed as to seeing a number of men fighting, who ran when he approached. He chased but missed them. When he went to the original place of the fight he still saw

---

[242] See CC No. 206. Stewart's previous comments had very recently led to the order being translated. See also Gillian Bickley, "Weights and Measures" in, ed., "Some Nineteenth Century Hong Kong Court Cases", 2009/2010, for a documented transcript of relevant material from *The China Mail*.

some men fighting; they also ran; heard no word of robbery.

The rest of the evidence, which extended to great length went to show that the whole affair had originated in a gambling quarrel and a fight had taken place in which complainant had got a smack across the fingers. The complainant and Li Atsai had added the robbery to the story.

Defendant fined $1, or four days' hard labour, for assault; complainant fined $25, or two months' hard labour, for preferring a malicious charge; and Li Atsai fined $5, or twenty one days' imprisonment with hard labour, for giving false testimony.

FRIDAY 14 OCTOBER 1881[243]
SUSPICIOUS CHARACTER
CC Number 287 📖 p. 231

Francis Xavier Sardrean (Brother Cyprian), said he was principal of St. Joseph's College. Defendant was second cook at the College until some time ago. He was then dismissed and ordered never to return to the premises. This morning he found defendant (Ho Apui) in the kitchen with the servants. Witness gave defendant into custody.

Prisoner was ordered to find two sureties in $25 each to be of good behaviour for six weeks, in default to be committed.

THEFT CC Number 288

Ling Amoi was charged with stealing two pieces of wood, the property of Li Kwan Yee.

Police Constable 161 said that on the 13th instant close upon midnight he was on duty in I Wo Street, East Point, when he saw defendant there. When he saw witness he went into a dark lane. Witness followed, and found the wood beside him. The Police Constable took defendant to complainant's shop as it was the only one there.

---

[243] "Police Intelligence," CM, Friday, 14 October 1881, p. 3, c. 6.

Sentenced to fourteen days' imprisonment with hard labour.

THEFT OF AN AWNING
CC Number 289

Chin Aheung was convicted of stealing an awning from a butcher's stall, and was sentenced to fourteen days' imprisonment with hard labour. A Police Constable had seen prisoner go into the stall, and come out with the awning, and as he could give no satisfactory explanation of how he got it, arrested him.

OBTAINING MONEY UNDER FALSE PRETENCES
CC Number 290

Un Ayun was charged as above.

It seemed that Wong Man Shan, fortune teller, had lost an opium pipe, some handkerchiefs, &c., and defendant, who was a water coolie, and had supplied the doctor with water, volunteered to go and find the pipe. He went, and in a short time returned with the information that he had seen it on a marine hawker's stall. The hawker wanted 10 cents for the pipe and the doctor gave this to defendant, who went, and never returned. The deluded fortune teller, who was not cute enough to foretell his own fate, went in search of the missing party and found him in an opium divan.

Prisoner was convicted of stealing the money and was sentenced to fourteen days' in gaol with hard labour.

THE STABBING CASE[244]
CC Number 291📖 p. 176

In this case H. Sewart [*sic*], Police Constable applied for a remand, as complainant could not get out of hospital before the 17th instant. The case was remanded till the 17th accordingly.

THE ALLEGED EMBEZZLEMENT CASE[245]
CC Number 292 📖 p. 226

This case, which was committed for trial at the Criminal Sessions,[246] was to-day reopened.

William Lynsaght said he was Inspector of Naval Police in H.M. Dockyards here. The members of the canteen comprise all the employees in the dockyard, workmen as well as police. The canteen was an association of a purely private character. As far as discipline went, witness was head of the canteen, but in other respects he was simply a member. The refreshments supplied to the canteen were got from the store and paid from the receipts at the end of the month. If any balance was over it was handed over to him for the benefit of the police mess. In return for this the police manage the canteen in turn. The police mess consisted of the unmarried members of the force, who stopped in the Yard. This mess was entirely unconnected with the canteen except in so far as he had already stated. Each policeman managed the canteen for six months at a time, and in addition to his privilege as a member he got the proceeds of the sale of empty hogsheads or barrels. Defendant

---

[244] The following is the complete set of reports in connection with this case in *The Complete Court Cases*: CC Nos 291, 296, 300, 388.

See also Gillian Bickley, ed., "The Stabbing Case" in, "Some Nineteenth Century Hong Kong Court Cases", 2009/2010, for a documented transcript of more complete material on this case, including the Inquest on the victim, the committal of the accused for murder and the Supreme Court trial.

[245] The following is the complete set of reports in connection with this case in *The Complete Court Cases*: CC Nos 255, 292, 293.

[246] See CC No. 255.

was a member of the canteen. Arrangements had been made for paying the bills which defendant ought to have paid. An advance for that purpose had been obtained from witness. The canteen was thus in debt, and the surplus funds will go to clear off this advance. On 2nd instant defendant was absent from duty at noon, at which time he should have gone on. When witness mustered the men at six o'clock, he found defendant still absent. He sent a Sergeant of the Police to look for defendant, but the Sergeant returned in about an hour without him. Latterly a reward was offered by the Commodore. Defendant was captured on the 5th *instant* by the Police. He had been absent from duty for three days and a half.

Remanded till 15th at ten o'clock a.m.

SATURDAY 15 OCTOBER 1881[247]
THE EMBEZZLEMENT CASE[248]
CC Number 293 📖 p. 227

This case, which was reopened yesterday,[249] again came before the Court to-day.

G. Northcote, Police Constable gave evidence as to arresting Conner. The Police Constable was in plain clothes at the time.

His Worship expressed his regret to find a man of his character, having ten years good character in the Artillery and four in the Naval Yard police, in the position in which he was. A legal technicality had arisen which had prevented the Supreme Court from dealing with the charge of embezzlement. Had he been in England he would have been amenable to the law, but such law did not affect this Colony, although he hoped it would soon. Had prisoner returned within 24 hours, the charge of desertion would probably not have been made. Although the charge of

---

[247] "Police Intelligence," CM, Saturday, 15 October 1881, p. 3, c. 5.
[248] The following is the complete set of reports in connection with this case in *The Complete Court Cases*: CC Nos 255, 292, 293.
[249] See CC No. 292.

embezzlement had been withdrawn he could not overlook the fact as an element in determining his punishment for the crime of desertion. He felt compelled to give him the full term of punishment laid down by the Ordinance, namely that he be imprisoned for six months.[250]

LARCENY BY A CONSTABLE[251]
CC Number 294 📖 p. 228
No. 433, Kong Asow, a Constable stationed at Yau-Mah-ti, was charged with the larceny of a quantity of clothing on the 14th instant.

Sultan Malak, Acting Sergeant of Police, said that he was on duty at half-past eleven o'clock last night on the Praya, Yau-ma-ti. He saw some one pass under a verandah, and as it was rather dark he threw the light of his lantern on him, when he saw the prisoner throw down a bundle and run. Constable No. 696, who was also present, pursued and apprehended the prisoner while witness picked up the bundle. On examination it was found to contain a number of jackets and other articles of clothing similar to a quantity which had been washed ashore from a wrecked junk. When arrested the prisoner said he was a lukong and on duty. He was wearing an oilskin coat over his uniform and was walking in an easterly direction, away from the station, when first noticed.

No further evidence was taken, and the further investigation of the case was postponed till Monday morning, the 17th instant.[252]

---

[250] Probably Ordinance No. 9 of 1862. "For the Establishment and Regulation of the Police Force of the Colony". Passed 3 May 1862. HKGG, 3 May 1862, pp. 140-145. Para. 15 allows for this sentence for desertion. (This Ordinance was repealed by Ordinance No. 14 of 1887.)

[251] See also Gillian Bickley, ed., "Storm", in, "Some Nineteenth Century Hong Kong Court Cases", 2009/2010, for a documented transcript of the complete original sources on this case and its background from *The China Mail*.

[252] On 17 October 1881, due to extensive coverage of the typhoon that had recently occurred, *The China Mail* has only a very brief

MONDAY 17 OCTOBER 1881[253]
COMMITTAL
CC Number 295
How Ayune was charged with the larceny of $400 in bank notes and jewellery.

The evidence given by Sergeant Fisher was to the effect that defendant's house was searched and that he found there $20 believed to be part of the plunder of a recent robbery. Certain circumstances excited his suspicion, and he handed the suspected person over to the female searcher who produced $244 which had been concealed about the prisoner's person. The jewellery which it was alleged the woman had stolen was found on the roof of her house.

The case was committed for trial.

The China Mail, 17 October 1881
THE STABBING CASE[254]
CC Number 296 📖 p. 176
The Stabbing Case [Deposition taken by F. Stewart
at the Civil Hospital]
The case in which a seaman named John Parry[255] was charged with stabbing a fellow-[sailo]r of the name of Thomas Finlay, aged [twenty-eight],[256] a native of

---

report from the Magistrates' Courts, and there is nothing about this case on this date, nor on the following day, 18 October.
[253] "Police Intelligence," CM, Monday, 17 October 1881, p. 3, c. 3.
[254] "The Stabbing Case", CM, Monday, 17 October 1881, p. 3, cc. 1 - 2. The following is the complete set of reports in connection with this case in *The Complete Court Cases*: CC Nos 291, 296, 300, 388. See also note to CC No. 291.
[255] This seaman is variably referred to as, "John Parry", "[John] Perry", "Powers" and "Power" in these Reports.
[256] This is the age given in the "Certified Copy of an Entry in a Register of Deaths kept in Terms of the Births and Deaths Registration Ordinance", dated 16 April 1999 [*sic*]. However, other details in this document are incorrect, probably due either to the physical condition of the original and/or difficulty in reading the handwriting of the original. Hence, the name of the District Registrar is given as "John Gerrad" for "John Gerrard".

Arklow, Ireland, on board [the] Canadian barque *Helen Marion*,[257] on the [] last, has now assumed a serious as[pect]. Today (17th), the wounded man's deposition was taken by Dr Stewart at the Government Civil Hospital, where he now [lies]. The Captain and a boy on board gave evidence, as the ship is ready to sail. Finlay is in a very weak state, and it was considered advisable under the circumstances, to take the precaution of securing his deposition: —

Thomas Finlay said he was an able seaman serving on board the Canadian barque *Helen Marion*. About dinner time on [Thur]sday the 13th instant, he went into the forecastle, when Powers [*sic*] (a nickname for the defendant Parry), came in after him [and] took a square-faced bottle of gin from [the] bunk. He held it in his hand for about a quarter of an hour and then broke it over witness's head. A portion of the broken [glass] remained in the prisoner's hand, and [on] witness trying to take it from him, he, [the] prisoner, drew a sheath knife from him [] and stabbed the witness in the right [breast]. There was no one else in the forecastle at the time. When he was stabbed [he] ran? out on deck and saw the Captain [.] Witness then fell and recollected nothing further. On recovering consciousness he found himself under treatment in the hospital. There was no previous row or [quarrel] between the two men. Prisoner was sober at the time and was talking to himself, but witness took no notice of what he said. He believed Power [*sic*] wanted to stow away the bottle, and was waiting till witness left the forecastle. Witness was not sober at the time. After having been struck with the bottle

---

The name of the Coroner is given as ("Tradehouse" for "Wodehouse". The cause of death is given as "Effects of a Normal respired in the chest"! The "Return of Inquests, 1881" lists "Died from the effects of a Wound received in the Chest" as one cause of death (HKGG, 18 March 1882, p. 303) and this seems to refer to this case.

[257] According to *The China Mail*, 22 August 1881 (p. 3, c. 7), the *Helen Marion* left Cardiff on 23 May 1881.

he took it from Power so as to prevent him repeating the blow. (Shows a small wound on the head). No conversation took place between us at the time. The knife produced was the one with which he was stabbed.

To prisoner —I still say that no words passed between us before I was struck with the bottle. I am sure I did not strike you before I was struck with the bottle. You had the knife in your hand when you stabbed me, but you took it from your belt. I did not see you cutting tobacco. You stood for a quarter of an hour with the bottle in your hand waiting for me to leave the forecastle before you stowed it away. You and I have been on friendly terms all the voyage, and have never had any words previous to this.

Captain R. J. Robinson, master of the *Helen Marion*, said that about half past one on the afternoon of the 13th instant he was in the hold. The boy Edward Jeavous came down and informed him that Thomas Finlay was cut. He immediately went on deck, and met Finlay who was wounded and bleeding from the right breast. He had the knife in his hand. Witness took it from him and dressed the wound, and then went to the *Victor Emanuel* for a doctor, who came on board, dressed the wound, and advised that the man be sent to hospital at once. Finlay was sent to hospital, and the case reported to the police authorities.

To the prisoner —You have behaved yourself on board to my satisfaction up to the time of this occurrence. You have been in trouble with others before this happened. You have been drunk on board ship in harbour before this.

To the Court. —Prisoner's general behaviour before coming to this harbour has been satisfactory. Had he not asked me I should not have thought it necessary to refer to his drinking.

Ed. Jeavous, ordinary seaman on board the *Helen Marion*, said that about dinner time on the 13th instant he was in the forecastle. After supplying Finlay with some things he wanted he left the forecastle. At this time Finlay, Power (Parry), and Brislan were in the forecastle. He heard Finlay ask where the bottle was, and say that he wanted to give Power a drop. He also heard Finlay say that he would hit the prisoner with a cane if he did not go away from him. Power then said that he would either go to gaol or to hospital for him. Witness then again entered the forecastle and when in the doorway he heard the crash of a bottle, and two seconds afterwards he saw blood flowing from Finlay's breast, and heard him say that he had been stabbed. Witness then jumped down the after hatch and told the captain.

To the Court: —Finlay looked as if he had been drunk and was just recovering. Power and Finlay had a few words before the bottle was smashed, and it was then I heard Power say that he would go to gaol or hospital for him. By this I understood that he would do something to Finlay, or that Finlay would do something to him. I saw no blow given, but I saw blood running from Finlay's breast. I saw no knife. I have not noticed any particular bad feeling between Finlay and the prisoner more than between any others on board.

To the prisoner: —I could see you when in the forecastle, but I could not see what you were doing. I saw nothing in your hands. Had you been cutting a pipe of tobacco I could have seen you. I did not see you with any bottle, you had nothing in your hands when I was looking at you.

At this point the enquiry was remanded till tomorrow morning at eight o'clock at the Magistracy, for the production of another witness.

TUESDAY 18 OCTOBER 1881[258]
THE TABLES TURNED
CC Number 297 📖 p. 279

Li Ayau, a coolie, was charged with stealing a jacket from one Cheung Yu Ming, this morning.

From the evidence of complainant it appeared that on his return from his ordinary employment yesterday evening he found prisoner and another man, who both occasionally visited him, sitting in an empty room in his house. When witness left home in the morning he placed a jacket he was not using in the cock loft, and on his return in the evening he missed it and accused defendant of having taken it. This was denied, but about five o'clock this morning he saw him come out of an adjoining house with the missing garment in his hand.

A watchman gave corroborative evidence as to prisoner having been seen with the jacket in his hand at an early hour this morning.

In defence, prisoner said complainant owed him half a dollar and gave him the jacket in payment. He also said complainant keeps a sly brothel, and he went to his house on invitation. He took the jacket to another house after it had been given to him, and when leaving there he was arrested. When he received the jacket complainant asked him to assist in removing some of his things as he was going to a fortune teller's house in Queen's Road. After carrying a few things he struck work and declined to carry any more.

Prisoner was then discharged, and complainant placed in the dock instead.

On being charged with preferring a malicious charge against the last defendant, he said that when he saw him with his jacket he thought it would be returned to him, and consequently did not give an alarm of thief. He also admitted having allowed him to sleep in his house.

---

[258] "Police Intelligence," CM, Tuesday, 18 October 1881, p. 3, cc. 4 - 5.

Fined $25, in default three months' imprisonment with hard labour.

TUESDAY 18 OCTOBER 1881[259]
A PREDILECTION FOR EDGED TOOLS
CC Number 298

Chan Afuk a fisherman, was charged with stealing a chopper and two brass ladles on the 17th instant.

Complainant, a street coolie, residing in a lane near the Recreation Ground, said he went to his work as usual yesterday morning, and on his return at one o'clock in the afternoon, he found the prisoner in his room, and as he was an entire stranger, he asked him what he did there, and immediately afterwards searched him, when he found his chopper and the two ladles concealed on his person.

Prisoner said in defence that he went into complainant's house under the impression that it was an opium divan. On leaving the place he was arrested and charged with stealing the things, and he now asserted that complainant brought them from the kitchen. He admitted having been three times in gaol on charges of larceny, two of which were for stealing choppers.

Sentence —Six months' imprisonment with hard labour, the first and last fortnight in solitary confinement; and to be exposed in the stocks at the scene of the offence for six hours.

TUESDAY 18 OCTOBER 1881[260]
THEFT FROM GOVERNMENT HOUSE
CC Number 299

Chu Achong, a bricklayer, was charged with stealing a water- bucket and a maul[261] from the verandah of Government House this morning.

---

[259] "Police Intelligence," CM, Tuesday, 18 October 1881, p. 3, cc. 4 - 5.
[260] "Police Intelligence," CM, Tuesday, 18 October 1881, p. 3, cc. 4 - 5.
[261] "Maul": A club or hammer. (*Oxford English Dictionary*)

A gardener, employed at the official residence, said that as he was returning from the market at half-past six o'clock this morning, he met the prisoner with the bucket and maul in his hand, and as he recognised the bucket as Government property, he gave prisoner into custody.

His defence was that he had only borrowed them for a little while.

Defendant admitted having taken the things, but said he was only going to use them for a little while at some work he had to do at the Slaughter House.

Sentence, twenty-one days' imprisonment with hard labour.

The China Mail, 18 October 1881[262]
THE STABBING CASE
Resumed Investigation at the Magistracy "before Dr Stewart"
CC Number 300 📖 p. 179
[No. 300]

This morning the investigation into the circumstances attending the stabbing of [sea?] man Thomas Finlay, by another sailor named John Perry [*sic*] (nicknamed Power) [abo]ard the *Helen Marion*, was resumed at the Police Magistracy before Dr Stewart.

Philip Breslin said he was an able seaman on board the *Helen Marion*. He remembered Thursday, the 13th *instant* About one o'clock witness was sitting outside the forecastle door; Thomas Finlay called him in [to the] forecastle, and asked witness if he knew anything about a bottle of grog. Witness [said] the bottle had been finished. Power had taken the last of it. When he said [this] defendant was present. A quarrel at once began between Power and Finlay concerning the bottle of whisky. Some very [bad] language passed between the two.

---

[262] "The Stabbing Case", CM, 18 October 1881, p. 3, cc. 1 - 2. The following is the complete set of reports in connection with this case in *The Complete Court Cases*: CC Nos 291, 296, 300, 388. See note to CC No. 291.

His Worship asked witness to tell him as nearly the exact words as possible as provocation might be an important element in the case.

Witness repeated some of the expressions [used.] Finlay gave Power a sort of shove [and] Power then said he would either go to gaol for him or make an hospital case of [him]. At this time Power deliberately put [his] hand on his sheath knife. After this [they] both sat down, but continued using [dirty?] expressions. Finlay had been drunk [up] to eleven o'clock, but the mate had [ob]jected to his moving about the deck, and [ordered] him to go in and rest himself. This he [did], and by the time of the affair witness would say he was sober or at least capable of doing his work. Power was sober. Witness had seen Power about eleven o'clock drink two glasses. After sitting some [time] still quarrelling, Finlay rose and [stepp]ed towards Power, and this time struck him; Power took up a large square- [sided] bottle and broke it on Finlay's skull. They continued pushing and struggling and witness heard Finlay say Power is [hold]ing a knife. Witness at once looked and saw the knife clenched in Powers's right hand and Finlay hanging on to his wrist. Finlay had been stabbed by this time. After Power struck with the bottle, witness was frightened, and did not look until he heard the man say he had been stabbed. [] was sitting on a chest between the [] about eight or ten feet separated the []. Witness did not see the knife used. Witness on hearing him cry out ran to his assistance and helped him to clutch the knife. Finlay showing his wound exclaimed, "Oh Lord bless us all; look at me! This blow he has used me." On seeing the wound witness let go the knife, and ran out of the forecastle. Finlay came out after him with the knife in one hand, and, holding the other on the wound. He went towards the [main] hatch with the knife in his hand.

Defendant said he had no questions to ask. He did not believe the witness had [exaggerated]. He had spoken no doubt according to his lights. He was sure he would not tell a lie.

His Worship said the witness had given his evidence in a most honest and straightforward manner. It was the most clear and straightforward evidence he had heard for a long time.

John Kavanagh, able seaman on board the *Helen Marion*, said he was sitting outside the forecastle door. He heard Finlay asking for Power. In two or three minutes Power went in; witness heard Finlay ask him where the bottle was. Witness did not hear the answer; Finlay said if he had the bottle he would not give Power a nip out of it. They had then some bad language, to which witness did not pay much attention. Finlay said if Power did not get out of his sight he would hit him with a tin he had in his hand. Power said if he hit him with the salt tin he would make a hospital case of him. Some short time afterwards he heard something else, a crash of glass. And then he heard Finlay sing out "He has struck me." Finlay then came out with the knife in his hand, bleeding from the breast.

Defendant did not wish to ask any questions.[263]

THURSDAY 20 OCTOBER 1881[264]
AN OLD OFFENDER
CC Number 301 📖 p. 352

Kwok Chut Sing was found by Police Constable 273 in Queen's Road this morning without a light or pass. Prisoner asked the Constable to take him to the station as he had no place to sleep. He had been six times previously convicted.

Sentence $50 or three months' imprisonment with hard labour.

---

[263] This reads abruptly; but *The China Mail* report really does end here.
[264] "Police Intelligence," CM, Thursday, 20 October 1881, p. 3, cc. 5 - 6.

A PECULIAR CASE
CC Number 302

Charles Swonson, a Swede, and Tse Aki were placed in the dock —the first being charged with being drunk and incapable, and the second with attempting to rob the tipsy individual. Swonson was seen by a Constable in Queen's Road in a very inebrious state, and the second defendant was busily engaged in searching his pockets. The Chinaman said the Swede had engaged his rickshaw and had not paid him, so he proceeded to search his pockets for a dollar to get it changed and pay himself. When the drunk man was arrested a Constable told the coolie to go to the station too, which he did. The first defendant was fined 25 cents or one day's imprisonment. He was then put into the box and sworn. He was an able seaman on board the German barque Adela; had come ashore on the 19th, and gone to Peter Smith's, where he got two dollars. He had some drinks, but had not engaged a rickshaw. The second defendant was discharged.

INSANE
CC Number 303

A case which has been before the Court since the 23rd of August, owing to the accused being in the asylum, was finished to-day. Accused had threatened the life of his wife in a fit of insanity and was placed in the asylum. Dr Ayres to-day said he could now be released, as he was perfectly harmless, but would require to have friends to look after him. The wife said she would take care of him, and the case was dismissed.

ROGUE AND VAGABOND
CC Number 304

Luk Ahing was convicted on the evidence of Police Constable 190 of having gambled in Upper Lascar Row, on the 19th *instant*, and was sentenced to twenty-one days' imprisonment with hard labour.

NUISANCE
CC Number 305 📖 p. 231

Leung Ahong was accused of leaving a number of stinking rice bags on the hillside, near High Street.

Inspector Cleaver said he had received a letter from Mr Percy [sic for "Piercy"] of the Diocesan Home complaining of the stench. Witness visited the spot and found a number of bags containing damaged rice, which had been laid there to dry. He reported the matter to Dr Ayres, who told him to take out a summons. The bags were on a vacant piece of Crown land.

Prisoner was fined $10, or seven days in gaol.

STRAGGLER CC Number 306

James Perkins, a straggler from H.M.S. *Magpie*, was ordered to be taken on board his ship.

BREACH OF THE OPIUM ORDINANCE
CC Number 307

U-Afu, 60 years of age, a pig dealer, was charged for being in possession of a quantity of opium, on the 19th instant, without a certificate from the Opium Farmer.

Police Constable No. 36, J. Johnston, said that by virtue of a warrant which he held he entered the prisoner's house in the village of Sai Wan at six o'clock yesterday evening, and on entering the premises he found a box containing one tael of prepared opium, as also two opium boxes containing traces of the drug, a brass boiler, and an opium strainer.

Wong Shing, master of a small huckster's shop in Queen's Road West, said that on the afternoon of the 17th instant he went to defendant's house in Sai Wan and there purchased six cents' worth of opium. Defendant sold the opium to witness, and he then laid an information with the police.

Antonio dos Santos, an excise officer, proved having accompanied the first witness to the prisoner's house and also the seizure of the opium found on the premises; also that the defendant was not in possession of a permit.

Prisoner denied having sold any opium, and said that what was found in his house was for his own use.

Fined $100, in default two months' imprisonment. The opium seized was also ordered to be given to the Opium Farmer.

A ROGUE AND VAGABOND
CC Number 308

Chun Afuk, a seaman, was charged with being a rogue and vagabond.

Police Sergeant 199, Pang Aloi, said he saw defendant and another man not in custody, in the Bonham Road this morning. They were looking at two rings but when they saw the constable approach they walked away rapidly. As witness knew prisoner to be a vagabond; he took him in custody, when defendant offered him $1 for his release.

Leung Tau, shroff at the Magistracy, said he had examined the rings which he found to be of brass with a little gilding over them.

In defence, the prisoner said that he came from Sham Shui Po this morning, where he keeps a gambling house. He gambled with people on the passage-boat, and the complainant wanted money from him, but as he had none to give him he was arrested. A man whom he met in the street showed him the rings.

His Worship sent him to gaol for three months' imprisonment with hard labour as a rogue and vagabond, and ordered the dollar he had offered to the constable to be paid in to the poor box.

BREACH OF THE DANGEROUS GOODS ORDINANCE
CC Number 309

The master of the Chai Ki Chan shop, Number 48, Queen's Road West, appeared on a summons at the instance of Inspector Orley, charged with unlawfully keeping a quantity of kerosine oil on his premises in breach of Section XI, of Ordinance No. 8 of 1873.[265]

---

[265] CC 309 identifies "The Dangerous Goods Ordinance", as, "Section XI, of Ordinance No. 8 of 1873". Related Ordinances are Ordinance No. 1 of 1848 and No. 4 of 1867, as the final paragraph of Ordinance No. 8 of 1873 states, "Nothing in this Ordinance contained shall be deemed to affect the provisions of Ordinances No 1 of 1848 and No. 4 of 1867."

Paragraphs 5 and 6 of Ordinance No. 8 of 1873 give a definition of "Dangerous Goods". "The goods commonly known as Petroleum, Nitro-glycerine or Glonoine oil, Gun Cotton, Fulminating Mercury, Dynamite, Lithofracteur and Horsley's Patent Blasting Powder shall be deemed to be dangerous goods within the meaning of this Ordinance.

"For the purposes of this Ordinance, the term, "Petroleum" includes Kerosene oil, Rock oil, Rangoon oil, Burmah oil, oil made from petroleum, coal, schist, shale, peat or other bituminous substance, and any products of petroleum, or any of the above mentioned oils."

(Phosphorus was added to the list of dangerous goods by an Order in Council dated 26 March 1877.)

The Ordinance required licences to be procured by those wishing to keep certain quantities of these dangerous goods. Each licence would specify the quantity covered by the license and take account of the mode of carrying and/or safe-keeping of the dangerous goods in question. Licenses cost one dollar each. However, except in the case of nitro glycerine, no licence was required if the dangerous goods were "kept in separate glass, earthenware, or metal vessels or cases each of which contains not more than a pint or pound, and is securely stopped or fastened."

As we see from CC 309, however, much more kerosene was kept in one container than was allowed.

There were additional regulations attached to this Ordinance as far as the storage of kerosene was concerned, sanctioned by the Governor in Council on 11 April 1881 (HKGG, 16 April 1881), over six months earlier than this case (CC 309) occurred. The regulations began as follows: "No premises will be licensed for the storage of kerosene within the City of Victoria, unldess they are built on approved sites."

This case was called in Court on the 13th *instant*, when Mr Orley proved having found in his shop one tin containing 5 gallons, and ten bottles containing 3 piculs each of kerosine oil. Defendant had no license. His Worship on that occasion remanded the case till this morning to enable defendant to procure a license.

On the case being again called to-day defendant said he had not applied for any license. He was now fined $10, in default two days' imprisonment. The oil was also ordered to be forfeited and handed over to the Superintendent of the Fire Brigade for public use; $2 of the fine, if paid, to be given to the informer, and also all his necessary expenses if duly certified.

FRIDAY 21 OCTOBER 1881[266]
A DARING OFFENCE
CC Number 310 📖 p. 280

Li Afuk was charged with damaging a blanket and some other articles belonging to the inmate of a brothel on the 17th *instant*, by throwing sulphuric acid over them.

Mr McCallum, public analyst, said he had examined the contents of the bottle, and found them to be strong sulphuric acid.

Of course, the Chai Ki Chan shop, Number 48, Queen's Road West, was within the City of Victoria, so these new regulations applied.

However, the Magistrate initially took a lenient view. On the occasion of the first hearing of the case, he remanded the case for a week, "to enable defendant to procure a license".

When the defendant said he had not applied for a licence, sentence was given.

The permitted penalty was the forfeit of the goods and containe(s) and a fine not exceeding twenty-five dollars. The sentence given was consistent with the provisions of the Ordinance.

(The text of Ordinance No. 8 of 1873 and related data, as used here, is that found in "The Historical Laws of Hong Kong Online".)

[266] "Police Intelligence," CM, Friday, 21 October 1881, p. 3, c. 4.

Defendant admitted throwing the liquid on the blanket. He said he had been a servant to Sir John Smale for nine years. He was employed in the Soda Water manufactory.

Prisoner was fined $25, and $5 compensation for the damage, in default two months' imprisonment with hard labour.

SATURDAY 22 OCTOBER 1881[267]
ASSAULT
CC Number 311 📖 p. 352

Tsang Ayui, Chu Aping, and Tse Akum were charged with assaulting one Li Asing, a tailor.

Complainant said he was a tailor in Sai-ying-pun. On the 21st instant in the forenoon he was in Caine Road. While passing an opium divan he saw defendants fighting with a fellow tradesman inside. Complainant went in and tried to separate them. Third defendant threw an earthenware pot at complainant and broke two of his front teeth; second defendant threw a pillow and cut his chin; third defendant broke his head with a bamboo. Complainant then thought it was high time to get a constable, and he gave the defendants into custody. He did not know defendants and none of them were concerned in a case recently in which complainant was fined 50 cents.

Chan Cheung said he was a fellow workman of the complainant. The quarrel in the divan arose about a pair of shoes. Complainant came to his rescue and got hurt.

A Police Constable gave evidence as to the arrest of the defendants.

According to the statements of the defendants some one in the divan had accused the second witness of stealing a pair of shoes. He left the divan and returned, accompanied with complainant and nine or ten others. A general fight ensued and the

---

[267] "Police Intelligence," CM, Saturday, 22 October 1881, p. 3, cc. 3 - 4.

things in the house were broken. The third defendant had been in gaol for three months as a rogue and vagabond, and on the 18th of July last entered into a bond to be of good behaviour for eight months.

Chan Ahoi said he was a cook in Tank Lane. On the 21st he saw the three defendants pursue the complainant and second witness into the street. He saw complainant struck with an earthenware pillow.

First defendant was fined $5 or fourteen days' hard labour, and in addition to find security, two householders, in $10 each to keep the peace for two months, in default to be committed; second defendant fined $5 or fourteen days' hard labour, and to find the same security as the first for the same period; third defendant had his bond estreated, in default of payment of $150 to be imprisoned for three months; fourth defendant (Chan Ahoi) was fined $25 or two months' imprisonment for giving false testimony. Complainant and his witness (Chan Acheung) to give personal security in $25 each to keep the peace for 3 months.

THEFT FROM THE PERSON
CC Number 312
Chu Ahing said that on the 21st instant, he was standing at the Sai-ying-poon Market, where there was a crowd of people. Suddenly he felt a hand at his purse, and looking he saw defendant withdrawing his hand from under his jacket. In his hand was a paper packet. Complainant seized defendant (Un Ayau), but he handed the packet to another man, who ran. Complainant took defendant to the station.

Defendant was sentenced to four months in gaol with hard labour.

EXTENSIVE THEFT
CC Number 313
Li Asing and Wong Achin were charged by Captain Miller, of the S.S. Catterthun, with stealing five bags of beche-de-mer on the 17th instant.

Captain Miller said that on delivering the cargo of the vessel he found he was five bags short of beche-de-mer. From the godowns the bags were delivered to the consignees, and again turned out five bags short. Witness spoke to his Indian storekeeper, and from what he said witness went and got some Indian firemen, who had been discharged on the expiration of their term. They would speak as to what they saw.

Four fireman said that on the night of the 16th instant, they saw the two defendants lowering bags over the side of the vessel, but took no very particular notice of it at the time, although thinking it a little strange. They were quite positive defendants were the men.

The case was remanded till the 29th *instant*.

THEFT FROM A WRECK
CC Number 314

Kong Asam, the police constable who stole the cloth at Yau-mah-ti during the gale of Friday, the 14th instant, was again before the Court to-day. Inspector Cameron spoke as to the circumstances of the case. The prisoner had been in the force for upwards of four years, and during that time had borne a most excellent character.

Prisoner was fined $20, (the value of the cloth), and $1 additional as a fine; in default fourteen days imprisonment with hard labour. The depositions were ordered to be sent to the Acting Superintendent of Police for his information.

THEFT
CC Number 315

Complainant (Fung Shing) was a seaman on board a junk. Defendant (Chan Afat) was also on the same junk. On the 22nd complainant went on shore to see a friend, leaving only the defendant on board. When complainant returned at midnight he missed his coverlet. Next morning he saw defendant with his coverlet in the Station. Some corroborative evidence was given, and defendant was sent to gaol for four months.

ROGUE AND VAGABOND
CC Number 316

Chan Ayau was convicted on the evidence of D.W. 15 of being a rogue and vagabond. It seemed that the watchman seeing prisoner with a long bamboo in his hand suspected him of stealing. He followed him, and when in East Street defendant saw him and started to run. Witness pursued and caught him. Defendant had been six times in gaol.

Sentence —Three months in gaol with hard labour as a rogue and vagabond.

WILFULL DAMAGE CC Number 317

Kwok Asum said he was an accountant at Number 28, Queen's Road West. Some coolies came to the shop and made a great noise, calling out "hurry up, hurry up." Defendant, who had been upstairs having tea came down, put out his hand and knocked down the kerosine lamp, very nearly setting the house on fire. Complainant believed that defendant wished to avoid payment.

Prisoner was fined $10, and $1 compensation, or two months' imprisonment with hard labour.

ROGUES AND VAGABONDS
CC Number 318

Inspector Corcoran said that having received information, he went to the back of some coolie houses opposite Number 2 Station. About thirty persons were there playing Po-tse. The two defendants were arrested. The others escaped; the second defendant seemed to be taking the principal part in the game, and he had been in gaol before.

First defendant was sentenced to six weeks' imprisonment with hard labour, as a rogue and vagabond; and second defendant three months' imprisonment with hard labour.

INDECENT ASSAULT
CC Number 319
Four Chinamen who have been several times before the Court, charged with indecently assaulting a Chinese female, were finally disposed of to-day.

First defendant was discharged; the second fined $25 or two months in gaol with hard labour; the third $5 or seven days with hard labour; and the fourth $10 or fourteen days with hard labour.

THEFT
CC Number 320
Ho Aki said he was a foreman of carpenters. He was now working at a house in Tai-ping-shan. He saw defendant coming out of the house with his quilt. Complainant at once seized him.

Sentence —Three months' imprisonment with hard labour.

TUESDAY 25 OCTOBER 1881[268]
CUTTING AND WOUNDING
CC Number 321
The case in which John Perry, seaman of the Canadian barque Helen Marion, was charged with cutting and wounding Thomas Fuidlay [*sic* for "Findlay"], a fellow seaman, on board the same ship on the 13th instant, in the Harbour of Victoria, was again called in Court to-day.

Police Constable Herbert Stewart [*sic*] said he had been to the Civil Hospital this morning, and was informed by Dr. Murray that the wounded man was recovering, but he would not be able to leave the hospital for some ten or twelve days yet.

On this the case was further remanded till the 1st proximo.

---

[268] "Police Intelligence," CM, Tuesday, 25 October 1881, p. 3, c. 3.

UNLAWFUL POSSESSION
CC Number 322

Chun Acheung, a coolie, charged with unlawful possession of a box and contents on the 17th instant, appeared on remand from the 18th, when the hearing was postponed to enable the police to make enquiries respecting the ownership of the property.

Police Constable No. 225, Ip Po, said he had examined the box and found the contents embraced a coverlet, a mosquito curtain, several articles of clothing, four packets of tea, a copy of the Koran, and a varied collection of odds and ends. The hinges of the box had been removed, but he had not noticed this, at the former investigation of the case, as the box was covered with canvas. He valued the box and its contents at $15. He believed the owner had gone to Singapore.

In defence the prisoner said he had been hired to carry the box from the Praya Central to the Recreation Ground. He admitted having no fixed place of abode, and sometimes slept in a friend's house in Tai-ping-shan.

Fined $5, in default two months' imprisonment with hard labour.

WEDNESDAY 26 OCTOBER 1881[269]
A SUSPICIOUS CASE
CC Number 323

Wong Mo, a jinricksha coolie, was charged with stealing a bundle of clothing on the 25th *instant*, valued at $25.

Ng Hung Kam, an elderly man who described himself as a necromancer, said he arrived here yesterday forenoon in a passage-boat from Sham Chun. On landing he engaged the prisoner's 'ricksha to convey him to a friend's house. He did not know the name of the street where his friend lived, but the house was named the Kwong Ying Cheong. He had

---

[269] "Police Intelligence," CM, Wednesday, 26 October 1881, p. 3, c. 2.

six bundles with him containing clothing and other articles, and on arriving at his friend's house he went in and left the bundles in defendant's trap. On leaving the house a few minutes afterwards the 'ricksha was still waiting for him, but his bundles were gone. On asking defendant about them he denied all knowledge of the things.

Defendant said he did not know how the bundles had disappeared. He also admitted a previous conviction of larceny in February last.

Remanded till Wednesday next, the 2nd proximo.

BREACH OF THE OPIUM ORDINANCE
CC Number 324

Chong Aping, a seaman, appeared on a charge of being in possession of a quantity of prepared opium on the 25th *instant*, without a certificate from the Opium Farmer.

Antonio dos Santos, an excise officer, proved arresting the prisoner yesterday afternoon on the arrival of the Canton steamer, and finding about seven taels of opium concealed in his pillow-box.[270]

Defendant admitted the charge, and was fined in the sum of $50, in default of payment six weeks' imprisonment with hard labour. The opium was also ordered to be forfeited to the Opium Farmer.

OBSTRUCTION
CC Number 325

Chan Ahau, of house Number 233, Praya West, appeared on a summons, charged with leaving one hundred bags of rice on a foot path, thereby unlawfully causing an obstruction to a public thoroughfare.

Defendant admitted the charge and was fined in the sum of $5, in default five days' imprisonment.

---

[270] See CC No. 329 for a similar ploy.

LARCENY
CC Number 326

Wan Asing, a coolie, was charged with being in unlawful possession of a number of carpenter's tools.

Defendant was found at an early hour this morning coming out of an unoccupied house in Bonham Strand, with thirty-four articles of carpenter's tools in his possession, and was arrested by a constable.

A contractor identified the tools as his property, and said he left them in the house yesterday evening. The house was under repair and he was at work there.

Defendant denied the charge, but admitted a previous conviction of child stealing, and was now sentenced to six months' imprisonment with hard labour.

ANOTHER OPIUM CASE
CC Number 327

Lung Au, 74 years of age, was charged with being in possession of a quantity of prepared opium on the 25th *instant*, without a valid certificate from the Opium Farmer.

Defendant admitted having boiled opium for his own use, but denied ever having sold any.

An informer however proved having purchased opium on the evening of the 24th instant, for which he paid in cash to the prisoner.

Fined $100, in default six week's imprisonment, and the opium to be forfeited.

[THURSDAY] 28 OCTOBER 1881[271]
BREACH OF ORDINANCE[272]
CC Number 328

Leung Ahi, a water boatman, was charged with being inshore before gunfire this morning without a permit, in contravention of Ordinance 14, of 1845.[273]

---

[271] "Police Intelligence," CM, Friday [*sic* for "Thursday"], 28 October 1881, p. 3, cc. 4 - 5.

[272] The present writer has seen a contemporary newspaper comment saying that all should be called to book for this offence, not just the little people, but the big shipping companies as well.

[273] Ordinance No. 14 of 1845 is entitled, "An Ordinance to repeal Ordinance No. 5 of 1844, entitled, 'An Ordinance for the preservation of good order and cleanliness within the colony of Hong Kong and its dependencies,' and to make other provisions in lieu thereof."

Section 3, division eight of No. 14 of 1845 refers to the period from 9.00p.m. and "gunfire in the morning", in connection with the required distance from low water mark of moored or anchored boats, during this period. It reads in full:

"Every owner, headman, or other person in charge of any boat which shall be found alongside of any public wharf or landing place (unless while taking on board or landing passengers or cargo,) or lying off the same so as to prevent the free access of other boats thereto, and the owner, headman, or other person in charge of any boat which shall be moored or at anchor at a distance of less than one hundred and fifty yards from low water mark, between the hours of 9 o'clock a night and gunfire in the morning: Provided always, that nothing herein contained shall be construed to extend to any boat moored or at anchor alongside of any private wharf with the consent of the owner thereof."

A manuscript note in the margin states that "one hundred and fifty yards" was "altered to 300 by Ordinance No. 9 of 1857, Section 10". Another manuscript note in the margin by Section 3, division eight of Ordinance No. 14 of 1845 reads, "Repealed by No. 8 of 1879".

See also Ordinance No. 10 of 1872, "An Ordinance enacted by the Governor of Hong Kong, with the Advice of the Legislative Council thereof, to prevent certain Nuisances", which was to be, "read as though incorporated with and forming Part of Ordinance No. 14 of 1845" (Section VIII). (HKGG, 7 September 1872, p. 388.) The nuisances concerned are, firstly, those which caused what we might now call "noise pollution", i.e. setting off fire-crackers, dressing stone for building works, street-cries, playing the game "Chai-Mui" at night and secondly, anyone "Carrying on or conducting . . . any noisy, noisome, dangerous, offensive, or noxious Trade or Business", without permission.

Inspector Corcoran proved finding the defendant's boat moored alongside the Praya wall, discharging water. He had no right to have his boat there between nine o'clock last night and gunfire this morning. The noise of the pumps had frequently formed the subject of complaint by the neighbours.

Fined $5, in default seven days' imprisonment.

BREACH OF OPIUM ORDINANCE
CC Number 329

Wong Ang, a carpenter, was charged with being in possession of a quantity of prepared opium on the 27th instant, without holding a certificate from the Opium Farmer.

Defendant was arrested on leaving the Macao steamer yesterday afternoon. On being searched a pillow box[274] which he carried was found to contain a tael of prepared opium.

Defendant said he came from Macao and knew nothing of the laws of this Colony. He smoked over a tael a day and what he had was for his own use.

Fined $25, in default ten days' imprisonment; the opium to be forfeited to the Farmer.

LARCENY CC Number 330

Kwok Afong, a coolie, and Kwan Alum, a bricklayer, were charged, the first, with stealing a pair of trousers on the 27th *instant*, and the second with being concerned in the same.

The first prisoner was caught taking the trousers from a line on which they had been hung to dry, and when perceived both prisoners ran away but were captured before they had gone very far.

First defendant said that complainant and a number of men assaulted him, and as they had no reason for so doing they had trumped up the present

---

[274] This is the second case of opium secreted in a pillow box over a short period of time. See also CC No. 324.

charge against him. He admitted six previous convictions for unlawful possession.

Second defendant denied having anything to do with the theft. He was on the hill side collecting herbs when he was arrested, and was not running at the time.

First prisoner, three months' imprisonment with hard labour; second, six weeks.

A RAID ON GAMBLERS
CC Number 331

A batch of twelve men and one woman, a widow, appeared on a charge of keeping a public gambling house on the ground floor of Number 17, Canton Bazaar, on the 27th instant.

Inspector Corcoran with a posse of police made an entrance into the house in question by virtue of a warrant he held for that purpose. He there found the whole of the prisoners seated round a table gambling with dominoes. At sight of the police they made determined efforts to effect their escape, breaking down partitions and upsetting the furniture in their endeavours to get away.

In defence the prisoners gave the usual excuses on such occasions. Some were looking for friends, others came to the house, while some were simply looking on.

First defendant, who was directing and managing affairs was fined in the sum of $200, in default six months' imprisonment with hard labour; one man who had been fined for a similar offence on a previous occasion was fined $50, in default six months' imprisonment with hard labour; and the others were each fined $25, in default, three months' imprisonment with hard labour.

Ng Ha, a coolie unemployed, who had given information to the police regarding the house being used by gamblers, was ordered to receive $10 from the fines should they be paid.

TRESPASSING ON THE RACE COURSE
CC Number 332

Three cattle owners appeared on summonses, charged with unlawfully permitting their cows to trespass on the Race Course at Wong Nei Chong, on the 26th instant, and were fined $2, $1, and 50 cents respectively, according to the number of delinquent animals they each owned, and the number of days the same had been in pound.

LARCENY FROM THE PERSON
CC Number 333

Tsang Ayan, a hat maker, was charged with stealing $7 in silver from the person of one Lam Li Sin, a shopkeeper, on the 28th instant.

Complainant said he was a shopkeeper in Penang. At nine o'clock this morning he was on the Praya, and while making inquiries about the Ichang wharf he felt some one put his hand in his pocket. On turning round suddenly he saw defendant running away, and on examining his pocket he missed a paper parcel containing the $7.

A watchman employed at the P. & O. Company's godowns who assisted in capturing the runaway gave evidence as to finding the money in the prisoner's hand when he was arrested.

Defendant said he picked up the packet on the road and a number of men chased him. He also admitted three previous convictions.

Six months' imprisonment with hard labour.

FRIDAY 29 OCTOBER 1881[275]
A ROGUE AND VAGABOND
CC Number 334

Yum Achun, a tailor, was charged with being a rogue and vagabond this morning.

Police Constable 651, Jewan Singh, said that about nine o'clock this morning he saw a number of

---

[275] "Police Intelligence," CM, Friday [sic], 29 October 1881, p. 3, cc. 4 - 5.

people gambling in Gap-street. On the constable presenting himself the defendant gave the alarm and a general stampede was the result, the prisoner alone being captured.

Defendant said he had been having his head shaved at the Recreation Ground where two men were playing chess. The constable beat these men and he, defendant, ran away and was arrested.

Twenty one days' imprisonment with hard labour, as a rogue and vagabond.

ASSAULT WITH A LETHAL WEAPON[276]
CC Number 335 📖 p. 280

Wong Acheuk, a tinsmith, was charged, first, with assault; second, with being in possession of a deadly weapon, to wit, two fighting irons, on the 28th *instant*, he not being in possession of a night pass.

Tam Atang, a carpenter, said he was passing along Square Street yesterday evening when the defendant knocked against him, and on being remonstrated with he drew a dagger and stabbed him in the hand. Complainant at once seized hold of him when he passed the weapon to another man. He could identify the man to whom the dagger was handed if he were to see him. On the prisoner being searched two fighting irons were found concealed upon his person. Complainant was alone at the time, but there was a number of other men with the prisoner.

Defendant said that he knocked against complainant accidentally and he at once began to beat him. He pulled out an iron bar and cut complainant's finger.

Remanded till Monday the 31st instant.

---

[276] The following is the complete set of reports in connection with this case in *The Complete Court Cases*: CC Nos 335, 339.

MONDAY 31 OCTOBER 1881[277]
PROVIDING FOR A RAINY DAY
CC Number 336

Ching Aleong, a servant, was charged with stealing an umbrella on the 28th instant.

Tsang Asau, a carpenter, said he missed his umbrella from his house on the evening of the 28th instant. Defendant had been out of employment for some time and had lived for the last three months with witness, and he was in his house when the umbrella was last seen there. Complainant reported his loss next morning, and on a search being made amongst the pawn shops that day the umbrella was found in a pawnbroker's in Queen's Road.

The accountant in the Him Kut shop identified the prisoner as the man who pledged the umbrella on the evening of the 28th.

Defendant denied the charge. He said he had been in the service of Dr. Wharry, and left when his master went to England.

Sentenced to four months' imprisonment with hard labour, under Section XVI, of Ordinance No. 3 of 1860.[278]

---

[277] "Police Intelligence," CM, Monday, 31 October 1881, p. 3, cc. 3 - 4.

[278] Section XVI of Ordinance No. 3 of 1860, "An Ordinance for amending and consolidating the Law respecting Pawnbrokers" (16 April 1860) reads as follows: "Every Person applying to borrow shall, at the Time of his Application in that behalf, give to the Pawnbroker to whom such Application is made true Information to enable him to comply with the Requirements of Sections Eight and Nine; And every Person applying to redeem Goods, or for a Copy of an Entry shall, at the Time of his Application, give to the Person to whom such Application is made a full and true Account of himself, his Name, his Place of Abode, the Name and Place of Abode of the Owner, and of the Circumstances under which his Application is made; And no Person shall pawn, or attempt to pawn, the Goods of any other Person without being duly authorized or employed in that Behalf." (HKGG, 21 April 1860, pp. 106-108, p. 107.)

MONDAY 31 OCTOBER 1881[279]
EMBEZZLEMENT
CC Number 337

Yum Atsun, a carpenter, appeared on remand, from the 24th, charged with embezzling the sum of $15, on the 14th *instant*.

It appeared that defendant's master had a contract with a shop in Wellington Street for the painting of a number of jinrickshas, and that he had collected the money for the work and appropriated it to his own use.

Sentence, four month's imprisonment with hard labour, the first and last fortnight to be spent in solitary confinement.

LARCENY FROM A DWELLING HOUSE
CC Number 338

Chan Alok, a boatman, was charged with stealing a box, containing a quantity of clothing from a shop in Yau-ma Ti, on the 27th instant.

So Cheung, the master of a salt fish store at Yau-ma Ti, said on the evening of the day in question he was outside his shop watching the boats arriving when he observed the prisoner walking off with his box, which had previously been on a shelf in the shop.

Defendant said he had salted fish for complainant for five months and when he called for his wages on the evening of the 27th he was beaten not only by his master but by a number of other shopkeepers. He also said he had a blanket and a pair of shoes in the shop.

Inquiries having been made since the first hearing of the case, it appeared that defendant was totally unknown to any one in Yau- ma Ti, and he was unable to identify either blanket or shoes as his property, nor could he name any friend in the village.

---

[279] "Police Intelligence," CM, Monday, 31 October 1881, p. 3, cc. 3 - 4.

Sentence, —Four months' imprisonment with hard labour, the first and last fortnight to be in solitary confinement.

MONDAY 31 OCTOBER 1881[280]
ASSAULT[281]
CC Number 339 📖 p. 281

The case in which Wong Acheuk, a tinsmith, was charged on Saturday last with assault, and with being in possession of deadly weapons without a light or pass, was again called to-day, when Sergeant Ip Nam said that he had since ascertained that this disturbance and assault on complainant arose out of a brothel row. The prisoner, he said, was once employed in a tinsmith's shop in Square Street, but was now a brothel bully and frequently mixed up with brothel rows.

Sentence twelve months' imprisonment with hard labour.

---

[280] "Police Intelligence," CM, Monday, 31 October 1881, p. 3, cc. 3 - 4.
[281] The following is the complete set of reports in connection with this case in *The Complete Court Cases*: CC Nos 335, 339.

BEFORE FREDERICK STEWART, ESQ.

THURSDAY 3 NOVEMBER 1881[283]
ASSAULTING A CONSTABLE
CC Number 340

Ho Asze, a carpenter, and two other men were charged with creating a disturbance at midnight last night, and also with assaulting a police constable in the execution of his duty.

From the evidence of Police Constable No. 139, U Atsai, it appeared that he heard a great noise in Lyndhurst Terrace last night, and on going to the place whence the noise proceeded he found the three defendants were the cause of the disturbance. He cautioned less noise but without avail, and he was compelled to seek assistance by blowing his whistle, when a European and an Indian constable came to his help. The first defendant assaulted the constable and tore his coat. He was very violent on his way to the station, but the others came of their own accord.

First defendant fined $5, in default seven days' imprisonment with hard labour, the others were discharged.

---

[282] **Note on all Court Case Reports for November 1882.** The Magistrates' courts were in session on Wednesday, 2 November 1881. ("Police Intelligence," CM, Wednesday, 2 November 1881, p. 3, cc. 5 - 6.) But no cases "Before Frederick Stewart, Esq." are reported. There is also no report of cases heard "Before Frederick Stewart, Esq.," in the CM for Tuesday, 1 and Tuesday 22 November, Thursday, 24 November 1881; or Wednesday, 30 November 1881.

[283] "Police Intelligence," CM, Thursday, 3 November 1881, p. 3, c. 4.

FOUND IN A HOUSE FOR A SUPPOSED UNLAWFUL PURPOSE[284]
CC Number 341

Chun Ayau,[285] a seaman, was charged with being found in a house in Wing Hing Street on the 2nd instant, for a supposed unlawful purpose.

From the evidence adduced it appeared that between eleven and twelve o'clock yesterday forenoon, defendant was found coming out of the cock-loft of the house in question, with the following articles in his possession — seven silver hair pins, a glass hair press, two Japanese ten-cent pieces, four cents, a $1 note and two cash. The house was occupied by an elderly woman and her daughter-in-law. The latter lives in this cock-loft, and she identified the things enumerated as her property. Neither of the women knew defendant, nor did they know how he came to be in the house.

Remanded till to-morrow.

FRIDAY 4 NOVEMBER 1881[286]
COMMITTED FOR TRIAL[287]
CC Number 342

Chun Ayan, a seaman, charged with being found in a dwellinghouse on the 2nd instant for a supposed unlawful purpose, again appeared before the Court to-day the case having been remanded from yesterday.

Mr E.L. da Rocha, receiving officer in the gaol, proved five previous convictions against defendant, by which it appeared that he was awarded three months' imprisonment in 1876 for larceny from a dwelling house; a second time in the same year for a similar offence he was awarded three months'

---

[284] The following is the complete set of reports in connection with this case in *The Complete Court Cases*: CC Nos 341, 342.

[285] In these reports, "Chun Ayau" is also named, "Chun Ayan".

[286] "Police Intelligence," CM, Friday, 4 November 1881, p. 3, c. 3.

[287] The following is the complete set of reports in connection with this case in *The Complete Court Cases*: CC Nos 341, 342.

incarceration with the addition of exposure in the stocks and two applications of the rod on the breech. In 1877 he was ordered to find security in $25 for three months for aiding and abetting a larceny, and three months afterwards he was sentenced to three years' penal servitude for larceny from the person of $1,063; and in April of the present year he was again convicted of larceny and sentenced to six months' imprisonment.

Defendant, having been duly cautioned, made a statement to the effect that the complainant and her witnesses had conspired against him and preferred a false charge. They know he had been in gaol before and that was why they wanted to get him into further trouble. The second witness beat him because he had had a quarrel with her husband about the redeeming of a jacket from pawn.

Committed for trial at the next Criminal Sessions of the Supreme Court.[288]

---

[288] This case is No. 4, Criminal Calendar -- November Sessions, 1881". (HKGG, 26 November 1881, p. 1043.) Chan A-yau, accused of 1) Larceny; 2) Previous conviction (felony); and 3) previous conviction (summary) was tried on 18 November and found guilty of an attempt to steal. He pleaded guilty of an attempt to steal and he also pleaded guilty to the second count. A Nolle prosequi was entered by the Attorney General on the third count. He was sentenced on 24 November to four years' penal servitude.

The following report appeared in CM, "In Criminal Sessions", Friday, 18 November 1881, p. 3, cc. 3 - 4.)
"In Criminal Sessions (Before his Honour, the Acting Chief Justice, Hon. Francis Snowden.)"
Friday, 18 November [1881]
The jury consisted of Messrs J. R. White, F. D. Bush, C. Danenberg, J. Gourlay, J. d'Almeida [sic], L. N. Collaço and J. Edgar.
Chan Ayau was charged with stealing seven silver hair-pins, and sundry other articles, on the 7th [sic] day of November. He pleaded not guilty. The evidence given in the case was of a most conflicting nature, and the jury returned a verdict of guilty of attempting to steal against him. Prisoner pleaded guilty to a previous conviction, Sentence deferred."

ALLEGED TRAFFICKING IN HUMAN BEINGS
CC Number 343 📖 p. 307

Ng Sam Mui, and Li Akwai , two elderly women, and Wong Awa, Kum Asam, and Lau Asam, coolies, were charged with having unlawfully detained one Pun Afung on the 1st instant, for the purpose of selling her.

This case has occupied the attention of the Court for several days, when evidence of the most conflicting nature has been adduced.

According to the complainant's story her husband, named Lau Ain, left her three years ago for Singapore, since which time she had resided in her native village Ka Ying-chau. He had recently sent her the sum of $15 to pay her passage to Singapore, and with that purpose she left her home by passage-boat. On this boat she met and became acquainted with a man named Wong Awa, the third prisoner, who represented himself as a clansman or distant relation. In due time (9th October), they reached Hong Kong, and on the recommendation of her pseudo friend she went to a house in the respectable locality of Ship Street to live until such time as an opportunity should offer of continuing her journey to Singapore. Wong Awa had discovered the fact that she was in possession of a few dollars, and she was induced to give them up to him for safe keeping. On the 31st ultimo, becoming suspicious at the delay in obtaining

---

The case was continued in the Supreme Court on 24 November 1881, and the following report appeared in *The China Mail*, 24 November 1881, p. 3, c. 4.

"Supreme Court

"In Criminal Sessions

"(Before his Honour, the Acting Chief Justice, Hon. Francis Snowden.) Thursday, 24 November 1881

"The Acting Chief Justice today sentenced the prisoners tried and convicted at the Criminal Sessions: --

Chan Ayau, convicted of an attempt to steal in a house, got four years' penal servitude."

conveyance to the Straits she asked for the return of her money, when her friend coolly informed her that he had spent the whole of it, and he further intimated that she would have to pay for her board and lodgings, which had now covered a period of over three weeks. She then expressed her willingness to pay the sum of $5, provided he would refund her the money she had entrusted to his care. This, however, he was unable to do, again telling her that he had spent the whole of it. Shortly afterwards, on the same day, the two female prisoners appeared on the scene, and in their presence and hearing, Wong Awa intimated his intention of disposing of her person by sale. To this she objected, and expressed her determination to go to Singapore to join her husband. Some disturbance was then raised about payment for her board and lodging, and during the afternoon her brother-in-law, who described himself as a fortune teller and necromancer, happened accidentally to pass, and he at once recognised her as his brother's wife. She then related to him the circumstances in which she was placed and he took her from the house. This caused a further dispute, as Wong Awa and the two women had been negotiating with a widower for the woman's purchase with a view to matrimony, and if the brother-in-law were allowed to interfere and spoil the interesting arrangement, they foresaw that they would be deprived of their commission as go-betweens. His Worship had occasion to remark yesterday, during the hearing of the case, that complainant had varied her after-statements very considerably from the story she told on the day of the first inquiry. He said her first tale was remarkably clear and explicit and appeared to be a truthful one, and remarkably well told for an ignorant country woman as she appeared to be. The case, however, was of too much importance for him to dismiss on account of any prevarications on her part, and after a tangled mass of evidence, which more or less implicated the whole of the prisoners, he decided to send the case to the next Criminal Sessions of the Supreme Court.[289]

---

[289] This case is No. 3 [*sic*] in the Criminal Calendar -- December Sessions, 1881. (HKGG, 31 December 1881, p. 1106.) Ng Sam Mui, Li A-kwei, Wong A-wa, Kam A-sam, and Lau A-sam, were charged with detaining, for the purpose of selling her, one Pun A-fung. The verdict was "not guilty". The following remarks are noted in the Calendar: "In this case, there was no evidence whatever that the woman was detained by force or fraud. The evidence showed that the prisoners wanted to obtain a sum of money by negociating to marry her to a man who was called as a witness." The notes are signed "F. S" (i.e. "the Hon. F. Snowden", Acting Chief Justice, who heard the case.)

The following report appeared in *The China Mail*, Monday, 19 December 1881, p. 3, c. 2
"Supreme Court
"In Criminal Sessions
"(Before the Hon. F. Snowden, Acting Chief Justice)
"Monday, 19 December 1881
"The Criminal Sessions were opened today.
"Unlawful Detention
"The first [*sic*] case was one of unlawful detention, in which Ng Sam Mui, Li Akwai, Wong Awa, Kam Asam, and Lau Asam, were charged with detaining, for the purpose of selling her, one Pang Afuk. The prisoners pleaded not guilty, and the following gentlemen were sworn as jurors: -- Messrs A. de Costa, T. Hashi, J. F. Broadbent, J. M. de J. P. Collaço, H. A. Ritchie, A. Soares, and C. F. Grossman.

"The Attorney General (the Hon. E. L. O'Malley) prosecuting, said the prisoners were indicted for taking part in the detention of a woman, unlawfully and by force, for the purpose of selling her. The complainant was a married woman whose husband had been in Singapore for three years, and with whom she corresponds. In the month of September last, she received money from him to pay her passage to Singapore. She made arrangements to leave her native place, and on the way had been detained by the prisoners who had promised to procure her passage, receiving in payment thereof $50 sent by her husband.

"The evidence led was substantially the same as that given in the Police Court.

"After evidence was heard, the Attorney General acknowledged that there had been very little evidence to sustain the charge of unlawful detention, and that there appeared to have been persuasion used rather than force. His Lordship agreed with the Attorney General that there was very little convicting evidence --

Complete Court Cases   269

SATURDAY 5 NOVEMBER 1881[290]
UNLAWFUL POSSESSION
CC Number 344

Leong Awang, a cooper, was charged with unlawful possession of two silver studs on the 4th instant.

Police Constable No. 78, W. Beckett, said he was in a jeweller's shop yesterday afternoon when defendant came in and offered the studs for sale. On being questioned respecting his possession of them he first said he found them at the bottom of the sea at Sham-shui-po, and afterwards that a man whom he did not know gave them to him.

In his defence to-day he said they belonged to a carpenter, but he did not know the man. The man wanted to sell them and defendant asked permission to look at them, and while doing so the other man ran away, and he was arrested by the constable by mistake.

Fined $3, in default, seven days' imprisonment with hard labour.

PUGILISTIC SEAMEN
CC Number 345

John Hanson, and Peter Garrald, seamen, were charged with fighting and creating a disturbance last night.

Police Constable 27, A. Macdonald, said he found the two men deeply engaged in a stand-up fight in East Street, about half-past eleven o'clock last night. They were both under the influence of liquor.

First defendant said he could not deny it, and the second remembered nothing about it.

Fined $1 each, in default four days' imprisonment with hard labour.

---

insufficient to justify him in laying the case before the jury. The jury found the prisoners not guilty. His Lordship then dismissed the prisoners advising them to inform all their friends that no person was allowed to sell another in this Colony."

[290] "Police Intelligence," CM, Saturday, 5 November 1881, p. 3, c. 2.

DRUNK AND INCAPABLE
CC Number 346
Thomas Drew, an American seaman, pleaded guilty to being drunk and incapable yesterday afternoon, and was also fined 50 cents, or two days' imprisonment.

WILFULL DAMAGE TO A GARDEN[291]
CC Number 347 📖 p. 367
Chang Apo, a gardener, was charged with wilfully damaging vegetables and flowers to the value of $40, on the 4th instant.

Mr T. H. Smith, partner in the firm of Messrs Blockhead & Company, said that defendant had been in his employment but was dismissed in September last. Yesterday morning from information he received from his present gardener, he went to Tsim-sha tsui, where his garden is situated, and there found that the whole of the vegetables and flowers had been pulled up and thrown about, and the garden rendered a complete wreck. The garden is about an acre and a half in extent and he estimated the value of the flowers and vegetables destroyed at $40.

Ng Alau, a gardener employed by Mr Smith, said he knew the prisoner, and when he was dismissed he said in witness's hearing "Well, I'll see who takes my place. I will beat him," and "If he plants any flowers or vegetables I will destroy them." Defendant said this when they were at work. He has had no employment since his dismissal from Mr Smith's service, and has lived with his mother at Yau-ma-Ti, about fifteen minutes' walk off. Witness said he lived in a house in his master's garden, and on getting up yesterday morning at six o'clock he found the door of the pig and fowl house broken. Nothing had happened to the pig or fowls. He then noticed that a large quantity of vegetables and flower seedings had been pulled up and destroyed. The

---

[291] The following is the complete set of reports in connection with this case in *The Complete Court Cases*: CC Nos 347, 356.

whole of the young seedings had been destroyed, and the seedlings in about 200 flower pots had been scooped out. Witness was sure the damage had been done by human hands, and not by fowls or pigs. The pigs and fowls were all safe in their shed, and there were the marks of human feet all over the flower beds. He went to bed the previous evening at nine o'clock, and everything in the garden was properly fenced and no animals could get in from outside, and the fence was not disturbed of yesterday morning. After further evidence of a similar nature had been given by another employé of Mr Smith's [sic], the case was remanded till Tuesday next the 8th instant.

MONDAY 7 NOVEMBER 1881[292]
A BATCH OF DRUNK AND INCAPABLES
CC Number 348

Samuel Edgar, a seaman unemployed, was charged with being drunk and incapable on the 6th instant.

Sergeant Grozart said he found defendant in Queen's Road yesterday evening helplessly drunk.

This is the same man who was committed for trial for habitual drunkenness and vagrancy last month, but whose case was sent back by the Attorney General to be dealt with summarily. He has scored no less than eleven convictions of this class of crime since December last.

He begged forgiveness this time, and promised to take the pledge.

He had to find security in two sureties of L10 [sic for "$10"] to be of good behaviour for three months, in default to be committed.

---

[292] "Police Intelligence," CM, Monday, 7 November 1881, p. 3, c. 2.

MONDAY 7 NOVEMBER 1881[293]
[A BATCH OF DRUNK AND INCAPABLES]
CC Number 349
Thomas Mede, a seaman of the American ship Helicon,[294] was fined twenty-five cents for being drunk and incapable yesterday evening.

A BATCH OF DRUNK AND INCAPABLES]
CC Number 350
Charles King, seaman unemployed, was fined fifty cents for being drunk, and was also ordered to pay fifty cents chair hire.

[A BATCH OF DRUNK AND INCAPABLES]
CC Number 351
J. C. de Young, seaman, of the Koningen Emmu der Nederlanden, who admitted he was too far gone to know what he was about, was fined fifty cents for being drunk and assaulting a constable.

[A BATCH OF DRUNK AND INCAPABLES]
CC Number 352
John Ryan, a Private in H.M.'s Royal Inniskilling Fusiliers, was also fined fifty cents for being drunk and assaulting a Sikh constable yesterday evening.

WATCHMAN TO GAMBLERS
CC Number 353
Man Ayau, a coal coolie, was charged with being a watchman to rogues and vagabonds engaged gambling on the Wanchai Road, yesterday forenoon.

Inspector Corcoran said he went to the back of some houses opposite Number 2 Station yesterday forenoon to look for gamblers, and when the prisoner saw him coming he gave an alarm, and from twenty to thirty men were thus enabled to make their escape.

---

[293] "Police Intelligence," CM, Monday, 7 November 1881, p. 3, c. 2.
[294] According to CM, 22 August 1881 (p. 3, c. 7), the *Helicon* left Cardiff on 31 May.

Six months' imprisonment with hard labour, as a rogue and vagabond.

DISORDERLY CONDUCT
CC Number 354 📖 p. 182

Edward Morris, seaman on board the American ship Stonewall Jackson, [295] was charged with being drunk and disorderly, and damaging property on the 6th instant.It appeared that defendant and some of his comrades went into a cigar and book-binder's shop in Queen's Road yesterday evening. He asked for two bundles of cigars, but declined to pay the proper price for them, upon which the shopman refused to let him have them. He thereupon took up a tray containing writing materials and threw it at one of the assistants in the shop, smashing a pane of glass in a show case, breaking the tray itself, and damaging some paper. His companions meanwhile drew their sheath knives and stuck them in the counter. A constable who witnessed the disturbance attempted to arrest the defendant, which resulted in a struggle taking place between them, and the other men who had their knives in their hands threatened to use them. Ultimately assistance was procured and defendant was locked up, his companions in the meanwhile decamping with the cigars without going through the formality of paying for them.

Defendant said he did not remember anything about it.

Fined $10 for disorderly behaviour, in default fourteen days' imprisonment with hard labour, and to pay $1 amends to complainant, or two days' further imprisonment.

---

[295] According to CM, 22 August 1881 (p. 3, c. 7), the *Stonewall Jackson* left Cardiff on 28 May.

TUESDAY 8 NOVEMBER 1881[296]
UNLAWFUL PAWNING
CC Number 355

Lok Ayau, a shop coolie, was charged with being in possession of a pawn ticket relating to stolen property.

From the evidence of Tsoi Acheung a carpenter employed at the Italian Convent, it appeared that a pair of trousers were stolen from his room on the 29th or 30th April last. The pawn shops were searched at the time and the trousers were found, but the pawnee was not discovered till yesterday, when the prisoner presented the ticket for the purpose of redeeming the trousers.

In defence prisoner said he bought the trousers last January in a shop in Jervois Street, but he did not now know the shop. He pawned them himself on the 30th April, and went yesterday to redeem them. He admitted three previous convictions, two of which were for larceny.

He was now convicted of pawning the trousers without being duly authorized, and was sentenced to six months' imprisonment with hard labour.

WEDNESDAY 9 NOVEMBER 1881[297]
WILFUL DAMAGE TO A GARDEN[298]
CC Number 356 📖 p. 368

The case in which Chang Apo, a gardner [sic] was charged with destroying his late employer's garden, was again before the Court yesterday, when some further evidence was heard.

Chan Anang, an apprentice fitter at Hung Ham [sic] Dock, said he had known defendant for some years. During a conversation which he had with defendant

---

[296] "Police Intelligence," CM, Tuesday, 8 November 1881, p. 3, c. 2.

[297] "Police Intelligence," CM, Wednesday, 9 November 1881, p. 3, cc. 2 - 3.

[298] The following is the complete set of reports in connection with this case in *The Complete Court Cases*: CC Nos 347, 356.

some days ago he told witness that a punti man had taken his situation,[299] but remarked that he would not keep the job, as when he planted his flowers defendant would destroy them, and this would be the cause of the punti man getting a thrashing from his master.

Lan Shui, [300] Police Sergeant 250, gave evidence as to complainant making a report at Yau-mah-ti Station, when Inspector Cameron sent witness to see the garden. He found that over 100 pots of flower seedlings had been destroyed, as also several beds of vegetables. Damage had also been done to the door of the house in which the goats, pigs, and fowls were kept. On being arrested on the Praya at Yau-mah-ti, defendant, when informed why he was apprehended, said "Oh that's a small matter. Let me go home; I want to consult with my mother about it."

Defendant wished to call some witnesses; but none of them knew anything about the case although they could speak as to his general conduct.

The case was then again remanded till the 9th *instant*.

On the case being called again to-day, Wang Wi Shi, a medical practitioner, said he had known defendant for about five years, but he knew nothing of the charge now preferred against him.

Two other witnesses were called upon by defendant, but they could not be found by the police.

Prisoner after having been duly cautioned, elected to defer his defence, and was duly committed for trial at the next Criminal Sessions of the Supreme Court.[301]

---

[299] It is notable here that resentment was felt particularly because the person who had taken the defendant's position was apparently from a different ethnic group (he was a "punti"), which had nevertheless been long resident in the location.

[300] Probably the same as Sergeant Lan Asui.

[301] The following information appears for case No. 5, "Criminal Calendar -- November Sessions, 1881". (HKGG, 26 November 1881, [p. 1043].) Chan A-po was charged with "unlawfully and maliciously destroying and damaging certain Saplings and Shrubs, the property of John Henry Smith" and tried on 18

WEDNESDAY 9 NOVEMBER 1881[302]
DAMAGING A 'RICKSHA
CC Number 357

Henry Johnson, a seaman unemployed, was charged with damaging a 'ricksha on the 8th instant.

Defendant, it appeared, was rather tipsy yesterday evening, and apparently felt inclined to quarrel with any one or anything that came in his way, and while in this mood he smashed the wheel of a 'ricksha standing near the Fire Engine House, Queen's Road.

Fined 50 cents for disorderly conduct, in default two days' imprisonment, and ordered to pay

---

November 1881. The verdict or plea was "guilty". Chan A-po was sentenced on 24 November 1881 to six calendar months' imprisonment with hard labour.

The following report appeared in CM, "In Criminal Session", 18 November 1881, p. 3, cc. 3 - 4.
"Supreme Court
"In Criminal Sessions (Before his Honour, the Acting Chief Justice, Hon. Francis Snowden.)
"Friday, 18 November 1881

"The jury consisted of Messrs J. R. White, F. D. Bush, C. Danenberg, J. Gourlay, J. d'Almeida [sic], L. D. Collaço and J. Edgar."

"Wilful Damage to a Garden
"Chan Apo, a gardener, was charged with destroying flowers and vegetables belonging to Mr J. H. Smith, of the firm of Blackhead & Company He pleaded not guilty. This case was fully reported when it was before the Police Court, and the evidence given today was to the same effect. The Jury returned a unanimous verdict of guilty, and sentence was deferred."

A further report appeared of the Criminal Sessions of the Supreme Court held on 24 November 1881 in *The China Mail*.
"In Criminal Sessions
"(Before his Honour, the Acting Chief Justice, Hon. Francis Snowden.) Thursday, 24 November 1881
"Chan Apo, convicted of wilful and malicious damage to the garden of his employer, received six months' imprisonment with hard labour."

[302] "Police Intelligence," CM, Wednesday, 9 November 1881, p. 3, cc. 2 - 3.

the sum of 50 cents compensation to the 'ricksha coolie.

JACK ASHORE
CC Number 358 📖 p. 183

George Hansen and Arthur Scott, firemen on board H.M.S. *Comus*, were charged with wilfully damaging paintings valued at $12, and also with assaulting the police, on the 8th *instant*.

Fong Chu Ching, photographer and painter, Queen's Road, said that the two defendants came to his shop at nine o'clock last night and wanted their portraits. He told them they had not had their portraits taken there, and they must have mistaken the shop, but they became very violent and smashed the four pictures produced. The assistance of the police was called for, but it took several men to take them to the station.

First defendant said he had given a photograph to complainant a fortnight ago to copy, and when he went for it last night it was refused. He denied having struck the complainant and had never seen the damaged pictures before.

Second defendant told a similar story, adding that there was not an angry word spoken in the shop.

Fined $5 for the assault, or seven days' imprisonment with hard labour, and to pay $6 each to complainant or suffer seven days' imprisonment.

A TASTE FOR LEGAL DOCUMENTS
CC Number 359

Un Ying Chung, a jinricksha coolie, was charged with stealing four summonses issued by the Summary Jurisdiction Court, on the 8th instant.

Mr Manuel Leon, Sheriff's Officer, said that he hired the defendant's jinricksha yesterday afternoon for the purpose of serving summonses in the Pok-fu Lam Road. He left the machine[303] in front

---

[303] "The machine": interesting term, then, to be applied to a "rickshaw". See also CC 365.

of Number 7 station[304] while he went to a house in the neighbourhood. He placed four summonses under the seat and told defendant to look after them, but when he returned they were gone. Each summons bore a stamp which witness would now have to repay, but he did not know the exact amount.

Remanded till the 10th instant to enable complainant to ascertain the value of the stamps; prisoner to be admitted to bail in one surety in $15.

ATTEMPTED SUICIDE[305]
CC Number 360

Chan Lin Ying, a single woman, was charged with attempting to commit suicide on the 8th instant.[306]

Police Constable 242, Tam Ashing said that about seven o'clock yesterday evening he found the defendant at the Harbour Master's Office dripping wet, and he was informed she had just been taken out of the water. He thought she was insane.

Defendant pleaded that a devil told her to jump in and she would be saved.

Remanded till the 10th instant for the opinion of the Colonial Surgeon.

WEDNESDAY 9 NOVEMBER 1881[307]
ROBBERY FROM THE PERSON
CC Number 361 📖

Lam Achoi and Lai Akum, cooks, were charged, with others not in custody, with robbing one Au Ayau of the sum of $8 on the 8th instant.

---

[304] According to Colin Crisswell and Mike Watson, Number Seven Police Station was located at the junction of Queen's Road and Pokfulam Road. ("Appendix 1", Colin Crisswell and Mike Watson, *The Royal Hong Kong Police (1841-1945)*, Hong Kong, Macmillan Hong Kong, 1982.)

[305] See also CC No. 366, where the single woman's name is given as, "Chun Lim Ying".

[306] NB The offence took place on 8 November, the defendant was charged the following day, 9 November and, somewhat unusually, the case was reported on 11 November 2008.

[307] "Police Intelligence," CM, Wednesday, 9 November 1881, p. 3, cc. 2 - 3.

Complainant said he had been employed as a fireman on board a German steamer, but was discharged from her yesterday at his own request as he did not feel well. When he left the steamer he went to live at the On Li boarding house, but the master there was very angry with him because some time ago he had recommended three men from another house for employment as firemen. He meant to explain the matter to the master of the On Li house and give him some money to appease him. Witness wanted the master to go and see the men he had recommended, but he declined and said he must be paid by complainant. He then left the house, but the master called on defendants and a number of other men to beat him. They did so and after the scuffle which ensued was over he found himself minus the sum of $8.

The witness prevaricated somewhat in his statement but adhered to the main facts of his story.

Chan Akok, a district watchman, said he saw a disturbance about seven o'clock yesterday evening at Webster's Bazaar, and the complainant making a great noise, saying he had been robbed. There were a great many people about, but complainant only pointed out the two defendants as having assaulted him.

Remanded till the 10th *instant*, bail, in one householder, each in $10.

A DISTURBANCE IN COURT
CC Number 362

Chun Atong, a married woman, was charged with creating a disturbance in the Police Court.

Sobail Singh, Police Constable 658, said that he was in charge of the dock in the Court this day. Defendant both in and out of the Court House was making a great noise. She wanted to go on the bench, and came there frequently for that purpose. She appeared to be insane.

Defendant said she came to take out a summons against her husband, who refused to let her live with him.

Remanded till the 10th instant, for the opinion of the Colonial Surgeon as to the woman's mental condition.

THURSDAY 10 NOVEMBER 1881[308]
A REFRACTORY SERVANT
CC Number 363 📖 p. 258

Fung Akai, a cook, was charged yesterday with leaving his employer's service on the 7th instant, without giving reasonable notice.[309]

Inspector Whitehead[310] said the defendant was in his employ. About half-past one on the afternoon of the 7th he was sent to market to procure some fish for dinner, but nothing more was seen of him till half-past eleven on the forenoon of the next day. Witness sent his interpreter to the prisoner's house to make enquiries respecting him, and he returned with a message that defendant had left because Mrs Whitehead would not let him have any firewood.

Defendant said that when he asked his mistress for firewood she ordered him to take some rails from the fence, but he said if the police saw him he would be arrested. She beat him and turned him away.

---

[308] "Police Intelligence," CM, Thursday, 10 November 1881, p. 3, cc. 2 - 3.

[309] It is interesting that servants were obliged by law to "give reasonable notice". With the advent of considerable numbers of non-Chinese domestic servants from the Philippines and elsewhere from about the 1970s onwards, the general public is, at the time of writing this, well aware of the tight regulations currently in force with reference to their employment.

[310] Inspector Whitehead is identified as Chief Inspector of brothels. (*A Magistrate's Court in 19th Century Hong Kong*, p. 239.) He appears as, "Whitehead, W. F. Inspector of Brothels, Lock Hospital. Foreman, Fire Brigade." ("List of Officers", HKBB1882, Section I3.)

At this point the case was remanded till this morning for the attendance of Mrs Whitehead, who now said she had sent the defendant to the market for fish and fowl. He returned without the fish and she declined to take the fowl which he brought. She then told him to send the coolie back to the market with the fowl, but he need not go himself. He then went away, and she saw nothing more of him till next day. She did not beat him, nor did she dismiss him from her service.

Fined L1 sterling,[311] or seven days' imprisonment with hard labour.

DISORDERLY CONDUCT
CC Number 364 📖 p. 281

Li Asui, a hawker, was charged with disorderly conduct, throwing crackers into a brothel, on the 9th instant.

The mistress of the brothel, a house in Square Street,[312] said some one threw a lighted cracker into her house yesterday evening, and it exploded with a

---

[311] It seems strange that the fine is stated as "L1 sterling", and not as a sum in Hong Kong dollars. Elsewhere in the cases, sums are occasionally stated in "£n". It is easy to assume that a compositor has substituted one currency symbol for another, in error. But it is less obviously a mistake when the whole word, "sterling" is given.

[312] For information about the brothel in Square Street, some four months later, see the following Editorial (*The China Mail*, Thursday, 9 March 1882):
"A somewhat alarming disclosure was made in the course of a case which came before Dr Stewart this morning. A native constable who had been told off to make inquiries into a row which occurred in a brothel in Square Street yesterday, stated that the defendant in the case, who when arrested was armed with a chopper of the class used by butchers and carpenters, belonged to a gang numbering about one hundred men, organised for the purpose of fighting. Inspector Fleming, who was in charge of the case, said the statement was merely founded on rumour. This may be so, but as Dr. Stewart remarked it is a rumour which should be most carefully inquired into, as the existence of gangs such as this is a danger to the peace of the Colony. One of the inmates of the brothel admitted, in reply to the Magistrate, that she had heard of the existence of such a combination."

loud noise. She did not see who threw it. Two Sikh constables, however, were able [to] give evidence on this point and identified the defendant as the perpetrator of the pyrotechnic display. Defendant of course denied the charge.

Fined $5, in default fourteen days' imprisonment with hard labour.

THEFT OF PUBLIC DOCUMENTS
CC Number 365 📖 p. 325

Un Ying Cheung, a jinricksha coolie, charged yesterday with stealing Summary Jurisdiction Summonses, was again placed in the dock this morning.

Mr. Leon, Sheriff's Officer, now detailed the documents missed, as also the value of the stamps they bore. He went to a school behind Number 7 Station, this morning, where some of the papers were given up to him by a boy. He was then taken to a shop near by were [*sic* for "where"] he had other missing papers given up to him. A boy attending the school said he picked up a number of papers scattered about in the middle of the street and gave them to shop people.

A constable residing at Number 7 Station said he was sitting in one of the windows playing chess[313] when he heard a noise outside, and both complainant and defendant came inside; the latter pointing to him said he had taken the papers. He had not been outside the station.

In defence the prisoner[314] said he just turned away his head and he saw the lukong come behind him and go to his machine,[315] but he did not see what he did.

---

[313] It is interesting that the police constable states that he was playing chess. Was he playing western or Chinese chess? Who was he playing with?

[314] "The prisoner": the rickshaw puller.

[315] "H[316] "Police Intelligence," CM, Friday, 11 November 1881, p. 3, cc. 4 - 5.

Ordered to find security in two householders in $10 each for his good behaviour for six weeks, in default to be committed.

FRIDAY 11 NOVEMBER 1881[316]
ATTEMPTED SUICIDES[317]
CC Number 366

Chun Lim Ying, a single woman, and Chun Atong, married woman, who were charged on the 9th instant with attempting to commit suicide, were again placed in the dock to-day.

Certificates from the Colonial Surgeon were put in, testifying as to the women's insanity, and they were ordered to be handed over to the Tung Wah Hospital.

DRUNK AND DISORDERLY
CC Number 367

John McCall, a private in the Royal Inniskilling Fusiliers, was charged with being drunk and disorderly on the 10th instant, and assaulting a police constable.

Police Constable 62, John Dick, said that he saw defendant at eight o'clock yesterday evening in the Queen's Road, opposite the Hong Kong and Shanghai Bank. He was drunk and very disorderly, knocking everybody about whom he met. He advised him to go home to barracks, but he would not go, and he was compelled to arrest him. Defendant became very violent, kicked the constable in a dangerous part and damaged his uniform coat and trousers.

Defendant said he had no recollection of what had happened.

---

[316] "Police Intelligence," CM, Friday, 11 November 1881, p. 3, cc. 4 - 5.

[317] See also CC No. 360, CM, 9 November 1881, where the single woman's name is given as, "Chan Lin Ying". Contrary to what is stated in CC No. 366, although the report appeared in *The China Mail* on 9 November 1881, the two women were in fact charged the previous day, 8 November 1881.

Find $5 for assaulting the constable, in default seven days' imprisonment with hard labour; and further to pay $5 for the damage to the constable's uniform, or suffer seven days' additional imprisonment.

BRIBING A CONSTABLE
CC Number 368 📖 p. 354

Wong Akwon, a servant, was charged with being at large in the streets at an early hour this morning without a light or pass, and also with attempting to bribe the constable who arrested him.

Defendant was arrested at half-past two o'clock this morning in Hollywood Road. He said he was going to a brothel; on the way to the station he slipped forty cents into the constable's hand.

Fined 50 cents or two days' imprisonment, the 40 cents bribe to be placed in the Poor Box.

GAMBLERS
CC Number 369

Three coolies were charged with gambling in an unoccupied house in Gap Street yesterday afternoon.

Police Sergeant 35, Mahomed Ali, went to the house in question and found fifteen or sixteen men gambling at fan-tan. The three prisoners were arrested, but the others escaped.

Fined $25 each, in default three months' imprisonment with hard labour.

UNLAWFUL POSSESSION
CC Number 370

Wong Afuk, a jinricksha coolie, was fined ten shillings, in default twenty-one days' imprisonment with hard labour, for being in unlawful possession of a bundle of firewood at five o'clock this morning. He had already five previous convictions recorded against his name, chiefly for larceny.

BREACH OF OPIUM ORDINANCE
CC Number 371

Kwok Yeung Ku, an opium dross dealer, was charged with being in possession of about two taels of prepared opium on the 10th instant, without a permit from the Opium Farmer.

Police Constable J. Morrison said that he searched the defendant's house, Number 9,Canton Bazaar, by virtue of a warrant he held for the purpose, yesterday evening. Defendant denied having any opium in the place, but the constable found a pot of prepared opium (produced) in a bed room. It had been upset after witness entered the house. Another pot with traces of opium in it was found under a bed, and three horn boxes containing opium and a quantity of opium dross were also found. There was a basket, containing 6 cents and 230 cash, which had been used as a till when sales of opium were being effected. There were ten or twelve men lying about smoking opium.

Antonio dos Santos, an excise officer, accompanied the last witness, when the house was searched, and he gave corroboratory evidence.

Fined $50, in default two months' imprisonment, and the opium found to be handed over to the farmer.

SATURDAY 12 NOVEMBER 1881[318]
A DANGEROUS LUNATIC
CC Number 372

Syed Ahmed, a seaman unemployed, was placed in the dock charged with being a lunatic and dangerous.

Rahamat, defendant's wife, said her husband kicked her yesterday evening, and threatened to kill her. He went into the kitchen for a knife, and as he could not get one he threw the Koran at her. She did not know why he beat her. He had been very quiet since he came out of the Asylum until about three

---

[318] "Police Intelligence," CM, Saturday, 12 November 1881, p. 3, cc. 1 - 2.

days ago, when he became very quarrelsome, and she is now afraid of her life.

It appeared that about six weeks ago the witness had occasion to complain of her husband's strange conduct, and he was put under restraint in the Asylum in Hollywood Road, but was discharged from that institution about three weeks ago apparently cured. He now asserted that it was his wife who was insane, and invited His Worship to go to his house, where he would see ever so many empty bottles that his wife had drank sam-shoo from.

Remanded till the 14th instant, to enable the Colonial Surgeon to report on defendant's mental condition.

DRUNK AND DISORDERLY
CC Number 373

Patrick Weir, a private in the Royal Inniskilling Fusiliers, was charged with being drunk and disorderly and assaulting a constable on the 11th instant.

Mr. G.W. Snelling, assistant in the Stag Hotel, said defendant came to the house yesterday afternoon and walked upstairs and out on to the verandah. He wanted a bottle of ale, but the boys would not serve him as he was in liquor. He became very rough with them, and witness told him to leave as he would not be served there. His clothes were disarranged, and on this being pointed out to him he became abusive and flourished a stick about in a threatening manner. He became so violent that it required two policemen to take him to the station. Witness saw him strike one of the constables and tear the other's turban off.

Defendant said he was very sorry indeed for what he had done. He had had no drink for a month, and what he had taken went to his head.

An officer from the regiment attended, and gave defendant a very good character.

Fined $1, in default four days' imprisonment with hard labour.

DISORDERLY CONDUCT ON BOARD A STEAMER

CC Number 374 📖

Chu Un Fuk, a clerk, was charged at the instance of Sergeant Campbell with disorderly conduct on board the steamer Powan on the 11th instant.

It appears that yesterday evening defendant went on board as a passenger bound for Canton.

He placed his mat in such a position that it was in the way of the Chief Officer, and when asked by him and the complainant to remove it, he worked himself into a high state of excitement. Sergeant Campbell, who was in plain clothes, told him through his interpreter who he was, and desired him to go to another part of the ship and be quiet. This seemed to wound his celestial dignity in a vulnerable point, and he proceeded to array himself in a long silk gown, adorned his face with a pair of spectacles as large as saucers, and stretching himself to his full height literally roared in the Sergeant's face. He explained, through the interpreter in the most grandiloquent language, that he did not care if witness was the Governor, and that he should not even open his eyes to look upon such a mighty man as he (defendant) was. He continued in this strain for some time, using defiant and abusive language, and attracting crowds round him, until it was found necessary to place him in restraint.

Defendant said he had been a schoolmaster, but was now employed as a clerk. He had been in the colony for six or seven years, and was on his way to Canton to attend the examinations now going on there. He was sorry for what he had done, and promised to behave himself in Canton.

Cautioned and discharged.

MONDAY 14 NOVEMBER 1881[319]
BREACH OF THE OPIUM ORDINANCE
CC Number 375

Tam Atak, a married woman, was charged with being in possession of a quantity of prepared opium on the 12th *instant*, without a permit from the Opium Farmer.

Inspector Perry said he executed a search warrant on defendant's house on Saturday evening, and found in the bedroom two tins containing fourteen taels of prepared opium, two empty tins bearing traces of opium and a pair of scales also bearing traces of opium. She admitted having no permit.

Defendant said the opium had been the property of her husband who died two months ago. She knew nothing about it.

To Aun, a servant unemployed, said he went to defendant's house on the afternoon of the 11th instant, and bought 50 cents' worth of opium from defendant's husband. He laid an information next day. Fined $50, in default two months' imprisonment.

SELLING SPIRITS WITHOUT A LICENSE
CC Number 376

Pang Afu, and Pang Fu Cheung, boatmen, were charged with selling spirits in the Harbour of Victoria on the 13th *instant*, without a license.

Frank Thornton, seaman on board the British ship Agnes Muir, said that defendants came alongside yesterday afternoon with liquor to sell. He bought two bottle [*sic*] of gin for a couple of shirts. He reported the matter, and a gig was sent after them and they were arrested. They had been selling liquor to the men nearly every day for the last week. One of the men got into trouble through getting drink supplied by defendants.

---

[319] "Police Intelligence," CM, Monday, 14 November 1881, p. 3, c. 2 only.

Alexander Clark, another seaman, said he was on the forecastle head when defendants were being pursued by the ship's gig, and he saw them throw overboard five or six bottles when the gig was nearing them.

Both defendants said they were only hawking fruit.

First defendant fined $20, or six months' imprisonment with hard labour; second, $100, or three months' imprisonment with hard labour.

ATTEMPTED SUICIDE[320]
CC Number 377

Fong Amui, a married woman, who was charged on the 7th *instant* with attempting to commit suicide, was again placed in the dock this morning.

Her husband said she had been ill lately and on the 6th instant attempted to cut her throat. She had been in hospital since then and he wished to take her home to Nam-hoi.

Defendant said she wished to go home with her husband, and promised not to attempt her life again.

Cautioned and discharged.

A ROGUE AND VAGABOND
CC Number 378

John Barry, a Russian seaman unemployed, was charged with being a rogue and vagabond.
He was seen by Detective Sergeant Fisher following Europeans begging and annoying them on Saturday evening. He had been twice convicted before of a similar offence during the present year.

Defendant said he was offered a 10-cent piece when he was arrested, but he did not ask for it.

Six months' imprisonment with hard labour.

---

[320] It seems that no report of CC 377 appeared in *The China Mail* earlier. This is a different case from CC 360/366.

TUESDAY 15 NOVEMBER 1881[321]
DRUNK AND DISORDERLY
CC Number 379

Ernest Hagger, seaman serving on board H.M.S. *Wivern*, was charged with being drunk, disorderly, and damaging a constable's uniform on the 14th *instant*.

Police Constable 502, Manah Singh, said he was on duty last night about eight o'clock near Number 4 Station, when he was suddenly seized from behind. On turning round he found himself in defendant's clutches. He tried to shake him off but prisoner held on to his clothes so tenaciously that his tunic was torn, and his entire clothing damaged to the extent of $5. Defendant struck and kicked the constable repeatedly until assistance arrived when he was finally arrested.

Defendant now said he remembered nothing about it.

A certificate of service was handed in to Court, showing defendant's character since 1875 to have been "very good."

He was fined in the sum of $5 for assaulting the constable, in default seven days' imprisonment with hard labour; and further to pay $5 for damaging the constable's uniform, in default to suffer seven days' further imprisonment.

DRUNK AND INCAPABLE
CC Number 380

Joseph Maxwell, of Australia, a printer unemployed, was charged with being drunk and incapable on the 14th instant.

He was found lying in the gutter in Queen's Road Central last night about ten o'clock by a constable who took him to the station in a jinricksha.

He had nothing to say, and admitted two previous convictions during October.

---

[321] "Police Intelligence," CM, Tuesday, 15 November 1881, p. 3, cc. 4 - 5.

Fined $1, or four days imprisonment with hard labour.

WATCHMAN TO GAMBLERS
CC Number 381

Chun Apo was charged with being a rogue and vagabond, having been caught in Pound Lane acting in the capacity of watchman to a nest of gamblers. When the constable appeared, he gave a preconcerted signal and called out "gather up and be off." By this means the gamblers were enabled to make their escape.Defendant said he had not the slightest idea why he had been arrested.

Six weeks' imprisonment with hard labour.

LARCENY
CC Number 382

Lau Afuk, a ropemaker, pleaded guilty to stealing a piece of timber from the slip at Lap-sap Wan, this morning, and was sentenced to twenty-one days' imprisonment with hard labour.

CREATING A DISTURBANCE[322]
CC Number 383

Leung Ahing, a jinricksha coolie, appeared on a summons at the instance of Mr. Franco, charged with creating a disturbance at his house on the 11th instant.

It appears that on the day in question, complainant, Mr. Phineas Mary Kerr Franco, Hong Kong Telegraph, engaged defendant's machine to take him from the City Hall to Wan-tsai. He remained there some time and drove home in the same trap. On finishing the journey he paid defendant five cents, as the two trips had occupied twenty

---

[322] An article on jinrickshaws also appeared in, *The China Mail* on 15 November 1881, clearly inspired by this case. See also Gillian Bickley, ed., "Rickshaws", in, "Some Nineteenth Century Hong Kong Court Cases", 2009/2010, for a documented transcript of this and other references from *The China Mail* which seem to derive from this (and similar) cases.

minutes, and two cents more as he had gone quickly. The jinricksha coolie was not satisfied with this and produced his table of fares, demanding more. This complainant declined to accede to as the scale referred to two coolies whereas he only had one. Defendant became noisy and troublesome, and he first gave him in charge, but to save time he afterwards took out this summons.

Defendant said he had been engaged with complainant over an hour, and seven cents was not enough.

Fined 50 cents or two days' imprisonment.

OBSTRUCTIONISTS
CC Number 384

Chan Shang, a shopkeeper, and seven others, appeared on summonses at the instance of Sergeant Hagarty, charged with unlawfully, and to the obstruction of passengers, setting out their goods on the public footpaths, in front of their respective places of business. The whole of the defendants admitted the offence with which they were charged, and as Chan Shang had been fined last week for a similar offence, he was now fined in the sum of $5, while the others were fined 50 cents each.

A LUNATIC
CC Number 385

Syed Ahmed, a seaman unemployed, was brought up on remand from the 12th instant, charged with being a lunatic and dangerous.

It may be remembered that defendant in this case had been under treatment in the asylum in Hollywood Road for a time, and though he was discharged, he again began to show symptoms of derangement, accompanied with violence to his wife.

Dr. Aryes attended to-day, and said that defendant had been under his observation for some weeks and he had not shown any signs of violence or excitement. He was quiet and harmless, and there was no reason why he should not be permitted to be at large.

Case dismissed.

BREACH OF THE OPIUM ORDINANCE
CC Number 386

Tsoi King Po, an accountant, was charged with being in possession of a quantity of prepared opium on the 14th *instant*, without a permit from the Opium Farmer.

Inspector Perry said he went to defendant's house in Hing Lung Lane yesterday evening, and searched for opium by virtue of a warrant he held for that purpose. In a small room he found an iron safe which he requested should he opened for his examination. Defendant said he had not got the key and sent a coolie for it. The coolie returned in a few minutes and said it could not be found. The Inspector then informed he [*sic* for "him"] that he would have to take him to the station, and that the safe would be broken open, upon which he produced the key from an inside pocket. When the safe was opened there were found two pots containing about three taels of opium, and two empty pots showing traces of opium, and under a counter in the same room there were ten balls of raw opium.

Tse Acheung, a coolie unemployed, said the defendant sold him ten cents worth of opium at the house on the evening of the 13th.

Defendant produced three certificates for the purchase of opium designed for shipment, but they bore others' names, and not the defendant's.

Prisoner said in defence that he bought the opium for the coolies on board Messrs Turner & Company's[323] barque which was going to a foreign country. The opium in Court was simply washings,

---

[323] According to E. J. Eitel, R. Turner of R. Turner & Company was one of the five members of the first British Chamber of Commerce in China, formed in Canton in 1834 (*Europe in China*, p. 35) and Turner & Company was among the first to purchase lots of land in Hong Kong (E. J. Eitel, *Europe in China*, p. 174).

and it was deposited in the safe to prevent his coolies from smoking it. About four years ago he bought some raw opium from a wreck. When boiled it was good for skin diseases. He denied having ever sold any opium.

Chan Sing Tai, accountant to the opium farm,[324] said he was well acquanited [*sic*] with opium and its preparation. He said the prepared opium in Court was made from the samples of raw [opium] shown, although it would be of poor quality unless mixed with some of a better kind.

Defendant said the raw opium in court would not produce opium at all if boiled, while the last witness declared he could boil the raw material and would realise the same quality of the drug as that in Court.

The case was then remanded till the 17th, bail being accepted in one householder in the sum of $50, the raw opium in the meantime to be boiled under the supervision of the police.

WEDNESDAY 16 NOVEMBER 1881[325]
PUBLIC OBSTRUCTION
CC Number 387 📖 p. 354

Kong Him, of the U-Lung salt fish lan,[326] appeared on a summons at the instance of Police Constable No. 306, charged with "that he, unlawfully and to the obstruction of passengers, did set out and leave 130 baskets and 50 casks of salt fish on a public foot-path on Praya Central, on the 11th instant, in contravention of Clause 11, of Section II, of Ordinance 14 of 1845."[327]

---

[324] The accountant to the opium farm seems to be present in court as an expert witness.

[325] "Police Intelligence," CM, Wednesday, 16 November 1881, p. 3, c. 3.

[326] "Lan": a business / combination / association.

[327] Clause 11 of Section II of Ordinance 14 of 1845 reads as follows:
"Every person shall be liable to a penalty not exceeding Five Pounds, who, within the Colony of Hong Kong, shall, in any thoroughfare or public place, or adjacent thereto, commit any of

The case was opened yesterday, when the constable, Lo Ayau, said the baskets and casks complained of were placed, some on the water side of the Praya, a number in the middle of the roadway, and others on the foot-path. There was room for one chair only to pass, two could not. The obstruction continued from ten o'clock in the morning till two o'clock in the afternoon. Defendant had been fined twice during the present year for a similar offence, and on the day now charged he told witness he was not afraid of any summons as he had plenty of money to pay any fine. Two other constables also saw the obstruction.

To-day, on the case being again brought before the Magistrate, Mr J.J. Francis appeared for the defence.

Lo Ayau, recalled, said he had been five years and four months in the Police Force. He was on duty on the Praya between the P.& O. Company's Godowns and the Gas Works from 10 a.m. to 2 p.m. on the 11th, and had been on the same beat for ten days previously. There are about twenty fish lans on that part of the Praya and all the fish boats come there daily to discharge their cargoes. The baskets and casks of fish complained of were in front of defendant's fish-lan only, and not in front of the others. The same baskets were there all the time. It was not a succession of baskets, and there were from ten to twenty men at work at them. None of them were empty. Witness was over his beat eight times. He told defendant to take away his fish, but he said, "Oh no; the Governor knows we always put some fish there." There were also fish there on the days when he was on duty prior to the 11th. He never at any time kicked defendant's empty baskets about.

---

the following offences; that is to say: -- . . . Every person who, upon any public footway, shall roll or carry any barrel, cask, butt, or other thing calculated to annoy or incommode the passengers thereon, except for the purpose of housing them or of loading any cart or carriage on the other side of the footway."

For another reference to this Ordinance, see note to CC 328.

Sergeant Nund Singh said he was on patrol on the Praya West at one o'clock in the afternoon of the 11th, and saw about 100 baskets of fish on the foot-path and the main road. They occupied the whole of the path and about one-third of the street. He gave last witness instructions to take out a summons.

By Mr Francis: — He did not see fish taken from a boat, but from the fish-lan. A number of men were packing the fish in the baskets. There were a number of empty baskets on either side. All the baskets were in front of defendant's premises. He was on duty there from 7 till 9 a.m., and went on again at noon.

The following witnesses were called by Mr Francis for the defence.

Lo Awai said he was accountant in a chandler's shop next door to defendant's. He was in his shop all day on the 11th, and at 8'clock that morning he saw about ten baskets of fish in front of defendant's lan, next the Praya wall. There were no baskets there between 10 and 11 that morning. He had been five years in his present shop, and he had no complaint to make of any obstruction; people could pass in and out of his shop. The baskets he saw only remained a few minutes.

Tam Acheung, accountant in a hardware shop, gave similar evidence. He was in his shop all day on the 11th, but did not see any obstruction caused by defendant's baskets of fish, and he did not see his men packing fish on the Praya. There were not 130 baskets and 50 casks on the Praya that day. If they had been there he must have seen them. Fish are generally landed before 9 o'clock, and they only remain a few minutes, when they are carried into the fish-lan.

E. J. Gomes, a watchman, also gave evidence to the effect that the baskets only remained a short time on the Praya, and that the men packed the fish in the doorway, and not on the road.

Sun Amui, defendant's head coolie, said there were not 100 baskets of fish on the Praya on the morning of the 11th. He had eight men at work in the shop, not in the street. About 80 or 90 baskets were landed that morning between five and six o'clock, and they were carried into the lan. About 100 baskets were sold that day. The purchaser sends his own coolies, and his master has nothing to do with them after they are sold.

The accountant in defendant's firm also gave evidence. He said business to the extent of $1000, was done that day, in exports and imports. The fish was packed inside the lan before being sent out, and there were not 100 baskets on the Praya. There were about ten men at work.

Mr Francis addressed the Court, and submitted that it had not been proved that any obstruction had occurred, and if there had, it was after the fish had been sold when his client was not responsible.

His Worship however held the charge proved, and fined defendant $10, in default two days' imprisonment.

The China Mail, Wednesday, 16 November 1881[328]
STABBING CASE ON BOARD THE *HELEN MARION*[329]
COMMITTAL FOR MURDER
CC Number 388 📖 p. 181
[John] Parry, a seaman on board the *Helen Marion*, charged with wounding Thomas [Finlay,] was again placed in the dock this morning — Dr Stewart on the bench — when [the char]ge was altered from wounding to [murder].

---

[328] "Stabbing Case on Board The 'Helen Marion'", [Police Magistrate's Court] CM, Wednesday, 16 November 1881, p. 3, c. 1.

[329] The following is the complete set of reports in connection with this case in *The Complete Court Cases*: CC Nos 291, 296, 300, 388.

Dr Murray, Acting Superintendent of the [Civil] Hospital, gave similar evidence to [that] tendered at the inquest some days [ago na]mely, that deceased was admitted to hospital suffering from a wound which [was in] the right lung, and that death had [resulted]. The knife he had seen was such [as] would produce the wound.

[In reply] to defendant, witness said that [in cases] of phthisis people sometimes lived [to a] considerable period with one lung []d with tubercles, provided these were [sewn?] up. Wounds in the lungs were not [necess]arily fatal, but were likely to prove [so even when as in] the case of the deceased no large [] vessel was damaged; if it had been [death] would have rapidly followed. The [fat]al wound had healed some time before [dec]eased died.

[Police Constable No. 4,] Herbert Servant deposed as to [taking] the deceased from a boat at Canton Wharf to the [Government Civil] Hospital. Deceased was wrapped in a large rug which was [covered] with blood. Witness afterwards [went on] board the *Helen Marion*, arrested [the] defendant, and received a knife from [the Cap]tain. Defendant was taken to the Police Station, where, after being cautioned by Inspector Mackie, he said, in answer [to the] charge, that "it was quite an accident."

He said he was in the forecastle on 13th of October cutting some tobacco, [when] Findlay [*sic*] came in with a bottle of [whisky] and said "You don't deserve any [of this]." Defendant answered that he [did] not wish any of it, upon which [Findlay] got up and struck him. He (defendant) told him to be quiet as he wanted no [quarrel] with him. Deceased then struck him [several] times with the bottle, upon which he (prisoner) picked up a bottle and struck [deceased] on the head with it thinking this might [stop] him, but it did not, for the deceased [laid] hold of him, and in struggling to get [the bottle] from deceased he accidentally stabbed [deceased] with the knife.

The prisoner was then cautioned that he [need] say nothing in answer to the charge [unless] he pleased. He reserved his defence, [and waived] his right of notice of trial, so [he] might be tried at the forthcoming [Criminal] Sessions.[330]

THURSDAY 17 NOVEMBER 1881[331]
LARCENY OF CLOTHING
CC Number 389 📖 p. 357

Kwong Akwong, a rice-pounder, was charged with stealing a pair of trousers from a house in Graham Street on the 16th instant.

It appeared that the trousers were hanging on a bamboo outside the door when defendant in passing appropriated them. A cry of "thief" was raised and the prisoner was captured with the trousers in his possession.

Defendant said a man brought him here to sell him and send him off to Singapore, but he refused to go. He had nothing to eat, so he stole the trousers to raise money to take him back to Canton.

Six weeks' imprisonment with hard labour.

---

[330] Listed as Case No. 4 in the Criminal Sessions -- December 1881 (HKGG, 31 December 1881, p. 1106), John Perry [sic] was tried for: 1) Murder; and 2) Manslaughter on 19 December 1881 and pleaded guilty to manslaughter. He was sentenced on 23 December 1881 to ten years' penal servitude. The Remarks note that a *Nolle Prosequi* was entered by the Attorney General on the first count.

The Supreme Court hearing, "In Criminal Sessions, "Before the Hon. F. Snowden, Acting Chief Justice", on Monday, 19 December 1881, was reported in *The China Mail*. (19 December, p. 3, c. 3.)
The China Mail also reports as follows the sentencing on 23 December 1881. Hon. Francis Snowden, Acting Chief Justice, sitting with a Special Jury, stated that the, "prisoner might be thankful that he had not been tried for murder, as the evidence given at the Police Court proved that the stabbing was not the result of an accident." The sentence was ten years' imprisonment. (CM, 23 December 1881, p. 3, c. 6.)
See note to CC No. 291.
[331] "Police Intelligence," CM, Thursday, 17 November 1881, p. 3, c. 4.

[ATTEMPTED SUICIDE]
CC Number 390

The same defendant was then charged with attempting to commit suicide in the Police Cells. Police Constable 280, Li Fan,[332] said he was on duty last night at the Charge Room gate, and when passing in front of No. 3 cell where defendant was confined, he saw him with his queue twisted round his throat, pulling very hard and trying to strangle himself. He at once called for assistance, and the European Constable on duty[333] came and removed the prisoner's queue and handcuffed him for the remainder of the night.

Inspector Lindsay, who was also on duty at the time, said he went to the cells when last witness called out, and he there saw the prisoner pulling very hard at his queue — which was twisted round his neck. When the queue was untied defendant fell back quite exhausted. He kept him handcuffed for the remainder of the night in the Charge Room. When told the charge that would be put against him he said "Yes, I should like to die; I have no money. I am very poor."

Defendant denied the charge. He just put his queue round his neck instead of round his head. He did not say he intended to die because he was poor.

Remanded till the 19th for the opinion of the Colonial Surgeon as to defendant's mental condition.

---

[332] The following is the complete set of reports which mention this policeman in *The Complete Court Cases*: CC Nos 390, 410. In these reports, "Li Afan" is also reported as "Li Afau". For an account of Li Afan's trial as head of a Triad Society, his jumping of bail and subsequent violent death, see Gillian Bickley, *A Magistrate's Court in 19th Century Hong Kong,*, pp. 219-222, and Gillian Bickley, ed., "Triads", in, "Some Nineteenth Century Hong Kong Court Cases", 2009/2010.

[333] Evidently, the "removal of the queue" was done to prevent further suicide attempts by the same method.

DRUNK AND DISORDERLY
CC Number 391

Joseph Periera, fireman unemployed, was charged with being drunk and disorderly in a boarding house in Lower Lascar Row.

Defendant admitted being drunk, and was fined $1, in default four days' imprisonment with hard labour.

A RIOTOUS YOUTH
CC Number 392

Walter Smith, 18 years of age, a seaman unemployed, was charged with creating a disturbance at the Sailor's Home on the 16th instant.

Mr J.R. White, steward of the Home, said defendant was making a great noise in the house at one o'clock yesterday afternoon. He was under the influence of liquor at the time and used very obscene language, and generally conducted himself in a most disorderly manner. Police Constable 11, Archibald McKane, said he was at the Home yesterday afternoon on duty. He did not see the disorderly conduct spoken to by Mr White, but when asked by him to take defendant into custody he used very filthy language, and resisted until assistance had to be sent for.

Defendant now had nothing to say further than to deny having used bad language.

Fined $5, in default seven days' imprisonment with hard labour.

NO LIGHT OR PASS
CC Number 393

Nine Chinese, embracing various professions, cooks, chair coolies, &c, were charged with being on the public streets at a late hour last night without either a light or pass.

One of the defendants had been somewhat saucy when apprehended, and was fined 50 cents, or two days' imprisonment; the others were each fined half that amount, or one day in durance vile.

LARCENY FROM THE PERSON
CC Number 394

Chong Asiu, unemployed, was charged with the theft of $2.15 from the person of one Leung Akit, on the 16th instant.

Complainant said he arrived from Canton yesterday afternoon. He came to look for a clansman, and as he did not know where to find him he walked westward. When at Lap-sap Wan he met defendant, whom he had never seen before, but at his invitation he went into a hut with him and remained there over night. He went to bed at half-past eleven, and at that time he felt a hand at his purse and on examining it he found his money gone. There were other two men in the hut besides complainant and defendant. He then at once said to defendant "My friend, return me my money," and he replied "This is truly a bad place." He again told him to return his money or he would inform the police, when defendant said "You need not trouble, we are safe here; this place is beyond the boundary. The police have nothing to do here." Witness identified the purse produced in Court as his. This morning he gave the prisoner in charge.

Defendant said he was a hawker of tea and lived at Lap-sap Wan. Complainant asked for a night's lodgings and he was allowed to come in to the hut. He afterwards accused him of stealing his money, but he had not done so; that in court was the proceeds of the sale of a coat. He told the Inspector he got it in an eating house.

Inspector Thomson said he caused the defendant to be searched when he was brought to the station this morning, and the moment the purse was produced containing the money, complainant claimed it as his property, and identified it by the character "Chung" on it.

Two months' imprisonment with hard labour.

SATURDAY 19 NOVEMBER 1881[334]
A ROGUE AND VAGABOND
CC Number 395

Tsoi Awa, a coolie, was charged with being a rogue and vagabond.

Sergeant Rae, who arrested the prisoner, said there was always a crowd of gamblers at work on the Praya near the Gasworks. Yesterday afternoon he caught the defendant while he was managing a game amongst a number of other men who made good their escape. On searching him he found $5 in silver, three $1 notes, and a number of copper cents and cash.

Defendant said he was not gambling, and the money found on his person had been obtained from a loan association. He saw a number of men gambling, but they ran away on the approach of the constable, and he alone was unfortunately caught. He lived in a house in Queen's Road West, but although he had been there two years he did not know the number.

Three months' imprisonment with hard labour.

TWO OLD CARD SHARPERS
CC Number 396

Un Ashui and Wong Asui, two women both over sixty years of age, appeared on a charge of being rogues and vagabonds.

An Indian constable found the old crones engaged with two others in a four-handed game at cards in the public street. On his approach the other two picked up the cards and some money that was lying on the ground and decamped, leaving the two dowagers to their fate.

They both admitted the card playing, but asserted that it was in the house and not on the street.

Convicted of obstructing the thoroughfare and fined $1 each, in default four days' imprisonment.

---

[334] "Police Intelligence," CM, Saturday, 19 November 1881, p. 3, cc. 3 - 4.

A FEEBLE CHARGE
CC Number 397

Edward Bracke, a seaman on board the British brig *Belham*, was charge [*sic*] with refusing to pay jinricksha hire.

It appeared that at an early hour this morning a cry of "police" was raised on the Praya, and on a constable proceeding to the place whence the sound appeared to come, he found the complainant and defendant disputing about a fare.

From the statements of both men it seemed doubtful whether the defendant had ever hired complainant's machine, and the case was dismissed.

MENDICANTS
CC Number 398

Ling Aho, 64, a married woman, and Tang Ashin, 78, a widow, were charged with begging in the public street yesterday.

Sergeant Hennessy said he had seen the two defendants daily for about a week begging in front of the Club, the Hotel, and the Central Market. The first defendant had some sewing in her hand, but this he described as only a blind. The second defendant now appeared to be both blind and helpless, but she was neither yesterday.

First defendant said she had been ten years in the Colony. Her husband was a street coolie, but she did not know where he was. The other prisoner was her adopted mother. They both denied begging.

Defendants were both ordered to be sent to the Tung-wa Hospital, with a letter to the committee giving their statements.

A RAID ON GAMBLERS
CC Number 399

Lo Achi, a tailor, Ng Wa King, a carpenter, and Un Awan, a cook, were charged, the first and second, with keeping a house for public gambling, and the third with acting as watchman.

Inspector Corcoran said he went with a party of police this morning to a house in Canton Bazaar, which he entered by virtue of a warrant he held. On account of the number of watchmen employed he had to adopt the ruse of landing his party at the Naval Yard, and, marching through there, was able to drop upon them unawares. The first defendant was arrested on the roof, the second in the house, and the third in the street. The ground-floor contained a quantity of the usual gambling paraphernalia, but no furniture. The second defendant had his tools with him, and was fitting up a strong door.

The constables who accompanied Inspector Corcoran gave corroborative testimony. First defendant said he only went to the house to look for a clansman, and when the police came he got frightened and took refuge on the roof.

The second defendant said he had been engaged to make a trap door and was at work when he was arrested. He lived next door, but did not know the man who employed him. Third defendant said he had nothing to do with the matter. He admitted a previous conviction for larceny.

From the evidence of an informer it was clearly proved that first defendant was manager of the establishment, and that the third was acting as watchman.

First defendant fined $100, in default six months' imprisonment, second $25, or two months, and third $50, or four months' imprisonment, $10 of the fines, if paid, to go to the informer.

MONDAY 21 NOVEMBER 1881[335]
DRUNK AND DISORDERLY
CC Number 400
Peter Carlson, seaman unemployed, appeared on a charge of being drunk and disorderly on the 20th instant.

---

[335] "Police Intelligence," CM, Monday, 21 November 1881, p. 3, c. 4.

Defendant it appeared went to the City of Hamburg Tavern about nine o'clock last night and demanded to be served with liquor. The manager considering that he had already had *quantum sufficit*[336] declined to supply him with more. This raised defendant's wrath, and he proceeded to violent measures to insure his orders being complied with, the result being that he was compelled to pay an involuntary visit to the cells.

Fined $1, in default four days' imprisonment with hard labour.

DRUNK AND INCAPABLE
CC Number 401

John William Harding, of the steamer Lord of Isles, pleaded guilty to being drunk and incapable yesterday evening, and was fined in the sum of twenty-five cents or one day's imprisonment.

LARCENY
CC Number 402

Tang Apo, unemployed, was charged with stealing four pieces of hard wood at Yau-mah Ti on the 20th instant.

Defendant was caught by a watchman at Yau-mah Ti at an early hour yesterday morning with a large piece of teak in his possession. He first betrayed his guilt by trying to run away when he saw the watchman.

He admitted five previous convictions since 1878, one of which *only*,[337] as defendant put it, was for larceny. Embezzlement and unlawful possession were however included in the interesting record, and

---

[336] Italics as in the original. This Latin phrase may be translated, "enough".

[337] "Only" is italicised in the original. The reason for the italics is indicated by, "as defendant put it". That is, it is not the writer who considers it a virtue that only one of five previous convictions was for larceny. It is the defendant who offers this value judgement. In contrast, the writer implies that he thinks one conviction for larceny is already too much.

he was now sentenced to three months' imprisonment
with hard labour.

DRUNK AND CREATING A DISTURBANCE
CC Number 403
Peter Lippe, Chief Mate of the German ship Mozart,
was charged with being drunk and disorderly on the
20th *instant*.

Police Constable 4, Herbert Servant, said he
was called to Graham Street at 3 o'clock yesterday
morning. There he found defendant making a great
noise saying that he had been robbed of $5. He was
taken to the station, where he was advised to go
quietly on board his ship, but instead of doing so he
followed a number of women about and commenced
blackguarding them. He was again advised to go
quietly on board, but preferred going to the station.
When locked up he made a great noise and smashed
up part of the furniture(!)[338] of the cell in which he
was placed.

Defendant had nothing to say further than to express
his regret for what he had done.

Fined $1, or four days' imprisonment with hard
labour, and further to pay 40 cents for the damage
done to the mahogany, or one day's additional
imprisonment.

THEFT OF CLOTHING
CC Number 404
Mok Mo, a jinricksha coolie, was charged with
stealing seven pieces of clothing on the 29th instant.

Un Sang Ying, wife of a cook employed by
Mr Holmes, said that she lived in Tank Lane.
Defendant lives on the ground floor of the same
house. Yesterday evening on going home she found
that a bundle of clothing which she had left on her
bed was untied, and several articles taken from it. On

---

[338] This exclamation mark is in the original. The implication is
that a prison cell cannot have much valuable furniture to smash
up. It seems to be Police Constable 4 who uses the term,
"furniture".

removing the bed quilt defendant was found concealed beneath. He jumped up and went into the cockloft. Shortly afterwards he came down and said he had not taken anything, and requested to be searched before he went away. After he left the house it was found that four jackets and four pairs of trousers were missing. One of the jackets has since been found.

No further evidence was taken and the case was remanded till the 28th instant.

WEDNESDAY 23 NOVEMBER 1881[339]
ANOTHER RAID ON GAMBLERS
CC Number 405

Cheung Shik Tsun, and four others, were charged with public gambling in Number 1 B., Peel Street, on the 22nd instant.

Inspector Mackie said that by virtue of a warrant he held he went into Number 1 B., Peel Street, yesterday afternoon in company with Inspectors Mathieson and Perry, and a party of police. On entering the house the utmost confusion at once prevailed. People were making their escape in all directions, some going by a ladder in the cookhouse on to the roof. The five prisoners were arrested as they were trying to leave by various means of exit. In the room were found the usual gambling implements, card boxes, counters, &c., and a quantity of cash strewn about on the floor.

Ching Akiu, a street coolie, said he went to the house on Monday afternoon where he saw ten men engaged at fan-tan. First prisoner was receiving and paying money, the second counting cash, and the other men, amongst whom were the third, fourth, and fifth defendants, were playing. Witness also played and lost fifty cents. He gave information to the police next day. He went there again yesterday, and the

---

[339] "Police Intelligence," CM, Wednesday, 23 November 23, p. 3, cc. 2 - 3.

same men were again playing when the police arrived.

Inspector Perry corroborated the evidence given by the first witness.

First defendant said he was a broker and only went to the house to look for a friend. He saw no gambling there. Second witness came in, and shortly afterwards the police arrived and arrested them. He admitted a previous conviction in 1879 of unlawfully purchasing a female child for the purpose of prostitution, for which he was awarded eighteen months' imprisonment with hard labour. One of the other prisoners said he was preparing medicine in the cookhouse when he was arrested, while the others were looking for friends.

First defendant was fined $200 or six months' imprisonment with hard labour; the others were each fined $50, in default three months' imprisonment with hard labour; and the cash found was ordered to be forfeited.

OBSTRUCTIONISTS
CC Number 406
Ip Achan, of 50 Queen's Road West, pleaded guilty to unlawfully causing an obstruction to the public thoroughfare by packing goods on a footpath on the 21st inst, and was fined in the sum of $2, or two days' imprisonment.

[OBSTRUCTIONISTS]
CC Number 407
Un Lam, a licensed hawker, appeared on a summons at the instance of Sergeant Hagarty, charged with unlawfully obstructing a public thoroughfare.

The Sergeant said defendant had been repeatedly warned without the slightest effect, and he had given the police much trouble.

Fined $2, or seven days' imprisonment.

A PUBLIC NUISANCE
CC Number 408
Li Alang, of Yee Wo Street, admitted having allowed an accumulation of filth to remain in an exposed situation in the neighbourhood of his residence yesterday. He also acknowledged having been twice previously fined for a similar offence, and was now mulcted in the sum of $10, or seven days' imprisonment.

ONLY TWO DRINKS
CC Number 409
Albert Carron, a seaman unemployed, was charged with being drunk and incapable on the 22nd instant.

Defendant said he had taken a couple of drinks and could not walk steadily.

Fined twenty five cents, or one day's imprisonment.

A ROGUE AND VAGABOND
CC Number 410
Un Apun, hawker, was charged as a rogue and vagabond and attempting to bribe a constable.

Police Constable 280, Li Afau [sic for "Li Afan"],[340] said he saw a number of men engaged gambling in Market Street this morning. Defendant offered him five cents to go away and take no notice of the gamblers.

Two months' imprisonment with hard labour, the five cents to be placed in the poor box.

---

[340] The following is the complete set of reports which mention this policeman in *The Complete Court Cases*: CC Nos 390, 410. For an account of Li Afan's trial as head of a Triad Society, his jumping of bail and subsequent violent death, see Gillian Bickley, *A Magistrate's Court in 19th Century Hong Kong,*, pp. 219-222, and Gillian Bickley, ed., "Triads", in, "Some Nineteenth Century Hong Kong Court Cases", 2009/2010.

STREET GAMBLING
CC Number 411

Chun Awo, a servant in a druggist's shop in Wellington Street, was sentenced to six weeks' imprisonment with hard labour for street gambling this forenoon, in Tung-man Lane.

FRIDAY 25 NOVEMBER 1881[341]
UNLAWFUL POSSESSION
CC Number 412

Wong Ayau, a marine hawker, was charged with unlawful possession of a quantity of oakum and copper on the 24th instant.

Police Constable 84, D. MacDonald said he met defendant at Hung Ham [*sic*] yesterday afternoon. He was carrying a basket containing oakum, old iron, and copper nails. When questioned as to how he got them he first said he bought them from a sailor and afterwards that he got them from some boys.

Fined twenty shillings, in default ten days' imprisonment with hard labour.

CAUSING AN OBSTRUCTION
CC Number 413

Tang Tsau, a hawker, was charged with causing an obstruction in a public thoroughfare on the 23rd instant.

Sergeant Hagarty said defendant had a large number of baskets on Queen's Road and East Street. Defendant and others had been frequently warned to discontinue obstructing the thoroughfare in the way they were doing, but without any result.

Fined $5, in default six weeks' imprisonment with hard labour.

---

[341] "Police Intelligence," CM, Friday, 25 November 1881, p. 3, cc. 3 - 4.

A ROGUE AND VAGABOND
CC Number 414

Lo Alah, a mat packer, was charged as a rogue and vagabond by acting as watchman to gamblers at the 24th instant.

Defendant had been frequently seen at work in the capacity of watchman to gamblers in Market Street, and was caught yesterday while passing signals to them.

Six weeks' imprisonment with hard labour.

STREET GAMBLERS
CC Number 415

Ho Asu, and Lo Achi, coolies, were charged with gambling in the public streets on the 25th[342] instant.

Police Constable 374, Li Achang saw a number of men gambling under the verandah in front of Messrs Douglas Lapraik & Company's premises. The first defendant was receiving and paying money, and the second was counting cash.

Both defendants were sentenced to six weeks' imprisonment with hard labour.

LARCENY
CC Number 416

Cheng Amui, a coolie, was charged with stealing a piece of leather, the property of the East Point Sugar Refinery, on the 25th instant.

Charles Larkin, a watchman employed by the company, said he saw defendant leaving the works this morning at half past six o'clock with the leather band over his arm. It had been cut from a wheel in the charcoal department where the prisoner was employed.

Defendant said that it was another man who had the leather and he threw it away as he approached the gate.

---

[342] It seems that the men appeared in court the same day as the offence.

Three months' imprisonment with hard labour.

SATURDAY 26 NOVEMBER 1881[343]
STREET GAMBLING
CC Number 417

Lam Achung, a hawker, was charged with street gambling on the 25th instant.

Police Constable 623, Kurrah Singh, said he was on duty yesterday afternoon at the Recreation Ground. Defendant had a number of men around his fruit stall gambling for money. Defendant pretended to sell oranges, but he is in reality managing the game.

Defendant denied gambling, but was convicted and sentenced to two months' imprisonment with hard labour as a rogue and vagabond.

OBTAINING MONEY UNDER FALSE PRETENCES
CC Number 418 📖 p. 357

Leong Achun, a hawker, was charged with obtaining the sum of $1.10 under false pretences on the 24th instant.

Wong Asam, a widow, said she lived in West Street. She met defendant on Thursday afternoon while on her way to the Western Market. He offered her two jade-stone drops for $1.60, but afterwards agreed to take $1.10 for them. Sometime afterwards she saw defendant in custody of a constable who called her and she produced the two drops she had purchased from the prisoner.

Li Atoi, an accountant in a shop in Wellington Street, said the jade stones were artificially coloured, and were only worth a few cents. If they had been real jade as he represented they would be worth about $4.

---

[343] "Police Intelligence," CM, Saturday, 26 November 1881, p. 3, cc. 1 - 3.

Ho Amang, a dealer in curios, said the stones were coloured to represent the best quality of jade. Real stones such as these professed to be would be worth $10, but they were only worth about twenty-five cents.

Police Constable 197, Wang Tsau, said he saw defendant offer the stones to several women for sale. He arrested him after a sale had been effected to the first witness, and he then offered to divide the money with the constable.

Defendant admitted having sold the drops to complainant, but denied having cheated her. She was willing to buy and he was willing to sell.

Six weeks' imprisonment with hard labour as a rogue and vagabond.

STEALING A GOLD FINGER RING
CC Number 419

Wong Ahong, a coolie, was charged on remand from yesterday, with stealing a gold finger ring on the 24th instant.

Kong Yuk Kun, a cook just returned from California, said that he was walking on the Praya Central on the afternoon of the 24th. His finger ring was too large and dropped from his hand and defendant picked it up. Instead of giving witness the ring he passed it on to another man who was standing by, and who at once decamped with it. He valued the ring at $28.

Police Constable 197, Wong Atsang, said he knew defendant to be a rogue and vagabond. He had been wandering about for some time without any visible means of subsistence.

Police Constable 586, Uttar Singh, said he saw complainant and defendant struggling together in Hollywood Road. They had hold of each other's queues. Complainant accused defendant of having taken his ring.

He took both to the station, and he produced a purse and pawn ticket which defendant had on his person.

Complainant, recalled, said the prisoner promised to return his ring to him, and he went up the hill with him, but seeing no prospect of finding the other man who had run away with it he seized hold of the prisoner near the Man Mo Temple and gave him into custody.

Defendant said he had not taken complainant's ring. The constable told lies in saying he had no employment. He had been searched and no ring was found on him, but complainant appropriated some money he had in his purse. He admitted a previous conviction for larceny.

Six months' imprisonment with hard labour, the first and last fortnight to be in solitary confinement.

PASSING COUNTERFEIT COIN
CC Number 420

Kwan Afuk , a carpenter, was charged with passing counterfeit coin on the 23rd instant. To Hi, an umbrella maker in Queen's Road, said defendant purchased an umbrella from him, at eight o'clock on the morning of the 23rd, for which he paid in silver dollars and ten-cent pieces. He returned several times that day and purchased umbrellas for some of his friends, each time paying for them in silver. In the afternoon of the 24th he came again and got another umbrella, making in all five. Soon after this witness sent his son to buy some steel ribs and gave him five of the dollars he had received from defendant in payment of the umbrellas. He came back and reported that the dollars were all bad. He then took the whole of the dollars he had received from defendant and a shroff pronounced them to be of copper. These were the only dollars witness had in coin, and he had made no mistake about their being the same he had received from defendant. On discovering the dollars were bad he told his son defendant was almost sure to return, and if he did so he was to be given in charge. On defendant coming back witness's son went out for a constable, and the prisoner, who evidently suspected something, make a rush out of the shop, but was pursued and arrested. When charged he offered to procure good dollars if he was released.

Witness's son gave corroborative evidence.

Leung Atsau, shroff at the Magistracy, [344] said he could detect good coins from counterfeit. On being shown fifteen dollar coins, those paid by defendant to complainant and others found on him when arrested, he pointed out eleven of them as spurious, being composed of copper and lead covered with silver.

Mr E. L. da Rocha, receiving officer Victoria gaol, proved three previous convictions against the prisoner, once in 1875 for larceny, and in 1875 and 1878 for uttering counterfeit coin, on the latter of which occasions he was sentenced to three years' penal servitude.

Defendant having been duly cautioned, said that as he was passing along Queen's Road he was seized by complainant who said "You bought these umbrellas from me, the money is all bad." He denied having bought any umbrellas from him, and then a constable took him in charge. Complainant wanted him to change the dollars, but he knew nothing about them. He came from Macao a few days ago, and was on his way to California. He never bought umbrellas from complainant. If he did so where were they now? He admitted having been in gaol before, but claimed to be a good man now.

Committed for trial at the next Criminal Sessions of the Supreme Court.[345]

---

[344] It seems that the shroff at the Magistracy here appears in court as an expert witness. See also CC No. 429.

[345] This case is No. 6 in the Criminal Calendar -- December Sessions, 1881. (HKGG, 31 December 1881, p. 1106.) Kwan A-fuk was tried before J. Russell, Acting Puisne Judge, on 19 December 1881 on four counts: 1) Uttering counterfeit coin; 2) Uttering counterfeit coin; 3) Previous conviction (summary); 4) Previous conviction (felony). He was found guilty on the first count, not guilty on the second count, and pleaded gjilty to the

WILFULL DAMAGE ON BOARD SHIP
CC Number 421 📖 p. 184

James Allen, a mariner unemployed, was charged with committing wilfull damage on board the steamer Crusader on the 25th instant. Mr W. Bryce, third engineer on board the Crusader, said he was speaking with defendant in the alley way, near the lamp-room on board, yesterday afternoon. Defendant was formerly second officer of the ship, but left yesterday. He complained of the Captain having stopped some of his wages, and threatened to take it out of him for so doing. Defendant then went into the lamp-room and smashed the lamp now in Court, which is generally used as the mast head light. Witness spoke to defendant about what he was doing, but he told witness to go to -----, and mind his own business. The lamps did not belong to his department. Witness then looked for the chief officer, but as he could not find him, he locked the lamp-room door, but defendant asked for the key, saying he was not done in there yet. Witness refused to give him the key, but gave it to the chief officer. The side lights were smashed during the three or four minutes he was looking for the chief officer. Defendant was slightly intoxicated.

Mr T. Occkerill, chief officer of the Crusader, said he was in the cabin writing yesterday afternoon when he was told something by the chief engineer. He at once went on deck where he saw defendant and asked him if he had damaged the ship's lamps. Defendant said "No." He then looked in the lamp-room and found the mast head light and the two side lights in court broken, and the glass strewn about the floor. He estimated the damage at L6 sterling. The lamps were the property of Messrs Baird & Brown of Glasgow. Defendant had been drinking, but he had his wits about him when he spoke to him.

---

third and fourth counts. He was sentenced the same day to seven years' penal servitude.

Defendant said he never had charge of the lamp-room key till yesterday morning when the chief officer ordered him to get it from the night watchman and with a padlock lock up the closet to keep the Chinese out. He did so and hung the key on a nail. A few minutes afterwards the chief officer bade him give it up for the purpose of issuing some oil to the coolies to clean brass work. He never saw it again till the third engineer had it. He met the captain ashore and was paid off. On going on board again he saw the third engineer in the alley way, and the lamp-room door was then open.

Sentence six weeks' imprisonment with hard labour.

MONDAY 28 NOVEMBER 1881[346]
THE ARMED ATTACK AT TAI TAM[347]
CC Number 422 📖 p. 369 (See also 📖 p. 370-373, p. 514, note 1083.)

Eight men, one of whom is described as a farmer, the others as coolies, were placed in the dock this morning, charged, first, with being concerned, with others not in custody, in an armed attack on the dwelling house of one Chang Au Fuk at Tai-tam village, and stealing therefrom property to the value of $128; second, unlawfully wounding and killing an Indian Constable named Easur Singh, No. 693, on the 27th instant, at Stanley in this Colony.

Sergeant J.C. Grant deposed: — I am a Sergeant of Police in charge of Pokfulum [*sic*] Police

---

[346] "Police Intelligence," CM, Monday, 28 November 1881, p. 3, c. 4.

[347] The following is the complete set of reports in connection with CC No. 422 in *The Complete Court Cases*: CC Nos 422, 444, 473, 482, 491. See also Gillian Bickley, ed., "The Armed Attack in Tai-Tam", in, "Some Nineteenth Century Hong Kong Court Cases", 2009/2010, for a documented transcript of other original sources related to this case, including Reports of the Inquest. See 📖, note 1083, for a reference to and description of the Criminal Sessions trial, in relation to this case, at the Supreme Court, and the sentences handed down. See also note to CC No. 491 below.

Station. On the 27th instant, at 3 a.m., I received a telegram from the Central Station. I took the European and Indian Constables in the Station with me and searched the roads and by-paths. About 5.20 a.m., while coming up the Aberdeen Road near Number 10 Bridge, I saw first and second defendants coming from the seaside towards the road. Soon afterwards I saw third, fourth, and fifth defendants coming in the same direction, but a little way behind the other two. I overtook these five men as they got on the Aberdeen Road near a place known as Kai-lung Wan. I asked them where they came from, and they said Aberdeen. I knew that was not correct as I had been on the road for two and a half hours; and besides, they did not come from the direction of Aberdeen. I searched the first defendant, and in the blue bag in court, which he had over his shoulder, I found the five charges of powder, two leaden bullets, percussion cap, slug shot, blue cotton trousers, black cotton trousers, and purse I now produce. I arrested the men, the first five prisoners, and took them to the station. On the morning of the 27th instant, about two o'clock, there was an armed attack at a small village called Tai-tam, near Stanley. An Indian constable was shot, and an inquest[348] is now being held on his body. I apply for a remand to enable me to produce further evidence, as I charge the first five prisoners with being concerned in the attack at Tai-tam.

Inspector Perry said — I charge sixth, seventh, and eighth defendants with being concerned in the armed attack at Tai-tam on the morning of the 27th instant, and I apply for a remand pending the inquest on the body of the Indian constable who was then shot, and pending further enquiries.

The case at this point was consequently remanded till the 5th proximo.

---

[348] See CC No. 444, for a reference to the inquest still being deferred.

A ROGUE AND VAGABOND
CC Number 423

Lai Asam, who described himself as a head coolie, was charged with being a rogue and vagabond on the 26th instant.

It appears that defendant was observed by a lukong on special duty accosting people in Queen's Road on Saturday afternoon, and offering them a ring for sale. On seeing the constable approach he walked off, and increasing his pace, gradually broke into a run. On being arrested, the ring worth about $1.20, and a bill, purporting to be for the sale of a ring for the sum of $85, were found on him.

Defendant said he bought the ring for $3.60 from a man in the street. He first wanted $8 for it, but afterwards reduced the price. Defendant pleaded that he did not know the man, nor where to find him. Had formerly been in European employ, but was now a head coolie.

Three months' imprisonment with hard labour, as a rogue and vagabond.

LARCENY BY A SERVANT
CC Number 424

Wai Acheung, a house boy, was charged with stealing several articles of clothing from his master on the 26th instant.

Mr J.H. Cox, of Messrs Turner & Company, said defendant was his house-boy. In consequence of the disappearance of several articles of wearing apparel he communicated with the police on the 25th *instant*. He identified the articles in Court, viz., towel, singlet, two pairs of socks, a pair of drawers, and a handkerchief, as his property. They were worth about $5.

Detective Sergeant Fisher said he went to Mr Cox's house to make enquiries respecting some missing articles of clothing, and from what the nurse told him he examined a basket standing outside of the defendant's quarters and found, amongst some wet linen, a pair of white socks marked "J.H.C."

Defendant claimed them as his own. Beneath the staircase he found the other articles enumerated. In reply to defendant, witness said he was quite sure prisoner claimed the socks as his. The other articles were not found in the house-coolie's room.

Li Alau, employed as a sick nurse to Mrs Cox, said that about the middle of the week her mistress complained of some clothes being missing. She saw defendant, and a Chinese stranger who came about the house, wearing socks matching those in the Court.

In defence the prisoner said he had never worn the socks. The washerwoman came to the house and washed the clothes just outside his room. The articles were found in the house-coolie's room.

Convicted of stealing one pair of socks, and sentenced to fourteen days' imprisonment with hard labour; and wages due to be forfeited.

TUESDAY 29 NOVEMBER 1881[349]
A SLEEPY WATCHMAN
CC Number 425

Santo Agar, a watchman, was charged with being asleep on duty on the 28th instant.

Police Constable No. 293, Wang Asam said he was on duty in Queen's Road Central between eleven and twelve last night. On passing Messrs Sale & Company's premises he saw no watchman about, and on looking into the kitchen he found the defendant asleep on a box. A European called attention to the prisoner and ordered him to be taken to the station.

Defendant admitted being asleep; he was sick.

Fined $2, in default seven days' imprisonment with hard labour.

---

[349] "Police Intelligence," CM, Tuesday, November 29, 1881, p. 3, cc. 4 - 5.

DRUNK AND DISORDERLY
CC Number 426

Richard Auguste, a seaman serving on board the French flagship Themis, was charged with being drunk and disorderly, and assaulting the police in the execution of their duty, and also with refusing to pay jinricksha hire on the 28th instant.

Police Constable 38, Richard Howell, said he was on duty in Queen's Road between seven and eight o'clock yesterday evening, when a coolie complained that defendant had refused to pay him for the hire of his jinricksha. Witness tried to induce him to pay, but without success. He only became very violent and struck him in the face, and on several other parts of the body. He lay down on his back in the road and kicked out with his feet. He was much under the influence of liquor. Witness's uniform trousers and cape were injured in the scuffle to the extent of $3.50. Assistance was called and defendant had to be carried to the station. He refused to walk.

Su Asam said the defendant engaged his jinricksha at Number 5 Station and he took him to a public house. Prisoner was very troublesome, continually rising up and sitting down again in the machine. On completion of the journey he refused to pay his hire.

The policemen who came to the first witness's help gave evidence as to the prisoner's violence on the way to the station.

Defendant said he did not know what he was doing.

Fined $5 for assaulting the police, in default seven days' imprisonment with hard labour; to pay $3.50 amends for damage to the constable's uniform; one-ten cents for jinricksha hire, or seven days' further imprisonment.

ROGUES AND VAGABONDS
CC Number 427

Yik Awong, unemployed, and Man Sun Pun, a coolie, were sentenced, the former to twenty one, the latter to fourteen days' imprisonment with hard labour; having been found engaged in gambling in the public streets on the 28th and 29th *instant*.

OBTAINING GOODS UNDER FALSE PRETENCES[350]
CC Number 428

E.F. Martin, a watchman, unemployed, was charged with obtaining goods to the value of $10.25 under false pretences on the 6th instant.

Hu Akong,[351] salesman in a piece goods shop in Jervois Street, said defendant came into the shop on the forenoon of the 6th instant, and asked to look at some grass cloth which he wished to select for a European. Witness sent a coolie with two rolls of cloth, worth $20, to go with defendant to show the stuff to the intending purchaser. Shortly afterwards the coolie returned with one piece only. From what he said the matter was at once reported to the police. The police sent for witness yesterday, and on his going to the station he identified the prisoner as the man who got away the grass cloth.

By defendant: — You never bought grass cloth from me before. You applied to me on a former occasion, and I asked the coolie to go with you, but I did not tell him not to part with the cloth until he got the money. The coolie told me you had not paid for the piece of grass cloth that was not returned. He has gone away to see his mother who is sick, and will not be back for three weeks.

Lai Achik, a servant in the shop, said he accompanied the coolie who carried the two rolls of grass cloth, with prisoner to the Roman Catholic Cathedral. Defendant went inside with one piece while they waited at the door, but seeing he did not

---

[350] The following is the complete set of reports in connection with this case in *The Complete Court Cases*: CC Nos 428, 449, 450.

[351] "Hu Akong", "Hu Akwong", "Afong" and "Tan Afun" are variations of this name found in reports of this case.

return within a reasonable time they gave information to last witness.

Remanded till to-morrow.

IN POSSESSION OF COUNTERFEIT COIN[352]
CC Number 429

Li Asang, a farmer, was charged with being in possession of two counterfeit dollars, and a quantity of spurious broken silver on the 28th *instant*.

Sergeant Lan Asui[353] said he was on special duty in Station Street, Yau-ma Ti, yesterday forenoon, when he saw defendant with something bulky under his jacket. Suspecting all was not right he asked defendant what he had got, and he replied "nothing." On being searched witness found three jackets, two pairs of trousers, and the silk turban now in Court on his person. In his purse were $3, three 10 cent pieces, and 5 pieces of broken silver now produced.

Leung Atsau, shroff at the Magistracy,[354] said he had examined the coins in Court. One was a good Mexican dollar, the second, a spurious trade dollar of the U.S. of America, consisting of silver and quicksilver, and worth about 20 cents. The third dollar was a bad Mexican, composed of copper and silver, and worth about 15 cents.

In defence, the prisoner said — I brought the dollars here to sell to people who collect bad dollars in order to extract the silver. The clothing in Court is mine. I was going to Yau-ma Ti to pawn the clothing, as there are no pawn-shops in Chang-sha Wan. My father told me the coins were bad. I am a farmer.

Remanded till 2nd December, bail being accepted in one surety in $25.

---

[352] The following is the complete set of reports in connection with this case in *The Complete Court Cases*: CC Nos 429, 433.
[353] Probably the same as Sergeant Lan Shui.
[354] It seems that the shroff at the Magistracy here appears in court as an expert witness. See also CC No. 420.

BEFORE FREDERICK STEWART, ESQ.,
December 1881[355]

THURSDAY 1 DECEMBER 1881[356]
INTENT TO COMMIT A FELONY
CC Number 430

Fong Atsin, a hawker, was charged with being found on the roof of a house on Praya Central with intent to commit a felony, on the 30th ultimo.

Pang Kaw, a servant in the I-Win Ku lodging house, Number 62, Praya Central, said that he went on the roof of the house yesterday afternoon at two o'clock to dry some clothes, and he found defendant crouching down there. He called up the shop coolie and they gave the prisoner into custody. Clothing had several times been lost from the roof on former occasions.

Defendant admitted being on the roof of the house in question. The next house is unoccupied and men are at work there, and he only went up to see one of the carpenters who owes him money, but as he could not see him where he expected to find him he went on the roof of Number 62.

Sentenced to three months' imprisonment with hard labour as a rogue and vagabond.

ATTEMPTED LARCENY
CC Number 431

Tang Aon, a coolie, was charged with being a rogue and vagabond on the 30th ultimo, [357] but, after

---

[355] **Note on December 1881 Court Case Reports in General.** There is no report of cases heard, "Before Frederick Stewart, Esq." in the CM for Thursday, 8 December 1881 or Friday, 16 December 1881. Monday, 26 December 1881 (Boxing Day) was a public holiday (HKGG, 17 December 1881, p. [1083]), and no courts sat on that day.

[356] "Police Intelligence," CM, Thursday, 1 December 1881, p. 3, cc. 5 - 6.

[357] There seems to be no report of the charge, here reported as having been made on 30th November 1881, in *The Complete Court Cases*.

evidence had been heard, was convicted of attempted larceny.

Police Constable 691, Mahomed Noor, said he saw two Manilamen in the Central Market yesterday afternoon, bargaining forfish. The prisoner stood beside one of them with a pair of scissors in one hand, and with the other under the man's jacket. He was just about to cut the man's coat when witness seized him. Prisoner at once dropped the scissors and put his foot on them. On the way to the station another man asked the prisoner why he did not throw the scissors away. Defendant said he had done so but the constable saw him. When he arrested the prisoner the Manilamen examined his pocket and said that he had lost nothing.

Defendant said the scissors did not belong to him. He went to the market to buy some small fish for his cat. He admitted two previous convictions for larceny in 1875 and 1877, for the latter of which he was sentenced to two years' imprisonment by the Supreme Court.

Sentenced to six months' imprisonment with hard labour.

LARCENY OF CLOTHING
CC Number 432

Li Akwai, a tailor, was charged with stealing an umbrella, five jackets, and two pieces of clothing on the 30th ultimo.

Li Shi Kwai, a tailor residing in East Street, said defendant was in his employ. Witness went to bed at four o'clock this morning and left the above clothing beside his bed, and the umbrella leaning against the wall. There is no bedroom separate from the shop, and defendant slept there as well as his (witness's) brother. Defendant was at work when witness went to bed. About six o'clock he woke up and found defendant gone, as also the clothing and the umbrella now in court. Witness went to the steamer to look for defendant, but not seeing him there he returned and found him in custody of the police.

Defendant admitted having taken the things as he had heard that his mother was dead, and he intended to tell his master by-and- bye. He now said his mother was not dead but ill, and she lives at Wan-chai.

Sentenced to three months' imprisonment with hard labour.

FRIDAY 2 DECEMBER 1881[358]
COUNTERFEIT COIN[359]
CC Number 433

Li Asang, a farmer, again appeared on a charge of being in possession of two counterfeit dollars and a quantity of spurious broken silver on the 28th ultimo.

Tsang Tsa-tai, wife of a man now in California, residing at Cheung Sha-wan, in Chinese territory, said defendant was her husband's cousin. He lives at a place called Cheung Cho Wan. His father is dead. (At the last hearing of the case defendant said his father told him the coins were bad). The articles of clothing found on defendant were her property, and her daughter's. She had them in a bag, but missed them on the 28th ulto. They were safe on her leaving for Hong Kong, but were missing on her return. She was positively sure the articles were hers, and defendant had no authority to take them, and if he had them in his possession when arrested he had them unlawfully.

By Defendant — He had pawned things belonging to me before without telling me, and I have always redeemed them.

Convicted of bringing into the Colony without lawful authority or excuse, one false or counterfeit coin, intended to resemble or pass for a

---

[358] "Police Intelligence," CM, Friday, 2 December 1881, p. 3, c. 5.

[359] The following is the complete set of reports in connection with this case in *The Complete Court Cases*: CC Nos 429, 433.

silver coin of the United States of America, knowing the said coin to be false or counterfeit.

Sentence, four months' imprisonment with hard labour, the first and last fortnight to be in solitary confinement.

SATURDAY 3 DECEMBER 1881[360]
BREACH OF THE OPIUM ORDINANCE
CC Number 434

Lum Atsoi, described as a driver, was charged with being in possession of a quantity of prepared opium on the 2nd instant without a permit from the Opium Farmer.

Sergeant Campbell said he went to Number 3 Tung-man Lane yesterday evening to search for opium by virtue of a warrant he held for that purpose. Defendant was sitting on a bed whenthe Sergeant entered, and immediately he became acquainted with the object of the visit, he put his hand behind him and upset a pot containing about four taels of opium. On the house being searched witness found two brass pans showing traces of opium, a bamboo strainer, a parcel, containing a quantity of opium refuse, and a pair of scales.

Defendant admitted having the opium and boiling utensils in his house, but he had nothing to do with them. Some man brought them from on board a ship.

An informer gave evidence to having seen defendant boiling opium at midnight on the 1st instant in the house Number 3, Tung-man Lane. Two balls of opium had been cut and put into a pan. He also said he had purchased opium from defendant about two months' ago.

Fined $100, in default six months' imprisonment with hard labour.

---

[360] "Police Intelligence," CM, Saturday, 3 December 1881, p. 3, cc. 4 - 5.

DRUNK AND DISORDERLY
CC Number 435

Thomas Sodaguest, a native of Finland, was charged with being drunk and disorderly on the 2nd instant.

Sergeant McKay proved that defendant was drunk and riotous in Queen's Road yesterday afternoon. He had a cane in his hand and was striking every one within reach. He was advised to go away quietly, but became still more riotous and noisy and made use of abusive language. He was then arrested but would not walk to the station, throwing himself down and kicking out in all directions.

Defendant admitted having been drunk and said he knew nothing about the matter. He had been here for two months and was out of employment.

Fined $1, in default three days' imprisonment for being drunk and disorderly; and $2, or four days' imprisonment with hard labour for assaulting the constable.

TOO MUCH SAMSHU
CC Number 436

Private P. Mackanery, Royal Inniskilling Fusiliers, was charged with being drunk and disorderly, and also with damaging private and public property on the 2nd instant.

From the evidence adduced it appeared that about half past eleven last night defendant and another man, not in custody, went into a house in Nullah Lane, Wan-chai. They were drunk and commenced knocking the furniture about by way of amusement. The occupants called the police and defendant was arrested in the street. Before consenting however, to submit to the kind attentions of the police he broke a Chinese constable's spear, and violently resisted his arrest.

Defendant called Sergeant Beales, of his regiment, to prove that he was in barracks at the time of the alleged offence, but the Sergeant only proved that defendant was present at a quarter to ten, adding that he might have gone out again afterwards without his (the Sergeant's) knowledge.

Fined $3, in default seven days' imprisonment with hard labour, and to pay 80 cents for damage to the spear and furniture.

UNLAWFUL POSSESSION
CC Number 437

Tsi Aki, a coolie, was charged with unlawful possession of a piece of wood on the 2nd instant.

Defendant was seen by a constable with a spar of timber in his possession, but when he observed the policeman he threw it down and ran.

In defence he now said he was only taking it home for firewood.

Fined 5 shillings, in default ten days' imprisonment with hard labour.

A PORTER BATH
CC Number 438

Chun Yung Kum, a cook, was charged with stealing a gallon of porter from the Commissariat Stores on the 2nd instant.

D.A.C.G. Hare, Commissariat Department, saw the prisoner fill a bucket with porter from a tub at the stores, and caused him to be arrested.

Defendant admitted having stolen the porter, but said it was only dregs and he intended to wash himself with it. He was employed by the Commissariat Compradore, and had probably acquired a taste for a bath of this description after the style of a celebrated Duke of Clarence.

Sentenced to one month's imprisonment with hard labour.

AN INFORMER
CC Number 439

Li Achin, a coolie, appeared on remand from the 1st instant charged with wilfully laying a false information before H.E. Wodehouse, Esq., Police Magistrate, on the 30th ultimo.

It appeared that on the 30th November the defendant laid an information before Mr Wodehouse, to the effect that on the previous day he had seen one Yuen Afat engaged boiling opium in house Number 193, Praya West. He said he saw about twenty taels of opium in course of preparation.

Consequent on this false information a warrant had been issued to Mr Santos, an Excise Officer, for the purpose of searching the premises and arresting the man against whom the information had been laid. On Mr Santos executing the warrant he found that no one of the name of Yuen Afat was known at the house, and that it was occupied by one Chan U Mun, a partner in the Opium Farm. It was quite a private house and he was offered every facility to prosecute a search but did not do so.

No further evidence was taken this morning and defendant was ordered to find two sureties in $10 each, to be of good behaviour for one month, in default to be committed.

MONDAY 5 DECEMBER 1881[361]
STEALING, AND RECEIVING STOLEN PROPERTY
CC Number 440

Wong Alui, and Fung Apui, coolies, were charged, the first prisoner, with stealing two buckets on the 4th instant; and the second, with receiving the same well knowing them to have been stolen.

Leung Akau, a shop coolie in the Fung-Wo mat shop, identified the buckets as his master's property. They originally bore the characters Fung Wo on each side, but these had been recently scraped off and others substituted. Early on the morning of the 2nd instant witness called the first defendant to bring him some water, and he gave him the two buckets for that purpose. Later on that morning from something that a fellow servant told him, he went to

---

[361] "Police Intelligence," CM, Monday, 5 December 1881, p. 3, cc. 1 - 2.

look for first prisoner but was unable to find him until yesterday morning when he met him in the Western Market. He asked where the buckets were, and prisoner took him to a house in the Hollywood Road, near the Po Lok Theatre. There he found the buckets outside the second defendant's door. This man said he had bought them from the first defendant for 20 cents, and if witness wanted them back he would have to pay 30 cents for them, as they had now been repaired.

The first prisoner admitted having sold the buckets. He had been employed to carry water, but the buckets were too big, and besides he was sick, and could not carry them. He admitted a conviction of larceny in September last.

Second prisoner said he bought them from the first prisoner, but did not know that they had been stolen. He put the characters on them which they now bore. He had mended the handles and that was why he wanted more than he had paid for them.

The prisoners were sentenced respectively to three months' and fourteen days' imprisonment with hard labour.

THEFT OF WOOD
CC Number 441
Wong Achui, a boatman unemployed, admitted having stolen a piece of timber from a house in course of undergoing repairs in Queen's Road, and was sentenced to twenty one days' imprisonment with hard labour.

PUBLIC GAMBLING
CC Number 442
A batch of three women and eight men, chiefly of the coolie class, were charged with public gambling on the 4th instant.

Inspector Corcoran said that yesterday evening he went with a party of police to house Number 39, Nullah Lane, by virtue of a warrant he held, and in a small room at the back of the house he found defendants engaged playing dominoes. As soon as they saw the Inspector they upset the table at which they were playing and tried to escape in all directions. The second prisoner, one of the men, was arrested as he was half way out of the window. He resisted frantically. The whole of the gamblers present were arrested. In the kitchen a ladder was found by which access could be obtained to the roof of the adjoining houses. The first defendant, one of the women, rented the house.

The defendants made the usual excuses, looking for friends, &c.

The whole of the defendants were convicted and were fined, the first in $100, or six months' imprisonment with hard labour; the eleventh $10 or twenty-one days; and the remainder $25, or three months each, with hard labour.

LARCENY ON BOARD SHIP
CC Number 443

Wong Amun, a stonecutter, was charged with stealing money and a quantity of sandalwood of the total value of $23, on board the steamship Lennox, while at sea between Singapore and this port, on the 3rd instant.

Yeung Ayim, a passenger by the steamer, said he was asleep on deck on the night preceding his arrival here, and about mid-night he had $22 in money in a jacket pocket, and $1 worth of sandalwood placed at his head. Before going to sleep defendant was sitting close by, and he, witness, was awoke by feeling his jacket being withdrawn from beneath his head. He then saw defendant running forward with it in his hand. The matter was reported to the Captain, but the property could not be found.

Lam Ali, another passenger also proved seeing the defendant running off with the jacket. It was moon-light, and he saw prisoner distinctly.

Defendant said he knew nothing about it, but was convicted and sentenced to six months' imprisonment with hard labour.

THE ATTACK AT TAI-TAM[362]
CC Number 444 📖 p. 373

The prisoners in this case were again brought up this morning, when Inspector Perry applied for a further remand till the 8th instant, as the witnesses were required at the inquest on the body of the Sikh constable still pending.

WEDNESDAY 7 DECEMBER 1881[363]
BREACH OF OPIUM ORDINANCE
CC Number 445

Wong Achoi, a fishmonger, pleaded guilty to boiling opium at Stanley without being in possession of the required certificate from the Opium Farmer. He pleaded, however, that he had shown the opium he had to the Inspector immediately on his producing the warrant.

Fined $10, in default seven days' imprisonment.

CREATING A DISTURBANCE
CC Number 446

Fung Atai and Chun Afuk were charged with fighting and creating a disturbance on the street on the 5th instant, and the first prisoner with being armed with a deadly weapon, he not being in possession of a night pass.

Defendants were found by a lukong in Centre Street. The first defendant was belabouring the second with a fighting iron. Second prisoner admitted five previous convictions, four of which were for larceny.

Fined $5 each, or fourteen days' imprisonment with hard labour, in addition six hours' exposure in the stocks at the scene of the disturbance.

---

[362] The following is the complete set of reports in connection with this case in *The Complete Court Cases*: CC Nos 422, 444, 473, 482, 491. See also note to CC 422 above and CC 491 below.
[363] "Police Intelligence," CM, Wednesday, 7 December 1881, p. 3, c. 2.

ROBBERY FROM THE PERSON[364]
CC Number 447
Wong Chan Wan, Wong Awai, and Ching Akan,[365] coolies, were charged with stealing from the person of one Chung Pak Shun, this morning, the sum of $30 in silver.

Inspector Lindsay charged the prisoners with having committed the theft near the Harbour Office at nine o'clock this morning, and applied for a remand to enable him to recover the stolen money if possible, and to make further arrests.

Case remanded accordingly till Saturday next, the 10th instant.

WILFULL DAMAGE
CC Number 448 📖 p. 185
Luigi Libretto, Band Sergeant, H.M.S. Iron Duke, appeared on a summons at the instance of one Mok Aping, a chair coolie, charged with that on the 5th instant [December], he did unlawfully, wilfully, and maliciously commit damage, injury, and spoil to a street chair to the extent of $1.50.

Complainant said defendant hired his chair at seven o'clock on the evening of the 5th instant, to take him from Queen's Road to Number 7 Station. Instead of paying him his proper fare he, defendant, proceeded to strike him and afterwards smashed his chair doing damage to the extent of $1.50. Defendant was not sober at the time.

Defendant said that he hired a chair on Monday evening, but not complainant's, to take him to the Central Station to visit a friend. Instead of bringing him here they took him over the hill, and on his asking them where they were taking him to they did not seem to understand him, but put him down and asked for their money. He told them they would not get any money until they took him to his proper destination. Defendant's coat was unbuttoned at this

---

[364] The following is the complete set of reports in connection with this case in *The Complete Court Cases*: CC Nos 447, 455.
[365] Also reported as, "Chin Akan".

time and one of the chair coolies put his hand inside his jacket and took all his money. Complainant and his mate were not the men who carried him, but the chair outside the Court is the one he engaged. He admitted smashing the chair after he found he had been deprived of his money.

Complainant's partner was called and gave corroborative evidence to that given by first witness.

At this point the case was remanded till Friday morning, the 9th instant, — defendant being admitted to bail in his personal security in $10.[366]

OBTAINING GOODS UNDER FALSE PRETENCES[367]
CC Number 449

The case in which E. F. Martin was charged on the 29th ultimo with obtaining goods under false pretences was again called in Court to-day.

Defendant this morning made a long statement in his defence, the leading feature in which was that he had been in the habit of buying things for Spanish seamen who could not speak Chinese. On the occasion on which he was now charged he got the complainant to send a man with him to take two pieces of grass cloth for approval, and that after the cloth had been rejected it was given back to the coolie, and he knew nothing more of it. As he was out of employment he went to Macao, with the intention of joining the Police Force there, but as he did not succeed he returned to this colony, and was arrested a few days afterwards. All the shipping compradores knew him, and he wished Father Burghignoli and Afong[368] called to speak to his character.

---

[366] There is no further report of this case in *The China Mail* reports of Frederick Stewart's court cases on this date.

[367] The following is the complete set of reports in connection with this case in *The Complete Court Cases*: CC Nos 428, 449, 450.

[368] "Hu Akong", "Hu Akwong", "Afong" and "Tan Afun" are variations of this name found in reports of this case.

The case was then further remanded till Friday morning, the 9th instant.

FRIDAY 9 DECEMBER 1881[369]
OBTAINING GOODS UNDER FALSE PRETENCES[370]
CC Number 450

E. F. Martin was again placed in the dock this morning, and [*sic* for "on"] charge of having obtained goods to the value of $10.25 from one Hu Akwong,[371] under false pretences, on the 6th ultimo.

This case, it will be remembered, was last called on the 7th instant, and was remanded till to-day to enable the Rev. Father Burghignoli and and [*sic*] a compradore to be called on the prisoner's behalf.

The Rev. Father on being interrogated by the prisoner said — I have no recollection of seeing a Spaniard about 11o'clock on the morning of the 6th ultimo.

Tan Afun, a ship compradore, said he had seen defendant come to his shop with Spanish seamen. He had a man in his shop who speaks Spanish and did not require an interpreter. He did not recollect any Spanish seaman buying grass cloth, and he had no knowledge of what defendant did with other shops.

His Worship held the charge proven and sentenced defendant to six months' imprisonment, the first and last fortnights to be in solitary confinement, the remainder with hard labour.

---

[369] "Police Intelligence," CM, Friday, 9 December 1881, p. 3, cc. 4 - 5.

[370] The following is the complete set of reports in connection with this case in *The Complete Court Cases*: CC Nos 428, 449, 450.

[371] "Hu Akong", "Hu Akwong", "Afong" and "Tan Afun" are variations of this name found in reports of this case.

WATCHMAN TO GAMBLERS
CC Number 451

Wong Akit, a jinricksha coolie, was convicted of acting as a watchman to a batch of street gamblers in Nullah Lane, Wan-tsai, about nine o'clock this morning, and was sentenced to one month's imprisonment with hard labour as a rogue and vagabond.

SATURDAY 10 DECEMBER 1881[372]
PIRACY ON THE HIGH SEAS[373]
CC Number 452 📖 p. 385

Wong Afuk and five others, the owner and seamen of the Kam-ki fishing junk, appeared on remand on a charge of piracy.

These men were originally arrested on charges of anchoring in a place not authorised by the Harbour Master, and further, with being rogues and vagabonds, and dangerous to the peace and good order of the Colony.

The first of these charges was withdrawn, and the more serious one of piracy entered against them.

Inspector Swanston said that from information he had received he now charged the six defendants with piracy on the high seas on the 28th and also on the 30th of November last. He now applied for a remand owing to two of the most important witnesses not being present.

Case remanded accordingly till the 17th instant.

---

[372] "Police Intelligence," CM, Saturday, 10 December 1881, p. 3, cc. 4 - 5.
[373] The following is the complete set of reports in connection with this case in *The Complete Court Cases*: CC Nos 452, 483, 508, 520. CC No. 452 seems to be the earliest Report of this case in *The China Mail*. The present writer has been unable to find any record of these men being charged, previous to CC 452, for anchoring in a place unauthorised by the Harbour Master and being rogues and vagabonds.

DOUBLE ASSAULT
CC Number 453
Kwok Ming Kong, a shopkeeper, and An Ashun, an accountant, were charged with assault this morning.

Mrs Theadora Francisca da Silva, residing at Number 58, Queen's Road East, said that the first prisoner assaulted her with a carrying pole this morning about nine o'clock in his own shop. He also assaulted her husband with a piece of wood.

No further evidence was taken and the case was remanded till Monday morning, both defendants being admitted to bail in $25 each.

ASSAULT WITH INTENT[374]
CC Number 454 📖 p. 205
Francis Wyley and Robert Whitley, Privates in H. M.'s Royal Inniskilling Fusiliers, were arrested on a warrant and charged with unlawfully assaulting Mr D. Byramjee and others with intend [*sic* for "intent"] to commit a felony on the 8th instant.

Lieutenant Davidson applied on behalf of the Military Authorities for a remand, and the hearing of the case was accordingly adjourned till two o'clock on Monday afternoon; the prisoners in the mean time to remain in Military custody.

ROBBERY FROM THE PERSON[375]
CC Number 455
The case in which Wong Chan Wan, Wong Awai, and Chin Akan, coolies, were charged with stealing the sum of $30 from one Chung Pak Shun, on the 7th instant, was again called in Court to-day.

It may be remembered that on the former hearing the case was remanded to enable a further search to be made for twenty-four dollars missing from the total amount alleged to have been stolen,

---

[374] The following is the complete set of reports in connection with this case in *The Complete Court Cases*: CC Nos 454, 456.
[375] The following is the complete set of reports in connection with this case in *The Complete Court Cases*: CC Nos 447, 455.

and to permit of more arrests being made. No further arrests, however, have been effected, nor has any more of the stolen money been recovered, and after hearing the evidence of the constables who arrested the three prisoners, the case was committed for trial at the Criminal Sessions of the Supreme Court.[376]

---

[376] Wong Chan Wan, Wong A-wai and Ching A-kan are listed in the December 1881 Criminal Calendar, as Case No. 8. (HKGG, 31 December 1881, p. 1108.) They were tried on 19 December, accused of Larceny. Wong Chan Wan was found guilty and sentenced to two years' imprisonment with hard labour. Wong A-wai and Ching A-kan each had a previous conviction (summary). Wong A-wai was found guilty and awarded the same sentence as Wong Chan. Ching A-kan was found not guilty by five jurors to two.

The following report appeared in *The China Mail*, Monday 19 December 1881, p. 3, c. 3.
"Supreme Court In Criminal Sessions
"(Before His Honour the Acting Puisne Judge, J. Russell, Esq.)
"Monday 19 December 1881
"Larceny
"The following jury was empannelled: -- Messrs J. I. Hughues, Chung Achoi, W. Scott, L. A. Rozario, C. Holliday, C. H. Siemund, A. Jorge."

"Wong Shan Wan, Wong Kwai, and Shing Akwan, were charged with stealing $30 belonging to Ching Pat Shang on the 7th *instant*.

"The man, from whom the money was stolen, was a farmer who had come on a visit to Hong Kong, and as reported in our columns at the time [CC 447 does not contain this detail. -- Ed.], while making some purchases the purse was snatched from his hand and the money either stolen or lost, a general scramble taking place when the money was scattered around. The three prisoners were arrested, but all the others concerned in the matter escaped. Two dollars were thrown on the ground by the second prisoner when arrested.

"The Jury returned an unanimous verdict of guilty against the first and second prisoners, and not guilty by five to two against the third prisoner.

"His Lordship in passing sentence said this was a bold case and came very near robbery with violence, and it was necessary to mark the gravity of the offence by giving a long term of imprisonment. The first and second prisoner would be sent to

MONDAY 12 DECEMBER 1881[377]
ALLEGED ASSAULT WITH INTENT[378]
CC Number 456 📖 p. 205

The case in which Francis Wyley and Robert
Whitley, Privates in H. M.'s Royal Inniskilling
Fusiliers, were charged with unlawful ly assaulting
Mr D. Byramjee and others with intent to commit a
felony on the 8th instant, again occupied the attention
of the Court this afternoon.

Lieutenant Davidson was again present [to]
watch the case on behalf of the Military Authorities.

Mr D. Byramjee said that on Thursday
evening last, the 8th instant, about a quarter-past six
when he was coming along the Kennedy Road in
company with Messrs Mehta and Billia, and when
near the last seat above the Racket Court, he came
upon four or five soldiers. Two or three of them were
stretched on their backs on the sloping bank, and two
others were crouching down by the side of the road.
Some of them had great-coats on, the others their
uniform. One of them had on [a] helmet. As witness
and his friends approached, all the men with the
exception of one, jumped up and stood in front of
them. One man did not stand in front of them, but
stood a little way off, and when asked for his
assistance he stood perfectly passive. The first
prisoner is that man, but I cannot say whether the
second defendant was there or not. One man caught
Mr Billia by the collar of his coat, but he could not
say if it was either of the defendants. Another man
caught witness by the sleeve, but he freed himself
from his grasp, and he and Mr Mehta ran. When
about ten yards off they stopped and called Mr Billia,

---

gaol for two years with hard labour. If they came up again they
would be certain to get penal servitude. Had the jury known, as
his Lordship knew, that the third prisoner had been eight times
previously convicted it might probably have had an effect on
their mind which would have produced different result."

[377] "Police Intelligence," CM, Monday, 12 December 1881, p. 3,
cc. 1 - 4.

[378] The following is the complete set of reports in connection
with this case in *The Complete Court Cases*: CC Nos 454, 456.

to come to them. Mr Mehta's chair was following, but neither Mr Billia nor Mr Mehta's chair coolies [c?/w?]ould come along. It was at this time that they called on first defendant for his assistance, but he remained quite passive. Ultimately Mr Billia got clear, and two of the men then chased witness and his companions as far as the second bridge. They were then loudly crying out for police. Soon after Mr Horspool and Mr Maconnochie came to their assistance from the opposite direction. Mr Horspool then gave chase to the men, and witness and Mr Billia followed. They met two men in dark clothes and on being asked for their assistance they at once joined in pursuit. Near the third seat, above Head-Quarter House, these two men passed the first defendant and asked him if he knew anything about the men who had attacked them, but he did not give any definite answer. The pursuit was continued till near the Magazine behind Victoria Barracks, when they met Mr Horspool returning. While speaking to him the first defendant came slowly along and was stopped. Mr Horspool enquired of him if he knew the men they were looking for, and where they had gone to. He said he knew them, but when asked their names he either would not or could not tell. Mr Horspool then asked him to come down to the barracks with them. The first defendant smelt of liquor, but he was sober. The other men were all intoxicated, more or less. Witness did not know what had become of the other men. (Mr Byramjee here illustrated how he had been seized — by one of the men catching hold of him by the left sleeve of his coat — not by the arm). Nothing was said to him when he was seized, but he could not tell what he had been seized for. On going eastward, about 5.45 p.m. at the commencement of the walk, they passed a number of men on the Kennedy Road, near its junction with the path leading to Head-Quarter House. One man was separated from the others, and witness thought it was the first defendant. At this time witness and Mr Mehta were alone. Two of them tried to throw their arms round Mr Mehta, apparently in a drunken frolic. He pulled Mr Mehta by the arm to enable him to avoid them. The men did not follow, and it was on the return walk that the as sault complained of took place. The first defendant kept by himself, and did not join in what the others were doing. He took no part whatever in the assault. Witness was unable to say whether the second defendant was present or not. He was unable to say whether the men were laughing at the time, or whether they were in a determined mood. They came upon them suddenly.

Mr D.R. Billia said that about a quarter past six on the 8th instant he was walking on the Kennedy Road where he saw Mr Mehta and Mr Byramjee occupying a seat. Before this he had passed four or five soldiers one of whom stood in front of him and held a stick over his head. Witness did not know whether it was in fun or whether he had any intent. The man did not speak and he did not know what he meant by it. Had he not ducked his head he would probably have been hit. He could not say whether it was a cane or a stick. Witness was unable to say whether either of the two defendants was one of the men he had seen on the Kennedy Road on the occasion. When he joined his friends he told them of what had occurred. On their way back he saw five or six soldiers, they were all in red coats, some of them were stretched on their backs on the bank, but he could not say if they were the same men that he had passed before. When the men jumped up one of them seized witness by the collar of the coat and said something which sounded like d----d fool. The button of witness's coat slipped from the button-hole and he stepped aside, while the man assumed a fighting attitude and attempted to stop him, but he avoided him and slipped by on the other side. Another of the men then tried to catch him and these two men collided and fell, and he then escaped. He could not say whether the men were drunk or sober. When they fell he escaped and joined his friends. The chair coolies gave no assistance. Taking all the circumstances into consideration, and looking at the thing calmly now that he had got over his fright, he could not say whether it was the result of a drunken frolic, or if with any malicious intent. He was unable to identify either of the two prisoners. It was dark and he only saw the men's white faces and that they were soldiers. He only noticed the first defendant when speaking to Mr Horspool afterwards, but he could not say that he saw the second defendant.

Mr D. M. Mehta said that on the evening in question when going out with Mr Byramjee a soldier jostled against him slightly. He had been drinking but was not drunk. Mr Billia joined them further on.

Witness then proceeded to detail what had occurred to him and his friends on returning from their walk, which was similar to that given by Mr Byramjee. He also corroborated Mr Billia's evidence as to two men trying to intercept that gentlemen. He heard nothing said by any of the men. He saw two of them come into collision and fall. They came against each other with great force, and would have fallen even if they had been sober.

Witness then left the witness box, and after closely inspecting the two men in the dock, said he could not recognise either of the two prisoners. It was very dark.

Mr. Hermann Aarons, clerk at Messrs. Vogel & Company's, said that on the evening of the 8th *instant* he was walking on the Kennedy Road at half-past six o'clock. When near the path leading to the barracks he met two soldiers. One of them was a tall stout man, and the other was short. The tall man rushed upon him in a violent manner and asked him who he was. Witness thought he was going to be robbed and defended himself by brandishing his stick to prevent him getting hold of him. Witness told him there was a policeman at hand, and he called out "Police," although he had no hopes of being heard. Witness walked quickly on till he met Inspector Horspool, but the men did not follow him. He told

Mr Horspool what had occurred and warned him, and he said he had already heard of the men. Witness joined Inspector Horspool in pursuing the men and he saw the man who had attempted to seize him make his escape. When he met the soldiers they were not running but walking along quietly as if enjoying an evening stroll. Mr Horspool told the shorter man that he was a police officer and took him to the barracks.

Witness having carefully inspected the two men in the dock could not say if either of them was on the road that night.

To Mr Horspool: I think the man who rushed on me had a cap on.

Mr G. Horspool Acting Deputy Superintendent of Police, said that about 6.20 p.m., on the 8th instant, he was walking with a gentleman on the Kennedy Road, in plain clothes. He heard a cried [*sic* for cry] of "Police" at some distance on the road. He at once turned to the eastward and when he had gone about 150 yards he met the three first witnesses. They were calling "Police," they appeared very much frightened, and Mr Byramjee told him something in consequence of which he proceeded some 300 yards further on when he met the last witness. Mr Aarons called out to be careful, as there were some soldiers on the road who had attempted to stop him. He also said something about a po liceman. Witness ran on till he came nearly to the path leading to Head-Quarter House where he came upon two soldiers. The first defendant was one of them. He was standing up with his belt on and properly dressed. The other man was sitting. He had no belt, and no hat, his coat was unbuttoned, and witness noticed he wore a dark shirt. Witness at this time heard sounds of two or three persons running down the footpath. He would say they were soldiers. He asked the two men what was the matter, and the one who was sitting got up and asked him what he meant. Witness told him he was a police officer, and that they would have to be careful of what they said. The four last witnesses came up directly afterwards, and when they got quite close the man who was sitting down made a bolt along the road. Witness left first defendant and followed the running man until he escaped down the hillside towards Victoria Barracks. Witness called out to an Artilleryman "Stop this blackguard," but they did not attend to him. On his, witness's, return he met the Artilleryman with the first defendant. Mr Byramjee, the first witness, then said, in the hearing of the first defendant, that he was with the party who had attacked him and his friends, but that he had taken no active part in the matter and had refused to render assistance when called upon. Witness then took the first defendant and handed him over to the Military authorities at the Victoria Barracks. The two Artillerymen and four witnesses came to the barracks. The Artillerymen said they thought witness had been only larking, or they would have paid attention to him. First prisoner was not sober. He said he did not know the other men's names, but they lived in Victoria Barracks. Witness could not swear that the second defendant was the man who escaped from him, but he corresponded with him in height and in build. He was tall and young, had a florid complexion, with dark hair, and taller than witness. He knew he was an Irishman by his voice.

Mr H. MacCallum, Apothecary and Analyst at the Government Hospital, said that shortly after six o'clock on the evening of the 8th instant he was walking along the Kennedy Road in company with a friend. When some little distance east of the first bridge they met a group of soldiers. They seemed to have been drinking, and were very merry. He heard one of them invite the others either to dinner or supper. Witness and his friend went as far as the Magazine, when he turned. On the way back he met two men running. The last one was shouting, "Stop that blackguard." Witness remarked to his friend that he thought they were soldiers amusing themselves. A little way further on they passed two soldiers who looked at them very intently, and from this he judged there was something wrong. Witness was unable to identify either of the two prisoners.

To Lieutenant Davidson: — The soldiers I first passed were not sober.

Sergeant T. Noble said he was Regimental Provost-Sergeant in the Royal Inniskilling Fusiliers. On the evening of the 8th *instant*, between seven and eight o'clock, he was present in the Guard Room when Mr Horspool and Mr Byramjee came there. A report had been made to the Sergeant-Major and he gave witness an order to get a lamp and search on the Kennedy Road for a cap that had been lost by one of the men. He got a lamp and searched the road, but did not find the cap. Two of the Regimental Police were left behind to see if any of the men might come to look for the cap, and to search for it themselves when the moon got up and it would be much lighter. They did so, and found the cap and brought it to the barracks. The cap was produced and bore the second defendant's regimental number.

T. Duffield, a private in the Regiment, said that on the evening of the 8th instant, about half-past seven o'clock, he was in his barrack room in Victoria Barracks. He saw second defendant come in without his cap. He was drunk and had his waistbelt under his serge jacket. His face was a little flushed with liquor but he did not seem to have been running. He came into the room, made down [sic] his bed and took off his jacket. He took his rug and lay down half an hour in [sic for "on"] the verandah. He was wearing a white cotton shirt. A corporal then came and took him to the guard room. Witness had no conversation with him, and he heard nothing to account for the loss of his cap.

First defendant said that on the evening of the 8th instant he was walking on the Kennedy Road for his own pleasure. He was alone and heard some one in front of him shouting for the police. He took no notice but walked on about his business, until he was apprehended by Mr Horspool. He asked defendant if he knew the men who had interfered with the gentlemen on the road, and he told him in reply that he did not. Defendant was then marched off to the Barracks and put in the guard room. He admitted having been drinking, but was not drunk. In reply to the bench: I heard no one ask me for assistance. Second defendant said that on the evening of the 8th instant, at twenty-five minutes to four o'clock he went to the Canteen, where he remained till five o'clock. He then went to his room, and as he had no braces on he put his belt beneath his serge. He returned to the canteen with another man, but left his cap lying on his bed. He remained in the Canteen till half past five but did not remember anything more until midnight, when he was woke up [sic], a prisoner in the Guard room, by the Sergeant-Major and Sergeant Noble, who asked him if he knew of anything that had happened on the Kennedy Road. He said he knew nothing at all about Kennedy Road, as he had been confined for being drunk. The Sergeant-Major then asked him his Regimental number and he told him. Defendant saw a cap in the Sergeant-Major's hand as he left the Guard room. The cap in court bore his Regimental number, and was his cap. He knew nothing more of this matter till he was brought up on Saturday. Any of the men who were about the room could see his cap on his bed. Any man could have taken his cap from the room. Defendant said he was very drunk, and did not remember being confined or anything that occurred that night.

W. J. McCormick, one of the Regimental Police, said that about eight o'clock on the evening of the 8th instant, he was ordered by Sergeant Noble to accompany him to Kennedy Road. After a time Sergeant Noble left him to continue the search, and he found it about half past eleven o'clock between the second and third bridges.

To the Bench: — Witness did not know that it was customary for one man to take another's cap. He had no doubt however that it often occurred, for instance if one man got the ribbons of his cap torn he might take another's.

Lieutenant C. J. L. Davidson, Royal Inniskilling Fusiliers, said he knew both defendants. The first prisoner bore a very good character; the second defendant also bore a very good character, and the charge against him of being drunk was the first against him in the service. He had served in the second battalion previous to his joining here twelve months ago.

To the Court: — I do not know that it is a customary thing for men to take each other's caps. No man is allowed to have another man's property, but I think it is a very likely thing to occur, that men may take the loan of each other's caps.

Mr Aaron, recalled, said that the prisoners resembled in size and general appearance the men who accosted him, but he could not swear to them. The tall man who tried to assault him most certainly wore a cap.

His Worship, addressing the men, said that under the circumstances there was nothing for it but for him to discharge them. He had gone into the case most fully both for the sake of the prisoners and of the public, and looking at it in every aspect as a jury would do,[379] he saw nothing for it, but to dismiss the case. At one time things looked very seriously against the second defendant, but from the place where the cap was found and where the alleged assault was made on Mr Aaron, who swore the man wore his cap, the man must have run a considerable distance before he lost it. He must look at the case as a jury would look at it, and there certainly was not enough evidence for him to convict them. There was no doubt soldiers had been there, and he would refrain

---

[379] In relation to another case (CC No. 656), Stewart sought a jury (a special sessions). For comments on legal matters such as this, see Garry Tallentire, "The Hong Kong (Police) Magistrate in the 1880s and 1990s", *A Magistate's Court in 19th Century Hong Kong*, pp. 147-158.

from making any remarks on the case, further than that they were now discharged.

DAMAGING A STREET CHAIR
CC Number 457

Luigi Libretto, Band Sergeant of H. M. S. Iron Duke, appeared on remand, charged with doing wilful and malicious damage to a street chair on the 5th instant.

Police Constable 37, W. McNeil, said he saw defendant in High Street with two chair coolies. He was in liquor and was very excited, and complained that he had been robbed of $25, but added that the chair coolies who were with him were not the men who had robbed him. He nevertheless wanted revenge out of them for the loss he had sustained. The coolies charged him with damaging their chair.

Fined fifty cents, and further to pay $1.50 for damage to the chair, in default seven days' imprisonment.

ROGUES AND VAGABONDS [Street Gambling]
CC Number 458

Mok Asang and Lo Ayau, coolies, were charged with being rogues and vagabonds on the 11th instant.

The two men were arrested from a crowd of street gamblers in Nullah Lane yesterday morning. The other men effected their escape.

First defendant said he was a new comer, and he was only managing the game while a friend of his was having his breakfast.

Second defendant said he was only passing when some one asked him to take up the cups and dice, when he was arrested.

Sentenced to three months' imprisonment with hard labour as rogues and vagabonds.

[GAMBLING]
CC Number 459

Chan Akung, a coolie, was also arrested at the same place later on in the day engaged in gambling transactions.

He pleaded that he was only looking on.

This man had four previous convictions recorded against him since 1874, two of being larceny, one of gambling, and another of being a rogue and vagabond.

Sentence — six weeks' imprisonment with hard labour.

LARCENY
CC Number 460 📖 p. 282

Ng Anam, a money changer, was charged with stealing a clock and two smoking pipes on the 10th instant.

Lai Su Lin, an inmate of a brothel in the Caine Road, said that on the evening of Saturday her attention was called to her room, and on looking to see what was the matter she found defendant there. He wanted to go away, but she would not allow him to do so until he had been searched. He then dropped from under his jacket the clock and two pipes in Court. She claimed them as her property, and valued them at $5.

Defendant said he thought it was Chinese custom to enter any room in a brothel, so he went in and wanted to have a pipe of opium. Complainant came in and wanted to turn him out, but he refused to go. He only came here two days ago from Shek Loong, and was now on his way to Foochow.

The mistress of the brothel corroborated the evidence given by the first witness, and defendant was ordered to find security of two householders in the sum of $5 each to be of good behaviour for six weeks, in default to be committed.

UNLAWFUL POSSESSION
CC Number 461

Li Ashun, a bricklayer, was charged with being in unlawful possession of a Government blanket on the 10th instant.

Police Constable 293, Wang Asum, said he saw defendant come out of a pawn shop in Hollywood Road on Saturday afternoon. He had a blanket in his hand which he said he had just redeemed, but on enquiries being made of the pawnbroker it appeared that he tried to pledge it. The blanket is the property of the police, and they refused to advance money on it.

Police Constable 14, Frederick Cookson from Number 9 Station proved that the blanket had been served out to him, and that it had been hung on a line in the Station yard to air.

Prisoner in his defence, said that he met a bricklayer on Saturday afternoon who sold him the blanket for eighty cents. Soon afterwards some one told him it was Government property, so he tried to get rid of it by pawning, but they refused to have anything to do with it. He knew the man who sold him the blanket, but if he was allowed a whole day to look for him he could not fined [*sic* for "find"] him.

Fined $2, in default six weeks' imprisonment with hard labour.

TUESDAY 13 DECEMBER 1881[380]
PREPARING FOR CHRISTMAS
CC Number 462

Lam Aping and Chung Akan, boys of 16 and 13 years of age, were charged with stealing a couple of dried ducks on the 12th instant.

Fang Asan, a dealer in poultry, said that at noon yesterday he had a lot of ducks drying on a piece of vacant ground below the Basel Mission Chapel. He was watching them, but on turning his head for a moment the two defendants took the opportunity to seize two of the ducks and make off with them.

Both prisoners denied the charge, although they were caught with the spoil in their possession.

---

[380] "Police Intelligence," CM, Tuesday, 13 December 1881, p. 3, cc. 5 - 6.

Ten days' imprisonment each, the last nine days to be in solitary confinement.

IMPROPER USE OF A HOUSEHOLDER'S CERTIFICATE
CC Number 463

Pun Aman, a shop coolie, appeared on a charge of attempting to use a Certificate of Registration on the 12th instant which was not duly obtained by him.

Mr James Parker, First Clerk at the Magistracy, said that at two o'clock yesterday afternoon defendant came to the office and produced a certificate from the Registrar General's office, to the effect that one Pun Yuk was the householder of Number 30 Jervois Street. The defendant offered himself as bail for a prisoner charged with unlawful possession, and represented that he was the person mentioned in the registration certificate as a householder. He said the certificate was his and that he had carried on the business of a draper for ten years. Mr Parker suspected all was not right and cautioned him very earnestly. On being pressed on the matter, he ultimately admitted that he was not the person he represented himself to be, and that the certificate belonged to his brother who had left the Colony.

Defendant admitted the charge, and said that he had come here to act for his brother.

Fined $20, in default six weeks' imprisonment with hard labour.

TUESDAY 13 DECEMBER 1881[381]
STREET GAMBLING
CC Number 464

Wong Afuk, Pang Akum, and Wong Kum Sing, were charged with street gambling on the 12th instant.

The prisoners were arrested yesterday forenoon while engaged gambling on the Praya near

---

[381] "Police Intelligence," CM, Tuesday, 13 December 1881, p. 3, cc. 5 - 6.

the foot of Tung Man Lane. The first defendant was managing the game.

First defendant said he had only gone to buy mangoes. He saw a number of men gambling, but they ran away and the constable arrested him. The second and third defendants were also arrested when the real gamblers made their escape. Second defendant admitted one previous conviction for gambling.

The first and second defendants were sentenced to three months, and the third to six weeks' imprisonment with hard labour.

[STREET GAMBLING]
CC Number 465
Ma Asam, a coolie, was also charged with gambling in the public streets on 12th *instant*.

Defendant was arrested yesterday afternoon while conducting a game of fan-tan in Market Street. The other men who were taking part in the game escaped.

Defendant said he was only taking a walk, while the gamblers ran away.

Sentence -- Three months' imprisonment with hard labour as a rogue and vagabond.

UNLAWFUL POSSESSION
CC Number 466
Lo Afuk, an unlicensed jinricksha coolie, was charged with the unlawful possession of a pair of shoes.

Defendant was seen skulking about in Wellington Street at an early hour this morning, and when questioned by the constable who arrested him he quietly dropped a pair of shoes from the sleeve of his jacket. He had not the slightest idea however of why he was arrested.

Fined five shillings, in default seven days' imprisonment with hard labour.

[UNLAWFUL POSSESSION]
CC Number 467

Wong Alo, a carpenter, was also charged with unlawful possession on the 12th instant.

He was seen in Hollywood Road carrying a spar of timber, but when he observed the constable he threw it down and ran into Square Street, where he was pursued and arrested.

He said he had been engaged by another man to carry the timber. He also admitted two previous convictions for larceny in 1879.

Fined L5 [*sic* for "$5"], in default six weeks' imprisonment with hard labour.[382]

ASSAULT
CC Number 468 📖 p. 326

Chun Awai, a boatman, was charged with assaulting a child about nine years of age on the 12th instant.

The boy, after promising to speak the truth, said he was walking along the Praya smoking a paper

---

[382] Wong Alo died in prison. See "Inquests", CM, 24 January 1882, p. 2, c. 6:

"An Inquest was held this afternoon in Victoria Gaol before the Coroner, H. E. Wodehouse, Esq., and the following gentlemen as a jury: -- Messrs G. D. Böning, J. F. Mardtfieldt and J. R. White, on the body of Wong A-lo, aged 28, a prisoner, who died in the Hospital Ward this morning.

"The prisoner was admitted to the gaol on the 13th December on a six weeks' sentence for stealing wood. Dr Ayres examined the deceased then and found him in a very emaciated condition, as he had found him twice previously within the last year. Instead of being placed on penal diet and condemned to hard labour, he was, on account of his debilitated condition, given an extra diet and only required to execute as much work as he was able to accomplish. He was removed to the Hospital Ward on the 10th of this month, suffering from bronchitis. He had recovered from that and had asked for some additional food, which was granted, and seemed to be improved yesterday, but this morning at half-past five, when the Hospital Warder visited him, he exhibited signs of extreme exhaustion. The Doctor was sent for, but before he arrived, at a quarter past six, the prisoner had died. During the whole confinement he had made no complaints, and yesterday was walking about along with some other patients. The Jury returned a verdict of death from natural causes. The prisoner's sentence expired today."

cigar when defendant slapped him so that he fell. On getting up he beat him again and threw him into the water.

Defendant said the boy threw sand at him, and he retaliated with orange peel. The lad fell into the water, and defendant at once stripped to take him out.

A Chinese constable said he saw defendant and the boy playing together on the Praya. The boy threw sand about him, and defendant threw the boy into the water. Some one jumped into the water and brought the boy out. When defendant was arrested he threw off his jacket to jump in also.

Sentence — Three months' imprisonment with hard labour.

DRUNKS
CC Number 469
Martin McGonell, a seaman unemployed, was charged with being drunk and refusing to pay jinricksha hire on the 12th *instant*.

Inspector Thomson said defendant was brought to the station about ten o'clock last night and charged with refusing to pay hire of a jinricksha, and also with damaging the machine.

Defendant said he knew nothing about it
Fined $1, or four days' imprisonment.

[DRUNKS]
CC Number 470
John Wilson, also a seaman unemployed, was charged with being drunk and incapable last night outside Number 7 Station.

Defendant said he was the worse of liquor and lay down.

Fined 25 cents or one day's imprisonment.

THEFT FROM THE DOCKS
CC Number 471

Tsang Asan, a carpenter, was charged with stealing a quantity of copper nails from the Aberdeen Docks yesterday morning.

Defendant was seen by a watchman with something bulky under his jacket, and on being searched was found with a quantity of nails concealed about his person.

Defendant denied the charge, and said he had only been charged because he refused to share some bananas he purchased with the watchman.

Sentence, six weeks' imprisonment with hard labour.

STRAYING CATTLE
CC Number 472 📖 p. 232

The Rev. R. Lechler, of the Basel Mission House, appeared on a summons at the instance of Mr Ford, Superintendent of the Government Gardens, charged with unlawfully permitting three cows to stray on Crown lands and destroy young trees planted there.

Mr Lechler said his cow-boy had allowed the cows to stray while he was taking his breakfast. He should not have done so, as he had been told to be careful not to allow the cows to touch the young trees.

Fined $2, in default one day's imprisonment.

WEDNESDAY 14 DECEMBER 1881[383]
THE TAI TAM ATTACK[384]
CC Number 473 📖 p. 373

This case again occupied a considerable portion of the time of the Court to-day. Most of the evidence given was precisely the same as that given at the

---

[383] "Police Intelligence," CM, Wednesday, 14 December 1881, p. 3, cc. 1 - 2.

[384] The following is the complete set of reports in connection with this case in *The Complete Court Cases*: CC Nos 422, 444, 473, 482, 491. See also note to CC 422 above and CC 491 below.

inquest. The following two witnesses had not been previously examined:--

Sawan Singh, Police Constable 584, said that on the 27th *ultimate* the deceased and witness went on duty at midnight. Deceased's beat was No. 1 and that of deceased was No. 2. [385] About two o'clock a.m. Police Constable Hill, who was on patrol duty, met witness and had some conversation with him, and then proceeded towards the village. About five minutes afterwards witness heard two musket shots, coming from the direction of the village. Witness ran in the direction of the sound, and while running he heard some eight or ten more shots. When near the junction of the footpath with the road witness saw Police Constable Hill standing there, and blowing his whistle. The deceased constable was lying near him. He ordered witness to remain there while he went and made a report. While standing there witness heard a noise in the bushes, and fired his carbine. The noise stopped but he saw no one. Witness spoke to the wounded man and asked him what was the matter. Deceased said four men fired at him and that he had fired in return. They had run towards Tai-tam village. Deceased said he was in much pain and that he was dying. Witness afterwards in company with Inspector Fleming and a party searched the roads leading to Victoria and Aberdeen. He afterwards returned to his beat. The sound which came from the bushes was "Tsau Tsau," ("run, run") —There were two or three distinct voices.

Kaiham Khan, Police Constable 562, said that on the morning of the 27th while in his own house in Stanley, he heard two musket shots. He ran out and went in the direction of the sound, and at the junction of the roads came upon a wounded man. It was the deceased. Last witness was standing beside him. He spoke to deceased. After some search on the road leading to Victoria, he returned to the station, and then searched in company with Chan Afoo, the

---

[385] One of these words, "deceased's" is a mistake for "witness's".

road leading to Aberdeen. They found a bed quilt on the road. It was lying as if it had been thrown down. There was fresh blood on it. About twenty yards further on they found another quilt. About forty yards further on still there were found a pair of trousers, a jacket, a handkerchief, and a child's headdress. They continued the search for another two miles, but finding nothing else they returned to the station. From where the blood-stained blanket was found for a distance of about a mile witness observed blood-stains, of about the size of a cent, and separated from each other by about a yard. About half-past one witness returned to the Aberdeen Road, and near the stone bridge found a hair pin. Witness knew two of the defendants (first and fifth) to be grass cutters at [a] place called Tsing Shui Wan (Shallow Water Bay) between Stanley and Aberdeen.

By Mr Holmes: —Witness had seen first defendant three times. Witness did not know where he lived. He had searched bundles of grass cut by the first and fifth defendants to see if there was any young branches.

A plan of the roads about Tai Tam, and of the house attacked, prepared by Mr G. J. King, Clerk in the Police Department, was then put in.

The case was adjourned till Saturday next [17 December 1881] at 11 o'clock.

THURSDAY 15 DECEMBER 1881[386]
LARCENY
CC Number 474

Wong Apo, a boatman, was charged with stealing a chopper valued at fifty cents, on the 15th instant.

Wang Fuk Chung, master of a cargo boat, said he saw defendant come on board at the Praya Central between five and six o'clock this morning, and after picking up the chopper walk off with it.

---

[386] "Police Intelligence," CM, Thursday, 15 December 1881, p. 3, cc. 2 - 3.

Defendant said he went to complainant last night to borrow a few candareens[387] from him, but as he was refused he took the chopper this morning.

Ten days' imprisonment with hard labour.

PUBLIC GAMBLING
CC Number 475

Chan Asz, and ten others, were charged with public gambling on the 14th instant in a house in Circular Pathway.

Inspector Mathieson said he went to Number 37, Circular Pathway yesterday afternoon in company with Inspector Lindsay and a party of police. He entered the house by virtue of a warrant he held, and found the whole of the defendants standing round a table. On the table were arranged a mat with dice, dominoes, counters, money basket, scales, cups &c., twenty cents in silver and a quantity of cash. The money was in a cup in front of the first prisoner who was managing the game, while the second prisoner was taking charge of the counters. Witness succeeded in getting into the house before he was observed, and was consequently able to arrest the whole of the men before any attempt was made to escape. None of the defendants belong to the house, and there was no furniture in the place except a sleeping bench.

Cheung Ting, a bricklayer unemployed, said he had gone to the same house on the 13th instant and there found over twenty men gambling. The first defendant was conducting the game on that occasion, and the second acted as banker. Witness lost $1.20, and reported the matter to the police the next day.

The excuses of the several defendants were of the usual varied character, playing for amusement, looking for friends, &c.

First defendant was fined $100, or six months' imprisonment with hard labour; the second and seventh, who had a previous conviction, $50 or

---

[387] "Candareen": A Chinese weight and money of account, equal to ten cash or one hundredth of a tael. (*Oxford English Dictionary*)

four months' imprisonment with hard labour; and the remainder $15 each or six weeks' imprisonment with hard labour. The money found in the place was also ordered to be forfeited, and $15 of the fines, if paid, to be given to the informer.

AN INCORRIGIBLE ROGUE AND VAGABOND
CC Number 476

John Murray, a seaman unemployed, was charged with being a rogue and vagabond.

Sergeant Hennessy said he found defendant lying asleep in Upper Lascar Row at half past two o'clock this morning. He had known defendant for the past fourteen months during which period he had been in gaol thirteen times for drunkenness and vagrancy, varied occasionally with an assault on the police. When not in gaol he slept in the street. He used to go to the Refuge, but that is now closed.

Defendant admitted that he was lying in the street, and also the previous convictions recorded against him.

Three months' imprisonment with hard labour.

NO JURISDICTION
CC Number 477

Cheung Anam, an accountant, was charged on suspicion of the larceny of $353 on board the steamship Helios on the 13th instant.

Chu Lam Ching, a passenger by the steamer from Malacca to this port, said he had a box on board with him which contained $353. He was on deck on the evening of the 11th, the day before arrival here, with a friend smoking opium. The box in question was only a short distance from where he was. It was covered with a mat, and when he went to his box it seemed to be all right, but he afterwards discovered that the hinges had been torn from it and were broken. Defendant was a passenger on board from Singapore. He slept on top of witness's boxes.

The case was on that occasion remanded till this morning, when, on its being resumed, Inspector Thomson said that the steamer was an Austro-Hungarian, and sailed under that flag. If the robbery complained of had taken place it must have been committed on the high seas, as the vessel arrived here about noon on the 12th, while the complainant reported the theft to the Captain of the ship at eight o'clock that morning, and at that time the vessel must have been from 30 to 40 miles distant from Hong Kong. From what the Captain had said to witness it seems that complainant had lost about $300 by gambling during the voyage; but whether any money had been stolen from him or not could not be ascertained.

The case was, under these circumstances, dismissed.

A PICKPOCKET
CC Number 478 📖 p. 358
Wong Achai, a barber, was charged with stealing $3 and some broken silver from the person of a junk master on the 14th *instant*.

Ngan Aming said that he was a passenger yesterday afternoon on board a steam-launch going from Victoria to Yau-ma Ti [*sic*]. When they arrived at the wharf he waited till the crowd of passengers had dispersed. A man belonging to the launch asked him if he had lost any money, and on his examining his purse he found the money gone. Defendant was arrested with the money in his possession, and witness identified it as his from the characters that were written on the wrapper.

Leung Anam, a seaman on the steam-launch, said that he saw the defendant with his hand under last witness's jacket while they were both on board as passengers.

Defendant said he saw the complainant take out his purse when he paid his passage money. He put the purse down beside him, and the last witness took it up. Last witness went ashore, and defendant followed him and asked him for a share, and as he would not divide the spoil he took it from him with the intention of returning it to complainant. He admitted a previous conviction of larceny in March last.

Sentence —six months' imprisonment with hard labour, the first and last fortnights to be in solitary confinement.

SATURDAY 17 DECEMBER 1881[388]
DRUNK AND DISORDERLY
CC Number 479

Robert Samuel Jerrard, seaman, on board the British barque Ribston was charged with being drunk and disorderly in Hollywood Road, on the 16th *instant*. Mahomed Hussean, Police Constable 520, said that defendant had received some drink at a large shop in Hollywood Road for which he refused to pay. He apprehended the prisoner, who then struggled with him and caused considerable disturbance.

Defendant said he wasn't drunk, and having only come out of gaol yesterday did not wish to go back. He admitted three previous convictions within the last three months for similar offences. Fined 20/ [*sic* for ?] or 21 days' imprisonment.

LARCENY
CC Number 480

Wong Aho was sent ten days to prison for having unlawful possession of two bundles of wood on Praya West, on the 16th instant.

DRUNK AND REFUSING TO PAY CHAIR-HIRE
CC Number 481

Robert Russell, seaman unemployed, was brought yesterday to Number 7 Station, drunk. Defendant was charged by coolies with refusing to pay chair-hire.

---

[388] "Police Intelligence," CM, Saturday, 17 December 1881, p. 3, cc. 2 - 3.

Defendant said he had no money. Fined 50 cents or two days' imprisonment.

THE TAI-TAM ATTACK[389]
CC Number 482 p. 375

The seven men charged with the armed attack on a house in the village of Tai-tam were again placed in the dock this morning.

Mr Holmes, of the firm of Stephens and Holmes, again appeared on behalf of the prisoners.

Chan Afoo, recalled at Mr Holmes' request, said he did not recognise many of these prisoners. He remembered the night of attack. The thieves remained in the house about five minutes. There was great confusion, but witness was not frightened. He was standing in a side room (witness here pointed out the room on the plan produced).

By Dr Stewart: —He knew the room.

By Mr Holmes: —He was standing there when the thieves entered. The door of the ancestral hall was opened by him and the prisoners had not come in in a rush, but one by one. The seventh prisoner attempted to stab him. There was a dim light given by a Chinese lamp in the doorway. He remained standing in the hall until the prisoners had left, and during that time was not frightened. Had never seen the seventh prisoner previous to that occasion nor any person like him. Saw the seventh prisoner again with the police on the 27th November. Had not seen any of the others at any time.

Mr Holmes then said he did not propose to examine the police and supposed that His Worship would probably remit the case, on the evidence given, to the Supreme Court. He reserved the prisoner's defence until then.

Police Constable Duncan, 21, [*sic* for "Duncan, Police Constable 21"] then corroborated

---

[389] The following is the complete set of reports in connection with this case in *The Complete Court Cases*: CC Nos 422, 444, 473, 482, 491. See also note to CC 422 above and CC 491 below.

Sergeant Grant's evidence as to the apprehension of five of the prisoners.

His Worship afterwards remanded the case till Tuesday next [20 December 1881].

PIRACY ON THE HIGH SEAS[390]
CC Number 483 📖 p. 385

Wong Afuk and five others, the owner and seamen of the Kam-ki fishing junk, again appeared on remand, on a charge of piracy. Four charges are now preferred against these men.

The first was that in which Lai Tsat Sing, a widow residing in the village of Ty Ho [*sic* for "Tai O"?], is the owner of a small boat with which she plies for hire. On the 28th ultimo she, in company with two other boatwomen, took a man as a passenger from Yu Kok to Mah Wan [*sic* for "Ma Wan"?]. On the return journey, after landing this man at his destination, she was attacked by a party of men in a fishing junk, some of whom she was able to identify amongst the prisoners in the dock.

In the second case, Chan Chung Hing, cattle dealer, of Tsing-mung, in the San-on district, said —I went to buy cattle at Tsing-mung on the 28th *ultimate*; but failed to make any purchases. When near Kwo-lo-wan, a boat came suddenly alongside mine. I was in the hold at the time. Besides myself there was a crew of three on board the boat, and a man named Tun Shun Fook a cattle dealer who was with us. Five men came down into the hold with swords in their hands, who commenced to rob the ship. They searched me, and took from me my purse, $25 in silver and 400 cash, and my bag in which they were contained. I also saw them take a pair of shoes, a blanket, and other things. The men came on deck, and cut the ropes of the sails, so that they could not be used, and after cutting the anchor rope, took away

---

[390] The following is the complete set of reports in connection with this case in *The Complete Court Cases*: CC Nos 452, 483, 508, 520.

the anchor. His Worship: Could you identify any of the men you see before you.

Witness: No, I cannot identify any of them because I have but one eye, which is not good, and it was very dark. We then made our way to Ping Chow, and the next day we had nothing to eat, as the pirates had all our food. We got to Ping Chow on the 30th *ultimate*, and the next day we left for home. I identify the hood, bag and shoe in court as some of my property which was taken from the junk by the pirate.

The third charge was made by Leung A-i a master of a stone junk, No. 252, belonging to Toong Kong [= "Tung Chung"?], [who] said[:] On the 28th *ultimate* my boat was anchored at Ping Chow to get in stone. We were asleep on board; I was in the cabin with my wife and daughter; and my crew of seven men were sleeping in the forehold. We went to rest at about six o'clock, and there were then no boats in sight. At midnight some men came into my cabin. I had no light, but I could see there were three men with swords. The leader searched me and took away 24 pieces of clothing value $28, four muskets, value $6, and also the rice bucket, rattan pillow, rice measure, brass ladle, blue cotton bag and the rice bag in court. They also took away my anchor, value $4, a rope, value $2.50, which I have seen on board the prisoner's boat used as a part of the tackle. They also damaged ropes on board the ship by cutting than [*sic* for "them"] to the extent of $8. Besides the three men who came to my cabin, there were others on board. How many I do not know.

Four muskets were here brought into Court which the witness identified as his property, taken as he described above. He was unable to identify any of the prisoners as being the men who plundered his boat. He never saw any of them before.

His Worship: Was anyone wounded on board your boat.

Witness: My wife's wrist was cut by having a jade bangle snatched from it, value $2.

By the fifth defendant: —Why did not you and your men resist the thieves.

Witness: There were 10 of them, and the hatches of the forehold were nailed down so that my crew could not help me.

The fourth charge was made by Puk Sing, master of the stone junk, No. 141, belonging to Hong Kong, [who] said: On the 9th moon Chinese, about the middle of November he had forgot the day but had reported it to the Police.

Inspector Swanston said the matter was reported, but he was unable to get the report as the office was closed.

The complainant continued: My boat was anchored at Ping-chow about a month ago. I went to sleep about dark, with my wife and seven children in the mainhold, my crew being asleep forward. About 10 o'clock I heard a noise, and I saw four men in the forehold, two with daggers and these two men holding their weapons at my chest asked me where my money was, adding, that I had better hand the money over or they would stab me. The fourth and sixth prisoners were the two men who did this.

By his Worship [sic]: —I had no light in the cabin, but the thieves lit matches, and I am perfectly certain that the fourth and sixth defendants were in the cabin. The men took away thirty-three pieces of clothing belonging to my wife and family, value about $35; three quilts, worth $6; a silver bangle, worth $3; and two pairs of ear-rings, value $2. I identify the two pans, opium pipe, opium lamp, also several articles of old clothing and bag as property removed. By the thieves: —A jacket belonging to myself I found the fourth prisoner wearing in Gaol on the 16th *instant*.

The first prisoner asked witness how he made up the value of $35 for the clothes he lost, to which the witness replied that two silk jackets were taken with two sets of silver buttons, worth $1.50; twenty pieces of black calico, value about $1.20.

Prisoner: Do you call an umbrella an article of clothing? No; I had forgot that. —How do you know there were ten men on board your junk? —I came up on deck as you were going away and saw about ten persons. What was the size of my boat?

His Worship pointed out to the prisoner that by the way in which the last question was put he admitted his presence there, and as he was undefended he would allow him to put the question as [to] the[391] boat. The prisoner wished the question to remain as he had stated it.

The witness then replied that he was unable to give the size of the boat.

In answer to the fourth prisoner, witness said he identified the jacket he (prisoner) was wearing in Gaol by the hole in the front. There were other holes in the jacket, but he could not say how many. The prisoner became angry on hearing this and addressed the witness in loud tones, but a threat from His Worship of being placed in the stocks outside silenced him.

The sixth prisoner asked witness why he did not report the matter to the mandarin at Ping Chow to which witness answered there was no mandarin there.

His Worship remanded the case till Saturday, 24th *instant*.[392]

---

[391] The word "the", here, is in italics. Perhaps this typographical irregularity arose because originally the name of the boat was going to be given (in italics), but was not in the end included, for some reason or other.

[392] According to *The Complete Court Cases*, this case was not in fact heard again until 31 December 1881.

MONDAY 19 DECEMBER 1881[393]
AN UNFOUNDED CHARGE [Keeping a public gambling house]
CC Number 484 📖 p. 340

Lau Aluk, a shopkeeper, was charged with being the keeper of a public gambling house on the 18th instant.

Inspector Thomson said he went to defendant's house yesterday evening to search for gamblers. The house had all the appearance of a respectable house, and on asking the informer where the gambling was going on, after some hesitation, he told him ["]upstairs["]. Witness went upstairs and found on a table the blanket produced, with dominoes, two trays, and two dice, but no fan-tan implements. While examining the house a cry of ["]thief["] was raised. There were seven or eight women in the place where the dominoes &c., were found. They had just finished a meal.

The witness believed the charge to be unfounded and His Worship dismissed the case.

GAMBLING INFORMERS
CC Number 485 📖 p. 340

Lum Afuk, seaman, Wong Atai, coppersmith, and Tse Acheung, coolie, were charged, the first prisoner with stealing an opium pipe and two brass smoking pipes, valued at $5, on the 18th instant; and the other two with being concerned in the same larceny.

Lau Aluk, defendant in last case, a shopkeeper on the Praya West, said yesterday evening the three prisoners came up into his house, to the top floor, and thinking they were customers he invited them to sit down and take a cup of tea. Shortly afterwards Inspectors Lindsay and Perry came in, accompanied by a party of police. As witness knew the two Inspectors he invited them also, to have a cup of a tea, but they refused and said they

---

[393] "Police Intelligence," CM, Monday, 19 December 1881, p. 3, cc. 3 - 4.

had come to search for gamblers. He told them they could search and see whether any gambling was going on there and they went up to the top floor. His family house was on the top floor, and in addition to his own family, there were also his wife's relations there, who had come from Macao for the Royal visit.[394] The blanket and dominoes in court were used by the women for their amusement. While the police were searching the house witness saw the first defendant pick up the opium pipe in court and put it up the sleeve of his coat when Inspector Thomson, who was also present, arrested him. The pipe was then dropped to the floor. Two other pipes were afterwards missed, one of which was in court, the other had not since been found.

Sergeant Rae gave evidence to the effect that he accompanied Inspector Thomson to complainant's house where they were met, according to appointment, by four informers. The police were led to expect that gambling was carried on and they had gone to the house armed with a search warrant. They found no one gambling, but while making the search a cry was raised that the first prisoner had stolen an opium pipe, and he was arrested by Mr Thomson. One of the four informers had since disappeared. The brass smoking pipe in court was found in a pawnbroker's shop in Queen's Road West.

Inspector Thomson said he went to the house to search for gamblers. He spoke to arresting the first prisoner when the cry of ["]thief["] was raised, and he saw the opium pipe drop on the floor from his sleeve. He had known the second and third defendants as gambling informers for the past twelve months, but he did not know the first prisoner.

Lo Asam, an accountant in a pawnbroker's shop proved the brass smoking pipe having been pledged by first prisoner. He knew the man well, as he often passed the shop.

---

[394] The "Royal visit" referred to here was that of the "Royal Princes", British Queen Victoria's two young sons, junior officers on the ship, *Bacchante*.

Sergeant Rae, recalled, said the information of gambling in this house had been given by second prisoner. He, and the second prisoner, and the man who had disappeared came to the station at six o'clock to conduct the police to the house. They went on a little in front and when the party arrived they found the three prisoners and the other man there.

First defendant said the house was a gambling house, he had lost $8 there. The opium pipe was thrown out into the street by the first witness. The inspector saw him do it.

Second defendant said he went to the house on Friday night where he played fan-tan, and lost $1. He gave information against the house to the police.

Third defendant said he accompanied the second prisoner to the house to arrest gamblers. He admitted a previous conviction for larceny in May of last year.

His Worship in sentencing the prisoners to six months' imprisonment each, with hard labour, said that the police were compelled to employ such men as defendants, but if they had been careful before, it would be necessary for them to be doubly careful in future.

SUNDAY CAROUSALS
CC Number 486

Hermann Kiske, Otto Olsen, and William Nelson of the American ship J. H. Bowers, was charged with being drunk and disorderly and assaulting the police on the 18th *instant*; and the first defendant with tearing a constable's jacket and causing him to lose his cap.

From the evidence of two lukongs it appeared that defendants were in the National Hotel yesterday afternoon. They were drunk and disorderly and the proprietor had to call in the aid of the police, and they in their turn had to get further assistance. Constables Servant and Hill joined the lukongs, and when the defendants were arrested the second prisoner bit Servant's finger severely, and as all three were violent the assistance of three man-of-war's men had to be obtained before they could be taken to the station. Hill's coat was damaged and his cap lost in the scuffle. He was in plain clothes at the time.

Defendants had nothing to say.

First prisoner was fined $2, in default seven days' imprisonment with hard labour, and further to pay $10.50 for damage to the constable's clothing, or seven days' imprisonment. The second and third were fined respectively $5 or fourteen days', and $2 or seven days' imprisonmentwith hard labour.

[SUNDAY CAROUSALS]
CC Number 487

Henry G. Nordland and William Walgren of the Russian ship Waltikka, for being drunk and refusing to pay jinricksha hire were each fined 25 cents, or one day's imprisonment.

[SUNDAY CAROUSALS]
CC Number 488

George Summers of the J. M. Bowers was fined 25 cents for being drunk and incapable; and William Nicol of the Blue Jacket was fined $2 or seven days' imprisonment for being drunk and assaulting the police.

THEFT OF CLOTHING
CC Number 489

Chu Asau charged Woo Apoo with breaking open a box and abstracting clothing to the value of $3 therefrom on the 19th *instant*.

Chu Asau, a coolie, said defendant and he lived together. He went out to his work yesterday, leaving defendant in the room. About noon, he heard something about defendant being apprehended, and on going to the Police Station, saw defendant and his box which was broken open.

Lai Apui said defendant and plaintiff both lived in his house. Yesterday morning at breakfast time he met defendant coming from the cockloft with some clothing in his hand; witness questioned him and he answered that they were his. Witness went to the cockloft and discovered the box now in Court broken up and everything taken away. He then gave information to the police.

Defendant said he owed some people some money, and getting excited did not distinguish his own clothing from plaintiff's. --Sentenced to 6 weeks' imprisonment with hard labour.

AN UNJUST ACCUSATION
CC Number 490 📖 p. 186

George H. Peters, seaman, accused George Oakes with stealing, along with another man, a bag containing $19 on the 16th *instant*.

George Henry Peters stated that on the 16th *instant*, he was in the Welcome Tavern, and was in the act of loaning a shipmate $1 which he took from his bag, when someone snapped [*sic*] the bag from him. Turning round, he observed defendant making for the door with something in his hand. He gave chase and followed him as far as the Sailor's Home, where he lost sight of him. On the 18th *instant*, plaintiff went in search of defendant, and while walking along Queen's Road saw him going towards the Sailor's Home along with two others. Stepping up to him, Peters asked defendant to accompany him to the Police Office. Defendant was then given into Sergeant Butlin's custody.

Sergeant Butlin gave evidence as to the apprehension of Oakes in Hollywood Road.

After several others had been examined Dr Stewart said that he was perfectly satisfied that defendant had nothing to do with the offence, and expressed sympathy with Oakes in his being placed in so hard a position. Dr Stewart also observed that the defendant left the court without a stain on his character, and thought that Peters had made a mistake and ought to apologise to Oakes for placing him in such a very hard position. The case was then dismissed.

THE TAI TAM CASE[395]
CC Number 491 📖 p. 376

This was again brought before the Magistrate, and some slight cross examination was made by Mr Holmes on recalled witnesses.

His Worship then committed prisoners for trial at the January Criminal Sessions,[396] and Mr Holmes reserved their defence.

WEDNESDAY 21 DECEMBER 1881[397]
BREACH OF THE OPIUM ORDINANCE
CC Number 492

Siu Akwan, a shop-coolie, was charged with having in his possession on the 20th instant, a quantity of prepared opium without a permit from the Opium Farmer.

Police Constable 85, James Forbes, said that he went yesterday evening to a house Number 12, Chi Mi Lane, by virtue of a warrant he held, to search the premises for opium. The defendant was pointed out by an informer who accompanied him as the master of the house, and on examining the place he found two earthenware jars, one of which contained opium, the other, what appeared to be medicine. There were other jars in the house, with opium dross and traces of opium in them.

---

[395] The following is the complete set of reports in connection with this case in *The Complete Court Cases*: CC Nos 422, 444, 473, 482, 491. See also note to CC 422 above.

[396] *The China Mail* report of the Criminal Sessions (19 January 1882, p. 3, c. 4; 23 January 1882, p. 3, cc.3-4) names three prisoners: -- Lai Aloi, Ng Akow, and Chun Atak. This enables us to identify the correct listing in the "Criminal Calendar -- January Sessions, 1882" (HKGG, 4 February 1882, p. 61), No. 11.

This states that Li A-loi, 'Ng A-kau and Chung A-tak were charged on five counts, the first of burglary, the second, third and fourth of larceny and the fifth of receiving stolen goods. The day of the trial was 19 January 1882 and all the prisoners were found guilty on the first count, and not guilty on the second, third, fourth and fifth counts. Sentence was given on 23 January 1882, and each was sentenced to twelve years' penal servitude.

[397] "Police Intelligence," CM, Wednesday, 21 December 1881, p. 3, c. 4.

Defendant admitted that the opium found had been boiled from opium dross, and that he had done so himself. He asserted however that it was only a medicine and could not be smoked. The dross had accumulated during the last twelve months.

Ho Aun, servant unemployed, said he had purchased opium from the defendant on the 18th instant, and next day he laid an information with the Opium Farmer at whose instance the search warrant had been issued.

Defendant was fined $25, in default six months' imprisonment with hard labour, and the opium found by the police was ordered to be forfeited to the Opium Farmer.

A BATCH OF GAMBLERS
CC Number 493

Un Achi, a baker, and fifteen others of the coolie class, were charged with public gambling on the 20th instant.

This was one of the usual cases in which a party of police under Inspector Thomson made a raid on a house, Number 107, First Street, and a gang of public gamblers was arrested. There was no furniture whatever in the place, and when the police arrived the men were found squatting on the floor busily engaged in their game and surrounded with the usual gambling implements. One of the defendants had been twice in gaol for gambling, and another had been twice convicted of a similar offence and once of larceny.

The first defendant said he had had a quarrel with the man who informed against him about three months' ago, and seemed to attribute this to spite on his part. The others made the usual trivial excuses for their presence, one only admitting that he was there gambling.

They were sentenced —one man, the master, to pay a fine of $50,[398] or four months' imprisonment with hard labour; three of the old offenders, to a fine of $25 each, or two months' imprisonment with hard labour; and the remainder to a fine of $10, or one month's imprisonment with hard labour; $5 of the fines, if paid, to be given to the informer.

A PICKPOCKET
CC Number 494 p. 283
Lan Aching, a hawker, was charged with picking the pocket of one Tam Awai, on the 20th instant.

Defendant was caught about eight o'clock yesterday evening in the Recreation Ground plying his trade on Tam Awai. He inserted his hand into complainant's pocket and succeeded in abstracting a handkerchief containing two $1 notes.

Defendant said he was standing near complainant when the cry of ["]thief["] was raised and he was arrested. He did not pick the man's pocket but he believed some one else did. He only came here a short time ago intending to become a hawker, but he had not yet commenced business in that line. In the meantime he had sent his wife to a brothel.

Three months' imprisonment with hard labour.

UNLAWFUL POSSESSION
CC Number 495
Tsang Afuk, a hawker, pleaded guilty to being in the unlawful possession of a piece of wood on the 20th instant. He also admitted four previous convictions of larceny and unlawful possession within a period of fifteen months, and was now sentenced to six months' imprisonment with hard labour.

---

[398] Under Ordinance No. 9 of 1876 (para. 4), the maximum fine for the "Master" was $200.

A ROGUE AND VAGABOND
CC Number 496

Chun Afuk, a cook, was charged with being a rogue and vagabond on the 20th instant.

Sergeant Pang Aloi said he saw the defendant following two seamen in the Queen's Road yesterday evening. He watched his operations for quite an hour and saw that when the seamen went into any shop he waited outside, and when they came out he followed closely behind them, and on one occasion he tried one of the men's pockets, but drew a blank.

Defendant admitted two previous convictions of larceny, and was now awarded three months' imprisonment with hard labour.

FRIDAY 23 DECEMBER 1881[399]
ALLEGED ATTEMPTED SUICIDE
CC Number 497

Patrick Doyle, of Ireland, described as a Surveyor, appeared on a charge of attempting to commit suicide on the 17th instant.

It appears that in this case defendant went to the bar of the Stag Hotel on the evening of the 17th instant and was served with a drink. A second was called for, but as he was then showing symptoms of already having had more than was good for him, the bar-keeper, Mr Snelling, declined to supply him with anything more. Upon this defendant drew from his pocket a small bottle which he placed to his lips, and after swallowing the contents, insensibility almost immediately ensued. He was then handed over to the police, who sent him to the Government Civil Hospital, where he has since remained under treatment.

On the case being called to day, no evidence to support the charge was produced, and His Worship dismissed the case.

---

[399] "Police Intelligence," CM, Friday, 23 December 1881, p. 3, c. 6.

SATURDAY 24 DECEMBER 1881[400]
ATTEMPTING TO STEAL A GOLD BANGLE
CC Number 498 📖 p. 233

Ho Apak was brought up on a charge of stealing a gold bangle, value $35, from Ip Apak, on the 23rd *instant* in Wing-lok Street.

Ip Apak, a fishmonger, said that while he was taking part in carrying the dragon in the fishmongers' procession[401] some one attempted to snatch the bangle from his arm but was prevented from doing this by it being attached to his arm by a string. He could not swear defendant was the person.

Soonderam Ramasammy, a master at the Wanchai Government School, while looking at the procession heard a cry of "stealing a bangle." He ran to the spot and seized a man whom some person pointed out. Defendant was not the man he handed

---

[400] "Police Intelligence," CM, Saturday, 24 December 1881, p. 3, c. 5.

[401] See "The Chinese Illuminations", CM, 23 December 1881, p. 3, c. 5.

"Last night was certainly not favourable for illuminations, being so drizzly and wet, that the roads were greasy and slippery in the last degree. The fireworks in the Parade Ground began about seven o'clock and were of various descriptions, the designs being mostly of a rather ludicrous and amusing design.

"The procession was the feature of the night's proceedings, and was certainly rather elaborate; -- fishes were supplied, as we mentioned, by the fish lans; the porkers, &c., by the butchers; and various other designs were carried by coolies, -- all the devices being illuminated by candles. A dragon, of monstrous length, wound up the whole affair. This in the crowding of the street was occasionally apt to get shortened and crammed up considerably, but its sinuous length of tinsel was a great attraction. ___

"Along Queen's Road decorations were, at intervals, suspended in front of various places of business. The Man On Insurance Office was tastefully illuminated, and otherwise by having plants placed all round the entrances; but the great point of the illumination was Bonham Strand, which was covered in from the one end to the other, and at intervals of about six yards were suspended historic figures sketches, which were done up in a very pretty and artistic style. Between the different sketches were 8l lamps which showed the figures to perfection, and certainly made the street brilliant in the extreme."

over to a European Police Constable, but witness had seen defendant before this time snatch at the bangle in Court.

Donald McDonald, Police Constable 84, apprehended defendant, whom he found in the custody of some Chinese, belonging to the procession, and who were using him roughly.

Defendant said he went to witness the procession and saw some people fighting with complainant's party, when some one seized him and he fell down. He had no employment at present.

Sentence of four months' imprisonment with hard labour was imposed.

GAMBLING
CC Number 499
Twenty Chinese were charged with gambling.

Inspector Thomson testified to going to 63, Second Street last night, and finding the prisoners gambling there; on his appearance they at once made a rush for the windows, by which several of them escaped. Counting sticks, a counting board, scales, cards, and dice were found on the premises.

The first defendant was fined $100, or six months' imprisonment with hard labour; the second, third, fourth and seventh were fined $40 each, or four months; the remainder $15 each, or six weeks in gaol with hard labour. The money was ordered to be confiscated,[402] and $10 was to go to the informer.

TUESDAY 27 DECEMBER 1881[403]
THROWING A PARCEL INTO GAOL
CC Number 500
Yesterday, while Peer Bhoy, Police Constable 613, was standing in Old Bailey Street he observed Li Aheung throw a parcel over the Gaol wall. He then followed and arrested him.

---

[402] Confiscating the money / security for money was authorized under Ordinance No. 9 of 1876, para. 7.
[403] "Police Intelligence," CM, Tuesday, 27 December 1881, p. 3, c. 5.

William Stanton, a warder, said he went with Peer Bhoy to the spot where he had seen the defendant throw the parcel over, but found nothing. Witness said it was very difficult to discover whether anything had been thrown over or not, as the prisoners were at work in the yard. Defendant was discharged on the 24th *instant* having just completed a sentence of 5 years' imprisonment.

Defendant said if he had thrown anything into the gaol it would have been found.

Fined $10 or 6 weeks' imprisonment with hard labour.

STREET GAMBLING
CC Number 501

Lo Apün and Chun Ayun were charged with street gambling before the Man Mo Temple in Hollywood Road yesterday. Lo Apün said he was playing for amusement and Ayun said he was only looking on, when they were arrested.

Sentence of 21 days' imprisonment with hard labour was imposed on each.

SNATCHING CAPS
CC Number 502

Pun Aching was charged with stealing two caps on the 24th *instant*.

Lai Shun stated that while returning from the fireworks[404] with his daughter in his arms, some one snatched his and his daughter's caps. Defendant was stopped by a Police Constablewhen the caps were found close to him. Alla Dhad, Police Constable 647,

---

[404] See "The Illuminations", CM, 27 December 1881, p. 3, cc. 1-4, c. 2. "The pyrotechnic display on the Parade Ground was of a similar description to those of the two preceding evenings and included rockets, crackers, and Catherine wheels, which kept up an incessant sputtering, at times resembling the file firing of an infantry platoon. Four large-sized stands were erected and provided with seats for the accommodation of ladies, which were fully occupied during the entire display, while the grounds of St John's Cathedral and every available spot were crowded by eager and delighted sight-seers."

was standing at the Clock Tower when he saw defendant snatch the caps from off complainant's and his daughter's head. Defendant in his defence said he was looking at the procession[405] and while walking away was seized by a policeman. Six weeks' imprisonment with hard labour.

STEALING TWO JACKETS AND A DOLLAR BANK NOTE
CC Number 503

Chan Man charged Lum Atak with stealing from his boat at the wharf, off the Harbour Office, two jackets and a dollar bank note.

Defendant denied the charge and said he was never near the boat. He was sentenced to two months' imprisonment with hard labour.

---

[405] See "The Illuminations", CM, 27 December 1881, p. 3, cc. 1-4, c. 3.

"The procession, which so hugely delighted the Chinese onlookers, was certainly of a unique description. The most noteworthy part of it was the designs of fishes illuminated inside with small lamps, and which were wonderful as specimens of constructive art. The immense, and somewhat unwieldy dragon kept up its antics during the most of the night to the apparently intense delight of the Chinese. Ornamental and illuminated pigs, and other animals were prominent in the procession. During the evening the Governor and party went through the streets and had a look at the illuminations and the procession.

The good humour of the vast crowds who moved among the street during the evening was most commendable, and we do not think that any European community of the same mixed class could have behaved in such an orderly and decent manner for such a length of time and similarly engaged. No case of crime of a serious nature is reported. . . . About twenty men from the Sailors' Home received employment, in case of emergencies, on the Fire Brigade, and were, we understand, most thankful for the favour of being allowed to do duty."

A PICK POCKET
CC Number 504

Lau-I while in Queen's Road West looking at the procession[406] had his pocket picked of his purse by the defendant Lo Ahin.

Defendant said the complainant trod on his foot, when he turned round and scolded him. Complainant then gave him in charge for stealing money. Sentenced to three months' imprisonment with hard labour.

ROGUE AND VAGABOND
CC Number 505

Lam Yau was charged with being a rogue and vagabond on the 17th instant.

Inspector Perry said he went to the hill side, above Kennedy Road, at 1 a.m. on the 27th instant, where he found defendant and three others in a mat-shed. The Inspector knew defendant as an old offender, who was branded and deported[407] in May 1874, and asked him if he had any employment, to which he answered that he had come from Canton four days ago. The two chisels in Court the Inspector had discovered in a box in which defendant was lying, but which he (defendant) knew nothing about.

Defendant acknowledged that he was a bad fellow, but had turned over a new leaf. He said he had been in gaol four times already. Sentence of three months with hard labour was passed.

---

[406] For further information about, "the procession", see CC 502 and related note above.

[407] For some account of the branding and deporting practices during 19th century Hong Kong, see *A Magistrate's Court in 19th Century Hong Kong*, pp. 61-62. The prisoner in CC 505 was branded and deported not long after the system was reintroduced in 1872.

THEFT OF PART OF THE "DRAGON"
CC Number 506
U Amui was charged by Chu Aon with unlawful possession of a pawn ticket, relating to stolen property.

Chu Aon, a butcher in the Central Market, said he was one of the managers of the Dragon in the late procession.[408] On the 25th he missed a piece of red silk from the Dragon's head, the silk in court was the same. The Dragon was placed in a new house near the P. & O. Company's premises on the 24th *instant*. When going to start next evening the silk was found wanting, the witness then made enquiries, but could find no trace of it, until the 26th, when defendant came to the market and said he had got a pawn ticket relating to the stolen part of the Dragon. Witness asked defendant where he got it, to which he replied a friend gave it to him. Defendant was then taken to the station.

Defendant in his defence stated that a man named Wong Atak offered to sell him the pawn ticket of a portion of the Dragon, which the butchers had lost in the Recreation Ground. Defendant said to this man that it was very wrong to deprive the butchers of their property, but he said he wanted some money. Defendant then bought the ticket for ten cents and took it to the butchers. Fined 15 shillings or 21 days' imprisonment with hard labour.

WEDNESDAY 28 DECEMBER 1881[409]
ASSAULT
CC Number 507
Wong Ashing was charged, on remand from the 19th *instant*, with assaulting Lai Ashing, hawker, and also damaging property to the value of $12.

Lai Ashing, hawker, said while walking in Queen's Road, Central along with Ip Afuk, defendant

---

[408] For further information about, "the procession", see CC 502 and related note.

[409] "Police Intelligence," CM, Wednesday, 28 December 1881, p. 3, cc. 3 - 4.

accosted his companion and asked for the loan of $3. On being refused this sum the defendant and five other men commenced to beat witness and Ip Afuk with iron bars. Witness was struck on the head by defendant, causing a serious wound. He was then taken to the Civil Hospital where he had remained until this morning.

Witness in answer to defendant said he had never picked his pocket, and did not throw the iron bar in court at the defendant. Ip Afuk said he came here a month ago on a visit to last witness and had brought sufficient money with him from Canton to support himself. He gave similar evidence to that of the previous witness.

Defendant said that the second witness had tried to pick his pocket but failed. He knew both witnesses as pickpockets.

His Worship, in sentencing prisoner to fourteen days' imprisonment with hard labour, remarked that on the evidence adduced he could hardly have committed him to prison, but after his own statement he had no doubt that prisoner had used the bar to strike the complainant,[410] and the use of those bars must be put down, they being almost as dangerous as knives were. [411]

PIRACY ON THE HIGH SEAS[412]
CC Number 508 📖 p. 389

Wong Afuk and 5 others were again brought up this morning, on remand, charged with 4 cases of piracy. Several fresh witnesses were examined, among whom was Li Pak Shing, who gave evidence as to identifying, a week ago, the boat by which he was

---

[410] This is an interesting comment on the practice of the law at this time. This defendant would not have been convicted on the basis of the evidence presented, but was convicted because of his own statement.

[411] This is one of the few occasions in these Reports when we hear Frederick Stewart's own voice and expression of opinion.

[412] The following is the complete set of reports in connection with this case in *The Complete Court Cases*: CC Nos 452, 483, 508, 520.

attacked and which belonged to the six defendants. This witness, also at this time, found some property belonging to him on board the boat. Another witness, a seaman on board a passage boat called I Li, identified a purse and anchor in court as belonging to the boat he was employed on, and which were found in the defendants' possession. The whole of the charges were again remanded till the 4th *proximate*

THURSDAY 29 DECEMBER 1881[413]
ALLEGED UNLAWFUL POSSESSION
CC Number 509

J. Dowling, a Sergeant in the Royal Inniskilling Fusiliers, appeared on a summons charged with that he did unlawfully have in his possession a small dog, the property of one Sergeant Vanstone of the Naval Yard Police, on the 23rd instant.

From the evidence adduced for the prosecution it appeared that the dog in question had gone amissing on the 22nd instant, and that after enquiries had been made at the various Police Stations about the animal, complainant accompanied by three Naval Yard Constables, applied to the Sergeant-Major of the Regiment for permission to search the barracks for his dog. This was at once granted, but before a search could be instituted, defendant, seeing the Naval Police, enquired what was wrong, and on being told what was wanted, at once informed complainant that there was a dog in his, defendant's, room, and if it was his he could have it. Defendant at this time was on duty and could not go to his quarters to give the dog up, but complainant got it himself without trouble, and next day he accused defendant, and another Sergeant who occupied the same room, of having taken a trinket from the dog's collar, adding that if they would admit that, no further notice would be taken of the unlawful possession of the dog. This defendant indignantly

---

[413] "Police Intelligence", CM, Thursday, 29 December 1881, p. 3, c. 3.

denied and threatened to have him locked up in the guard room if he persisted in making any such assertion. Evidence of a conflicting nature was adduced on both sides, and his Worship, without hearing the whole of the witnesses for the defence, said that he had quite made up his mind on the subject, and considering there was not the slightest foundation for the charge, dismissed the case.

FRIDAY 30 DECEMBER 1881[414]
CUTTING AND WOUNDING
CC Number 510 📖 p. 258

Ngau was charged with cutting and wounding Chu Atam, a woman under his protection, on the 8th November.

Chu Atam said she was a widow, living under the defendant's protection in Number 33, Upper Lascar Row. On the 8th Nov. the defendant asked her for some money but was refused, he then went out and did not return that day. On the following night defendant returned and she opened the door to him, and while proceeding upstairs before him, felt a stab in the right shoulder. The wound bled very much, but she was able to go and make a report at the Station, whence she was taken to the Civil Hospital, where she remained twenty-seven days. Defendant ran away after stabbing the complainant, and she only discovered his return to the Colony on the 28th when he was taken in charge.

Chü Apin, sister of the complainant, said she lived with her sister and witnessed defendant strike her but thought it was with his hand and not with a knife. On hearing her sister's cries she ran downstairs and went to the door, but defendant was gone.

Dr. Marques, Assistant Superintendent at the Civil Hospital, gave evidence as to admitting Chü Atam on the 8th Nov. suffering from an incised wound, one inch deep and one inch in length, and

---

[414] "Police Intelligence," CM, Friday, 30 December 1881, p. 3, cc. 4 - 5.

said the wound had probably been inflicted with a knife or some sharp instrument.

Defendant denied the charge but had no witnesses to call.

Sentenced to six months' imprisonment with hard labour.

ILLEGAL POSSESSION OF OPIUM
CC Number 511

Kwok Ahung and Lum Awai appeared charged with having possession of prepared opium without having [a] permit from the Opium Farmer.

Inspector Perry said he went to the servant's quarters, at the back of the Hong Kong Club, possessed of a warrant to search the premises. He searched the room and found, at the foot of the bed, the 25 tins of opium produced in Court. The Inspector also saw other traces of prepared opium and the defendants admitted they had no permit.

Antonio dos Santos, an excise officer, said he accompanied the former witness and while the Inspector was speaking to the defendants, he observed first defendant crawl under the bed, when witness caught him with two boxes of opium in his hands. Witness valued the opium in Court at $30, and had been trying to bring a conviction against defendants for some months past.

Chan Chung, an unemployed coolie, went to the Hong Kong Club on the 28th instant. He had known the first defendant to sell opium for several years and had purchased some opium from him on the 28th instant. He received the opium from first defendant and paid the money to the second.

First defendant admitted selling the opium without a license but said the second defendant had nothing to do with the matter. He did not live at the Hong Kong Club, but only kept his opium there. A fine of $200, in default two months' imprisonment with hard labour was imposed on first defendant, and the second discharged; the opium being handed over to the Opium Farmer.

OBTAINING MONEY BY FALSE PRETENCES
CC Number 512

Lau Akiu, Lum Awong and Lau Aping were charged, on remand, with obtaining money by false pretences from Li Atsun, accountant, on the 20th instant.

Li Atsun said he was the accountant at the Fuk Shang Pawnshop in East Street. He said the first defendant offered a gold bangle for pawn on the 19th instant. He gave her $20 for the article thinking it was all gold, but on her leaving he pierced it and found it only partly gold. He then went to her house and informed her of this. She took him to second defendant's house from whom she said she had received it. The second defendant had received it from some other woman they could not find. He then had them removed to the Station.

First defendant said she received the bangle from the second to pawn, who in turn had got it from a woman named Sau Tsai, who was due her [*sic*] for "owed her"] $5, borrowed three years ago. Out of the $20 given for the bangle, the second defendant only received $3, the rest going to this third woman, Sau Tsai, who had never been found. The second defendant said she had got the bangle from Lau Aping, the third defendant, who had told her to say Sau Tsai instead of Lau Aping.

His Worship sentenced each of the prisoners to three months' imprisonment with hard labour.

ROGUES AND VAGABONDS
CC Number 513

Wong Asing was observed, on the 29th *instant*, in Praya Central inviting people to gamble. He lived in an opium den in Gilman Street, and had been in prison three months already for gambling. He had no employment at present. He was committed to prison for three months with hard labour.

[ROGUES AND VAGABONDS]
CC Number 514

Wong Atsoi was charged with being a rogue and vagabond on the 29th instant.

Mungal [*sic*] Singh, Police Constable 692 said he saw about 15 persons gambling in Second Street yesterday, with the prisoner acting as watchman. He was unsuccessful several times in apprehending prisoner, whom he had watched for some time and failed in procuring any of the others.

Defendant said he was employed in a shop at Number 9, Shung Fung Lane, but on this being inquired into it was found he had left ten days ago, without warning his master.

Sentenced to three months' imprisonment with hard labour.

SATURDAY 31 DECEMBER 1881[415]
ROGUE AND VAGABOND
CC Number 515

Tse Ip was charged with being a rogue and vagabond, and also with creating a disturbance on the 30th *instant*.

Lo Ayan, Police Constable 306, observed defendant and 20 or 30 others sitting on the footpath in First Street yesterday, playing at Fan-tan. Defendant was managing the game. In apprehending him he attempted to escape, and tried to strike the constable, but was prevented by another constable coming to his assistance.

Defendant said he was buying something to eat when the constable apprehended him, and was not engaged in gambling. Sentenced to 3 months' imprisonment with hard labour.

---

[415] "Police Intelligence," CM, Saturday, 31 December 1881, p. 3, cc. 3 - 4.

PICKPOCKET
CC Number 516 📖

Chan Afuk, coolie from Canton, was charged with stealing a one dollar note from Leong Akan, cook, on the 29th *instant*.

Leong Akan said he was standing in front of a Second Hand Clothes' stall in East Street, defendant and two others being close by. Suddenly his pocket was picked of a dollar note, and his handkerchief was dragged half out and defendant at that moment started to run,[416] but was seized by witness. On the way to the station some friends of defendant came and urged him to give witness a dollar, but of course the constable refused to allow him to do this.[417]

Chan Sing, District Watchman, said, while on duty in Hollywood Road he found defendant in complainant's custody. While conveying defendant to the station some of his companions offered to pay the dollar; defendant also asked permission to pawn his jacket to raise sufficient money to pay the sum.

Defendant denied the theft but admitted having undergone 6 months' imprisonment for an offence similar to the one he was now charged with. He was committed to prison for nine months with hard labour.

ASSAULT
CC Number 517

Yau Ayam, chair coolie, was charged with assaulting Ching Aling, another chair coolie, and Yau Alok,[418] with being armed with a deadly weapon, and without a pass on the 30th *instant*.

---

[416] Interesting information about the working practices of pick-pockets.

[417] In other words, by-standers urged the person who was arrested to bribe the person whose handkerchief he had snatched so that he would withdraw his complaint. However, the policeman, very properly would not stand by and permit this to be done.

[418] According to the complainant, Yau Ayau and Yau Alok work as a team, carrying a sedan chair. Yau Ayau denies this.

Ching Aling said while in Queen's Road Central on the night of the 29th the defendants' chair and his came into collision. Both then abused him, but he said nothing and went home. Next morning at breakfast time defendants came to his house, the first seizing him, and the second striking him with the iron bar in Court. Some of his friends seized them and had them given in charge.

Police Constable 145 said he went to 119, Second Street by the request of some one who said a man had been killed. He saw complainant bleeding, who pointed out defendants as having assaulted him with the iron bar. First defendant stated that the second defendant and complainant had a fight, and he was only a witness to the affair. They did not carry the same chair; and the second defendant said complainant was due him [*sic* for "owed him"] a sum of money and on asking this money complainant struck him. Then the Police Constable came and arrested him.

Heung Achun, a barber, who resided next door to the complainant corroborated the complainant's evidence.

First defendant was fined $2, in default, 7 days' imprisonment with hard labour; and the second was fined $5, in default, 21 days' imprisonment. The iron bar was forfeited to the Crown.

THEFT OF SILK
CC Number 518

Ho Tai, hawker, was charged with the theft of a piece of silk from Lau Ayuk, on the 30th *instant*.

Lau Aut said she lived at 33, Caine Road and on the 30th *instant*, returning from the kitchen found defendant in her room and in the act of putting the unfinished petticoat in Court under his jacket. She was making the petticoat for his wife. She seized defendant and gave him in charge. Fung-hoi Ki, master of a tailor's shop in Queen's Road Central said the silk belonged to him but he had given it to last witness to make into a petticoat. Defendant said he was decoyed here, and happened to enter this house when several men there beat and nearly killed him. He was afterwards given in charge by first witness, who forbade the men to beat him.

Shuk Ranjan, Police Constable, found defendant in possession of part of the petticoat, and was trying to take the other part from the complainant.

Leung Hing Hi, landlord of Number 33, Caine Road, gave evidence in support of the charge, similar to that of the complainant.

The prisoner was sentenced to 4 months' imprisonment with hard labour.

BEFORE FREDERICK STEWART, ESQ.,
January 1882[419]

WEDNESDAY 4 JANUARY 1882[420]
DISOBEDIENT CHAIR COOLIES
CC Number 519
Lam Lun and Fung Fat, chair coolies, were charged with disobedience of orders on the 3rd instant.

Mr James Henry Cox said that defendants had been ordered to take his wife out yesterday afternoon, but they failed to put in an appearance when ordered.

Kwok Aming, house-boy to Mr Cox, proved delivering a message from his mistress for them to take her out in her chair. They refused because they had not received their wages for last month. Fined $1, in default, four days' imprisonment each.

PIRACY[421]
CC Number 520 📖 p. 389
Wong Afuk, owner of a fishing junk, and five fishermen were again placed in the dock this morning on four separate and distinct charges of piracy on the high seas in the month of November last.

The prisoners having been duly cautioned elected to reserve their defence, and were committed to take their trial at the next Criminal Sessions of the Supreme Court.[422]

---

[419] **Notes on Court Case Reports for January 1882 as a whole.** Monday, 2 January 1882 was a public holiday (HKGG, 17 December 1881, p. [1083]), and no courts sat on that day. There is no report of cases heard "Before Frederick Stewart, Esq.", in the CM of Thursday, 5 January 1882 and Wednesday, 11 January 1882.

On Tuesday, 3 January 1882 and Friday, 13 January 1882, *The China Mail* reports cases heard by H. E. Wodehouse only.

[420] "Police Intelligence", CM, Wednesday, 4 January 1882, p. 3, cc. 4 - 5.

[421] The following is the complete set of reports in connection with this case in *The Complete Court Cases*: CC Nos 452, 483, 508, 520.

[422] The following information appears in the Criminal Calendar for the January Sessions, 1882, HKGG, 4 February 1882, p. 61,

CUTTING AND WOUNDING
CC Number 521

Tsoi On, a hawker, again appeared on a charge of cutting and wounding one Kau Muk Yau, on the 14th ultimo.

The complainant is now in hospital suffering from a severe wound on the left side of his neck, and a certificate was put in to the effect that he would not be able to attend the Court for another week.

The case was accordingly remanded till next Wednesday.

---

where this case, tried on 18 January 1882, appears as CC Nos. 9 and 10.

As Case No. 9, 1) Wong A-fuk [*sic*], 2) Lung A-fong, 3) Wong A-yiu, 4) Wong Mun Tong, 5) Wong A-hoi and 6) Ching A-u were tried on the two counts of 1) Piracy and Assault and 2) Receiving goods piratically stolen.

1) Wong A-fuk [*sic*], 2) Lung A-fong, 3) Wong A-yiu and 5) Wong A-hoi were found guilty of receiving goods piratically stolen and not guilty of piracy and assault. 4) Wong Mun Tong and 6) Ching A-u were found guilty on both counts.

Sentence was given on 23 January 1882.

4) Wong Mun Tong and 6) Ching A-u were sentenced to six years' penal servitude each on 1st count, and four years' penal servitude each on 2nd count to be concurrent with sentence on 1st count. This sentence to take effect after expiration of the sentences past [*sic*] on the same prisoners in case No. 10.

1) Wong A-fuk [*sic*], 2) Lung A-fong, 3) Wong A-yiu and 5) Wong A-hoi were sentenced to four years' penal servitude each to take effect after expiration of sentence passed on the same prisoners, in case No. 10.

As Case No. 10, 1) Wong A-fuk [*sic*], 2) Lung A-fong, 3) Wong A-yiu, 4) Wong Mun Tong, 5) Wong A-hoi and 6) Ching A-u were tried on the two counts of 1) Piracy and Assault and 2) Receiving goods piratically stolen.

1) Wong A-fuk [*sic*], 3) Wong A-yiu, 4) Wong Mun Tong and 5) Wong A-hoi were found guilty of 2) Receiving goods piratically stolen and not guilty of 1) Piracy and assault.

2) Lung A-fong and 6) Ching A-u were found guilty of both 1) Piracy and Assault and 2) Receiving goods piratically stolen.

2) Lung A-fong and 6) Ching A-u were sentenced to six years' penal servitude for 1) Piracy and Assault and four years' penal servitude for 2) Receiving goods piratically stolen to be concurrent with their sentence for 1) Piracy and Assault.

1) Wong A-fuk [*sic*], 3) Wong A-yiu, 4) Wong Mun Tong and 5) Wong A-hoi were sentenced to four years' penal servitude each.

A DETERMINED GAOL BIRD
CC Number 522

Chan Ayau, 23 years of age, was charged with snatching from the person a blue bag containing ten earthenware spoons and other articles.

The complainant in this case is the master of a firewood junk trading between Kowloon City and Hong Kong: yesterday afternoon he was walking along the Praya when the prisoner snatched his bag from his hand and made off with it. Complainant pursued him and he was ultimately arrested by a lukong.

He had no less than six previous convictions recorded against his name since 1877, five of them being for larceny.

Prisoner having been duly cautioned reserved his defence, and was committed to take his trial at the next Criminal Sessions of the Supreme Court.[423]

---

[423] The following information appears in the Criminal Calendar for the January Sessions, 1882, HKGG, 4 February 1882, p. 61, where this case is No. 6.
Chun A-yau [*sic*] was tried on 18 January 1882 and pleaded guilty to three counts: 1) Larceny from the person; 2) Previous conviction (summary); 3) previous conviction (felony). He was sentenced the same day to three years' penal servitude.
A *Nolle prosequi* was entered by the Attorney General on the second and third counts.

A report in *The China Mail* reads as follows (Wednesday, 18 January 1882, p. 3, cc. 3-4, c. 4.):
"Supreme Court
"In Criminal Sessions
"(Before His Honour the Acting Puisne Judge, J. Russell, Esq.)
"Wednesday, 18 January 1882"

["The following jury were impanelled: Messrs A. W. Mactavish, E. A. Jorge, A. H. M. da Silva, J. M. do Rozario, G. A. Wieler, J. B. Gomes, and E. Holst.
"Mr Mackean prosecuted on behalf of the Attorney General.]"

"Larceny
"Chan Ayau pleaded guilty to stealing ten earthenware spoons, a bag, and some cash, from the person of Li Tsun Tsz, on the 3rd of January.

FRIDAY 6 JANUARY 1882[424]
BLUE JACKETS ON THE WAR PATH
CC Number 523 📖 p. 187

James Caine, William Haines, and George Murphy, seamen of H.M.S. *Carysfort*, were placed in the dock to-day, and charged with disorderly conduct in the Temperance Hall at an early hour this morning.

Mr E. Shillibeer, Manager of the Hall, said that a complaint was made to him between one and two o'clock this morning by a boarder in the house. From what he was told he got up and went to one of the rooms which he found locked on the inside. He knocked at the door, but getting no reply he ultimately burst it open. In the room he found the three prisoners, two of whom were in bed, the other sitting up. They had no business there and he ordered them out, but they declined to go and abused him. One of them threw him down on the bed, another struck him on the head, and the third assaulted him in a dangerous part of the body, from which he had since suffered much pain. He called for assistance, and eight or ten of the boarders came and released him, and he gave defendants in charge of the police.

The first and second defendants expressed a desire to see any marks of assault which complainant bore, and they were shown accordingly.

Lo Ai, a coolie employed at the Hall, said the three prisoners came there about midnight and asked for some place in which to sleep. He told them the beds were all occupied, and they commenced to beat him with their fists. He ran away from them, and they went upstairs, after which he saw no more of them. The first prisoner was drunk, but the other two were sober.

John Glaholm, a mate unemployed, residing at the Temperance Hall, said that some time between midnight of last night and two o'clock this morning,

---

"His Lordship said he found there were seven previous convictions against the prisoner. He would sentence him to three years' penal servitude."

[424] "Police Intelligence", CM, Friday, 6 January 1882, p. 3, c. 4.

the three prisoners came into his room there. He told
them it was a private room and they could not be
permitted to remain. They however evinced no
intention of leaving and he went to last witness's
room and roused him. Mr Shillibeer accompanied
him back to his own room, which was then found
locked inside. On last witness bursting open the door
and going inside he heard a scuffling going on, but he
did not see any assault. There was not much light in
the alley-ways. The Manager sent for the police, but
before a constable arrived the three prisoners had
come out into the Hall. Several of the boarders came
from their rooms, but he did not see them do
anything, and he did not think Mr Shillibeer required
any assistance.

Police Constable No. 5, George Rogers, said
he was called to the Temperance Hall about two
o'clock this morning, and the Manager asked him to
take the three prisoners into custody on a charge of
entering one of the rooms for an unlawful purpose.
One of the men had a stick in his hand, which was
said to have been taken from the room in question
and was claimed by last witness. He refused to give
up the stick to the man who claimed it, but gave it up
to the constable. The men went quietly to the station,
and there a charge of disorderly conduct and assault
was preferred against them by Mr Shillibeer.

In defence, the first prisoner said that when
they went to the Hall shortly after midnight they saw
the Manager whom they asked for beds. He did not
know whether there were any vacant, and told them
they could go round the house and see for
themselves. They did so and found an unoccupied
bed in Number 10 Room. Two of them turned in and
the other lay down on the floor. The third witness
occupied another bed in the same room and ordered
them out, but they refused to go as they had been sent
there by the Manager and had paid for a bed. When
the Manager came to the room to turn them out, he
struck him, first prisoner, over the arm with a stick in
Court (shows swelling on arm).

The other two prisoners made a somewhat similar defence.

Complainant, recalled, denied having seen the defendants till he was called by the third witness. He went to bed at half-past eleven o'clock, and left no one in charge except some coolies to let in boarders who might be out late.

An officer from the ship gave the prisoners bad characters, and His Worship fined them $3 each, in default, seven days' imprisonment with hard labour.

THEFT OF TROUSERS
CC Number 524

Ip Acheuk was convicted of stealing a pair of trousers, belonging to Yau Ip He, a widow residing in Gutzlaff Street. The trousers were found concealed in prisoner's sleeve when caught in Gage Street. He pleaded that another man stole them, and gave them to him. He had no occupation at present. Sentenced to six weeks' imprisonment with hard labour.

COUNTERFEIT COIN[425]
CC Number 525 📖

Kan Akut, marine hawker, was charged with selling two pieces of counterfeit coin and also with being in possession of twenty-six other pieces.

Inspector Perry said on the 3rd January he met Ng Ahoi who gave him information, which led him to give this person a one-dollar note, which he returned the following day with the two counterfeit coins in Court. From the same informant's statement, he went accompanied by other officers to Number 95, Second Street, where after search he discovered all the other coins produced resembling dollars; fourteen of which were new, and the remainder old and chopped. He also found 30 copper coins which when silvered would look like Japanese twenty-cent pieces.

---

[425] The following is the complete set of reports in connection with this case in *The Complete Court Cases*: CC Nos 525, 529.

In a table in the room, which had a false bottom, were found a packet of powder, and four steel chops. Defendant said to the witness while engaged doing this that he was a collector of coins.

Ng Ahoi, a tailor, said on the 28th December he, along with an acquaintance, went to Number 95, Second Street, where his friend gave defendant $12, and received in return 24 coins resembling dollars. On the same occasion witness himself gave defendant 50 cents and received one of those coins in return, but going home and piercing it, he found it was not good and took it back to the house and said so to the defendant, who only returned him 40 cents, instead of 50 as he had paid. He then did as Inspector Perry related.

In answer to defendant witness admitted that he had been told the coins were copper.

Leung Atsau, shroff, employed at the Magistracy, said he had examined the coins and valued some of the dollars at 35 cents, some at 10 cents, and others at less. The powder presented was used for the purpose of giving copper coins the appearance of silver.

Bedell Lee Yun, interpreter [426] at the Magistracy, said the wooden label in Court was that used by persons who collect old silver ornaments and bad dollars, and the words on it meant "I collect silver taels;" that is, adulterated silver.

The case was then remanded till the 9th *instant*.

---

[426] Here, Frederick Stewart clearly referred to the Court Interpreter as an expert witness. This is a practice that continues today. See Garry Tallentire, "The Hong Kong (Police) Magistrate in the 1880s & 1990s: A Flavour of the Times", in *A Magistrate's Court in 19th Century Hong Kong*, pp. 147-158, p. 151.

SATURDAY 7 JANUARY 1882[427]
ROBBING A SHIPWRECKED SEAMAN
CC Number 526 📖 p. 189

William Blood, a seaman unemployed, was charged with stealing an overcoat on the 6th instant from one William Lecky, a ship's boy.

William Lecky said he had been on board the British barque Forward Ho, which was recently wrecked, and he was now living at the Sailor's Home. The prisoner was also staying there but he was not acquainted with him. He identified the overcoat in Court as his. It was worth $4. Yesterday afternoon he went out for a walk, leaving the coat under his bedclothes. On returning to his room about six o'clock he observed that the pillow of his bed was very low, and on making an examination he found that the coat was missing. Enquiries had been made at the Home without any result, and he afterwards asked several policemen if they had seen any sailors with a bundle of clothes. Amongst others he asked constable Servant who gave him certain information, and took him to a shop where he was shown the missing coat.

Police Constable No. 4, Herbert Servant[428] said he apprehended the prisoner at the Sailor's Home this morning. When charged with stealing the coat he replied that he had nothing to say. Witness had seen the prisoner selling a coat in a shop in East Street yesterday evening, and on questioning him about it, he said it was his own property, that he had brought it here from Manila, and that he was obliged to part with his clothes as he was staying at the Sailor's Home and had no money. About half an hour

---

[427] "Police Intelligence", CM, Saturday, 7 January 1882, p. 3, c. 6.
[428] In *The Complete Court Cases*, we find "Herbert Servant", "H. Sewart" and "H. Stewart". Quite possibly these are one and the same. However, the number is given only with "Herbert Servant, Police Constable No. 4". The Index of, *A Magistrate's Court in 19th Century Hong Kong*, lists, "Servant, Herbert, Police Constable" and, "Sewart, H., Police Constable" but not, "H. Stewart".

afterwards he met the complainant from whom he heard about the missing coat.

Defendant admitted the charge, saying that he was very hard up. He had no tobacco and no soap.

Sentence — two months' imprisonment with hard labour.

STEALING CLOTHING
CC Number 527

Leong Alai charged Yu Aput with stealing clothing to the value of 40 cents.

Defendant admitted the charge but said the property did not belong to the complainant, but to another person, who owed him some money.

Leung Aching said the property was his, and Leong Alai was his landlord, and had charge of it and the defendant was not authorized to take it.

Defendant said that the last witness gave him permission to use the things and he therefore took them. This he did while Leung Aching was in the country. — Six weeks' imprisonment with hard labour.

MONDAY 9 JANUARY 1882[429]
DRUNK AND ASSAULTING THE POLICE
CC Number 528

Vassuly Nicolon and Michael Spragin, of the Russian steamer Wladvostok [*sic*], pleaded guilty to being drunk and disorderly and assaulting the police on the night of the 8th instant, and were fined, the first defendant in twenty-five cents, and the second in $1, or three days' imprisonment, and both to pay twenty cents chair hire.

COUNTERFEIT COIN[430]
CC Number 529 📖 p. 360

The case in which Kan Akut, a marine hawker, was charged with dealing in counterfeit coin on the 5th

---

[429] "Police Intelligence", CM, Monday, 9 January 1882, p. 3, c. 6.
[430] The following is the complete set of reports in connection with this case in *The Complete Court Cases*: CC Nos 525, 529.

instant, again occupied the attention of the Court to-day.

Mr H. McCallum, analyst at the Government Civil Hospital said that he had examined a small parcel of a powder which he received from Inspector Perry, and found it to be finely divided tin. A similar powder is used in India for burnishing ornaments and it gives them a silvery appearance. He then produced a small piece of copper which he had burnished with the powder in question, and which had all the appearance of silver.

Defendant having been duly cautioned reserved his defence, and he was committed for trial at the next Criminal Sessions of the Supreme Court.[431]

---

[431] The following information appears in the Criminal Calendar for the January Sessions, 1882, HKGG, 4 February 1882, p. 61, where this case is No. 8.

Kan A-kut was tried on 18 January on two counts, 1) Selling counterfeit coin and 2) Being in possession of counterfeit coin.

He was found not guilty of 1) Selling counterfeit coin and not guilty of 2) Being in possession of counterfeit coin. The jurors voted six to one on the second count.

Kan A-kut was discharged.

The following report appeared in *The China Mail* (Wednesday, 18 January 1882, p. 3, cc. 3-4, c. 4.):
"Supreme Court
"In Criminal Sessions
"(Before His Honour the Acting Puisne Judge, J. Russell, Esq.)
"Wednesday, 18 January 1882

["The following jury were impanelled: Messrs A. W. Mactavish, E. A. Jorge, A. H. M. da Silva, J. M. do Rozario, G. A. Wieler, J. B. Gomes, and E. Holst.
"Mr Mackean prosectued on behalf of the Attorney General.]"

"Counterfeit Coin Case
"Kow Akut [sic] was charged with selling two counterfeit dollars to one Ng Ahoi, at less value than they purported to bear, on the 3rd of January; and on a second count, with having in his possession a number of counterfeit coins.

ASSAULT AND ROBBERY
CC Number 530

Wong A Fuk, a coolie, was charged with three others not in custody, with assaulting and robbing one Chun Amu on the Pok-fu Lum [sic] Road on the 7th instant.

The case was investigated at some length, but was ultimately remanded till the 11th instant.

TUESDAY 10 JANUARY 1882[432]
DISOBEDIENT SERVANT
CC Number 531

Wong A-I and three others, chair coolies, were charged with disobedience of orders on the 9th instant.

Mr J. H. dos Remedios, residing in Caine Road, said the four defendants were in his employment. They took him and his wife to the City Hall last night about nine o'clock, and when he went into the Hall he gave his coat to the second defendant, who was the head coolie, and gave them instructions to return at eleven o'clock. On leaving the concert at fifteen or twenty minutes past that hour, there were neither his chairs nor chair coolies to be found. He was concerned for his wife's health, as she had been unwell lately, and after waiting ten minutes or so he had to borrow a chair for her use. On the way home he met the defendants.

"Evidence was given by an informer to the effect that the prisoner had sold him two counterfeit dollars, and Inspector Perry proved finding the coins in his possession.

"The defendant said he went about teaching the occupation of shroffing, and two witnesses attested to this statement.

"His Lordship pointed out to the jury that there was not much reliance to be placed on the statement of the informer, as it was unsupported.

"The jury after some deliberation found the prisoner not guilty unanimously on the first count; and not guilty by six to one on the second."

[432] "Police Intelligence", CM, Tuesday, 10 January 1882, p. 3, c. 5.

All the men made the same defence. They admitted having been ordered for eleven o'clock, but they went to sleep, and the watchman who had been told to wake them had also fallen asleep.

Fined $1 each, or four days' imprisonment.

AIDING AND ABETTING GAMBLERS
CC Number 532

Chun Asing, a cook, and another man bearing the same name, described as a hawker, were charged with being watchmen to gamblers on the 9th *instant*.

Police Constable 523, Mahomed Jan, said that he was on duty yesterday afternoon in Gilman Street. The two prisoners were standing in front of a house, but as soon as they saw him they rushed upstairs and called out "Police coming." He followed them and arrested them on the staircase. In the house, which was not furnished for dwelling in, he saw about fifty persons, who at once made a rush to the cookhouse and escaped by means of a ladder on the roof, but before this they fastened down a trap- door. Witness blew his whistle, and on assistance being obtained the trap door was forced open, and inside the room were found a large quantity of gambling implements. When they were arrested the second prisoner said the first defendant was watchman to the gamblers; and he was only going upstairs to get some money, and had nothing to do with the gambling. The first prisoner also said he had nothing to do with it.

Defendants made the usual lame excuses generally put forth on such occasions, but were convicted of aiding and abetting public gambling, and were each fined in the sum of $25, in default two months' imprisonment with hard labour.

A CHAIR COOLIE IN LIQUOR
CC Number 533 📖 p. 234

Lai Asu, a chair coolie, was charged with being drunk and unfit for duty on the 9th instant.

Mr George Piercy, head schoolmaster of the Diocesan Home and Orphanage, said that defendant was ordered to take his wife's chair to West Terrace about five o'clock yesterday evening. He had been on leave at three o'clock, but returned to duty at the proper time, but he was so drunk that his wife was compelled to leave the chair.

Defendant admitted the charge and said he had taken a little samshoo.[433]

Fined $1, in default four days' imprisonment with hard labour; and to forfeit what wages were due.

LARCENY OF CLOTHING
CC Number 534

Lau Cheung, a tailor, was charged with stealing a jacket on the 8th instant, valued at $2.50.

Cheung Kau, an employé in an opium divan, said that on the night of the 8th instant the prisoner was admitted at half-past ten o'clock. He wanted to smoke, and on finishing that enjoyable operation he seized complainant's jacket off a bed and ran. Witness got up and ran after him, but failed to catch him and reported the matter to the police. Next day he found the prisoner in another opium divan and gave him in charge.

A fellow servant of the complainant gave similar testimony.

Defendant admitted a previous conviction of larceny in 1878, and was now sentenced to six months' imprisonment with hard labour.

THURSDAY 12 JANUARY 1882[434]
BREACH OF THE OPIUM ORDINANCE
CC Number 535

Cheung Ashu, unemployed, was charged with being in possession of a quantity of prepared opium on the 11th instant, without a permit from the Opium Farmer.

---

[433] "'Chinese spirits' shall mean the intoxicating liquor commonly known as samshoo". (HKGG, 11 June 1879, p. 306.)

[434] "Police Intelligence", CM, Thursday, 12 January 1882, p. 3, c. 4.

Acting Sergeant T. Campbell said that he went to defendant's house, Number 40, Wellington Street, yesterday evening, in company with an informer and two Excise officers. He was armed with a search warrant under which authority he searched for opium and found two horn boxes, a tin box, and three earthenware pots, all containing quantities of prepared opium or opium dross. Defendant said they had been left there by some of his friends. In an adjoining room there were some eight or ten men smoking opium, and the place generally was fitted up for that purpose.

Defendant produced a number of certificates, but on examination by the Court Interpreter they were all found to be obsolete and of no value.

The informer who accompanied the police gave evidence of having purchased opium from the prisoner on the 8th *instant*.

Defendant denied having sold any opium to last witness, but admitted having opium in his possession, some of which he had purchased from the Opium Farmer, and the remainder he had received from friends.

Fined $25, in default six weeks' imprisonment. The opium found in prisoner's house to be forfeited.

UNLAWFUL POSSESSION OF WARLIKE STORES
CC Number 536
Leong Ashoo, a fishmonger, was charged on remand with being in the unlawful possession of a 64 pr.[435] common shell, on the 10th instant.

Defendant was arrested by one of the Water Police in the harbour, and on his boat being examined an iron shell was found, which the constable believed to be Government property.

Sergeant Crawford, R. A., Armstrong Armourer in the Ordnance Store Department,

---

[435] Presumably, an abbreviation for, "pounder".

identified the shell as War Department property from the marks it bore. Shells like the one in question were fired at targets at sea, but this one had never been so fired, and witness could not account for its being in defendant's possession.

On the case being again called to-day, the constable who arrested the prisoner said he had visited the Ordnance Department, as well as all the war vessels in harbour, but those responsible for such stores said they were not deficient of any shells of the description of the one in Court.

Defendant said he found it when fishing off the Long Pier at Wanchai.

Fined 7s. 6d., or four days' imprisonment for unlawful possession. The shell to be returned to H. M.'s stores.

DRUNK AND INCAPABLES
CC Number 537
George Hartfield, Charles Johnson, and Henry Dunn, seamen unemployed, were each fined fifty cents, for being drunk and creating a disturbance yesterday.

A STRAGGLER
CC Number 538
Thomas Cowdrey, of H.M.S. Tourmaline, was ordered to be sent on board his ship as a straggler.

A PICKPOCKET
CC Number 539
Fong Acheung, a shop coolie, was charged with picking the pocket of one Ng Amui of a watch, valued at $9, on the 11th instant.

Complainant's story was that he was at the Harbour Office yesterday to be examined prior to embarking for San Francisco, when he felt some one in the crowd take something from his purse.

A man in the crowd saw what defendant had done and pursued him and gave him into custody. Complainant identified the watch, and said he bought it about eight years ago in California.

Defendant said he had a clansman who was going to California, and he went to the Harbour Office to look for him, when he was arrested. He admitted having been in gaol in September last for larceny, and since he left that establishment he had been unemployed. His uncle supported him.

Sentenced to six months' imprisonment with hard labour.

A SLEEPY WATCHMAN
CC Number 540
Chu Sz, a watchman at Mr Scott's bungalow, Albany Road, was fined $1, or four days' imprisonment, for going to sleep when on duty at two o'clock this morning.

SATURDAY 14 JANUARY 1882[436]
THROWING BRICKS
CC Number 541
Su Yu, a street coolie, was sentenced to seven days' imprisonment with hard labour, for assaulting Mahomed Jan, with a brick in Gilman's Bazaar. The prisoner and some others were told to move on by the constable, but instead of that, some of them commenced to throw bricks, which they took from an adjoining building. Defendant said he was beaten by the constable and did not throw any of the bricks; but several witnesses testified otherwise, and he was committed.

STEALING COPPER NAILS
CC Number 542
Chun Cheung, a coolie, was convicted of conveying away some copper nails in his shoes, covered with oakum, from Sham Shui Po Dock, where he was employed. Defendant said the shoes were used for holding nails in when at his work, and while in the act of removing them before going out, he was

---

[436] "Police Intelligence", CM, Saturday, 14 January 1882, p. 3, c. 2.

apprehended. Imprisonment for six months with hard labour was imposed on him.

A STRAGGLING SAILOR
CC Number 543

Frederick Victor Muller, seaman on board the Alert, from which he had deserted, was brought up and charged with this offence. George Durrant, Police Constable discovered defendant in the Welcome Tavern, after searching for him for some time. Defendant admitted leaving the dingy at the wharf. His Worship gave orders to have him conveyed on board the Alert, where very likely a just punishment would be inflicted on him for this misdemeanour.

MONDAY 16 JANUARY 1882[437]
WHOLESALE THEFT
CC Number 544

Loh Ayau, a coal coolie, was charged with stealing a pair of shoes, a cotton jacket, and a purse, containing $3.60 silver, 350 copper cents, and 1,000 cash, on the 21st October last.

Wong Alung, a head coolie living at 23, Ni Hing Lane, said that on the 21st October he took all his coolies out to discharge coals. Defendant complained of a sore eye and was allowed to remain in the coolie house. Going back some time afterwards witness found on entering his room, and opening his box, which was unlocked, that the above money was gone, as also the property. Though the room door was locked any person could have access to it by climbing over the partition, which was not very high. Defendant was gone by this time and though information was lodged at the station, he was not apprehended till yesterday. Witness seized him while standing at a house door in Queen's Road East. Defendant admitted taking the money when brought

---

[437] "Police Intelligence", CM, Monday, 16 January 1882, p. 3, c. 5.

to the station, but said he did not think there was so much of it.

Defendant said he stole the money but thought there was not the amount stated by complainant, as it disappeared so quickly. He had been sick, and had had no work for some time.

Six months' imprisonment with hard labour was imposed.

A BATCH OF ROGUES
CC Number 545

Leong Atai and four others were charged with being suspicious characters.

John Butlin, Police Constable, discovered the five defendants in Sui Hing Lane early yesterday morning four of them sleeping under mats and the other one keeping watch. He had been watching this lane as he had information there were thieves in it. The first defendant had on a false queue.

The defendants all made excuse that they had no place to sleep in. The first defendant said that his queue had been cut off by some person, while he was lying in the street. They were each sentenced to three months' imprisonment with hard labour as rogues and vagabonds.

THEFT OF TROUSERS
CC Number 546

Ming Afat was charged with stealing ten pairs of trousers from Wong Shing's shop in Jervois Street.

The complainant said defendant and two others came and wanted to purchase some shoes. They did not purchase any and after they left he missed a bundle, containing ten pairs of trousers, from the counter, where it was lying. He went to the station and reported the matter, and while there defendant was brought in by a watchman with the bundle under his jacket.

Defendant said he was an unlicensed hawker, residing in Third Street, Sai-ying-pun. He was going to pawn the trousers, which belonged to him, and had been brought from his native place, Kwei Shin. He said he was not running when arrested and always carried his bundles under his jacket.

He was sentenced to four months' imprisonment with hard labour.

THEFT BY AN ACTOR
CC Number 547

Chu Awa, an actor, was convicted of stealing a box containing property to the value of $20, from a fortune-teller's house Number 17, High Street. This morning defendant said to the fortune- teller's brother that he could not sleep and thought he would go out for a short time. The box in question was placed in an inner room of the house, and defendant had not been seen near it, but shortly after he had left, he was brought back by a constable with the box under his arm. He was then taken to the Police Office and charged with the theft. He admitted taking the box, and stated that his company was broken up and in order to raise money to go home he had taken the box. His departure for home will be delayed for six months, he being sentenced to imprisonment for that period with hard labour.

AN OPIUM CASE
CC Number 548

Ho Ayu, shopkeeper, was charged with being in possession of prepared opium, without a permit from the Opium Farmer.

Inspector Perry, along with two excise officers and an informer went to Number 80, Wellington Street, and by virtue of a warrant searched the premises and discovered two tins, containing 5 taels of prepared opium, 73 catties of the same, and scales and other utensils bearing traces of raw opium. Defendant showed him the six permits produced in Court, when one was asked for.

Lai Akim, an unemployed coolie, said he went to Number 80, Wellington Street on the 11th *instant*, and purchased from defendant 10 cents worth of opium. He then went and gave information to the police, and accompanied Inspector Perry to the place.

The two excise officers gave evidence similar to Inspector Perry, and valued the opium at $205. They also identified some of the articles produced as being used in the preparation of opium.

The interpreter at Court stated that of the six permits only two belonged to Ho Ayu, and were only to the amount of 10 taels.

Defendant stated that he bought the two tins of prepared opium on the 1st instant from the Opium Farm. He also said he was a dealer in Malwa Opium, and had bought the raw opium from Hadjee Ali, Yuk-ün and U-ün. He denied selling any opium to the informer. The pans in Court he used for boiling his food and the scales were used for weighing raw opium.

The case was remanded to allow of defendant bringing forward the parties he bought the opium from.

Bail in two sureties of $100 each was accepted.

TUESDAY 17 JANUARY 1882[438]
LARCENY AND UNLAWFUL POSSESSION
CC Number 549

Ng Aloi, unemployed, was charged with stealing a hat, and with being in unlawful possession of a cap and shirt.

Chu Alok said, while talking to some Indians in his shop in Lower Lascar Row, defendant came and snatched the hat in Court. Witness gave chase, captured him, and handed him over to a constable.

Police Constable 520, who apprehended defendant, said complainant was handed over to him on the charge of stealing the hat, which complainant had in his hand at the time. Defendant had in his

---

[438] "Police Intelligence", CM, Tuesday, 17 January 1882, p. 3, c. 3.

possession the cap and shirt, and gave no account of how he came by them.

Defendant asserted that he bought all three articles from a stall opposite to complainants, but on this stall keeper being brought to Court, he stated he had never seen defendant.

Sentence, -- larceny of hat, one month's imprisonment; unlawful possession of other articles, fined ten shillings or 14 days' imprisonment with hard labour. Sentence to be cumulative.

WEDNESDAY 18 JANUARY 1882[439]
A COLLECTOR OF HERBS
CC Number 550

Chun Sing, a coolie, appeared on three charges, stealing water cresses, assaulting the owner of the cresses, and damaging the police cell in which he had been incarcerated. Cheung Apo, a market gardener, said that yesterday afternoon he was returning to his country residence, a hut on the hillside near Pok-fu-lam, and when getting within sight of his garden he found defendant busily engaged rooting up his water cresses. He at once seized him and a fierce combat was the result, in which he sustained several severe blows on the face and lower extremities adminis tered by a bamboo. Defendant made his escape but was afterwards captured by a policeman.

Defendant admitted taking water cresses from a stream on the hillside. Complainant came and beat him and the injuries he had received were the result of a fall.

Sergeant Rae said that at 9 o'clock last night he was called to the cell in which defendant was confined and found that he had removed three bricks from the wall of the building. He had used a small piece of bamboo to pick out the mortar.

---

[439] "Police Intelligence", CM, Wednesday, 18 January 1882, p. 3, c. 4.

Defendant said the chunam fell from the wall and he took out the bricks. He described himself as a collector of herbs.

Sentence -- Twenty-one days' imprisonment with hard labour for larceny of the water cresses, and to be fined $10, in default fourteen days' further imprisonment with hard labour, for attempting to escape from custody.

COUNTERFEIT COIN
CC Number 551

Choi Akiu, a fisherman, was charged with tendering two counterfeit dollars knowing the same to be false or counterfeit coins, on the 17th instant.

Police Constable 38, Frederick Howell, stationed at Stanley, said that from information he received from a shopkeeper there he searched the village and on finding defendant in the street he arrested him. When defendant saw the constable approaching he turned and ran.

Chan Afu, a shopkeeper, gave evidence to the effect that the prisoner came to him and purchased fifty cents' worth of opium. He paid for the opium with a dollar receiving 50 cents change, which was afterwards found to be of copper. Witness then went to look for defendant and found him in another shop some distance from his own. He was making purchases there, and he, witness, told him that the dollar he had previously received from him was a bad one. He received back the change formerly given to prisoner as well as the opium he had supplied to him, and he offered to go to his boat and procure a good dollar in place of the bad one.

Wong Aon, another shopkeeper, said defendant, who was not a resident in Stanley, also came to his shop there and tendered a bad dollar in payment for goods he had purchased. On his attention being called to the fact that the dollar was bad he at once offered to procure a good one in place of it.

The constable recalled, said that when he first met defendant he was coming up from the direction of the beach, but when he saw witness he turned about and went back again.

Mr Kwan Chak Lum, Usher to the Court, said he had examined the two dollars produced and found that they both purported to be Mexican dollars, but they were of spurious metal and were worth twenty-five and thirty cents respectively.

Defendant said he did not know that the dollars were bad. His boat was lying off Stanley and he went into the village to purchase opium and other things. He also admitted a conviction of larceny in 1879.

Six months' imprisonment, the first and last fortnights to be in solitary confinement, the remainder with hard labour.

The two counterfeit coins were also ordered to be destroyed.

THURSDAY 19 JANUARY 1882[440]
VAGABONDS AND INCAPABLES
CC Number 552 📖 p. 234

James Robert Ransome, unemployed telegraph operator, and Wyra Boory, an unemployed steward belonging to Penang, were charged with being rogues and vagabonds, and also with being drunk and incapable on the 17th instant.

Police Sergeant[441] Butlin said he found the two defendants lying drunk in East Street yesterday. Neither defendant had any visible means of subsistence and they were without any place of abode. The first defendant had been once previously convicted as a rogue and vagabond. The first defendant said he lived in Francis Street, Wanchai, and made his living by teaching some Gun Lascars

---

[440] "Police Intelligence", CM, Thursday, 19 January 1882, p. 3, c. 5.

[441] "Police Sergeant". See Geoffrey Roper, "The Police Role in Magistrate Frederick Stewart's Court", in, ed. Gillian Bickley, *A Magistate's Court in 19th Century Hong Kong*, pp. 117-130, on the changed policy of appointing expatriates to the rank of "Inspector" only.

the English language. He was put in gaol before as a matter of charity.

Police Sergeant Butlin said he had made enquiries about the truth of this statement and found it to be untrue.

Second defendant admitted the charge.

Each sentenced to 14 days' imprisonment with hard labour.

FRIDAY 20 JANUARY 1882[442]
THEFT FROM THE BARRACKS
CC Number 553

Cheung Afoo, a coolie, was charged this morning with stealing a razor from one of the men of the Inniskillings quartered in Whitfield Barracks, Kowloon, on the 19th instant.

Inspector Cameronpreferred the charge, and requested a remand as the complainant, Private Robert Moore, was employed on special duty and was unable to attend.

Remanded accordingly till to-morrow morning.

STEALING A SAMPAN
CC Number 554

Wong Yuk, a coolie, was charged with stealing a sampan from Aberdeen, and further with being armed with a dagger, at an early hour this morning.

Complainant, a fishmonger at Aberdeen, said that he had a small sampan at the back of his house, which was on the beach in the village. Yesterday evening the prisoner came to his house and requested the loan of the sampan, but complainant declined to let him have it at that hour, as junks came in then with fish and he required it himself. About midnight he was roused by a constable who had the prisoner in custody, and on his looking for the sampan he found it in the water.

---

[442] "Police Intelligence", CM, Friday, 20 January 1882, p. 3, c. 5.

Police Constable Macdougall said that at half past twelve this morning he found defendant sculling about in a small boat which was new to the place. He hailed him several times but got no answer and he then gave chase and overtook him. Defendant would give no account of himself and the constable arrested him and found him armed with a dagger. Defendant said he had borrowed the boat from complainant, but this was denied. He was an old offender, having no less than six previous convictions recorded against him, all of a serious nature.

Remanded till Monday next, the 23rd instant.[443]

UNLAWFUL POSSESSION
CC Number 555

Chin Achang, a saltfish dealer, pleaded guilty to being in the unlawful possession of portions of an unfinished jacket. He was arrested while trying to dispose of the pieces to a pawnbroker.

Three months' imprisonment with hard labour.

ROGUE AND VAGABOND
CC Number 556

Lum Afat, a hawker, was charged with being a rogue and vagabond, having been found, along with about fifteen others not in custody, sitting on the footpath in First Street gambling.

Defendant denied gambling, and said the money found in his hand, twenty cents and about fifty cash, was not for gambling purposes but to buy something. He admitted two convictions for breaches of the Gambling Ordinance[444] in May and June of last

---

[443] There is no further report of this case in *The Complete Cases*.
[444] "The Gambling Ordinance" was probably No. 9 of 1876, passed 11 December 1876. "To consolidate and amend the law relating to Public Gambling." (HKGG, 16 December 1876, pp. 553-554.) For the text of Ordinance No. 9 of 1876, see University of Hong Kong, "The Historical Laws of Hong Kong Online", and HKGG, 16 December 1876, pp. 553-554. This Ordinance was

year, and was now sentenced to three months' imprisonment with hard labour, and the money found on him was ordered to be deposited in the Poor Box.

SATURDAY 21 JANUARY 1882[445]
ROBBERY[446]
CC Number 557 📖 p. 283

Cheong Yak Fong and Tsung Yang Kiu, [447] doctors, were charged with being concerned, with others not in custody, in robbing Chow Young Chan of $205 on the 9th instant.[448]

This case was again brought up on remand from the 17th *instant*.[449] The complainant stated on that date that he had been a gold-miner in Portland for 25 years and had returned from San Francisco on the 7th *instant*. He took his abode at the I-wai-kü

---

amended by Ordinance No. 27 of 1888, passed 12 November 1888. (See HKGG, 24 November 1888, pp. 1067, 1070-1071.) In several places, the text of Ordinance No. 9 of 1876, as given in "The Historical Laws of Hong Kong Online", states, "Repealed by Ordinance No. 27 of 1888 . . ."
It seems then, that Ordinance No. 9 of 1876 is the Ordinance that prevailed during the period when these Court Cases were heard. The official name was, the "Public Gambling Amendment Ordinance, 1876".
In the context of the present study, it is interesting to note that the covering notice published in HKGG 24 November 1888 (p. 1067) reporting that assent has been received to five Ordinances, including No. 27 of 1888(was signed by Frederick Stewart, then Colonial Secretary.

[445] "Police Intelligence", CM, Saturday, 21 January 1881, p. 3, c. 1.
[446] The following is the complete set of reports in connection with this case in *The Complete Court Cases*: CC Nos 557, 593.
[447] In the reports of this case, the first name is given as both "Cheong Yak Fong" and "Cheong Tak-fong" and the second name as both "Tsung Yang Kiu" and "Tsung Yang-kin". (See *A Magistrate's Court in 19th Century Hong Kong,*, p. 486, n. 747.)
[448] There is no report of this case being heard before Frederick Stewart on this date in *The Complete Court Cases*.
[449] There is no report of this case being heard before Frederick Stewart on 17 January 1881 in *The Complete Court Cases*.
A further search in *The China Mail*, 17 January 1882, has also not proved successful.

Lodging house on the Praya. He handed over his property to the master of the house to take care of. On the day of his arrival he met the second defendant, who accosted him and offered to get a person to cure a sore eye, which had been bad for sometime. At that time the second defendant, after enquiring where he came from, said he belonged to a village close to the complainant's and they agreed to go home together by the Canton steamer. On the 11th instant he packed up his traps, and along with the second defendant proceeded to go to the steamer, but on the way he was enticed to go to a brothel by him. A man whom the second defendant knew asked some money from complainant, but being refused they seized him, along with some others, and abstracted his gold from his pocket, where it was concealed. He then returned to the Lodging house and afterwards reported the matter.

Tung Chung Man, the master of the Lodging house, stated that the complainant had given him a bag to keep, said to contain some gold coins, but after living 4 days with him, complainant received the bag and other property as he said he was going to live with a clansman of his. Complainant did not mention to him his intention of going to Canton. Three or four days after he had left witness's house he came back and said some men had cheated him. He said nothing about gambling nor of his having been enticed into a brothel and robbed. Judging by the weight of the bag, witness imagined there would be about $200 worth in it.

A constable gave evidence as to apprehending the second defendant in his own home in Po-yan Street; and the first in Hollywood Road. Both were pointed out to him by the complainant as being concerned in the robbery. He heard some of the crowd, who were at the door say, "They have promised to give him back [450]80," but he could not

---

[450] It is impossible to read clearly up to the margin of the copy supplied to the present Editor. Maybe a first digit is missing from this number. (See *A Magistrate's Court in 19th Century Hong*

say who "They" referred to. He knew the second defendant to be the first defendant's apprentice, and they both practised in the Recreation Grounds.

Tsui Yat Ko, a dentist, residing in the same house as the two defendants, said he heard complainant accusing them of stealing $200.

The case was again remanded till Monday, 23rd January.

STEALING A COVERLET[451]
CC Number 558

Au Afat was charged, on remand, with stealing a coverlet from Chung Aheung, a coolie, residing in 56, Third Street, Sai-ying- pun. Complainant, while asleep on the 13th January, was awakened by feeling his coverlet being taken away. The defendant had entered the house quietly and with the aid of a bamboo with a hook on the end, had drawn the coverlet to him from the top of the stairs. He ran off with it, but was arrested before getting any distance.

The Receiving officer of the Gaol proved six previous convictions against the defendant.

Defendant having been cautioned, reserved his defence, and was committed for trial at the Criminal Sessions of the Supreme Court.[452]

Kong,, p. 486, n. 750.) Or possibly, it is simply a dollar symbol that can't be seen, making the sum referred to "$80".

[451] "Police Intelligence", CM, Saturday, 21 January 1881, p. 3, c. 1.

[452] For the February 1882 Sessions, held on 27 February 1882, two courts were sitting, each with its own jury. One was before the Hon. F. Snowden, Acting Chief Justice and the other was before the Hon. J. Russell, Acting Puisne Judge. For cases heard before the Hon. F. Snowden, the Attorney General (The Hon. E. L. O'Malley), instructed by the Crown Solicitor, Mr Sharp, prosecuted. For cases heard before the Hon. J. Russell, Mr Mckean, on behalf of the Attorney General, prosecuted.

The following information about this case appears in the Criminal Calendar for the February Sessions, 1882, HKGG, 11 March 1882, p. 258, where the case is No. 3.

MONDAY 23 JANUARY 1882[453]
LARCENY
CC Number 559

Chun Achim, Chun Akwa, William Cottrell (American), and Wong Ahok, were charged, the first and second with being in unlawful possession of a quantity of rope, and the third and fourth with having stolen the rope from the Annamese gunboat Li-tai, on the 22nd *instant*.

A police boat saw the first and second defendants land at the Patent Slip at Lap-sap-Wan on

---

Au A-fat [*sic*] was tried before J. Russell, Acting Puisne Judge, on 27 February and charged on three counts of 1) Larceny, 2) Previous conviction (summary), and 3) Previous conviction (summary). He was found guilty on 1) Larceny, and pleaded guilty on the second and third counts. He was sentenced the same day (27 February 1882) to three years' penal servitude.

The following report appears in *The China Mail* (Monday, 27 February 1882, p. 3, cc. 2-3, c. 2):
Supreme Court
In Criminal Sessions . . .
(Before the Hon. J. Russell, Acting Puisne Judge.)

Monday, 27 February 1882
The following jury was empannelled: Messrs W. S. Ramsay, S. R. Rozario, G. M. de Carvalho, J. Rooke, C. W. Richard, F. J. V. Jorge, W. H. Gaskell.
Mr Mackean, on behalf of the Attorney General, prosecuted.

Larceny
Au Afat was found guilty of stealing a coverlet belonging to Chung Sui Ping, from his bed. The complainant's companions had gone to the theatre and left the room of their door open, so that easy admittance could be gained on their return. The complainant had been asleep, when he was roused by feeling his coverlet being taken away. He immediately rose and gave chase. The defendant had attempted to take the coverlet away with a bamboo pole, with a hook on the end of it. Six previous convictions were recorded against him. He was sentenced to three years' penal servitude.

The Sessions were then adjourned until Thursday, the 2nd March, at half-past ten o'clock.

[453] "Police Intelligence", CM, Monday, 23 January 1882, p. 3, c. 2.

the 21st instant. The second defendant landed and was followed by some of the police, but noticing this he turned back and made for his boat and threw something overboard. The boat was seized and a quantity of rope and some gratings found on board. From information received the police went on board the Li-tai and apprehended the third and fourth defendants.

Ching Ku Shing, partner in the Shun Wo Un Hong in Wing Lok Street said that he, along with Mr Kwok Yin Kai, was proprietor of the Li-tai, and that the third defendant was employed by them as a head watchman on board. Third defendant had no authority to sell any of the belongings of the vessel. Witness identified the rope and gratings as belonging to the ship. The fourth defendant was also a watchman, employed under the third.

The first defendant said he had sold the third defendant some oranges, who had then asked him to purchase the rope, which he did, paying him $1.50 for it. The gratings he purchased from the fourth defendant for 300 cash.

The second defendant said he was a partner of the first in a fruit selling business, and knew nothing about this matter.

Cottrell, the third defendant, said he was asked to sell the rope for as much as he could get by Lam Ashing. He had not accounted for the money to his owner, as he had had no opportunity. The greater part of the money was already spent in provisions as they had run short of them. He sold the rope to the first defendant. He admitted two previous convictions of being a rogue and vagabond.

The fourth defendant admitted selling the gratings, but said he had been ordered to do so by the third.

Lam Ashing, a coolie in the Shun Wo Un Hong, said he did not authorize the third defendant to sell the material, as he had no power to do so.

The first and second defendants were convicted of receiving stolen goods; and the third and fourth of larceny. They were each sentenced to four months' imprisonment with hard labour, the first and last fortnight to be passed in solitary confinement.

UNLAWFUL POSSESSION OF A JACKET
CC Number 560
Li Aho, marine hawker, was charged with being in unlawful possession of a jacket. Yesterday the defendant presented the jacket for pawn to the Tai Chang pawn shop, at the corner of Caine Road. A constable, who was in the shop at the time, heard the prisoner say the jacket belonged to his brother. The constable requested him to take him to the brother, but the defendant then said he had bought it from a man he could not find. The jacket was proved to belong to the master of the Kwong Li Un Hong[454] and was missed, along with a pair of silk trousers, on the 20th *instant*.

Defendant admitted two previous convictions and was then fined L10 [*sic* for "$10"], or three months' imprisonment with hard labour.

A NOVEL USE OF A QUEUE
CC Number 561
Ip Atai was charged with snatching a hat from Pang You. Pang You was engaged listening to a story-teller in the Recreation Ground on Saturday, when he felt some one snatch his hat. On getting up to give chase, he found his queue was tied to his neighbour's, but he observed defendant running off with his hat. He broke his neighbour's queue string and gave chase. The defendant ran to the Praya, where he threw the hat into the harbour, and there being no boat handy the hat was lost. Defendant offered at the time to repay complainant, but this was refused, and he was apprehended and convicted of the crime. Six months' imprisonment with hard labour was imposed.

---

[454] The name of this ship is not in italics in the original.

THEFT OF WOOD
CC Number 562
Chung Achi was found guilty of stealing a piece of wood belonging to Chung Fu. The defendant admitted two previous convictions and was sentenced to six months' imprisonment with hard labour.

TUESDAY 24 JANUARY 1882[455]
AN OFFENCE UNDER THE POST OFFICE REGULATIONS
CC Number 563
Yau Chung Ping, shopkeeper of Fokien, was charged by the Postmaster General with neglecting to give intimation of an alteration in the date of sailing of the steamship Plainmeller, bound for Singapore on the 20th January.[456]

Mr Wotton, who appeared for the defendant, expressed his regret that the neglect should have taken place; and on behalf of his client promised to avoid such a neglect in future. He said his client was

---

[455] "Police Intelligence", CM, Tuesday, 24 January 1882, p. 3, cc. 1 - 2.

[456] See CM, 19 January 1882, p. 2, c. 5 for the following listing under "Shipping: Arrivals":
"19 January. 'Plainmeller', British steamer, 1195, Wm McKenzie, Swatow 18 January, General. — BUN HIN CHAN."
"Bun Hin Chan" seems to be the name of the agent.
It is of course clear that it was essential that residents should know accurately the dates when ships left for various desinations, so as to plan their mail accordingly. But it is at first difficult to see why it was "Yau Chung Ping, shopkeeper of Fokien", who was "charged by the Postmaster General with neglecting to give intimation of an alteration in the date of sailing of the steamship 'Plainmeller', bound for Singapore on the 20th January", or why he was in Hong Kong.
Perhaps he had come on the ship in some official capacity which included the responsibility to report the up-to-date sailing schedule.
Also in *The China Mail*, 19 January 1882, p. 2, c. 5 under "Shipping: Cleared", we find:
"'Plainmeller', for Singapore, &c."
In the information about passengers, we find that 594 Chinese were to depart on the "'Plainmeller'" for "Singapore, &c.".
The China Mail of 20 January 1882 lists 'Plainnmeller' under Shipping "Departures" (p. 2, c. 4).

not a person who would willingly behave in an offensive manner, and would ask his Worship to be as lenient as possible.

His Worship said he would leave the matter in the Postmaster's hands, and would dismiss the summons if he did not press the charge.

The Postmaster agreed to relinquish the charge if the defendant would promise to prevent the recurrence of the offence.

The defendant then apologised, and promised to pay attention to the requirements of the Post Office regulations.

His Worship pointed out that the defendant might have incurred a penalty not exceeding $500. Such a neglect was a serious matter as the Postmaster was responsible for the correct transmission of mails, and was likely to be accused of negligence when anything went wrong through such a cause as this. He dismissed the summons, but cautioned defendant as to future conduct in reporting correctly the hour of sailing of his vessels.

THEFT OF TWENTY CENTS
CC Number 564
Mok Shin, while on board the Canton steamer yesterday, dropped two 10 cent pieces from his purse, and Ki Awo picked them up and ran off, but was quickly captured. He was convicted and sent to prison for twenty-one days.

THEFT OF SCALES
CC Number 565
Chun Apu, unemployed, was observed by a constable walking along the Praya yesterday with a pair of scales in his hand. Defendant immediately turned and was in the act of running off when the constable, suspecting him, seized him, and had him taken to the station. The scales were afterwards found to belong to Ayai Chan, hawker, who had missed them for a short time. Defendant was sent to gaol for six weeks.

UNLAWFUL POSSESSION OF RICE
CC Number 566
Tse Atak was fined five shillings or four days' imprisonment for having in his possession a bag containing about 20 catties of rice, and for which he could not satisfactorily account.

ROBBERY FROM THE PERSON
CC Number 567
Yeung Afu was charged on remand, with stealing from Cheung Sam, gold digger, the sum of $20.

Complainant had returned from California a few days ago, and while walking in Queen's Road Central the defendant had abstracted the money from his pocket. Defendant was apprehended while in the act. Five previous convictions were proved against him, and he was committed for trial at the next Criminal Sessions.[457]

---

[457] The following information appears in the Criminal Calendar for the February Sessions, 1882, HKGG, 11 March 1882, p. 258, where this case is No. 4.

Yung A-fu was tried before J. Russell, Acting Puisne Judge, on 27 February 1882 on three counts: 1) larceny, 2) Previous conviction (summary) and 3) Previous conviction (summary). He was unanimously found guilty. The same day (27 February 1882), he was sentenced to five years' penal servitude. A "*Nolle prosequi*" was entered by the Attorney General on the second and third counts.

The following report appeared in *The China Mail*. (Monday, 27 February 1882, p. 3, cc. 2-3, c. 2.)
"Supreme Court
"In Criminal Sessions
"(Before the Hon. J. Russell, Acting Puisne Judge)
"Monday, 27 February 1882
"[Stealing from the Person]

"The following jury was empanelled: Messrs W. S. Ramsay, S. R. Rozario, G. M. de Carvalho, J. Rooke, C. W. Richard, F. J. V. Jorge, W. H. Gaskell.

"Mr Mackean, on behalf of the Attorney General, prosecuted."

PASSING COUNTERFEIT COIN
CC Number 568

Ho Yau, barber, and U-sheung, hawker, were charged with passing counterfeit coin on the 23rd instant.

A constable who knew both defendants as bad characters, watched their operations in Queen's Road Central yesterday. The first defendant went into the Lai-on pawnshop and quickly came out carrying a jacket. The constable went into the shop and was shown the counterfeit coin the defendant had passed. He followed them to the entrance of the Central Market, when they turned, and the second defendant entered the same shop and tendered a bad dollar in payment of some purchase. The constable then arrested them, when some more coins were found in their possession.

The first defendant denied having given in payment the dollar produced in Court. Some found in his sleeve, he said, had been given him by his aunt, now in the country.

The prisoners were both convicted and sentenced to six months' imprisonment with hard labour, the first and last fortnight to be passed in solitary confinement.

"Yeung Afu was charged with snatching a bag, containing $30, from the person of Cheung Asam, a gold digger, in Queen's Road on the 21st January.

"The evidence of the complainant and the constable, who arrested the prisoner, proved that he had snatched the bag while the complainant was in a crowd, and that some person unknown pinioned the complainant's arms, but was unable to hold him. The complainant then seized the prisoner.

"He was found guilty, unanimously, by the jury.

"His Lordship, in passing sentence, remarked that the prisoner, who was a young man of about 21 years of age, had had a terrible career. No less than five previous convictions were already recorded against him, the first occurring when the prisoner was thirteen yeas of age. His Lordship said he must impose a heavy sentence, and he would therefore commit him to prison for five years' penal servitude."

WEDNESDAY 25 JANUARY 1882[458]
OPIUM CASE
CC Number 569

Pun Amui, compradore, belonging to Canton, was charged on Monday with being in possession of prepared opium without a permit from the Opium Farmer.

On Monday evidence was given as to the finding of a large quantity of prepared opium in the house Number 15, Stanley Street, the defendant being the proprietor. He produced a permit for a portion of the opium, but some of it being proved to be eight or nine years old, no permit could have been procured for it as the Opium Farmer did not have the monopoly at that time, and as he had failed to inform the Opium Farmer of having it in his possession since, an offence was proved. The case was remanded till to-day to allow the defendant to procure a permit, as he said he had forgot about its being on his premises. The Opium Farmer, however, [c?/w?]ould not grant the permit at this late date, as the rules would be infringed by doing so. The defendant should have applied for a permit when the notice was issued.

He was fined $10 or two days' imprisonment -- the opium to be confiscated.

THURSDAY 26 JANUARY 1882[459]
LARCENY
CC Number 570 📖 p. 326

Ly Aying, a lad of fifteen, employed as a shop boy by Messrs Kelly and Walsh, Queen's Road, was charged with the theft of a $25 note on the 25th instant.

Mr. C. Grant, Manager of the business in Hong Kong, said that yesterday afternoon he put a $25 note in the till. A short time afterwards he sent the prisoner to clear away a quantity of waste paper

---

[458] "Police Intelligence", CM, Wednesday, 25 January 1882, p. 3, c. 1.

[459] CM, Thursday, 26 January 1882, "Police Intelligence", p. 2, c. 5.

from behind the counter in which the till had been placed. Later on Mr Davidson, one of the assistants, had occasion to go to the till for change, and after getting what he required he omitted to lock the drawer. About five o'clock when the cash was balanced it was found that the $25 note in question was missing, and on the boys in the shop being searched, it was found in the prisoner's purse, on his person.

Defendant said he picked the note up from the floor. He did not know why he had not given it to his master.

Mr Grant, recalled, said the defendant had been in his service for three years. He bore a good character and was liked very much as a servant.

Sentence -- Four months' imprisonment with hard labour.

A GAMBLER'S HAUNT
CC Number 571

Un Aho, rice-pounder, was charged with being a rogue and vagabond and with being in possession of a deadly weapon on the 25th instant.

Defendant was found watching outside a door on the first-floor at house Number 1, Tai Hing Lane, with an iron bar in his hand, apparently guarding the house. The police while arresting him heard a noise as if a number of people were making their escape by the roof. All the articles employed in gambling were found in the room and brought to the station. Some time ago a gambling assembly was broken up in the same house.

Defendant admitted gambling and said if the lukong caught him with an iron bar in his hand he could not help it.

Fined $50, or three months' imprisonment with hard labour. Money and gambling implements were ordered to be confiscated.[460]

---

[460] Confiscating the money and gambling implements was authorized under Ordinance No. 9 of 1876, para. 7.

DAMAGING TREES AT THE RACE COURSE
CC Number 572
Ling Ayau was convicted of damaging trees at the race course on the 25th instant by cutting down branches. Defendant was previously convicted of the same offence. He was ordered to pay $5, or be imprisoned for fourteen days with hard labour.

A VAGRANT
CC Number 573
Leong Atsun was discovered asleep in an unfinished building in Lower Lascar Row by a watchman last night.

Defendant stated that he had no money to pay his board, and his landlord turned him out. He had no friends or relations to help him or speak as to his character. He had undergone six weeks' imprisonment already for the same offence.

Sentenced to six weeks' imprisonment.

FRIDAY 27 JANUARY 1882[461]
LARCENY
CC Number 574
Wong Aki, a coolie, was charged with the larceny of a pair of trousers on the 25th instant.

From the statement of complainant it appeared that on the morning of Wednesday last the defendant came into his house and asked for a light to his cigar. He got this, but was scarcely satisfied with the civility thus extended to him, and increased his obligations to the complainant by appropriating a pair of cotton trousers that were hanging on a bamboo in the passage; and further had the audacity to put them on, and was wearing them when apprehended.

In his defence the defendant said that complainant wanted to send him to Singapore where he was to be sold "like a pig." He was afraid at this and ran, and through this he excited the suspicions of the police and was arrested. He admitted that the

---

[461] "Police Intelligence", CM, Friday, 27 January 1882, p. 3, c. 1.

trousers he was then wearing were the property of complainant, as also to having been a former resident in Victoria Gaol.

Sentence -- Three months' imprisonment with hard labour.

KIDNAPPING[462]
CC Number 575 📖 p. 308

Pang Asun and Chan Acheung, aged 21 and 22, married women belonging to Canton, were charged, on remand from yesterday, with bringing Chan Nui into this colony for the purposes of prostitution.

Chan Nui, the complainant, said she was the wife of Chung Tai-fuk, a coolie working in a chandler's shop in Canton, and who used to visit her in the village of Lo-kong, where she lived with her father-in-law, on Chinese Festivals. On the 23rd September an old woman, who lived in the same village but whose name she did not know, came to her father-in-law's house and asked her to accompany her to Canton, which she did in the expectation of meeting her husband. The old woman said the object of her visit to Canton was to make some purchases. When they arrived in Canton the old woman placed her on board a small boat, and told her to remain there until she returned. This boat was occupied by two women, and she remained there until the 28th September, but still her friend did not return. On that date the first defendant came on board the boat and asked the boatwomen if they had a woman for sale, to which they replied in the affirmative and pointed to the complainant. After some disputing the bargain money was settled as $245, and this woman left in the boatwomen's hands three gold rings, and the gold earring as earnest money. This woman did not come back to the boat,

---

[462] The following is the complete set of reports in connection with this case in *The Complete Court Cases*: CC Nos 575, 587, 600, 619. See also *A Magistrate's Court in 19th Century Hong Kong*, pp. 496-497, notes 867-890, where variations in personal and place names are noted.

but on the 4th October an old woman, which [s]he now knew to be the first defendant's mother-in-law, came and paid the money in silver dollars. Complainant at first refused to proceed with the first defendant's mother-in-law, but on her promising to find her husband she consented. She was then brought to Hong Kong and taken to the Kiu-lan brothel, where she was furnished with a new dress, and told to make herself agreeable to visitors. The second defendant, who is a servant, she did not see until she was taken to the brothel. The mother-in-law went back to Canton a few days ago. Her husband came to the brothel on the 23rd *instant*, with a friend in search of her. He stayed all night, went out early in the morning and returned at noon alone, and told her that he intended to petition the Court for her release. On the [25]th[463] instant her husband, in company with Inspector Lee,[464] re moved her from the brothel and took her to the Tung Wa Hospital.

In answer to the Magistrate she said she had not been brought by physical force, but had been deluded and deceived. She had not communicated with her relations, as she had no means of doing so.

The case was then remanded till the 31st instant.

ATTEMPTED LARCENY OF A SAMPAN
CC Number 576

Mok Ngan was charged with larceny of a boat belonging to Wong Afu.

A brick junk belonging to complainant was anchored off Praya West on Wednesday night, when defendant was observed by him cutting the ropes of their sampan, which was attached to the boat. The complainant along with some of his men gave chase

---

[463] Original defective. Supplied by reference to CC No. 587.
[464] Inspector John Lee was Assistant Inspector of Brothels, Lock Hospital. ("List of Officers", HKBB1882, Section I3.) Geoffrey Roper has suggested that Inspector Lee was apparently European, as he was accompanied by an interpreter on his brothel visits.

and captured defendant. He had only managed to sever a rope at one end of the boat and threw the detached portion and the chopper he used into the water, when he became aware that he was seen. There was about 30 feet of rope.

The defendant was convicted of stealing the rope and sentenced to six weeks' imprisonment.

SATURDAY 28 JANUARY 1882[465]
COMMITTAL OF NUISANCE
CC Number 577 📖 p. 361

Kong Ayuk was convicted of committing a nuisance at the back of Number 1 Police Station to-day and was fined 25 cents or two days' imprisonment.

DRUNK AND DISORDERLY
CC Number 578

Charles King, unemployed seaman, was convicted of being found drunk in Lower Lascar Row and creating a disturbance by annoying people and making a considerable noise. He was fined 50 cents or two days' imprisonment.

THEFT OF JACKETS
CC Number 579

Lai Aping was sentenced to six weeks' imprisonment with hard labour for appropriating a jacket belonging to Tam Sam, blacksmith, Queen's Road West. The jacket had been hung out on a bamboo to dry and the defendant while passing had been tempted to remove it, with the expectation of enjoying undisputed possession.

[THEFT OF JACKETS]
CC Number 580

Tse Lai, coolie, was charged with stealing a jacket belonging to Leung Tsai on the 27th instant.

---

[465] "Police Intelligence", CM, Saturday, 28 January 1882, p. 3, c. 2.

Defendant had taken the jacket from the complainant's stall in Queen's Road West, but had been captured before getting away.

Six weeks' imprisonment with hard labour was imposed.

[THEFT OF JACKETS]
CC Number 581

Yung Yau, cook, was charged with stealing two jackets from Chan Kwai Ya on the 27th instant.

The complainant said she lived in Sam To Lane, off the Praya; and had been engaged washing in the cook-house when she heard a foot on the stairs. On going to see who it was she saw defendant coming down from her bedroom with two jackets under his arm. She had him arrested by a constable and charged him with the crime.

Defendant said he went out for a walk and while walking through Sam To Lane a woman invited him to drink a cup of tea. After staying some time they had a dispute and he was pushed out and given in charge by the complainant. He denied taking the jackets.

Sentenced to two months' imprisonment with hard labour.

UNLAWFUL POSSESSION
CC Number 582

Wong Kwan, unemployed, was charged with being in unlawful possession of 2 lbs. of potatoes on the 26th *instant*.

Police Constable McDonald said while on duty in Hung-hom village he met defendant and as his proportions looked rather bulky he stopped him. Defendant sat down when the constable tried to search him, and also tried to throw the potatoes away. He gave a great deal of trouble while being conveyed to the station.

Defendant said he picked the potatoes up in the Western Market, and as he had no place to cook them carried them round his waist. His reason for resisting the constable was because he did not know him, and was not aware what object he had in stopping him.

He was convicted of larceny and committed to prison for six weeks.

MONDAY 30 JANUARY 1882[466]
DRUNK AND INCAPABLES
CC Number 583

William Baker, seaman unemployed, Paul Schulte, seaman on board the German steamer Electra, Barney Bennet, seaman unemployed, and Bernard Nicklesen of the British ship Hindostan, were fined in sums varying from twenty-five cents to $1, for being drunk and incapable in the public streets yesterday.

UNLAWFUL POSSESSION
CC Number 584

Cheong To Kwai and Cheong Yau Choi, boatmen, were charged with unlawful possession of a quantity of rope on the 29th *instant*.

Police Constable Thomas Ryan said that about eleven o'clock last night he was on duty near the P. & O. Company's Wharf, when he saw defendants in a large boat. They had a shrimp net down and he hailed them. On searching their boat he found in the fore compartment a quantity of old rope, and in the cabin several coils of new, as also two pieces of lead piping. First defendant told him he had picked the things up in the harbour, and he used them for fishing purposes.

First prisoner said he bought the piping in a shop in Queen's Road, but he neither knew the number nor designation of the shop. He intended to use the lead as sinkers for his nets. The old rope he said he had picked up in various places in the harbour; and with regard to the new rope, he had made that himself out of old material which he had

---

[466] "Police Intelligence", CM, Monday, 30 January 1882, p. 3, cc. 4 - 5.

been collecting during the past three years. He had hooked it all up from time to time from the bottom of the harbour.

The second defendant made a somewhat similar statement, with this difference, that he said he had purchased the lead piping from a sampan lying off Jardine's.

Inspector Cradock valued the lead pipe at sixty cents, the old rope at $1.92, and the new rope at $16.00. He said he had seen old rope fished up from the bottom of the harbour. He did not think the new rope had ever been in the water. It had all the appearance and colour of new Manila rope with no trace of dampness about it.

Fined L5 each [*sic* for "$5"], in default two months' imprisonment with hard labour.

ROGUES AND VAGABONDS
CC Number 585

Chun Fuk, stone-cutter, and Tsai Awa, silversmith were charged with being rogues and vagabonds.

The defendants were heard soliciting money from a man at the back of the Ko Shing Theatre. The first defendant was known to deal among [*sic*] false rings and had been in the act of palming one off on this man when he was arrested. He had just completed a term of three months' imprisonment for a similar offence; and was without any visible means of subsistence. Both were proved to be the associates of thieves; and otherwise men of a bad character. They were each sentenced to undergo three months' imprisonment.

[ROGUES AND VAGABONDS]
CC Number 586

Kwan Po, Li Kap Sau, and Wong Su Sing were charged with a similar offence. They were all caught gambling, the first defendant being manager of the game. The offence was proved and the first defendant was fined $5 or 10 days' imprisonment with hard labour; the second $2 or three days' imprisonment, and the third 50 cents or 1 day's imprisonment.

TUESDAY 31 JANUARY 1882[467]
ALLEGED KIDNAPPING[468]
CC Number 587 📖 p. 310

Pang Asun, and Chun Acheung, married women belonging to Canton, were charged, on remand, with bringing to this Colony and detaining one Chan Nui for the purposes of prostitution.

In the previous examination the complainant declared that the first defendant had paid $245 to some boatwomen at Canton, into whose keeping she had been decoyed by an old woman belonging to her native village, on the 23rd September. She was brought to Hong Kong by the first defendant's mother-in-law and detained in a brothel until the 23rd of this month.

To-day Inspector Lee said that on the 25th instant, a man named Chung Tai Fuk came to his house with a petition and instructions from the Acting Registrar General to investigate the grievance of which he complained. He went to the brothel, called Mui Lan, Number 32 West Street, of which the second defendant was the registered keeper, and entered a room on the ground floor, where he saw the complainant and the first defendant. The latter ran towards him, fell on her knees, and protested vigorously that she and her children would be ruined. Complainant was weeping, and after he had called the keeper and demanded the list of inmates, he asked what was her name, which she said was Chan Nui.

Mr Holmes, of Messrs Stephens & Holmes, at this point appeared for the two defendants.

Inspector Lee, continuing, said that on examining the list he found no name corresponding

---

[467] "Police Intelligence", CM, Tuesday, 31 January 1882, p. 3, cc. 5 - 6.

[468] The following is the complete set of reports in connection with this case in *The Complete Court Cases*: CC Nos 575, 587, 600, 619.

to complainant's. He then asked her how her name did not appear, to which she made no reply, but some one in the room cried out that Kwok Ching-kam was her name. This complainant denied, but said her mistress had told her to answer to that name when the Inspector came. On the previous evening he made an official visit to the brothel and read out the names on the list, to each of which an answer was made by one of the inmates. The number of names on the list corresponded with the number of inmates. He asked them in a body if they were all there as voluntary prostitutes, to which no answer was made.

The case was again adjourned till the 4th February, — Bail being allowed in the sum of $100 each.

BEFORE FREDERICK STEWART, ESQ.,
February 1882[469]

WEDNESDAY 1 FEBRUARY 1882[470]
AN UNLICENSED VEGETABLE HAWKER
CC Number 588

Chun Aman admitted having hawked vegetables
without being in possession of a license, and also
with obstructing the street traffic to-day. He was
fined 50 cents or two days' imprisonment.

WEDNESDAY 1 FEBRUARY 1882[471]
ASSAULT ON BOARD THE "GLENELG"
CC Number 589

Chan Afung, a coolie, charged Hugh McMillan, a
fireman on board the S.S. Glenelg, with having
assaulted him on the 31st *ultimate*

Chan Aping said while waiting on a coal boat
coming from shore the complainant, who was under
the influence of drink, came and struck him a blow
on the eye with his fist.

The defendant said he was supplied with
some native liquor, which had the effect of turning
him into the condition of a man bereft of reason. He
humbly expressed his regret for what had occurred
and said it was his first appearance in a Police Court.
He had been all round the world and never had been
in such a predicament before.

The leniency of the law was extended to him,
and he was fined $2, or four days' imprisonment.

---

[469] **Note on the Court Case Reports for February 1882 as a
whole.** The courts were sitting on 8 February 1882, (see CM, p.
3, c. 4), but there is no report from Frederick Stewart's court. As
for 28 February, there is a very brief Police Court section (less
than two column inches), but it omits to state which magistrate's
court is being reported on. The dedicated database used by the
current writer has no hard copies for 23 February 1882. One case
has been added to the sequence and is numbered [635a].

[470] "Police Intelligence", CM, Wednesday, 1 February 1882, p. 3,
cc. 5 - 6.

[471] "Police Intelligence", CM, Wednesday, 1 February 1882, p. 3,
cc. 5 - 6.

OBTRUSIVE CHAIR COOLIES
CC Number 590

The bearers of 7 licensed chairs were charged, on remand, with unlawfully, when unengaged, standing ready for hire at a place other than that directed by the Registrar General, namely, in Queen's Road Central.

Au Aching, a constable, said that on Sunday the 29th *ultimate* he was on duty near the Clock Tower, when he observed the defendants all with their chairs placed on the wrong side of the road. He heard an European call for a chair and they all rushed forward inviting him to enter their chair, and entirely blocking up the thoroughfare. Although the defendants had been repeatedly warned that it was an offence they still persisted in the annoyance.

Charles Osmund, Registrar General's clerk, said there were stands at the entrance to the Hong Kong Hotel, the Supreme Court and Peddar's [*sic*] Wharf; and at these stands the number allowed must not be exceeded. There were a larger number of chairs than the provided stands could accommodate.

The Magistrate cautioned the defendants and then discharged them.

DESTRUCTION OF TREES
CC Number 591

Lo Kui Mui and Tau Mui were convicted of cutting the branches of some trees at Tai Tam Tuk village. While the prisoners were being conveyed to the station the villagers made a slight attempt to rescue them, but were unsuccessful. The defendants were fined $2 each, or four days' imprisonment with hard labour.

THEFT OF A PIECE OF WOOD
CC Number 592

Mo Sam Hing was sentenced to fourteen days' imprisonment for stealing a piece of wood at Stanley on the 31st *ultimate*.

ROBBERY[472]
CC Number 593 📖 p. 285

Cheong Tak-fong and Tsung Yang-kin, doctors, who were charged with being concerned in robbing Chow Yang Chan of $205 were to-day discharged. The case had been remanded to allow of the inmates of the brothel in which the complainant said he had been robbed to appear as witnesses, but the complainant had been unable to point out the house to the police. The defendants acknowledged supplying him with some medicine for a sore eye on the 9th December, but knew nothing further about his actions until he came to the second defendant and said he had been cheated of the $205.

ASSAULT
CC Number 594 📖 p. 285

Ho Achi, a tailor, was charged with assaulting Chan Ayan.

The complainant said that he had no occupation and had been here five months on a visit to a friend. On the 31st *ultimate* he was in a brothel in Square Street, when the defendant along with some others commenced to beat him and drove him out. The defendant struck him on the head and arm with an iron bar. The wounds bled freely and he had to visit the Hospital to have his head dressed. The constable who apprehended the defendant said he saw him beating the complainant with his fists, but did not observe any others assisting him.

Defendant said he was on the way to his shop, when he saw the complainant fighting. The complainant seized hold of him thinking he was one of his assailants.

He was fined $1, or suffer [*sic*] 4 days' imprisonment with hard labour, and required to give personal security in the sum of $10 to keep the peace for two months.

---

[472] The following is the complete set of reports in connection with this case in *The Complete Court Cases*: CC Nos 557, 593.

A DESTITUTE SEAMAN
CC Number 595

William Jacks, seaman of St. Helena, unemployed, went into the charge room of the Central Station and gave himself up as a destitute. He had frequently done this before, and received some food and a night's lodgings, but as he was drunk on this occasion he was locked up and charged with being a rogue and a vagabond. He had been twice imprisoned, once for larceny, and once for being a rogue and a vagabond. Defendant said he had been in the colony over 9 months and could find no employment; the drink was given to him.

He was sent to prison for 21 days, the imprisonment to be accompanied by hard labour.

THE TABLES TURNED
CC Number 596

Un Asui, a shopkeeper, was charged on a warrant with being in possession of stolen property.

The Hon. Ng Choy[473] appeared for the defence.

Chan Kan, keeper of an opium divan at Number 93, Hollywood Road, said that a man named Yang Tai, formerly cook to his family, who reside at Number 30, West Street, came and visited him. During the visit he went to the roof to dry some clothes, leaving this friend in his room alone. When he came down the friend was gone, as also two cotton jackets, a jade bangle, and a silver watch and chain. He went in search of Yang Tai and found him in a gambling house in Market Street. The defendant was standing near the gamblers and had the witness's jackets, bangle, and watch in his hands. He seized Yang Tai, but some party assisted him in his

---

[473] Ng Choy (1842-1922), was the first Chinese to be appointed a Member of the Legislative Council in Hong Kong and (for a brief period under Governor John Pope Hennessy) Acting Police Magistrate. aka Wu Ting Fang. Also known as Wu Ting Fang, he was originally from Singapore, studied in Hong Kong at St Paul's College and was the first Chinese to be called to the English bar.

struggles to get away and witness was unable to detain him. Defendant left the house, and witness followed him to Number 7, Station Street, and ascertained that $12 had been lent on the property; and he refused to allow them to be redeemed, saying that only the party who pledged them would be allowed to redeem them. The same day he returned to the house with Constable, 190, and asked admittance, but a woman called from inside that it was too late to redeem things. Next day he accompanied two inspectors, the house was searched and a jacket was found which he claimed as his. Defendant said to witness in the hearing of Sergeant Wong Ayau, "If you will say nothing about me at the Court, I will give you back your things; if not, I will spend money in the matter."

In answer to the Hon. Ng Choy, defendant said the jacket was his, and he identified it by a tear in the pocket, and that it fitted him. (He was asked to put it on, when it was found that the collar of the jacket did not fit him.)

Inspector Perry said he went with the last witness and a party of police to Number 7 Upper Station Street, on the 31st ultimo. He there saw defendant in a small room, and found some portions of Manila lottery tickets, some books, money amounting to $25, and 60 or 70 pieces of clothing on a shelf above a bed, many of which were labeled. While he was searching in another part of the room the complainant picked out one jacket from among them as belonging to him.

In answer to the Hon. Ng Choy, the Inspector said that the defendant only recognised the jacket when they were about to leave. He also said that the defendant had the reputation of being an inveterate gambler.

Police Constable 190 said, complainant went to the Central Station and represented that Yang Tai had stolen his property, and then lost it in gambling. He was instructed to enquire into the matter, and he on leaving the Station asked complainant where Yang

Tai was. Complainant then said that Yang Tai had gone away, and that the real case was that he, the complainant, had gone with Yang Tai, to a gambling house, and lost his property. Witness then accompanied the complainant to Number 7 Station Street to allow him an opportunity of redeeming the things, but they could not gain admittance; a child's voice from the inside telling them to come back next day as its father was at the Theatre. He then went back and told the Inspector that the charge was a false one. He accompanied Inspector Perry in his search. He had previously arrested the complainant in a gambling house in Gilman Street.

Sergeant Wong Ayau, who also accompanied the Inspectors, said the complainant had to be asked to go over the clothes a second time, and be certain that none of the articles were his, before he pointed out the jacket in Court. He heard the defendant say to the complainant that he had not been robbed of his things but had lost them in gambling.

The Hon. Ng Choy said that it was quite evident that the defendant ought to be discharged as the charge was not one of gambling, but that of being in possession of stolen property. The whole evidence went to prove that the complainant had lost his property in gambling, and that by the statements he had made he had committed gross perjury.

The Magistrate then discharged the defendant, and the complainant was charged with perjury.

This man averred that his statement was true, but asked the Magistrate if he did punish him to extend mercy towards him.

He was fined $25, in default two months' imprisonment.

THURSDAY 2 FEBRUARY 1882[474]
ALLEGED ROBBERY OF $100
CC Number 597

Chan Aleong and Yeung Acheong, of Wai Chau, were charged, along with two others not in custody, with robbing one Tang Ashing of $100 on the 27th January.

Tang Ashing said he was a tin miner in Klanga [*sic* for "Klang"], and had come from Singapore on the 26th *ultimate* on his way to his native place Kwai Shin. On his arrival he went to a doctor's shop in Wing Lok Street, kept by Chan Ayu, and handed over his money, $130, for safe custody. The following day he asked Chan Ayu for $100 in order to purchase some gold ornaments. He received the sum and went to the Queen's Road, where a man of the name of Leung Afuk, and whom he had never seen before, accosted him and asked whether he had returned from Singapore. He said to complainant that he had a friend in Klang, which friend had a sweetheart in the Colony, and invited him to visit the sweetheart. They went to a house in Tsing-sau Lane, West, and there he partook of some tea along with Leung Afuk. They were the only persons in the room at the time, but there were some women in the passage. Defendants and another man came in after he had had tea, and on his rising to leave they pinioned him, laid him on the floor, removed his money belt and abstracted his money, which was in two parcels of $50 each. He identified twenty-five out of the twenty-nine dollars as being a portion of his money. Although he had cried for assistance none came. The first defendant seized him by the throat with the one hand and with the other assisted Leung Afuk to take away the money belt. Leung Afuk and the other man left the house immediately after the robbery, and the two defendants still confined him. The first defendant at this time was in possession of

---

[474] "Police Intelligence", CM, Thursday, 2 February 1882, p. 3, cc. 3 - 4.

all the money. Latterly after a severe effort he escaped and went direct to the Doctor's shop in Wing Lok Street and got the proprietor to accompany him to the house he was robbed in. There they found the money belt under the bed, but no one in the room. They then went to the Police Station, reported the matter and returned to the house along with a detective, where they waited two hours and were just about to leave when the first defendant came in and was arrested. He saw the first defendant searched and the large purse in Court taken from his person.

Wong Tai Loi, a constable gave evidence as to the arrest.

Some more evidence was taken, and the case then remanded till the 6th February.

FRIDAY 3 FEBRUARY 1882[475]
THE ATTRACTIONS OF A CLOTHES LINE
CC Number 598

Li Akum, a bricklayer, was charged with stealing clothing belonging to Yan Yau-sau, a cook, on the 3rd February.

The defendant had entered the yard of the Basel Mission House, and seeing some clothes hung up on a line to dry had been so overpowered by the temptation that he lowered the line and attempted to decamp with some clothing, but was detained by a constable. A previous conviction was admitted by the defendant, and he was then sentenced to four months' imprisonment.

AN OLD AND DANGEROUS OFFENDER
CC Number 599

Chan Akun, a hawker, was charged with cutting and wounding Lau Asing, and with being at large without a night pass and in possession of a dagger.

Lau Asing said while standing at the door of the shop in which he was employed, in Jervois Street, he heard a cry of "Robbery" and saw the defendant

---

[475] "Police Intelligence", CM, Friday, 3 February 1882, p. 3, c. 3.

running with a constable after him. He stepped in front of him and held out his arm to stop him, but the defendant drew a dagger and inflicted a severe wound on his arm, and so got past. He took up the chase, but had to desist on account of the pain from the wound. He saw a constable arrest the defendant.

Two other witnesses gave similar evidence, and both had received slight wounds from the dagger. All three had had to visit the Hospital to have their wounds dressed.

There are eight previous convictions for various crimes standing against the defendant.

The case was remanded till the 10th *instant*.[476]

SATURDAY 4 FEBRUARY 1882[477]
ALLEGED KIDNAPPING[478]
CC Number 600 📖 p. 311

Pang Asum and Chun Acheung, married women, were charged, on remand from Tuesday, with bringing one Chan Niu into this colony for the purposes of prostitution, and also with detaining her.

Mr Holmes, of Messrs Stephens & Holmes, appeared for the defendants.

The complainant after changing hands several times had at last been brought to Hong Kong from her native village on the 5th October, and since that time had been detained by the defendants. Mr Holmes examined the complainant this morning, and in answer to him, she said that though her husband did not send money regularly, she was not in need of it at the time she left her village in the expectation of seeing her husband. Although there had never been any violence used in bringing her here, yet they always deceived her by promising to find her

---

[476] There is no further report of this case on 10 February 1882.

[477] "Police Intelligence", CM, Saturday, 4 February 1882, p. 3, c. 3.

[478] The following is the complete set of reports in connection with this case in *The Complete Court Cases*: CC Nos 575, 587, 600, 619.

husband. She never heard the Chinese Interpreter, who accompanied the Inspector, ask her if she were willing to stay in the brothel.

The Interpreter was called, and in answer to Mr Holmes said that he positively asked the complainant whether she was a willing inmate of the brothel or not, and that she answered him in the affirmative.

The case was again remanded till the 11th of February.

SATURDAY 4 FEBRUARY 1882[479]
ATTEMPTED SUICIDE
CC Number 601

Tam Chu, hawker, was charged with attempting to commit suicide by drowning on the 27th *ultimate*

The evidence did not show clearly whether he had fallen or jumped into the water, and as it was stated that he was not of a melancholy disposition, nor giving [*sic* for "given"] to gambling and other bad practices; and as his father appeared and promised to look after him, he was cautioned and discharged.

MONDAY 6 FEBRUARY 1882[480]
DESTROYING TREES
CC Number 602

Ng Atoi was sentenced to four days' imprisonment with hard labour for committing the offence of cutting trees on the Aberdeen Road, on the 4th instant.

A STRAGGLER
CC Number 603

Gilbert Merren was brought up on the charge of being a straggler from the American ship Importer.

---

[479] "Police Intelligence", CM, Saturday, 4 February 1882, p. 3, c. 3.

[480] "Police Intelligence", CM, Monday, 6 February 1882, p. 3, c. 3.

The defendant said the Captain told him outside the Harbour Master's office, when he had brought a charge against the second mate, that he had killed better men than him and would kill him also if he again came on board the ship.

He was ordered to be conveyed on board his ship and to have an opportunity of speaking to the U.S. Consul.

[ROBBERY]
CC Number 604

Chan Aleong, trader, and Yeong Acheong, unemployed, were charged on remand, from the 2nd instant, with having along with others not in custody, robbed Tong Asing of $100.

The complainant had arrived from Singapore and had been strolling in Queen's Road, when a man named Tung Fuk had come and made his acquaintance. His friend took him to a house in Tsung Sau Lane, where this man, the two defendants and another man had forcibly taken the money from him.

There was some other evidence of a corroborative nature led to-day. The prisoners were then cautioned, reserved their defence and were committed for trial at the next Criminal Sessions.[481]

TUESDAY 7 FEBRUARY 1882[482]
LARCENIES
CC Number 605

Chun Aon, hawker, was convicted of stealing an earring and two drops from Ho Sam, widow, at the Tung Hing Theatre on Monday night. Sentence --

---

[481] The following information appears in the Criminal Calendar for the February Sessions, 1882, HKGG, 11 March 1882, p. 258, where this case is No. 7.
Chan Lung [sic] and Yeung [sic] A-cheung [sic] were tried on 27 February 1882 for Robbery with violence and were unaminously found not guilty and discharged.
[482] "Police Intelligence", CM, Tuesday, 7 February 1882, p. 3, c. 5.

Three months' imprisonment with hard labour was imposed.

[LARCENIES]
CC Number 606 📖

Leong Atuk, a shop coolie, had snatched an earring from Hu Chung, married woman, on the 6th instant. The complainant had been bestowing some cash on a beggar when the defendant had come up behind and violently snatched the earring. Defendant confessed to snatching the earring, but pleaded as an excuse that he thought the woman was his mistress, and as his mistress owed him some money he made off with the article. He was sentenced to three months' imprisonment with hard labour.

UNLAWFUL POSSESSION
CC Number 607

Shum Atsat, a hawker, was charged with being in unlawful possession of two pieces of clothing belonging to Ip Acheung, and after hearing evidence was convicted. He had been in the act of entering a pawn shop in Gage Street when apprehended and had acted in a suspicious manner. He was fined L3 [*sic* for "$3"] or suffer 6 weeks' imprisonment with hard labour.

THURSDAY 9 FEBRUARY 1882[483]
A SEAMEN'S FIGHT
CC Number 608

William Baker, of Scotland, and Michael Hanna, of Ireland, seamen unemployed, were charged [with] being drunk and fighting in the street on the 8th instant.

The defendant admitted being drunk and pummelling each other on the Praya yesterday. They had indulged in abusing each other to such an extent that they were found rolling on the ground by the

---

[483] "Police Intelligence", CM, Thursday, 9 February 1882, p. 3, cc. 3 - 4.

constable, who had to engage the assistance of several other constables to convey them to the station. The first defendant also admitted two previous convictions.

The first defendant was fined $1 or, in default of payment, to suffer four days' imprisonment; the second defendant was cautioned and discharged, the Police to convey him on board his vessel, the Anjer Head.

STREET GAMBLING[484]
CC Number 609

Hung Awo, a Canton coolie, was found amusing himself by gambling with a number of others in Caine Road yesterday. According to the defendant's version he was watching some children playing when he was arrested, but the constable stated that he distinctly saw him gambling. He was sentenced to seven days' imprisonment with hard labour.

FRIDAY 10 FEBRUARY 1882[485]
UNLAWFUL POSSESSION
CC Number 610

Wong Asaw, a coolie, was charged with being in unlawful possession of wood and had, in the charge room, stated that he picked it off the street, but when brought before the Magistrate averred that one of the workmen, who along with him was working to a contractor, had given the defendant the wood to take home. He said the contractor's name was Tak Cheung and was erecting buildings at Bowrington, but he had not wish [sic for "wished"] to have him called. The man who gave him the wood, he said, had

---

[484] See CC 644 below. As reported in CC 644 (21 February 1882) the defendant in CC 644, "Chun Afuk, a hawker" was also arrested, probably on 9 February ("twelve days ago") for gambling, and was also sentenced to seven days' imprisonment but the offence took place on the Recreation Ground,not Caine Road.

[485] "Police Intelligence", CM, Friday, 10 February 1882, p. 3, c. 5.

gone home to his native place. The Police had made enquiries, but could not discover any contractor of that name. The defendant's latter version of his coming into possession of the wood not being proved to be true he was fined ten shillings or in default to be imprisoned for fourteen days.

BREACH OF RECOGNIZANCE
CC Number 611 📖 p. 190

Charles Ring, seaman, who was allowed out on his own recognizance in the sum of $5 last Saturday, by the Magistrate, was again brought up yesterday; he having failed to quit the Colony as he had distinctly avowed to do.

George Rogers, Police Constable said he had been to Messrs Butterfield & Swire's where the Captain of the Ajax had volunteered to give the defendant a passage home to England, on condition that he went to the Sailors' Home sober, to-day at 11 o'clock.

Defendant could not show cause why his recognizance should not be estreated [sic] and said he could offer no explanation of his non-appearance on Monday.

The Magistrate then remanded the case till to-day.

Police Constable Rogers volunteering to-day to convey the defendant to the Sailors' Home; and if necessary see him on board the vessel he was discharged.

SATURDAY 11 FEBRUARY 1882[486]
DRUNK AND DISORDERLY
CC Number 612

John Nelson, a Dutch seaman, on board the Atjeh, was found drunk and refused the kindly attentions of a European Constable who offered to get a sampan to take him off to the ship. Instead of that he showed

---

[486] "Police Intelligence", CM, Saturday, 11 February 1882, p. 3, cc. 3 - 4.

fight and created a disturbance. He was fined 50 cents or suffer two days' imprisonment.

[DRUNK AND DISORDERLY]
CC Number 613

Antonio Gomes, a watchman unemployed, was found lying in the roadside in Elgin Street yesterday. He admitted the charge and also nine previous convictions. He was ordered to be bound over with two sureties in one recognizance of L10 [sic for "$10"], with condition to be of good behaviour, in default to be committed for six weeks.

[DRUNK AND DISORDERLY]
CC Number 614

Martin McDonald, an English seaman, unemployed, was fined 25 cents or in default of payment to suffer one day's imprisonment. He was found in Queen's Road drunk, lying in a jinricksha. He stated that he was drunk, but had not engaged the jinricksha in which he was found, the hire of which was claimed but not granted.

MENDICANCY
CC Number 615

Wong Asz, Wong Asing and Wong Afuk all admitted begging in various parts of the town. The first and third were ordered to be sent to their native country, and the second to be sent to the Tong [sic] Wah Hospital.

A YOUTHFUL PICKPOCKET
CC Number 616 📖 p. 327

Tse Afuk, 11 years old, was convicted of picking a knife from the pocket of U Fuk, school boy. The complainant had been looking at some tricks being performed in the Recreation Ground, when the defendant had picked his pocket, actuated most likely by a desire to learn the profession he was looking at. He was ordered to be imprisoned for seven days, six of these to be in solitary confinement.

ROGUE AND VAGABOND
CC Number 617

Vyeapoory, of Madras, was found by a constable drunk in a jinricksha. The constable took him to a house, where the defendant had said he lived, but the keepers of the house refused to have anything to do with him. The offence being proved and the defendant admitting a previous conviction he was sentenced to twenty one days' imprisonment.

ASSAULT BY A SHIP CAPTAIN
CC Number 618 📖 p. 191

A. Roper, Captain of the steamer Anjer Head, at present lying in harbour, appeared on a summons charged with assaulting, on board that vessel, John Dare, chief officer, on the 10th instant.

John Dare, the complainant, said he went to the Harbour Master's Office yesterday morning regarding a claim he had on the ship, and returned to the ship about half past two in the afternoon, when the Captain asked him if he was going in the ship. He answered yes; and the Captain then got hold of him, shoved him against the cabin door sill, threw him into the cabin and locked the door. Witness opened the door with a key he had under his charge and said to the Captain that he had no right to imprison him. The Captain struck him on the shoulder, tore his coat and broke his watch chain, and by so doing made witness lose pendants to the value of $65. He was also struck with a bamboo by the Captain and ordered to leave the vessel.

In answer to the defendant the complainant said he was disappointed at Capt. Thomsett's decision, which was that he had no claim against the Captain. He denied shaking a key in the captain's face and saying that it was a master key.

The second mate of the vessel said he was at the gangway of the ship keeping order, and had heard the complainant and defendant talking together very loudly, but had seen no blows struck. He never heard anything of the watch chain being injured until he came to the Court. The witness had heard the parties have some angry words at the breakfast table about stowaways being on board, at which time the complainant laughed in the defendant's face, when he was checked for allowing the stowaways on board.

The defendant denied assaulting the complainant, but admitted taking a master key from the complainant as he did not care to have anyone on board his vessel in possession of such an article. The Magistrate expressed his regret that the case had not been tried before the Harbour Master, who would have been much more conversant with all the sides of the question. It was quite apparent to him that there had been a good deal of temper displayed and provocation given, on both sides, but the evidence showed him that some assault had been committed and he therefore ordered the defendant to pay a fine of $5, or, in default, to be imprisoned for two days. The fine was paid.

ALLEGED KIDNAPPING[487]
CC Number 619 📖 p. 312

Pang Asum and Chun Acheung, married women, the first, the keeper of the Mui Lan Brothel, 32, West Street, and the second an assistant, were charged on remand from the 4th instant, with bringing into and detaining in this Colony one Chan Niu for the purposes of prostitution.

Mr Holmes, of Messrs Stephen & Holmes, appeared for the defendants; and Mr Sharp, of Messrs Sharp, Toller & Johnson, the Crown Solicitor, appeared to prosecute.

Some of the witnesses were re-examined, but no further facts were elicited. The defendants were then Committed for trial at the Criminal Sessions of the Supreme Court, Mr Holmes reserving their defence.

---

[487] The following is the complete set of reports in connection with this case in *The Complete Court Cases*: CC Nos 575, 587, 600, 619.

The complainant had been decoyed from her native village, Lukong, by an old woman, who resided in the same place, to Canton, where the complainant expected to see her husband, who was then working there. Arrived at [*sic* for "on arrival at"] Canton she was kept in close confinement in a small boat until the first defendant came and bargained, with the proprietors of the boat, for her purchase. The complainant saw the purchase money paid by the first defendant's mother-in-law, who conveyed her to Hong Kong, where she was taken to Mui Lan Brothel and detained until her husband discovered her on the 25th January. It was stated in evidence by the complainant that no violence had been used and that she had not made any complaint to the Inspector of Brothels, when he visited the place.

The case will come up on Saturday, the 18th instant.[488]

MONDAY 13 FEBRUARY 1882[489]
THE CRACKER NUISANCE
CC Number 620

Ng Asum was fined $1, with the option of suffering 4 days' imprisonment, for firing crackers in the street on Sunday.

UNLAWFUL POSSESSION
CC Number 621

Chun Achau, coolie, was apprehended by a constable at half-past twelve last night in Hong Hing Street. He was carrying a bundle of children's clothes, which he said he had picked up at Wantsai. In the charge room he stated that he had found it lying at the Clock Tower; and before the magistrate he gave a third version of the story, and said he had seen a woman

---

[488] No report of this case, reported as to be heard on 18 February 1882, has been traced, whether in *The China Mail* or *The Daily Press*. The "Criminal Calendar -- February Sessions, 1882", shows that nine cases were heard on 27 (not 18) February 1882.
[489] "Police Intelligence", CM, Monday, 13 February 1882, p. 3, c. 3.

drop the bundle from a jinricksha, and that he was going after the vehicle to return the parcel, when he was arrested.

The Magistrate ordered [him] to pay 10 shillings, or suffer fourteen days' imprisonment with hard labour.

THEFT OF AN ANKLET
CC Number 622

Wong Akan, a coolie, was arrested by Sergeant Fisher in Queen's Road Central, where he was struggling with a woman, who accused him of stealing a child's anklet. The defendant was known to be an associate of thieves, and had no visible means of subsistence, having been frequently seen by the Police engaged watching people more attentively than he should have been doing. He was committed to gaol for twenty-one days.

LARCENY
CC Number 623

Cheung Sau, coolie, was apprehended last night about 12 o'clock in St. Francis Street with a bag of rice on his back, which he was apparently carrying off to the hillside. The property was identified as belonging to Wong Ai, who had a great many of his articles removed on account of the fire.[490] The defendant had taken advantage of the unprotected

---

[490] For references to a fire, see CC Nos 623, 626, 652, 685. Each of CC No. 623 and CC No. 626 clearly indicates that the reference is to a fire that took place on 12 February 1882. In CC 652 (Case heard on 27 February 1882), there is a reference to, "the late fire . . . on Praya East". CC 685 (re a case heard on 15 March 1882) refers simply to "the fire".

Quite naturally, in contemporary writing, the degree of specificity in referring to the same event decreases over time. For this reason, it is perhaps useful to point out that there was another fire in early1882, this one near the Central School. (CM, 13 January 1882, p. 3, c. 7.) This is probably the same fire as is referred to in the caption, "The Kelly and Walsh Fire Case", among the reports of the cases heard by H. E. Wodehouse on Saturday 14 January 1882.

state of the rice and made off with it. Six weeks' imprisonment with hard labour was imposed.

A DRUNKEN CHINAMAN
CC Number 624

Yau Ming Cho, shopkeeper, admitted being drunk and, in company with some prostitutes, creating a disturbance in Hollywood Road early this morning. He was fined 50 cents with the option of two days' imprisonment.

THEFT OF COTTON
CC Number 625

Ip Wai, jinricksha coolie, was sentenced to six months' imprisonment with hard labour, the first and last fortnight to be in solitary confinement, for stealing a piece of cotton cloth, value 50 cents, from the Tse Ying on the 12th instant. The defendant had abstracted the calico from the complainant's basket, which was lying beside her on the Praya, while she was looking about for a boat to take her home.

TUESDAY 14 FEBRUARY 1882[491]
ALLEGED THEFT IN THE POLICE QUARTERS
CC Number 626

Chan Aheung, servant, was brought up on suspicion of stealing $7, from the box of Chunda Singh Police Constable, on the 12th instant.

Chunda Singh said the complainant was employed as a boy by the Indian Constables. On the 12th instant when the fire bell[492] rang the first time, the complainant, after putting on his uniform had got the length of the verandah, remembered that he had left his keys under the pillow, and went back and told the defendant, who was cleaning boots, to look after them, which he promised to do. After standing in the Barrack compound a quarter of an hour the Inspector

---

[491] "Police Intelligence", CM, Tuesday, 14 February 1882, p. 3, c. 4.
[492] See note above to CC 623.

on duty released him as he was not required to go to the fire.[493] He went back to his room, found the keys where he left them, put them in his pocket, and went and cooked his breakfast. About 9 o'clock he opened his box and found seven one dollar notes missing; these he had seen at half past six the same morning all secure. He spoke to the defendant about the matter, who denied all knowledge of the affair. Witness saw the last man leave the room before he went to the compound, and when he returned no one was in the room. Witness also stated that a good deal of money and many articles of clothing had been missed lately from the Indian quarters.

The Barrack Sergeant said when the complainant preferred the charge he stated that he had gone to his box at half past six, taken some money out, and gone to market, leaving his keys under his pillow; but complainant, recalled, said he did not go to market at that time, though he was uncertain whether he had said so to the Barrack Sergeant or not.

The defendant said he was not cleaning boots at the time stated, but that Un Leung (another servant) was. He was in the complainant's room when the fire bell rang, but did not hear him say anything about the keys. He went to the fire and returned in about half an hour.

The defendant denied the charge and was then discharged.

WEDNESDAY 15 FEBRUARY 1882[494]
SNATCHING DOLLARS FROM A STALL
CC Number 627

Chun Ayau, hawker, was charged with stealing $2 from the stall of Li Lok, money changer, on the 14th *instant*.

The complainant's case was proved by the following statement; about 8 o'clock at night when

---

[493] See note above to CC 623.
[494] "Police Intelligence", CM, Wednesday, 15 February 1882, p. 3, cc. 2 - 3.

the defendant went pastthe money changer's shop in Queen's Road West, he snatched up the $2, which were just going to be weighed [and] ran off, but was quickly stopped by a constable who was in the vicinity.

The defendant admitted taking the money and stated that he had been in the Colony ten days without having any employment. He was sentenced to one month's imprisonment with hard labour.

GAMBLING
CC Number 628

Chan Awai, a carpenter belonging to Sun On, was, along with others, engaged in some illegal purpose in an unoccupied house in Pound Lane yesterday. Sundah Singh, a constable, happened to be passing through the lane, when he heard some one crying "Police coming," and saw several people rushing out of the doorway. He handed the defendant over to another constable, went upstairs and found a counting stick, cup, matches, scales, a money tester and a quantity of bad cash. The constable knew the defendant to be a frequent gambler in Pound Lane and Gilman Bazaar. Fined $10, or suffer fourteen days' imprisonment with hard labour.

OBTAINING WATCHES BY FALSE PRETENCES
CC Number 629

Li Alun, a tailor, was charged with obtaining two silver watches from Wong Ying Kut, watchmaker, 155 Queen's Road Central, by false pretences on the 5th instant.

The complainant stated that he was visited by the defendant on the 5th instant. After some conversation two watches were handed over, one worth $5.50, and the other $3.50. The defendant agreed with witness to bring the money at once if he sold them to a friend.

Ip Akong, accountant in the Yuk Shang pawnshop, Queen's Road Central, said he remembered distinctly that the defendant, who was a customer of the Pawnshop, pawned the watch in Court on the 5th instant, and received $4.45 on the articles.

Defendant stated that he got two watches from the complainant, on loan, one to carry and one to sell. He became hard up and pawned one and sold the other, for which he received $1.50, and the promise from his friend to pay another $2.50, on the friend's return from Canton.

The complainant, recalled, said further that he had told the defendant that he was scarce of money and wanted to sell his two watches.

The Magistrate sentenced the prisoner to six weeks' imprisonment with hard labour.

AN EVASIVE PASSENGER
CC Number 630

Leong Aki, barber, was seen by a constable sitting on the stair of the house Number 34 East Street at three o'clock this morning. A gimlet was found in one of his stockings and a chisel on the stair. When questioned by the constable the barber said he went up the stair to be out of the constable's way. He was without light or pass.

The defendant with much simplicity said he was with a friend until late and wishing to avoid the constable went up the stair. He bought the gimlet, but did not know why he had put it in his stocking. He admitted two previous convictions, six months for breaking into a house, and three months for being found in possession of a chisel.

He was sentenced to six months' imprisonment with hard labour; the first and last fortnight to be spent in solitary confinement.

AN UNHAPPY INMATE OF A BROTHEL
CC Number 631 📖 p. 286

Lo Chun, of Canton, was charged with attempting to commit suicide on the 12th instant.

John Lee, Inspector of Brothels, said he went at the instance of the keeper, to the brothel Number 44, Caine Road, and there found Lo Chun sitting on a bed, in one of the rooms, vomiting. In reply to him she said she had taken opium dross. He took her to the Government Civil Hospital, where Dr. Marques, in the witness' presence, gave her an emetic.

Defendant stated that she had had a quarrel about some money and took the opium dross, but did not state her object in doing so.

The defendant's mother appearing and asking for her release, in order to take care of her, the Magistrate cautioned and discharged her.

NIGHT PROWLERS
CC Number 632

Sui Acheung and Lam Amun were charged with stealing a basket of vegetables value $2 belonging to Wong Chan Sing, shopkeeper.

The complainant, whose shop is in the Central Market, left the basket all safe outside his door last night. At three o'clock, a constable roused him and told him the defendants had been stealing his vegetables. He knew the defendants, who were fishmongers, and whose stall adjoined his. The constable, attracted by the sound caused by the basket being pulled along the pavement, caught the defendants in the act of removing it to their own stall.

Both defendants stated that they had no intention of stealing, but were only moving the hamper out of their way as it was an obstruction.

They were each sentenced to one month's imprisonment with hard labour.

A DANGEROUS FISHMONGER
CC Number 633

Chun Apo, a fishmonger, was yesterday committed for trial at the March Criminal Sessions[495] of the

---

[495] This case can not be identified in "Criminal Calendar -- March Sessions, 1882". There is a "Chiu A-po listed with two others on five different charges as Case No. 6 in, "Criminal Calendar --

Supreme Court for being in possession of burglarious instruments and deadly weapons. A constable apprehended him about 5 o'clock on the morning of the 13th in Fish Street, when there was found on his person two swords, a pair of pincers, and a large boring iron. He has undergone eight years' imprisonment already for the commission of various crimes.

16 FEBRUARY 1882[496]
LARCENY OF PIPES
CC Number 634

Chan Ayau, shoemaker, was charged with stealing two smoking pipes from Wong Kut, accountant, on the 14th instant.

The complainant, an accountant in the Yau Hang money changer's shop, Bonham Street, said the defendant came into the shop about eight o'clock at night, and snatched up two brass pipes, value $4, which were lying on a table near the door. The defendant was pursued by some of the other shopmen, who were at the back of the premises at the time, and apprehended.

Constable 311, on duty in Queen's Road at the time of the theft, arrested him, while he was running with some persons in pursuit; the complainant coming up shortly afterwards and accusing him of the theft. The constable then took the defendant to the station. Seven previous convictions are recorded against the defendant. He was cautioned, reserved his defence, and was then committed for trial at the March Criminal Sessions of the Supreme Court.[497]

April Sessions, 1882", but Case No. 633 concerns a man charged alone on a quite different charge. No Criminal Calendar for May to December 1882 appears in the HKGG and it has not been possible tot race his

[496] "Police Intelligence", CM, Thursday, 16 February 1882, p. 3, c. 5.

[497] This case is No. 13 in Criminal Calendar -- March Sessions, 1882. (HKGG, 15 April 1882, p. 386.) On 22 March, Chan A-yau [sic] was tried on three counts: 1) Larceny; 2) previous

FRIDAY 17 FEBRUARY 1882[498]
[LOCAL AND GENERAL]
ADDITIONAL 635 p. 192

A case of a peculiar nature was brought before Dr Stewart this morning, in which Samuel Simons, fireman on board the British steamer Gleniffer, was charged with cutting and wounding James Whitley Simson whilst the ship was lying at the Tanjong Pagar wharf at Singapore on the 5th *instant*. It seems from the evidence heard that the defendant, who had been working some time extra, had been asked by the

---

conviction (summary); 3) Previous conviction (summary). He was found guilty on the first count and pleaded guilty to the second and third counts. On 27 March, he was sentenced to two years' imprisonment with hard labour.

The following report appeared in *The China Mail*. (Wednesday, 22 March 1882, p. 3, c. 5.)
"Supreme Court
"In Criminal Sessions (Before the Hon. G. Phillippo, Chief Justice.)
"Wednesday, 22 March 1882

"LARCENY
"Chau Ayow [*sic*] was found guilty of stealing two brass opium smoking pipes on the 14th February belonging to Wong Akat from the complainant's house in Wing Lock Street. He admitted two previous convictions. Sentence was reserved."

The following report appeared in *The China Mail*. (Monday, 27 March 1882, p. 3, c. 4.)
"Supreme Court
"In Criminal Sessions (Before the Hon. G. Phillippo, Chief Justice.)
"Monday, 27 March 1882

"The prisoners found guilty on Wednesday and Thursday last were sentenced this morning by His Lordship."

"Chun Ayan, convicted of stealing two brass smoking pipes from the house of Wong Akat in Wing Lok St. on the 14th February, was sentenced to two years' imprisonment. Two previous convictions were admitted."
[498] "Local and General", CM, Friday, 17 February 1882, p. 3, cc. 2 - 3.

chief engineer, the complainant, to turn to again, when defendant used some indecent language, with the result that complainant struck him on the mouth. Defendant had then struck complainant with a knife, and wounded him slightly on the shoulder.

Defendant, in his statement, admitted having done so, but said he went ashore and intended to deliver himself up to the police, but as it was a holiday in Singapore, it was advised that the case should be brought on here and tried. The Captain of the Gleniffer said that on the way up he allowed the defendant, on a promise to behave properly, to return to his work, and he had conducted himself very well. The case was discharged through want of jurisdiction.

FRIDAY 17 FEBRUARY 1882[499]
[LOCAL AND GENERAL]
ADDITIONAL 635a

The Kowloon barracks seem to be a mark for many of the thieves in the Colony. Today Ngai Im was charged before, and sentenced by, Dr Stewart to twenty one days' imprisonment for stealing six pounds of beef from these barracks. The only defence he had to give was that he wished the beef for food.

MONDAY 20 FEBRUARY 1882[500]
THEFT
CC Number 636

Li Acheung, bricklayer, was committed to prison for four months for stealing four jackets, two pair of shoes, and one pair of stockings belonging to Leung Shing, bricklayer. During the absence of the complainant at the theatre, the defendant had entered his room and stolen the articles, and on the following day the complainant accidentally discovered the defendant in an opium smoking den in Hollywood

---

[499] "Local and General", CM, Friday, 17 February 1882, p. 3, c. 1.
[500] "Police Intelligence", CM, Monday, 20 February 1882, p. 3, cc. 3 - 4.

Road with the jackets on, and the shoes below the bed on which he was lying.

ROGUES AND VAGABONDS
CC Number 637

Chun Ayau, hawker, was sentenced to six weeks' imprisonment with hard labour for being a rogue and vagabond. He was without a place of residence, had no occupation, and was known by the Police to have done little else than gamble for the last three years.

Cheung Acheung was arrested by Police Constable Servant who found him along with 20 or 30 others engaged gambling, the defendant occupying the position of manager of the game. Two previous convictions were recorded against him. Considering these and the present offence the Magistrate sentenced him to twenty one days' imprisonment with hard labour.

PICKPOCKET
CC Number 638 📖 p. 327

Luk Akun, a hawker, was charged with picking from the pocket of Wong Chung Kan, school boy, a silk handkerchief and a one-dollar note on the 19th instant.

Last night on the Praya West the defendant had been grasped in the act of putting his hand into the complainant's pocket, who held on to him until his finger was bitten. The defendant then ran off, but complainant followed and got a constable to arrest him. During the struggle the handkerchief and bank note had been handed over by the defendant to a confederate. Three previous convictions are standing against him.

The Magistrate sentenced him to three months' imprisonment with hard labour.

DRUNK
CC Number 639

Leonard McKnight, private of the Royal Inniskilling Fusiliers; Andrew Anderson, seaman on board the *Andromeda*; and Vincent Zabra, seaman on board the *Ashington*, were charged, separately, with being drunk. The first and second were fined 50 cents in default of payment two days' imprisonment, and the third 25 cents, in default of payment one days' imprisonment.

A JUVENILE THIEF
CC Number 640 📖 p. 328

Leong Asing, coolie, was charged with stealing a silver bangle from Ip Fung Yeung, a child, on the 19th instant.

The defendant, a lad of 14 years of age, stole the bangle from the child, which was being carried on her elder sister's back. His mother appeared and stated that he had never committed any theft before and begged the Magistrate to release him, and promised to look after him in future.

The Magistrate ordered him to pay 50 cents to the complainant, in default to suffer three days' imprisonment, two of them to be in solitary confinement.

TUESDAY 21 FEBRUARY 1882[501]
THEFT OF LUCIFERS
CC Number 641

Ching Chung, a coolie engaged in removing the contents of the Wanchai Godowns, was observed by a constable stowing 2 bundles of matches, containing 24 boxes, under his jacket. Defendant tried to exonerate himself by saying that he saw the boxes lying about and believing that they were not wanted appropriated them. He was sentenced to ten days' imprisonment with hard labour. The property was

---

[501] "Police Intelligence", CM, Tuesday, 21 February 1882, p. 3, c. 4.

ordered to be returned to Messrs Arnhold, Karberg & Company.

OBSTRUCTIONISTS
CC Number 642
Lai Asin, Chung Sam Yau and Tsang Asau were each fined 50 cents, with the alternative of undergoing two days' imprisonment for sitting, along with 20 others, on a mat in High Street, Sai Ying-p'un, and gambling, thereby obstructing the traffic.

ATTEMPTED LARCENY FROM THE PERSON
CC Number 643 📖 p. 328
Tse Atai, cook, was charged with attempting to pick the pocket of Chun Tim, hawker, on the 20th instant.

The evidence given proved that the defendant had made an attempt to steal something from the complainant, who was standing looking at some persons boxing on the Recreation Ground. The defendant when seized by the complainant struck out with his fists and made great endeavours to get off, but was unsuccessful. His character was not good, and he was known to be a notorious gambler. He has been frequently noticed playing with boys and allowing them to win, and by this ruse inducing grown up persons to take up the game, when they were generally cheated by the rascal.

He was sentenced to six weeks' imprisonment with hard labour.

[GAMBLING][502]
CC Number 644
Chun Afuk, a hawker, was apprehended by Police Constable Servant on the Recreation Ground, while he was engaged gambling along with a great many others. The defendant threw away some gambling articles when he was arrested, but these were picked up by the constable and produced in Court as evidence against him. Twelve days ago he was

---

[502] See note to CC 609 above.

sentenced to seven days' imprisonment for a similar offence. He was now sentenced to 10 days' imprisonment with hard labour.

WEDNESDAY 22 FEBRUARY 1882[503]
UNLAWFUL POSSESSION
CC Number 645

Li Aching, washerman, was charged with unlawful possession of two blankets, one flannel shirt and one pair of cotton trousers, on the 20th instant.

The defendant was apprehended by a constable at the Clock Tower with the articles in his possession. When asked for an explanation he said the articles belonged to the Commissariat Department and that they were being taken to be washed. He did not know his master's name when the constable questioned him, and so was taken to the Station. From further evidence it was proved that the articles belonged to the Commissariat Department, and the defendant not being apparently aware of the impropriety excused himself by saying that he only intended to loan them to a friend for a night or two. He was convicted of unlawful possession of a pair of drawers and a handkerchief, and was ordered to pay a fine of L1 [*sic* for "$1"], or be imprisoned for ten days.

FRIDAY 24 FEBRUARY 1882[504]
BREACH OF OPIUM ORDINANCE
CC Number 646

Ho Ahung and Ng Akau, were found in possession of prepared opium without a permit from the Opium Farmer, on the 16th instant. The first defendant's case was remanded till the 24th instant; bail being admitted in two sureties of $120 each. The second defendant was fined $50, in default six months' hard labour. All the opium found to be confiscated.

---

[503] "Police Intelligence", CM, Wednesday, 22 February 1882, p. 3, c. 6.
[504] "Police Intelligence", CM, Friday, 24 February 1882, p. 3, c. 3.

SATURDAY 25 FEBRUARY 1882[505]
[STEALING]
CC Number 647

Chun Achün, bricklayer, was charged with stealing from Cheung Kum, a girl, two silver hair pins on the 24th *instant*, in Queen's Road East.

The defendant snatched the silver hair pins from the complainant, who was proceeding to the Theatre. He ran off, but was followed and apprehended by some soldiers on the Praya. The hair pins were thrown into the water. The defendant also cut one of the soldiers, who had pursued him, on the hand with some sharp instrument.

He tried to defend himself by saying that a brick had fallen on his foot, and he was running home to get some medicine.

The magistrate sentenced him to three months' imprisonment.

STRAGGLER
CC Number 648

Patrick Gorman, seaman on board the American ship Cashmere was ordered to be sent on board his vessel for being found straggling on the streets.

A VIOLENT LASCAR
CC Number 649

Alli Second, a barber, was charged with disorderly conduct and assaulting Ching Fuk and Essur Singh, at the Race Course, on the 24th *instant*, and also with assaulting the constable in the execution of his duty.

Ching Fuk testified that on the 24th *instant*, at the Races, the defendant had three cards and was trying to get people to pick out a certain card at 5 cents a trial. Witness did so and lost several times; then he raised the sum to 11 cents, when witness again took a chance and won. Defendant then refused to pay, and on witness insisting on payment, the

---

[505] "Police Intelligence", CM, Saturday, 25 February 1882, p. 3, cc. 4 - 5.

defendant struck him several times, as also the constable who interfered.

The defendant was fined L1 [*sic* for "$1"], with the alternative of seven days' imprisonment, on each count.

MONDAY 27 FEBRUARY 1882[506]
STEALING A COTTON JACKET AND FOUR SILVER BUTTONS
CC Number 650

Li Akut stole a cotton jacket and four silver buttons, total value $1.40, on the 26th *instant*, from a tailor at 42, Bridges Street. Complainant declared that on the 26th *instant*, at 10 a.m., he washed his jacket and put it upstairs to dry. At 2 p.m. of the same day he went up to get it and found it had disappeared. He then proceeded up the hillside and saw defendant sitting there. Complainant accused him of stealing the jacket. He denied stealing it, but said another man stole it. He took complainant to a place close by, where, under a piece of tin, the jacket was found.

Defendant had no question to ask, and received six months' imprisonment with hard labour.

RIOTOUS SEAMEN
CC Number 651

Agust Limbury and Charles Jones were charged -- the first with being drunk and fighting in the streets, and the second prisoner with attempted rescue, on the 26th instant.

Ng Kin, Police Constable No. 318, stated that on the 26th instant, at 4 p.m. he was on duty near Number 5 Station where he saw defendant and ten other seamen drunk and fighting. He called for assistance and Police Constable 650 came; the other Europeans tried to rescue the prisoners. Police Constable 62 went and assisted them, and two men were arrested; the others succeeded in getting away.

---

[506] "Police Intelligence", CM, Monday, 27 February 1882, p. 3, cc. 3 - 4.

John Dick Police Constable 62 said that on the 26th instant, at 4.20 p.m., hearing a whistle he proceeded to the spot, and saw complainant struggling with first defendant. When he told second defendant to go away he came up to witness and said "I will never allow a black man[507] to take a white man." He then arrested him as he tried to rescue first defendant. The prisoners were fined $1 each, or four days' imprisonment with hard labour.

THEFT OF MATCHES
CC Number 652
Ho Achan was sentenced to six weeks' imprisonment with hard labour, for stealing 48 boxes of matches from the godowns where the late fire occurred on Praya East.[508] He acted as a watchman on the premises.

CREATING A DISTURBANCE
CC Number 653
F. Victor, an unemployed seaman, was fined $1, with the alternative of seven days' imprisonment with hard labour for creating a disturbance. Three previous convictions were admitted.

LARCENY
CC Number 654
Li Akut was convicted of stealing a cotton jacket belonging to U. Lok, tailor, and was sentenced to six weeks' imprisonment with hard labour for committing this crime.

---

[507] This report does not make it very clear who said and did what, as pronouns are used so much more often that personal names. However, it seems unlikely that any person involved in this affair was black. Quite likely, all that was meant by "black" was "non-white". The editor has come across a similar usage in unpublished material from a similar period.

[508] For references to a fire, see CC Nos 623, 626, 652, 685. See also note above to CC No. 623.

ALLEGED ATTEMPTED SHOOTING[509]
CC Number 655 p. 193

John Bryant, boatswain on board the steamship *Ashington*, at present in harbour, with assaulting Samuel Bryant, fireman, and also with firing a revolver at the complainant on the 26th instant on board that vessel.

The complainant said that while in the forecastle on the morning of the 26th, between 8 and 9 o'clock, along with another man, the defendant came along and asked the complainant and the other man to accompany him to the chief engineer's room to have a dispute settled. The dispute arose from the defendant accusing the complainant of taking sails. The second engineer, who was in the engineer's room, when appealed to, said he believed that the complainant's statements were true. The defendant then ordered the complainant away from the engineer's room, which order the latter complied with, followed by the defendant. The complainant, when they reached the alley way, told the defendant, that if he was again insulted he would have to speak to the Captain, whereupon the defendant struck the complainant a blow on the eye with his fist, which blow the complainant returned in self defence. Defendant then went to his berth and fired a revolver at the complainant from the door-way; how the shot missed the complainant was unable to say.

James Bath, chief engineer, said he was present when the two parties came to the room, shortly after which he heard a pistol shot. He then went out of his room and asked defendant what he fired for, to which he received the reply "Oh, it's all right. I only did it to frighten him." Questioned by defendant, the witness was forced to confess that he, the defendant, was considerably intoxicated and

---

[509] The following is the complete set of reports in connection with this case in *The Complete Court Cases*: CC Nos 655, 660. See also, "Attempted Shooting", in, ed. Gillian Bickley, "Some 19th Hong Kong Criminal Cases", 2009. The report starts rather abruptly. This is a correct transcription, however.

excited at the time, although witness had said to the court that he was but slightly drunk.

Edwin Allison, Captain of the *Ashington*, said he heard a report at the time of the occurrence, but thought it was a Chinese cracker, until he was informed of the affair. He then sent for the Police. On Saturday he gave the defendant a half day's liberty, but this time was exceeded. In answer to the defendant, the Captain said that he did not think it possible that a shot fired from the defendant's berth could injure any person standing before the galley, and that defendant had been a steady, persevering man during the time he had been in witness' employ, 8 or 9 months.

The case was remanded till Wednesday, the 1st March.

BOTH MAGISTRATES SITTING
MONDAY 27 FEBRUARY 1882[510]
THEFT AT THE RACES
CC Number 656

Choi Kwan was charged with attempting to steal from the person of Henry Millar, Police Constable 16, one silver watch, on the 24th instant, while the complainant was at the Race Course.

The complainant stated that he was on duty at the Races, and in plain clothes. While standing inside the rails something made him draw back and look downwards, when he found the defendant with the watch in his hands.

The offence was proved, and two previous convictions for offences of the same nature were recorded against him.

He was sentenced to two years' imprisonment with hard labour.

---

[510] "Police Intelligence", CM, Monday, 27 February 1882, p. 3, cc. 3 - 4.

BEFORE FREDERICK STEWART, ESQ.,
March 1882[511]

WEDNESDAY 1 MARCH 1882[512]
ASSAULTING A HOUSE-BOY[513]
CC Number 657

Captain Burnie, Marine Surveyor was charged, on a summons, with assaulting Chun Yung, a house-boy, on [.....].

The complainant stated that he was the house-boy to the defendant [.....] mistress had, before [.....] him to give the [.....] 1 p.m. Defendant [.....] why he had [.....] him [fou...] [.....] black [.....] cautioned him, but apparently without effect. The complainant, when spoken to, denied that he had been told to give the children their dinner, and that he had not been insolent. Defendant then boxed his ears.

The Magistrate imposed a fine of $1, with the alternative of one day's imprisonment.

LARCENY
CC Number 658

Li Asu was accused by Lam Sun Chan with stealing a jacket and a silver chain, valued at $1, on the 28th *ultimate*. Defendant entered complainant's house Number 128 Hollywood Road, and stole the articles.

---

[511] **Note on Court Case Reports for March 1882 as a whole.** In the *China Mail* Court Reports for 2 March, 8 March and 22 March 1882, Police Court cases are reported only as "Before H. E. Wodehouse, Esq.". On 22 March, the Criminal Sessions were being held at The Supreme Court and the reporting occupied more than two columns. There is no report of cases heard, "Before Frederick Stewart, Esq.", in the CM of 24 March.

[512] "Police Intelligence", CM, Wednesday, 1 March 1882, p. 3, cc. 2 - 3.

[513] Page torn in original. This text presented here is somewhat edited.

[LARCENY]
CC Number 659

Mak Aun was convicted of stealing a blanket from Am Fuk's room in Bridges Street, and was sentenced to six months' imprisonment with hard labour, the first and last fortnight to be spent in solitary confinement. Five previous convictions for committing the same offence were recorded against him.

ATTEMPTED SHOOTING[514]
CC Number 660 📖 p. 194

John Bryant, boatswain, on board the S.S. *Ashington*, was again charged with assaulting, and firing a revolver at, Samuel Bryant, fireman, on board that vessel on the 26th *ultimate*.

Mr Wotton, of Messrs Brereton and Wotton, appeared for the defendant.

John Stafford, the second engineer of the vessel, said he was in the chief engineer's berth when the defendant along with the complainant and a seaman, came to the berth and asked the witness to settle some dispute. The defendant asked witness if the complainant and the seaman had said the defendant carried tales. To this the witness replied that the complainant had said so. Defendant accused the complainant of this, whereupon a disturbance ensued. The chief engineer then turned the men out and locked the door. Witness then heard some disturbance going on forward and shortly afterwards heard a shot fired. The Chief opened the door and went forward. The witness followed and found the chief holding the boatswain by the hands. The chief told witness to go inside the boatswain's berth and get the revolver. He did this and found it at the inner end of the table. The chief engineer succeeded in persuading the boatswain to go to bed. Witness was of opinion that if the defendant had not been drunk,

---

[514] The following is the complete set of reports in connection with this case in *The Complete Court Cases*: CC Nos 655, 660.

the revolver would not have been fired. In answer to Mr Wotton he stated that he along with others had made a search for the mark of a bullet all over the alley way and found none. He was of opinion that if there had been any marks they would have been discovered.

Some further evidence was taken of a similar character.

The constable who arrested the defendant said that the revolver was loaded in five chambers, and that one was empty.

Mr Wotton in reserving the defendant's defence said that he did not think that there was any necessity for sending the case to the Supreme Court.

The Magistrate said he thought the question of the defendant's intention was one which he would like to be left to a jury,[515] and he would endeavour to have the case brought up before a special sessions.[516]

FRIDAY 3 MARCH 1882[517]
AN OLD MAN'S TROUBLES
CC Number 661 📖 p. 259

Liu Him, Liu Hing, and Liu Luk were charged with assaulting Liu Fuk on the 2nd *instant*.

Liu Fuk stated that he was unemployed. Between 5 and 6 p.m. while he was walking in Centre Street the third defendant, an uncle of his, seized him and took him to his father's shop. There his legs and hands were tied up by the three defendants. A Police Constable seeing this entered the house and arrested them, though the witness was not calling out. His father and mother were in the

---

[515] Magistrate Frederick Stewart is being rather careful in seeking to refer the matter to a special sessions.

[516] A Special Session was held on 10 March 1882. As reported in HKGG (18 March 1882, p. 296), John Bryant was unanimously found not guilty of shooting with intent to murder and not guilty of shooting with intent to do some grievous bodily harm but guilty of common assault. The sentence, also dated 10 March 1882, was three months' imprisonment with hard labour.

[517] "Police Intelligence", CM, Friday, 3 March 1882, p. 3, cc. 4 - 5.

house at the time. These measures were taken to prevent him going out to play, which his father would not give him permission to do.

Liu Hip-kat said the complainant was his son, the 1st defendant his cousin, the 2nd and 3rd nephews. His son was a very bad youth, spending witness's money in gambling and other bad practices. His intention was to send the son to his native country to school, and thereby remove him from temptation. The witness cried bitterly while giving his evidence and stated that he would be without hope in his old age if the son emigrated as he threatened to do. The defendants had used no unnecessary violence.

The Magistrate cautioned and discharged the defendants.

DRUNK AND INCAPABLE
CC Number 662
John Jason, of the S.S. Hong Kong, admitted being found drunk on the Praya, near the Central Market, and was fined 25 cents, or one day's imprisonment.

LARCENY
CC Number 663
Cheung Ayau, coolie, was sentenced to twenty one days' imprisonment for stealing a piece of wood from the Yau Ch'eung shop, Queen's Road Central, which was lately burnt.

STEALING HIS MASTER'S GOODS
CC Number 664
Su Asz, an apprentice tailor, admitted stealing a roll of blue silk, two pieces of fur and two silk waistcoats, worth in all $17, alleging as his reason for so doing that his master had scolded him. After the scolding he took the articles and ran off, hiding the two pieces of fur, the only things that had not been recovered, among some timber in Gough Street. Going back the day after, the things were missing. The complainant, Au Asam, stated that he had scolded the defendant lately for his laziness, the only thing he had to

complain of. Sentenced to three months' imprisonment with hard labour.

CHARGE OF STEALING COTTON JACKETS
CC Number 665

Chun Sz, boatman, was charged with stealing six cotton jackets belonging to Wong Kwok, tailor, Wanchai Road, on the 2nd *instant*.

The complainant, master of the Wo Lung clothing shop, said while on the floor above his shop having his head shaved, he observed, through the skylight, the defendant and three other men, not in charge, bargaining with the shopman left in charge. The defendant went to one of the shelves, took a bundle of clothing and put it under his jacket, during the time that the others were conversing with the shopman. The complainant called out to the shopman, who seized the defendant. The others ran off.

The shopman corroborated the complainant's statement.

Three previous convictions were produced against the defendant.

After being cautioned the defendant stated that he entered the shop with his friends. After they had been bargaining for some time one of the friends had a quarrel with the shopman. He then walked off, the shopman followed with the bundle and made the constable believe that he had stolen the clothes.

He was committed for trial at the next Criminal Sessions.[518]

---

[518] This is listed as Case 14 in "Criminal Calendar -- March Sessions, 1882" (HKGG, 15 April 1882, p. 386). On 23 March 1882, Chun Sz was tried befoe Chief Justice George Phillippo on three counts: 1) Larceny; 2 and 3) Previous conviction (summary) and pleaded guilty on all three counts. On 27 March 1882, he was sentenced to five years' penal servitude.

The following report appeared in *The China Mail*. (Thursday, 23 March 1882, p. 3, c. 1.)

"Supreme Court

UNLAWFUL POSSESSION
CC Number 666

Li Ashik, fisherman, was fined 20 shillings, with the alternative of 21 days' imprisonment with hard labour, for being in unlawful possession of one pair of trousers belonging to Pang Ahi, station coolie at Stanley, on the 2nd *instant*. He was likewise fined in the same sum, with the alternative of the same imprisonment for being in unlawful possession of wood stolen from the military barracks at Stanley.

"In Criminal Sessions (Before the Hon. G. Phillippo, Chief Justice.)
"Thursday, 23 March 1882
"Shop Lifting

"The following gentleman were empanelled as a jury: -- E. H. Joseph, D. Rustomjee, I. G. Geddes, H. A. L. James, H. A. do Rosario, A. B. da Souza, H. Muirhead. [Presumably this applies to all cases on this day under Phillippo. -- Ed]

The Attorney General (The Hon. E. L. O'Malley), instructed by Mr Sharp, the Crown Solicitor, prosecuted."
        "Chun Asz was found guilty of stealing six cotton jackets from the shop of Wong Kwok, tailor in Wanchai Road, on the 2nd March.
        "The defendant and three others entered the complainant's shop, and while the three others were engrossing the attention of the assistant, the defendant lifted a bundle of clothing and was making off; when the master of the shop, who was on the first floor, and saw the defendant's movements through a trapdoor, called the attention of the assistant who ran after the defendant and held him until a constable came up.
"The defendant admitted two previous convictions. Sentence was reserved."

Another report in *The China Mail* (Monday, 27 March 1882, p. 3, c. 4) reads as follows:

"Monday, 27 March 1882
"The prisoners found guilty on Wednesday and Thursday last were sentenced this morning by His Lordship.
        "Chun Asz, proved to have stolen six cotton jackets from the shop of Wong Kwok, tailor, on the 2nd March, and who had already undergone a sentence of two years' imprisonment, was sentenced to five years' penal servitude."

Complete Court Cases   481

ASSAULT BY A CONSTABLE
CC Number 667

Sohail Singh,[519] Police Constable 658, was charged with assaulting Au Ahap, chair coolie to Mr Remedios, on the 2nd instant.

The complainant stated that he was, until yesterday, in the employ of Mr Remedios, when he was fined $3 for neglect of duty. While leaving the court he was struck by the defendant on the eye.

The defendant stated that after the complainant had paid his fine he came into court in a hurried manner and stamped on his foot. He felt the pain and pushed the complainant, but he did not know how he got his discoloured eye. He said he had been ten years in the force and never been so charged before.

The constable was fined $2, with the alternative of two days' imprisonment.

MONDAY 6 MARCH 1882[520]
GAMBLING
CC Number 668

Inspector Perry charged Cheung Acheung and four others with public gambling at 17, Market Street, on the 5th instant.

The Inspector, accompanied by Inspector Matheson, while passing down Market Street, and while approaching Number 17, heard a sudden rush. He saw several people rushing downstairs. He remembered he had a warrant,[521] although not in his possession, to enter this house. When he got in, he observed a number of persons going through the smoke hole on to the roof. He arrested four of them in the house and the other one while coming down a ladder which was in the cook house of Number 11. All the usual articles used by gamblers were found in the house.

---

[519] Also "Sobail Sing" (CC 362).
[520] "Police Intelligence", CM, Monday, 6 March 1882, p. 3, c. 5.
[521] Under Ordinance No. 9 of 1876, para. 7, a warrant was needed to enter or break into a suspected location.

One of the defendants was discharged, but the other four were each fined $15, with the alternative of suffering six weeks' imprisonment with hard labour.

TUESDAY 7 MARCH 1882[522]
FIRING CRACKERS
CC Number 669
Seven Chinese admitted the charge of firing crackers, and were each fined 25 cents, with the alternative of one day's imprisonment.

DRUNKS
CC Number 670
Robert Reedman, seaman on board the American barque W. H. Besse, was found drunk in Queen's Road Central about 11 o'clock last night. He said he had tried to get on board, but had to give in and lie down. He was fined 25 cents[523] or one day's imprisonment.

[DRUNKS]
CC Number 671
Charles Wilcox, seaman on board the Glenelg, was found drunk and incapable in Lower Lascar Row late last night. He expressed his regret for the occurrence, but was fined the customary sum of 25 cents,[524] with the option of one day's imprisonment.

UNLAWFUL POSSESSION
CC Number 672
Lo Fuk, a coolie, was charged by James Holland, private of the Royal Inniskilling Fusiliers, with the

---

[522] "Police Intelligence", CM, Tuesday, 7 March 1882, p. 3, c. 4.

[523] It is interesting that, in the Report for CC 671, either the Magistrate or the Court Reporter takes care to point out that 25 cents was the usual fine at the time for being "drunk and incapable" in the street. On 7 March 1882, the same fine sentence was awarded for "firing crackers" (CC 669).

[524] Either the Magistrate or the Court Reporter takes care to point out that 25 cents was the usual fine at the time for being drunk and incapable in the street.

unlawful possession of one pound of tea, the property of the Regimental band.

Pte. Holland observed the defendant coming from the Murray Barracks cookhouse with a basket over his arm. There was something bulky under his jacket, and when asked to stop Lo Fuk said "No can." He was stopped and the tea found there. The defendant was a coolie employed by the band. His defence was that he was not aware who had put the tea where it was found.

This innocent excuse was hardly sufficient to exonerate him from the charge, and he was fined ten shillings, with the option of fourteen days' imprisonment with hard labour.

THEFT
CC Number 673

Wong Alun, Yau Akap and Wong Aku, coolies, were charged with the theft of some coffee, the property of a fireman on board the Russian ship Vladivostock.

The complainant had gone ashore some days ago to the Central Market to purchase provisions for the ship. The purchases finished, he engaged the defendants to carry them to the wharf, where one of the defendants ran off with 81b. of coffee. The first carried the beef, and the complainant could not say which of the other two carried off the packet. He missed a $5 note at the same time, but how it disappeared he was unable to say.

The first defendant was discharged, the second and third were sentenced to twenty-one days' imprisonment with hard labour.

GAMBLERS
CC Number 674

Sum Aying and Su Akwon, coolies, were each fined $15, with the alternative of six weeks' imprisonment with hard labour, for being found gambling, along with others, in an unoccupied house in Gilman's Bazaar yesterday. The defendants averred that they were looking at the house to see if it was suitable for a coolie house. The gambling gear found, they said, had been used at the race-course.

THURSDAY 9 MARCH 1882
EDITORIAL[525] [ADDITIONAL 674a] 📖 p. 286
A somewhat alarming disclosure was made in the course of a case which came before Dr Stewart this morning. A native constable who had been told off to make inquiries into a row which occurred in a brothel in Square Street yesterday, stated that the defendant in the case, who when arrested was armed with a chopper of the class used by butchers and carpenters, belonged to a gang numbering about one hundred men, organised for the purpose of fighting. Inspector Fleming, who was in charge of the case, said the statement was merely founded on rumour. This may be so, but as Dr. Stewart remarked it is a rumour which should be most carefully inquired into, as the existence of gangs such as this is a danger to the peace of the Colony. One of the inmates of the brothel admitted, in reply to the Magistrate, that she had heard of the existence of such a combination.

FRIDAY 10 MARCH 1882[526]
ROGUE AND VAGABOND
CC Number 675
Chan Hong, remanded from yesterday, was sent to gaol for fourteen days with hard labour as a rogue and vagabond. Defendant had been acting as watchman to gamblers in Gilman's Bazaar, and on seeing the police coming called out, and thus enabled the gamblers to escape.

---

[525] See a reference to the Square Street Brothel in Court Case Number 364.
[526] "Police Intelligence", CM, Friday, 10 March 1882, p. 3, c. 5.

SATURDAY 11 MARCH 1882[527]
CHINESE FEMALE ROWDIES
CC Number 676

Wong Aho, married woman, for assaulting Hou Alin, also married, was fined 50 cents with the alternative of two days' imprisonment. The females commenced a quarrel, in which the complainant accused the other of having several husbands, and from abuse they proceeded, after the customary habit of rowdies, to scratch, and otherwise ill-treat each other. They were bound over in personal security of $2, to keep the peace towards each other for two months.

A MISCHIEVOUS SEAMAN
CC Number 677

Henry James, an unemployed seaman belonging to Jamaica, about 10 o'clock, maltreated Cheng Yik Yu, a tailor, to such an extent that the Magistrate ordered him to pay the sum of $1, otherwise to be imprisoned for four days. Defendant kicked the tailor, smashed his lantern, and, when the constable tried to arrest, him ran off, putting the policeman to the trouble of running after him.

ROBBING A WIDOW
CC Number 678

Chun Tai stole a brass smoking pipe from Wong Chat, widow, while the latter was in the female compartment of the Gallery of the Ko Shing Theatre on the 10th March; to this he pleaded guilty, and was sentenced to three months' imprisonment with hard labour.

ABUSING A FRIEND'S HOSPITALITY
CC Number 679

Leung Chak was accommodated with a night's lodgings by Li Kwai and Chun Yun, carpenters, fellow workmen of his, and when leaving in the

---

[527] "Police Intelligence", CM, Saturday, 11 March 1882, p. 3, c. 7.

morning took with him three jackets, two trousers and one silver dollar belonging to his friends. He admitted taking part of the clothing, but stated that the complainants had placed the other articles in his room, where they were found, to make the offence appear more serious. He was sentenced to six weeks' imprisonment with hard labour.

TUESDAY 14 MARCH 1882[528]
THE ATTACK ON THE POLICE SERGEANT
CC Number 680

Wong Akong, 24, carpenter, was charged on remand from yesterday, with assaulting Sergeant Hanson, with attempt to commit a felony on the 12th instant.

The case was adjourned till Wednesday, but in order to have the evidence of the Naval Officer whose attention was first attracted, the case was resumed this morning.

Paul W. M. Rich, mate of the German gun vessel Iltis, said he started yesterday about 2 p.m., alone, for a trip to the Peak. As it was rather warm he unbuttoned his uniform coat, thus exposing to view his gold chain and locket. About one-third of the way up he met the defendant and inquired of him the shortest path to the Peak. The defendant, who had been proceeding downwards, directed him by signs to ascend a by-path, he believed in continuation of one he had been on before. The defendant followed; suspecting him, witness ordered him to desist, but he paid no attention. Finding that the man would not turn back witness allowed him to go ahead of him. At a sharp bend of the path the defendant disappeared. The Officer continued on his way, but the path after going a little further came to an end and he had to return. At the sharp bend the defendant was standing there with his hands behind his back. Witness took a sharp- cornered stone from the defendant, which the latter had in his hand and made him go along with

---

[528] "Police Intelligence", CM, Tuesday, 14 March 1882, p. 3, cc. 4 - 5.

him, expecting to find a constable. On reaching the main road the defendant refused to mount the road with witness, and he went alone, reporting the matter to Sergeant Hanson at the Gap Station. The Sergeant accompanied witness down part of the way, but no trace of the defendant was seen.

The case was then again adjourned till to-morrow, when Sergeant Hanson will likely be able to appear and give his evidence.[529]

STEALING A SHIPMATE'S CLOTHING
CC Number 681

Joseph Laila, 18, of Chili [*sic* for "Chile"], fireman on board the steamer Hong Kong, was accused by John Hamilton, fireman, and a shipmate of the accused, of stealing clothing to the value of L1 [*sic* for $1] 8s.

According to the complainant, he and the defendant went on board a steamer on the 28th February intending to go to Singapore, but they afterwards decided to remain and returned on shore. The sampan man got the complainant's clothes and took them to Number 46 Third Street. Some days after he went to this house in the expectation of receiving his clothes back, but was told his friend had visited the place and got them.

The defendant said he lived with the complainant, and as they had no money to supply them with necessaries, he, after selling out his own stock, took the complainant's clothes, with the latter's permission.

This last statement the complainant stated was not true. He never was without food, and did not require money.

The Magistrate sentenced the Chilian to twenty one days' imprisonment with hard labour.

---

[529] "The case in which Wong Akong is charged with assaulting Sergeant Hanson was adjourned today till the 23rd instant, owing to the Sergeant being still unable to leave the hospital." ("Local and General", CM, 16 March 1882, p. 2, c. 7.)

WEDNESDAY 15 MARCH 1882[530]
LARCENY
CC Number 682

Lam Foi Tsoi, hawker, was sentenced to fourteen days' imprisonment with hard labour for stealing a fish from a fishmonger in Yau-mah Ti [sic] yesterday night. He averred that he went out to look for his uncle after dark. The fishmonger passed him, and then turned round and accused him of stealing his fish. This was too lame a defence to relieve him of the charge.

ALLEGED ASSAULT
CC Number 683 📖 p. 287

Christini [sic] Brown, of Germany, single woman residing at 22, Gage Street, was charged with unlawfully assaulting Luk Achü, tailor, on the 14th instant.

The complainant said he went to 15, Gage Street in the forenoon yesterday to ask for payment of a $100, which a woman was due him [sic]. The defendant was present in this house; after making his request to the woman, who said she had no funds and who promised to pay him next month, he protested that he was in urgent need of the money. The defendant then pulled his ear, called him a thief, and said he had cheated her friend. The complainant warded off her blows, and took to his heels.

The defendant asserted that while on a visit to her friend, who was lying on a couch indisposed, the complainant entered the house and asked for payment, which her friend promised in a few days. The complainant, however, persisted on having immediate payment, and said "You must pay me money just now, what for you keep me? You wantee things, you must pay money!"[531] Witness then interfered, and asked him why he made such a noise,

---

[530] "Police Intelligence", CM, Wednesday, 15 March 1882, p. 3, cc. 4 - 5.

[531] This is one of a few examples of pidgin English recorded in *The Complete Court Cases*.

when he commenced to abuse her, necessitating her taking him by the collar of the coat and showing him the door. Complainant slapped her in the face; she then took hold of him, and threatened to summons him for assault, but he had anticipated her.

The Magistrate dismissed the summons.

LARCENY OF CLOTHING
CC Number 684
Chung Kai, boatman, was committed to prison for two months for stealing property to the value of $7, belonging to Lo Ayau on the 14th instant.

UNLAWFUL POSSESSION
CC Number 685
Li Atim, shop-keeper, was convicted of the unlawful possession of one lamp and a quantity of books, the property of Henry Duright Stiles, book-seller, Number 2, Blue Buildings, Wanchai. The property went amissing at the time that the fire took place,[532] and the complainant, who was absent at Canton[533] on that occasion, missed them from a book-case he had left in Mrs. Snelling's charge. He gave information of the loss to the Police, and Inspector Perry succeeded in discovering some of the books in the possession of the defendant, who is a second-hand furniture-dealer in Hollywood Road. The defendant was unable to find the party from whom he bought the books, for which he had paid $1, and who had made a profit of $7 or $8 on the sale of two of them, one of them having been sold to Mr. Staunton, the prison warder, from whom the first clue of the property was obtained. The shopkeeper was now sentenced to six weeks' imprisonment with hard labour; and the books were returned to the owner.

---

[532] For references to a fire, see CC Nos 623, 626, 652, 685. See also note above to CC No. 623.

[533] It is interesting to note that there is no hint that it was anything strange for a European to be away from Hong Kong in Canton.

A DRUNK AND VIOLENT DARKIE[534]
CC Number 686

James Solomon, an African seaman, unemployed, was apprehended by Police Constable Dick, yesterday evening, having been seen soliciting alms from passing sailors. The African refused to go to the station, lay down and kicked at all and sundry people who attempted to approach him; ultimately, he was accommodated with a chair and removed. His defence was, that the Police Constable beat him, making his arm stiff. The case was remanded till to-morrow.

A FREQUENT OFFENDER
CC Number 687

Lam Afuk, an unemployed coolie, who is charged with the larceny of two brass smoking-pipes was committed for trial at the April Criminal Sessions.[535] He was seen to enter the I-Shun Hong, Number 42, Bonham Strand yesterday evening, and observed secreting the two pipes in his sleeve. One of the accountants of the Hong caught him just as he was getting into the street. If convicted his sentence will likely be severe as he has been already imprisoned five times for committing the same offence.

---

[534] The following is the complete set of reports in connection with this case in *The Complete Court Cases*: CC Nos 686, 688.

[535] See No. 9, "Criminal Calendar -- April Sessions, 1882", HKGG, 6 May 1882, p. 461.

Lau A-fuk was charged with 1) Larceny; 2) Previous conviction (Criminal Sessions); 3) Previous conviction (Criminal Sessions); and tried on 19 April 1882. He pleaded guilty on all three counts. Sentence was given on 24 April 1882: three years' penal servitude.

THURSDAY 16 MARCH 1882[536]
ROGUE AND VAGABOND[537]CC Number 688

James Solomon, the African seaman, charged with being a rogue and vagabond yesterday, was sentenced to seven days' imprisonment with hard labour.

THEFT OF COPPER
CC Number 689

Leung Kam, Captain of a lighter, was charged with stealing a quantity of copper, value $27, on the 8th instant at Hung Ham Dock, belonging to the Hong Kong and Whampoa Dock Company.

Adam Hogg, a watchman, gave evidence to the following effect: -- On the 3rd March a lighter belonging to the Messageries Maritimes Company, and of which the defendant is Captain, entered the Hung Ham [*sic*] Dock to be re-coppered. By agreement the old copper was to be the property of the Dock Company, but on the 8th instant, when the repairs had been completed, a quantity of the copper was missed. A search was made on board the lighter and about 230 lbs. were found concealed below the ceiling. When the property was found six men forming the crew and a woman, believed to be defendant's wife, departed, leaving the defendant to bear the onus of the whole transaction.

Joseph Smith, foreman carpenter, under whose supervision the work was carried out, said, that not being aware of the exact terms of the agreement he allowed the defendant and his men to store away the old copper in the hold.

The defendant said he was unaware at first that the property belonged to any other than his master, but after being told that it was the property of the Dock Company, he ordered it ashore. He had landed so much of it, and was to have removed the

---

[536] "Police Intelligence", CM, Thursday, 16 March 1882, p. 3, cc. 2 - 3.

[537] The following is the complete set of reports in connection with this case in *The Complete Court Cases*: CC Nos 686, 688.

quantity discovered under the ceiling, but the watchman would not allow him.

The defendant was sentenced to three months' imprisonment with hard labour.

FRIDAY 17 MARCH 1882[538]
LARCENY OF A BOAT
CC Number 690

Li Ngan and Wong Aping, marine hawkers, convicted of having in their unlawful possession a boat and about nine cwt. of coal, value $6, were each fined L10 [*sic* for $10], with the alternative of undergoing three months' imprisonment with hard labour. They were seen by Police Constable McDonald going from the Hong Kong side to Yau Mah Ti [*sic*] this morning, about half-past five, but as soon as they saw the Police boat, the first defendant jumped into the water, although about 200 yards from the shore, and tried to escape; and the second got on board a fishing junk, leaving the boat they were in to look after itself. The first defendant swam to the same junk, and Constable McDonald apprehended them both, and though the property had not been claimed, they could not give an explicit explanation of how they became the possessors, and were accordingly found guilty of the misdemeanour.

BANGLE STEALING
CC Number 691 📖 p. 329

Lui Ahoi, hawker, and Chun Tak, money-changer, were sentenced -- the first, to twenty-one days' imprisonment with hard labour for stealing a bangle from the child of Lai Akum, on the 15th instant, in Ng Kwai Lane; and the second to one month's imprisonment with hard labour for receiving the same, knowing it to be stolen property.

---

[538] "Police Intelligence", CM, Friday, 17 March 1882, p. 3, c. 4. Mention is made in a small article that this was St Patrick's Day. (See CM, p. 3, c. 2).

A BAD FIT
CC Number 692

Kung Achi, hawker, was proved to have been in the unlawful possession of a pair of shoes. He was arrested by a Police Constable in Ladder Street this morning, at four o'clock, on account of his attempt to retrace his steps[539] on seeing the constable. The defendant asserted that the shoes belonged to him, but his inability to put them on proved otherwise. He had been so often within the precincts of the prison walls that he could not remember the number of his visits, but the prison officials produced six convictions against him, and the Magistrate then fined him twenty shillings, giving him the option of enduring six weeks' hard labour.

ALLEGED ASSAULT AND ROBBERY
CC Number 693

Wong Kong Yau, and three other coolies were, along with the complainant Cheung Kui, ordered to give personal security in $10 each to keep the peace for the next three months. The defendants were accused by the complainant with assaulting and robbing him at Quarry Bay on the 13th instant, but the evidence showed that a man who was along with the complainant, his friend, had disappeared with the property, and that the complainant had only been taken hold of and tied up after he began brandishing a knife.

ROBBERY
CC Number 694 📖 p. 235

Chu Azing, Wong Awing and Chiu Apo were charged with receiving two pieces of bark and a large leather box, knowing the same to have been stolen, on the 7th [*sic* -- see below (ed.)] *instant* the property of the Rev. Marcus Leang [*sic*],[540] part of articles stolen to the value of over $200.

---

[539] "Attempt to retrace his steps": i.e. he attempted to run away.
[540] *The Daily Press*, Thursday, 20 April 1882, spells the name "Leong".

Rev. Marcus Leang said he was a Roman Catholic Priest and lived in the parsonage in St. Francis Street. On the 7th of February he went to the chapel about ten minutes to six, leaving the large box in Court in his room near his bed. The box which was locked, was the property of a friend, the Rev. Chü Tak Mong, and had been in his custody for two months and a half. He was not aware of the contents nor their exact value, but he knew the two pieces of cinnamon were part of the contents. The small teak box in Court was part of his own property, and was left unlocked, at the same time as he left his friend's box, and contained a quantity of valuable books. He missed the articles on his return from the chapel, but next morning found his own box and some of the small books on the hill side.

The defendants were arrested by Inspector Corcoran, and each of them was proved to have been implicated in the affair.

Rev. Chü Tak Mong, missionary, identified the brown leather box, a tin of medicine, the empty tin, two pieces of cinnamon, two show-cases and some valuable books as belonging to him, which he valued at $400.

The second defendant admitted being concerned in the robbery, and the third defendant was proved to have pawned several of the articles. The second defendant has one previous conviction against him, and the third five previous convictions.

After being cautioned the prisoners were committed for trial at the April Criminal Sessions.[541]

---

[541] The following information appears in the Criminal Calendar for the April Sessions, 1882, HKGG, 6 May 1882, p. 461, where this case is No. 6.

Chu A-ying, Wong A-wing and Chiu A-po were tried on 19 April 1882 on five counts: 1) Larceny, 2) Larceny, 3) Receiving stolen goods, 4) Previous conviction (summary) and 5) Previous conviction (summary).

Chu A-ying was found not guilty on all counts and discharged. Wong A-wing pleaded guilty to 1) Larceny and 2) Larceny, and was found guilty on 3) Receiving stolen goods and was sentenced on 24 April 1882 to nine months' imprisonment with hard labour.

Friday 17 March 1882[542]
[DISTURBANCE AT THE SUPREME COURT]
"Local and General"
ADDITIONAL 695 📖 p. 361

Wong Leong-Tak, an old man of 65 years, and who is known by many in the Colony as the "King of Siam", and who is the possessor of a medal for distinguished services in some unheard-of warlike encounters, was this morning brought before Dr Stewart, charged with disorderly conduct at the Supreme Court, a place which he constantly haunts, and is frequently a considerable annoyance to those conducting the business. This morning he was turned away by a constable, but with his usual cunning he effected an entrance by the other passage; this led to the old man being ejected a second time, during which he raised a considerable row. It was stated before Dr Stewart that his passage had been frequently paid to Swatow from the Poor's Box, but he always retraces his steps to the Queen's Dominions. His object in visiting the Supreme Court this morning was to receive payment of the modest sum of $100,000, which, he said, the Judge had promised him. Dr Stewart remanded the case till tomorrow, to allow of some means being devised to relegate the King to some quarter where his claims to distinction will be more fully recognised.

Chiu A-po was found guilty of 3) Receiving stolen goods, and pleaded guilty to 4) Previous conviction (summary) and 5) Previous conviction (summary) and was sentenced on 24 April 1882 to three years' penal servitude.

The present writer has not been able to find any report in *The China Mail*, but has found one in *The Daily Press*. See Gillian Bickley, Ed, "Robbery", in, "Some Nineteenth Century Hong Kong Court Cases", 2009/2010.

[542] "Local and General," CM, 17 March 1882, p. 3, c. 2.

MONDAY 20 MARCH 1882[543]
BOTH MAGISTRATES SITTING

THEFT AT THE SAILORS' HOME
CC Number 696 📖 p. 195

James Howard, an unemployed English seaman, was charged with stealing $6 from A. Anderson, seaman, on the 19th instant.

The complainant said he was a seaman on board the Oneida, and was at present residing at the Sailors' Home. Yesterday about 11 o'clock in the forenoon he went out with the defendant, who resided in the same room, and returned in about an hour, slightly the worse for liquor. He immediately went upstairs, leaving the defendant downstairs, and went to bed with all his clothes on. At that time he had six one-dollar notes in his trouser pocket for certain, but how much more he was unable to say. He awoke at four o'clock in the afternoon and found his money missing. The defendant, who knew of him having money in his possession, he had reason to think, had stolen the dollars.

Henry Grastin, who also occupied the same room, said he saw the defendant go to the complainant's bed and take some money out of the former's pocket, about half-past one yesterday afternoon. He did this without knowing that witness had seen him, and acted all through in a very suspicious manner. Witness did not mention the matter to the complainant because he thought the defendant had taken the money to look after it; the men being great friends.

William Blood, seaman, entered the room about half-past one on his bare feet, and just as he got inside he saw the defendant jump away from complainant's bed and put something in his pocket. At the time he did not suspect that anything was wrong.

---

[543] "Police Intelligence", CM, Monday, 20 March 1882, p. 3, cc. 4 - 5.

The defendant when searched had in his possession one five-dollar note and some cents, and averred that the money had been given him by various men. He had got the note by changing four notes and one silver dollar for it at the Welcome Tavern.

Peter Joyce, seaman on board the Glenelg, said he knew that the defendant had money previous to the 19th instant, he having given to him five dollars some nine days ago. He also saw the defendant return $30, to James Dalton, a shipmate, on the same day. This money Dalton handed to the defendant to keep while the former was in a state of intoxication.

Another witness said he knew the defendant to have had money in his possession previous to the 19th.

The defendant said he went upstairs about dinner-time to awaken the complainant, but changed his mind thinking that Anderson was too drunk. He bought a looking-glass from the second witness who was lying in his bed, and then went downstairs again. He was just leaving the room when the third witness came in. He protested that he did not take the money, and pointed out that the third witness had just finished two months' imprisonment for larceny. He admitted having suffered four months' imprisonment for cutting the tackle of the P. & O. steamer, which he was discharged from about the middle of November last.

The Magistrates imposed a sentence of eighteen months' imprisonment with hard labour.

MONDAY 20 MARCH 1882[544]
BEFORE FREDERICK STEWART, ESQ.

ASSAULT ON A CONSTABLE
CC Number 697
Kwok Tai, fireman unemployed, was ordered to pay
a fine of 50 cents or suffer two days' imprisonment,
for assaulting Odum Singh Police Constable, in
Queen's Road on Saturday, and was also ordered to
pay 50 cents as amends for tearing the constable's
uniform.

UNLAWFUL POSSESSION OF BRANCHES
CC Number 698
Ho Afat, a farmer, was convicted of having in his
possession, unlawfully, a quantity of freshly-cut
branches on the 19th instant, and was fined $2, in
default of payment to suffer seven days'
imprisonment with hard labour.

Lam Asau, coal coolie, was fined $3, with
the alternative of suffering ten days' imprisonment
with hard labour for unlawful possession of newly
cut branches, and Fu Hi was fined $2, with the option
of seven days' imprisonment for damaging trees, on
the 19th instant.

HARD UP FOR A DRINK
CC Number 699
James Sands and Cornelius McEroy, privates in the
Royal Inniskilling Fusiliers, were arrested by Police
Constable James about 11 o'clock on Saturday night,
at the back of the National Hotel, at the instance of
the proprietor, John Olson. The defendants were
found by the proprietor of the Hotel sitting in a
window at the back of the premises and when asked
what they wanted, said they would like something to
drink. The proprietor also noticed that the back gate
was broken. The second defendant confessed to

---

[544] "Police Intelligence", CM, Monday, 20 March 1882, p. 3, cc.
4 - 5.

doing this. They were told they could get no drink and asked to go away, but this they refused to do, and the constable was called for.

The constable said when he came on the scene the defendants were cursing and swearing, and on the way to the station, they used obscene and abusive language.

The Magistrate found them guilty of disorderly conduct and fined each, $2 with the alternative of four days' imprisonment with hard labour.

INSENSIBLY DRUNK
CC Number 700
Peter Joyce, an unemployed seaman, did not remember being picked up in Queen's Road Central about midnight on the 18th instant by a constable, thus proving himself to have been in a drunk and incapable condition. He was fined 25 cents, and given the option of suffering one day's imprisonment.

NO PERMIT
CC Number 701
Lau Sam, in whose house, Number 78, Jardine's Bazaar, Acting Police Sergeant Smith found 8 boxes of prepared opium, one pair of scales, two pipe bowls and some other opium utensils, was fined $25, and given the option of suffering six weeks' imprisonment with hard labour, for retailing prepared opium without having a permit from the Opium Farmer.

THEFT OF AN UMBRELLA
CC Number 702
Chan Wong was convicted of stealing an umbrella from Chan Ching, on the 18th *instant*, and having three previous convictions against him, was sentenced to six months' imprisonment with hard labour, first and last fortnights in solitary

confinement, and six hours in the stocks at the scene of the offence.

THEFT OF RICE
CC Number 703
Li Tai and Chan Sui Kan were charged at the instance of Christian Fulling, chief officer of the Fyen, with the theft of rice.

Both defendants were tally-men on board the vessel which was discharging rice in two sorts of bags -- gunny bags and mat bags. The chief officer saw two gunny bags of rice in [*sic*] thrown into a boat alongside. This boat had nothing to do with rice packed in that way.

The prisoners were sentenced to two months' imprisonment with hard labour each.

TUESDAY 21 MARCH 1882[545]
DRUNK
CC Number 704
William Smith, engineer, after admitting a charge of drunkenness was fined 25 cents, with the option of one day's imprisonment.

[DRUNK]
CC Number 705
Henry Edward, an American without occupation, was fined $1, and given the option of suffering two days' imprisonment for being drunk and disorderly in the Police Canteen yesterday.

AN HABITUAL LOITERER
CC Number 706
Edward Phelan, an English seaman without any fixed residence, was sentenced to twenty-one days' imprisonment, with hard labour as a rogue and vagabond.

---

[545] "Police Intelligence", CM, Tuesday, 21 March 1882, p. 3, cc. 1 - 2.

Police Constable Dick saw Phelan about half-past six o'clock in Hollywood Road loitering, and ordered him to move away, which he did. About seven o'clock the constable again saw him at the corner of Tank Lane, and when turning to come away two stones were thrown at him. Shortly afterwards the defendant was apprehended in Upper Lascar Row. The defendant had been put on board his ship, but had come ashore again, and resumed his old practice of loitering. A charitable constable gave him a suit of clothes the other night, but the defendant immediately sold them.

LARCENY OF WOOD
CC Number 707
Ten days' imprisonment was imposed on Ng Atai for stealing three pieces of wood from a carpenter's shop in D'Aguilar Street yesterday.

AN INEFFECTUAL ATTEMPT TO ESCAPE
CC Number 708 📖
Tang Fuk, hawker, along with another man, seized hold of Li Tse, gardener, who was on his way back to Amoy from Penang, and snatched one pair of trousers, and took two silver dollars from the complainant's hand yesterday, on the Praya. When caught by the complainant the defendant cut away part of his queue, but the complainant retained his hold until a constable relieved him. Four previous convictions were recorded against the defendant who was sentenced to six months' imprisonment with hard labour, first and last fortnight in solitary confinement, and six hours in the stocks on the Praya.

A NEEDY HAWKER
CC Number 709 📖 p. 236
Hou Asze, admitted attempting to steal $18 from the pocket of Agha, schoolmaster, on the 20th instant. He had no money, he said, to purchase articles to trade in and tried to pick complainant's pocket for that reason. Four previous convictions were also

admitted. Sentenced to six months' imprisonment with hard labour, first and last fortnight in solitary confinement.

THEFT FROM THE NAVAL YARD
CC Number 710

Chun Hi and Chan Chun Chi were ordered to pay $6, or suffer one month's imprisonment each for stealing two and a half pounds of lead; two blocks, and a piece of copper wire from the Naval Yard on the 20th instant.

THURSDAY 23 MARCH 1882[546]
THEFTS
CC Number 711

Ip Ashun was charged with stealing a pair of cotton trousers from another Chinaman, and was convicted on evidence and sentenced to one month's imprisonment with hard labour.

[THEFTS]
CC Number 712

Ip Muk and Ip Yang-kui were charged with stealing one bag, three bells, two rings and one key, &c., from Mr Kennedy's Horse Repository on the 23rd.

It appeared that Mr Kennedy met the first defendant on the bridge near the Repository with a bag, and having lost several things of late he stopped him, and made him turn out his bag, when he found the property in Court. He took defendant to the station; on the way to which they met the second defendant with whom the first defendant wanted to speak. Second defendant was in Mr Kennedy's employ.

The theft was proved, and the defendant sentenced to six weeks' imprisonment with hard labour. Second defendant's wages to be forfeited.

---

[546] "Police Intelligence", CM, Thursday, 23 March 1882, p. 2, c. 7 - p. 3, c. 1.

SATURDAY 25 MARCH 1882[547]
LARCENY
CC Number 713

Lam Ling, coolie, admitted stealing a quantity of brass, the mountings of a jinricksha, and some canvas covers. He said his mother was sick, and that he stole the articles to raise cash to purchase a jacket to go home with, apparently intending to appear respectable before his parent. The visit will be delayed for two months, the magistrate sending the coolie to prison for that period.

MORE PAY
CC Number 714

Man Asz and three others were fined 25 cents, with the option of one day's imprisonment, and ordered to give personal security in $10 each, to keep the peace for three months.

A. Police Sergeant Smith [*sic* for "Police Sergeant Smith"?] yesterday, was on his way from Wantsai to the Central Station, and when passing the Commissariat an officer made a complaint to him. About 150 coolies were hanging about making a disturbance and calling out "Ta." He tried to get them to move on, but failing, he apprehended two of the defendants, who seemed to be the ringleaders, and Police Constable Lyon arrested another two, after which the crowd dispersed.

The defendants stated that they were engaged at the rate of 18 cents a day. They worked for three hours and demanded 18 cents, but on only receiving 9 cents they objected, and there being so many of them, and each one saying something there was a considerable noise.

The Magistrate advised them in future not to attempt to extort more than was actually due them.

---

[547] "Police Intelligence", CM, Saturday, 25 March 1882, p. 3, c. 5.

MONDAY 27 MARCH 1882[548]
LEAVING SERVICE WITHOUT NOTICE
CC Number 715 📖
Leong Acheung was charged by Lieutenant Gordon
Barclay with leaving his service without giving
notice, and on the evidence of complainant, was
convicted and fined $5, or ten days' imprisonment
with hard labour.

A DISORDERLY AMAH
CC Number 716 📖 p. 260 (See also 📖 p. 262.)
Yau Akan, an amah, was charged with leaving her
employment without leave, and also with creating a
disturbance in her employer's house on the 23rd
instant.

    The case was adjourned from Saturday, on
which occasion the following evidence was given:

    T. N. Driscoll, tailor and outfitter, Queen's
Road Central, said that defendant was told to go and
get her dinner about 6 o'clock on the evening of the
23rd. Shortly after, his little girl seemed to have told
the defendant to make haste, at which the defendant
had become angry, made some disturbance, and used
very bad language. Witness went downstairs to know
the cause of the disturbance, when the defendant
abused him and wanted to know why the child was
sent down to tell her to make haste. He corrected the
child before the defendant, told her to finish her food
and go upstairs. A few minutes after this the
defendant went upstairs and commenced to yell.
Witness put her in her room, but several times she
renewed the disturbance. When wanted to put the
children to bed she could not be found in the house.

    The defendant said she wanted her dinner,
the boys and coolies were busy and she could not get
it, and her mistress wanted her to take the child.
Witness went for her dinner, and when she returned
her mistress checked her, slapped her face, and

---

[548] "Police Intelligence", CM, Monday, 27 March 1882, p. 3, cc.
3 - 4.

kicked her. Witness then asked her wages, and said she would leave, but these were refused. After the children were bedded she told her master, mistress, and all the servants that she intended to leave. Her master seized hold of her and would not let her go. She afterwards reported the matter at the station, and had come to Court next day to take out a summons, but instead she received a letter to take to her master's, where she was given into custody.

The case was resumed this morning when Mrs Driscoll said she returned from a walk about 6 o'clock, asked the defendant if she had had dinner, told her, after being answered in the negative, to go and get it. Witness gave the child no orders to the amah; defendant became angry, and made use of abusive language. Witness said defendant was very noisy and abusive for some time and tried to get on to the verandah to scream and attractthe attention of neighbours.

Kwok Akau, coolie, said he saw the last witness slap defendant on both sides of the face, while the latter held the baby. The master then took the baby from defendant and then the mistress kicked defendant, who fell down.

James Parker, first clerk at the Magistracy, said the defendant came to the Court on the 23rd or 24th instant and applied for a summons against Mrs Driscoll. As the Court was closed he bade the defendant return next day. She came back next day and renewed her application, adding that she would be content to let the matter drop if her clothes, registration ticket, wages and testimonials were given her. Witness reported the matter to Dr Stewart, (the Sitting Magistrate) who asked witness to write Mr Driscoll to see whether the matter could be amicably arranged.[549] He wrote, and soon afterwards Mr Driscoll came to the office and said he had given the defendant into custody.

---

[549] NB: The magistrate tried to get the matter settled out of court, but did not succeed in doing so.

The Magistrate found the charge proved and fined the defendant $2, with the option of two days' imprisonment.[550]

DRUNK
CC Number 717
Thomas McDonald admitted being drunk and incapable on the 26th instant, and was fined 25 cents with the option of suffering one day's imprisonment.

LARCENY
CC Number 718
Ng Acheung, painter, was sentenced to twenty-one days' imprisonment for stealing one pair of shoes belonging to Chan Asz, widow, from the sill of the window of her house, 32, Stanley Street, on the 26th *instant*.

---

[550] See "Mr Driscoll's Amah Again", CM, 29 March 1882, p. 3, c. 5. This case was brought before H. E. Wodehouse.
"Mr T. N. Driscoll charged Kun Ayan with disorderly conduct in his house on the 28th instant. He stated that he went from his store to his house, 3 West Terrace, with the intention of partaking of luncheon. At the entrance to the Terrace he saw a crowd of several coolies and the defendant, who was talking very loudly and was very excited. On noticing the complainant the defendant ran up the hill in the direction of Robinson Road. From what he afterwards learned, he took out a summons against the defendant. He also stated that Mrs Driscoll was ill and unable to appear.
"Leung Alai, house-boy to Mr Driscoll, said the defendant was an amah with his master until the other day, when she was fined $2 by the Magistrate for leaving service without notice. Yesterday she came to the house and applied for a pair of stockings, a tin of tea, and a small bamboo, which things she had left behind. Witness admitted her, and she followed upstairs to his mistress's room, where her mistress told the defendant the articles were not in the house. The latter persisted that they were in the house. His mistress told the defendant to leave, and dragged her downstairs. The defendant on this called out "save life" and made a considerable noise.
"After the defendant stating that what she really wanted was her wages, and that she had gone there at that hour because she knew her late master had luncheon at that time, the magistrate discharged her."
The two magistrates seem to have had a similar opinion about this case.

DISTURBERS OF THE PEACE
CC Number 719

Hassim and Joseph Young, were each fined 50 cents, or two days' imprisonment for being found fighting and creating a disturbance in Upper Lascar Row on the 26th instant.

ATTEMPTED ROBBERIES ON BOARD THE "MARY TATHAM"
CC Number 720

Chan Sing Fuk and three others were sentenced to four months' imprisonment for larceny of clothing. This morning the four defendants had, on board the Mary Tatham bound for Portland, attempted to steal bundles of clothing from four passengers in different parts of the ship, but each had been promptly detained by the complainants. The men had imagined that they could provide themselves with the articles without any fear of detection on account of the confusion on board.

TUESDAY 28 MARCH 1882[551]
SPENCER COMMITTED FOR TRIAL
CC Number 721

Anthony Santos Spencer[552] was committed for trial at the next Criminal Sessions of the Supreme Court,[553]

---

[551] "Police Intelligence", CM, Tuesday, 28 March 1882, p. 3, c. 3. NB *The China Mail* of 28 March 1882 announces Frederick Stewart's appointment as Acting Colonial Secretary. (See p. 2, cc. 6-7; p. 3, c. 1.)

[552] Antonio Spencer was probably a former pupil of the Hong Kong Government Central School for Boys and in this case, Magistrate Stewart had been his headmaster some years past. (See *A Magistrate's Court in 19th Century Hong Kong*, p. 49 and p. 441, n. 78.) Antonio Spencer had an Irish father, William Henry Spencer, born in New York, who married in turn three women, all with Portuguese surnames. Of these, the first wife, Antonio's mother, may have been a Chinese who had been brought up in a Portuguese household, and given a Portuguese name. (See Gillian Bickley, unpublished file [WhoPupls], with some biographical data, such as this, derived from Revd Carl

on the charge of stealing a clock from the house of Dr. Eastlacke on the 27th November last. The evidence given was to the effect that the defendant and another boy went to the house of Dr. Eastlacke in Wyndham Street, and enquired for Dr. Van der Hock, the defendant saying that he came from Mr Woodford of the Hong Kong and Shanghai Bank. The defendant agreed to wait until the doctor returned, he being out at the time. He also solicited permission to wait in the parlour, which was ultimately granted. Some short time afterwards Dr. Eastlacke's son entered the parlour, and the clock and the defendant were missed.

Spencer was also committed for trial at the Criminal Sessions on the charge of obtaining goods

---

Smith's card index of individuals who have lived along the China Coast.)

[553] The following information appears in the Criminal Calendar for the April Sessions, 1882, HKGG, 6 May 1882, p. 461, where Nos. 1, 2, 3 and 4 refer to Spencer.

Anthony Santos Spencer was tried on 19 April 1882, pleading guilty to "Obtaining goods on forged instrument", "Attempting to obtain goods by false pretences" and "Obtaining goods on forged order". He was found guilty of "Larceny in a dwelling-house".

He was sentenced on 24 April 1882 as follows.

For "Obtaining goods on forged instrument" he was sentenced to three months with hard labour, for "Attempting to obtain goods by false pretences", he was sentenced to "three months with hard labour, sentence to commence at the expiration of sentence in Case No. 1" (Obtaining goods on forged instrument).

For "Obtaining goods on forged order", he was sentenced to "Three months' imprisonment with hard labour, sentence to commence at the expiration of sentence in Case No. 2" (Attempting to obtain goods by false pretences).

For "Larceny in a dwelling-house" he was sentenced to "Three months imprisonment with hard labour, sentence to commence at the expiration of sentence in Case No. 3 ["Obtaining goods on forged order"]. The first week and last month of imprisonment to be passed in solitary confinement. Prisoner to be once privately whipped fifteen strokes with a rattan on the breach."

by fraudulent means from Messrs McEwen Frickel & Company, Queen's Road, on various dates.[554]

[OBTAINING GOODS ON FALSE PRETENCES]
CC Number 722

Inspector Lindsay applied for the discharge of Tang Asze, one of the coolies charged with obtaining goods by means of chits, the Inspector stating that he was satisfied that the coolie did not obtain the goods on false pretences. The coolie was discharged.

TUESDAY 28 March 1882
"Police Intelligence"
The China Mail

A brief notice comments on Magistrate Frederick Stewart's re-appointment as Acting Colonial Secretary, to the effect that: "Everything will run smoothly again now!"[555]

The following is the last in this series of *The Complete Court Cases of Magistrate Frederick Stewart as Reported in The China Mail, July 1881 to March 1882.*

WEDNESDAY 29 MARCH 1882[556]
GAMBLERS' WATCHMAN
CC Number 723

Tse Aleung, was sentenced to seven days' imprisonment after having been convicted of being a watchman to gamblers this morning in Market Street. He had also tried to bribe the Police Constable who apprehended him.

---

[554] For a transcript of further material about Anthony Santos Spencer's cases, see, Gillian Bickley, ed., "Spencer's Cases" in, "Some Nineteenth Century Hong Kong Court Cases", 2009/2010.

[555] "Police Intelligence", CM, 28 March 1882, p. 2, cc. 6, 7; p. 3, c. 1. See also *A Magistrate's Court in 19th Century Hong Kong*, p. 34.

[556] "Police Intelligence", CM, Wednesday, 29 March 1882, p. 3, c. 5.

~~~~~~

END OF THE *CHINA MAIL* COURT CASE
REPORT TRANSCRIPTS

~~~~~~

Cases brought for alleged Offences against
"The Excise Ordinance (Opium) 1858-1879,
Amendment Ordinance 1879":
their results, the sentences given & notes on the
relevant legislation[557]

With a Table showing, for each opium case,
the amount of the fine and the alternative period
of imprisonment,
showing whether the latter was with, or without,
hard labour.

The Ordinance applicable to these 1881-1882 court cases is Ordinance No. 7 of 1879, "The Excise Ordinance (Opium) 1858-1879, Amendment Ordinance 1879".[558]

All the offences against the Opium Ordinance in this set of reports concern possession of opium, unlicensed by the Opium Farmer.

Based on a study of these court case reports and from searching the legislation which relates to them, the following picture has emerged.

The term, "possession", was defined by Ordinance No. 1 of 1879, para. 1 as follows: "for the purposes of this Ordinance, any boiled or prepared opium, or utensils or vessels used for preparing the same shall be deemed to be in possession of any person if he knowingly have them in actual possession, custody, or control by himself or by any other person."

Broadly speaking, the position was that no-one in Hong Kong or in Hong Kong waters could have in their possession, whether for their own use or for sale, any prepared opium at all unless they had obtained it

---

[557] See also the Appendix, "The Excise Ordinance (Opium) 1858-1879, Amendment Ordinance 1879: Selections to explain the opium and opium-related cases before Frederick Stewart, July 1881 to March 1882". Referred to after this as, "The Excise Ordinance (Opium) 1858-1879".

[558] See also the Appendix, "The Excise Ordinance (Opium) 1858-1879".

from the current Opium Farmer or from any of the licensed agents of the current Opium Farmer. Since the law was very strictly enforced, it would have been prudent for anyone, even with authorized possession of prepared opium from an authorized source, to keep available, in case he or she was ever requested to show it, the certificate, which it was the legal responsibility of the seller to provide each purchaser.[559]

The position of Opium Farmer was obviously well-known and "The Opium Farmer" (less often, "the Farmer") is referred to in some twenty-one of the twenty-three cases. (CCs 19, 91, 111, 124, 178, 210, 307, 324, 327, 329, 371, 375, 386, 434, 445, 492, 511, 535, 548, 569, 646.)

Almost all the cases refer to *prepared* opium, a few refer to *raw* opium (e.g. CCs 124, 178, 386, 548) and a similar number to opium *dross* (e.g. CCs 19, 124, 178, 371, 492) or opium refuse (CCs 178, 434). One only refers to *crude* opium (CC 124). In three cases, there is reference to opium *balls* (CCs 91, 386, 434). The term, "*boiled*", is used seldom and then only as a verb (CCs 327, 492). In one case Malwa Opium and Patna opium are named (CC 91) and in another case Malwa Opium only (CC 548). In one case, there are no details at all about the type of opium that was found (CC 264). In another, the

---

[559] The amendments to section 7 of Ordinance No. 2 of 1858, effected by Ordinance No. 7 of 1879, had resulted in the following wording: "It shall be the duty of every person selling or retailing prepared opium under this Ordinance [i.e. Ordinance No. 2 of 1858], to deliver therewith a sealed certificate, specifying the amount so sold; which certificate shall be evidence of the facts therein stated, and shall not be transferable and shall contain a notice printed in English and Chinese, in the following form: — 'Notice is hereby given that the monopoly of the Hong Kong opium farm, at present held by the undersigned, expires on the ...., and that the boiled or prepared opium now purchased and sold cannot be legally used or retained in your possession after noon of the 3rd day from the above date, without the consent of the new holder of the monopoly or of the Governor. [There follow three blank lines for signatures.]'"

opium could be described in none of these ways, as the defendant was in the process of boiling it (CC 445).

The charge in most cases was being in possession of prepared opium without a (valid) permit or a (valid) certificate from the Opium Farmer.

There was a legal reason for the overwhelming majority of references in these reports to "prepared" opium. Under the Ordinance, the finding of prepared or boiled opium, as well as utensils for preparing or boiling it, in unauthorized possession or unauthorized circumstances, was not only the primary offence but it was also a prerequisite for seizing raw opium.

> "All boiled or prepared opium offered or exposed for sale or retail by any unauthorized person and all boiled or prepared opium found in the possession or custody or control of any unauthorized person or in any unauthorized place, except as in the last section mentioned, [560] and any utensils or vessels which have been used or which are manifestly intended to be used in boiling or preparing opium by any unauthorised person or in any unauthorized place, may be seized by a police or excise officer, and shall be forfeited and may be by a Magistrate delivered and adjudged to the holder of the exclusive privilege for the time being, and any unauthorized person in whose possession any such boiled or prepared opium or utensils or vessels are found may be apprehended and taken before a Magistrate by any police or excise officer." (Ordinance No. 1 of 1879, para. 7.)

---

[560] This relates to Paragraph 6, which was repealed by Ordinance No. 7 of 1879 and so does not apply to these 1881-1882 cases.

"Wherever boiled or prepared opium is so seized as last aforesaid and any such utensils or vessels are also seized as aforesaid [present writer's emphasis], the police or excise officer seizing the same may also seize any raw opium [present writer's emphasis] that may be found in the custody or control of such unauthorized person or in such unauthorized place and such raw opium shall be subject to the order of the Magistrate before whom the case is brought." (Ordinance No. 1 of 1879, para. 8.)

There was also provision under the Ordinance for an officer to seize raw opium under special circumstances, where no boiled or prepared opium was found in the possession of an unauthorized person or place.

"Whenever from any other cause [i.e. beyond that provided for in Ordinance No. 1 of 1879, paras 7 & 8] there is reasonable ground to believe that boiled or prepared opium is manufactured by any unauthorized person or in any unauthorized place within this Colony it shall be lawful for a police or excise officer to seize any raw opium found in the possession of such unauthorized person or in such unauthorised place." (Ordinance No. 1 of 1879, para. 9.)

This would have given authority in relation to CC 124, where the charge was, "possession of crude opium without a certificate", for the report quotes the Police Constable as stating that he found, "five empty tins in one of which there were traces of prepared opium".

Inadequate certificates
Some defendants produced documentation which was considered inadequate. In one case, the defendant produced three certificates for the purchase of opium

designed for shipment, saying that the opium had been bought for coolies on board a barque, "which was going to a foreign country", but the certificates bore others' names, not the defendant's (CC 386). In one case the Defendant produced a number of certificates, but on examination by the Court Interpreter they were all were found to be obsolete and of no value (CC 535). The Defendant showed the Inspector six permits when he was asked to show a permit (CC 548). However, the Court Interpreter stated that, of the six permits, only two belonged to the defendant, and were only to the amount of ten taels. But the Defendant stated that he bought the two tins of prepared opium from the Opium Farm. This case was remanded to allow the defendant to bring forward the parties he said he bought the opium from, and bail was accepted. In a final case of this type, the Defendant, "a compradore, belonging to Canton", "produced a permit for a portion of the opium, but some of it being proved to be eight or nine years old, no permit could have been procured for it as the Opium Farmer did not have the monopoly at that time, and as he had failed to inform the Opium Farmer of having it in his possession since, an offence was proved. The case was remanded till to-day to allow the defendant to procure a permit, as he said he had forgot about its being on his premises. The Opium Farmer, however, [c?/w?]ould not grant the permit at this late date, as the rules would be infringed by doing so. The defendant should have applied for a permit when the notice was issued." (CC569). The sentence in this last case was relatively low — $10 or two days' imprisonment and confiscation of the opium — and this maybe reflects that the Magistrate was taking into consideration that the Defendant lived outside Hong Kong (in Canton), as well perhaps as indicating his view that the Opium Farmer was being rather literal in his application of the rules.

The sentences

In most of the cases, it is stated that the unauthorised opium found was to "go to", "be handed over to", "be delivered to", "be given to", or "be forfeited to" the Opium Farmer. In those cases where the opium was "to be forfeited" (CC 327, 535), it seems likely that this is shorthand for, "forfeited to the Opium Farmer". Presumably the same may be true of the two cases where the opium was to be "confiscated". (CC 569, 646) In some reports, nothing is said about what was to happen to the opium. (E.g. CCs 264, 375, 434, 445.) Possibly this was an oversight on the reporter's part or maybe the editor cut these reports.

In several cases, the sentence was a fine or a period of imprisonment, but, unlike the cases involving offences against the gambling ordinance, where most give an alternative of imprisonment with hard labour, in a few only of these opium cases (e.g. CCs 324, 434, 492, 200, 646) does the sentence mention imprisonment, "with hard labour".

The following table shows the amounts of the fine in each case, together with the alternative penalty available. It seems that there was no standard equivalence between the amount of the fine and the length of the alternative period of imprisonment. In one case the alternative to a fine of $15 was five days (CC 19), in another, the alternative to a $5 fine was seven days (CC 33). The alternative to a $25 fine was in one case one month's imprisonment (CC 91), and in another, 21 days (CC 124). In one case, the alternative to a $100 fine was six months with hard labour (CC 434); in another, the alternative to $200 fine was two months with hard labour.

It seems unlikely that the alternatives were set, based on how the Magistrate was feeling on any particular day. (This is a claim that E. J. Eitel made about cases relating to paupers.) [561] Probably there were other considerations, practices of the court at

---

[561] "Treatment of Paupers in Hong Kong", 22 April 1880, in HKGG, 9 June 1880, pp. 466-473.

the time, not indicated in the Ordinances, in which the alternative sentences were carefully based on the particulars of each and every individual case, including the evidence and the Magistrate's view of the witnesses in court. Some of the witnesses, the Magistrate would have known better than others — the members of the Police Force, the excise officers, possibly even the informers — and he would have built up over time an impression of their reliability as witnesses.

As for the primary sentence, did it match the apparent offence? In one case, where only a tael of opium was found (in a house in Sai Wan village), the sentence was $100 or two months' imprisonment, which seems to a lay person exceptionally severe (CC 307). Perhaps there were other circumstances, not mentioned in the report, but hinted at by the presence of a brass boiler and opium strainer at the premises.

Sentences for Opium Offences

CC	Fine	Alternative jail time	CC	Fine	Alternative jail time
19	$15	5 days	33	$5	7 days
91	$25	1 month	111	$10	14 days
124	$25	21 days	178	$20	14 days
210	$20	21 days	264	$20	14 days
307	100	2 months	324	$50	6 weeks w. hard labour
327	$100	6 weeks	329	$25	10 days
371	$50	2 months	375	$50	2 months
386	Rdd		434	$100	6 months w hard labour
445	$10	7 days	492	$25	6 months w. hard labour
511	$200	2 months w. hard labour	535	$25	6 weeks
548	Rdd		569	$10	2 days
646	1st Def.	Rdd	646	2nd Def. $50	6 months w. hard labour

KEY:
CC: Court Case
Rdd: Remanded
Def: Defendent

Repeat offenders?

None of the defendants is said to have been sentenced for the offence before. It is true that this point is mentioned in a case, where the defendant, having unlawful possession of stolen goods, had gone with them to an opium divan. (CC 232.) But this is an opium-related case, not an opium case as such.

Informers, Excise Officers and Police

Some of the defendants in these cases are explicitly stated to have been informed against and subsequently arrested by a member of the Police Force, with a warrant in his possession. In one case, an Inspector of police, excise officer and informer all gave evidence (CC 91); in another, an Inspector, two excise officers and an informer had searched the premises together (CC 548); in another it was an Acting Sergeant, an informer and two Excise Officers (CC 535). In one case, an informer purchased opium from the defendant, informed the Opium Farmer and laid information (CC 124). In another case, we are told that the informer bought opium from the defendant, "laid an information" with the Opium Farmer, and the search warrant was then issued at the instance of the Opium Farmer (CC 492). In another case, the informer purchased opium from the defendant, and then, "laid an information" with the police (CC 307).

Informers

Why did the informers act as they did? — The answer seems simple. Rewards were evidently involved and presumably they did it for the money. It seems no coincidence that several of the informers were unemployed. More than one was an unemployed servant (e.g. CCs 375, 492). At least three were unemployed coolies (CCs 386, 511, 548).[562] However, unlike in some of the cases dealing

---

[562] "If any charge or complaint shall be preferred under 'the Excise Ordinance (Opium) 1858-1879' or under any of the said regulations made thereunder and upon the said charge or

with other offences, none of these opium case reports state explicitly that any of the fine was going to an informer. Did Frederick Stewart really not award any part of any fine to informers in these cases? (He was entitled to award up to one half of the fine to an informer under Ordinance No. 7 of 1879, para. X.) Similarly, although he is reported as awarding the opium, the subject of the cases in question, to the Opium Farmer, no report states that he awarded any of the fine to, "the holder of the exclusive privilege", that is, the Opium Farmer. Again, under Ordinance No. 7 of 1879, para. X, any part of the fine not awarded to an informer was to be paid over to the Opium Farmer. Had the law changed? Or the practice of the law? Was it simply too complicated for the Court Reporter or too lengthy for the Editor to include this information in the published reports?

Excise Officers
As for the Excise Officers, they were not government officials as such but "agents or servants" of the Opium Farmer, appointed or licensed by the Governor of Hong Kong. (Ordinance No. 1 of 1879, para. 11.) Consistent with this, there is no listing of Excise Officers in the "Index to Establishments" in the Hong Kong Government Blue Books, during the relevant period; which tends to confirm that they were not remunerated by the Hong Kong Government. The names and places of residence of every excise officer "were to be posted in a conspicuous place at the Police Court." (Ordinance No. 1 of 1879, para. 12.) They were to wear a badge, "bearing such sign or mark of office as may be

---

compliant the accused shall be convicted, the pecuniary penalty imposed upon the offender shall, after the adjudication of a portion of the same not exceeding one half at the discretion of the Magistrate to the informer, be paid to the holder of the exclusive privilege, and all the boiled or prepared opium to which the same relates shall be forfeited and by the magistrate adjudged and delivered to the holder of the privilege." (Ordinance No. 7 of 1879, para. X.)

directed by the Governor". Before acting against any person under the provisions of the Ordinance, every excise officer was to declare his office and show his badge to the person against whom he was about to act." (Ordinance No. 1 of 1879, para. 13.) Impersonation of an Excise Officer was punishable by, "a penalty not exceeding one hundred dollars." (Ordinance No. 1 of 1879, para. 11.)

Police

Police acting in such cases were also to show evidence of their position. "Every Police officer acting under the provision of this or the said recited Ordinance [i.e. Ordinance No. 2 of 1858], if not in the uniform proper to his service[,] shall in like manner [i.e. similar to what the Excise Officers were required to do] declare his office and produce to the person against whom he is about to act such part of his public equipment as the Captain Superintendent of Police shall have directed or may direct to be carried by Police officers when employed on secret or special service." (Ordinance No. 1 of 1879, para. 13.)

Warrants

A warrant is mentioned in eight of these opium cases. (CCs 371, 375, 386, 434, 445, 492, 511, 535.)

Search warrants could be issued by a Justice of the Peace as follows:

> Seizure under search warrant. "Any Justice of the Peace may issue a search warrant under section 9 of the said recited Ordinance [i.e. Ordinance No. 2 of 1858],[563] and such

---

[563] Section 9 of Ordinance No. 2 of 1858 reads as follows:
"Power to issue search warrants upon lawful evidence of facts."
"Upon lawful evidence being first given to the reasonable satisfaction of a Stipendiary Magistrate or the Superintendent of Police (duly constituted under Ordinance No. 12 of 1844), that any person within this Colony or the waters thereof hath in his possession or custody any opium contrary to section 8, or any

search warrant may be executed by any
police or excise officer and the person
executing any such search warrant may seize
and hold any utensils or vessels which have
been used or which are manifestly intended
to be used in boiling or preparing opium and
in any case where boiled or prepared opium
is found under the circumstances mentioned

---

opium prepared, sold, or retailed, contrary to this Ordinance, it
shall be lawful for the said Magistrate or Superintendent to issue
a search warrant in that behalf, and under such warrant any
member of the Police Force may enter any tenement, place, or
vessel, within this Colony or the waters thereof, and search for,
and (if found) seize and hold, subject to the order of the Court
hereinafter mentioned, any prepared opium within such tenement,
place, or vessel, and whereof no satisfactory explanation shall
have been given by the person aforesaid." (Section 9 of
Ordinance No. 2 of 1858.)

NB Section 8 of Ordinance No. 2 of 1858 was partly repealed by
and partly amended by Ordinance No. 7 of 1879. Section 8 of
Ordinance No. 2 of 1858, among other points, refers to Section 7
of Ordinance No. 2, which was itself amended by Ordinance No.
7 of 1879.

The amendments resulted in the following wording: "No person
shall bring into this Colony, or the waters thereof, or (except in
cases to which section 7 applies) have in his possession or
custody within the same, any boiled prepared opium without
having a valid certificate under section 7 of Ordinance No. 2 of
1858, as amended."

And the amendments to section 7 of Ordinance No. 2 of 1858,
effected by Ordinance No. 7 of 1879, resulted in the following
wording: "It shall be the duty of every person selling or retailing
prepared opium under this Ordinance [i.e. Ordinance No. 2 of
1858], to deliver therewith a sealed certificate, specifying the
amount so sold; which certificate shall be evidence of the facts
therein stated, and shall not be transferable and shall contain a
notice printed in English and Chinese, in the following form: —
'Notice is hereby given that the monopoly of the Hong Kong
opium farm, at present held by the undersigned, expires on
the ...., and that the boiled or prepared opium now
purchased and sold cannot be legally used or retained in your
possession after noon of the 3rd day form the above date, without
the consent of the new holder of the monopoly or of the Governor.
[There follow three blank lines for signatures.]'"

Complete Court Cases   524

in the said section of the said recited Ordinance [i.e. Ordinance No. 2 of 1858] or any such utensils or vessels as last aforesaid are found, may also seize any raw opium found in the possession of any person having such boiled or prepared opium, utensils, or vessels, or in any such tenement, place, or vessel as is mentioned in the said section." (Ordinance No. 1 of 1879, para. 10.)

It seems likely that, when there is no mention of a warrant but an Informer or Excise Officer or both are mentioned (e.g. CCs 91, 124, 327), the search was in fact conducted under the authority of a warrant.

In some circumstances, action could be taken by a Police Inspector without a warrant.

"It shall be lawful for an Inspector of Police having reasonable ground for believing that there is boiled or prepared opium in any ship within the waters of the Colony contrary to the provisions of the Opium Ordinances, (such ship not being a ship of war or vessel having the status of a ship of war) to proceed without warrant on board such ship and search for boiled or prepared opium and seize any boiled or prepared opium so found, and it shall be lawful for such Inspector to take the opium so found together with the person in whose custody possession or control it is found before a Police Magistrate, to be dealt with according to law." (Ordinance No. 7 of 1879, VIII.)

There is one case where Police Inspector Swanston was clearly acting under this authority. For, although he boarded a junk at sea and seized the opium that he found there, as well as arresting the Defendant, no mention is made of any search warrant (CC178). In fact, no direct evidence is reported in *The China Mail*, to the effect that he had "reasonable ground for believing" that there was "boiled or prepared opium" on the ship, "contrary to the provisions of the Opium Ordinances", unless the statement, "Had known defendant for two years as the master of the junk", is intended to convey this.

In this same case (CC 178), it seems that the opium equipment was seized under Ordinance No. 1 of 1879, para. 7, which reads as follows:

> "All boiled or prepared opium offered or exposed for sale or retail by any unauthorized person and all boiled or prepared opium found in the possession or custody or control of any unauthorized person or in any unauthorized place, except as in the last section mentioned,[564] and any utensils or vessels which have been used or which are manifestly intended to be used in boiling or preparing opium by any unauthorised person or in any unauthorized place, may be seized [present writer's emphasis] by a police or excise officer, and shall be forfeited and may be by a Magistrate delivered and adjudged to the holder of the exclusive privilege for the time being, and any unauthorized person in whose possession any such boiled or prepared opium or utensils or vessels are found may be apprehended and taken before a Magistrate by any police or excise officer." (Ordinance No. 1 of 1879, para. 7.)

In other circumstances, action could be taken by any Police or Excise Officer without a warrant.

> "It shall be lawful for any Police or Excise Officer to arrest, without warrant, any person within the Colony whom he reasonably suspects [present writer's emphasis] to be conveying or to have concealed on his person boiled or prepared opium which has not paid duty to the holder of the exclusive privilege,

---

[564] This relates to Paragraph 6, which was repealed by Ordinance No. 7 of 1879 and so does not apply to these 1880-1881 cases.

and to convey such person to the nearest Police Station, there to be dealt with according to law." (Ordinance No. 7 of 1879, IX.)

The above would seem to be the authority under which an excise officer arrested the defendant arriving from the Canton steamer (CC 324).

The attendance of an Excise Officer at the arrival of steamers from Canton or Macau (rather like Customs Officers at some ferry piers and airports today) was clearly appropriate, given the nature of their official duties. The following wording was particularly appropriate to their doing so: "No person shall bring into this Colony, or the waters thereof, or have in his possession or custody within the same, any boiled prepared opium without having a valid certificate under section 7 of Ordinance No. 2 of 1858, as amended." (Ordinance No. 7 of 1879, para. V.)

There are several cases where there is no mention of a warrant, of an informer or an excise officer. We cannot speculate by what authority the defendant in each of these cases came to appear in court. But the evidence suggests that the Opium Ordinances were well understood and conscientiously acted upon by those enforcing the law. It seems unlikely that there was any illegality in the arrests that had been made.

Pleading guilty, co-operating with the police, being caught in a lie

Some may have improved their situation by pleading guilty. The man who pleaded that he had shown the opium he had to the Inspector immediately on his producing the warrant (CC 445) may have improved his position by doing and stating this.

However, several defendants were caught in a lie, either in court, or (according to witnesses) in what they said during the search that had been made. Most spectacular perhaps is the case of the woman who, admitting that she had no permit, claimed that the opium had been that of her husband, who had died two months previously. However, the informer stated that he had bought opium from her husband only a few days previously (CC 375). Perhaps reflecting her lie, her sentence (HK$50 or two months' imprisonment) was relatively severe. In another case, which could have been one of absent-mindedness or forgetfulness when under pressure perhaps, the defendant, when visited in his house and asked to open a safe, sent a coolie to find a key. But the coolie returned saying he could not find it. After the Police Inspector said that the safe would have to be broken open and the defendant would have to go along to the Police Station, the defendant produced the key from an inner pocket! (CC 386.)

Denials, excuses and defences

Some defendants denied they had any opium. Some defendants offered excuses. Some may include what defendants understood to be mitigating circumstances. One, admitting that he had boiled the opium, stated that it was for his own use (CC 327). Two denied selling the opium that had been found and each said that what was found was for his own use (CCs 307, 323). One said that it really had been bought from the Opium Farmer, by his son, and produced tickets showing the purchase of opium (CC 178). One said some friends had brought it from Macau and given it him (CC 210); another that some man brought the opium and boiling utensils that had been found, from on board a ship; and that he himself had nothing to do with them (CC 434). Another denied having sold any opium to the informer, admitted having opium in his possession, but explained that some of this he had purchased from the Opium Farmer and the remainder he had received from friends (CC 535). This last defendant was fined $25 or six weeks imprisonment.

A traveler from Macao said that he came from Macao and knew nothing of the laws of Hong Kong. He smoked over a tael a day and what he had was for his own use (CC 329). He was still fined $25, in default ten days' imprisonment; the opium to be forfeited to the Farmer. He seems to have been treated no differently from other defendants, despite his non-resident status and his plea of ignorance about the laws of Hong Kong.

In one of the cases where the defendant's documentation was said to be inadequate (CC 548), the Defendant nevertheless stated that he bought the two tins of prepared opium from the Opium Farm. He also said he was a dealer in Malwa Opium, and had bought the raw opium from Hadjee Ali, Yuk-ün and U-ün. He denied selling any opium to the informer. The pans in Court he used for boiling his food and the scales were used for weighing raw opium. This case was remanded to allow the defendant to bring forward the parties he said he bought the opium from, and bail in two sureties of $100 each was accepted. It seems that the Magistrate entertained the suspicion at least that the informer might have been telling a lie and was willing to believe that the man was an opium dealer and might therefore indeed have purchased opium in a legal manner.

One defendant offered what seems to have been an informed defence, stating that the material found was for medicinal use (CC 386) (which was allowable under Ordinance No. 2 of 1858, para. 5, still current at the time). Another — the master of the junk (CC 178) — said that, "the pan was only used when they were at sea"; apparently showing knowledge that it was an offence to be found in possession of unauthorized opium at sea only in Hong Kong waters and apparently hoping therefore that this statement would somehow help him to be exempt, even though it was in fact in Hong Kong waters that he had been found with unauthorized opium and equipment for preparing it.

Who were these defendants?

All the names mentioned are Chinese names and it seems that, in these cases as a whole (as in the gambling cases), no-one other than a Chinese is arrested for opium or opium-related offences. One only was a woman (CC 375), described as a, "married woman". Her fine was relatively heavy, probably influenced by the strong indication that she told a lie, stating that the opium had belonged to her husband who had died two months previously, whereas the informer said that he had bought opium from her husband some days previously.

Generally, the age of defendants is not mentioned. We do know, however, that at least some were youngish men and some fairly elderly. Of the four described as "unemployed", one was twenty-two, one was thirty-two and one was sixty-eight years old. Another (no occupation given) was seventy-four. The occupations of the men were fairly varied. One was master of a licensed fishing junk. There was a cook, a sixty-year old pig dealer, a seaman, a carpenter, an opium dross dealer, an accountant, a driver, a fishmonger, a shop-coolie, a shopkeeper and a compradore belonging to Canton.

Time of day and place where the opium was found

The time of day is mentioned in several of these cases, usually the evening, but in a couple of cases, the afternoon. This detail appears to be a means of making the witness's statement more realistic, rather than for any other reason.

The place of the offence is not detailed with the same frequency as in the gambling cases, although the following are mentioned, mainly in the central area of Hong Kong Island or less often in Wanchai: Number 9, Canton Bazaar; Number 12, Chi Mi Lane; top floor of Number 8, Shin Hing Lane; Hing Lung Lane; Number 15, Stanley Street; Number 3, Tung-man Lane; Number 51, Wanchai Street; Number 80, Wellington Street; Number 40, Wellington Street. It is interesting, however, that one raid took place following information at Sai wan village (CC 307) and another at Stanley (CC 375). In some cases, the actual floor of a building or the room is mentioned: bedroom; top floor. From today's perspective, it is amusing to read that some opium was being kept in the servants' quarters at the back of the Hong Kong Club. In some cases, the opium was found in a dwelling: — defendant's house; defendant's bedroom; a junk. In one case, although the place searched was described as the defendant's house, there were ten or twelve men "laying about smoking opium" (CC 371).

One place is significant though. As mentioned above, it seems that the excise officer made it a practice to go to meet both the Canton steamer (CC 324) and the Macau steamer (CC 329). Sometimes however, opium was successfully brought in. In one case the defendant said that the opium that had been found had been brought from Macau by some friends and given to him (CC 210).

In another case, discussed in other contexts in this essay, including under the sub-heading, "An unusual case", immediately below, the arrest was made at sea, on board a junk in Shau-ki-wan Bay (CC 178). (As this was, "Within the waters of the Colony", this was allowed under Ordinance No. 7 of 1879, VIII.)

An unusual case
In the case where opium was found on board a junk in Shau-ki-wan Bay (CC 178), the charge was, "unlawful possession of a quantity of prepared opium without a valid certificate from the Farmer". But the Defendant said that the opium belonged to his son, who bought it from the Opium Farmer. He produced in court two tickets showing the purchase of 2 taels, 6 mace, 3 candareens[565] on August 11, and 1 tael, 2 mace on August 26th. There was another ticket for 2 taels in June.

---

[565] See the Glossary for measurements of weight.

It is not explained whether there was a difference between a "permit from the Opium Farmer", which the Excise Officer, Mr Santos, said that the Defendant did not have, and "tickets showing purchase", such as the Defendant produced in court.

The amount of opium was reported in different ways by the Police Inspector who made the seizure and Mr Santos, the Excise Officer. The Inspector said there were two sets of scales bearing traces of opium, two horn boxes nearly full of prepared opium, a pillow box containing three other horn boxes, nearly full of prepared opium, five earthenware jars containing more or less opium; a tin box with opium dross, and a piece of about four oz. of raw opium, several empty pots containing traces of prepared opium, a small box three parts full of prepared opium, a strainer containing opium refuse, and a large horn box containing about three taels of opium. The Excise Officer said there was about ten or twenty taels of prepared opium, and three taels of raw opium. The tickets produced by the Defendant related to a total of five taels, eight mace and three cadareens. As the Table of weights shows,[566] one cadareen = ten mace and one mace = ten taels. It is clear from this that the amount of opium found was much less than the amount which the tickets showing purchase accounted for.

The ticket for the largest amount was dated 11 August, that for the next largest quantity was dated 26 August, and the ticket for the smallest amount was dated 2 June. Was the court sceptical about this evidence? Did Frederick Stewart feel that the tickets belonged to another person than the Defendant? Did he feel that the amounts were greater than could be consumed by one person (the Defendant's son, whose opium the Defendant declared it to be)?

It seems that the most damning evidence was the finding of equipment for preparing opium, particularly the strainer containing opium refuse and

---

[566] See the Glossary.

the brass pan, which the Defendant clearly admitted using, as his evidence was that, "the pan was only used when they were at sea".

The Defendant was fined $20 or 14 days' imprisonment; and all the opium, raw and prepared, was to go to the Opium Farmer.

Medicinal Use (CC 386)

In one case, the Defendant made the defence that the opium found was for medicinal use only. "The opium in Court was simply washings, and it was deposited in the safe to prevent his coolies from smoking it. About four years ago he bought some raw opium from a wreck. When boiled it was good for skin diseases. He denied having ever sold any opium." (CC 386.)

The accountant to the opium farm, Chan Sing Tai, was present in court, apparently as an expert witness. Having first stated that he was well acquainted with opium and its preparation, he expressed the opinion that the prepared opium in Court was made from the samples of raw opium shown, although it would be of poor quality unless mixed with some of a better kind.

This was disputed by the Defendant, who said that the raw opium in court would not produce opium at all if boiled.

Disputing this view in turn, the accountant to the opium farm declared he could boil the raw material and realise the same quality of the drug as that in Court.

The decision made by the Magistrate was a practical one, first to determine which of the statements — the accountant's or the Defendant's — was correct. He instructed that the raw opium should be boiled under the supervision of the police. To allow time for this to be done, the case was then remanded until a set date, bail being accepted "in one householder in the sum of $50".

If the evidence was that the material was for medical use (because it could not be used for smoking), then the case would perhaps be dropped, because this was allowed by Ordinance No. 2 of 1858, para. 5, which was still current.[567]

Opium equipment
Equipment for making and using opium, as well as containers bearing evidence of having contained opium is mentioned in several cases.

Attempts to avoid discovery
There is no doubt that most of the defendants knew that possession of opium without a license from the Opium Farmer was illegal. Some took measures to avoid discovery of the opium. While an Inspector was speaking to the defendants in the servants' quarters at the Hong Kong Club, an excise officer observed the first defendant crawl under the bed, and caught him with two boxes of opium in his hands. (511) In another case, immediately the defendant became acquainted with the object of the Sergeant's visit, he put his hand behind him and upset a pot containing about four taels of opium. (CC 434) This seems to have been a common ploy. The Defendant in another case first denied having any opium, but the constable found a pot of prepared opium (produced) in a bed-room, that had been upset after witness entered the house. (CC 371) One man kept opium in an earthenware jar, similar to one in which he kept medicine (CC 492) and, although admitting that the opium found had been boiled from opium dross, and that he had done so himself, he asserted that it was

---

[567] "From henceforward, no person not holding any such privilege or licence, or save as he may be by such privilege or licence in that behalf authorized, shall, within this Colony or the waters thereof, boil or in any way prepare opium, or sell, retail, or offer or expose for sale or retail, any boiled or prepared opium; yet so that no medical practitioner, chemist, or druggist, not being a Chinaman, or (being such) not having an European or American diploma, shall be prevented from preparing or selling opium *bona fide* for medicinal purposes, the burthen of proof whereof shall be upon any person alleging the same in his defence." (Ordinance No. 2 of 1858, para. 5.)

only a medicine and could not be smoked. The dross had accumulated during the last twelve months." However, an informer testified that he had bought opium from the man recently.

Interestingly, none of the defendants showed the terrible fear of arrest that the gamblers in the gambling cases show.

Not surprisingly, at least some of those professionally concerned with the provision of opium could be associated with other offences and knew some pretty tough characters. A fifty-two year old licensed opium dealer, who kept an opium divan at 45, Praya at Yau-mah-ti, British Kowloon, was charged with receiving stolen goods there. (CC 170 & CC 200) The *China Mail* Editor was in no doubt what this said about him. "Thieves Friend", the caption to the report on the second hearing proclaims. A seventy-year old man, living at Number 63, Temple Street, Yau-mah-ti, a fellow clansman's house that he said he was looking after, deposed that three men came in there. One seized him by the throat, rubbed his face with pepper, tied a cravat round his throat and nearly strangled him. The other two men in the meantime ransacked the house, taking—with other goods—some of his property. After the theft, the thieves went to the Defendant's opium divan and the stolen goods were later found in his possession there. He refused to say who brought them. He also refused to give the police any information to enable them to get hold of the thieves, saying it would cause too much trouble. So firmly did he believe in the trouble that his giving information would case, that he was willing to incur a sentence of six weeks' imprisonment with hard labour to avoid it.

This was not the only case in these Reports where stolen goods were taken to an opium divan. One man was informed on for taking two bundles to an opium divan in Square Street in the middle of the night and was found on a bed there, using the stolen blanket for a pillow, with one of the bundles, containing two jackets, under the bed (CC 232). This defendant seems to have lived on the fringes of society, for he had been in gaol three times before and the arresting policeman said he often saw him prowling about the streets. On this occasion, he tried to avoid arrest by pointing out a blind boy as their owner of the goods. In spite of this, the sentence seems to have been relatively light for the time, thirty days with hard labour or a fifteen shillings fine.

The opium habit gave rise to other offences. It seems that people carried opium boxes about their person[568] — in a purse or pocket maybe — and that others might pickpocket them to obtain these.[569] And as we have just seen (in relation to CC 232), those in possession of stolen goods might think of an opium establishment as a good place to hide them.[570]

~~~~~~~~~~

---

[568] See CC 127.
[569] See again CC 127.
[570] E.g. CC 232.

Gamblers' encounters with the police and the magistrate's court,
forms of gambling, gambling venues and equipment:
information derived from the gambling and gambling-related cases heard before Frederick Stewart, July 1881 to March 1882.
With quotations from relevant ordinances.

All the cases in the Table, "Showing gambling and gambling related cases, numbers involved, results of the cases, sentences given", based on the database of Court Case Reports published here, concern gambling in one way or another. In one case only, is there an accompanying offence, "Causing an Obstruction" (CC 14); but in several cases, defendants are convicted as "Rogues and Vagabonds".

None of these defendants appeared in court on a gambling or gambling-related charge as a result of a complaint. All were there because they had been informed against and subsequently arrested by a member of the Police Force.

A decision of guilty or otherwise seems to have been assisted by circumstantial evidence. If an individual or a group tried to run away when a policeman approached, that tended to suggest guilt. If, as happened in one case, those in court called out, "theft", while a raid was taking place, this suggested innocence. The finding of gambling equipment (sometimes stated to be produced in court as evidence) tended to suggest that the offence had occurred, but the absence of fantan equipment and a statement that such gambling equipment as was found was for the amusement of the women of the house suggested innocence (CC 485). If defendants were arrested as a result of a raid, the place where they were arrested was important. Were they arrested in the gambling place or elsewhere? (See CC 668.)
As for the sentence handed out, it appears that, if one was an organizer of the illegal activity or a person

involved in the management of it in any way (for example, acting as watchman, receiving the money and/or giving it out), the punishment was greater. Prior convictions were clearly taken into account and resulted in heavier sentences. Being reported to be previously known (even if never arrested or punished) for the activity for which they were presently in court (e.g. CC 628) seems to have been a negative contributing factor.

Perhaps those few defendants described in such a way as to indicate that they are visiting from the Chinese Mainland (CC 609, CC 628) were given lighter sentences because of their non-resident and visitor status. The rice-pounder in CC 571 may have improved his situation by pleading guilty. But how would his comments — "If the lukong caught him with an iron bar in his hand he could not help it." — have been to his advantage or otherwise, or of no effect at all?

Some defendants offered excuses. Apart from more general excuses, such as, "looking at the house to see if it was suitable for a coolie house" (CC 674), "looking for friends" (CC 331), visiting the house (CC 331), other excuses given may include what defendants understood to be either mitigating circumstances or circumstances which, if believed, would render them not guilty of the charges: e.g. playing for amusement (CC 501), only looking on (CC501, 331). Some said that the gambling equipment found "had been used at the race-course" (CC 674). The "Canton" coolie might not have known what the useful excuses were, but said he was "watching some children playing" (CC 609).

In the case of those gamblers whose occupations are mentioned, most are coolies (including the only three women identified, and a visitor from Canton). Two are specifically identified, one as a "coal coolie" and the other as a "jinricksha coolie". Also identified are three hawkers, a couple of bakers, two cooks, two servants (including one servant in a druggist's shop) and two carpenters (including one from Sun On). There is one tailor, one rice-pounder, one shopkeeper. When groups are mentioned, if their ethnicity is mentioned at all, it is always Chinese and it seems that, in these cases as a whole, no-one other than a Chinese is arrested for gambling or gambling-related offences. Most are men. Of the very few women (CC 442, CC 368), one rented the place for gambling and was heavily fined (CC 442).

Generally, the age of defendants is not mentioned. We do know, however, that at least some were young men. One coolie was aged twenty-six and two other coolies were each twenty-eight.

The most popular place for gambling was Market Street or nearby. Close second were Gilman's Bazaar, Canton Bazaar and at Nullah Lane. Also resorted to were Caine Road, Centre Street, Circular Pathway, First Street, Gap Street, Lower Lascar Road, Park Wharf, Peel Street, Po Yan Street, Pound Lane, the Praya, the Recreation Ground, Second Street, Tai Hing Lane, Tung-man Lane or the Praya near the foot of Tung Man Lane and Wanchai Road. They might gamble near the Harbour Office or in front of the Man Mo Temple in Hollywood Road. People might congregate under a verandah or around a fruit stall on the Recreation Ground.

In several cases people were found gambling in an empty or unoccupied house (once at each of Gap Street, Gilman's Bazaar, Gilman Street, and Pound Lane), or in a house described as bare of furniture.
The gambling took place at any time of day. One case occurred at about 8.00 in the morning, another at about 9.00 am. Oher times of day were less specific. Five offences occurred in the morning, two in the forenoon, two about noon, eight in the afternoon and four in the evening.

Playing was with dice, cards or dominoes. Fantan is frequently mentioned and in one case it was being played with small stones and a square piece of tile.[571] Quite a lot of other equipment was needed: Counting sticks, a counting board, scales, cards and dice (CC 498), a blanket and trays (CC 492) are mentioned.

There is no doubt that gamblers and organizers were entirely aware that gambling was an illegal activity. Careful measures were made for preventing arrest. Trap-doors were put in place (e.g. CC 532); strong doors constructed (CC 399). Lookouts were posted and when the police approached, they called out, "Police coming" (CC 531, CC 532, CC 643) or made a signal with a bamboo hat (CC 150). Most striking was the fear of arrest that gamblers showed, demonstrating both their strong desire to take part and the desperate stakes that were involved. Seeking to evade arrest, people ran over the roof-tops or jumped from buildings, sometimes falling and putting themselves in hospital for several days.

The evidence of these Court Cases as to the practice of gambling is consistent with what has been previously described, but it adds detail, life and emotion.

Ordinance No. 9 of 1876

Ordinance No. 9 of 1876 states that the definition of "Gambling" "shall apply to and include lotteries, as well as those known as Wai-sing, Pak-kop-piu, Tsz-fa, as all others." (Ordinance No. 9 of 1876, para. 2.) None of these are mentioned in these Reports.

Under Ordinance No. 9 of 1876, fines were authorized as follows:

"Any person who shall keep any house, room, or place, boat, vessel, or any place on land or water, for public playing or gambling, or shall permit any person to play within such house, room, boat, vessel,

---

[571] The posed archival photograph in *A Magistrate's Court in 19th Century Hong Kong* (p. 337) shows Chinese people playing Fantan and well illustrates what indoor gambling would have looked like.

or any place on land or water as aforesaid, shall forfeit a sum not exceeding two hundred dollars on conviction thereof in a summary manner." (Ordinance No. 9 of 1876, para. 4.)

"Any person who shall use, haunt, or be found within such house, room boat, vessel, or any place on land or water as aforesaid, shall forfeit a sum not exceeding fifty dollars on conviction thereof in a summary manner." (Ordinance No. 9 of 1876, para. 5.)

"The person appearing, or acting as master, or as having the care and management of any such house, room, office, agency or place aforesaid, shall be taken to be the keeper thereof, and shall be liable as such to the penalty aforesaid." (Ordinance No. 9 of 1876, para. 6.)

<u>Entering or breaking into a location, arresting the people there and (on conviction) confiscating the equipment and gambling money was authorized by Ordinance No. 9 of 1876, para. 7.</u>

"It shall be lawful for any Justice of the Peace or constable of the Police, duly authorized by warrant of any Justice of the Peace, to enter, and if necessary to break into any house, room, boat, vessel, or any place, either on land or water, within which such Justice of the Peace shall be credibly informed on oath, or shall have reasonable grounds of his own knowledge to suspect and believe that public gaming or playing is or has been commonly carried on, and to arrest all persons within such house, room, or place as aforesaid and to seize all tables, dice, or other implements of gambling, or which shall be used as such, and also all monies or securities for money which shall be in actual use for the purpose of gambling, and which said implements of gambling, and money, or securities for money, on conviction of the offender, shall be, and they are hereby declared to be forfeited to Her Majesty's the Queen, Her Heirs and Successors." (Ordinance No. 9 of 1876, para. 7.)

"All penalties herein mentioned shall be recovered, and levied, on conviction of the offender, before any Magistrate of Police, or any two Justices of the Peace, in the manner provided by Ordinances No. 10 of 1844, and No. 7 of 1866." (Ordinance No. 9 of 1876, para. 10.)

Table 2: Showing gambling and gambling related cases, numbers involved, results of the cases, sentences given[572]

KEY
R&V / R(s)&V(s) = Rogue(s) and Vagabond(s)
Def. / Defs = Defendant / Defendants
periods of time indicate periods of imprisonment to which a defendant was sentenced
"OR default" / "OR": If a defendant could not or did not wish to pay the fine which he was sentenced to pay, the alternative punishment ("default" / "in default") was a period of imprisonment, sometimes stated to be, "with hard labour", sometimes with no such stated provision.
NS = Not specified
PC = Police Constable
PS = Police Sergeant
ref. = reference
w. = with

Notes on the presentation of the Table
The date is given, for clarification, only in a few cases.
Where a penalty, awarded by the court, concerns all those arrested or the activity as a whole (e.g. the confiscation of equipment or money found at the place of the offence), this is presented in a separate row.
Where there is more than one defendant and his or her circumstances or sentence varies from that of others, a different row is provided for each.

---

[572] See also the following: 1) "Gamblers' encounters with the police and the magistrate's court, forms of gambling, gambling venues and equipment: information derived from the gambling and gambling-related cases heard before Frederick Stewart, July 1881 to March 1882. With quotations from relevant ordinances." 2) "Editor's Introduction".

Table 2: Showing gambling and gambling-related cases, the numbers involved, the results of the cases, the sentences given.

Case No. (w. date in some cases)	Charge / Conviction	Location	Time of Day	Sentence	Prior Convictions?	No. of others not arrested also doing same thing.	No. and Profession/ Occupation of Defendants
128	Watchman to Gamblers, standing near Market Street, wearing a bamboo hat w. which he made a signal & called out a warning.	Near Market Street.	NS	Fourteen days in gaol with hard labour.		NS	
151	Watchman to Gamblers.	Footpath near Market Street.	NS	14 days w. hard labour.		A crowd of gamblers.	
353	Watchman to Gamblers.	Wanchai Road.	Fore-noon	Six months w. hard labour as R&V.		20-30, who made their escape because of the alarm Def. gave.	A coal coolie

381	Watchman to Gamblers. R&V.			Six weeks w. hard labour.	"nest of gamblers"	
399	Watchman to Gamblers. See 399 below.					
451	Watchman to Gamblers.	Pound Lane.	About 9 o'clock in the morning.	One month w. hard labour as R&V.	"batch of street gamblers"	Jinricksha coolie
532	Convicted of, "Aiding & Abetting public gambling". Watchman to Gamblers. Standing in front of a house in Gilman Street; rushed upstairs & called out, "Police coming".	Gilman Street.	Afternoon	$25 fine OR 2 months w. hard labour.	About 50 who escaped via the cookhouse & a ladder on the roof, fastening a trap-door behind them.	Hawker
532	Convicted of, "Aiding & Abetting public gambling".	Upstairs in a house in Gilman Street.	Afternoon	$25 fine OR 2 months w. hard labour.	About 50 who escaped via the	Cook

No.	Offence	Location	Time	Sentence		
	Watchman to Gamblers. Standing in front of a house in Gilman Street; rushed upstairs & called out, "Police coming".				cookhouse & a ladder on the roof, fastening a trap-door behind them.	
723	Watchman to Gamblers.	Market Street.	Morning	7 days in prison. Also tried to bribe the arresting PC.		
14	Street Gambling & Causing an Obstruction.	Po Yan Street.	Morning	Six weeks w. hard labour as R&V.		
15	Gambling.	NS	NS	14 days w. hard labour as R&V.		
25	Street Gambling playing at Fan Tan.	Marketing Street, Tai-ping-shan.	Afternoon	1st & 3rd Defendants, 6 weeks w. hard labour as Rs&Vs.		
25	Street Gambling, playing at Fan Tan.	Marketing Street, Tai-ping-shan.	Afternoon	2nd Def: 3 months w. hard labour as rogue & vagabond.	in Gaol before	
38	Street Gambling.	Gilman's Bazaar.	NS	6 weeks hard labour.	convicted last March	Coolie, aged 26

					of keeping a public gambling house		
38	Street Gambling.	Gilman's Bazaar.	NS	$2 fine or 7 days' w. hard labour.			Coolie, aged 28
39	Street Gambling.	NS	NS	$2 fine.			Coolie, aged 28
43	Street Gambling.	NS	NS	6 weeks w. hard labour as R&V.			
58	Public Gambling.	Number 22, Lower Lascar Road.	NS	1 Def. only. Fined $50 OR 3 months w. hard labour. Gambling implements found in the house to be forfeited.			
116	Street Gambling. Playing fantan w. small stones & square pieces of tile.	Near the Harbour Office.	NS	2 no. Defs. 14 days w. hard labour as R&V.		Forty or fifty others who escaped.	
117 (Same event as CC 116? - no	Street Gambling. Playing fantan.	Near the Harbour Office.	Evening	14 days (hard labour not mentioned) as R&V.			

connection made by The China Mail)							
125	Street Gambling. Playing fantan.	Market Street.	NS	Def. 1: 6 weeks w. hard labour as R&V.	In gaol twice before	5 or 6 others.	
125	As above.	As above.	NS	Def. 2: 2 weeks (w. hard labour perhaps implied) as R&V.		5 or 6 others.	
126	Street Gambling. Playing fantan.	Praya.	Evening	2 Defs. 14 days w. hard labour as R&V.		About 13-14 others	
146	Public Gambling.	Number 11, Centre Street.	About noon	18 (of 22) Defs. $20 or six weeks w. hard labour.			
146	As above.	As above.	As above.	General penalty. All gambling implements to be forfeited.			
146	As above.	As above.	As above.	1st Def. counted cash. $100 OR four months w. hard labour.			
146	As above.	As above.	As above.	2nd Def. received the money. $100 OR four months w. hard labour.			
146	As above.	As above.	As above.	3rd Def. paid the money. $100 OR four			

146, 157. 9 Sept 1881 / 16 Sept 1881	As above.	As above.	As above.	months w. hard labour. 8th Def. in hospital. Remanded. He was well enough to appear in Court seven days later, on 16 September. $10 OR three weeks w. hard labour.
147	Playing fantan.	NS	NS	14 days (no mention of hard labour) as R&V.
157 See No. 146 above. 9 Sept 1881 / [16 Sept 1881]	Public Gambling, 9 August.	Number 11, Centre Street.	About noon.	See 146 above.
176. 25 August 1881 / 20 Sept 1881	Haunting a gambling house.	Gilman's Bazaar.	NS	Def. jumped, found insensible w. dagger in his hand. Had been in Hospital, legs still swollen & walked w. difficulty.

				"Ordered to find 2 householders, each to be surety in $20 to be of good behaviour for two months; in default 14 days imprisonment."		
[176]. 25 August 1881	[Haunting a gambling house.]		NS	Def. jumped w. him. Still (20 Sept 1881) in hospital. Sentence unknown.		
[176] 25 August 1881	[As above.]		NS	17 others [fined]		
199	Street Gambling	NS	NS	14 days as R&V.		
208. 25 Sept 1881 / 26 Sept 1881	Street Gambling w. dice.	Market Street.	NS	1st and 2nd Defs one month w. hard labour as R&Vs.	About 8	
222	Street gambling.	Market Street.	About 8.00am.	14 days w. hard labour as R&V.	9 or 10	
231	Street gambling w. cards.	Park Wharf.	NS	2 Defs. 7 days w. hard labour as R&V.	2	
256	Street gambling w.	Peel Street.	NS	$1 OR 7 days in gaol.	w. some	Servant

	dice.				other men w. some other men	
257	Street gambling w. cards.	NS	Morning	14 days as R&V.		
331 (raid)	Keeping a public gambling house. Gambling at a table w. dominoes.	Number 17, Canton Bazaar.	NS	1st Def., directing & managing affairs, fined $200 OR in default six months w. hard labour.		
331 (raid)	As above.	As above.	NS	One Def., Fined $50 OR in default three months in gaol w. hard labour.	had been fined for a similar offence previously	
331 (raid)	As above.	As above.	NS	All other Defs (totally 10 other men and one woman): fined $25 OR in default three months in gaol with hard labour.		
369	Gambling at fan-tan.	Unoccupied house in Gap Street.	Afternoon	3 Defs fined $25 OR in default three months' in gaol w. hard labour.		12 or 13 Coolies
399	Keeping a pubic gambling house;	Canton Bazaar.	Morning	1st Def., $100 fine OR in default six months.		Tailor

	manager of the establishment.			(No mention of hard labour.)			
399	Keeping a pubic gambling house.	As above	As above	2nd Def., $25 OR 2 months. (No mention of hard labour.)			Carpenter
399	Watchman to Gamblers. See also 399 above under "Watchman to Gamblers".	Canton Bazaar	As above.	3rd Def., $50 or 4 months (No mention of hard labour.)	previous conviction for larceny		Cook
399	As above.	As above.	As above.				
405	Public Gambling.	In Number 1, B, Peel Street.	Afternoon	5 Defs.. 1st Def fined $200 or 6 months with hard labour.			
405	As above.	As above.	As above.	General penalty. Cash found was ordered forfeited.			
405	As above.	As above.	As above.	5 Defs. 2nd, 3rd, 4th and 5th fined $50 OR in default 4 months with hard labour.			
411	Street gambling.	Tung-man Lane.	Fore-noon	Six weeks w. hard labour.			Servant in a druggist's shop
415	Street gambling.	Under the	NS	1st Def. receiving &			

No.	Charge	Location	Time	Sentence		People	Notes
		verandah in front of Messrs Douglas Lapraik & Company's premises.		paying money. Six weeks w. hard labour.			
415	As above.	As above.	NS	2nd Def. counting cash. Six weeks w. hard labour.		"a number of men"	
417	Street gambling, managing the game.	Recreation Ground around fruit stall.	Afternoon	Two months w. hard labour as R&V.		"a number of men"	Hawker. Pretending to sell oranges at his fruit stall.
442	Public gambling, playing dominoes.	Number 39, Nullah Lane.	Evening	1st Def (woman) rented the house. $100 OR six months w. hard labour.			3 women and 8 men, "chiefly of the coolie class"
442	As above.	As above.	As above.	11th Def. $10 or 21 days.			As above.
442	As above.	As above.	As above.	2 women & 7 men, $25 fine OR three months each w. hard labour.			As above.
458	R&V, street gambling.	Nullah Lane.	Morning	1st Def. managing the game. 3 months w. hard labour as R&V.		"Crowd of street gamblers"	

458	As above.	As above.	As above.	2nd Def. holding cups and dice. 3 months w. hard labour as R&V		as above	
459	Gambling.	"At the same place", [i.e. Nullah Lane].		Six weeks w. hard labour.	4 priors recorded against him since 1874, two of larceny, one of gambling, one of being a R&V		Coolie
464	Street gambling	The Praya, near the foot of Tung Man Lane.		1st Def., managing game, 3 months.			
464	As above.	As above.		2nd Def., 3 months.	prior conviction for gambling		
464	As above.	As above.		3rd Def., six weeks w. hard labour.			
465	Street gambling. Conducting game	Market Street.	NS	3 months w. hard labour as R&V.		others escaped	Coolie

475	of fan-tan. Public gambling. On the table were arranged a mat w. dice, dominoes, counters, money basket, scales, cups &c, twenty cents in silver and a quantity of cash. The money was in a cup in front of the first prisoner.	At Number 37, Circular Pathway.	Afternoon	1st Def., managing the game. Fined $100 OR 6 months w. hard labour.		
475	As above.	As above.	As above.	2nd Def., taking charge of the counters., $50 or four months hard labour.		
475	As above.	As above.	As above.	7th Def., $50 or four months hard labour.	one prior not specified	
475	As above.	As above.	As above.	The remaining 8 Defs (nb 11 Defs in all), $15 each or 6 weeks w. hard labour.		
475	As above.	As above.	As above.	General penalty.		

484	Keeping a public gambling house.	NS	evening. NB believed to be unfounded. Case dismissed	Money found to be forfeited. 7 or 8 women had just finished a meal in the place where were found a blanket, dominoes, two trays, two dice, but no fan-tan implements. While the witness was examining the house, a cry of "thief" was raised. Charge believed unfounded. Case dismissed.		Shop-keeper
493	Public gambling.	Number 107, First Street.	NS			1 Baker & 15 Coolies.
493	As above.	As above.	NS	1st Def., "The master", $50 fine OR four months w. hard labour.		Baker
493	As above.		NS	One, "old offender", $25 fine OR two months w. hard labour.	twice in gaol for gambling	Coolie
493	As above.		NS	One, "old offender",	twice	Coolie

No.	Charge / Items	Address		Penalty	Conviction	Notes	People
				$25 fine OR two months w. hard labour.	convicted for gambling, once for larceny.		
493	As above.		NS	A third, "old offender", $25 fine OR $25 fine OR two months w. hard labour.	not specified		Coolie
493	As above.		NS	Remainder, $10 OR one month w. hard labour.			12 Coolies.
499	Gambling. Counting sticks, a counting board, scales, cards & dice found on the premises.	Number 63, Second Street.	NS	General. Money [i.e. the gambling money] to be confiscated.		Several escaped through the windows.	20 Chinese
499	As above.	As above.	NS	1st Def., $100 OR 6 months w. hard labour.			
499	As above.	As above.	NS	2nd Def., $40 fine OR 4 months in gaol (hard labour not mentioned). No reason given for being given a different			

					sentence from the majority. Judging from other cases, it may be because he had prior convictions.
499	As above.	As above.	NS		3rd Def., $40 fine OR 4 months in gaol (hard labour not mentioned). No reason given for being given a different sentence from the majority. Judging from other cases, it may be because he had prior convictions.
499	As above.	As above.	NS		4th Def., $40 fine OR 4 months in gaol (hard labour not mentioned). No reason given for being given a different sentence from the majority. Judging from other cases, it may be because he had prior convictions.

499	As above.	As above.	NS	7th Def., $40 fine OR 4 months in gaol (hard labour not mentioned). No reason given for being given a different sentence from the majority. Judging from other cases, it may be because he had prior convictions.	
499	As above.	As above.	NS	All other Defs, $15 fine each OR 6 weeks w. hard labour.	
501	Street Gambling.	"Before the Man Mo Temple, Hollywood Road".	NS	21 days w. hard labour.	
571	Watchman to gamblers. R&V. In possession of a deadly weapon. Def. was found watching outside a door on the first-floor at House Number 1, Tai	First-floor at House Number 1, Tai Hing Lane.	NS	Def. admitted gambling and said if the lukong caught him with an iron bar in his hand he could not help it. $50 fine OR 3 months hard labour. General. Money & gambling implements	A number of people apparently escaped by the roof. Rice-pounder.

No.	Details	Location	NS	Sentence	Remarks	Escaped	Description
	Hing Lane with an iron bar in his hand, apparently guarding the house. The police while arresting him hear a noise as if a number of people were making their escape by the roof. Some time ago a gambling assembly was broken up in the same house.			to be confiscated.			a Canton coolie
609	Street gambling.	Caine Road	NS	7 days w. hard labour.			
628	[Public gambling.] Sundah Singh happened to be passing when someone called out, "Police coming," and several people rushed out of the	In an unoccupied house in Pound Lane.	NS	$10 OR 14 days w. hard labour.	Known by the PC as a frequent gambler in Pound Lane & Gilman Bazaar.	Several others apparently escaped.	Carpenter from Sun On.

	doorway. Evidently he arrested one of these. Handing over the man he had arrested to another PC, he went upstairs and found a counting stick, cup, matches, scales, a money tester and a quantity of bad cash.						Hawker
644	Street gambling. Def. threw away gambling articles when he was arrested but these were picked up by the constable and produced in Court as evidence against him.	Recreation Ground.	NS	10 days w. hard labour.	Twelve days previously (i.e. 9 February 1882?), was sentenced to 7 days also for gambling	"a great many": does not state whether they all escaped or not.	
668	Public gambling.	In Number 17,	NS	One was discharged			

"The Inspector, accompanied by Inspector Matheson while passing down Market Street and while approaching Number 17, heard a sudden rush. He saw several people rushing downstairs. He remembered he had a warrant, although not in his possession, to enter this house. When he got in, he observed a number of persons going through the smoke hole on to the roof. He arrested four of them in the house and the other one	Market Street.		(presumably the one who was, "arrested . . . while coming down a ladder which was in the cook house of Number 11.")		

Ref	Description	Location	Time	Outcome	Notes
668	while coming down a ladder which was in the cook house of Number 11. All the usual articles used by gamblers were found in the house." As above.	As above.	NS	4 Defs fined $15 OR 6 weeks w. hard labour.	
674	Gambling. Gambling gear found.	In an unoccupied house in Gilman's Bazaar.	NS	2 Defs each fined $15 OR 6 weeks w. hard labour.	"Others." NS if they escaped or not. Coolies
Gambling Informers, 485	Good, graphic story told.	Praya West. NOT CONVICTED	Evening	All four informers were convicted. (Charge not clearly stated, but mention is made that things were missing from the premises and one admitted a previous conviction for larceny "in May of last year".)	

All sentenced to 6 months w. hard labour.

Table 3 : The "Light and Pass" Rules in Frederick Stewart's Court, 1881-1882[1]

Date	Case Number	Number and Profession or Occupation of Defendants	Number of Prior Convictions	Accompanying Offence/Infelicity of Manner/ Personal Circumstance(s)	Time of Day or Night	No Light and / or No Pass	Sentence	Order of severity of punishment
08/08/1881	CC47	1	2 (gaol)	Sleeping on mat	NS	Both	3 weeks in prison w. hard labour	10
14/08/1881 and 17/09/1881	CC155 and CC165[2]	4	Def. 1: 3 (gaol) Def. 2: 3 (gaol) Def. 3: 1	All pretended to be asleep	3:10am	Both	$10 or 3 months in prison w. hard labour each	11

---

[1] For a Key to abbreviations used in this Table, see "Table, Showing gambling and gambling related offences . . .", above.

[2] Originally, all four defendants were additionally sentenced to three months in prison with hard labour as Rogues and Vagabonds and the two sentences were to be cumulative. The sentence was amended to $10 and three months in prison with hard labour for having no pass, only; by reference to Section 11 of Ordinance No. 5 of 1850.

Date	Case							
20/09/1881	CC179	1 (Coolie)	(gaol) Def. 4: 9 (gaol) 1 (6 months for breaking into a dwelling house)	In possession of housebreaking instrument	a NS	Both	3 months in prison w. hard labour	13
22/09/1881	CC184	2	Def. 1: Nil stated Def. 2: Nil stated	Def. 1: Pushed Policeman Neither gave a satisfactory answer.	after midnight	Both	Def. 1: $1 or 4 days in prison Def. 2: discharged	4 0
10/10/1881	CC267	3	Nil stated		10:15 p.m.	Both	$2 or 6 days in prison w. hard labour each	5
12/10/1881	CC275	2 (Def. 2: chair coolie to	Def. 1: 1 Def. 2: Nil		night	Both	$2 or 7 days in prison	6

20/10/1881	CC301	1 (Mr Johnson)	6	Requested place to sleep	[after midnight]	Both	$50 or 3 months in prison + hard labour	12
31/10/1881	CC339 CC335	1 (Tinsmith)		Assault, possession of deadly weapons (fighting irons)	Evening	Both	12 months in prison w. hard labour	15
11/11/1881	CC368	1 (Servant)		Trying to bribe constable. Said he was going to a brothel.	early morning 2:30 a.m.	Both	$0.50 or 2 days in prison *and* $0.40 cents bribe to poor box	3
17/11/1881	CC393	9 (Cooks, chair coolies, etc.)	Nil stated	Def. 2: - I (8 of the 9) Def. 1: (1 of the 9): was somewhat saucy when apprehended	a late hour/ "last night"	Both	Def. 1: $0.25 or 1 day in prison Def. 2: $0.5 or 2 days in prison	1 2
07/12/1881	CC446	2 No profession or	Def. 1: Nil Def. 2: 5 (4 for larceny)	Def. 1: Fighting and creating a disturbance in the street and armed with a deadly	NS	Def. 1: No	$5 or 14 days in prison w. hard labour each and 6 hours in stocks at night scene of disturbance	8

		occupation given				pass	each.	
				weapon. B Fighting and creating a disturbance in the street.				
31/12/1881	CC517	2 Chair coolies		Def. 1: assault Def. 2: armed with a deadly weapon on 30 January 1882	Night	Def. 1: Both. Def. 2: No pass	Def. 1: $2 or 7 days in prison w. hard labour Def. 2: $5 or 21 days in prison Iron bar confiscated.	7 9
03/02/1882	CC599	1	8 (various crimes)	Cutting and wounding possessing a dagger			?	?
15/02/1882	CC630	1 (Barber)	2 (six months for breaking into a house;	Burglarious instruments	3:00 a.m.	Both	Both 6 months in prison w. hard labour. / The first and last fortnights to be in solitary confinement.	14

		three months for being in possession of a chisel.)

Among the above cases, there are sixteen different sentences (for one additional case, the sentence is not known). The degree of severity is indicated by the numbers 0 to 15.

The Light and Pass Rules, as evident from and applied in Frederick Stewart's court, are discussed in *A Magistrate's Court in Nineteenth Century Hong Kong* (pp. 99-116).

It is slightly ambiguous as to whether there were one, two, three or four offences, i.e. "Without a Pass", "Without a Light", "Without a Pass and also without a Light", "Without a Pass or a Light". A report for 1881 lists five cases of a Chinese with no light at night, and 805 cases of Chinese with no pass at night. (HKGG, 26 February 1881, p. 132.) The Hong Kong Government Police Reports for 1882 (HKGG, 3 March 1883, pp. 176-184, p. 177) itemise among the list of cases, "no pass or light". A similar phrase is used in HKGG, 19 February 1881 and HKGG, 11 March 1882, p. 261. Those reported as without pass or light during the years 1878-1881 inclusive are 335, 762, 840, 566 respectively. (See HKGG, 19 February 1881 and HKGG, 11 March 1882, p. 261.)

Earlier notices are equally ambiguous. See, e.g. HKGN No. 52 of 1865 (HKGG, 1 April 1865, p. 175), which reads:

"The following Notice to the Chinese Inhabitants of Victoria, inserted in the Chineese Gazette, is published for general information.

"Every Chinese going out after dark must carry a light.

"From 8pm till morning Gunfire, any Chinese found without a Pass and light will be taken into custody.

"Any Servant who may be sent out during the above period must be furnished with a Pass and light by his Employer."

A summary of cases deserving notice decided at the Magistracy of Hong Kong, from 12 to 18 July 1879 inclusive, includes one "Breach of 'The Night Passes Ordinance'". Three men were convicted "of being at large in the public streets without lights or passes". (HKGG, 23 July 1879, p. 444.)

Table 4: Sentences to the Stocks (or Cangue) in Frederick Stewart's Court, 1881-1882[3]

Date	Case Number	Number and Profession/Occupation of Defendants	Number of Prior Convictions	Accompanying Offence/Infelicity of Manner/Personal Circumstance(s) OR mitigating circumstance(s)	Charge/Con-viction	No. of hours in the stocks and place where sentence to be carried out	Any Accompanying Sentence?	Description of complainant	Order of severity of punishment
28/07/1881	CC16	1	Nil reported		Larceny from the person	6 hours place not given	6 weeks [sic] prison with hard labour	Chinese girl	5
28/07/1881	CC17	1	Nil reported		Attempted pick-pocketing	6 hours place not given	6 months prison with hard labour.	Chinaman	6
17/08/1881	CC85	1	4 (gaol sentences)		theft	2 [sic] hours place not given	6 months prison with hard labour.	Ship's cook	6
8/09/1881	CC138	2	Nil		Def. 1 and	6 [sic] hours	Def. 1 and Def.	Mr Watts	3

---

[3] For a Key to abbreviations used in this Table, see "Table 2, Showing gambling and gambling related offences . . .", above.

		One is explicitly referred to as an earthworker	reported		Def. 2: Cutting earth, undermining a wall	place not given	2: each: £1 = [$1?] fine or 14 days in prison with hard labour.	of the Survey Department	
10/09/1881	CC145	1	Nil reported	assaulted PC	disorderly conduct	4 hours at the Commissariat (the place near where offence occurred) for disorderly conduct	For assaulting the PC: $1 or 4 [sic] days prison with hard labour. Nothing for the disorderly conduct.	Police Constable	2
8/10/1881	CC265	2 [By implication, Coolies]	Nil reported	Def. 1: and Def. 2: "unfortunates" (but this may refer to the sentence?)	Def. 1: and Def. 2: assault	Def. 1: and Def. 2 each: 6 hours at public hydrant, where assault occurred.	Def. 1: and Def. 2: each: $1	Chinaman	1
13/10/1881	CC281	1	Nil reported		Undermining a wall	6 hours at place where	$5 or 14 days prison with hard	H. Gustave,	4

Date	CC No.		Prior convictions	Offence		Sentence	Description	No.
					offence occurred	labour.	scholar at St Joseph's College	7
18/10/1881	CC298	1 Fisherman	3 (gaol sentences for larceny)	Stealing a chopper and two brass ladles	6 hours at place where offence occurred	6 months hard labour, first and second fortnights in solitary confinement.	Street coolie	
4/11/1881	CC342	1 Sea-man	5 (In 1876, alone, two sentences of three months gaol for breaking into a dwel-ling house. The second of these carried the additional sentence of	Found in a dwelling house for an alleged unlawful purpose		**Committed to Criminal Sessions**	Woman	

7/12/1881	CC446	2	Def. 1: Nil reported Def. 2: 5 (4 for larceny)	two applications of the rod and unspecified time in the stocks.)	Def. 1: Fighting and creating a disturbance B: Fighting and creating a disturbance; armed with a deadly weapon; no night pass	6 hours at place where offence occurred	Def. 1 and Def. 2: $5 or 14 days in prison with hard labour	Lukong	4
17/12/1881	CC483	6 Sea-men	Nil reported	[In court, one was threatened by the	Four charges of piracy		**Committed to the Supreme Court** on 31	1. widow 2. cattle dealer	

[... Magistrate with being removed to the stocks aside for shouting out during the court proceedings.]

December 1881.

Date	Case			Offence	Punishment (stocks)	Punishment	Occupation	
							3. junk master 4. junk master	
20/03/1882	CC702	1	3	Stealing an umbrella	6 hours at place where offence occurred	6 months hard labour, first and second fortnights in solitary confinement.	Chinese	7
21/03/1882	CC708	1	4	Snatching a pair of trousers and two silver dollars	6 hours at Praya (the place of the offence)	6 months hard labour, first and second fortnights in solitary confinement.	hawker	7

Among the thirteen cases in Table 4, in one case, the defendant had previously been sentenced to the stocks; and in one other case (CC 483), a defendant was threatened with being removed from the court room to the stocks outside, for disorderly behaviour (calling out) in court. Both these cases were committed to the criminal sessions. In the remaining eleven cases, there are a total of fourteen defendants, and the number of sentences, therefore is fourteen. The degree of severity of these cases is indicated by the numbers one to fourteen, one being the lightest sentence.

For some discussion of the information presented in this Table, see, *A Magistrate's Court in Nineteenth Century Hong Kong*, pp. 68-71.

Table 5: Court Cases heard by Frederick Stewart and Reported more than once in *The China Mail*.

20, 93, 235, 238	341, 342
60, 65	347, 356
66, 67	390, 410
86, 87, 94.	422, 444, 473, 482, 491
92, 113	428, 449, 450
155, 165	429, 433
169, 205	447, 455
191, 236	452, 483, 508, 520
224, 242, 250	454, 456
233, 237	525, 529
234, 247	557, 593
251, 255a	575, 587, 600, 619
255, 292, 293	655, 660
291, 296, 300, 388	686, 688
335, 339	

Total number of cases concerned: twenty-nine; total number of reports: seventy-three.

Appendix I

The Excise Ordinance (Opium) 1858-1879, Amendment Ordinance 1879: Selections to explain the opium and opium-related cases before Frederick Stewart, July 1881 to March 1882.

A discussion of opium is often regarded as central to a discussion of the early relations between China and the West. An early discussion appears in J. R. Eames, *The English in China* (1909). He states that, after the signing of the treaties of Nanking, "the opium traffic took a new lease of life", although the law against the importation of opium into China remained unaltered.[573]

> "At every Treaty Port a flourishing trade in opium arose, connived at by the officials and openly prosecuted by the Foreigners. The new colony of Hong-kong became the centre of illicit trade, the smugglers finding no difficulty in transporting across the frontier goods that could lawfully and openly be taken into the port. So great became the scandal, that in 1858[574] Lord Elgin came to

---

[573] J. R. Eames, *The English in China*, London, Curzon Press, 1909, new impression, 1974, p. 564. Referred to after this as, "J. R. Eames, *The English in China*".

[574] Eitel — inaccurately, it seems — gives 1853 as the date when the "present state of legitimate commerce" began, attributing it as arising "through the decision of the Chinese Government to legalise the importation of opium." (*Europe in China*, p. 274.) But this may quite possibly be a typographical error. A later historian, G. B. Endacott implies that legalization occurred during the Governorship of Sir Hercules Robinson (for which he gives the dates, September 1859 to March 1865) (G. B. Endacott, *A History of Hong Kong*, Oxford University Press, 1964, p. 327). The Index to Geoffrey Robley Sayer, *Hong Kong 1841-1862: Birth, Adolescence and Coming of Age*, Hong Kong University Press, 1980, reprint of the original 1937 edition, published by Oxford University Press under the title *Hong Kong: Birth, Adolescence and Coming of Age*, lists, "Opium: legalized by tariff convention of 1858" (p. 229). The text referred to reads as follows: "In 1858, consequent, one presumes, on the legalization of the import of opium into China, an opium monopoly was

Complete Court Cases   581

the conclusion that legalization was the only remedy. In this view the Chinese acquiesced, and opium was admitted subject to a duty of 30 taels per chest, on the same footing as general imports under the Treaty of Nanking. After importation it was to pass into Chinese hands and become subject to such duties as the Government should think proper. Since that date opium has been more and more grown in China, with the result that the importation from abroad is but a fraction of the whole."[575]

Eames specifically refers to the later Chefoo Convention of 1876,[576] which had provisions relating to opium, [577] which were modified by a supplementary agreement made on 18 July 1885 in London,[578] ratified 6 May 1886. But he states that soon after, 11 September 1886, "the Opium Convention was signed, by which the importation of opium into Hong-kong was further regulated."[579]

The cases of breaches of the Opium Ordinance, reported in *The Complete Court Cases*, took place after the legalization of the opium trade in 1858 and the much later Chefoo Convention of 1876 on the one hand and the supplementary agreement of 18 July 1885, ratified 6 May 1886 on the other hand.

There are several nineteenth-century local Hong Kong Ordinances relating to opium, including Ordinance No. 11 of 1844, No. 5 of 1845, No. 4 of 1853, No. 2 of 1858, No. 7 of 1858, No. 1 of 1879, No. 7 of 1879, No. 4 of 1883, No. 8 of 1883, No. 1 of 1884, No. 17 of 1886 and No. 22 of 1887.[580]

---

reintroduced in Hong Kong for the first time since its abandonment in 1848." (G. R. Sayer, p. 185.)

[575] J. R. Eames, *The English in China*, 1909, pp. 564-566.

[576] J. R. Eames, *The English in China*, 1909, p. 542.

[577] J. R. Eames, *The English in China*, 1909, p. 543.

[578] J. R. Eames, *The English in China*, 1909, p. 543.

[579] J. R. Eames, *The English in China*, 1909, p. 543.

[580] Of Ordinance No. 22 of 1887, Traver and Gaylord write that it was passed in response to treaty requirements and they take the

The Ordinance applicable to these 1881-1882 court cases before Frederick Stewart is clearly Ordinance No. 7 of 1879, "The Excise Ordinance (Opium) 1858-1879, Amendment Ordinance 1879".

A reading of the relevant Opium Ordinances, together with the opium cases among the Court Cases of Frederick Stewart, July 1881 to March 1882, helps to illuminate each.

The purpose of the Opium Ordinances during the period in question was clearly to protect the monopoly of the Opium Farmer, [581] and thus to protect also the revenue which the Hong Kong Government obtained by means of selling the monopoly.[582] — In 1879, the monopoly was sold for three years for the annual sum of $205,000.[583] In

---

view that its role was entirely symbolic. Its net effect was, they write, "an incease in the flow of opium to China and a rise in the value of the opium monopoly." In their view, the next major piece of legislation on this topic was the Ordinance passed in 1909. (Traver, Harold H. "Colonial Relations and Opium Control Policy in Hong Kong, 1841-1945", in Traver, Harold H and Mark S. Gaylord, *Drugs, Law and the State*, University of Washington Press, 1991, pp. 135-148, p. 142.)

[581] See Ordinance No. 1 of 1879, paras 2, 3, 4, 5, 6; and Ordinance No. 7 of 1879, sections III, IV, V, VI, VII.

[582] E. J. Eitel has useful information about the sums gained by the Hong Kong Government through the sale of the opium monopoly and he also refers to a Commission appointed by Governor Sir Arthur Kennedy on 8 June 1872, "to enquire into the working of the opium monopoly, because there was very good reason to suppose that the amount received from this farm was far short of what it ought to have realized." (*Europe in China*, p. 485.) Eitel states that from 1858 until 1878, the monopoly had been "held by a Chinese syndicate in Hongkong at an unfairly low rate". (*Europe in China*, p. 536.)

[583] See HKGN No. 12, dated 21 January 1879, HKGG, 22 January 1879, p. 28. With effect from 28 February 1879, The Opium Farm was leased for 3 years to Mr Banhap by his Attorney, Mr Tan-King-Sing, for the sum of $205,000 p.a. (Presumably this means that Mr Tan-King-Sing acted for Mr Banhap in this transaction.) E. J. Eitel describes Mr Tan-King-Sing as "a partner of the SingaporeSyndicate" and states that the public was not satisfied with the manner in which the monopoly was sold. (*Europe in China*, p. 536.)

1882, the monopoly was sold for one year for HK$210,000.[584]

If any case, infringing the Ordinance, was proved, some recompense was to be given to the Opium Farmer. "If any charge or complaint shall be preferred under 'the Excise Ordinance (Opium) 1858-1879' or under any of the said regulations made thereunder and upon the said charge or complaint the accused shall be convicted, the pecuniary penalty imposed upon the offender shall, after the adjudication of a portion of the same not exceeding one half at the discretion of the Magistrate to the informer, be paid to the holder of the exclusive privilege, and all the boiled or prepared opium to which the same relates shall be forfeited and by the magistrate adjudged and delivered to the holder of the privilege." (Ordinance No. 7 of 1879, para. X.)

Several paragraphs in the Ordinances are aimed at protecting the interests of an incoming Opium Farmer, ruling as to what should and should not be done by the outgoing monopoly holder towards the end of the period during which he held the license. For example, he was not to produce more opium than usual at that particular time of year or to sell off stock at prices less than the current going price.

Thus, Ordinance No. 7 of 1879, paragraph 7, reads:

> "Neither the holder of the exclusive privilege nor his licensees shall, during the three months preceding the end of his term, manufacture more than the usual quantity of boiled or prepared opium, or during the said three months sell any boiled or prepared opium at less than the average current prices of the day, or in greater quantities than usual at the time of the year, and at the end of his term shall not sell, export, or otherwise make away with, or dispose of any of his stock of

---

[584] HKGN No. 55, "Sale of the Opium Farm", HKGG, 11 February 1882, p. 126.

boiled or prepared opium, but shall make over to the new holder of the said exclusive privilege the full and complete stock of raw or boiled and prepared opium then in his possession at the marketable value thereof and in the event of any difference arising as to quantities of boiled and prepared opium manufactured or sold during the last three months of the term and the price of the same and of the nature and quantity of the raw or boiled or prepared opium so to be purchased or made over and the prices thereof such difference shall be determined by three arbitrators, one to be appointed by the new holder of the exclusive privilege, one by the person whose exclusive privilege has expired or is about to expire, and one by the Governor, and the award of such arbitrators or a majority of them shall be final, and the arbitration or such other settlement shall be held at such time after the end of the term of the outgoing holder of the exclusive privilege as to the Governor may seem reasonable, and any award made may be filed in Court pursuant to the provisions of 'the Hong Kong Code of Civil Procedure.'" (Ordinance No. 7 of 1879, paragraph 7.)

This concern extended to those to whom the outgoing Opium Farmer had issued a certificate and to their own stock of opium. Their certificate would cease to be valid after noon of the third day from the date of the expiration of "his privilege" (Ordinance No. 7 of 1879, section 4.)

Shortly after Frederick Stewart had heard his last case as Police Magistrate, when he was Acting Colonial Secretary, he issued a Government Notification of "Supplementary Conditions, made by the Governor in Council, to which licenses granted under the Excise Ordinances (Opium), 1858-1879, are to be subject".[585] Clearly there was concern that the Opium Farmer was being cheated by those to whom he granted licences. From now onwards, among other regulations, licensees were to pay the Opium Farmer a monthly fee in advance and report to him daily "the quantity of Opium sold per day".[586]

Preamble to Ordinance No. 1 of 1879

The Preamble to Ordinance No. 1 of 1879 refers to Ordinance No. 2 of 1858 which re- established an Opium monopoly.[587] (Presumably it is no coincidence that this was the year when the opium trade was legalized.)

> "Whereas by Ordinance No. 2 of 1858 it is enacted (amongst other things) that the Governor in Council may grant unto any persons for such considerations and upon such conditions and for such terms and periods and in such form as from time to time shall be by the Governor in Council regulated and determined and also previously notified to the pubic in the *Hong Kong Government Gazette* the sole privilege of boiling and preparing opium and of selling and retailing within this Colony or the waters thereof opium so boiled and prepared".

---

[585] HKGN No. 221, HKGG, 13 May 1882, p. 475.

[586] "Supplementary Conditions, made by the Governor in Council, to which licenses granted under the Excise Ordinances (Opium), 1858-1879, are to be subject", HKGG, 13 May 1882, pp. 475-476.

[587] E. J. Eitel describes the establishment in 1844 of a short-lived earlier Opium Monopoly, replaced in 1845 by a system of opium retail licences (*Europe in China*, pp. 235-236, 265) and refers to the re-establishment of the opium monopoly by Governor Sir John Bowring on 1 April 1858 (*Europe in China*, p. 336).

The first holders of the renewed monopoly seem to be those named in HKGN No. 26, 23 March 1858, *Gazette Extraordinary*, 23 March 1858, pp. 1-5, p. 5, where we read: "Privilege for Sale of Prepared Opium" granted to Chun-Tai-Kwong of the Man-Cheong shop for Twelve Months from 1 April 1858.

The Preamble also states that Ordinance No. 2 of 1858 enacts, "that the person, if any, actually holding any such privilege is thereby empowered to grant licenses to all proper persons authorizing them to boil and prepare opium and to sell and retail opium so boiled and prepared".

Among those provisions of **Ordinance No. 2 of 1858** which were still current up to and beyond 1881-1882, some are particularly relevant to the "The Complete Court Cases of Magistrate Frederick Stewart as Reported in *The China Mail*, July 1881 to March 1882". For instance: —

> "From henceforward, no person not holding any such privilege or licence, or save as he may be by such privilege or licence in that behalf authorized, shall, within this Colony or the waters thereof, boil or in any way prepare opium, or sell, retail, or offer or expose for sale or retail, any boiled or prepared opium; yet so that no medical practitioner, chemist, or druggist, not being a Chinaman, or (being such) not having an European or American diploma, shall be prevented from preparing or selling opium *bona fide* for medicinal purposes, the burthen of proof whereof shall be upon any person alleging the same in his defence." (Ordinance No. 2 of 1858, para. 5)

Some of the paragraphs of Ordinance No. 1 of 1879 are as follows

Defining the terms, "Excise Officer" and "Possession": --

> "The term 'Excise Officer' shall mean the person appointed by the Governor under section 11 of this Ordinance, and for the purposes of this Ordinance, any boiled or prepared opium, or utensils or vessels used for preparing the same shall be deemed to be

in possession of any person if he knowingly have them in actual possession, custody, or control by himself or by any other person." (Ordinance No. 1 of 1879, para. 1.)

Prepared opium, &c., found in possession of unauthorized persons, or in unauthorized places may be seized.

"All boiled or prepared opium offered or exposed for sale or retail by any unauthorized person and all boiled or prepared opium found in the possession or custody or control of any unauthorized person or in any unauthorized place, except as in the last section mentioned, [588] and any utensils or vessels which have been used or which are manifestly intended to be used in boiling or preparing opium by any unauthorised person or in any unauthorized place, may be seized by a police or excise officer, and shall be forfeited and may be by a Magistrate delivered and adjudged to the holder of the exclusive privilege for the time being, and any unauthorized person in whose possession any such boiled or prepared opium or utensils or vessels are found may be apprehended and taken before a Magistrate by any police or excise officer." (Ordinance No. 1 of 1879, para. 7.)

Raw opium found in possession of unauthorised persons or in unauthorised places may be seized.

"Wherever boiled or prepared opium is so seized as last aforesaid and any such utensils or vessels are also seized as aforesaid, the police or excise officer seizing the same may also seize any raw opium that may be found in the custody or control of such

---

[588] This relates to Paragraph 6, which was repealed by Ordinance No. 7 of 1879 and so does not apply to these 1881-1882 cases.

unauthorized person or in such unauthorized place and such raw opium shall be subject to the order of the Magistrate before whom the case is brought." (Ordinance No. 1 of 1879, para. 8.)

Officer may seize raw opium under special circumstances.

"Whenever from any other cause there is reasonable ground to believe that boiled or prepared opium is manufactured by any unauthorized person or in any unauthorized place within this Colony it shall be lawful for a police or excise officer to seize any raw opium found in the possession of such unauthorized person or in such unauthorised place." (Ordinance No. 1 of 1879, para. 9.)

Seizure under search warrant.

"Any Justice of the Peace may issue a search warrant under section 9 of the said recited Ordinance [i.e. Ordinance No. 2 of 1858],[589]

---

[589] Section 9 of Ordinance No. 2 of 1858 reads as follows: "Power to issue search warrants upon lawful evidence of facts." "Upon lawful evidence being first given to the reasonable satisfaction of a Stipendiary Magistrate or the Superintendent of Police (duly constituted under Ordinance No. 12 of 1844), that any person within this Colony or the waters thereof hath in his possession or custody any opium contrary to section 8, or any opium prepared, sold, or retailed, contrary to this Ordinance, it shall be lawful for the said Magistrate or Superintendent to issue a search warrant in that behalf, and under such warrant any member of the Police Force may enter any tenement, place, or vessel, within this Colony or the waters thereof, and search for, and (if found) seize and hold, subject to the order of the Court hereinafter mentioned, any prepared opium within such tenement, place, or vessel, and whereof no satisfactory explanation shall have been given by the person aforesaid."

NB Section 8 of Ordinance No. 2 of 1858 was partly repealed by and partly amended by Ordinance No. 7 of 1879. Section 8 of Ordinance No. 2 of 1858, among other points, refers to Section 7 of Ordinance No. 2, which was itself amended by Ordinance No. 7 of 1879.

and such search warrant may be executed by any police or excise officer and the person executing any such search warrant may seize and hold any utensils or vessels which have been used or which are manifestly intended to be used in boiling or preparing opium and in any case where boiled or prepared opium is found under the circumstances mentioned in the said section of the said recited Ordinance [i.e. Ordinance No. 2 of 1858] or any such utensils or vessels as last aforesaid are found, may also seize any raw opium found in the possession of any person having such boiled or prepared opium, utensils, or vessels, or in any such tenement, place, or vessel as is mentioned in the said section." (Ordinance No. 1 of 1879, para. 10.)

The amendments resulted in the following wording: "No person shall bring into this Colony, or the waters thereof, or (except in cases to which section 7 applies) have in his possession or custody within the same, any boiled prepared opium without having a valid certificate under section 7 of Ordinance No. 2 of 1858, as amended."

And the amendments to section 7 of Ordinance No. 2 of 1858, effected by Ordinance No. 7 of 1879, resulted in the following wording: "It shall be the duty of every person selling or retailing prepared opium under this Ordinance [i.e. Ordinance No. 2 of 1858], to deliver therewith a sealed certificate, specifying the amount so sold; which certificate shall be evidence of the facts therein stated, and shall not be transferable and shall contain a notice printed in English and Chinese, in the following form: -- 'Notice is hereby given that the monopoly of the Hong Kong opium farm, at present held by the undersigned, expires on the ...., and that the boiled or prepared opium now purchased and sold cannot be legally used or retained in your possession after noon of the 3rd day from the above date, without the consent of the new holder of the monopoly or of the Governor. [There follow three blank lines for signatures.]'"

Excise officer. Warrant of appointment.

"The Governor may, for the purposes of this Ordinance, grant his warrant in form of schedule (B)[590] to such agents or servants of the holder of the exclusive privilege for the time being as may be approved of by him to act as excise officers: and no persons except those so appointed shall be competent to act as excise officers under this and the said recited Ordinance [i.e. Ordinance No. 2 of 1858]. Such warrants may at any time be withdrawn by the Governor and any person without lawful authority assuming to act as an excise officer under this Ordinance shall be liable to a penalty not exceeding one hundred dollars." (Ordinance No. 1 of 1879, para. 11.)

Excise officers' names to be posted at Police Court [sic].

"The names and places of residence of every excise officer so appointed as aforesaid shall be posted in a conspicuous place at the Police Court." (Ordinance No. 1 of 1879, para. 12.)

Excise officers to be supplied with badges.

"Every excise officer appointed under this Ordinance shall be supplied with a badge bearing such sign or mark of office as may be directed by the Governor and before acting against any person under the provisions of this Ordinance every such excise officer shall declare his office and produce to the person against whom he is about to act his said badge.

---

[590] A template for appointing such an excise officer is given in Schedule B.

Police officer to produce part of his public equipment when acting as excise officer.

Every Police officer acting under the provision of this or the said recited Ordinance [i.e. Ordinance No. 2 of 1858], if not in the uniform proper to his service[,] shall in like manner declare his office and produce to the person against whom he is about to act such part of his public equipment as the Captain Superintendent of Police shall have directed or may direct to be carried by Police officers when employed on secret or special service. (Ordinance No. 1 of 1879, para. 13)

Penalties to be recovered summarily.

"All penalties under the said recited Ordinance [i.e. Ordinance No. 2 of 1858] or under this Ordinance may be recovered in a summary way before any Magistrate. (Ordinance No. 1 of 1879, para. 14.)

Proceedings in case of prepared opium, &c., found without being apparently in possession of any one.

"In case any boiled or prepared opium or utensils or vessels used for preparing the same are found without being apparently in the possession of any one, it shall be lawful for the Magistrate to cause a notice to be affixed at the place where any such article may be found calling upon the owner thereof to claim the same, and in case no person shall come forward to make a claim within one week from the date of such notice, the same together with any raw opium that may be found in the same place shall be forfeited and may be handed over by the Magistrate to the holder of the exclusive privilege for the time being." (Ordinance No. 1 of 1879, para. 15.)

Forfeiture of raw opium found where opium is
unlawfully boiled or prepared.

"Where any boiled or prepared opium, or
utensils or vessels used for preparing the
same are found in the possession of any
unauthorized person, or in any unauthorized
place, and it appears to a Magistrate that such
boiled or prepared opium was boiled or
prepared by such person, or in such place, or
if any utensil or vessel used for boiling or
preparing opium be found in the possession
of such person or in such place, it shall be
lawful for such Magistrate to declare any raw
opium found in the possession of such person
or in such place to be forfeited and to direct
that the same shall be delivered to the person
holding the exclusive privilege at the time
when the same was so found as aforesaid."
(Ordinance No. 1 of 1879, para. 16.)

Ordinance No. 7 of 1879
Under Ordinance No. 7 of 1879, action without a
warrant was permitted as follows on certain ships:

"It shall be lawful for an Inspector of Police
having reasonable ground for believing that
there is boiled or prepared opium in any ship
within the waters of the Colony contrary to
the provisions of the Opium Ordinances,
(such ship not being a ship of war or vessel
having the status of a ship of war) to proceed
without warrant on board such ship and
search for boiled or prepared opium and seize
any boiled or prepared opium so found, and it
shall be lawful for such Inspector to take the
opium so found together with the person in
whose custody possession or control it is
found before a Police Magistrate, to be dealt
with according to law." (Ordinance No. 7 of
1879, VIII.)

Under Ordinance No. 7 of 1879, action without a
warrant was also permitted as follows:

> "It shall be lawful for any Police or Excise
> Officer to arrest, without warrant, any person
> within the Colony whom he reasonably
> suspects to be conveying or to have
> concealed on his person boiled or prepared
> opium which has not paid duty to the holder
> of the exclusive privilege, and to convey
> such person to the nearest Police Station,
> there to be dealt with according to law."
> (Ordinance No. 7 of 1879, IX.)

Under Ordinance No. 7 of 1879, fines were
authorized as follows:

> "If any charge or complaint shall be preferred
> under 'the Excise Ordinance (Opium) 1858-
> 1879' or under any of the said regulations
> made thereunder and upon the said charge or
> complaint the accused shall be convicted, the
> pecuniary penalty imposed upon the offender
> shall, after the adjudication of a portion of
> the same not exceeding one half at the
> discretion of the Magistrate to the informer,
> be paid to the holder of the exclusive
> privilege, and all the boiled or prepared
> opium to which the same relates shall be
> forfeited and by the magistrate adjudged and
> delivered to the holder of the privilege."
> (Ordinance No. 7 of 1879, para. X.)

~~~~~~~~~~~

Appendix II
Comparing the work of Frederick Stewart and his equivalent Scottish contemporaries

by Dr Ian Grant[591]
Head of Court and Legal Records
The National Archives of Scotland,
HM General Register House,
Edinburgh, Scotland.
1999

There was no direct, or even directly comparable, Scottish equivalent to Hong Kong's stipendiary magistracy until, under a special Act of Parliament, George Neilson, a noted legal scholar, was appointed in 1910 to a unique post as a stipendiary magistrate in Glasgow.

Jurisdiction, at the lowest level, in Scotland had been, effectively, feudal. As one of the perks of being a significant landowner, holding "in free barony" (*"in liberam baroniam"*), or, with greatly increased power, in free regality (*"in liberam regalitatem"*), landowners could act, in all save the most serious crimes, for centuries as judges within their lands. Much more frequently they appointed baron-baillies, who exercised jurisdiction on their behalf. In both, however, of the Jacobite Rebellions of 1715-16 and 1745-46, some landowners used their feudal power over tenants and other landholders to encourage them to join with the rebellious. After the later Rebellion, accordingly, an Act for abolition of heritable jurisdictions stripped landowners of all save very

---

[591] All notes are by the present writer, the editor of *The Complete Cases of Frederick Stewart.*
Dr Ian Grant is "an expert legal historian" (Dr Margaret McBryde, Publications and Education Branch, letter to the present writer, dated 22 April 1999). Dr Grant says this of himself, "Having embarked at Edinburgh University on a joint degree in Scottish History and Law Dr. Grant made the financially unrewarding choice of specialising in the former rather than latter. He is currently Head of the Court and Legal Records Branch at the National Archives of Scotland."

minor functions and powers. Some heritable courts, despite their being virtually powerless and continued only as "museum-pieces" survived until modern times. Within recent years there has been an appointment of a "Baron-Baillie of the Lordship of Strathnaver". It is unlikely, however, that the post-holder actually exercised criminal jurisdiction, as opposed to proudly proclaiming on letter-headings the holding of that post.

In rural Scotland, from the reign of King James VI and I[592] downwards there were Justices of the Peace, who dealt with minor crimes, besides dealing such other matters as authenticating legal deeds and licensing, from 1753, premises for sale of alcohol. James VI had, of course, imported into Scotland contemporary English practice. In the ancient royal and baronial burghs, and later in the police burghs, which were created as new centres of population came to exist, there was commonly a "Provost", who acted as chairman of the councillors and magistrate and a senior and junior "Bailie", acted as unpaid magistrates, holding meetings of the burgh court. Guidance on the emergence of the earlier Scottish burghs may be found in George S. Pryde's *The Burghs of Scotland: A Critical List*, ed. A. A. M. Duncan, 1965, while the later burghs are dealt with by R. M. Urquhart in a series of typescript publications dealing with 19th century civic legislation.

A nearer equivalent than these unpaid magistrates to the Hong-Kong stipendiary magistrates might be found in the Scottish sheriffs. Many functions, both in Scotland and England, had originally been exercised by the "earls" or "ealdormen" or "comitates". At a very early period, certainly not later than the reign of King David 1 (1128-1153) there appeared "vice-earls", sheriffs or "vice-comitates", roughly parallel to English county

---

[592] This monarch was James VI of Scotland and James I of England. (Ed.)

court judges, and treating both civil and criminal actions. Some of these sheriffdoms became, in due course, hereditary appointments, much detailed information on these being contained in the late Professor William Croft Dickinson's introduction to a Scottish History Society's publication of an early sheriff court book from Fife. From 1747, however, as above-noted, in the aftermath of one of the several Jacobite Rebellions, sheriffships became Crown appointments, occupied by lawyers who normally spent most of the year pleading, at Edinburgh, civil or criminal actions, but regularly visiting the shires which were their particular charges. In most instances, initially, a sheriff had responsibility for only one county or shire, and were known simply as the "sheriff" for the county. Legislation from 1853 and 1870 meant, however, that, by the late 19th century, many of the smaller Scottish shires or counties were grouped together with the responsible judge described as a "Sheriff-Principal", to whom one or more "Sheriff-Substitutes" might be answerable. Civil and criminal actions might be initiated before the sheriff. In more important cases they might be begun or appealed to a single judge in the Outer House of the Court of Session in Edinburgh or panel of Judges in the Inner House. There had, though numbers varied slightly downwards, or latterly upwards, traditionally been fifteen judges of the Court of Session, also styled as "Senators of the College of Justice". From their number the Lord Justice-Clerk and five others were, traditionally, with enhanced salary and allowances, chosen to act also as judges in major criminal causes, described as "Commissioners of Justiciary", who, either conducted trials at Edinburgh or, from 1747, on circuit in the Southern, Western, and Northern Circuits. Normally they worked in pairs, with two judges appointed to each circuit, although each had the authority to work singly or in tandem. Within recent years the growth in criminality has resulted in all of the (now twenty-six) supreme court judges being designated as Commissioners of Justiciary. The Lord Advocate has, and uses, authority to hold hearings of Justiciary courts in many venues which were not part of the traditional "circuits". Only a small proportion of criminal cases, however, reached even the Sheriffs or Sheriff-Principals, far less troubling the Commissioners of Justiciary. Most of the work was in the courts was carried out by the "Sheriff-Substitutes". These had, initially, been appointees of the Sheriffs or Sheriff-Principals, paid from their salaries, and, during the 18th century, were accordingly, mostly both ill-remunerated and ill-qualified. Following a number of Royal Commissions enquiring into the operation of the Scottish Courts, however, and particularly from 1838 downwards, payment and appointment of the Sheriff-Substitutes became a Crown responsibility. By the late 19th century almost all were advocates (the Scottish equivalent of barristers) with at least five years practice, although a minority were appointed from the ranks of solicitors (usually "Writers to the Signet", or "Solicitors to the Supreme Court"), elites practising in Edinburgh rather than before the local courts.

Before the Sheriff Courts there were, as noted, both civil and criminal actions. Some actions were designated as "privative" to the sheriff courts, excluding jurisdiction of the higher courts, as involving only comparatively small sums of money. Some actions had to be heard in the Court of Session because defenders were resident outwith Scotland and did not admit jurisdiction of the Sheriff Court. With some actions there was a choice of court, and in which it was pursued might depend on how actively the agent was milking the action for fees. On the civil side the sheriff, or sheriff-substitute, exercised administrative, as well as normally understood, judicial. Supervision of local and national elections, correction of errors in registration of births, deaths, and marriages, alteration of administrative boundaries, designation of, and closure of cemeteries, were among their many possible responsibilities. Criminal actions, which gradually came to be distinguished as treated under "summary procedure" and "solemn procedure" were heard before them. Under "summary procedure" they heard cases without a jury, with normal limit of 3 months imprisonment. Under solemn procedure, following a finding of guilt by a jury, the sheriff could, in the late 19th century, imprison up to two years. If charges were of a gravity where this seemed inadequate, there was a power to remit to the High Court of Justiciary for sentence.

Some of the more serious criminal charges, such as murder, had to be dealt with by the High Court of Justiciary, either at Edinburgh or on circuit, rather than by the Sheriff Courts. The sheriff courts had, however, a substantial jurisdiction. As late as the 1780s sheriffs had condemned criminals to death for house-breaking and seen the sentences carried into effect. Practice as to hearing particular actions before the High Court of Justiciary or sheriff courts, and as to remitting for graver sentences in the more serious crimes, has varied, often inexplicably.

During the later 19th century there was some, but sporadic, reporting of the civil and criminal actions in sheriff courts, as opposed to reporting of processes in the House of Lords/Outer or Inner House of the Court of Session/High Court of Justiciary, or, very rarely, in magistrates' courts. A system of appointment by the Faculty of Advocates (equivalent to English barristers) of law "reporters" should, from the late 17th century, have ensured all actions in the Superior Courts in which deliberations of the judges might provide guidance to inferior courts were highlighted. Clearly, however, many of those appointed as "reporters" lacked competence. Doubts must always, remain, therefore, as to as to how far relevant precedents were effectively picked up or ignored. Some of the series of law reports restricted themselves deliberately to the House of Lords and Court of Session/High Court of Justiciary.

Others included reports of what were deemed important Sheriff and magistrate court cases. With these, however, only a minuscule proportion of cases were considered worthy of noting and publication, much smaller than the proportion of supreme courts actions reported in print.

The role of a stipendiary magistrate in Hong Kong in the late 19th century seems, accordingly, more akin to that of a Scottish sheriff-substitute or sheriff-principal rather than that of any unpaid and voluntary Scottish magistrate. From the sheriff court, appeal, both in criminal and civil matters, would, in many cases, in the late 19th century, lie to the Court of Session/High Court of Justiciary in Edinburgh. If, in civil litigation, a litigant was unhappy with the decision of the Court of Session, both before a single "Outer House" judge on initial hearing, or before a panel of judges in the "Inner House" there was a final appeal to the House of Lords at Westminster.

The Scottish sheriff-substitute, as opposed to magistrate, exercised a wide-ranging jurisdiction, subject, in some instances, to appeal to the Sheriff-Principal or to the Court of Session and House of Lords or the High Court of Justiciary. By the late 19th century it is probable that between eighty and ninety per cent of appointees were members of the Faculty of Advocates with at least five years practice. Most of the remainder were Writers to the Signet or Solicitors to the Supreme Court, with extensive experience before the Edinburgh courts, although there was a small minority who had been appointed after acting over lengthened periods as procurators in local sheriff courts.

~~~~~~~~~~~

Referencing Conventions and Key to Abbreviations

Referencing Conventions

The method of referencing used is based on the MLA (Modern Language Association of America) Style Sheet.

Key to Abbreviations used in editorial comment and notes in this publication.

a.k.a: also known as
CC / CCs: Court Case Report / Court Case Reports
CM: *The China Mail*
CMG: Order of Saint Michael and Saint George
"Court Cases 1881-1882": Bickley, Gillian, compiler & editor, "Before Frederick Stewart, Esq: The Court Cases of Frederick Stewart, Police Magistrate, Hong Kong, July 1881-March 1882", unpublished typescript, 1998-1999.
GN: Hong Kong Government Notification
HK: Hong Kong
HKGG: *The Hong Kong Government Gazette*
HKPRO: Hong Kong Public Records Office
HKGBB: Hong Kong Government Blue Book(s)
HKRS: Hong Kong Records Series, HKPRO
HMS: Her Majesty's Ship
LH: Left hand
No. / Nos: Number / Numbers
OED: *Oxford English Dictionary*
Personal Archive: Gillian and Verner Bickley personal archive
Revd: Reverend
Rt Revd: Right Reverend
SCMP: *South China Morning Post*
St: Saint
The Complete Court Cases: *The Complete Court Cases of Magistrate Frederick Stewart, as Reported in The China Mail, July 1881 to March 1882*, Proverse Hong Kong, December 2008.
TS: Typescript

Glossary

After hatch: after hatchway: "the hatchway nearest the stern" (*<http://www.marineterms.com>*)

amissing: missing (colloquial)

candareen: A measurement of weight. See "Measurements of weight" below.

Cash: The cash was a currency denomination used in China between 621 and 1948. It was the chief denomination until the introduction of the yuan in the late 19th century. (*Wikepedia*)

Chek: A measurement of length. Seems to mean the same as, "Covid", *q.v.* (See note to CC 206. See also *A Magistrate's Court in Nineteenth Century Hong Kong*, p. 362 for, "Schedules of Standard Weights and Measures . . . republished in October 1881".) Both "chek" and "covid" = 14 1/16 English inches.

Covid: "a lineal measure formerly used in India: its length varied, at different times, from 36 to 14 inches" (OED).

fan-dagger: A 1996 auction listing describes a 19th Japanese fan dagger as having a 7 1/2 inch blade with false edge. The lacquer-decorated scabbard was in the style of a folded fan. A 2007 auction lists another Japanese fan dagger, with a 16.5cm blade, the *saya* (scabbard) and *tsuka* (hilt) of wood and carved in the form of a closed fan.
fantan: reputed to be an ancient game, based on guessing the number of porcelain buttons placed under a cup.

Forecastle: a short raised deck at the fore end of a vessel. In early vessels, raised like a castle to command the enemy's decks. (*OED*)

I-cheung shop [CC 206] It seems that, "I-Cheung" or "I-ts'z" is a place to house death tablets and coffins awaiting shipment. This was a service provided in Hong Kong particularly by the Tung Wah Hospital. Historically, Chinese people living overseas wished their remains to be returned in China. When they died outside China, including in Hong Kong, their remains were stored, waiting for arrangements to be made for their final resting-place in their family home in China.

instant: Latin for "now", e.g. as in, "this month".

kept woman: mistress.

Lan: guild, guild's premises, warehouse.

Lascar [from the Urdu and Persian word, "laškar" (meaning "army")]: (as defined by Ordinance No. 4 of 1864) includes and comprehends all seamen, natives of India, Malays, natives of Manila, or of any other part of Asia, except Chinese. (Although Ordinance No. 4 of 1864 was repealed by Ord. No. 6 of 1852, the latter does not change this definition.

Lukong/lukwong: green jackets = during the period of these reports, this term refers to Chinese police constables. However, the word came into use in the 1840s when the European police force wore green coats and this is the meaning of the nickname. (Crisswell and Watson, *The Royal Hong Kong Police*, *op. cit.*, p. 14.)

mace: A measurement of weight. See "Measurements of weight" below.

machine: jinricksha ("machine" is consistently used with this meaning in these Court Cases)

proximo: Latin for "next", e.g. as in, "next month".

Purlin: a horizontal beam along the length of a roof, resting on principals and supporting the common rafters or boards. (*Oxford Encyclopedic English Dictionary*, 1991.)

Samshu (CC 533): 1) "'Chinese spirits' shall mean the intoxicating liquor commonly known as samshoo." (HKGG, 11 June 1879, p. 306.) 2) "The generic name for Chinese spirits distilled from rice or sorghum." (OED) 3) "A diabolical mixture of alcohol, tobacco juice, sugar and arsenic." (Arthur Hacker)

Shroff: cashier.

tael: A measurement of weight. See, "Measurements of weight" below.

'Tween decks = "between decks": "the space between any two decks of a ship" OR "the name of the deck or decks between the ceiling and main deck." (*<http://www.marineterms.com>*)

ultimo: Latin for "previous", e.g. as in, "the previous month".

~~~~~~~~~~~

Measurements of weight[593]

16 taels = 1 catty = 1 1/3 lbs = [1] kin
120 catties = 1 stone = [1] shik
10 taels = [1] mace = 57.984 grains = [1] seen
[1] leang = [1] tael = 579.84 grains troy
10 mace = [1] candareen = [1] fun
100 catties = [1] picul = 133.5 lbs = [1] tam

~~~~~~~~~~~

---

[593] See, "Schedules of Standard Weights and Measures . . . republished in October 1881", in *A Magistrate's Court in 19th Century Hong Kong*, p. 362. Also HKGG, 8 October 1881, pp. 915-919, pp, 918-919.

Spelling Conventions

The romanisation of Chinese personal and geographical names in the Court Case transcriptions remains as it appears in the original newspaper reports. Elsewhere in the text, the Wade-Giles system of romanization is normally followed.

~~~~~~~~~~~~

References

"Abstract of Cases brought under Cognizance at the Police Magistrates' Court during a period of Ten Years, from 1st January 1875, to 31st December, 1882, inclusive", HKGG, 7 April 1883, p. 315.

Bickley, Gillian, compiler & editor, "Before Frederick Stewart, Esq: The Court Cases of Frederick Stewart, Police Magistrate, Hong Kong, July 1881-March 1882", unpublished typescript, 1998-1999. (Referred to as, "Court Cases 1881-1882".)

Bickley, Gillian, Ed. *The Development of Education In Hong Kong, 1841-1897: As Revealed By The Early Education Reports of The Hong Kong Government, 1848-1896*, Hong Kong, 2002.

— *The Golden Needle: The Biography of Frederick Stewart (1836-1889),* David C. Lam Institute for East-West Studies, Hong Kong Baptist University, 1997.

— *The Golden Needle: The Biography of Frederick Stewart (1836-1889).* Full audio version on 14 CDs. Read by Verner Bickley. ISRC HK-D94-00-00001-40.

— "The 'Light and Pass' Rules: Unenlightened Law?", in, Gillian Bickley, Ed., *A Magistrate's Court in Nineteenth Century Hong Kong"*, Hong Kong, Proverse Hong Kong, 2005, *q.v.*, pp. 99-116.

— *A Magistrate's Court in Nineteenth Century Hong Kong: Court in Time: Court Cases of The Honourable Frederick Stewart, MA, LLD, Founder of Hong Kong Government Education, Head of the Permanent Hongkong Civil Service & Nineteenth Century Hongkong Police Magistrate*, edited by Gillian Bickley, indexed by Verner Bickley, with chapters contributed by Gillian Bickley, Verner

Bickley, Christopher Coghlan, Tim Hamlett, Geoffrey Roper and Garry Tallentire, and with a Preface by former Hong Kong Chief Justice Sir T. L. Yang. Hong Kong, Proverse Hong Kong, 2005, 1st edition. ISBN-10: 9628557041, ISBN-13: 9789628557042.

—*A Magistrate's Court in Nineteenth Century Hong Kong: Court in Time: Court Cases of The Honourable Frederick Stewart, MA, LLD, Founder of Hong Kong Government Education, Head of the Permanent Hongkong Civil Service & Nineteenth Century Hongkong Police Magistrate*, Ed. Gillian Bickley, indexed by Verner Bickley, with chapters contributed by Gillian Bickley, Verner Bickley, Christopher Coghlan, Tim Hamlett, Geoffrey Roper and Garry Tallentire, and with a Preface by former Hong Kong Chief Justice Sir T. L. Yang. Hong Kong, Proverse Hong Kong, 2006, revised 1st edition. E-book, Mobipocket. ISBN-10: 962-85570-7-6; ISBN-13: 978-962-85570-7-3.

—*A Magistrate's Court in Nineteenth Century Hong Kong: Court in Time: the Court Cases Reported in* "The China Mail" *of The Honourable Frederick Stewart, MA, LLD, Founder of Hong Kong Government Education, Head of the Permanent Hong Kong Civil Service & Nineteenth Century Hong Kong Police Magistrate. Modern Commentary & Background Essays with Selected Themed Transcripts and Modern Photographs of Heritage Buildings of the Magistracy, Prison and Court of Final Appeal.* Ed. Gillian Bickley, indexed by Verner Bickley, with chapters contributed by Gillian Bickley, Verner Bickley, Christopher Coghlan, Tim Hamlett, Geoffrey Roper and Garry Tallentire, and with a Preface by former Hong Kong Chief Justice Sir T. L. Yang. Hong Kong, Proverse Hong Kong, 2nd edition (w. new photographs), 2009. E-book, Mobipocket. ISBN-13: 978-988-17724-4-2.

— "Magistrate Frederick Stewart", in, Gillian Bickley, Ed, *A Magistrate's Court in Nineteenth Century Hong Kong"*, Hong Kong, Proverse Hong Kong, 2005, *q.v.*, pp. 33-73.

— "Some Nineteenth Century Hong Kong Court Cases", scheduled 2009/2010. (Will contain full documentation of "The Kicking Case", "Triads", "Chinese Students Returned from America", "False Report: The British Ship, "The Bolton Abbey"", "Weights and Measures", "The Stabbing Case", "The Storm", "The Tai Tam Murder", "'Rickshaws: The New Machine", "Spencer's Cases", "Larceny of Cinnamon and Silk".)

— *The Stewarts of Bourtreebush*. Aberdeen, UK, Centre for Scottish Studies, University of Aberdeen, 2003.

— unpublished file [WhoPupls].

Bickley, Verner, "Differing Perceptions of Social Reality in Dr Stewart's Court", in, Gillian Bickley, Ed, *A Magistrate's Court in Nineteenth Century Hong Kong"*, Hong Kong, Proverse Hong Kong, 2005, *q.v.*, pp. 75-85.

— *Searching for Frederick and Adventures along the Way*, Hong Kong, Asia 2000, 2001. pbk. 420pp., inc. bibliography, index. ISBN-10: 962-8783-20-3; ISBN-13: 978-962-8783-20-5.

The China Mail

Coghlan, Christopher, "Thoughts about the Practice of Law in Hong Kong arising from the Court Cases of Fredreick Stewart, Esq.: White Gloves and Patience", in, Gillian Bickley, *A Magistrate's Court in Nineteenth Century Hong Kong"*, Hong Kong, Proverse Hong Kong, 2005, *q.v.*, pp. 87-97.

Crisswell, Colin and Mike Watson, *The Royal Hong Kong Police (1841-1945)*, Hong Kong, Macmillan Hong Kong, 1982.

Criminal Calendar for January to December 1881, inclusive: HKGG 1881, pp. 120, 212, 233, 303, 411, 562, 674, 817, 875, 950, 1043, 1106.

Criminal Calendar for January to April 1882, inclusive. HKGG 1882, pp. 61, 258, 296, 461. (NB No Criminal Calendar appears in HKGG 1882, May to December, inclusive.)

"Criminal Statistics. 1881", HKGBB 1881, pp. Y1-Y14.

The Daily Press.

Eames, J. R., *The English in China*, London, Curzon Press, 1909, new impression, 1974.

Eitel, E. J., (Ernst Johann), *Europe in China: the History of Hong Kong, from the beginning to the year 1882*, Hong Kong, Oxford University Press, 1983 (first published by Kelly and Walsh, Ltd., 1895).

— "Treatment of Paupers in Hong Kong", 22 April 1880, in HKGG, 9 June 1880, pp. 466-473.

Endacott, G. B., *A History of Hong Kong*, Oxford University Press, 1964.

"Gaols and Prisoners. Hong Kong. 1881," HKGBB 1881, X2-X6.

Hamilton, Sheilah, *Watching over Hong Kong: Private Policing 1841-1931*, Royal Asiatic Society (Hong Kong Branch), 2008.

Hamlett, Timothy, "Reporting the Cases of Frederick Stewart'", in, Gillian Bickley, Ed, *A Magistrate's*

Court in Nineteenth Century Hong Kong", Hong
Kong, Proverse Hong Kong, 2005, *q.v.*, pp. 131-145.

Hong Kong Government Blue Books.

Hong Kong Government Gazettse.

Hong Kong University Libraries Digital Initiatives.

Index To CO/129, 1842-1926, History Department,
University of Hong Kong, 1997, CD publication,
1997.

Jury List for 1881, HKGG, 5 March 1881, pp. 158-
165.

Jury List for 1882, HKGG, 25 February 1882, pp.
201-210.

"List of Officers", HKBB1882, Section I3.

Munn, Christopher, "'An Anglo-Chino [*sic*]
conspiracy in crime': the Caldwell Scandal,
1857-1861", TS, nd.
— "The Criminal Trial under Early Colonial Rule",
in *Hong Kong's History*, ed. Tak-Wing Ngo, London
and New York, Routledge, 1999, pp. 46-73.

— *Chinese People and British Rule in Hong Kong,
1841-1880*, Routledge, 2001.

Norton-Kyshe, James William, *The History of the
Laws and Courts of Hong Kong*, London, Unwin,
1898, 2 Vols.

National Archives of Scotland, *Crime and
Punishment in Scotland from the 16th to the 20th
century,* exhibition text, 28pp.

"PoliceForce", Section I, HKGBB, 1880, 1881, 1882.

"Return of Serious and Minor Offences reported to have been committed during the Year 1881, with the Results of such Reports", Police Department, Hong Kong, 30 January 1882, signed W. M. Deane, Captain Superintendent of Police. Table A, HKGG, 11 March 1882, p. 259.

Roper, Geoffrey, "The Police Role in Magistrate Frederick Stewart's Court", in, Gillian Bickley, Ed, *A Magistrate's Court in Nineteenth Century Hong Kong"*, Hong Kong, Proverse Hong Kong, 2005, *q.v.*, pp. 117-130.

Sayer, Geoffrey Robley, *Hong Kong 1841-1862: Birth, Adolescence and Coming of Age*, Hong Kong University Press, 1980, reprint of the original 1937 edition, published by Oxford University Press under the title *Hong Kong: Birth, Adolescence and Coming of Age*.

Sinclair, Kevin and Nelson Ng Kwok-cheung, *Asia's Finest Marches On: Policing Hong Kong from 1841 into the 21st century*, Hong Kong, Kevin Sinclair Associates Limited, 1997, p. 227. (Earlier version, Kevin Sinclair, *Asia's Finest*, Hong Kong, Unicorn, 1983.)

"Statistical Return for the Prisons of Hong Kong for 1882", HKGBB 1882, X2-X6.

Tallentire, Garry, "The Hong Kong (Police) Magistrate in the 1880s and 1990s: A Flavour of the Times", in, Gillian Bickley, Ed, *A Magistrate's Court in Nineteenth Century Hong Kong"*, Hong Kong, Proverse Hong Kong, 2005, *q.v.*, pp. 147-158.

Traver, Harold H. "Colonial Relations and Opium Control Policy in Hong Kong, 1841-1945", in Traver, Harold H and Mark S. Gaylord, *Drugs, Law and the State*, University of Washington Press, 1991, pp. 135-148.

—, Mark S. Gaylord, "Colonial Relations and Opium Control Policy in Hong Kong, 1841-1945", in *Drugs, Law and the State*, University of Washington Press, 1991, p. 159.

Tsai Jung-fang, *Hong Kong in Chinese History: Community and Social Unrest in the British Colony, 1842-1913,* New York, Columbia University Press, 1993.

University of Hong Kong Digitial Initiatives. "The Historical Laws of Hong Kong Online". Comprises a total of six consolidations of the laws of Hong Kong: 1890, 1901, 1912, 1923, 1937, 1950, and 1964 (last updated to 1989)."
http://xml.lib.hku.hk/gsdl/db/oelawhk/browse.shtml

University of Hong Kong Digitial Initiatives. *Hong Kong Government Gazettes* in, "Hong Kong Government Reports Online, 1853-1941". Website: http://sunzi1.lib.hku.hk/hkgro/index.jsp

Welsh, Frank, *A History of Hong Kong*, HarperCollinsPublishers, 1993.

Checklist of A) Compilations and Indices of Hong Kong Ordinances, and B) Hong Kong Ordinances which have been researched and found relevant to 1) the present publication, *The Complete Court Cases*, or 2) to *A Magistrate's Court in Nineteenth Century Hong Kong* (2005), or to both these publications. Including some information as to where these materials may be found.

Also two groupings from the above: 1) "The Gambling Rrdinance" and related legislation; 2) "The Opium Ordinance" and related legislation & HKGG references.

Compilations and Indices of Hong Kong Ordinances
NB: Shelf numbers as noted are included for reference as well as some comments.

Chronological Table of Ordinances. Laws of Hong Kong. Index. [HKU Law Library. PR KT 4353.1 H7 F90.]

Laws of Hong Kong, 1923 edition with Index of Short titles Vols 1-5. v. 1, 1844-1890; v. 2, 1891-1900; v. 3, 1901-1903; v. 4, 1904-1912; v. 5, 1913-1923. HKU Special Collections. HK 348.5125 H7 5vols. [NB These do not include all ordinances within these periods.]

"Chronological Table of Ordinances. Laws of Hong Kong. Index." In *Laws of Hong Kong*, Vol. 1. [HKU Law Library.]

"The Historical Laws of Hong Kong Online", University of Hong Kong Libraries.
http://xml.lib.hku.hk/gsdl/db/oelawhk/browse.shtml

"Hong Kong Government Reports Online (1853-1941)", University of Hong Kong Libraries.
http://sunzi1.lib.hku.hk/hkgro/index.jsp

The Ordinances of Hong Kong for the years 1844-1846. [HKU Law Library.]

The Ordinances of Hong Kong for the years 1847-1859. [HKU Law Library.]

The *Ordinances of Hong Kong 1886.* [HKU Law Library.]

The Ordinances of Hong Kong, 1888, printed by Noronha and Co., Government Printers, Hong Kong, 1889. [HKU Law Library.]

The Ordinances of Hong Kong, 1889, printed by Noronha and Co., Government Printers, Hong Kong, 1890. [HKU Law Library. KT 4351 H7 S1]

The Ordinances of Hong Kong, 1897, printed by Noronha and Co., Government Printers, Hong Kong, 1898. [HKU Law Library.]

The Ordinances of Hong Kong, 1930, printed by Noronha and Co., Government Printers, Hong Kong. [HKU Law Library.]

1844[594]

Ordinance No. 5 of 1844. "An Ordinance for the preservation of good order and cleanliness within the colony of Hong Kong and its dependencies." Passed 20 March 1844.

Ordinance No. 10 of 1844. "An Ordinance to Regulate Summary proceedings before Justices of the Peace and to protect justices in the execution of their office." Passed, 10 April 1844.

---

[594] Some sources include in the title of an ordinance, "An Ordinance enacted by the Governor of Hong Kong, with the Advice of the Legislative Council thereof". Others exclude this element. Where present, this formula is omitted in the list below.

Ordinance No. 11 of 1844. "An Ordinance for licensing Public Houses and for regulating the retail of fermented and spirituous liquors in the colony of Hong Kong." Passed 1 May 1844.

Ordinance No. 14 of 1844. "An Ordinance for the Suppression of Public Gaming in the Colony of Hong Kong". Passed, 10 June 1844.

Ordinance No. 17 of 1844. "An Ordinance for the better securing the Peace and Quiet of the Inhabitants of the Town of Victoria and its vicinity during the night-time." "Peace and Quiet Ordinance." Passed 11 September 1844.

Ordinance No. 21 of 1844. "An Ordinance for licensing the Sale of Salt, and the Sale of Opium, Bhaang, Ganja, Paun, Betel, and Betel-leaf, within the Colony of Hong Kong, and for the Licensing of Pawnbrokers and Auctioneers, with a Table of Fees on official Licences and Signatures." Passed 26 Nov 1844.

Ordinance No. 22 of 1844. "An Ordinance for Establishing Standard Weights and Measures, and for preventing the Use of such as are false and deficient". Passed 30 December 1844. Republished in HKGG, 8 October 1881, pp. 915-919.

1845
Ordinance No. 1 of 1845, "An Ordinance for the suppression of the Triad [*sic*, i.e. the word "Society" is absent] and other secret Societies within the Island of Hong Kong and its Dependencies". Passed, 8 January 1845.

Ordinance No. 3 of 1845. "An Ordinance for licensing the retail of tobacco and snuff, within the colony of Hong Kong and the waters thereof." Passed 7 July 1845.

Ordinance No. 5 of 1845. "To repeal Ordinance No. 21 of 1844, and to make better Provision for licensing the Weighing and Brokerage of Salt, and the Sale of Opium, Bhaang, Ganja, Paun, Betel, and Betel-leaf, within the Colony of Hong Kong, and for the Licensing of Pawnbrokers and Auctioneers, with a Table of Fees on official Licences and Signatures." Passed 12 July 1845.

Ordinance No. 12 of 1845. "An Ordinance to amend No. 1 of 1845"[595] for the Suppression of the Triad Society and other Secret Societies in the Island of Hong Kong and its Dependencies." Passed 20 October 1845.

Ordinance No. 14 of 1845. "An Ordinance to repeal Ordinance No. 5 of 1844, entitled, 'An Ordinance for the preservation of good order and cleanliness within the colony of Hong Kong and its dependencies,' and to make other provisions in lieu thereof." Passed 26 December 1845.

1847

Ordinance No. 1 of 1847. "An Ordinance for Licensing Markets and for preventing Disorders therein." Passed 30 January 1847.

Ordinance No. 4 of 1847. "An Ordinance to Repeal and Amend Ordinance No. 1 of 1847 entitled 'An Ordinance or Licensing Markets and for preventing Disorders therein'." Passed 12 August 1847.

1848

Ordinance No. 1 of 1848. "To regulate the Manufacture and storage of a certain description of gunpowder within the Colony of Hong Kong". Passed 31 August 1847.

---

[595] Chronological Table of Ordinances. Laws of Hong Kong. Index. HKU Law Library. PR KT 4353.1 H7 F90.

1850

Ordinance No. 5 of 1850. "Ordinance to regulate Proceedings before Justices of the Peace". Passed 17 December 1850.

1853

Ordinance No. 1 of 1853. "An Ordinance for the Regulation of the Gaol of Hong Kong". Passed 20 September 1853. HKGG, 1 October 1853, pp. 7-8.

Ordinance No. 4 of 1853. "An Ordinance to Amend Ordinances No. 11 of 1844 and 5 of 1845, and to improve the Regulations for the Sale of Spirituous Liquors by Chinese, and the Regulations for the Retail and Preparation of Opium." Passed, 22 December 1853. HKGG, 24 December 1853, pp. 59-60.

1854

Ordinance No. 2 of 1854. "Market Ordinance". Passed 29 August 1854. HKGG, 2 September 1854, pp. 177-178.

1855

Ordinance No. 1 of 1855. "An Ordinance to enforce neutrality during the Contest now existing in China". Passed 15 January 1855. HKGG, 20 January 1855, pp. 239-240.

"The Chinese Passengers Act, 1855". Passed 14 August 1855. See HKGG, 11 February 1882, pp. 83-120.

1856

Ordinance No. 12 of 1856. "An Ordinance to regulate the Chinese burials, and to prevent certain nuisances within the colony of Hong Kong." Passed 12 June 1856. HKGG, 14 June 1856, pp. 5-6.

1857

Ordinance No. 9 of 1857. "An amended Ordinance for better Securing the Peace of the Colony." Passed 15 July 1857. HKGG, 18 July 1857, p. 2.

Ordinance No. 12 of 1857. "An Ordinance for Checking the spread of Venereal Disease." Passed 24 November 1857. HKGG, 28 November 1857, pp. 1-3.

1858

Ordinance No. 2 of 1858. "An Ordinance for licensing and regulating the Sale of prepared Opium." Passed 17 March 1858. HKGG, 20 March 1858, pp. 1-2.

Ordinance No. 6 of 1858. "To amend Ordinance No. 9 of 1857". Passed 27 March 1858. Please see HKGG, 30 March 1858, p. 1. It is explained that Ordinance No. 9 of 1858 is re-numbered as Ordinance No. 6 of 1858.

Ordinance No. 7 of 1858. "An Ordinance for amending Ordinance No. 11 of 1844. [q.v.]" Passed 5 April 1858. HKGG, 10 April 1858, p. 90.

Ordinance No. 8 of 1858. "An Ordinance for Regulation of the Chinese People, and for the Population Census, and for other Purposes of Police." "To regulate Chinese people".
Passed 10 May 1858. HKGG, 15 May 1858, pp. 2-5.

Ordinance No. 9 of 1858. "To amend Ordinance No. 9 of 1857". Please see HKGG, 30 March 1858, p. 1. It is explained that Ordinance No. 9 of 1858 is re-numbered as Ordinance No. 6 of 1858. Passed 27 March 1858.

1860

Ordinance No. 3 of 1860, "An Ordinance for amending and consolidating the Law regarding Pawnbrokers". Passed 16 April 1860. HKGG, 21 April 1860, pp. 106-108.

1862

Ordinance No. 6 of 1862. "An Ordinance to abolish the Offices of Chief Magistrate and Assistant Magistrate, and to appoint and define the Duties of Two Police Magistrates." Passed 22 March 1862. HKGG, 29 March 1862, pp. 94-96.

Ordinance No. 9 of 1862. "For the Establishment and Regulation of the Police Force of the Colony". Passed 3 May 1862. HKGG, 3 May 1862, pp. 140-145.

1863

Ordinance No. 1 of 1863 (Police Magistrates). First reading, 17 January 1863. (See HKGG, 31 January 1863, pp. 33-34.) "An Ordinance to amend certain provisions in Ordinance No. 6 of 1862, intituled [sic], 'An Ordinance to abolish the Office of Chief Magistrate, and to appoint and define the duties of two Police Magistrates'". Passed 6 February 1863. HKGG, 7 February 1863, p. 40.

Ordinance No. 4 of 1863. "An Ordinance to repeal Ordinance No. 1 of 1853 and to provide Gaols and Debtors' Wards, and for the due control of Prisoners therein." Passed 26 May 1863. HKGG, 30 May 1863, pp. 145-147.

1865

Ordinance No. 4 of 1865, "An Ordinance to consolidate and amend the Enactments in Force in this Colony relating to Offences against the Person". Passed 2 June 1865. HKGG, 10 June 1865, pp. 291-300.

Ordinance No. 7 of 1865. "An Ordinance to consolidate and amend the Enactments in Force in this Colony relating to Larceny and similar Offences". Passed 3 June 1865. HKGG, 24 June 1865, pp. 355-373.

Ordinance No. 12 of 1865. "An Ordinance for the Further Security of the Residents in this Colony from Personal Violence". Passed 14 June 1865. HKGG, 1 July 1865, p. 400 only.

Ordinance No. 13 of 1865. "For the Rendition in Certain Cases of Chinese subjects charged with Piracy". HKGG, 8 July 1865, p. 410 only.

1866
Ordinance No. 6 of 1866. "An Ordinance for the better Regulation and Control of certain Vessels frequenting the Waters of Hong Kong, "The Harbour and Coasts Ordinance Hong Kong 1866". Passed 14 August 1866. HKGG, 18 August 1866, pp. 325-329.

Ordinance No. 7 of 1866. "An Ordinance dividing the City of Victoria into Districts, and for the better Registration of Householders and Chinese servants in the Colony of Hong Kong." "The Victoria Registration Ordinance 1866". Passed 16 August 1866. HKGG, 25 August 1866, pp. 336-340.

Ordinance No. 8 of 1866. "An Ordinance to make further Provision for the Maintenance of Order and Cleanliness within the Colony of Hong Kong." Passed 16 August 1866. HKGG, 25 August 1866, pp. 340-343.

Ordinance No. 9 of 1866. "An Ordinance to make Provision for the more effectual Suppression of Piracy." "Suppression of Piracy." Passed 16 August 1866. HKGG, 25 August 1866, pp. 343-347.

Ordinance No. 12 of 1866. "For imposing and regulating Stamp Duties in the Colony." "The Stamp Ordinance, 1866." Passed 8 September1866. HKGG, 1866, pp. 374 - 381.

1867

Ordinance No. 4 of 1867. "To Regulate the Importation and Storage of Gunpowder". Passed 22 May 1867. (HKGG, 25 May 1867, pp. 177-178.)

Ordinance No. 5 of 1867. "An Ordinance to amend Ordinance No. 9 of 1858" (q.v.). "The Markets Ordinance 1867". Passed 22 May 1867. HKGG, 25 May 1867, pp. 179-180.

Ordinance No. 9 of 1867. "An Ordinance to make further Provision for the Maintenance of Order and Cleanliness within the Colony of Hong Kong." Passed 17 June 1867. HKGG, 22 June 1867, pp. 228-231. Followed by related "Rules and Regulations", HKGG, 22 June 1867, p. 232.

Ordinance No. 10 of 1867. "An Ordinance for the better Prevention of Contagious Diseases." "The Contagious Diseases Ordinance, 1867." Passed 23 July 1867. HKGG, 27 July 1867, pp. 268-281. (Proformas are shown at pp. 277-281.)

1868

Ordinance No. 1 of 1868, "To make Provision for the more effectual Suppression of Piracy". Passed 22 May 1868. HKGG, 23 May 1868, pp. 199-202.

Ordinance No. 3 of 1868. "To Empower the Supreme Court to direct Offenders to be Whipped and to be kept in Solitary Confinement in certain specified Cases". Passed 22 May 1868. HKGG, 23 May 1868, pp. 203-204.

1869

HKGN No. 87 of 1869, 27 July 1869. "Additional Conditions for holding the Opium Grant Privilege for the preparation and sale of Prepared Opium within the Colony of Hong Kong". HKGG, 31 July 1869, p. 335. Refers to Sections II and III of Ordinance No. 2 of 1858
(Regulations for constructing Opium Furnaces and Boiling-houses.)

Ordinance No. 2 of 1869. "To make further provision in relation to Criminal law and proceeding". Passed 24 September 1869. HKGG 25 September 1869, pp. 450-451.

1870

Ordinance No. 14 of 1870. "An Ordinance to amend and consolidate the Law in relation to the Issue of Passes for Chinese, and to provide for the better Security of the Residents of the Colony." Passed 9 September 1870. HKGG, 13 September 1870, pp. 453-456.

1872

Ordinance No. 2 of 1872. "To prevent Certain Nuisances". Passed 5 April 1872. HKGG, 6 April 1872, p. 194. (Section VII states: "This Ordinance shall be read as though incorporated with and forming part of Ordinance No. 14 of 1845 [q.v.].")

Ordinance No. 4 of 1872. "An Ordinance . . . to make provision for the branding and punishment of criminals in certain cases." Passed 5 April 1872. HKGG 6 April 1872, pp. 195-196.

Ordinance No. 10 of 1872. "An Ordinance to prevent certain Nuisances." Passed 5 September 1872. HKGG, 7 September 1872, p. 388.
See Section VIII, which reads: "This Ordinance shall be read as though incorporated with

and forming Part of Ordinance No. 14 of 1845 [q.v.]."

1873
Ordinance No. 6 of 1873. "For the better Protection of Chinese Women and female Children, and for the Repression of certain Abuses in relation to Chinese Emigration." Passed 8 May 1873. HKGG, 10 May 1873, pp. 221-222.

Ordinance No. 8 of 1873. "An Ordinance for the Amendment of the Law with respect to the carriage and deposit of dangerous goods." Passed 9 July 1873. (CC 309 identifies "The Dangerous Goods Ordinance", referred to in "The Complete Court Cases of Magistrate Frederick Stewart", as, "Section XI, of Ordinance No. 8 of 1873".)

1875
Ordinance No. 2 of 1875. "An ordinance for the better Protection of Chinese Women and Female Children and for the Repression of certain Abuses in relation to Chinese Emigration". Passed 18 March 1875. HKGG, 20 March 1875, pp. 105-106.

Ordinance No. 11 of 1875. "An Ordinance to provide for the more convenient administration of the Extradition Acts, 1870 and 1873." Passed 2 September 1875. HKGG, 4 September 1875, p. 358 only.

Ordinance No. 16 of 1875. "An Ordinance to amend and consolidate the laws concerning the jurisdiction of Magistrates over indictable offences and for other purposes." "The Magistrates Ordinance, 1875." Passed 25 November 1875. HKGG, 27 November 1875, pp. 471-473.

1876

Ordinance No. 8 of 1876. "An Ordinance to consolidate and amend the Ordinances relating to Deportation, Conditional Pardons, the Branding and Punishment of certain Criminals, and the Ordinance No. 9 of 1857, entitled 'An amended Ordinance for better Securing the Peace of the Colony' [q.v.]". "The Deportation and Conditional Pardons Consolidation Ordinance, 1876." Passed 11 December 1876. HKGG, 16 December 1876, pp. 551-553.

Ordinance No. 9 of 1876. "An Ordinance to consolidate and amend the Law relating to Public Gambling." "The Public Gambling Amendment Ordinance, 1876". Passed 11 December 1876. HKGG, 16 December 1876, pp. 553-554.

1879

Ordinance No. 1 of 1879. "Ordinance to amend Ordinance No, 2 of 1858 entitled 'An Ordinance for Licensing and Regulating the Sale of Prepared Opium'". Passed 18 January 1879. HKGG, 22 January 1879, pp. 23-27.

Para. 18 states as follows: "This and said recited Ordinance [No. 2 of 1858 (q.v.]] may be cited as 'The Excise Ordinance (Opium), 1858-1879'". Bill to establish a Spirit Farm, HKGG, 11 June 1879, pp. 305-330.

Ordinance No. 7 of 1879. "An Ordinance to amend 'The Excise Ordinance (Opium) 1858-1879'". Passed 9 December 1879. "The Excise Ordinance (Opium) 1858-1879, Amendment Ordinance 1879". HKGG, 10 December 1879, pp. 813-815. [Also sometimes referred to as, "Excise Ordinance (Opium) 1858-1879" (See e.g. HKGG, 10 February 1881, p. 818.)]

Ordinance No. 8 of 1879. "An Ordinance to consolidate and amend the laws relating to merchant shipping, the duties of the Harbour Master, the control and management of the waters of the Colony

and the regulation of vessels navigating the same."
"The Merchant Shipping Consolidation Ordinance."
Passed 30 December 1879. HKGG, 14 January 1879,
pp. 19-55.

1880
Ordinance No. 5 of 1880. "To amend Ordinance No.
9 of 1857 [q.v.]". Passed 31 August 1880. Sent to
London, 10 September 1880. See HKBB, 12
February 1880 which refers to HKGG, 12 February
1880.

1881
Ordinance No. 3 of 1881. An Ordinance entitled,
"The Penal Ordinances amendment Ordinance, 1881".
Passed 24 June 1881. HKGG 1881, pp. 513-514,
1006-1009.

Draft Ordinance, "to amend and repeal certain
Ordinances relating to Branding and to the
punishment of Flogging." As published in HKGG, 19
November 1881, pp. 1006-1007.

"Penal Laws Amendment Ordinance. Abolition of
Branding and Public Flogging, &c." Extracts of
despatches, 17 October 1880 to 4 October 1881,
published 19 November 1881, HKGG, 19 November
1881, pp. 1006-1009.

Ordinance No. 12 of 1881. "An Ordinance entitled
the 'Banishment and Conditional Pardons Ordinance,
1881'". Passed 23 August 1881. HKGG, 27 August
1881, 738-740.

1882
Ordinance No. 8 of 1882. "The Banishment and
Conditional Pardons Ordinance, 1882". Passed 1
March 1882. HKGG, 4 March 1882, pp. 225-226.

"Supplementary Conditions, made by the Governor
in Council, to which licenses granted under the

Excise Ordinances (Opium), 1858-1879, are to be subject". Passed, 27 April 1882. HKGG, 13 May 1882, pp. 475-476.

Ordinance No. 24 of 1882, "The Jurors and Juries Ordinance". Passed 19 December 1882. HKGG, 13 January 1883, pp. 14-15.

1883
HKGN No. 67 of 1883. HKGG, 21 February 1883, pp.122-123. (Signed Frederick Stewart, Acting Colonial Secretary.)

"Conditions made by the Governor in Council, under the provision of the Excise Ordinances (Opium), 1858-1879". Dated 21 February 1883. These follow HKGN No. 67 of 1883. Dated 21 February 1883. (HKGG, 21 February 1883, p. 122.)

Ordinance No. 4 of 1883. "The Excise Ordinances (Opium) 1858-1879, Amendment Ordinance 1883". Passed 7 March 1883. HKGG, 10 March 1883, pp. 210-211.

Ordinance No. 8 of 1883. "The Excise Ordinances (Opium) 1858-1879, Amendment Ordinance 1883, (No. 2)." Passed 20 July 1883. HKGG, 21 July 1883, pp. 626-627.

1884
Ordinance No. 1 of 1884. "The Opium Ordinance, 1884." Passed 26 March 1884. HKGG *Extraordinary*, 27 March 1884, np.

1885
[Weights and Measures Ordinance of 1885. -- Not seen. -- Ed]

1886

Ordinance No. 17 of 1886. "The Opium Ordinance, 1886". Passed 21 May 1886. HKGG, 22 May 1886, p. 443.

Ordinance No. 19 of 1886. "Ordinance entitled 'The Reformatory Schools Ordinance'". Passed 21 May 1886. (*Ordinances of Hong Kong 1886* (q.v.).) Announcement of confirmation of this Ordinance dated 8 September 1886, HKGG, 11 September 1886.

1887

Ordinance No. 16 of 1887. "An Ordinance Empowering the Courts to Award Whipping as a Further Punishment for Certain Crimes." Passed 24 June 1887. HKGG, 25 June 1887, pp. 691-692.

Ordinance No. 22 of 1887. "An Ordinance for the better regulating of the trade in Opium." Passed 27 May 1887. (1890), HKGG, 28 May 1887, 601-604 (text).

1888

Ordinance No. 13 of 1888. "The Regulation of Chinese Ordinance, 1888". Passed 21 March 1888.

Ordinance No. 27 of 1888. [Can't find using an online search so as to determine the name of this Ordinance.] Passed 12 November 1888. HKGG, 24 November 1888, pp. 1070-1071.

1889

Ordinance No. 8 of 1889. "To amend the Powers of Police Magistrates". (*The Ordinances of Hong Kong, 1889* (q.v.))

1891

Ordinance No. 2 of 1891. (A note says this was originally Ordinance No. 7 of 1891.) Gambling.

1897

Ordinance No. 6 of 1897, "An Ordinance to amend The Regulation of Chinese Ordinance, 1888". (*The Ordinances of Hong Kong, 1897* (q.v.).)

1898

Ordinance No. 3 of 1898. "An Ordinance for the more effectual punishment of bribery and other misdemeanours". "The Misdemeanours Punishment Ordinance, 1898". Passed 23 February 1898. HKGG, 5 March 1898, p. 213.

1930

Ordinance No. 25 of 1930. Passed 5 December 1930. Repeals Ordinance No. 13 of 1888, "Regulation of Chinese".

1971

Prevention of Bribery Ordinance. Passed 14 May 1971.

1974

"Independent Commission against Corruption Ordinance". Passed 15 February 1974.

"The Gambling Ordinance" and related legislation

Ordinance No. 9 of 1876 (q.v.).

Ordinance No. 27 of 1888 (q.v.). In several places, The "Historical Laws of Hong Kong Online" text states, "Repealed by Ordinance No. 27 of 1888 . . ." Also the Index to HKGG, 1888, refers to Ordinance No. 27 of 1888 as amending Ordinance No. 9 of 1876. Also HKGG, 24 November 1888 (p. 1067) reports (signed by Frederick Stewart) that assent has been received to five Ordinances, including No. 27of 1888.

All suggests that the next relevant Ordinance after Ordinance No. 9 of 1876 is Ordinance No. 27 of 1888. Therefore Ordinance No. 9 of 1876 must be the one referred to as "The Gambling Ordinance" in these 1881-1882 Court Cases.

Examples of earlier Ordinances, which refer to gambling, are: Ordinance No. 14 of 1844 (q.v.), Ordinance No. 8 of 1866 (HKGG 1866, pp. 340-343). So does Ordinance No. 7 of 1866 (HKGG, 25 August 1866, pp. 336-349) and Ordinance No. 9 of 1867 (HGGG, 22 June 1867, pp.228-232).

An example of a later Ordinance, which refers to gambling are: Ordinance No. 2 of 1891 (a note says this was originally Ordinance No. 7 of 1891).

"The Opium Ordinance" And Related Legislation & HKGG References

Ordinance No. 10 of 1844. q.v.
Ordinance No. 11 of 1844. q.v.
Ordinance No. 17 of 1844. q.v.
Ordinance No. 21 of 1844. q.v.
Ordinance No. 3 of 1845. q. v.
Ordinance No. 5 of 1845. q.v.
Ordinance No. 4 of 1853. q.v.
Ordinance No. 2 of 1858. q.v.
Ordinance No. 7 of 1858. q.v.
HKGN No. 87 of 1869. q.v.
Ordinance No. 1 of 1879. q.v.

[Bill to establish a Spirit Farm, HKGG, 11 June 1879, pp. 305-330.]

Ordinance No. 7 of 1879. q.v.
Ordinance No. 4 of 1883. q. v.
Ordinance No. 8 of 1883. q.v.
Ordinance No. 1 of 1884. q.v.
Ordinance No. 17 of 1886. q.v.
Ordinance No. 22 of 1887. q.v.
Ordinance No. 7 of 1879. q.v.

"Supplementary Conditions, made by the Governor in Council, to which licenses granted under the Excise Ordinances (Opium), 1858-1879, are to be subject". Passed, 27 April 1882. q.v.

HKGN No. 67 of 1883. HKGG, 21 February 1883, pp.122-123. q. v.

"Conditions made by the Governor in Council, under the provision of the Excise Ordinances (Opium), 1858-1879". Dated 21 February 1883. q.v.

INDEX

327, 384, 428,
463, 479, 484
Central Police
Station, 46, 110,
221
Central School, 39,
43, 226, 458, 509
Central Station, 110,
131, 133, 140,
209, 336, 443,
444, 505
Centre Street, 203,
335, 478, 540;
No. 11, 161
Chai Aping (aged
68), 146
Chai Awing, 108
Chai Ki Chan shop,
246, 247
chair coolie(s) /
chair-coolie(s), 40,
116, 126, 145,
156, 222, 223,
225, 302, 391,
394,404,405, 482
chair stands, 441
Chan Acheung, 249
Chan Acheung
(married woman,
aged 22, of
Canton), 432
Chan Achiu, 197
Chan Achung
(unemployed),
111
Chan Afat (seaman),
250

Chan Afoo, 359,
365
Chan Afu
(shopkeeper), 415
Chan Afuk, 150,
226
Chan Afuk (coolie
from Canton),
391
Chan Afuk
(fisherman), 239
Chan Afung (coolie),
440
Chan Agan, 186
Chan Ahau, 254
Chan Aheung
(servant), 459
Chan Ahing, 152,
219
Chan Ahoi (cook),
249
Chan Akan, 159
Chan Akau, 107,
184
Chan Akok (district
watchman), 280
Chan Akun
(hawker), 447
Chan Akung
(coolie), 351
Chan Alam (cook),
169
Chan Aleong
(trader), 450
Chan Aleong of Wai
Chau, 446
Chan Alok
(boatman), 262

Chong Asiu
(unemployed),
303
Chow Atuk, 158
Chow Yang Chan,
442
Chow Young Chan,
419
Chu Achong
(bricklayer), 239
Chu Ahing, 249
Chu Alok, 413
Chu Aon (butcher at
Central Market),
384
Chü Apin (female),
387
Chu Aping, 248
Chu Asau (coolie),
373
Chü Atam
(protected woman),
387
Chu Awa (actor),
412
Chu Azing, 494
Chu Kun (cook on
Thales ship), 213
Chu Lam Ching
(passenger on a
steamer), 362
Chu Sz (watchman),
409
Chuk Hing Lane,
128
Chun Achau (coolie),
457

Chun Acheung
(coolie), 253
Chun Acheung
(married woman
belonging to
Canton), 438
Chun Acheung
(married woman),
448
Chun Acheung
(married woman),
assistant at the
Mui Lan Brothel,
456
Chun Achim, 422
Chun Achün
(bricklayer), 471
Chun Afuk, 335
Chun Afuk (cook),
378
Chun Afuk (hawker,
469
Chun Afuk (hawker),
452
Chun Afuk (seaman),
245
Chun Akwa, 422
Chun Aman, 440
Chun Amu, 404
Chun Aon (hawker),
450
Chun Apo, 292
Chun Apo
(fishmonger), 463
Chun Apu
(unemployed),
426

coolie (shop-), 188, 406, 431, 275, 326, 332, 354, 375. *See also* Leong Atuk, Leung Akau

coolie (street-), 239, 305, 309

coolie (water-), 230

coolie(s). *See also as descriptions following personal names.*

coolie house(s), 251, 485

Cheang Asz (aged 42), 206

Fak Acheong (aged 28), 111

Leung Atsin (aged 26), 111

Kwan Atsan (aged 28), 111

Li Akin (aged 35), 142

Leong Ahi (aged 36), 145

Leong Akai (aged 29), 176

Wong Aon (aged 23), 183

Lam Acho (aged 54), 195

Ho Achoi (aged 30), 196

Ching Ku Shing (partner in the Shun Wo Un Hong, 423

Corcoran, Inspector of Police, *See Inspector of Police Corcoran*

Cottrall, William, 162

Cottrell, defendant, 423

Cottrell, William (American), 422

counterfeit coin(s), 316, 317, 328, 399, 402, 403, 415, 416, 428

Court Interpreter, 400, 407, 413, 518

cow-boy, 358

Cowdrey, Thomas (of HMS *Tourmaline*), 408

Cox, Mr James Henry, 394

Cox, Mr. J.H. of Messrs Turner & Co., 321

Cox, Mrs, 322

Cradock, Inspector of Police. *See Inspector of Police Cradock*

Crawford, Sgt., R.A. (Armstrong Armourer, Ordnance Store), 407

Fleming (Inspector).
*See Inspector of
Police Fleming*

Flin, Benjamin, 166

Fokien, 425

Foley, J.E., PC No.
1. *See PC No. 1,
J.E. Foley*

Fong Acheung (shop
coolie), 408

Fong Achi, 212

Fong Akum, 126

Fong Amui, married
woman, 290

Fong Atsin (hawker),
326

Fong Chu Ching
(photographer and
painter), 278

food and a night's
lodgings provided
for a destitute,
443

Forbes, James, PC
No. 85, 375. *See
PC No. 85 James
Forbes*

Ford, Mr.
(Superintendent,
Government
Gardens), 358

fortune teller, 230,
238, 268

fortune-teller's
house, 412

Forward Ho, British
barque, 401

Francis Street, 416

Francis, Mr. J.J.,
112, 165, 199,
296, 297, 298

Franco, Mr., 292

Franco, Mr. Phineas
Mary Kerr [*sic*],
292

Fredreson, Frederick,
224

Fitzpatrick, John
(steward), 198

Fu Akwai, 152

Fuk Lun draper's
shop, 190

Fuk Shang
Pawnshop, 389

Fukeera, Abdoola,
170

Fulling, Christian
(chief officer of
the *Fyen*), 501

Fung Ahing, 116

Fung Akai (cook),
281

Fung Apui (coolie),
332

Fung Atai, 335

Fung Awai, 171,
189

Fung Fat (chair-
coolie), 394

Fung Kwok Tai, 208

Fung Man Lane, 182

Fung Shing
(seaman), 250

Fung-hoi Ki (master
of a tailor's shop

in Queen's Road Central), 392

Fung-Wo mat shop, 332

Fyen, 501

Gage Street, 399, 451; (No. 15), 489; (No. 22), 489

gale, 223, 250

Gamble, Sergeant, 96

Gamblers, 49, 56, 74, 76, 77, 78, 81, 83, 91, 94

gambling, 13, 30, 31, 34, 61, 62, 63, 65, 66, 67, 68, 69, 71, 78, 79, 80, 81, 82, 87, 88, 89, 91, 100, 101, 105, 106, 111, 113, 117, 123, 145, 152, 162, 163, 174, 181, 186, 194, 195, 196, 201, 205, 220, 229, 245, 258, 260, 273, 285, 304, 306, 309, 310, 311, 312, 313, 314, 324, 351, 352, 354, 355, 361, 363, 370, 371, 372, 376, 380, 381, 389, 390, 405, 418, 420, 430, 437, 444, 445, 449, 452, 467, 469, 479, 484, 519, 538, 540, 541, 542, 544

gambling cases, 531, 536

gambling equipment / implements, 430, 538, 539, 542

gambling house, 174, 245, 372, 445; Gilman Street, 445; Market Street, 443

Gambling Ordinance, 14, 418

gang, 166, 282, 376, 485

Gap Station, 488

Gap Street / Gap-street, 260, 285, 540

Apo (aged 17, 277

Garfit, A.S. (juror), 165, 199

Garrald, Peter (seaman), 270

Gas Works / Gasworks, 296, 304

Gaskell, Mr W.H., juror, 422, 427

German Tavern, 122

Gilman / Gilman's Bazaar, 111, 174,

Gustave. H. (scholar at St Joseph's College), 226

Gutierres, Mr. J. A., 125

Gutierrez, Augusto Aureliano, 125

Gutzlaff Street, 399

H.M. Consul at Nagasaki, 218

H.M. Dockyards, 231

HMS *Carysfort*, 397

HMS *Comus*, 278

HMS *Iron Duke*, 336, 351

HMS *Magpie*, 244

HMS *Tourmaline*, 408

HMS *Wivern*, 291

Ha Wan Market, 228

Hadjee Ali, 413, 530

Hagarty, Police Sgt, 293, 310, 312

Hagger, Ernest (seaman on HMS *Wivern*), 291

Haines, William (seaman on HMS *Carysfort*), 397

Hamilton, John (fireman on steamer *Hong Kong*), 488

Hang Cheung shop, 190

Hanna, Michael (seaman unemployed of Ireland), 451

Hansen, George (fireman on board *Comus*), 278

Hanson, John (seaman), 270

Hanson, Police Sgnt., 487, 488

harbour, 123, 128, 146, 181, 188, 226, 236, 407, 408, 424, 436, 437, 455, 474

Harbour Department, 202

Harbour Master, 143, 339, 456

Harbour Master's Office, 19, 143, 144, 166, 279, 450, 455

Harbour Office, 123, 149, 202, 336, 382, 408, 409, 540

Harding, John William (seaman of steamer *Lord of Isles*), 307

Hare, D.A.C.G. (of Commissariat Dept), 331

Harry Wicking, 156

Company, Limited, 159, 183, 492

Hong Kong Club, 388; servants' quarters, 532, 535

Hong Kong Harbour, 214

Hong Kong Hotel, 441

Hong Kong Police Force, 32

Hong Kong Telegraph, 292

Horspool, Mr., 218, 220, 343, 345, 348; Horspool, Mr G., Ag Deputy Superintendent of Police, 346. *See Inspector of Police Horspool*

Hospital, 66, 174, 356, 442, 448

Hospital Road, 66, 157

Hospital Ward, 356

Hotel de l'Univers, 140

Hotel(s) *See National; Stag.*

Hou Alin (married woman), 486

Hou Asze, 502

How Ayune, 234

Howard, James (English seaman, unemployed), 497

Howard, Joseph (American seaman), 156

Howell, Frederic, PC No. 38 [*sic*]. *See PC No. 38 [sic] Frederick Howell*

Howell, Richard, PC No. 38 [*sic*]. *See PC No. 38 [sic] Richard Howell*

Hu Akong (salesman in piece goods shop), 324

Hu Akwong, 324, 337, 338

Hu Asai (chair coolie to Hon. Mr Johnson), 225

Hu Asheung (bean curd manufacturer), 184

Hu Chung (married woman), 451

Hughues, J.I., juror, 341

Hung Ahok (widow), 127

Hung Awo (coolie from Canton), 452

Hung Ham [*sic*], 183, 312, 492

Hung Ham [*sic*] Dock, 275

Hung Ham [*sic*] Dock Company, 492

Hung-hom village, 435

Hunter, Herman (a steward from San Francisco), 221

Hutchison, J.D. (John Du Flon) (merchant), 126

I Awan (pawnshop coolie), 182

I Azs (wife), 171

I Li, 386

I Wo Street, 229

Imperial examinations, 288

Chu Un Fuk (clerk; formerly schoolmaster), 288

Impersonation of an Excise Officer, 524

Importer (American ship), 449

Indian, 46

Indian (police) quarters, 460

Indian constable(s), 32, 131, 139, 264, 304, 320, 459

Indian Police Constable No. 693, Easur Singh, 319

Indian storekeeper, 250

Indians, 413

informer(s), 32, 102, 117, 135, 151, 161, 192, 247, 255, 306, 329, 362, 370, 371, 375, 377, 380, 404, 407, 412, 413, 522, 523, 528, 529, 530, 531, 536, 585, 595; informers (gambling-), 371

informers (named), Ng Hoi (q.v.), Wong Man Yu (q.v.), Wong Way Fu (q.v.)

Inland Lot No. 420, 226

Inniskillings, 417

Inspector of Brothels, 433, 439, 457, 463; *See also* Lee, John; Inspector of Brothels; Whitehead, W.F.

Inspector of Markets Orley, 190, 227, 246, 247

Inspector of Nuisances, Mr Adams, 138, 186

Inspector of Police, 39, 54, 110, 112,

Lo Chun (of Canton), 462

Lo Fan, Sam Shui District, 210

Lo Fuk, 484

Lo Fuk (coolie), 483

Lo Kui Mui, 441

Lo Lai Hi (fisherman), 124

Lo Li Ui, 203

Lo Yuk Yung, 186

Lock Hospital, 281, 433

Loh Ayau (coal coolie), 410

Lok Achun, 106

Lok Ayau (shop-coolie), 275

Lo-kong (village), 432

London Mission Chapel, 162

Long Pier, Wanchai, 408

Loong Ai (woman), 125

Lopes, Antonia (aged 48; widow), 174

Lorberg, T.H.E. (juror), 165

Lorberg, F.H.G. (juror), 199

Lord of Isles, steamer, 307

Louis, Pellici (seaman on the *Adonis*), 116

Loureiro, Mr Jose (Portuguese Consul), 158

Love, R., PC No. 32. *See PC No. 32, R. Love*

Lower Lascar Road, 116, 540; No. 22, 116

Lower Lascar Row, 413, 431, 434, 483

Luck Atsin, 224

Lui Ahoi (hawker), 493

Lui Tung (carpenter), 224

Luk Achü (tailor), 489

Luk Ahing, 243

Luk Akin, 113

Luk Akun (hawker), 467

Luk Apong, 126

lukong(s) (i.e. Chinese constables), 119, 177, 233, 283, 321, 335, 372, 396, 430

Lukong (village in China), 457

Lul Singh, PC No. 530. *See PC No. 530, Lul Singh*

Lum Afat (hawker), 418

Lum Afuk (seaman), 370

Lum Ahun (servant), 188

Lum Akan (aged 22, 195

Lum Alap, 109

Lum Among, 198

Lum Amui, 200, 201

Lum Ashing, 194

Lum Atak, 382

Lum Atsoi, 159

Lum Atsoi (driver), 329

Lum Awai, 388

Lum Awong, 389

Lum Kwai Mui, 204

Lun Heong (of Fung Tai old clothes shop), 191

Lung Ahing, 127

Lung Au (aged 74), 255

Ly Aying (shop boy, aged 15), 429

Lyndhurst Terrace, 264

Lynsaght, William (Inspector of Naval police in HM Dockyards), 231

Lyon, PC, *See also* PC Lyon

M'Breen, James Joseph (clerk, Irish), 128, 129, [130], [132], 136, 137, [139], [140]

M'Breen, Jane Francis (wife of James Joseph M'Breen), 128, 129, 130, 138, 139

M'Leane, W., *See* PC No. 76, W. M'Leane

Ma Asam (coolie), 355

Macao, 195, 216, 257, 317, 337, 371, 529

Macao steamer, 155, 257, 532

Mathias, Maria (aged 24; wife), 174

MacCallum, Mr. H. (Apothecary and Analyst Government Hospital), 347

Macdonald, A., *See* PC No. 27

MacDonald, D., PC No. 84, 312; *See* PC No. 84, D. MacDonald

MacDonald / McDonald, G., *See* PC No. 82, G. MacDonald / McDonald

Macdougall, *See* PC
    Macdougall, 418
MacDougall, *See* PC
    No. 50 [*sic*]
Mackanery, Private
    P. (Royal
    Inniskilling
    Fusiliers), 330
Mackean, Mr. (ag
    on behalf of
    Attorney General),
    396, 403, 422
Mackean, Mr.,
    barrister [?], 427
Mackie, Inspector.
    See Inspector of
    Police Mackie
Maconachie, Mr.
    (manager, Gilman
    & Co.), 214
Maconnochie, Mr.,
    343
Mactavish, Mr.
    A.W., juror, 396,
    403
Made, James, 223
Magazine (*military,
    not media outlet*),
    343, 347
Magistracy, 73, 130,
    132, 137, 194,
    208, 212, 237,
    240, 245, 317,
    325, 354, 400
Magistracy, first
    clerk at, 507
Magistrate, 36, 41,
    45, 57, 106, 118,

119, 136, 138,
    139, 140, 141,
    174, 185, 190,
    192, 196, 207,
    247, 282, 296,
    375, 433, 441,
    445, 452, 453,
    456, 458, 462,
    463, 467, 468,
    476, 478, 479,
    483, 485, 486,
    488, 490, 494,
    500, 505, 507,
    508, 511, 516,
    518, 519, 526,
    527, 530, 534,
    585, 589, 590,
    593, 594, 595,
    604
Magistrate of Police,
    543
Magistrate,
    Stipendiary, 590
Magistrate, the, 517,
    523
Mah Achiu (servant),
    220
Mah Wan [*sic for
    Ma Wan?*], 366
Mahomed Ali, PS
    35, 285
Mahomed Hussean,
    PC No. 520. *See
    PC No. 520,
    Mahomed
    Hussean*
Mahomed Jan, PC
    No. 523, 405, 409

Mahomed Noor, PC No. 691, 327

Mahomedan Cemetery, 146

Mak Alui, 150

Mak Aun, 477

Mak Lung (of Fuk Tai draper's shop), 192

Malacca (place), 362

Malacca, P&O Steamer, 148

Malak, Sultan (Ag PS), 233

Malwa Opium, 413, 515, 530

Man Achin, 164

Man Ali (aged 70), 187

Man Asz, 505

Man Ayau (coal coolie), 273

Man Kong village, 110

Man Mo Temple, 316, 381, 540

Man Sun Pun (coolie), 323

Man, Abdoolah (watchman), 178

Manah Singh, PC No. 502. *See PC No. 502, Manah Singh*

mandarin, 369

Manila, 401

Manila lottery tickets, 444

Manilamen, 327

Marçal, Capitulino Priamo (unemployed compositor), 204

Mardtfieldt, J.F., juror, 356

marine hawker. *See Tong Achi*

Market Ordinance, 30, 31, 64, 65, 66, 69, 71, 221, 619

Market Street, 152, 153, 163, 194, 201, 311, 313, 355, 443, 482, 511, 540

Market Street (No. 17), 482

Marketing Street, 105

Marques, Dr. / Mr. (Assistant Superintendent, Civil Hospital), 120, 387

Marques, Dr. (Government Civil Hospital), 463

married woman, 109, 125, 206, 269, 280, 284, 289, 290, 305, 451, 486, 531

Ling Aho (aged 64), 305

Martin, E.F., 337, 338

Martin, E.F. (unemployed watchman), 324

Mary Tatham (vessel), 509

Wong Kwok (tailor, 480

Mathias, Lorenço, 174

Mathieson, Police inspector. *See* Inspector of Police Mathieson

Maurente, Ramon (merchant), 108

McCall, John (Private, Royal Inniskilling Fusiliers), 284

McCallum, Mr. (public analyst), 247

McCallum, Mr.H. (Govt Civil Hospital analyst), 403

McCormick, W. J. (of regimental police), 349

McDonald, Donald, PC No. 84, 380

McDonald, G., PC No. 82, 160

McDonald, Martin (seaman, English), 454

McDonald, PC No., 493

McDonald, Police Constable, 435

McDonald, Thomas, 508

McEroy, Cornelius (private, Royal Iniskilling Fusiliers), 499

McGonell, Martin (seaman uemployed), 357

McKane, Archibald, PC 11, 302

McKay, Police Sergeant 330

Mckean, Mr., ag for Attorney General, 421

McKnight, Leonard (private, Royal Inniskilling Fusiliers), 468

McMillan, Hugh (fireman on SS *Glenelg*), 440

McNeil, W., PC No. 37. *See PC No. 37, Wm McNeil*

Mede, Thomas (seaman, *Helicon*), 273

medical diploma, European or american, 535

Mehta, Mr., 342, 343, 344, 345

Merren, Gilbert of American ship *Importer*, 449

Messageries Maritimes Company, 492

Messrs Arnhold, Karberg & Company, 469

Messrs Baird & Brown of Glasgow, 318

Messrs Blockhead & Company, 271

Messrs Brereton and Wotton, 156, 477

Messrs Butterfield & Swire's, 453

Messrs Douglas Lapraik & Company, 313

Messrs Gilman & Company, 214

Messrs McEwen Frickel & Company, 511

Messrs Sale & Company, 322

Messrs Sharp, Toller & Johnson, 456

Messrs Stephen(s) & Holmes, 365, 438, 448, 456

Messrs Turner & Company, 294, 321

Messrs. Vogel & Company, 345

Mexican dollars, 416

Military Authorities, 340, 342

military barracks, 481

Millar, Henry (PC No. 16). *See PC No. 16 Henry Millar*

Miller, Captain, 250

Miller, Captain of SS *Catterthun*, 249

Ming Afat, 411

Mo Sam Hing, 441

Mok Aping (coolie (-chair)), 336

Mok Asang (coolie), 351

Mok Awa (Harbour Dept boatman), 202

Mok Awang (boy aged 12), 202

Mok Chin Ki, 181

Mok Kai, Po Leung Kuk detective, 212

Mok Mo (jinricksha coolie), 308

Mok Ngan, 433

Mok Shi (of Yin Cheung old clothes shop), 191
Mok Shin, 426
Mong Sing Chan, 115
Moodien / Mooideen (aged 40 or 38; seaman, belonging to Malacca / Malacca-man), 135, 147
Moore, Private Robert, 417
Morris, Edward (seaman on American ship *Stonewall Jackson*), 274
Morrison, J. (PC). *See PC J. Morrison.*
Mosque, 147
Mossop, (Mr.), 118, 119, , 120, 121, 128, 129, 132, 136, 137, 138, 139, 140
Mozart, German ship, 308
Mr. Kennedy's Horse Repository, 504
Mr. Armstrong's Auction rooms, 168

Mui Lan brothel, 438, 457
Mui Lan Brothel, 32 West Street, 456
Muller, Frederick Victor (seaman, *Alert*), 410
Mung Ahing (aged 35), 146
Mungal Singh, *See* PC No. 692
Murphy, George (seaman, HMS *Carysfort*), 397
Murray Barracks, 484
Murray, Dr, 252; Ag Superintendent of the Civil Hospital, 299
Murray, John (of steamer, *Anjer Head*), 223
Murray, John (seaman unemployed), 362
Nam-hoi, 207
Nam-hoi (place), 290
National Hotel, 372, 499
Finlay, Thomas (aged 28; able seaman, 234
Naval Officer, 487
Naval Yard, 71, 93, 131, 219, 232, 306, 504

Nicklesen, Bernard (of British ship, Hindostan), 436

Nicol, William (of Blue Jacket), 373

Nicolon, Vassuly (of Russian steamer *Wladvostok* [sic]), 402

night watchman, 319

Noble, Sergeant T. (Regimental Provost-Sergeant in the Royal Inniskilling Fusiliers), 348, 349

Nordland. Henry G. (of Russian ship *Waltikka*), 373

Northcote, G., PC, 232

Nullah Lane, 330, 333, 339, 351, 540

Number 10 Bridge, 320

Number 2 Station, 147, 204, 251, 273

Number 4 Station, 291

Number 5 Station, 112, 323

Number 6 Station, 175

Number 7 station, 279

Number 7 Station, 120, 200, 283, 336, 357, 364

Number 9 Station, 353

Number Seven Police Station, 279

Nund Singh, Police Sgt, 297

Oakes, George, 374

Occkerill, Mr.T. (chief officer on the steamer, *Crusader*), 318

Octava (steamship), 105

Odum Singh, PC. *See PC Odum Singh.*

Maxwell, Joseph (printer), 291

Old Bailey Street, 380

old Sugar Refinery, East Point, 204

Olsen, Otto (of American ship *J.H. Bowers*), 372

Olson, John (proprietor, National Hotel), 499

O'Malley, Hon. E.L., 421, 481;

opium dross dealer, 286, 531

opium equipment, 527

Opium Farm, 35, 295, 332, 413, 515, 518, , 525, 530, 534, 584, 585, 591

Opium Farmer, 101, 135, 146, 151, 175, 176, 195, 244, 245, 254, 255, 257, 286, 289, 294, 329, 335, 375, 376, 388, 406, 407, 412, 429, 470, 500, 514, 515, 516, 518, 519, 522, 523, 529, 532, 533, 534, 535, 584, 585, 586, 587

opium habit, 537

opium, medicinal use, 534

Opium Monopoly, 582, 584, 587

Opium Ordinance(s), 31, 71, 73, 74, 76, 77, 79, 81, 84, 89, 526, 527, 528, 583, 584, 594

opium (Patna), 515

opium pipe, 141, 230, 370, 371, 372

opium refuse, 176, 329, 515, 533

opium retail licences, 587

opium shop, 156

opium smoking pipes, 465

opium trade, 35, 582, 587; legalisation of, 583

Ordinance, 74, 192, 193, 233, 234

Ordinance No. 10 of 1844, 543

Ordinance No. 12 of 1844, 524, 590

Ordinance No. 22 of 1844, 193

Ordinance No. 14 of 1845, 256, 295

Ordinance No. 5 of 1850, 169

Ordinance No. 2 of 1858, 35, 515, 524, 525, 528, 587, 588, 590, 591, 592, 593

Ordinance No. 2 of 1858, para. 5, 530, 535, 588

Ordinance No. 3 of 1860, 261

Ordinance No. 7 of 1865, 176

Ordinance No. 7 of 1866, 543

Ordinance No. 9 of 1876, 174, 377,

Indian constable(s);
Indian Police
Constable No.
693, Easur Singh
Peddar's Wharf, 156,
441
Peel Street, 220, 309,
540
Penang (place), 259,
416, 502
Penedo (vessel), 185
Percy [*sic* for
"Piercy"], *See
Piercy, Mr.
George*
Periera, Joseph
(fireman
unemployed), 302
perjury, 445
Perkins, James
(straggler from
HMS *Magpie*),
244
Perry (Police
inspector), *See*
Inspector of
Police Perry.
Perry [*sic* for
"Parry"], John
(seaman, *Helen
Marion*), [aka
"Power(s)"], 240,
252. *See also*
Parry
Perry, John (beggar),
215
Peter, 193, 194

Peters, George
Henry (seaman),
374
Petersen's /
Peterson's
Boarding House,
173, 224
Phelan, Edward
(English seaman
w. no fixed
residence), 501
Phillippo, Hon. G.,
Chief Justice, 465
Phillips, Thomas
(seaman on the
American ship,
Invincible), 124
Piercy, Mr. George
(headmaster,
Diocesan Home
and Orphanage),
244, 405
Ping Alung
(hawker), 185
Ping Chow / Ping-
chow [= Peng
Chau?], 367, 368,
369
Po Leung Kuk, 21,
51, 102, 109, 207
Po Leung Kuk
detective(s), 32,
102, 109, 212
Po Leung Kuk
detective, Wong
Man Yu, 208. *See
also* Wong Man
Yu.

Po Lok Theatre, 158, 333

Po Yan Street, 100, 540

Pok-foo-lum [*sic*] / Pok-fu Lam / Pok-fu Lum Road, 167, 278, 404

Pok-fu-lam, 414

Police Canteen, 501

Police Constable(s), 32, 97, 100, 104, 110, 116, 117, 133, 134, 142, 158, 159, 170, 178, 185, 195, 200, 213, 228, 229, 248, 264, 283, 284, 392, 491, 511, 517, 544

Police Court, 121, 155, 269, 277, 280, 300, 440, 476, 523, 592

Police Force, 21, 22, 233, 296, 337, 520, 522, 525, 538

Police Force, member of, 590

Police Magistrate, 39, 42, 586

Police Office, 374, 412

Police Station, 137, 197, 204, 299, 373, 447, 528, 529, 595

Police Station (Central), 320

Police Station (Pokfulam), 320

Police Station No. 1, 434

Police Station No. 2, 135

Police Station No. 5, 472

See also "Number [N] Station".

Pong Atin, 221

poor box, 101, 151, 152, 196, 201, 245, 311

Poor Box / Poor's Box, 51, 285, 419, 496

Portland (place, USA?), 419

Portland (destination), 509

Portuguese Consul, 158

possession of stolen property, 149, 443, 445

Post Office, 85, 426

Postmaster General, Mr Lister, 425, 426

potatoes, 435

Po-tse (game of chance), 251

Pottinger Street, 125, 131, 136, 140, 166

Pound Lane, 203, 292, 461, 540

Powan (steamer), 288

Powers (nickname for "Parry", q.v.), 234, 235, 237, 240, 241, 242

Po-yan Street, 420

Praya, 120, 152, 179, 187, 202, 227, 233, 253, 254, 257, 259, 276, 295, 296, 297, 298, 304, 305, 315, 326, 332, 354, 356, 357, 360, 364, 370, 389, 396, 420, 424, 426, 433, 435, 451, 458, 459, 467, 471, 473, 479, 502, 536, 540

Praya Central, 107, 253, 295, 315, 326, 389

Praya East, 458, 473

Praya West, 254, 297, 332, 364, 370, 433, 467

Prehn, Marcus (ship-carpenter), 122

PS (Police Sergeant) No. 6, 164

PS No. 35, Mahomed Ali, 285

PS No. 69, Rae, 371 *See also Rae, G., Police Sergeant No. 69.*

PS No. 199, Pang Aloi / Pang Loi, 213, 245

PS No. 250, Lan Shui, 276

PS No. 524, 215

PS Butlin, 374, 416

PS Pang Loi, 211

PS Smith, 505

Police Sergeants (PS): See also: Campbell, Campbell, T., Fische, Grozart, Hagarty, Hanson, Hennessy, G., Ip Nam, Lan Shui, Mahomed Ali, Malak Sultan, McKay, Nund Singh, Smith, Wong Ayau

public coolie, 106

public gambling, 81, 111, 161, 305, 309, 333, 361, 370, 376, 405, 482

Public Gambling,
162
public gambling
house, 258, 370
Puk Sing (master of
stone-junk No.
141), 368
Pun Aching, 381
Pun Afat, 184
Pun A-fung, 269
Pun Afung (female),
267
Pun Aman (shop
coolie), 354
Pun Amui
(compradore of
Canton), 429
Pun Lun (of Lim
Cheung old
clothes shop), 191
Pun U District, 110
Pun Yeuk (of Shing
Ki draper's shop),
191
Pun Yuk
(householder),
354
Quarry Bay, 494
Queen's Road (No.
208), 131
Queen's Road, 97,
98, 127, 132, 154,
157, 162, 182,
215, 238, 242,
243, 261, 272,
274, 277, 278,
279, 284, 312,
316, 317, 321,

323, 330, 333,
336, 374, 378,
379, 428, 429,
436, 446, 450,
454, 464, 499,
511
Queen's Road
Central, 130, 164,
291, 322, 384,
392, 427, 428,
441, 458, 461,
479, 483, 500
Queen's Road
Central, tailor and
outfitter, 506
Queen's Road East,
106, 147, 216,
340, 410, 471
Queen's Road West,
145, 244, 246,
247, 251, 304,
310, 371, 383,
434, 435, 461
Race Course, 74, 85,
259, 471, 475
Racket Court, 342
Rae, G., Police Sgt
No. 69, 161, 304,
371, 372, 414
Rahamat (wife), 286
Ramasammy,
Soonderam (Govt.
school-master),
379
Ramma, Salomon,
123
Ramsay, Joseph
(constable of the

Naval Yard Police), 133
Ramsay, Mr. W.S., juror, 422, 427
Ransome, James Robert (unemployed telegraph operator), 416
raw opium, 151, 175, 176, 294, 295, 413, 517, 530, 533, 534, 590, 591, 593, 594
Receiving officer of the Gaol, 421
Recreation Ground, 100, 239, 253, 260, 314, 377, 384, 424, 452, 454, 469, 540
Recreation Grounds, 421
Reedman, Robert (seaman on board American barque *W.H. Besse*), 483
Refuge, 362
Regiment Sergeant-Major, 386
Regimental band, 484
Regimental Police, 348, 349
Registrar General's office, 354
Remedios, Mr., 482

Remedios, Mr.J.H. dos, 404
Remedios, R. dos, 156
Remedios, S.V. dos (juror), 165, 199
Rev. Chü Tak Mong (missionary), 495
Rev. Marcus Leang [*sic*], 494
Rewards, 522
Ribston (British barque), 364
Ng Ajuk (aged 26), 141
Chun Tai Hing (aged 25), 120
Rich, Paul W. M. (mate of the German gun vessel, *Iltis*), 487
Richard, Mr.C.W., juror, 422, 427
Ring, Charles (seaman), 453
Robinson Road, 178, 508
Robinson, Captain R. J. (of *Helen Marion*), 236
Rocha, Mr. E.L. da (receiving officer, Victoria gaol), 265, 317
rod on the breech, 266

Sam Amui (head coolie), 298

Sam Shui (District), 209, 210

Sam To Lane, off the Praya, 435

Samshui, 207

Samuel, William (watchman, Surveyor General's Dept.), 174

San Francisco (place), 221, 419

San Francisco (destination), 408

San Lane, off Caine Road, 172

Sands, James (private, Iniskilling Fusiliers), 499

Santos, Antonio dos (excise officer), 176, 245, 254, 286, 332, 388, 533. *NB Not the same as Anthony Santos Spencer, forer pupil at the HK Govt Central School*

Sardrean, Francis Xavier (Brother Cyprian) (principal, St Joseph's College, 229

Sau Tsai (woman), 389

Sawan Singh, PC No. 584. *See PC No. 584. Sawan Singh*

Schulte, Paul (seaman on board the German steamer *Electra*), 436

Scott, Arthur (fireman on board *Comus*), 278

Scott, Mr.George (manager of the O.B.C.), 181, 211, 409

Scott, W., juror, 341

Smith, Walter (aged 18), 302

search warrant(s), 289, 371, 376, 407, 522, 524, 525, 526, 590

Second Hand Clothes' stall, 391

Second Street, 380, 390, 392, 540

Second Street, No. 95, 399, 400

Second, Alli (barber), 471

secret or special service, 524, 593

Seimund, 137, 141

Seimund, Mr., 141

Simson, James Whitley, 465
Sin Akiu, 164
Sin Alum, 157
Singapore, 126, 166, 223, 253, 267, 269, 300, 334, 362, 425, 431, 443, 446, 450, 465, 488. *See also Tanjong Pagar wharf*
Singapore (destination), 425
Singapore Syndicate, 584
Siu Akwan (shop-coolie), 375
Slaughter House, 240
sly brothel, 238
Smale, Sir John, 248; (former servant of, Li Afuk), 247
Smith (Police Sgt), 505
Smith, Frederick (seaman on steamship, *Africa*), 124
Smith, J., PC No. 31. *See PC No. 31, J. Smith*
Smith, Joseph (foreman carpenter), 492
Smith, Mr. T.H. (partner in Messrs Blockhead [*See also Blackhead*] & Co.), 271, 277
Smith, [?], PC No. 47 *See PC No. 47 Smith*
Smith, Peter, 243
Smith, William (engineer), 501
Snelling, Mr. G. W. (assistant in the Stag Hotel), 287, 378
Snelling, Mrs, 490
Snowden, Hon. Francis, Ag Chief Justice, 155, 266, 267, 277, 300; Attorney General, 421
So Cheung (salt fish store master), 262
Sobail / Sohail Singh, PC No. 658. *See PC No. 658, Sobail/Sohail Singh*
Soda Water manufactory, 248
Sodaguest, Thomas (native of Finland), 330
sold "like a pig." (people trafficking), 431
soldiers, 46, 342, 344, 345, 346,

Stephens and Holmes. *See Messrs Stephen(s) and Holmes*

Stewart, Dr Frederick, 40, 73, 102, 217, 218, 220, 235, 240, 282, 298, 365, 374, 465, 466, 485, 496

Stewart, Dr Frederick (Magistrate), 19, 24, 32, 33, 34, 35, 36, 37, 38, 39, 40, 41, 42, 43, 44, 45, 46, 47, 106, 139, 140, 145, 193, 374, 385, 400, 419, 476, 478, 507, 509, 514, 523, 533, (*practical and careful decision*, 534), 538, 544, 581, 582, 584, 586, 596

Stewart, Frederick (Magistrate), Ag Col. Secy, 511

Stewart, Frederick (Magistrate), appointed Ag Col. Secy, 509

Stewart, Herbert [*sic*] PC, 252 [= *PC No. 4, Herbert Servant?*]

Stiles, Henry Duright (bookseller), 490

Stipendiary Magistrate, 524

stocks, 8, 100, 128, 158, 161, 222, 227, 239, 266, 335, 369, 501, 502

stone junk (No. 141), 368

stone junk (No. 252), 367

Lai Asau (aged 32), 177

Stonewall Jackson (American ship), 274

story-teller, 424

street coolie, 409

Su Akwon (coolie), 484

Su Asam (rickshaw coolie?), 323

Su Asz (apprentice tailor), 479

Su Atai (district watchman), 160

Su Yu (street coolie), 409

Sui Acheung, 463

Sui Hing Lane, 411

Sum Aying (coolie), 484

watchman, 123, 159,
160, 161, 174,
178, 183, 238,
251, 259, 297,
306, 307, 313,
322, 324, 358,
405, 409, 411,
431, 473, 492,
493; See also
Ismail

Watchman/men to
Gamblers, 65, 66,
75, 77, 79, 292,
305, 313, 339,
405, 485, 511

watchman to rogues
and vagabonds,
273

watchman (head-),
423

watchman
unemployed, 454

Water Police, 407

Watts, Mr. (Survey
Dept), 157

Watts, Mr. William
(overseer at
Survey Dept), 226

Waugh, George, 124

Webb, Emma, 167,
168

Webster's Bazaar,
280

Weir, Patrick
(private, Royal
Inniskilling
Fusiliers), 287

Welcome Tavern,
374, 410, 498

Wellington Barracks,
135, 147

Wellington Street,
262, 312, 314,
355; (No. 40),
407, 531; (No.
80), 412, 531

West Street, 314;
(No. 30), 443;
(No. 32), 438, 456

West Terrace, 406;
(No. 3), 508

Western Market,
314, 333, 435

Whampoa, 110

Wharry (Dr), 261

White, J.R., juror,
266, 277, 356

White, Mr. J.R.
(steward of the
Sailor's Home),
302

Whitehead, Mrs,
281, 282

Whitehead, W.F.
Inspector of
Brothels, 281

Whitfield Barracks,
Kowloon, 417

Whitley, Robert
(army private,
Royal Inniskilling
Fusieliers), 340

Whitley, Robert
(private, Royal